Spoiling for a Fight

Micah L. Sifry

Spoiling for a Fight

Third-Party Politics in America

Routledge
New York   London

Published in 2003 by
Routledge
29 West 35th Street
New York, NY 10001
www.routledge-ny.com

Published in Great Britain by
Routledge
11 New Fetter Lane
London EC4P 4EE
www.routledge.co.uk

First Routledge hardback edition, 2002
First Routledge paperback edition, 2003
Copyright © 2003 by Routledge

Routledge is an imprint of the Taylor & Francis Group.

Printed in the United States of America on acid-free paper.

10 9 8 7 6 5 4 3 2 1

Library of Congress Cataloging-in-Publication Data
Sifry, Micah L.
    Spoiling for a fight : third-party politics in America / Micah L. Sifry.
        p.   cm.
    Includes bibliographical references and index.
    ISBN 0-415-93142-8 (hb) / 0-415-93143-6 (pb)
    1. Third parties (United States politics).
    2. United States—Politics and government—1993–2001.
    I. Title
    JK2265 .S56   2002
    324.273—dc21   2001048181

For Mira, Jesse, and Leslie

Contents

Section IV. Organizing from the Bottom Up

Section V. The Future

Our movement needs both its pragmatists and its dreamers, its inside-players and its utopian outsiders. We would never have begun without the dreamers, and never have lasted without the pragmatists.

—*Barbara Ehrenreich*

Author's Note and Acknowledgments

I have long been fascinated by the path less traveled: short-cuts through a neighbor's backyard, aqueduct trails, blue highways, river beds, cobble-stone paths in the heart of a modern city, abandoned railway lines that have been converted to bike trails. There's something in me that loves anything that doesn't conform to the rigid grid of checkerboard property lines and suggests a different, more interesting, way of getting from here to there.

My interest in third-party politics stems from a similar root. I don't believe the path to wisdom leads solely through the Democratic and Republican parties, far from it. If anything, history makes clear that many of the innovations and improvements in this country that we hold dear began at the margins, in the campaigns and pressures mobilized by third parties. Periodic explosions of third-party sentiment have forced the major parties to change direction and attend to new issues.

For the last ten years, we have been living through such a moment in American history, one that I believe is still unfinished. The issue is not simply getting government spending under control, which many believe was the signal contribution of Ross Perot's 1992 campaign and the third-party movement centered on his Reform Party. The issue is putting the people in greater control of the decisions that affect their own lives, and whether we will be a plutocracy or a democracy.

The thesis of this book, which was completed well in advance of September 11, 2001, was that the public wanted greater choices in politics than were currently on offer from the Democrats and Republicans, but that America's leading third parties still had a long way to go before they could fill that vacuum.

Now the stakes for everyone seem higher. In the days after the attacks on the World Trade Center and the Pentagon, public distrust in our national leaders—so long a staple of post-Vietnam, post-Watergate politics—took a dramatic drop. People were impressed with the initial actions of their leaders, and there also seemed to be a yearning for something we were not sure we would get: wise leadership capable of handling the twin crises of international terrorism and economic recession. On first glance, this would suggest that the moment for third-party organizing had suddenly gotten much less ripe.

Maybe yes and maybe no. In my opinion, faith in government after September 11 also rose because the long-standing gap between our ruling elites and average voters seemingly disappeared in the days and weeks after the attacks. To most Americans, government no longer meant a faceless bureaucrat or an arrogant politician; it meant a courageous rescuer or brave soldier. Instead of serving special interests, we seemed to have a government serving our common interest. Instead of distant representatives hobnobbing with Fortune 500 fatcats, we had senators and mayors who walked among the people. We were all humbled, equally, by the horrendous events of the 11th, and in that newfound equality many glimpsed new promise for American democracy.

Our current leaders could keep this moment going. Nothing is forcing them to return to their old habits. But the underlying fundamentals of America's political economy were not changed by September 11. Elections were not cancelled by the attacks, and big money certainly did not stop dominating campaigns and distorting legislation. The messy struggles of politics, of who gets what and who doesn't, continued, only now with choices that seemed starker. The tragedy elevated the national leaders of the Republican and Democratic parties, from President Bush on down, but it also presented them with greater challenges. Success may give the major parties new life and a greater hold on the electorate; failure may topple them faster than we can imagine.

Still, past history suggests a pessimistic prospect for third parties, at least in the short term. Life in America during wartime, whether cold war or hot, has never been welcoming of dissenting voices or minority groups. The nation quite naturally rallies around the flag and its elected leaders. Official censorship commingles with self-censorship, and people who ask inconvenient questions are tarred as disloyal, even traitorous.

On the other hand, our recent experience with other wars and national tragedies, from the Gulf War to the Oklahoma City bombing, suggests that moments of national unity and sky-high popularity for the President can be quite fleeting. In the spring of 1991, after President George Bush "won" the Gulf War and enjoyed a 91 percent approval rating, no one predicted that the next year an independent billionaire and then an obscure southern Democratic governor each would be topping him in the polls.

If anything, September 11 represents the end of an era of American complacency and the beginning of a new public ethos of engagement. Where that will take us is impossible to predict, but if more people are now paying attention to politics because they understand in a new, visceral way, how politics can affect their lives, then third parties, independent voices and the struggle to expand the boundaries and depth of American democracy will have a lively and relevant future.

This book is the product of nearly a dozen years of research and writing for a variety of publications starting with *The Nation*, my longtime home; and ranging from newspapers and magazines including the *American Prospect*, the *New York Times*, the *Los Angeles Times*, *Newsday*, and *Tikkun* to electronic pioneers like *HotWired*, *Salon*, *TomPaine.com*, and *Newsforchange.com*. It has been nurtured by many editors, fellow writers, activists, foundations, friends and family. To everyone who has assisted me in this long process, my everlasting thanks for your patience, your ideas and your support.

These kindred souls include many intellectual mentors, some who I have been fortunate to know and befriend and others whose work I only know their writings: Douglas Amy, Richard Cloward, E. J. Dionne, Barbara Ehrenreich, Gloria Emerson, Tom Ferguson, Tom Frank, Larry Goodwyn, William Greider, Doug Henwood, Jim Hightower, Christopher Hitchens, Arianna Huffington, Walter Karp, Naomi Klein, Andy Kopkind, Ted Lowi, C. Wright Mills, Kevin Phillips, Frances Fox Piven, and Robert Sherrill.

Many of the leaders and activists featured in this book, without whom there would be no third-party story, have been tremendously generous with their time. Perotistas, Reformers, Independents—whatever you want to call them, Tom D'Amore, Jack Gargan, Dean Barkley, Phil Madsen and the many United We Stand America dissidents who fed the *Perot Periodical* have been critical to shaping my understanding of the angry middle. Among the Greens, I must thank David Cobb, Mike Feinstein, Anne Goeke, Abe Guttman, Tabitha Hall, Greg Kafoury, Tom Linzey, Damacio Lopez, Linda Martin, Carol Miller, Ross Mirkarimi, Cris Moore, Dean Myerson, John Rensenbrink, Steve Schmidt, Norm Shatkin, Sam Smith, and Xubi Wilson. I owe a special thank you to Ralph Nader for being so accessible and open for so many years, and to his many lieutenants, including Theresa Amato, Steve Cobble, George Farah, Carl Mayer, Tarek Milleron, Russell Mokhiber, John Richard, and Harvey Rosenfield. Harriet Barlow, Secky Fascione, Ericka Bozzi Gomez, Jonathan Green, Tom Hucker, Bertha Lewis, Bill Lipton, Bob Master, Zach Polett, Joel Rogers, Karen Scharf and Peter Shapiro have all been terrifically helpful guides into the New Party and Working Families Party universes, and I have to especially express my appreciation to Daniel Cantor for all his time and friendship. Conversations with all of these people have woven themselves into my analysis of the third-party prospect, but it is probably David Cobb, Steve Cobble, and Daniel Cantor who have had the most influence on my thinking. Sorry guys, but you'll have to take your lumps with me.

For nurturing my curiosity about independent politics, giving me a place to write about it and always sharpening my prose, I have to single out my colleagues at The Nation—Roane Carey, Marc Cooper, David Corn, Elsa Dixler, Robin Epstein, Doug Ireland, John Leonard, Richard Lingeman, Judith Long, Peter Meyer, Victor Navasky, Richard Pollak, Betsy Reed, Bruce Shapiro, Katrina vanden Heuvel, and JoAnn Wypijewski. David, Marc, Doug, Katrina, and Victor have in particular been stalwart supporters and valued friends. I also must thank a few editors at other publications that shared my vision in the importance of this unfolding story and were there with a check and a freelance assignment whenever it took a new turn. David Weir, who picked me up at *HotWired* and carried me to *Salon*; Chris Scheer, who sent me on the Nader 2000 trail for *Newsforchange.com*, and John Moyers, who embraced me at *TomPaine.com*—my great thanks.

This book wouldn't exist if it weren't for the good graces and financial support of George Soros and his Open Society Institute, which gave me an independent fellowship in 1998 that allowed me to conduct much of the on-the-ground reporting at its heart. My everlasting gratitude as well to OSI's Gail Goodman, Gara LaMarche, Aryeh Neier, and Mark Schmitt. In the same vein, I also must add huzzahs to Bill Moyers and the Schumann Foundation for stepping in with vital additional support that allowed me an extended leave of absence from work in early 2001, and to Miles Rapaport, David Callahan and their organization Demos: A Network for Ideas and Action for offering the book a home in the midst of their growing web of pro-democracy work. E. Joshua Rosenkranz of the Brennan Center for Justice at New York University and Arianna Huffington also each helped defray some of my research costs; thank-you again.

James Ciment, David Levine, Chris Malone, Lori Minnitte, Manny Ness, and Frances Fox Piven—my colleagues in the Independent Politics Group at the City University of New York/Graduate Center—thanks for being my de facto "dissertation support group," for putting on two great conferences, and most importantly, for getting out on the limb with me. You show that there can be a vibrant life inside academia.

Similarly, I have to salute journalists Rebecca Bershadker of ABC News, John Nichols of the *Capitol Times* and Maria Recio of the *Fort-Worth Star-Telegram* for showing that the mainstream media can take third parties seriously and cover them consistently. Plus I must thank them for always being willing to compare notes with me. Likewise, my hat is off to Tom Gogola and "subcomandante" Mark Spencer, who contributed so much to the *Perot Periodical*, and especially helped shape its vision. In the same category, but on a pedestal all his own, I must bow to Richard Winger and his indefatigable newsletter *Ballot Access News*. If someone someday gives out Oscars to the real heroes of American democracy, then Richard deserves a lifetime achievement award. No one else in America knows more about the hard facts of third-party life, and Richard has played a critical and unheralded role in prying open state ballots to more choices. And he was always there to cheerfully and selflessly answer all my arcane questions.

Then there are my invaluable colleagues in the pro-democracy movement, starting with fellow Public Campaign staffers Susan Anderson, Rick Bielke, Margaret Engle, Michael Ettlinger, Robyn Garnett, Gail Gomez, Randy Kehler, Brian Leiken, Ellen Miller, Addrana Montgomery, Nick Nyhart, Donna Parson, Annie Perezchica, Deb Ross, Eric Schmeltzer, Jodie Silverman, Tracy Sturdivant, and Nancy Watzman. I feel like I have had a whole cheering section helping me along through the writing grind. And I especially must thank Ellen and Nick, not only for being so supportive, but also for allowing me so much freedom and time to pursue this project. It is a privilege to work shoulder-to-shoulder with such people, as well as with organizer-strategists like Betty Ahrens, John Bonifaz, Roger Bybee, Marc Caplan, George Christie, David Donnelly, Janice Fine, Becky Glass, Tory Griffith, Janet Groat, Bob Hall, Pete MacDowell, William McNary, Len Norwitz, Dan Petegorsky, Jamin Raskin, Jim Reed, Rob Richie, and Alison Smith.

I owe a special thanks to Marc Cooper, Janice Fine, and Doug Ireland for having somehow found the time to read and comment on an early version of this manuscript, as well as to the various participants in each third-party project who also evaluated the final product for historical accuracy. Thanks also to Joey Parnes, Ellen Tattelman, Ken Devine, Anita Softness, Debbie Swiderski, Richard Steinman, and my other friends in the Mishkan Ha'Am, Riverdale and Goldens Bridge communities for all your support. Finally, I would be in big trouble if I didn't give a huge hug to Robbie Friedman and Chris Dugas, who have stood by me through every step of the process, from finding an agent and a publisher to proofreading the galleys. You are all family.

Speaking of agents and publishers, Kim Witherspoon and David Forrer of Witherspoon Associates—thanks for being such constant boosters and dogged allies. And Eric Nelson of Routledge has been all I could ask for in a book editor—confident of the value of this project, expansive in his vision of the book, and shrewd in his advice. My thanks as well to production editor Jeanne Shu and copy editor Norma McLemore, who did a phenomenal job polishing my prose in ways that I didn't know were even possible.

Finally, my family. My parents, Anna Levendel and Benny Sifry, and my parents by marriage, Mike and Faye Lieman, have been constant champions and role models for us all. Likewise all my siblings, Rachel Sifry, David Sifry, Ben Lieman, Dorrie Lieman and Harold Lieman. Many, many times, each of these family members pitched in for me while I was burrowed away, writing, or listened sympathetically as I described the work in progress. No one could ask for better. My daughter Mira and son Jesse are constant inspirations to me and a joy to live with. Thanks you two for understanding when I needed to work, for asking good questions, and for being so much fun to play with.

Last, and most, I have to thank my partner in all things, Leslie Lieman. More than anyone else, she has been with me at every stage of this project, nurturing my earliest writing and supporting my vision. Her wisdom and common sense have touched every page.

Micah L. Sifry
New York City, October, 2001

Introduction

Harbingers of Change

Getting into the hotel elevator at 7:00 A.M. on the morning of Election Day, November 7, 2000, Green Party presidential candidate Ralph Nader looked a little more tired than usual. He had just finished a sixteen-hour run of last-minute get-out-the-vote rallies starting with a meeting with the Reverend Al Sharpton in Harlem at 3:00 the previous afternoon, continuing with a flight up the coast to Boston University, where he addressed thirty-five hundred college students at a rally organized on two days' notice, followed by a late-night drive to speak to seven hundred up at the University of New Hampshire in Durham (outdrawing Democratic vice presidential candidate Joe Lieberman, who visited the school three hours earlier) and ending with a 1:30 A.M. Maine rally at the University of South Portland with three hundred semidelirious students and older folks crammed into a sweltering and smelly lecture hall. He and his small entourage of advance men and reporters had rolled into the Hampton Inn in South Portland at 3:00 in the morning. The Roman legion drumbeat that Nader playfully taught a group of drummers at the last rally—"Boom-boom-buh-buh-buh-buh"—was still ringing in my ears as Nader ambled beside me in the elevator. We had a plane to catch at 7:45 A.M.

"So, do you want to hear my prediction?" Nader asked. "Mmmhmm," I answered, half-awake. "Oh, you mean about the election," I said. The question was whether Nader would reach 5 percent of the vote, qualifying the Green Party for millions in federal funding for its 2004 presidential efforts. This was a central goal of his candidacy.

"Three percent," Nader declared, with just a touch of resignation in his voice. "Oh, really?" I answered. "Why do you think that?" I had been guessing that his final tally would be anywhere between 4 and 6 percent. This, based on the fact that most national polls had shown him hovering between 5 and 6 in the week before the election and optimistically assuming that although maybe half of those voters would melt away on Election Day, the polls were undercounting his real base of support by leaving out the proverbial unlikely voters who might be attracted to his uncommon honesty and candor.

"Did you hear the early New Hampshire vote?" Nader answered as the elevator took us down to the lobby. "I got just one vote out of eighty in Dixville Notch," he reported, citing what he thought were the results from a tiny mountain hamlet that always votes at the stroke of midnight on Election Day. "I usually do better there," he said. "Maybe we should have made a visit," he added sardonically, no doubt thinking of all of the corners of the country he had covered over the course of his eight-month run for the presidency. I mumbled something about how the Dixville Notch vote was meaningless, that it was a tiny group of voters and far from representative of the electorate. But although it turned out that Nader was wrong about the actual returns from Dixville Notch,[1] his prediction for the rest of the country was dead-on.

Should Nader have run? What did his campaign accomplish, both in terms of affecting the national political debate and in terms of building the Green Party? Could anything have been done differently to produce a better outcome? And where do Nader and the Greens go from here? After successfully getting on forty-four state ballots, raising almost $9 million, hiring one hundred campaign workers, mobilizing one hundred fifty thousand volunteers, and starting five hundred local Green groups and nine hundred campus chapters, Nader's 3 percent showing—2.7 percent, to be precise, or about 2.8 million votes out of a little more than 100 million cast—was a big disappointment to many of his supporters. Though Nader didn't have Ross Perot's billions, and he was excluded from the presidential debates (unlike Perot in 1992 and John Anderson in 1980), he was widely known and highly respected for his decades of selfless service as the country's leading public advocate. If this was the best a third party could do in the presidential sweepstakes with a candidate of such high public standing, maybe it was a mistake for activists to try to challenge the two-party duopoly at the presidential level, where it was most entrenched. Maybe the whole Nader gamble was a huge mistake.

And maybe it wasn't. After all, what else are political dissidents supposed to do— submit to the dominating power of big money in both major parties? Or abandon the national electoral playing field—the one place where the largest number of Americans participate in politics? Nader and the Greens were doing what every true believer in democracy would do: making their best effort, despite the obstacles erected by the two-party duopoly, to address their fellow Americans with a serious, alternative message about important issues facing the country. Close to a million new or previously discouraged voters responded, on top of ones that Nader took from Gore and Bush, judging from exit polls that found about one-third of Nader's voters saying they wouldn't have participated in the election if he had not been running.[2] Several hundred thousand people saw Nader in person and not only heard a thoroughgoing critique of the corporatization of America but discovered that they were not alone in wanting the revival of civic values that was at the core of Nader's crusade. His was the best showing of any progressive third-party presidential candidate since 1924. The energy unleashed by his campaign was evidenced by the tens of thousands of people who actually paid to attend one of his "super-rallies." With the two major parties continuing to neglect the issues that Nader and the Greens raised it is clear this dissident movement is not going away anytime soon.

Is America ripe for more outside-the-box politics? And can this enthusiasm produce real changes in the country's direction? Certainly, in the last ten years there has been a surge of interest in independent and third-party candidates. The corruption, dishonesty, and sheer ossification of the two-party duopoly are producing its antithesis: the search by millions of Americans for a meaningful alternative.

At the presidential level the most visible of these developments was, of course, the emergence of Ross Perot, who received nearly 20 million votes in 1992 and 8 million in 1996. The total vote for other third-party presidential candidates—those without the kind of attention that Perot was able to command thanks to his wealth—also doubled, from 1 million to 2 million, between 1992 and 1996 and doubled again, to 4 million, in 2000. Less noticed, but of equal importance, has been the increasing success and sophistication of minor political parties at the state level. The Greens and the New Party established real roots, actually electing and holding onto local offices in more than twenty states, swinging a number of key races, and pushing important initiatives on such issues as the right of workers to a living wage.

The last few years have been full of harbingers. For the first time in decades, a third-party candidate who was not a high-profile refugee from one of the two major parties—Jesse Ventura—won election to statewide office, as the governor of Minnesota. The 1998 elections also saw Maine's independent governor and Vermont's independent member of Congress win reelection by substantial margins. Third-party candidates also drew substantial fractions of the vote, into the double digits, in several gubernatorial races and in a smattering of congressional battles, with a noticeable effect on the local political debate. In addition to many tiny sectarian groups, at least six minor parties—the Reform Party, the Greens, the New Party, the Libertarian Party, the Natural Law Party, and the U.S. Taxpayers Party (now called the Constitution Party)—were active in a coordinated and growing fashion across several states.

In 2000, the third-party presidential candidacies of TV commentator Patrick Buchanan and consumer advocate Ralph Nader drew national attention, with the press falling over itself to cover the infighting within the Reform Party and, to a lesser degree, the chances that Nader would swing the race from Gore to Bush. Below the radar, Greens won thirty-two races, swelling their presence in local politics to eighty officeholders spread over twenty-one states. Several Progressive Party state legislators were returned to office in Vermont, while their gubernatorial candidate drew a respectable 10 percent of the vote and participated in all the statewide debates. In Minnesota, Jesse Ventura's Independence Party showed that it had legs, with nearly two dozen candidates for the state legislature getting respectable chunks of the vote, and one congressional contender reaching 20 percent in a three-way race. The New Party continued to rack up its victories in a half-dozen cities, while a newly created effort based on its model, the Working Families Party of New York, emerged as a fresh force in state politics.

The rise of these new parties and independent candidates has offered the hope that something like full-blooded competition might be brought to the electoral arena and with it the possibility that new ideas, alternative policies, real accountability and fresh perspectives might prevail. With voter turnout continuing to hover at barely half the eligible electorate, disaffection from the major parties has become a central fact of political life. Many people believe the moment is, indeed, ripe for more independent, third-party bids in American politics.

A One-Party System Shared by Two Parties

There is another reason why this resurgence of interest in third parties is important. We need more choices outside the two-party framework that has governed American political life for more than a century. And we need those choices both in physical terms, as viable candidates on state and federal ballots, and in philosophical terms, as alternative ways of thinking about and solving our nation's problems. Right now, we have neither.

America's seemingly perfect two-party duopoly has produced a politics of near-total paralysis. Few elections are competitive. Most are dominated by whoever has the most money. The expensive top-down art of using market research to produce manipulative TV ads has replaced bottom-up campaigning. Big issues, whether they are related to problems we will face in the future or accountability for mistakes made in the past, are rarely addressed honestly. As a result more citizens are giving up on the franchise, or, as we will see in this book, rebelling against the rotten and dysfunctional two-party system and trying to open it up.

A duopoly is defined as a market with just two sellers. Picture a beach with just two ice cream stands selling essentially similar products. While the vendors may start out

Of course, there were also some substantial differences between Bush and Gore, and not just in personality or character. They disagreed about how much military spending should be increased, for example. They parted ways on aspects of tax policy. And they clashed on other issues of importance, such as abortion and gun control. But on many fundamental questions about the direction of America and the quality of life of its citizens, they were in total, numbing agreement.

For a country that prides itself as the heartland of free-market capitalism, this lack of competition in the political arena is not just perverse. It is positively unhealthy. The essence of democracy is the ability to hear and decide among opposing views. But the political duopoly—two parties tacitly agreeing to divide the market up and not seriously challenge each other 90 percent of the time—is producing a special kind of civic paralysis. In order to move in a different direction, we need to be able to see an alternative path and hear someone telling us why this is the better way to go. But the duopoly stifles meaningful debate about the big choices facing the country, with rare exceptions (such as the fights over the nomination of Robert Bork to the Supreme Court and the NAFTA accord). Instead, most day-to-day politicking in Washington and many statehouses has become a subtle, grinding war of position aimed at a tiny number of so-called "swing" districts and voters, while those special interests with the resources to hire lobbyists and finance campaigns play an insider's game of dividing up the spoils.

Alternative points of view do not lack support in American public opinion. Substantial numbers of Americans—in some cases majorities—support aid to poor children, cuts in corporate welfare, reductions in military spending, universal health care insurance, alternatives to the drug war, labor and environmental protections in trade agreements, tougher measures to guarantee clean air, water and food, a living wage, more democratic oversight of federal banking policy, burden sharing with our overseas allies, more investment in energy conservation and alternative fuels, and a comprehensive overhaul of the campaign finance system, to take some of the major issues that were not raised in the 2000 presidential election.[14]

But these choices are rarely presented to the voters for ratification because the two major political parties, the Democrats and the Republicans, have made it exceedingly difficult for parties and candidates with dissenting views to share space with them on the civic stage. It's as if two football teams had agreed to play only between their respective 40-yard lines—and to keep other teams that want to use the whole field out of the stadium.

The Third-Party Prospect

Other political parties—what we commonly call third parties[15]—(and independent political candidates) are those other teams. Historically, third parties have led the way in opening up discussion of new issues. The abolition of slavery, women's right to vote, the direct election of U.S. senators, initiative and referendum powers, the progressive income tax, shorter working hours, child labor laws, federal farm aid, and unemployment insurance—all these changes came about because of the pressures first mobilized by minor political parties. While most of the concerns raised by third parties have been progressive, they have sometimes also been repositories of resentment—pushing for restrictions on immigrants or crackdowns on crime. In general, third (and fourth and fifth) parties broaden the permitted boundaries of public discussion. When they are politically successful, third parties also offer protection to their supporters from the tendency, always present, of the holders of power to use the state to suppress unwanted dissent.

At different times, third parties have had a substantial presence in Congress and state capitols. The People's Party elected two senators and eight congressmen in 1890, a number that peaked at five senators and twenty-two congressmen six years later. In all, between 1890 and 1902, the states of Kansas, South Dakota, Montana, Nebraska, California, Colorado, North Carolina, Idaho, Alabama, and Arkansas all sent People's Party representatives to Congress. During the same period, People's Party members also held governor's offices in Colorado, Kansas, and South Dakota. The Socialist Party had a member of Congress from either New York or Wisconsin in nearly every election cycle from 1910 to 1928, along with a substantial number of municipal officials, even mayors of major cities, until 1960. The Farmer-Labor Party of Minnesota thrived in the 1920s and 1930s, electing a number of senators and representatives to Congress and holding the governor's mansion from 1930 to 1938. Prohibitionists elected the governor of Florida in 1916 and sent a representative to Congress from Los Angeles for three consecutive terms between 1914 and 1920; they also helped push through the Eighteenth Amendment to the Constitution banning the manufacture or sale of liquor (which was repealed thirteen years later). The party was, moreover, the first to demand women's suffrage (in 1872); it was joined later by the short-lived women's Equal Rights Party (1884–1888) and later by the Socialists (in 1904).

Teddy Roosevelt's Bull Moose Progressives were elected to Congress from the states of Washington, Illinois, Michigan, New York, Pennsylvania, and Louisiana between 1912 and 1918; later, followers of Wisconsin's "Fighting Bob" LaFollette would send a number of their Progressive Party leaders to Congress and the statehouse between 1934 and 1946. In New York City, the American Labor Party sent two representatives to Congress at its height between 1946 and 1948. (And thanks to the brief use of proportional representation, the ALP elected several members to New York's city council, and even the Communist Party had two council members at one point in the early 1940s.) Popular pressures mobilized by Upton Sinclair's 1934 "End Poverty in California" gubernatorial campaign, along with the Huey Long and Francis Townsend populist movements, undoubtedly helped push President Franklin D. Roosevelt to the left and aided the passage of the Social Security Act of 1935. Similarly, the Progressive presidential campaign of Henry Wallace in 1948 prompted Harry Truman to tack left on housing, health care, and civil rights.[16]

But third parties, even regionally based parties, have not played such a substantial role in American politics for more than fifty years. Why? Because the two major parties, often acting in concert, took steps to close down the third-party option. Laws regulating ballot access were tightened, giving the Democrats and Republicans a tremendous advantage; rules governing voter registration were toughened so as to disenfranchise poor and minority citizens; fusion, in which smaller parties cross-endorsed candidates of other parties but had their votes counted on their own line, was banned; membership in third parties, especially of the left, was stigmatized as fringe and unpatriotic. As television came to dominate public life, the costs of campaigning and gaining visibility also worked to deter and suppress third-party candidates.

Mainstream political scientists like to say that the American two-party system is a natural product of something called "Duverger's Law"—the claim, made by Maurice Duverger, that winner-take-all systems that award representation by single-member districts cause voters to congregate around one of two parties in almost mechanical fashion. The actual history of American politics shows that despite such structural choices we had a thriving multiparty system until the early 1900s, when most of these deliberate steps were taken to suppress insurgent third parties and disruptive voters. In addition, it's hardly correct to say that we have a two-party system today, outside of the fight for the presidency and the balance of control in Congress. Most Americans live in defacto one-party districts, where even a vote for a second party is a so-called wasted vote.[17]

An honest appraisal of the future of third parties in America must start by admitting that the path ahead is still strewn with obstacles. Though we need more choices, it isn't clear that we will get them. Money dominates elections as always in all but the few states with "Clean Money/Clean Elections" full public financing systems for candidates.[18] Winner-take-all elections force most candidates into a "spoiler" role, causing many potential supporters to fear "wasting" their vote. The mainstream media haven't changed their tendency to marginalize all third-party candidacies, regardless of the candidates' actual chances. And in most states the rules written by the major parties hinder other parties' access to the ballot and make it harder for people to simply find their candidates on the actual ballot.

More subtly, anyone trying to create a political alternative is swimming against a powerful cultural tide of declining expectations about politics itself. Why bother with a new party if you think nothing good can be achieved through politics, that wealthy special interests will win out no matter what, or that career politicians will sell out to protect their own incumbency regardless of which party they belong to? The victories of a few independent candidates are certainly suggestive of the potential for efforts outside the two-party box. But they are not the same thing as creating a durable third party. A political party, defined as an ongoing, self-conscious organization of individual voters and officeholders with a common identity and ideas that seeks to win and exercise power, is a rare thing. Building one—even at the local level where most of the real work of politics happens—takes endurance and social solidarity.

We Americans, accustomed to the instant gratifications of consumer capitalism, have little patience for the inevitable trials and tribulations that come with supporting any fledgling political enterprise. In addition, we are atomized as never before by forces of modern life—television, exaggerated fear of crime, social architecture that separates people into isolating cocoons, the flowering of Internet chatrooms devoted to every subgroup imaginable. As a result, there are few places where large groups of people can develop the essential bonds of trust and common interest that serious party organizing requires.

Third party efforts are also hindered by an unseen process of social self-selection. The people most drawn to them tend to be well meaning but politically inexperienced, along with a good number of ideological and single-issue zealots. Many savvy political organizers also tend to stay away from third parties for pragmatic reasons—the odds are long, and they worry about helping the party they most detest by taking away votes from the party they only somewhat dislike. This process of self-selection often leaves third-party efforts bereft of basic organizing smarts and scrambling to hold onto an ever-fluctuating cast of volunteers. Inexperience is as much a killer of third-party prospects as the structural obstacles erected by the two-party duopoly.

Class, race, and gender are also hidden obstacles. As I discuss in chapter 2, indexes of political alienation show that the potential base for outside-the-box politics is disproportionately concentrated among people of lower incomes, darker skin color, and women. But third-party activists are often middle-class whites; frequently the leaders are men. The deliberate and unconscious choices they make about how to organize themselves and what issues to emphasize often have the effect of narrowing their appeal to the very constituencies that they need most to build their ranks.

And yet the impulse to seek out new choices has not died. In this book, we will meet many of the people who have tried, despite the obstacles, to take on the duopoly in recent years. However, I have paid only passing attention to the Libertarian Party, the Natural Law Party, and the Labor Party, and none whatsoever to even smaller, more sectarian parties. None of these efforts, however well intentioned, have yet had major effects on our electoral process. A number of Libertarians have been elected to local office, but the only partisan races in which they have managed to draw into the double digits have been those with only one major party candidate on the ballot. Nor have the party's presidential candidates managed to climb out of the 1 percent ghetto. Libertarians managed to "spoil" two U.S. Senate races for the Republican Party, one in 1998 in Nevada and one in 2000 in Washington state, but in both cases this was by getting in the middle of a very tight major-party battle, not by getting a large vote on their own.[19] Like the Libertarians, the Natural Law Party has managed to recruit a good number of local and congressional candidates. But that party, too, has had no significant effect on the process. The party's close and curious ties to the "transcendental meditation" movement of Maharishi Mahesh Yogi also seems to destine the party to the margins of mainstream politics, even as that connection provides it with a steady source of volunteers. The Labor Party has yet to field any candidates for office. Thus it is simply impossible to judge its influence or potential.

Rather, the focus here is on three concurrent third-party projects that all started at the beginning of the 1990s and played out, sometimes spectacularly, over the course of the last decade. The Reform Party was the biggest and most significant of the three. Though its founder, Perot, has quit the scene, and the party itself disappeared into fringe-land with the divisive candidacy of Pat Buchanan, the essence of the original Perot phenomenon continues in a potentially more viable form in Minnesota. Governor Ventura is still highly popular in his state and across the country, despite (or because of?) his constant self-aggrandizing. From its beginning in the anti-incumbent fervor of the early 1990s to its semirevival under Ventura's banner, this third-party project has been self-consciously "centrist," seeing the opportunity for a new political movement positioned in the middle of what it sees as the extremes of the two major parties. That may well be one way forward for third-party advocates. Chapter 1 explains how Ventura achieved his stunning victory; chapters 3 through 5 trace the rise and fall of the whole Perot phenomenon, from its roots in the early 1990s, through the construction and destruction of Perot's grass-roots base and finally into the party's one moment of revival in 1999 and then implosion.

The second movement explored here is that of the Greens, the party that "spoiled" the 2000 election in the eyes of many Gore backers, but whose de facto leader, Ralph Nader, and supporters believe fervently that you can't spoil a system that is rotten to the core. The Greens are fundamentally a reaction to the overall rightward drift of both of America's major parties in the last generation; they see the opportunity and need for a new political movement not in some imaginary "center" but on the progressive left. Theirs is a front-on confrontation with the entire duopoly, a challenge to all the rigging so eloquently described by Theodore Lowi and a demand for dramatic political and economic reforms. As some social and environmental conditions worsen, or as the moral intensity of the antiglobalization movement spreads, the Green Party's banner may well rise. But for it to do so the Greens will also have to find a way beyond their current base of progressive college towns and similar locales. Chapter 6 charts the origins of the Greens and the party's entry into serious electoral organizing in the mid-1990s, with a focus on New Mexico, its biggest success. Chapters 7 and 8 zero in on Ralph Nader's presidential efforts and close with a detailed postmortem on his 2000 campaign.

Finally, there is the New Party and a state party that developed out of its model, the Working Families Party. Though founded by progressives and led by veteran labor, feminist, environmental, and social justice organizers, the New Party does not buy the Green vision of "organizing the left." Rather its goal is to "organize from the bottom up," reaching those Americans who are most disenfranchised by the existing order, with a deliberate emphasis on inner-city constituencies and organized labor. Its leaders have also chosen to focus on nonpartisan electoral work at the local level and a "changing the rules" strategy to eliminate the "spoiler" problem for third-party efforts in partisan races. Until those rules are changed, it may well be that no durable third-party effort can survive in America's emaciated political culture, and we will be left with chronic explosions of anti-incumbent sentiment and independent celebrity bids for office as the only alternatives to the duopoly. Chapter 9 looks at the New Party's local victories and ultimately unsuccessful Supreme Court bid to revive the nineteenth century practice of fusion, or cross-endorsement. Chapter 10 shows what a thriving modern third party might look like if more states were to follow New York's example of allowing fusion, with a detailed portrayal of the state's newest and most promising minor party, the Working Families Party.

What Works and What Doesn't

Fish need to be their own oceanographers—especially those that want to travel through turbulent waters and reach safe harbor. So before plunging into the narrative of third-party activity in America from the 1990s to the present, let me offer some guideposts. A general clarification is needed first. Though most people commonly think of parties as national organizations, nearly all party building happens at the state and local levels. Third parties get the most attention when they run someone prominent for president, and a presidential campaign may be a good way for a party to advertise its message to a large number of voters all at once and to identify pockets of concentrated support. But thanks to America's federal system, almost all the work of constructing a party—getting a line on the ballot, registering voters into the party, building chapters, nominating candidates, raising money, qualifying for public subsidies, holding annual conventions—takes place at the state level, under laws that vary greatly in their receptiveness to new political projects. Thus, third-party prospects are greatly influenced by local conditions beyond their control. Across the country, branches of a particular third party can also differ a great deal in their internal makeup. This has been most true of the Reform Party, which began in some states as a spontaneous, grass-roots outgrowth of Ross Perot's 1992 campaign, and in others as a centrally driven product of Perot's wallet. But Greens and New Party chapters also have their idiosyncrasies, shaped by local conditions and accidents of history.

Third parties succeed when people get elected under the party's banner or the party's candidate gets enough votes to affect the larger political debate and change people's political awareness. A third, more subjective measure of success is when a third party shows that it is not a flash-in-the-pan phenomenon but actually builds an enduring organization that is self-supporting and growing. Third-party failures are equally interesting (and far more prevalent). Instead of focusing outward on talking to voters and trying to convince them to support a new political direction by backing their candidates, third-party activists often turn inward. A core group of devotees is often enough to keep a third-party project going for quite some time without any meaningful victories at the ballot box. Success comes to be defined in other ways, such as winning internal leadership fights or ideological arguments. These may give activists some satisfaction, but they do little to reach a larger public. Starting on the periphery of politics, many third-party activists thus unwittingly participate in their own self-marginalization.

The fact that a party has a line on the ballot, an organizational structure, and maybe even a little media attention can make its supporters think it exists in the more meaningful sense of reaching voters—when actually it is not. Of course, minor political parties can serve other purposes, giving their members a sense of identity, like small churches and obscure clubs. Scholar J. David Gillespie refers to these groups as "continuing doctrinal parties" because they derive their support "more from their activists' faithful commitment to party doctrine or creed than from any genuine hope of electoral victory."[20] The idea of "bearing witness" against a corrupt and seemingly impenetrable political system can be noble. But it is usually not very political in the sense of actually affecting the direction of the country. That requires a willingness to engage in dialogue with real voters, not just true believers, no matter how hard that may be. So one critical element of third-party growth is whether the party's activists are outward focused (on winning elections or moving issues) or inward focused (on often irrelevant organizational or ideological battles).

Once a third party enters the electoral playing field, there are many factors—external and internal—that affect its potential. These include legal requirements for getting and keeping a place on the ballot, the timing and intensity of election contests, whether races are partisan or nonpartisan, limits on voter registration, access to public subsidies for candidates or parties, and whether the party is allowed to cross-endorse (or fuse with) other party's candidates. Third parties have to clamber through many discriminatory hoops just to get their candidates on the ballot. To take one extreme example, in a number of states the deadline to turn in petitions is so early that activists have to be out on the streets in the dead of winter. This test of endurance is all the more appalling when you realize that most private shopping malls and businesses legally prohibit petitioning on their property. People can no longer even circulate petitions on the premises of post offices.[21] Thus the sheer costs of getting on the ballot are a constant problem for many third-party efforts. Most states also require that voters register well before Election Day, another hindrance to outsider bids that often don't catch people's attention until the final weeks of campaigning. Of the six states that allow Election Day voter registration, four (Maine, Minnesota, New Hampshire, and Wisconsin) also have significant levels of third-party activity. A correlation also exists between the availability of public financing and third-party strength. Of the nineteen states overall that offer some form of public subsidy to candidates and/or parties, twelve have seen recent or ongoing surges of third-party activity.[22]

In addition to these kinds of structural, fixed factors affecting the climate for third-party organizing, there are also more variable, fluid conditions at play. These include changing local economic circumstances, the quality (or lack thereof) of the major party candidates, the dynamics of competition between the two major parties, the chances of recruiting an already prominent candidate (even a refugee from the major parties) to run on the third-party line, and local demographic changes. People often turn to third parties when the major parties are seen as failing. An economic downturn or a spate of scandals involving local politicians may give a third party an opening, particularly if the major party that is not in power is not very active, or if it is possible to credibly pin blame on both major parties. Economic growth can also upset existing political balances, particularly if its benefits are not spread evenly. Then there are the opportunities that arise as the public turns away from some of today's harsh campaign tactics. In races in which the two major-party candidates spend most of their time focused on negative attacks on each other, a third-party candidate can benefit from a "pox-on-both-your-houses" reaction.

Separate from these external factors are the internal choices that third-party activists make themselves. Parties need leaders, activists, and adherents. Leaders represent the party on the ballot, in the media, and stand in the forefront of internal decision-making. Activists, who are usually volunteers but also can be paid organizers, do nearly all the nuts-and-bolts work of building the party, supporting its candidates, spreading the word, participating in its internal structures, and so on. And adherents are the base of voters, generally passive, who mostly express their support by voting for the party's candidates, and sometimes make a financial or other contribution to the party's efforts. But there are many different ways to combine these ingredients, some more successful than others. A party can be built around charismatic leadership, a common vision, or the plain old self-interest of its members (with a membership and decision-making structure that reflects real levels of individual and institutional affiliation).

Parties also have to make choices about where they want to position themselves on the political spectrum, what kind of issues to emphasize, and whom to aim their efforts at. The three third parties to be explored in this book have each pursued a blend of strategies. There is the "nonideological" approach that portrays the two major parties as out of touch, with the third party in the sensible middle. There is the more explicitly ideological effort to rally either the left or the right against the two-party establishment. And there is the populist call to the bottom against the top. These appeals can be aimed broadly at the whole populace or in a more targeted way at constituencies that might be more sympathetic, such as people in the declining middle class, the urban poor, students, talk-radio listeners, working-class people living in inner-ring suburbs, even readers of specific political magazines. Organizing a real base—voters, volunteers, and donors—is the toughest challenge that third-party activists face. But it is only when they face that challenge that today's third parties have a life in American politics beyond acting as momentary repositories for the electorate's unhappiness with the status quo.

A close look at the trajectories of the Reform Party, the Greens, and the New Party shows that each has strengths and weaknesses. In chapter 11, I conclude with a look at the prospects for the future. As I write, leading actors like Nader and Ventura are laying in their plans for 2002 and 2004, Greens and the remnants of the Reform Party are trying to move ahead, and the New Party and Working Families Party are still hoping to export their model to more states. The future of America's third parties is still open. If they are to be successful, what's needed is serious attention to what works and what doesn't.

Challenging
the Duopoly

*Jesse Ventura and
Finding the Third-Party Voter*

The People Want
More Democracy

Election Night: November 3, 1998. Television viewers around the country are startled by the image of excited teenagers bodysurfing over the heads of a crowd of well-wishers in flannel and jeans while the camera zeroes in on the shaved and glistening head of Minnesota's new governor. "We shocked the world," shouts the Reform Party's Jesse Ventura, a former Navy Seal, professional wrestler, small-town mayor, and talk-radio host, punching the air with his fist for emphasis.

An Unlikely Messenger

I remember when I first heard of Jesse Ventura's campaign for governor of Minnesota. As a subscriber to a mailing list for people interested in the American Reform Party, a splinter of Ross Perot's Reform Party that broke away over disagreements about Perot's authoritarian tendencies, I received an e-mail message on March 1, 1998, from Ventura's fledgling campaign. It announced the creation of a Ventura website and invited me to sign up on the JesseNet, a list for campaign volunteers. "A pro wrestler for governor?" I thought, amused. A young colleague of mine in Washington, D.C., who was a pro wrestling fanatic, jumped with glee when he heard about Ventura's run. "This shows that wrestling is moving into the mainstream," he crowed. After hearing that, I'll admit that I didn't take Ventura very seriously, at first.

One item in the Ventura campaign's message did catch my attention, however. The *Minneapolis Star-Tribune* had conducted a poll on all eleven major party candidates running for governor—keep in mind, this was months before the primaries—and because the Reform Party had achieved major-party status in Minnesota in 1994, Ventura was included. He came in fourth out of eleven—in a field that included the sons of two former vice presidents, the son of a governor, and the son of a department store mogul, as well as the current mayor of St. Paul.[1] Not bad. Having high name recognition is a basic rule for success in politics. I decided to open a "Jesse Ventura" file.

Three months later another e-mail from Ventura's volunteer press coordinator, Gerry Drewry, caught my eye. Two concurrent polls by the state's leading newspapers, the *Star-Tribune* and the *St. Paul Pioneer-Press*, gave Ventura anywhere between 7 and 23 percent of the vote in the general election, depending on which Democratic-Farmer-Labor (DFL) and Republican candidates he was matched up against. The *Pioneer-Press*'s numbers were generally lower because its pollsters screened out people who had not voted in the last election, a bias that Drewry complained "eliminates all of the discouraged voters who didn't like either of the two biggest parties." The *Star-Tribune* also attempted to focus on likely voters, but evidently left more Ventura supporters in the tally. Its conclusion:

> Jesse Ventura, the Reform Party candidate for governor, attracted double-digit support in each of the three-way general-election matchups featuring him, a DFLer and a Republican. Those results should invigorate Reform Party activists. No other candidate in the party's brief history in Minnesota has received more than 5 percent of the votes in a statewide election. The results suggest that Ventura could be a spoiler, at the very least, in the final outcome if he takes more votes from one candidate than the other.[2]

"Double-digit support." At that level, third-party and independent candidates become worth watching. After all, in every election for Congress and lower-level offices hundreds of minor-party contenders regularly draw 1 to 3 percent of the vote—and have little impact. Getting more than 10 percent, even if only in a poll or two, means becoming a factor in any three-way race. Maybe even the deciding factor. With 10 or 15 percent of the vote, a third-party candidate can force one or both of the major candidates to pay attention to neglected issues or constituencies. That alone is an unusual and invigorating role to play. And if by some combination of circumstances that candidate manages to attract 20 percent or more in the polls, he or she is no longer just a "factor." "Contender" is more accurate, since by definition if one candidate has more than 20 percent, the others are splitting less than 80 percent. Which means the third-party candidate is now within striking distance of at least one, if not both, of the major candidates. I decided to take a trip out to Minnesota sometime after the party primaries in mid-September, when the general election would be in full swing.

Minnesota and Jesse Ventura belonged on the political radar screen for one other reason, beyond Ventura's healthy name recognition and poll standing. Minnesota was one of the only states in the country with a lively third party that had grown directly out of Ross Perot's presidential campaign of 1992. In most other states the Reform Party was implanted from above when Perot decided, three years later, after most of his grass-roots support had dwindled away, to form a new political party. Here it had grown organically from the bottom up. In 1992, Perot got 24 percent of the vote in

Minnesota, well above his national average of 19 percent. In a number of counties, he topped 30 percent—even pushing then-president George Bush into third place in several cases.[3] Back in July of that turbulent year, after Perot had abruptly dropped out of the race, a group of volunteers working for "Minnesotans for Perot" decided to form a new political party to pursue Perot's reform agenda regardless of whether he stayed in politics.[4] The fact that this seed had been planted so long ago made Ventura's appearance more significant.

In November of 1992, this new party, then called the Independence Party, played an informal role supporting one independent candidate for Congress in the Sixth Congressional District, mainly comprising the suburbs around the Twin Cities. That candidate, lawyer and businessman Dean Barkley, got a surprising 16.1 percent of the vote with a campaign that blended social liberalism and fiscal conservatism. His plan for reducing the federal deficit, for example, combined means-testing of entitlements like Medicare and Social Security with big cuts in defense spending. His middle-of-the-road approach earned him the endorsement of the *Star-Tribune*.[5] Two years later, Barkley, by then a formal candidate of the party, ran for U.S. Senate and cleared an important hurdle by garnering 5.4 percent of the vote. This qualified the Independence Party as a major party under state law and made its candidates eligible for a modest amount of public financing for their campaigns. (It also drew the attention and support of Ventura, who was then a radio talk-show host.)[6] In 1996, Barkley ran again for Senate, and this time, after being allowed into one of the major candidate debates, he won 7 percent of the vote.

I had gotten to know Phil Madsen, a computer trainer who was the founder of the Independence Party, during the 1996 presidential campaign, while covering developments within the Reform Party for magazines like *The Nation* and HotWired's *Netizen*. In the fall of 1995, Perot had surprised many by deciding to support the creation of a third party after years of saying that he wanted to stick to nonpartisan efforts to influence the system. As Perot's hired hands moved out across the country coordinating state party-organizing drives, they soon collided with the handful· of preexisting Perot-inspired parties like Minnesota's Independence Party that had their own autonomous structures and leadership. Most of these conflicts were resolved more or less amicably as these parties made the pragmatic decision to join up with Perot's fledgling Reform Party. But activists like Madsen and Barkley continued to push for more democracy and accountability within the national Reform Party. They even led a walkout from a founding convention of the party that took place after the 1996 election, when it became clear that Perot loyalists were calling all the shots. Their tenacity and their independence were impressive. Most important, they had created an organization that rested on a shared vision among a group of activists, rather than the singular talents of a charismatic leader.[7]

By 1998, Barkley needed a break from carrying the Reform Party's flag in Minnesota; he was now chairing Jesse Ventura's campaign. In fact, he was the person responsible for convincing Ventura to run for governor in the first place.[8] And Madsen was in charge of the campaign's website and, as he put it, "virtual field operations." With these kinds of connections, it would be hard, if not impossible, to tar Ventura with the Perot brush. And that boded very well for Ventura. Perot, who lost more than half of his voter support between 1992 and 1996, was obviously damaged goods. At the same time, the antipolitical phenomenon that propelled him to prominence in the first place had not gone away. Colin Powell's near candidacy in the fall of 1995, when he soared past front-runners Clinton and Dole in the opinion polls, showed the public's hunger for fresh, honest, outsider candidates hadn't disappeared.[9] The fact that Ventura came out of Perot's grass-roots base but owed nothing to the Texan's top-down operation meant that he was perfectly positioned to tap into that same market.

If he was a credible campaigner.

Working-Class Hero

The first major poll after the September 15 party primaries in Minnesota showed Democratic Attorney General Hubert "Skip" Humphrey III with a commanding lead over his rivals. He was the top choice of 49 percent of likely voters, while Norm Coleman, the Republican mayor of St. Paul, was the pick of 29 percent, and Ventura, 10 percent.[10] While these numbers suggested that Ventura would not be a deciding factor in the race, he was soon to benefit from a major strategic error by the front-runner. The Humphrey campaign had evidently decided that it could only gain by insisting on Ventura's inclusion in all the major debates, reasoning that the muscleman's appeal would cut predominantly into Coleman's support among suburban men, sportsmen, and hunters in particular. Ventura seemed to oblige by showing up a few days later for a candidates forum at the Governor's Economic Summit dressed in a camouflage jacket, black jeans, hiking boots, and an Australian bush hat—the same one, he noted, that he wore in the movie *Predator*.

Ventura had actually been snubbed by the event's organizers but was invited to attend by Roger Moe, the Senate majority leader who was Humphrey's running mate and his stand-in at the forum. "We're doing this in the interest of fairness," Moe said. "His party has earned major party status, and he deserves as much a chance to speak as any of us." Moe gave most of his speaking time to Ventura, who used it to talk up the value of third parties and to attack his opponents as the captives of special interests. A reporter covering the event for the *Minneapolis Star-Tribune* noted the contrast between Ventura's getup and "the crowd of suits" watching him speak. "You're going to find me a little different from the other candidates," Ventura said.[11]

That difference was on full display the day I flew into Minneapolis to interview Ventura at length. It was Thursday, October 8, almost a month before the election and a week after Ventura had appeared with Humphrey and Coleman at a televised debate in St. Paul and at a local debate in the city of Hibbing, in the heart of the heavily Democratic Iron Range. According to reports, Ventura had made a strong impression at the first debate and received a standing ovation at the second.[12] His campaign was at a cusp.

That day, Ventura and Moe were speaking at a luncheon forum sponsored by the Minnesota High Technology Association at the Radisson Hotel near the airport. Norm Coleman had been invited as well, but he declined to come or send a representative. Even without the Republican, Ventura and Moe made a great study in contrasts. Ventura, dressed in a black V-necked short-sleeve shirt and black pants, used most of his opening speech to introduce himself to the all-white audience of phone utility executives, high-tech entrepreneurs, and small businessmen and -women. Moe, in a standard politician's gray suit, was more of a known quantity to the people there and focused primarily on their parochial concerns: wiring the state, dealing with the high-tech industry's shortage of skilled labor, and the like.

Judging by the crowd's response, Ventura made the better impression. Moe's speech was a standard, low-key presentation that dwelled primarily on mundane matters like maintaining funding levels for higher education and changing pension and tax laws so more retirees could participate in the state's booming economy. He was politely applauded, especially after he impressed the audience with his personal acknowledgment of several leading businessmen among them. But Ventura drew a stronger response when he reminded the crowd of the mess in Washington (special prosecutor Kenneth Starr's report on President Clinton's affair with Monica Lewinsky had come out the month before) and the problems created by "career politicians" more concerned with what it takes to get reelected than serving the public.

"I believe people should come from the private sector, go into government, and then get out and go back to the private sector rather than become professional politicians," he declared in his deep, gravelly voice. "When the state has a $4 billion budget surplus, you're being overtaxed," he said, hitting his number one issue. "It's easy for my opponents to say now that they will cut taxes—my, my, it's thirty days before the election," he added, playing into voter skepticism about election-season promises.

"It's high time for a third party," he said, his voice getting even lower. "Let's look at Washington. I'm embarrassed. We've got a lot of problems that government should be dealing with, but instead, for the next nine months, the focus of this nation will be on despicable behavior by career politicians. If this isn't the right time for a third party, then when?" The well-dressed audience listened, taken by Ventura's plainspoken approach. His strategy of standing with the public and its dislike of partisan politics was clearly working. "It doesn't make any common sense or logic to elect the top exec-utive from one of the two legislative parties. That's putting the proverbial fox in the henhouse, isn't it? And then you've got an adversarial relationship with the other party. Just like in Washington, right now. Party lines, battling for party agendas—not doing what's best for the country. Here in Minnesota you'll get the same thing. In the end, what happens to Minnesotans? Well, like I tell people, there's more Minnesotans than there are Democrats or Republicans." At this statement, a wave of applause broke across the room.

As people in the audience nodded at each other, Ventura concluded by addressing the main obstacle facing any third-party candidate. "They're going to tell you that vot-ing for a third party is a wasted vote. Well, not voting your heart or your conscience, that's a wasted vote. Imagine if a hundred fifty years ago, we held to that mind-set today. Guess what, Abraham Lincoln would have never been our president, because Abraham Lincoln was a third-party candidate."[13] Again, another strong round of applause.

After the luncheon broke up, I walked with Ventura to a table far from the hotel's main lobby, at the corner of an interior courtyard where we thought we wouldn't be interrupted much. On our way there, he was arguing with a member of the audience who disagreed with his insistence that the state return the budget surplus to the voters. Ventura was ragging on him as a "socialist from the 'U' [university]" who was just the sort of elitist he hated. This led him, unprompted, to start our conversation with an angry diatribe.

"I'll tell you what pisses me off," Ventura growled. "You see, I grew up in the '60s, and I grew up in south Minneapolis, where if you didn't have money you got drafted. You got sent to Vietnam. And where do these college [types] get off saying that just because they can go to college, they're not faced with that? That's how bogus and bull-shit the draft was. It gave out college deferments. Why? Why should you be penalized just because maybe you don't want to go to college, so then you have to go fight and die? That's why when I got out of the service I vehemently supported the stop-the-draft movement. My best friend graduated from technical school, he graduated that morn-ing, came home to shower and change clothes to his graduation party, and there it was: 'Greetings, you've been selected.' On the very day he finished technical school to be a tool-and-die man. Why should school get you out of it? I'll tell you why—cause that protected the wealthy. Even if their kid wasn't even qualified to go to school, they could pay for him and get him to go, just to get him deferred. But the poor people, they got drafted, they had to go. Why do you think it was so heavily minorities being drafted?"

For all his personal wealth and success, Ventura at heart was still a working-class guy from south Minneapolis. And average people sensed this. Every few minutes dur-ing our conversation, a janitor or deliveryman or repairman—the guys who wear shirts with their names stenciled on the front pocket—would interrupt to shake Ventura's hand and promise to vote for him. "Tell ten friends," Ventura replied each time. Young women and a few young guys in suits stopped by as well. A group of teenagers were leaning over the balcony above us to eavesdrop. "This happens to me all day long," he told me. "People drive by my car and give me the thumbs up." Leaning in conspiratorially, he declared, "I'm going to win this thing. You know why? Voter turnout. They can't poll those 50 percent who don't vote. If I get 20 percent of them to come back, I'll win. And don't believe the Republicans when they say I only take Republican votes because of my fiscally conservative ideas. I'm also socially liberal."

This was true. While Ventura made cutting taxes and shrinking government his primary concern, his second-biggest issue was reducing public school class sizes. In speeches and debates, he always brought up public schools and went out of his way to point out that he sent his kids to public school, unlike Coleman and Humphrey. He also opposed incumbent Governor Arne Carlson's push to give parents vouchers to send their children to private school. Later in the campaign, Humphrey dropped out of a debate that had been arranged to be held before a handpicked group of Minnesota high school students, choosing instead to attend a football game and sit in a private box. During their next debate on statewide television, Ventura took full advantage of the opportunity to ask Humphrey about it, saying "Attorney General Humphrey, throughout your entire campaign, you've been stating that you're the education candidate and that young people and education are so important to you. Then I ask you, sir, why, a week ago, when we had a debate scheduled in front of a hundred high school students from across the state of Minnesota, did you choose to cancel that debate, and instead go to a football game and sit in a luxury suite?"[14]

In addition to backing public schools and taking not-so-subtle digs at the elitist tendencies of his opponents, Ventura favored public investment in building a light-rail system to relieve traffic congestion in the Twin Cities, supported most environmental efforts, backed a woman's right to choose, advocated decriminalizing marijuana, favored gay rights and same-sex marriage, opposed the death penalty (in favor of life in prison without parole), and even said he would allow burning the flag as a form of free expression. His commonsense instincts were essentially progressive. Not only had he returned from Vietnam and demonstrated against the draft for its bias against the poor, he took his wife to a state rally for the Equal Rights Amendment, and he had tried to form a union of pro wrestlers. Only when it came to guns and crime did he take a position to the right of center, favoring laws allowing people to carry concealed weapons and calling for extended prison terms for convicts who behave badly in jail. He told me he disliked Pat Buchanan "because he carries too much of a religious agenda. And I'm a firm believer in separation of church and state."

He was also a vociferous supporter of political reform, calling for term limits and the creation of a unicameral state legislature to end the backroom deals of conference committees. Everywhere he went, he made a point of attacking lobbyists and special interests, often waving his hands over his head to show that he had "no strings attached." And he had far-reaching, even radical ideas about how to reform campaign finance. After hearing him rail against bloated government spending on the state university system, I asked him why he thought government often gave away subsidies to big business. "Two words," he answered. "Campaign finance. That's how it happens. Because all of these professional politicians are owned. And they have to pay back, in order to further their career, all their sugar daddies out there." Then he surprised me. "I want socialism to come into campaign finance," he said. "If you've achieved major-party status, I think you should be given a block of money from the government and that is all you can spend to get elected. How you choose to spend it is up to you. But that way you'll have a fair [system], and it comes down to who sells their soul to rock 'n' roll, if you get what I mean."

Ventura also had big ideas about taxes. First, he wanted to freeze property taxes, which he said punished people for improving their properties and rewarded those who let their homes go to seed. "What kind of message does that send to citizenship and core values?" In addition, he said, property taxes were an arbitrary and unfair way to fund education spending, as opposed to income taxes. More broadly, he advocated switching from the income tax to a national sales tax. "That would make you the number one entity again in our country, rather than the government," he said. Average tax-payers, he argued, would no longer be penalized for making money, only for spending it. "With a national sales tax, you'd get that mystical number on your paycheck that says 'gross.'" And since government revenues would become more tied to economic fluctuations, the government would have more reason to pay attention to the economy. With an exemption meant to cover spending by low-income people, he reasoned that a consumption tax would capture revenues from a lot of illicit income. "You have a multibillion dollar industry that pays no taxes. But if you have a national sales tax, drug dealers will pay because they buy things." He admitted that he hadn't hammered down all the details, saying, "I don't claim to be the expert on this, but it makes common sense."

He was also harshly critical of most of the nation's drug policies. "I believe the war on drugs is a miserable failure. They're trying to stop supply. But drugs even get into prison, so how are you going to stop them from getting on the streets then?" In his view, prohibition was "just creating a revenue source for the gangs." His bottom line: "Addiction should be treated medically, not criminally." Ventura's views on victimless crimes like personal drug use extended as well to prostitution, for which he got into some trouble later in the campaign. "It's a lot easier to control something when it's legal than when it's illegal," Ventura told reporters. "Nevada doesn't seem to have a problem with it, do they?" After a rush of criticism from the Humphrey and Coleman campaigns, as well as from women's groups, Ventura insisted that he was not advocating legalizing prostitution, just suggesting that alternative approaches should be studied. "We need to look at solving these social problems in a different way," he said.[15]

Clearly, Ventura was running to inject new ideas into the political debate and shake up the status quo. But why do so as a third-party candidate, especially in the face of two major parties that he himself admitted "work together to make sure any third party gets snuffed"? You're banging your head against a huge wall, I told him. Why do it? "For the experience," he answered. "Why did I do thirty-four parachute jumps out of an airplane? The experience. Why, last spring, did I rappel down from the top of the Civic Center before the Sonics playoff game started? For the experience. If you look at my background, I live life to the fullest."

But then he grew more serious. "Also I see the need. Say what you will, but I served my country. I served as mayor [of Brooklyn Park, a small Twin Cities suburb]. Maybe I'm a softie when it comes to challenging the system, and I've challenged the system a lot in my life. I like challenging the system. I'm a rebel. An article just described me as a cross between James Dean and Mr. Clean." He chuckled at the image. "I found that interesting. I believe a third party should have a chance and should rise up. As I said at the luncheon, if not now, then when? I mean with this *disgusting* display going on in Washington right now, tying our entire government up. All they practice is partisan politics, what's good for their party, not what's good for the country, the people, or the state of Minnesota. And this [the Lewinsky mess] has opened my eyes even more to it. These career politicians do nothing but run to further their careers. And their agendas are simply created by the people who bankroll them. End of story. I'm a rebel. No one's bankrolling me." Then he paused, and his eyes seemed to tear up a bit. "And I also want to see if the American dream has died. My version of the American dream. And that is this: Must one be a professional politician to lead the state of Minnesota? I just have to challenge to see if that's what our country has evolved to now."

For someone who had framed his campaign against the powers-that-be so starkly, Ventura exuded a startling amount of confidence about his chances. "The scenario for how I win is I keep gaining momentum. The race is won in the last three weeks. And I just believe that my message is strong enough, and I think there's enough anti–career-politician sentiment out there. And I create a vision of 'you know what? Jesse Ventura, why not?' Rather than why, why not." At that point in the campaign, he had raised enough money in small contributions to qualify for more than $300,000 in public financing. That money, however, was due him only retroactively, after the election, and his organization was having trouble securing a bank loan in order to pay for critical TV and radio ads. He had only one paid staffer, campaign manager Doug Friedline, who previously ran a pull-tab gambling operation for a Minneapolis bar, and had managed Barkley's 1996 run for the Senate and worked on Ventura's mayoral race in Brooklyn Park. There was no formal field operation. No polling or focus groups, just a small circle of advisers who helped Ventura prepare for debates. But hundreds of volunteers had signed up, coordinated by a core group of about twelve unpaid organizers, and knitted together through the surprisingly effective and vibrant use of the Internet.

"Won't it be a shock when I win," he laughed, recalling the response to his performance in the debate earlier that week in Hibbing, up north. "The Democrats have made a major mistake, assuming I would just cause the defeat of the Republican. The Iron Range has always been traditionally DFL, but I'm winning up there. They're not tax-and-spend liberals up there; they're conservative, workin'man DFL up there," he growled, with an emphasis on "workin'man." Already, he knew something that would become clear to the Humphrey campaign only very late in the race, that he was siphoning away the votes of many union members. "Mae Schunk [his running mate, a teacher] and I are both vested union members, but the unions will not endorse us. Rank and file I win. For example, the letter carriers in one of the major districts took a vote, and I won going away, and that was with all the other Democratic candidates in there. The only ones we can't win with are the phony union leaders. But the upper echelon doesn't win elections. It's the rank and file that goes in and votes." He even predicted that the unions' vaunted get-out-the-vote operations would "backfire on them. They're going to get there and vote for me."

Why Not?

Three days after that conversation with Ventura, the New York Times ran a front-page story headlined "Angry Voters Aren't Sure Where to Place the Blame: Clinton Inquiry Raises Ire in a Bellwether State." The article, reporting on the preelection mood in Washington state, described how the partisan war over the Lewinsky affair had alienated many voters. "The whole sense of anger out there is very real, but it's also like a heat-seeking missile that's missing a target," said a Seattle-based Democratic political consultant. "It's really complicated, and people don't quite know who to blame. But if they do lock onto something in these next few weeks, God help the target."[16] Even though the Clinton-Starr mudfest wasn't the main issue in the Minnesota race, something told me that Ventura's timing couldn't be better. Across the country, the political circus in Washington was turning off voters—leading to predictions of another drop in turnout on Election Day. But in Minnesota, voters had a viable way to thumb their noses at both parties.

That second week in October was a turning point for the Ventura campaign, it is now clear in retrospect. Surprised by Ventura's effective performance in earlier debates, and undoubtedly worried by internal polls that showed him rising, the Humphrey and Coleman campaigns started quietly pulling out of many of the commitments they had made for other joint appearances. The Ventura campaign put out a news release October 11 blasting its opponents for "blow[ing] off these events." It charged, "As Jesse shows increasing voter support, the career politicians are trying to shut him out of the public spotlight."[17] Still, there were a handful of major televised debates to come, including one the weekend before the election that would be seen across the state, and Humphrey and Coleman didn't dare risk skipping those.

Published polls soon confirmed the pro-Ventura trend. On October 20, the *Star-Tribune*/KMSP-TV Minnesota Poll reported that support for Ventura had jumped to 21 percent, while Humphrey crashed 14 points to 35 percent, in a statistical tie with Coleman's 34 percent. The next day, Ventura's comments about possibly legalizing prostitution splashed across the news pages. But even with the critical coverage, a poll done between October 23 and 25 by the *Pioneer Press*, KARE-TV, and Minnesota Public Radio found him inching upward to 23 percent of likely voters, with Humphrey and Coleman each sagging slightly and remaining in a dead heat.[18]

One year earlier, Barkley and campaign manager Doug Friedline had outlined with Ventura what they thought it would take to win the race:

1. Beat the [Ross] Perot vote percentage of 1992 of 24% in the polls in October of 1998.
2. Be included in all of the debates and do well in those debates.
3. Pray that a pro-life candidate such as [state Sen.] Doug Johnson wins the DFL primary so as to make Jesse the only pro-choice candidate on the ballot.
4. Raise $400,000 to $500,000 to spend on paid media for the last 2 weeks of the election to motivate enough of the non-voting public to carry him past the 35% to 38% that would be needed to win.
5. Motivate the young voters to vote.[19]

While they obviously hadn't drawn the Democratic opponent they had hoped for—Humphrey was a staunch supporter of choice—the other pieces of their plan were falling into place.

Assisted by Minnesota's progressive campaign finance law, which gives individual refunds to voters who make political contributions of up to $50, the campaign had already raised more than $75,000 by early October. Under that same law, Ventura stood to receive $327,000 in public financing after getting at least 5 percent of the vote in the general election. Success now hinged on getting a short-term loan against that retroactive financing. After being turned down by Ross Perot and dozens of Minnesota banks in its search—Ventura sarcastically charged in his autobiography that their rejections might have had something "to do with the fact that the head of the Republican Party in Minnesota is the head of one of the banks"—the campaign obtained the money from tiny Franklin Bank.[20] Located in inner-city Minneapolis, the bank specializes in making high-risk business loans to minorities. Boosted by fund-raising through its web-site, the Ventura campaign ultimately raised and spent more than $600,000—a frac-tion of the $13 million spent by the Humphrey and Coleman campaigns and their party committees, but enough to be heard and seen by most voters.

The adman for the Ventura campaign, Bill Hillsman, who had produced the funny and eye-catching commercials that helped propel maverick Paul Wellstone to his 1990 upset Senate win, made the most of his modest budget. His first TV ad showed two prepubescent boys playing with action figures—one was Jesse Ventura in a suit and the other was "Evil Special Interest Man." The announcer spoofed children's Saturday morning toy commercials. "New, from the Reform Party, it's the Jesse Ventura action figure! You can make Jesse Ventura battle special interest groups!" One of the boys tells the special interest doll, "I don't want your stupid money." Special Interest Man responds, "We politicians have powers the average person can't comprehend." Jesse Ventura will lower taxes and improve public education, the announcer intoned, con-cluding, "Don't waste your vote on politics as usual." (The ad was a hit, and campaign contributions starting pouring in at the rate of $10,000 a day after it started running.)[21] On the radio, Hillsman reinforced the same themes, interposing Ventura's growling "I'm no career politician," with music from the theme of the movie *Shaft*.[22]

Replayed on news programs, these quirky commercials got a lot of free attention, especially against the backdrop of the more conventional advertising deployed by Humphrey and Coleman.[23] Humphrey's TV ads had all the visual clichés familiar from years of political campaigns: the candidate in shirtsleeves, sitting blandly in a playground while declaring his toughness on crime; the candidate reading to school-children and holding a basketball as the narrator emphasizes his efforts to improve education. One of Coleman's ads tried to give him a "Rocky"-like appeal, showing him triumphantly walking the floor of the Republican convention. Another attacked Humphrey for voting to raise Minnesotans' taxes, promising that Coleman was "the only one" of the three candidates who would deliver lower taxes.

Two weeks before the election, public polls showed that Ventura was a viable can-didate. He had produced a strong message focused on cutting taxes, improving public education, and putting the elites in their place; and he had raised enough money to put that message on television and radio. Additionally, hundreds, if not thousands, of grass-roots volunteers were cheaply knitted together via the Internet. These were all crucial factors in building the Ventura victory. But the final, and most unsung, piece of the puzzle was voter targeting. Ventura's broad-based support—including youthful and blue-collar voters, unlikely voters (who might better be called discouraged voters), and huge numbers of suburbanites—cannot be explained entirely by his message, his money, and his volunteers. In Ed Gross, a veteran of both victorious Wellstone cam-paigns as well as those of numerous other populist-style Democrats, the Ventura campaign had access to the kind of sophisticated voter research and analysis common to top-flight political efforts but rare in third-party bids.

"We had no chance of winning without Ed," Hillsman later told me.[24] "I was extrapolating counties where Perot had high votes in 1992 plus where Doug Johnson, my populist candidate, did well in the '98 DFL primary." Buoyed by Hillsman's quirky ads, Johnson—the least well-known candidate in the Democratic gubernatorial field, had gone from 5 to 19 percent of the vote precisely by galvanizing many unlikely voters. Of the Ventura campaign, Hillsman said, "I just didn't see how we could win. I thought Jesse would top out at 29 to 31 percent. But I had a gut feeling that something was going on. I knew he had a chance if he could pull off Republican votes from Coleman, but that was my blind spot. Finding independents and populist Democrats I knew from my past work, but that wasn't enough."

"Hillsman called me four weeks out," Gross recalled.[25] "We weren't sure Jesse could win. So let's go after Coleman, we thought. If we could keep Coleman under 35 [percent], easily Skip [Humphrey] could run 35 and win. Ventura was putting together a middle coalition, drawing from both the Democratic and Republican bases. Democrats were coming his way, but no one had done a study of who would make up the Republican piece. My modeling, which involves studying election results overlaid over time with demographics, showed us where they were. And once I started looking at the numbers, I realized that with Humphrey running such a poor campaign, we could win."

The Coleman campaign had realized this, too. Brian Sweeney, a consultant who worked on the Coleman campaign, recalled that eight days before the election, his candidate's tracking polls showed the Republican leading Humphrey for the first time as support for the Democrat rapidly eroded. Two days later, Sweeney said, "the numbers were holding, with one nuance. Jesse now had surpassed Skip. Skip could finish third, we mused. It was on this Wednesday, just six days from the election, that I made a late-night call to Chris Georgacas, Coleman's manager. There is only one dynamic, I said, that could stop our victory: If people realize how close Jesse is, they just might—like Curly, Moe, and Larry—put two fingers into the collective eyes of the two parties and say, why not?"[26]

Both major candidates, Sweeney noted, had at this point retooled their advertising to counteract their fear that Ventura had become, to voters, a plausible choice—not just a spoiler or a protest vote but a serious leader who would deliver on their main concerns, taxes and education. "'Norm Coleman: The Only One' was appearing against 'Only Humphrey.' If Jesse had a chance, we were both perfect foils for his campaign. But Jesse didn't have a chance. Still, this reminded me of several multicandidate primaries in which I'd been involved. The two leading candidates beat each other up, and the well-liked third candidate ran up the middle and won."

The final dynamics of Ventura's upset were a little more complicated than that. As reconstructed by conversations with Barkley, Hillsman, Gross, Friedline, and Madsen—the campaign's core staff—there were actually four overlapping constituencies they targeted in the last days before the election: women, moderate Republicans, blue-collar suburbanites, and alienated people in their 20s and 30s.

"If Jesse does extremely well, we will have to have a lot of women voting for him," Hillsman told me ten days before the election. "They don't really like the Republican agenda and Coleman cozying up to the right, plus they're really confused by Clinton—they like what he's doing, but they don't like the creature very much. Liberal women are especially in a quandary. If Skip continues to hold his dominance among women it will be almost impossible for anybody else to win this thing. Otherwise, either of the other candidates could win." At the time, Hillsman was worried that Ventura's comments about prostitution, taken out of context to make it sound as though he favored its legalization, would really hurt him. But it turned out that Hillsman's last television ad, designed to reaffirm Ventura's bona fides, saved the day.

Titled "The Mind," the ad quickly became known as the "Rodin ad" for its portrayal of a very buff and seemingly nude Ventura, seated still as a statue on a pedestal in the pose of Rodin's sculpture "The Thinker." As violins played and a woman's voice sang, the camera circled Ventura, cutting to different angles of his muscular physique[27] while the voice-over summed up his attributes: "Navy Seal, union member, volunteer high school football coach, outdoorsman, husband twenty-three years, father of two. A man who will fight to return Minnesota's budget surplus to the taxpayers, who will fight to lower income and property taxes, who doesn't accept money from special interest groups, who will fight to lower public school class sizes." After a final wide-angle shot from a distance, the camera zoomed in on Ventura's rugged face. And he winked.

"This was the last major decision that we had to make," Barkley wrote in his diary of the campaign. "We needed a closing ad that would show the voters the warm, real family man that Jesse was. We had to reach the women voters that had not yet warmed up to Jesse. We were worried that the ad might offend the very people that we were trying to attract. I spent two days showing the ad to my friends and neighbors in the suburbs. The ad was enthusiastically received by everyone who saw it." In fact, Barkley told me later, each time he screened the ad, all the women in the room insisted on seeing it again!

To attract moderate Republican voters and keep Norm Coleman's total vote down, the campaign took several steps. One was to run radio ads asserting that Abraham Lincoln was a third-party candidate and to rebut the feeling that a vote for Ventura might be a wasted vote—or worse, the equivalent of a vote for Humphrey. A lot of emphasis went to targeting voters in the First and Second congressional districts in the rural southern part of the state, which had elected conservative Democrats as well as moderate Republicans to Congress. And to counteract Coleman's efforts to get close to

Ventura and thus peel off his voters—at all the debates Coleman's refrain was "Jesse's right about that"—the Ventura campaign took out an unusual full-page ad in the *Star-Tribune* and a lot of local newspapers contrasting Ventura with Coleman head-to-head. (Without the benefit of internal polling, they knew that Coleman was the last obstacle to victory and didn't even bother running a second ad comparing Ventura to Humphrey.) "Norm Coleman: Democrat, Republican? All of the above," the text read, reminding readers of Coleman's recent and opportunistic switch from the DFL to the Republicans. "Jesse Ventura: Democrat, Republican? None of the above." "Coleman: Used to work for Skip. [Coleman was an aide to Humphrey before he switched parties to run for mayor of St. Paul.] Ventura: Takes votes away from Skip." The ad also noted their differing positions on abortion rights.

In addition, in what was also a move to reach blue-collar suburbanites, the campaign put all its resources into a final seventy-two-hour "Drive to Victory" tour through the bedroom communities ringing the Twin Cities. It rented an RV for Ventura to travel in, posted the itinerary on the campaign's website (they didn't have, or need, an advance team), and sent regular updates and photos of the tour to the site for people to follow as they traveled. A sampling of the stops they made gives the flavor of the crowds they were after: sports bars like Champs in St. Paul and the New Brighton Eagles Club; the TC West Auto/Truck Stop in Rogers and the Albert Lea Trails Truck Stop; the Anoka Burger King on Main Street and the River Hills Mall food court in Mankato, both centers of what the campaign called the "Independent Belt"; the shift change at the MinnTac mine in East Hibbing, a Democratic stronghold; a final rally in a ballroom in Medina, a Republican stronghold.

Meanwhile, on the airwaves, the campaign was doing its best to target disaffected and younger voters. On one radio ad, Ventura told what he believed: "I believe in returning the entire $4 billion surplus to the hardworking people who paid it in. I believe Led Zeppelin and the Rolling Stones are two of the greatest rock bands." Instead of concentrating its commercials during TV news programs, which presumably reach more likely voters, Ventura's ads were running during programs like the *X-Files*, *The Simpsons*, and *Cops*. Said Bill Hillsman, "we skewed our buy slightly to reach those independent/skeptical voters with the Fox media buy." He also bought ad time on cable channels like CNN and Lifetime, as well as some country stations. And yes, he did not neglect Ventura's wrestling fans, placing some ads on World Wrestling Federation programs on TNT.

A Political Earthquake

The stage was set for Ventura's victory. And yet, many of the state's leading political observers and opinion shapers had no idea what was coming. In September, Wy Spano, the publisher and coeditor of the newsletter "Politics in Minnesota," had predicted Humphrey would win "because he was most like an incumbent."[28] Days before the vote, the editors of the MN-Politics website, David Erickson and Blois Olson, wrote that "the only way for Jesse to win is if Skip and/or Norm alienate the electorate in the final days of the campaign, allowing him to squeak through the middle. Is this likely? No."[29] Political scientist Steven Schier of Carleton College, a frequent commentator on Minnesota politics in the national media, told *USA Today*, "The Reform Party has very limited prospects. It's at best a vehicle for interesting personalities."[30]

The editorials in the *Star-Tribune* were indicative of elite attitudes toward the untested, third-party contender. One published the Friday before the vote had the condescending title, "It's Been Fun, but the Election's Near." Scolding voters for not taking the election seriously enough, for indulging in their "enduring appetite for the political sideshow, for campaigns as entertainment," the editors tried to shame the public into behaving. Much of Ventura's support, they claimed, "is simply the appeal of a candidate who campaigns in warmup clothes, sprays crowds with one-liners and dismisses tough questions as irrelevant." "Of course, it's fun to tell friends and neighbors—or pollsters, especially pollsters—you're voting for Ventura," they concluded. "It's another matter to explain, in a sentence or two, why he'd actually make a better governor than either of his opponents."[31]

Both parties also brought in their big guns to help their beleaguered standard-bearers. Former vice president and U.S. senator Walter Mondale stumped for fellow Minnesotan Humphrey, as did Vice President Al Gore. Bob Dole and Jack Kemp, the 1996 Republican nominees for the White House, flew in to help Coleman. Even First Lady Hillary Rodham Clinton came in on the final weekend, and, echoing the *Star-Tribune*'s "It's Been Fun" editorial, called Ventura's campaign a "circus sideshow act."[32]

Voters paid no attention to the sermons from on high. A political earthquake was under way. In Anoka County, a blue-collar suburban area that was the epicenter, the county commission got a thousand phone calls the day before the election from new voters asking how to register to vote.[33] (Minnesota allows voters to register as late as Election Day.) The night before the election, ACORN, a hardworking grass-roots group that focuses on organizing people of low and moderate incomes, actually shut down its get-out-the-vote phone operation in the Twin Cities when it became apparent that most of the people it was reaching were planning to vote for Ventura instead of Humphrey, the Democrat.[34] "I could tell going into the election," said Doug Williams, head of an electrical workers union. "I was getting requests for information on him from my members. People were wearing his T-shirts and bumper stickers—people who hadn't really participated before."[35]

Al Garcia, a criminal defense lawyer and twenty-year veteran of numerous DFL races, was up in Anoka County managing the campaigns of two candidates for the state House. "I could sense it coming," he recalled. My wife told me early on that she would support him, and she hates politics. And all my legal clients were supporting Jesse, from the first-time DWI offenders to the major dope dealers! And he was pulling at me, in my gut. I'm a blue-collar guy who grew up in north Minneapolis. My dad's a dockworker, my mother's a waitress. Like the folks in Anoka. And he was saying things that average people could connect with."

The polls opened at 7:00 A.M. "At 7:45 in the morning on Election Day," Garcia said, "I'm number 250 at my polling place in Coon Rapids [a city in Anoka County]. Six people were registering to vote, and they had already registered eighty people. At 8:00 P.M. you had lines of people waiting to vote. When the first Coon Rapids numbers came in, I got a chill. Humphrey 120, Coleman 35, Ventura 340. The election was over."[36] Donna Handel, a church secretary who worked as an election judge in Coon Rapids, said the experience that day "was staggering." At least twelve hundred people voted at her site, and perhaps three hundred were new registrants. "I've lived here thirty-seven years, and I didn't know half of them. Some were people that my kids had grown up with. Others were new people who had moved into new homes. And others were from the old part of the precinct. You could just feel the energy."[37]

The day after the election, even Ventura, who had boasted that he would win, was at an uncharacteristic loss for words when asked to explain his stunning triumph. "Ask *them*," he told reporters, meaning the voters.[38] Looking at the voters is a good place to start. Ventura won with 37 percent of the vote; Coleman drew 34 percent, and Humphrey 29 percent. But the day before the election, the *Star-Tribune*/KMSP-TV Minnesota Poll showed him tied with Humphrey at 29 percent each, with Coleman leading at 36 percent. What happened?

A huge surge of new voters, many of them newly enthusiastic young people, showed up at the polls. Turnout exploded. According to state election officials, it was as if a presidential election was taking place. Typically, about 53 percent of eligible voters come out for a midterm election in Minnesota, but that Tuesday's turnout was just over 60 percent, head and shoulders in front of the rest of the country, where the overall average slumped to barely 36 percent. Twenty-eight percent of the people who voted for Ventura said they wouldn't have voted had he not been on the ballot, according to exit polls. Of the 15 percent of the voters who registered on Election Day, 78 percent voted for Ventura. And it was the mobilization of these "unlikely voters" that made all the difference.

None of the state's four major polling organizations predicted Ventura's victory because they all factored out these voters.[39] Underlying this error is a deadly assumption about the habits of American voters: that they're apathetic and predictable and easily manipulated. None of the experts bothered to imagine such a huge surge and shift in voting patterns because, in a way, they have been lulled by the stifling effects of the two-party duopoly into thinking that ordinary people couldn't possibly retain their own reserves of independent political energy. But in fact, alongside voter cynicism and abysmal turnout habits, there is a deep desire for greater self-rule. Whatever else we may learn from Ventura's victory, his election shows more clearly than any other event in recent American history that the people want more democracy.

The shape of Ventura's vote was as important as its size. He did well with all the age groups except those over sixty, and won a whopping 46 percent of the eighteen- to twenty-nine-year-olds. (Everywhere else in the country, people under forty-four made up just 40 percent of the electorate; in Minnesota they were 51 percent.) He won strong pluralities from all the income groups except those making more than $100,000. Women were almost equally likely to vote for him as men. About the only group he did poorly with were people with postgraduate degrees, who, along with the elderly, strongly supported Humphrey, the only blocs to do so.

It is also telling that Ventura's vote, rooted in a majority of ballots cast by political independents, drew more from the left than the right. He won a full one-third of Democrats voting, compared to 28 percent of the Republicans. And he got 44 percent of self-identified liberals, compared to 29 percent of conservatives. In the end Coleman held on to more of his conservative base, mainly by bashing gay rights and stressing on his pro-life position, while Humphrey experienced a near total meltdown in the face of Ventura's working-class populism.[40]

The major party candidates had no idea what hit them. On Election Night, as local reports showed Ventura in the lead with half the votes counted, Humphrey told people at his nonvictory party, "We're just coming around the corners. I think they're going to be showing a Humphrey victory." Across town, Coleman was telling his supporters to "keep the faith."[41] A day later, Dane Smith, the *Star-Tribune*'s chief political reporter, said that local Democrats and Republicans had gone into hiding. "We can't find any of them today," he told NPR's *All Things Considered*. "They're not answering their phones."

Ed Gross said the secret of his candidate's success was rooted in class and message. "The voters saw Jesse as someone who's an outsider who's going to change things. Watching the TV debates, they saw two 'suits' and one nonsuit—and most of them don't wear suits. Not only that, one of the 'suits' had worked for the other, and they both were owned by big money." Gross recognized the dynamic from the 1990 and 1996 Wellstone campaigns for Senate. "I told Ventura: in a lot of ways, to the voters, you are a Wellstone. And voters went for Wellstone because they want to have a connection. They've felt disconnected for a long time. They want to feel like the guy up there knows how they live."

Blue-collar, working-class voters, Gross added, were critical to Ventura's coalition of political independents, disaffected Democrats, and moderate Republicans. "People want to be represented, not just the money interests," he said. "People who make less than $40,000 a year, working hard to fulfill their dreams." As one writer summed up their rebellious mood, drenched in the wild scene of slam-dancing and beer cups held high at Ventura's victory party: "It was the cultural elites' worst nightmare. . . . These people did not realize that it was the job of beer drinkers to elect wine-drinkers, who then work with scotch-drinking lobbyists."[42]

The geography of Ventura's vote is illustrative. "In the high-income professional suburbs, Jesse did poorly," said Myron Orfield, a Democratic member of the Minnesota House and an expert on political demography and regional planning. "In the less affluent suburbs, which are full of households making less than $50,000 a year, often on two jobs or more, he did very well." For instance, in House District 50A, in the northernmost exurbs of Anoka County, Ventura got 58 percent of the vote. In contrast, one of his poorest showings was in District 42A, in affluent Edina, where he finished third and got just 22 percent of the vote. Orfield continued, "He also won northeast Minneapolis, which is blue-collar land. And he did better in poor parts of the city than he did in the yuppie areas. The only place where the Democrats held their base was in the Iron Range, where he wasn't that strong."[43]

Even more stunning, in a half-dozen suburban counties ringing Minneapolis–St. Paul to the north and west, Ventura won an absolute majority of the vote. All six of these counties—Anoka, Chisago, Isanti, McLeod, Sherburne, and Wright—voted for Bill Clinton over Bob Dole in 1996. They are full of politically independent swing voters coveted by both major parties. Indeed, Paul Wellstone spent a great deal of time in these counties during his 1996 reelection campaign. In each one, Ventura actually got more votes than Clinton. The "Drive to Victory," which was focused on these very counties, paid off.

Why? Why, for instance, did Ventura get 64,100 votes in Anoka County, compared to 37,111 for Coleman and 24,975 for Humphrey? Dean Barkley said it was because the county is full of Ventura's target group: "younger married couples, both working, with a moderate income." More important, it's full of people who "don't think that the other parties represent their interests anymore. They see the Republicans as being for wealthy Republican suburbanites, and the Democrats for inner-city dwellers who want what the rich have." The critical fact about these disaffected voters, Barkley said, is that "nobody cares about them. They think that all they hear from politicians is talk, while nothing ever changes. Taxes keep going up, and meanwhile they're wondering how they're going to retire or pay for college."[44]

"It's a changing county," said Dave Mann, then the co-director of the Minnesota Alliance for Progressive Action. "It's got a lot of working families who are comfortable but not far from being uncomfortable."[45] While Minnesota doesn't formally register voters into parties, internal party surveys show Anoka with a high percentage of independents, more than the state average of one-third, he added. "There's a lot of fluctuation of turnout there, but they come out for the big ones." "Don't forget, this is Jesse's home turf," said Mike Kaszuba, a reporter for the *Star-Tribune* who has long covered the Twin Cities suburbs. "And the northern suburbs are a lot different from the south and west. There you'll find Jeep Cherokees, big malls, fancy restaurants. In the north it's more pickup trucks, beer stores instead of wine stores."[46]

Two days after his inauguration, I interviewed Governor Ventura in his new office at the state Capitol and asked him if he knew why he had done so well in the blue-collar suburbs. "I don't know, I don't know," he repeated. "All we did was go off of past numbers"—places where third-party candidates Ross Perot and Dean Barkley had done well in previous campaigns—"and said these are counties we can take and take strongly." Ventura's honest answer—and his insistence that as the state's top executive he now had to govern "for all of Minnesota"—suggested that he might not understand the full nature of his appeal, or that with his libertarian, entrepreneurial leanings, he might not feel comfortable with the implications of leading a working-class movement.[47]

On the other hand, one hint of a more shrewd sense of politics came from Dean Barkley, now installed by Ventura as the director of the Minnesota Planning Agency. I visited with him in the basement of the state Capitol, where the Ventura transition team had its offices. The past weeks had been a blur of planning their state budget proposal, screening job applicants, and picking top appointees. "When you see our tax plan and you see where we are targeting who gets the rebates, you'll see that we know where we come from," Barkley said, his feet on his desk with the confident air of someone in the catbird seat. "Jesse just said to me, 'I'm representing the middle class working guy who's just surviving and no one's lookin' out for them.'"[48]

Still, when we spoke, Ventura seemed far more at ease casting himself as the guardian of the hopes of a new generation than a working-class hero. In his inaugural remarks, he also talked a lot about young people. In the name of "these new young people, this generation that came on board, and yes, might well have elected me," he called on the state's politicians to "put down the partisan party politics and look at the bigger picture. . . . We cannot fail, we must not fail, because if we do, we could lose this generation, and we dare not let that happen."[49]

The Politics of Rising Expectations

By opening up the closed two-party political system and forcing fresh air into stale debates, third-party victories like Ventura's can dramatically change the public mood and its expectations about politics. In his book *Indispensable Enemies, The Politics of Misrule in America*, political essayist Walter Karp described how easily this process can unfold. He wrote:

There is in this Republic one great wellspring animating citizens to act in their own behalf: their own understanding that by means of politics and government what is wrong can be righted and what is ill can be cured. In a word, political hope.

The very opposite condition, the condition safest for party power, is public apathy, gratitude for small favors and a deep general sense of the futility of politics. Yet there is nothing natural about political apathy, futility and mean gratitude. What lies behind them is not "human nature" but the citizens' belief that politics and government can do little to better the conditions of life; the belief that they are ruled not by the men whom they have entrusted with their power but by circumstances and historical "forces," by anything and everything that is out of human control; the belief that public abuses and inequities are somehow inevitable and must be endured because they cannot be cured.

The condition of public apathy and futility, however, is swiftly undone by reform and even by the convincing promise of reform. Every beneficial law reminds the citizenry anew that the government—which is their government—can help them remove evils and better the conditions of life. Every law which remedies an abuse reminds the citizenry that other abuses can be remedied as well. Every beneficial law rips the cover of inevitability from public inequities and rouses the people from apathy. Reform in America does not bring passive contentment to the citizenry. It inspires active hope.[50]

To sense that hope renewed among ordinary people is a wonderful feeling. Plenty of it was in air the day of Ventura's inauguration, when hundreds of average Minnesotans came to the state Capitol's rotunda to witness Ventura's swearing-in, many of them waiting hours in the subzero cold for a chance to meet the new governor and shake his hand. There was a bus driver from the east side of St. Paul, a twenty-nine-year-old single father who was raising his kid on his own, who said he was excited about the Reform Party because "we need something new." There was a middle-aged car dealer in a sweatshirt who voted for Jesse because "he's real people." A seventeen-year-old in a leather jacket with his cap down over his eyes, who said he had attended Champlain High School, where Ventura was a volunteer football coach, shyly admitted that it was pretty unusual for someone his age to come to the state Capitol but he wanted to be there to help the governor. Scott Jameson, a scruffy-looking thirty-three-year-old from Ventura's old stomping grounds in Brooklyn Park, said he believed the election would "give state government back to the people—giving us more input in decision making." A forty-ish woman who said she voted for Humphrey took the day off from work to stand in the receiving line. She praised Ventura for "the fact that he challenged all of us to be more civic minded." There were lots of families with young children in tow. People were dressed as if they were going to a hockey game, not an inauguration.

The next day, when I offhandedly told a middle-aged shuttle van driver at my hotel that I was headed up to Anoka County to find out why so many people there voted for Ventura, he leapt to respond. "You should ask me—I voted for him! If you had a choice between a guy who kept his childhood nickname, Skip, a turncoat who switched parties from Democrat to Republican [Coleman], and someone who spoke honestly, who would you pick? My sixteen-year-old son is proud of my vote." I asked him what he expected from Ventura, and he responded in terms of his hopes of ending his alienation from politics, not the substance of governing. "I don't know what he'll do. But he's going to tell all those Bible thumpers on the right and the tree huggers on the left to vote for their own, and he'll unite all the disaffected voters in the middle in a new party. I'm a lifetime DFL-er, from the 'L', but I'm sick of union heads who negotiate contracts that sell out the workers, and I've had it with these professional politicians. We don't have workers running for office anymore, just people who never worked a real forty-hour week in their lives."

The Reverend Jerry O'Neill, pastor of a working-class Lutheran church in Anoka, told me over coffee and blueberry cream-cheese muffins that he thought Ventura had reached deep into the working class, past the "winners with good jobs" and the "respectables who may not have good jobs but compensate by seeking respect in their community and church," touching the "survivors who just get by and the hard-living, rootless folks who have completely given up on trying to be successful or live by conventional norms." O'Neill observed that this was a tough community to minister to— "we in the clergy aspire to a middle-class, white-collar mentality, and when I came here 15 years ago I had to prove to my congregation that I wasn't uppity." He criticized politicians for "not relating to and serving with working-class people."

O'Neill directed me to a book that had influenced his thinking: *Blue-Collar Ministry: Facing Economic and Social Realities of Working People*, by Tex Sample, a pastor and theology professor. In it, Sample analyzed what it is like for ordinary people to grow up in a country where individual freedom and equality of opportunity is assumed and winning is everything.[51] Of course, there is no such thing as equality at the starting gate of life. While some working-class people manage to succeed (the "winners") and others maintain their self-respect by holding fast to the values of family and flag, church and community, for many the experience of losing shapes their worldview. To these, the survivors and dropouts from mainstream society, voting and participating in politics are seen as pointless exercises in a rigged game that takes place far from their lives.

"I think Jesse Ventura stirred up the hard-living people and the survivors," O'Neill said, "rekindling their faith in the American dream and giving them a new sense of empowerment. He showed them what it means to work at yourself." In Sample's terminology, Ventura was a blue-collar aristocrat, a prince of the working class who had won the rat race using his body and his street learning, not book learning. Ventura had not renounced his roots. He flaunted them, wearing his track suit to a candidates' debate on the way to his regular gig coaching a high school football team. "It's not an appeal to abstract principles or programs as much as down-to-earth issues, which leaves all sorts of questions," O'Neill added. "And I love his response: 'What harm can I do in four years?' It's almost as if he's done it already, and now he can enjoy the ride. That's got me a little worried since we want to know what his agenda will be. But freeing people to believe that the political system can work is great. And I think he'll force the political system to address the needs of working people."

Ventura's victory was also embraced by such unlikely bedfellows as then-Republican columnist Arianna Huffington and progressive Democratic senator Paul Wellstone. "What if we suddenly started seeing others, inspired by the new governor, seeking political office without submitting to the strictures of either party?" Huffington wrote in her syndicated column. "What if candidates, instead of weighing whether to please the unions or the new Democrats, James Dobson or the Log Cabin Republicans, just decided to play outside the parties' box?"[52] "Many voters yearn for populist voices, and they're willing to look outside the box to find them," Wellstone wrote in an op-ed piece after the election. "While [Ventura] won by capturing only 37 percent of all votes cast—hardly an electoral mandate—it is significant that his campaign captured the imagination of many voters with energy, humor, and a strong populist, antiestablishment message that drew heavily on themes of political reform."[53]

In the early weeks after his election, amid a deluge of media attention, Ventura continued to signal that he would be not be a conventional officeholder. For example, appearing on the CNN program *Late Edition with Wolf Blitzer* to discuss the Clinton impeachment, he laughed out loud as former New York governor Mario Cuomo, another guest on the show, insisted that "there is no proof that President Clinton lied before the grand jury." When he got a chance to comment, he said, "I hope Governor Cuomo is listening. [President Clinton] lied to his wife; he lied to his family; and he lied to the American people. And that is undeniable. Whether the grand jury he lied to or not, fine, you can bicker over that, but guess what? Keep this up and you're going to see a lot more Jesse Venturas elected throughout the country because I can see that happening very quickly."[54]

Ventura's victory shows that, under the right conditions, a third-party candidate for high office can build a winning electoral coalition. Ventura's base was grounded in the mythical center of American politics and drew on suburban Republicans and working-class Democrats alike, along with a powerful number of new, youthful voters. But the key was his message, which was socially liberal or libertarian, fiscally conservative, antiestablishment, pro–campaign finance reform, and working class.

Ventura is all of these. So are the majority of Americans. Most Americans support choice, the separation of church and state, and better public schools. They think that what goes on in the bedroom is no one else's business, and they even favor the medical use of marijuana. They want lower taxes and fewer of their tax dollars wasted on corporate welfare. A majority believe that special interests have more influence over elected officials than do their real constituents, and super-majorities favor far-reaching changes in the campaign finance system. And despite the prevailing myth, more Americans define themselves as working class than middle class.[55] When Minnesotans saw three candidates on stage—two in business suits talking like politicians and one in jeans talking in plain English—they connected with the one who was most like them in style and philosophy.

But having a strong message isn't sufficient; the public has to be able to hear the person delivering it. To reiterate, it helps to have some name recognition among voters from the start. Second, it is essential to be included in widely televised debates with the other major candidates. And third, no matter how many volunteers pitch in, the candidate needs money to get his message onto television. Minnesota has a fairly progressive campaign finance law that gives individual voters refunds for small contributions to candidates, and even third parties can get some public financing. Ventura's campaign chairman Dean Barkley said, "Without the $325,000 in public financing that we got two weeks before the election, we couldn't have won."[56]

Such a campaign can rally an electoral coalition lethal to the Democratic and Republican parties.

2

The Moment
Is Ripe

Cracks in the Facade?

Jesse Ventura's victory had an unsettling effect on conventional politics. By the summer of 1999, a year before the political conventions that would select the Democratic and Republican nominees for president, the mainstream media were busily speculating about the chances of a third-party candidate entering the race. Lowell Weicker, former independent governor of Connecticut and three-term Republican senator, appeared on CNN's *Crossfire* and talked about the possibility of seeking the Reform Party's nomination.[1] Patrick Buchanan went on *Inside Politics* to deny rumors that he was thinking of the same option, but as fellow Republican George W. Bush outdistanced the rest of the GOP field in fund-raising, expectations continued to rise that Buchanan would run as a third-party candidate.[2] Speculation about the third-party gambit was so intense, two hundred reporters traveled in mid-July to Dearborn, Michigan, to cover the Reform Party's midterm convention, a ratio of one journalist for every two delegates.

While much of the attention was on the avowedly "centrist" Reform Party and the chances that Ventura would run for president, splinters also started to appear on the right and the left of the major parties. That summer, Republican Senator Bob Smith of New Hampshire quit the GOP and dallied with a presidential candidacy with the antiabortion U.S. Taxpayers Party. Veteran consumer advocate Ralph Nader let it be known that he would probably try to run again as the Green Party's candidate. And film actor Warren Beatty, a longtime liberal activist, toyed publicly with throwing his hat in the ring either as a Democrat or as a maverick independent.[3]

Some of this speculation was of course just the press looking for something to write about during a slow period in the presidential news cycle. Self-promoters quickly smelled an opportunity for free publicity, and soon people like real-estate developer Donald Trump and actress Cybil Shepherd were advertising their supposed interest in a presidential bid. In a matter of weeks the press was even puncturing its own bubble, publishing surveys showing that actress Heather Locklear—who was definitely not a candidate—could get as many votes as Trump and not that many fewer than Buchanan.[4] But all this speculation was based on a real fact: Forty-six percent of those surveyed during those summer doldrums said they would want a third-party choice on the ballot in 2000 if the only choices were George W. Bush and Al Gore.[5]

Such outbreaks of third-party speculation have become increasingly common, happening on an almost cyclical basis with every national election. In the fall of 1995, retired General Colin Powell was showered with media attention as the bigfoots of the national press fed rumors that he was considering a run for the presidency, possibly as an independent. Indeed, the same thing may well happen again in 2003, a year before the next presidential election, especially if the likely major candidates are again Bush and Gore. Picture an independent candidacy by someone like John McCain, decrying both major parties for having undermined America's national security and its economic health because they were too enthralled to weathly special interests.

These eruptions are not random events, but reminders of deep turbulence in the American electorate. Patriotic surges notwithstanding, the Democratic and Republican parties are not as solid or dominant as they seem. Their ties to average voters through local political clubs and chapters have almost entirely disappeared, replaced by thirty-second TV ads driven by political consultants and expensive market research. Local patronage systems and ethnoreligious loyalties still produce a habitual partisan reflex on Election Day on the part of many voters, but much current voter identification with either major party seems based more on dislike for the perceived flaws of the other party than in any positive feeling for their own. That, plus the weakness of the Democrats' and Republicans' current leaders, their inability to articulate a clear philosophy or govern effectively, their penchant for petty feuds and negative campaigning, and their common subservience to special interest campaign contributors, have all produced a pervasive sense of disenchantment and disgust on the part of many citizens, coupled with a yearning for authentic democratic representation and strong, honest leadership.

As a result, several times in the last decade, large numbers of voters have stepped out of the box called "two-party politics" in search of an alternative. This phenomenon first surfaced with the anti-incumbent term limits movement, and the election of independents like Vermont's Bernie Sanders to Congress and Connecticut's Lowell Weicker to the governor's office in 1990. Then came Perot's independent campaign for president in

1992, which drew a stunning 19 percent of the vote. More harbingers followed, including the election of independent Angus King to the governor's office in Maine in 1994 and showings in the double digits for Green Party congressional candidates in two districts in New Mexico in 1997 and early 1998 that effectively spoiled the chances of Democratic candidates in both races. Jesse Ventura's election to the Minnesota governor's office in November 1998, more than anything else, made the impossible seem possible.

But is the impossible really possible? The idea of a new, major political party competing with the Democrats and Republicans is supported by somewhere between half to two-thirds of the public, according to recent polls.[6] This public sentiment in favor of more choices makes sense, not only as a way to force new issues into the mainstream debate but as a means of holding the major parties accountable.

Today's third parties and independent candidates also seem to be appealing to something deeper—the simple and understandable desire for something new and different in American politics. After all, it seems as if both major parties have been around forever. Partisan posturing and gridlock are the norm, while in the back rooms fund-raising and influence peddling have become the real business of most elected officials. Meanwhile, pressing national concerns are never addressed except maybe during a crisis. To borrow an image from advertising—a field all too intimate with today's mainstream politics— the Democratic and Republican "brands" are becoming stale. More Americans are ready to party with someone new—if that person and his or her party seem credible.

But that doesn't mean it will be easy. In the last ten years, in addition to Jesse Ventura of the Reform Party, third parties like the Greens, the Libertarians, and the New Party have elected several hundred members to numerous nonpartisan lower offices such as city council, county commission, and school board. Of the ninety thousand or so elective offices in this country, approximately 70 percent are officially nonpartisan, which means no party label appears on the ballot. Such races, which are more prevalent west of the Mississippi, are somewhat more hospitable to third parties. They can organize themselves around a particular candidate (as the major parties often still do), but since the barrier to getting on the ballot is lower, there are usually many more than two candidates running. Thus these races can be won with a fairly low percentage of the vote, assuming no runoff is required. The issue of "spoiling" is also muted when there are no party labels on the ballot.

On the other hand, the number of third-party candidates who have won partisan elections and currently hold offices such as state representative or county commissioner can be counted on two hands.[7] One genuine independent, Bernie Sanders, is still representing Vermont in Congress, and Angus King remains governor of Maine. Weicker's term as governor of Connecticut and Walter Hickel's term as governor of Alaska both ended in 1994. Third parties have a long way to go.

Understanding the prospects of today's third parties requires knowing which voters might be most tempted to leave the two-party box, what messages might reach them, and how one organizes a new party in the current political environment.

A Word of Caution

Over the last ten years, I have met and interviewed many third-party activists. Some, like Steve Schmidt of the New Mexico Green Party, have traveled fairly straightforward journeys from the liberal-left wing of the Democratic Party out to the further left of the Greens. Before becoming a Green in 1994, Schmidt worked for Democratic presidential candidates Michael Dukakis in 1988 and Jerry Brown in 1992. As a co-drafter of Brown's "Take Back America" platform, Schmidt accompanied Brown to the Democratic platform hearings, and it is there that he experienced his personal epiphany. "There I had Ron Brown [then the Democratic national chairman] tell me 'get lost,' that what we were urging was not in the cards, that increased fund-raising was, there would be no "unilateral disarmament" and so on," he recalled. "There are a lot of stories here but the bottom line is that the Democratic leadership moved to get back the 'Reagan Democrats' and re-align itself with business interests."[8] Schmidt wanted no part of such a right-leaning Democratic Party, so he left.

Others, like Californian Char Roberts, have traveled a more complicated path. "I've been both a registered Democrat and a registered Republican (not at the same time!) and an unpredictable, independent voter," she told me several years ago, when she was busy hosting a website ("Charlotte's Web," one of the earliest activist sites, focused on trade and globalization issues) and working hard on behalf of Ross Perot's United We Stand America movement, which later became the Reform Party. "I was in college in the sixties—was on the staff of the U.C. Berkeley newspaper, the *Daily Cal*, moderately liberal, and I married the editor of the *Daily Cal* who was quite conservative, and we've been amending each other's politics ever since," she said. "One of our first efforts was to try to help elect a young black Republican to state assembly from Berkeley, something we thought would be a winning combination—but wasn't. I'm conservative fiscally and anti–Big Government, but also anti-Big Business, very pro-labor and pro–small-business."

Roberts's political education is a study in eclecticism. When I asked her age, she said, "I'm old enough to have been there when this was said at Sproul Hall, U.C. Berkeley":

> There's a time when the operation of the machine becomes so odious, makes you so sick at heart, that you can't take part—you can't even passively take part—and you've got to put your bodies upon the gears, and upon the wheel, upon the levels, upon all the apparatus, and you've got to make it stop, and you've got to indicate to the people who run it, to the people who own it, that unless you're free, the machine will be prevented from working at all!

After citing this speech by Mario Savio, the leader of the Berkeley Free Speech Movement and one of the early avatars of the rebellious 1960s, Roberts spoke admiringly of

Martín Gross, a prominent conservative writer who has called for a "velvet revolution" against Big Government. Later, she told me her politics had also been shaped by such progressive writers as William Greider, Ben Bagdikian, and Noam Chomsky, along with conservative Kevin Phillips and economic nationalist Pat Choate.[9]

San Franciscan David Wiesner is another independent activist whose politics has bounced all over the map. I got to know him after he conceived and led a powerful grass-roots effort in the mid-1990s, "Ban Bribery Now," calling Congress to pass legislation banning all gifts from lobbyists to legislators. Asked how he got involved in political activism, he said, "When I was 14, I became an anti-Vietnam activist. I campaigned for Eugene McCarthy before I could vote." But as far as how he would identify himself politically, he said, "Tough call. I registered Republican to vote against Nixon, but then I stayed that way. I voted all Democrat [in 1994] to punish the Republicans for filibustering lobbying reform. The best answer is that I am an independent."[10]

Encounters like these demonstrate that for many Americans, politics does not move in a straight line. Certainly many people are "hereditary voters," in that they identify with the party their parents belonged to. But they also swing all over the map, responding to events and charismatic individuals, changing their minds, and not worrying whether they've moved in a consistent direction from point A to point Z.

I say all of this as a preface to the rest of this chapter, which is the only place in this book where I will turn to survey research and public opinion polls rather than the real world of on-the-ground reporting and analysis. Public support for new political initiatives like third parties is not random. It comes from somewhere, or rather, it is concentrated in some parts of the electorate more than others. For that reason, we need to look at empirical data exploring voter attitudes toward politics. But, as the stories of people like Char Roberts and David Wiesner suggest, statistics inevitably miss the human element. People's political identities are not frozen in stone. They change over time, they change in intensity, and they change in response to specific appeals and events. A graph line cannot capture those nuances—if anything, straight lines on a chart tend to fool us into thinking that those wrinkles don't even exist. So take the rest of this chapter as a rough sketch of the big picture, but by no means the only way of seeing the full story.

Finding the Third-Party Voter

Surveys show that political alienation in America has risen steadily since the 1950s. Identification with both of the major parties is on the decline. Compared to Democrats and Republicans, political independents show twice the inclination to vote for third-party candidates. While nonvoting has risen, the few polls of nonvoters show that many, perhaps half, are abstaining because the major parties and their candidates fail to appeal to them. This suggests they might respond to new parties. All of these trends indicate that the market is ripe for more independent, alternative candidacies.

Third-party candidates attract votes when the major parties fail. "To be sure, third parties can help their own causes by selecting high caliber candidates or by building a loyal following over the years," write academics Steven Rosenstone, Roy Behr, and Edward Lazarus in their book, *Third Parties in America*. "But, overwhelmingly, it is the failure of the major parties to do what the electorate expects of them—reflect the issue preferences of voters, manage the economy, select attractive and acceptable candidates, and build voter loyalty to the parties and the political system—that most increases the likelihood of voters backing a minor party." [11]

Thus, the first indication of third-party potential is, ironically, Americans' declining trust in government and in their representatives in Washington—precisely because the executive and congressional branches have been controlled by the Democrats and Republicans for so long. For almost fifty years, political scientists at the University of Michigan have been asking a cross section of Americans about their attitudes toward the political system. Their responses, as compiled in the National Election Studies, reveal much about the rising tide of public alienation from politics and government as practiced by the two major parties. Most measures of public trust have been dropping since the 1950s,[12] but the decline has been most pronounced among certain social groups, particularly people with lower levels of education, income, and social status.[13] This suggests that although the major parties retain substantial support among some groups, third parties and independent candidates may do better among those Americans who feel the least faith in the current electoral system.

In general, between half and six-tenths of the population says there are important differences between the major parties. But here again, a socioeconomic breakdown is revealing. In 1998, about 46 percent of people in the bottom two-thirds of income distribution thought there was no difference between the parties. Much smaller percentages of people in the top brackets agreed with that sentiment. Similarly, 62 percent of those with minimal education (less than a high school diploma) and 51 percent of those with a high school diploma said there was no difference between the parties in 1998, compared to just over a third of those with at least some college education. Blue collar workers were almost twice more likely than professionals to agree with the assertion (55 to 31 percent).

The Rise of Independents

The decline in public trust in government and our elected representatives in Washington has been mirrored by an increase in those Americans identifying as political independents. The rise of the independent vote has not gone unnoticed by political professionals; independents are the most sought-after "swing voters" coveted by both parties. What few have noted is that independents are also far more likely to vote for third-party candidates.

According to the Committee for the Study of the American Electorate, in the twenty-four states (and the District of Columbia) in which voters formally register by party, the percentage of the eligible electorate enlisting as independents or with third parties reached approximately 13 percent in 1998, up from 8.3 percent in 1990, 3.5 percent in 1970, and 1.6 percent in 1962.[14] From 1990 to 1998, the proportion of voters registered as independents or third-party has increased approximately 57 percent, while the number of registered Republicans has decreased almost 5 percent and the Democrats almost 14 percent. Considering that many voters often keep their major party registration so as to have a voice in party primaries, these trends are quite significant. Many voters may also never bother to change their party registration, even when their voting habits have changed, making it likely that the registration figures cited above undercount the number of real independents in the electorate.

Voter statements of their political preference—a looser definition than party registration—show the same trend. The proportion of people identifying as independents went from 23 percent in 1952 to an average of 25 percent in the 1960s, 35 percent in the 1970s, 33 percent in the 1980s, and 35 percent in the 1990s, according to the National Election Studies.[15] A socioeconomic breakdown shows that these voters are somewhat more likely to be of lower income, education, and occupational status than party partisans, though the correlation is not as strong as that between socioeconomics and alienation from government. In fact, many hard-core partisans—most likely black Democrats—can be found in the lower income and education groups, the NES survey shows.

The trend toward independence seems most pronounced among new registrants and young voters. Anecdotal reports from state voter registration offices indicate a surge in people registering as independents as a result of the implementation of the 1993 National Voter Registration Act (known as "motor-voter" because it enables people to register at their motor vehicle offices as well as social service agencies), which has simplified and expanded registration procedures. In the first five months of the law's implementation in Iowa, for example, twenty-six thousand voters registered as independents, compared to seventy-two hundred Republicans and sixty-two hundred Democrats.[16] In the first month of motor-voter in Kentucky, 37 percent registered as Democrats, 30 percent as Republicans, and 33 percent as independent or minor party.[17] Two years after the motor-voter took effect in Florida, the number of registered Republicans, Democrats, and nonaffiliates/third-party registrants had each risen about half a million. Since 1996, however, the number of major party registrants declined slightly, while the number of non–major-party registrants rose an additional quarter of a million.[18]

Younger voters in general have weaker party allegiances than their elders. In all of the last four presidential elections with a major third-party candidate on the ballot (John Anderson in 1980, Ross Perot in 1992 and 1996, and Ralph Nader in 2000), voters under the age of thirty-five were far more likely to support that candidate than were their elders.[19] Jesse Ventura's 1998 win in Minnesota was driven by younger voters: forty-six percent of those between the ages of eighteen and twenty-nine voted for him, as did 43 percent of those between thirty and forty-four, compared with 37 percent overall.[20] A 1999 Gallup poll found that 41 percent of eighteen- to twenty-nine-year-olds identified themselves as independents, compared to 34 percent of people over the age of sixty-five.[21]

There are very good reasons for third-party activists to pay attention to the rise of independent voters. All exit polls since the third-party candidacy of George Wallace in the 1968 presidential election show that voters who identify themselves as independents are about twice as likely as other voters to support third-party candidates. In drawing 13.6 percent of the popular vote, Wallace got 25 percent of the vote of independents, compared to 14 percent of Democrats and 5 percent of Republicans, according to the Gallup poll. In 1980, John Anderson got 7 percent of the overall vote, but 13 percent of the independents, according to the CBS News/New York Times exit poll. In 1992, Ross Perot got 19 percent overall, but 30 percent of the independents. In 1996, he got 8 percent overall, but 20 percent of the independent vote. And in 2000 Ralph Nader, the Green Party candidate, got 3 percent overall, but 6 percent from independents. The same trend appeared in the gubernatorial races of 1998 and 2000, according to exit polls.[22]

Nonvoters or Discouraged Voters?

But maybe these signs of voter alienation and disaffection from the two major parties are not good news at all for third parties and independent candidates. Maybe they signal a "great turnoff" from politics in general, a statement of resignation rather than protest. Maybe Americans are so inured to partisan mudslinging and legislative gridlock and their own sense of distance from politics and lack of power that any third-party candidate seeking their support is on a fool's errand.

After all, as the measures of political alienation have risen, turnout in national and state elections has declined. According to the Committee for the Study of the American Electorate, turnout in the 1998 elections dropped to just 36 percent of the eligible voters, a steep decline from a high of 49 percent in 1966. Similarly, turnout in presi-

dential elections has also dropped, from 63 percent in 1960 to 51 percent in 2000. Significantly, the only time turnout has substantially risen in presidential elections in the
last forty years was in 1992, when Ross Perot was on the ballot, included in the nationally televised candidate debates, and spent millions of his own money on television ads
in the last weeks of the campaign.[23]

Political scientists and pollsters have long known of the relationship between socioeconomic status and voter participation. The higher the income and education level,
the more likely a person is to vote. In 2000, more votes were cast by the two-fifths of
the population that make more than $50,000 a year than by the three-fifths that make
less than that.[24] It was not always thus in America. Scholars and pundits who blame
low turnouts on the personal characteristics of the people not voting are confusing
causes and effects. The problem isn't that people don't vote because they lack a sense
of personal political efficacy, or because their relative lack of education causes them to
pay less attention to politics and makes them more impatient with the bureaucracy of
registering and voting. After all, in other Western countries there are no correlations
between education, class, age, and turnout. In Sweden, 95 percent of the least educated voted in 1979, compared with 97 percent of the most educated; in Italy, about 90
percent of those with five years or less of schooling voted in 1968, compared with just
38 percent of Americans with a similar education level.[25]

Actually, until the late 1890s, poor and less educated people used to participate in politics at the same level as other social groups in America.[26] Turnout in presidential elections regularly hit the high 70s and low 80s, in percentage terms, between 1840 and 1896.
Average people were drawn into politics by strong ethnic and religious identities (and
conflicts), by local machines that rewarded votes with patronage, and, especially after the
Civil War, by movements and parties that raised new issues of concern to the growing
ranks of impoverished farmers and exploited workers as the country was transformed by
the industrial revolution and the rise of the first great concentrations of economic power.
But these new parties, with names like the Greenback-Labor Party and the People's Party,
and movements of organized labor and farmers' alliances, posed a grave threat to regional
economic elites. In the North, manufacturing interests came to dominate the Republican Party; in the South, commercial and landowning interests ran the Democratic Party.
And they moved rapidly to smother these challenges to the status quo.

As Frances Fox Piven and Richard Cloward, two scholar-activists who are leading
experts on why Americans don't vote, write:

> Step by step, the elites crafted the institutional arrangements which narrowed the elec-
> torate, and they did so precisely to demobilize the groups whose politics were becoming
> threatening and disruptive. Voter registration arrangements were targeted specifically at
> the cities where the immigrant working class was concentrated. Literacy tests, stricter

naturalization procedures, and burdensome voter registration procedures were not so likely to bar the rich as they were the poor, or the well-educated as they were the uneducated. At the same time, the local parties with a motive to enlist these voters were weakened by reform campaigns.[27]

They were assisted by a deceptively simple change in the technology of voting. Until 1892, parties printed their own ballots listing their candidates and distributed them to supporters to deposit at the polls. But concerns about fraud led to the introduction of the so-called Australian ballot, which was printed in advance by the state, making the process of deciding whom to support a genuinely private decision. This change meant that, as one historian of elections put it, "disgruntled citizens could no longer simply organize themselves spontaneously and enter the political arena independently by issuing their own party ticket."[28] It also prompted states to define procedures regulating access to the ballot. Soon, not only did legislatures make it harder for poor and working-class people to vote, they set voting thresholds and petitioning hurdles that were intended to prevent minor parties from even appearing before the voters and to make it much tougher for those parties to maintain themselves once there.

Over the next twenty-four years, from 1896 to 1920, turnout in presidential elections crashed from 79 to 49 percent. In the South, write Piven and Cloward, "blacks and poor whites virtually disappeared from the polls." Voter participation there hit an astonishing low of 19 percent in 1924. In the rest of the country the decline wasn't nearly as steep, but it was concentrated among the immigrant young, who were primarily working class. And both major parties adapted quite happily to the new political environment that they had created. In each region of the country, one major party held a monopoly on local politics, making efforts to mobilize voters far less important to party success. Appeals to the economic interests of poorer voters became less frequent, with only a partial remobilization occurring during the Depression years as a result of the New Deal. In a process that was mutually reinforcing, the parties tended to ignore people with lower levels of education and income, and these people tended to ignore the parties, and politics.[29]

It may be that the new decline in turnout that started after the 1960 elections is just the footprints left behind by the American working class as it finishes checking out of politics. In *Politics and the Class Divide*, a study of the differing attitudes toward political activism among working-class and middle-class white New Englanders in the early 1990s, sociologist David Croteau points out that

With some notable exceptions, most working people do not see politics as being particularly relevant to their lives. They do not have a great deal of interest in public affairs nor do they have a clear motivation for becoming involved in politics since they do not see political involvement advancing their interests or making a positive contribution to their existence. Workers also do not feel an especially strong obligation to participate in public life or act on abstract values. Finally, they do not see potential political participation as an intrinsically rewarding activity.[30]

According to the National Election Studies, 42 percent of all Americans identify as "average working class" compared with 37 percent who identify as "average middle class." If you add in those who called themselves "upper working class" (8 percent) and "upper middle class" (12 percent) you still have the same, counterintuitive picture: more Americans think of themselves as working class (50 percent) than middle class (49 percent).

But these proportions have shifted significantly from the 1950s, when 63 percent of Americans thought of themselves as working class, compared to 30 percent as middle class and 7 percent as upper middle. Voter turnout was also substantially higher then, hitting its postwar high in 1960 and dropping ever since. If lower voter participation was simply a symptom of working-class alienation, then turnout should be trending upward as fewer people identify themselves in that class. Clearly, more must be going on than just the disengagement Croteau describes.[31]

Perhaps not all nonvoters are just signaling their apathy when they fail to vote. Perhaps they are more specifically alienated from the Democratic and Republican establishments and their candidates. Recall the zigzag political paths of people like Char Roberts and David Wiesner. Perhaps the word "nonvoter" is too black-and-white a term. In fact, much like political independents, a significant number of nonvoters—as many as one-third of them—show clear signs of wanting more choices than are offered by the major parties. This subset of nonvoters might better be called "unlikely voters" or, to put a sharper point on it, "discouraged voters."

Who are these unlikely or discouraged voters? It's rare to find any detailed inquiry into the backgrounds and attitudes of nonvoters that might allow us to discern between apathetic and angry abstainers. In May of 1996, the League of Women Voters released a poll that showed nonvoters were no more distrustful of the federal government than regular voters—similarly high percentages of each group said, for example, that government is run by "a few big interests." Voters were, however, far more likely to see significant differences between the parties on major issues, and to believe that elections matter and that their vote makes a difference. The poll also suggested that efforts to mobilize voters were highly important: about three-quarters of voters said they had been contacted by a candidate or party, compared with less than half of the nonvoters.[32] (According to the NES, the likelihood of someone reporting that they have been contacted by either major party rises with the person's level of education, income, and occupation.)

This still doesn't tell us much about the political leanings of nonvoters, except that they don't see much difference between the two major parties or have much meaningful contact with them. More answers can be found in two little-noticed surveys, one conducted in the summer of 1983 by ABC News, and the second done after the election of 1996 by Republican pollster Kellyanne Fitzpatrick. ABC News polled more than twenty-five hundred voting-age Americans and then compared the characteristics of highly likely voters (people who were registered to vote who said they always vote) with very unlikely voters (people who were not registered to vote and gave little inclination that they were planning to vote in the next election). The Fitzpatrick poll compared a sample of eight hundred voters with four hundred nonvoters. Here are some of the highlights of the two surveys:

- About a third of nonvoters aren't apathetic, and their failure to vote can't be explained by personal reasons like illness or work or family responsibilities. They're angry and feel shut out by the choices offered.[33]
- In the Fitzpatrick survey, women were more likely than men to give political reasons for their nonparticipation, a reflection perhaps of the gender gap or, more precisely, of women's greater likelihood to feel abused or neglected by the political system. (Perhaps a woman at the top of the ticket would alter this trend.)
- Nonvoters have weaker party loyalties, identifying as political independents at nearly twice the rate of regular voters (47 percent compared to 20 percent in the ABC News poll, 30 percent to 16 percent in the Fitzpatrick survey).
- There is a subtle but significant tilt toward liberalism among nonvoters. In the Fitzpatrick poll, 38 percent of nonvoters identified as conservatives, compared with 48 percent of the voting public. And while 17 percent of voters called themselves liberals, 22 percent of nonvoters chose that label.[34]
- Nonvoters overall tend to be working class, as opposed to middle class. They identified as such by two-to-one in the ABC News study. In the Fitzpatrick study, 36 percent of the nonvoters made less than $25,000 a year, compared to 22 percent of the voters.
- Nonvoters show much greater interest in having more choices in elections. In the ABC News poll, nonvoters were more likely to agree that "TV news departments should include all presidential candidates in any televised debate even if that means dozens of minor candidates will appear along with the major ones." Forty-six percent of nonvoters agreed compared with 38 percent of likely voters.[35]

A survey done by Harvard University's Vanishing Voter Project just before the 2000 presidential election that asked people about their intentions to vote found a very similar picture. The project reported that "Half of the likely non-voters believe that 'most politicians are liars or crooks,' nearly 90 percent say that 'most political candidates will say almost anything in order to get themselves elected,' and 43 percent claim that 'Republicans and Democrats are so alike that it does not make much difference who wins.'" People who said they were planning to go vote were generally less skeptical of politicians, but not by much. More than a third questioned politicians' honesty; three-fourths doubted the campaign promises that they make; and one-fifth said that Republican and Democratic politicians are too much alike.

The Vanishing Voter Project's survey also confirmed the Fitzpatrick and *ABC News* poll findings that nonvoters were markedly more liberal on issues than regular voters. "When asked about the federal budget surplus, likely voters are more inclined than nonvoters to say it should go to a tax cut, debt reduction, or strengthening social security," the project's survey reported. "Non-voters are more likely to say it should be spent on domestic programs in such areas as health, education, and welfare." [36]

Breaking the Two-Party Lock

These survey results suggest that politicians are making a big mistake if they ignore all nonvoters and focus their energies solely on people who vote regularly. Al Garcia would tend to agree. He managed the campaigns of two candidates for the Minnesota state house of representatives in 1998. Both were in Anoka County, where Jesse Ventura received more than 50 percent of the vote. One candidate, Jerry Newton, a decorated Vietnam veteran and small-business owner, fiscally conservative but very supportive of public schools and the environment, lost badly to a far-right pro-lifer as the Ventura voters swung Republican down-ballot. The other, Luanne Koskinen, an incumbent with strong labor backing, barely held on to her office. [37]

This was no isolated phenomenon—across the state the Ventura voters ended up costing Democrats control of the state house of representatives. Over lunch at Billie's, a popular Anoka restaurant, a few months after the election, Garcia spilled out his postmortem: Democrats got whipped because they didn't reach out to new voters, and there were a lot of them. "I think Luanne kept her core base, but other, new people came out. We were too focused on the regular voters," Garcia says. "If you hadn't voted in two out of the last four elections, you didn't get anything [in the mail] from Luanne or Jerry." [38] Targeting likely voters, of course, is standard practice in most campaigns these days. But Garcia says he knew that that strategy wouldn't be enough.

There's actually nothing special about Al Garcia's story. In most cases, campaigns at all levels of American politics these days are focused narrowly on likely voters, people who vote regularly. Eric Johnson, campaign manager to Skip Humphrey, the

Democratic candidate who lost to Ventura, admitted as much after the election. "We didn't see Ventura coming because our polling screened out unlikely voters," he told the *Wall Street Journal*.[39]

But do most politicians, particularly comfortable incumbents in either of the two major parties, really want to reach these voters—for all the platitudes we hear about their devotion to democracy and the importance of every vote? Many experts who have studied the problem of low voter turnout think this situation is not an accident. "Low turnout is the compound consequence of legal and procedural barriers intertwined with the parties' reluctance to mobilize many voters, especially working-class and minority voters," said Frances Fox Piven, who with her husband, Richard Cloward, built the movement that passed the motor-voter act. "I've come to the conclusion that party competition takes the form of demobilizing, not mobilizing, voters, because new voters threaten incumbents, raise new issues or create the incentive to raise new issues," she added. "One political scientist even called them 'discordant voters.' You need mavericks, outsiders, to try to mobilize new voters—nobody else wants to take the risk."[40]

"Nonvoters matter a lot," agreed Democratic pollster Stanley Greenberg, "though most candidates act as if they don't. There's no question that you can change the shape and size of the electorate, though that is more true for presidential elections than for individual, even statewide, campaigns." For example, turnout increased by 5.5 percent in the three-way presidential race of 1992. "There's reason to believe that the populist economic issues that Clinton was raising and the independent-libertarian issues that Perot was raising were at work there," Greenberg argued. "By comparison, in 1994 conservative definitions of the issues brought in more rural, conservative portions of the electorate while the health-care reform failure led many non–college-educated women to drop out."[41]

Republican pollster John Zogby, whose firm made highly accurate predictions of the outcome of 1996 and 2000 presidential elections, concurred. "If there's a strong independent candidate in the race, you begin to see the numbers of undecided voters in those groups who often don't vote—younger voters, registered independents—start to decline in our surveys, a sign they are planning to vote," he said. "You will also see an increase in those who call themselves liberal or progressive if there's a credible Green Party candidate in the race. We saw that in New York with Ralph Nader, for example, in 1996."

But Greenberg cautioned that this is hard to do. "It's not often that an election creates the kind of issue definition that brings in the groups that dropped out," he said. Translation: Most candidates tend to blur the differences between themselves and their opponent, making it less likely for discouraged voters to notice that an important race is under way. It's the duopoly at work, again. What's needed is almost something like a crusade. "In the past social movements have had a big effect on turnout," noted Frances Fox Piven, "as would a revival of Democratic politics or third-party efforts."

Rep. Jesse Jackson Jr. harkened back to his father's 1984 and 1988 campaigns as further proof that discouraged voters can be effectively mobilized. Indeed, the number of Democratic primary voters rose from 18 million in 1984 to nearly 23 million in 1988, with the Reverend Jesse Jackson's total share rising by 3.4 million. "If you're able to tap into the people who aren't consciously involved in politics or following it," the younger Jackson said during an interview in his Capitol Hill office, "and show how everything they do has something to do with politics—that shirt they wear, the stop sign, the taxes they pay, the schools they attend, the police officer on their street, the fire department . . . you can inspire them and give them reason to participate." Of course, that doesn't mean people stay involved. "I know some people who participated in 1984 and '88 who say they haven't participated since the reverend ran," Jackson added. "The reverend brought them in, and the reverend's *not* running has taken them out."

It takes a certain kind of candidate, message, and campaign to reach these voters, Jackson argued. "There is a relationship between the dynamism of a candidate, the charisma of the candidate, the countercultural nature of a candidate and their appeal to a nonvoter," he said. "Now the price that one has to pay in order to go after a nonvoter is to be a nontraditional candidate, which means you're not going to be able to cater to traditional economic forces that have significant influence—you have to have some relationship to them, but you can't be seen as beholden to them. You have to be seen as a real American: you have to be someone who can look the press right in the face and tell them exactly how it is. You have to be Beattyite, almost Bulworthian."[42]

Speaking the People's Language

Not many American politicians are trying to run this kind of campaign or can convincingly pull it off, for reasons that are all too familiar. However, there are a number of recent successful examples that predate Jesse Ventura. What seems to matter most is that the candidate have a populist message and style—someone who wants to empower ordinary people versus the establishment, who is blue collar as opposed to buttoned down, who favors effective government on behalf of the interests of average working people, and who supports sweeping efforts to clean up government and reform the electoral process itself.

Those were Paul Wellstone's attributes in 1990, when he won a U.S. Senate seat. The Minnesotan, a former university professor and political activist, not only drew more Democratic votes than the party's candidate in the previous Senate contest, but he generated more activity at the polls: more voters came out in 1990 than did in 1988, a presidential election year. Such an increase in turnout is a sure sign that discouraged voters are being reached. Similar populist attributes helped push Jesse Jackson's 1988 presidential campaign onto the front pages, particularly after he beat front-runner Michael Dukakis head-to-head in the Michigan Democratic primary—a victory rooted in the fact that Michigan allowed people to register to vote on the same day as the election.

And just as those attributes can encourage voters to support a maverick within their own party, they can also inspire voters to cross traditional party lines, as many Democratic union members evidently did in support of Pat Buchanan in 1996. Buchanan's vote totals in union strongholds like Racine, Wisconsin, and Dubuque, Iowa, jumped dramatically between his 1992 and 1996 campaigns.[43] The difference: in 1992 Buchanan ran primarily as a hard-core social conservative with a nativist, even racist, tinge; in 1996 he had added a broad critique of corporate greed and footloose capital that was pitched directly at workers displaced by the amoral forces of globalization. Buchanan's billboards in the rusted-out old industrial district of Dubuque, where the only other signs of political activity were tattered "Perot '92" stickers, didn't say "Save the unborn." They said, "He'll bring our jobs back."[44]

More evidence of the appeal of working-class populists among discouraged voters can be found in the campaigns of Bernie Sanders. In 1988 and 1990, Bernie Sanders—the former socialist mayor of Burlington—sought Vermont's lone seat in Congress as an independent.[45] He ran on such issues as instituting national health care, establishing tax fairness, protecting the environment, addressing the needs of the poor, and involving working people in the political process. He came close in the three-way race in 1988, drawing 37.5 percent of the vote to 41.2 percent for Republican Peter Smith and 18.9 percent for Democrat Paul Pourier. Two years later he won a solid victory with 56 percent of the vote, beating the incumbent Smith, who got 39.5 percent, and Delores Sandoval, the Democratic nominee, who got only 3 percent. In both races, the total vote was way up—13 percent higher—compared with the previous election cycle. (Since then Sanders has been reelected five times, usually with a healthy margin of victory.)

And while Sanders did well in his breakthrough victory in 1990 with the college-educated, alternative-lifestyle types who have moved up to Vermont in the last generation, his strongest support actually came from the poor, conservative hill towns and farm communities of the state's "Northeast Kingdom." For example, Sanders's strongest showing statewide that year came in the rural county of Orleans, on the border with Canada, where he pulled 62 percent of the vote.[46] The same pattern of support for Sanders among Vermont's blue-collar working families could be found in Bennington County, the only one he lost in 1990. He got only 38 percent of the vote in the town of Dorset, where median household income was very high ($42,200) and 40 percent were college graduates. By comparison, he got 53 percent in the town of Woodford, where incomes were much lower ($25,200) and only 8 percent were college graduates. Another indication of how Sanders's independent and working-class oriented campaign succeeded: in 1990 he won a majority of the vote in all four of the conservative-leaning counties that had been lost two years earlier by Democratic gubernatorial candidate Madeline Kunin, who had run more as a traditional liberal than as a populist. People would say to him, "I don't really know what socialism is, but if you're not a Democrat or a Republican, you're OK with me."[47]

According to this analysis, Jesse Ventura, a socially liberal, fiscally conservative, pro–campaign finance reform, antiestablishment hero with a working-class style, hit discouraged voters—as well as disaffected Democrats and Republicans—on the bull's-eye. His campaign deliberately targeted "unlikely voters" by focusing his public appearances in an "Independent Belt" of suburbs to the north and west of Minnesota's Twin Cities, and by placing his offbeat TV ads on offbeat shows. Helped by same-day voter registration, his candidacy drastically boosted turnout, and most of those new voters pulled his lever.

In several other ways, Ventura's vote corresponded with those groups least satisfied with the existing political system. Far more self-identified liberals than conservatives voted for him. Women voted for him almost as much as men. In the high-income professional suburbs, Jesse did poorly. In the less affluent suburbs, he did very well. Turnout in many of these blue collar districts was more than 70 percent, with as many as 20 percent of the total registering on Election Day. For good reason, many third-party activists point to the "Minnesota model"—public campaign financing, same-day voter registration, access to televised debates, and a populist message—as *the* way to win more races without changing the underlying winner-take-all system. As I mentioned in my introduction, states with Election Day voter registration or some form of public financing for candidates or parties have also tended to have more active third-party efforts.

Seizing the Opportunity

It would be misleading to end this discussion of the opportunities for third-party and independent victories without a brief look at one other critical piece of the puzzle, which is what the major parties and their candidates actually do during each election cycle. Most elections start out as the Democrat's or Republican's to lose, not the third-party candidate's to win. Missteps by the major candidates, dissension within one or both major party's ranks, the abandonment of a major party nominee by the party's leadership or base, overly negative campaigns—all of these unpredictable elements can contribute to an alternative candidate's breakthrough. Those factors—along with special assets each candidate brought to their race—go a long way in explaining the gubernatorial victories of Lowell Weicker in 1990 and Angus King in 1994.

In leaving the Republican Party after three terms as a U.S. senator and running as an independent, Weicker signaled that he was not going to be a friend of the establishment in his run for governor of Connecticut. He also cast himself as someone who would do more to address educational inequities and the problems of the state's urban poor—though not with any of the programmatic fervor of a Bernie Sanders. The three-way race clearly stirred up voter interest, with turnout climbing 5 percent over the previous cycle. In general Weicker did best in the less well-off eastern half of the state (where Perot got more than a quarter of the vote two years later), and he took far more votes from the Democratic base than the Republican base.[48] Like Sanders and Ventura, Weicker's outside-the-box run energized many previously discouraged voters.

Though Weicker made much of his independence from the major parties, it would be a mistake to argue that his election success could be easily copied. When he declared his candidacy, he had the highest name recognition of any of the candidates in the race—an advantage gleaned from eighteen years in the U.S. Senate. The Democratic nominee, U.S. Rep. Bruce Morrison, was hurt by the unpopularity of the incumbent Democratic governor—William O'Neill, who left office with a billion-dollar budget deficit and the economy in a recession—and by O'Neill's open unwillingness to rally the Democratic Party machine to Morrison's aid. And the Republican nominee, U.S. Rep. John Rowland, came across as unseasoned (he was only thirty-three at the time of the race) and inconsistent (noteworthy was his midcampaign decision to become pro-choice after years of opposing abortion). Weicker was well financed, he had important endorsements and backing from Republican and Democratic officeholders alike, and he led in the polls from the beginning of the race until Election Day.

The victory of Angus King in Maine may also have more to do with local political circumstances. When he won his four-way race in 1994, he did so without increasing turnout, and mainly by appealing to high-income and high-education voters—unlike Sanders, Ventura, and Weicker. His strongest counties were along the coast up from Portland; these tended to be better off than his weakest counties in the far rural corners of the state. In general he took more votes from Republicans than Democrats. Perhaps this is not surprising, as his prime issues were tax cuts, getting government out of the way, and creating a more business-friendly environment in the state; he was known for hosting a highbrow public policy TV show for many years, and he was a successful self-made businessman.

King was also fortunate in having two relatively weak major-party opponents in former Democratic governor Joe Brennan and Republican Susan Collins, as well as a strong third-party contender alongside him in the Green Party's Jonathan Carter. Collins, who came in third in the race, won the eight-way Republican primary with only 22 percent of the vote. She was hampered on her right throughout the campaign by attacks from religious conservatives opposed to her moderate views on abortion and gay rights, and she got no help from the state's incumbent Republican governor. Brennan had lost his previous race for governor and nearly lost an earlier congressional reelection battle; while he led the race with King and Collins for much of the year, ultimately he could not expand his support beyond the Democrats' core one-third of the electorate. Meanwhile, King—the wealthiest candidate in the race—was also the best financed, using a million dollars of his own money to run a strong television advertising campaign. And he was helped by Maine's notoriously independent voters, who had already elected an independent governor in the 1970s, and who gave Ross Perot his best showing—30 percent of the vote—in the 1992 presidential race.

And yet, both Weicker and King's victories explode the argument that you can't win if you leave the two-party framework. Most important, each time an independent or third-party candidate wins a high-profile race, it lowers the psychological bar for other victories elsewhere. As voters across the country see alternative candidates win elections and govern effectively, they may decide that it is safe to take chances on such people in their own elections. "The conventional analysis we're fed is that people are happy with politics, and they like the politicians they have," says Patrick Caddell, one-time political adviser to a host of maverick Democrats ranging from Jimmy Carter to Jerry Brown. "Victories by people like Jesse Ventura suggest that's not true. The fact that he won is like a can opener. It says to other people in other states 'why can't we have people like this?' It's a dangerous example."[49]

Organizing the Angry Middle

Ross Perot and the Reform Party

3

Mad as Hell, Used and Abused

The only party I'm for is the huge party this nation is going to throw on election day when we throw these arrogant bums out on their collective butts.

—Jack Gargan

"Patient Zero" of the Perot Epidemic

If it's hard to devise a winning strategy for a single outsider seeking to defeat the duopoly, either as a third-party candidate or as an independent, it's even more difficult to build a successful new institution—a party with a coherent structure and message that can attract votes. Over the last ten years, three different third-party efforts have arisen seeking to attain that goal—the Reform Party, the Greens, and the New Party. Each has had an important impact and can teach us much about the future of third parties in America.

Third parties often rise when the major parties stumble. So it's not surprising that the biggest third-party movement to shake American politics in the last ten years started in 1990, as the economy began to slide into recession, the budget deficit began to soar, the Democrat-controlled Congress bickered with Republican President George Bush, and the word "gridlock" came into political fashion.

But third parties, like any political project, do not appear out of thin air. Ripe social conditions help, of course, but new political parties, like social movements, arise only when they are organized. Previously little-known people take unusual steps, reaching out to find like-minded citizens, presenting petitions and voicing grievances. If they are lucky and if they are skilled, far-reaching connections are made, and a whole new form of social activity begins to occur. Key decisions made by these central organizers—what kind of base they try to build, what kind of internal decision-making process they

65

adopt, and what set of issues they choose to emphasize—can have a huge effect on the future of the fledgling party.

Thus, in exploring the trajectory of the Perot phenomenon, it makes sense to start where it really began, two years before most Americans ever heard of the checkbook populist from Texas. In the summer of 1990, Jack Gargan was a recently retired professional financial planner living in Florida—and, as he put it, "one ticked-off granddad"—who had grown appalled at the mushrooming federal debt and the arrogance of Congress in voting itself pay raises in the middle of the night while blithely wasting taxpayers' money. He wasn't a politician, though he had tried running for local office once without spending any money, to make a point. He was upset, however, about the drift of the country. So he took a gamble and spent nearly $50,000 of his life's savings on full-page ads in six newspapers across the country, calling on his fellow citizens to "Throw the Hypocritical Rascals Out!" and asking for help in spreading his call.[1]

In big, bold-face capital letters, he declared "I'M MAD AS HELL AND I'M NOT GOING TO TAKE IT ANYMORE!" The ad featured a stern photo of Gargan, silver haired and open collared, above a pungent list of his complaints against Congress. His language was simple and evocative of an earlier time. And every synonym for "angry" was deployed, to good effect: The ad's text read, in part:

Hello, my name is Jack Gargan. I'm just a recently retired "working stiff." Like most of the people I talk with, I'm fed up with members of Congress who care more about getting re-elected than they do about what's happening to our country.

Specifically, I'M APPALLED that Congress continues to hock the future of our children and grandchildren. Our national debt is now over 3 TRILLION dollars, and going higher by the minute. ENOUGH IS ENOUGH!

I'M BITTER that more than half of all our income taxes go just for the annual interest on that national debt (it's not just some outrageous amount we stuck our children with).

I'M OUTRAGED that Congress even talks about further raises in our taxes while totally ignoring the ONE HUNDRED AND EIGHTY BILLION DOLLARS IN SHEER GOVERNMENT WASTE as documented by the Grace Commission report.

I'M ANGRY that, after being told by the American public that their existing salary was already an overpayment on their abilities, they turned right around and arrogantly voted themselves the biggest raise in history! Then they had the gall to insult our intelligence and call it a "vote for ethical government." If they have to be paid to be ethical they have no business being in public office. . . .

I'M INCENSED every time I stand in the checkout line behind someone with designer sunshades, designer jeans and $100 sneakers who pay their bill with food stamps, their vote bought and paid for by a congressman who knows how to use federal giveaway programs to keep themselves in office! (I have no quarrel with food stamps going to truly needy people.)

I'M LIVID when I recall how, in typically gutless congressional style, they let an "outside commission" stick the younger American workers with a raise in Social Security taxes (over $15,000 per year for some couples!) to bail out a bankrupt Social Security system to "make it a sound program for our retired senior citizens," knowing full well that there will not be enough money to fund that same "baby-boom" generation who will be footing most of the bill.

I'M EVEN MORE LIVID when I discovered this same Congress then screwed our retired senior citizens by taking 52 BILLION dollars out of the Social Security Trust Fund using voodoo economics to make the federal deficit look not quite as outrageous, while slipping the trust fund an I.O.U. in return. God forbid we have even a mild recession, or our retired folks will also end up holding the bag!

I'M ENRAGED when I see money pouring in to incumbents from PACs, special interest groups who use their money to stifle public interest, to congressmen who will sell their soul for another term in office.

I'M DISGUSTED by the number of shady dealings by members of Congress who get nothing more than a slap on the wrist from their peers when they get caught in the act. Something's mighty wrong with the system when 98% of incumbents are re-elected. The other 2% don't lose. They either go out feet first, or in total disgrace for conduct too embarrassing even for congressional standards!

I'M SHOCKED that the world's richest nation can become the world's biggest debtor nation, all within the space of one generation!

I'M REALLY HACKED OFF that Congress has permitted, and in some cases actually abetted, the S&L rip-off which will now cost every American family an estimated EXTRA $30 per month for the next 30 years . . . and not even prosecuting the scoundrels, their friends, who have stuck us with this bill!

I'M TIRED of paying for the "franking privileges" (postage) and printing costs of blatant advertising disguised as newsletters to the voters back home, subsidizing congressmen for everything from haircuts to lunches to health insurance plans, and paying for an army of over-paid congressional "aides" (more than 32,000 at last count). Talk about an "aides epidemic"!

I'M INSULTED that Congress, who exempted themselves from Social Security laws, has set up a pension plan that will pay a congressman in six years what the average American under Social Security must work a lifetime for (and there are 14 CON-VICTED FELONS currently drawing fat congressional pensions—up to $80,000 per year!—and 6 more waiting in the wings to reach retirement age).

But mostly, *I'M SAD* that we as a nation have thrown up our hands in surrender to the politicians and bureaucrats who have put us in this predicament.

BUT I'M NOT GOING TO GIVE IN TO THOSE CLOWNS! Maybe one person can't make a difference, but you and I together can! And here's what we must do: The root of all our problems is elected officials who use their incumbency to put a stranglehold on their office. They devote most of their time and energy to raising money for re-election, rather than to running the country properly. I propose that we simply rise up and VOTE EVERY INCUMBENT SENATOR AND CONGRESSMAN OUT OF OFFICE! Further, that we only elect new people who will pledge to strictly limit the term of their office and to prohibit the federal government from spending money it does not have, except in a bonafide national emergency.[2]

Gargan's "Grassroots Petition" ended by telling readers that he had set up a nonprofit organization, THRO Inc. (for "Throw the Hypocritical Rascals Out") and borrowed from his life's savings to get the venture going. He also said that he had placed his ad in several major newspapers and appealed for small donations to run it in more places. He assured readers that this was not connected in any way to the Democrats or Republicans. "The only party I'm for is the huge party this nation is going to throw on election day when we throw these arrogant bums out on their collective butts!" Gargan roared in his text.

Then, like the famous TV anchorman in Paddy Chayefsky's movie *Network*, who also raged "I'm mad as hell, and I'm not going to take it anymore," Gargan pulled the cork out of an angry America. Donations started to pour in, even though people at first had no way of knowing if Gargan was for real, or just a scam artist. "As fast as the money did come in, I'd go buy an ad in another paper," he recalled as we sat together in his study at his home in Cedar Key, a necklace of islands on Florida's Gulf Coast. The local airstrip abuts his front driveway. Gargan looked and sounded uncannily like Jerry's retired father on the 1990s TV sitcom *Seinfeld*, though he took himself a lot more seriously. "When people saw I really was doing what I'd said I'd do, the money started pouring in."[3] Soon he had more than a full-time job running THRO, appearing on hundreds of TV and radio shows and traveling across the country to hundreds of town hall–style meetings.

Perot came later. More precisely, the Perot explosion of 1992–93—which engaged hundreds of thousands of Americans in a supposedly quixotic effort to get the Texas billionaire on the ballot in all fifty states, at one unbelievable moment found him leading in some presidential polls, drew 19.7 million votes in the presidential election, and then enlisted approximately 1.5 million dues-paying members into a new government reform group called United We Stand America (UWSA)—was actually catalyzed by Gargan and his organization. Late in the fall of 1990, Perot had called Gargan offering to help with THRO, and the two men started a friendly relationship. Gargan soon resolved that, while Congress controlled the nation's purse strings, it would help a lot to have a sympathetic ear in the White House. He began a quiet effort to draft Perot, which burst into public view when the Texan addressed a roaring crowd of three thousand that Gargan had gathered in Tampa on November 2, 1991. "Run, Ross, Run," read the signs Gargan had planted in the audience. It was more than three months before Perot's historic appearance on Larry King's television show.

Not long after Perot officially threw his hat into the ring on that program, the two men had a unpublicized falling-out. Gargan was upset by Perot's manhandling of his rapidly growing base of grass-roots supporters. "People used to call my office Dallas East, because when they couldn't get through to Perot—all these people that were doing the petitioning—at the time I had his ear, they would all come in through me," he said.[4] Gargan tried to warn Perot of problems brewing within the burgeoning movement, first advising him that anything genuinely grass roots could not be controlled from above. When it became clear that Perot's lieutenants, whom many volunteers referred to as "white shirts" (as opposed to the "brown shirts" favored by Mussolini's fascist followers) for their old-fashioned style of dress and authoritarian style, Gargan wrote Perot a prophetic and angry letter. "The press will get this story eventually," he told Perot. "And it is your own group who are shipwrecking your campaign. Instead of a corps of young tigers they are coming off as a gang of young nazis. I think you need some urgent damage control here."[5] Perot's authoritarian behavior still rankled Gargan years later. "What really pisses me off," he said to me in 1998, "is that there were so many thousands of just good people who had never been involved in politics before, who saw this golden opportunity—'we can get involved'—and they were squashed like bugs."[6]

Perot's paranoia and megalomania also deflated the support he had attracted from the upper reaches of American capitalism. Before he famously pulled out of the race in July 1992, his supporters and contributors included many leading figures from the financial sector, including Theodore Forstmann and William Simon, prominent

Republican investment bankers; Felix Rohatyn, a Democrat who worked the other side of Wall Street; Robert Hormats of Goldman Sachs; and A. C. Greenberg of Bear Stearns. Computer industry leaders like Scott McNealy, president of Sun Microsystems, and Charles Sporck, a founder of National Semiconductor, also came out for him. The supply-siders in this group were interested in Perot's support for cutting capital gains taxes and reducing government spending to balance the budget; the others were attracted to Perot's interest in some form of government intervention to enhance industrial competitiveness, in the manner of the much-touted "organized capitalism" then in vogue in Japan and Germany. These seemingly contradictory interests were never resolved, thanks to Perot's crack-up; what was significant about them is that powerful economic actors were prepared to throw their support behind a nascent third-party bid.[7]

Meanwhile, Gargan's campaign to shake up Congress continued unabated. Over three years, he ran a total of 633 advertisements in newspapers across the country. Nineteen ninety-two was a banner year for independent and third-party candidates for Congress, many of whom Gargan says THRO had helped recruit. A large number of incumbents actually decided to retire from Congress that year rather than face a reelection fight (though there is always more than the average rate of retirements in a year when incumbents have to run in newly reapportioned districts).[8] More than three hundred thousand people had written him, and most sent money. The average donation was a humble ten dollars.

The people who flocked to THRO were, in general, a lot like Gargan—mostly white, heading toward or in retirement, culturally on the "square" side but with a "live-and-let-live" attitude toward others, and working in non-elite fields. That is to say, these were people who were more likely to be self-educated than Ivy League graduates. They tended to work in second-tier professions like engineering or sales rather than high-status fields like medicine or the law. Few, if any, had backgrounds in politics or political organizing. And though some had participated in earlier protest movements, especially the movement against the Vietnam War in the 1960s, they had almost no awareness of the strong tradition of antiestablishment reform efforts on the American left. For example, there was no cross-fertilization with Vermont Rep. Bernie Sanders, Congress's sole independent, even though he broke into Washington the same year that THRO took off. (I'd often ask people in the anti-incumbent movement if they even knew who Sanders was, and few did.) Some people active on the conservative fringe, like Howard Phillips of the U.S. Taypayers Party and Alan Keyes, then head of Citizens Against Government Waste, showed up at THRO's early rallies in 1991, but for the most part the group was not aligned with the political right, either.

It was as if Gargan had found a whole new vein in the body politic, one that was independent of the long-standing grievances of the left and right, as well as the cultural baggage of its leaders and organs. This, I'm convinced, was part of the anti-incumbent movement's original charm—people could come to a meeting and not be immediately reminded of whatever allergies they had to the standard politicking of the right or left. It's not a coincidence, I think, that this happened at a time when organized labor was still deep in the doldrums of the George Meany and Lane Kirkland years and when many movements on the left and right were played out by the ideological struggles that occurred under Reagan.

Some, like Joe Klein writing in *Newsweek*, called Gargan and Perot's followers the "radical middle" in an attempt to convey this group's contradictory nature—radical in the sense of wanting to go to the roots of the nation's problems, and middle in the sense of not being from the ideological extremes.[9] *Washington Post* columnist E. J. Dionne preferred the term "anxious middle," to describe the worries of a group stressed by rapid economic and cultural change, "angry at government but uneasy over the workings of the economic system," as well as to convey the fact that this large bloc of voters had swung back and forth between the two major parties in the last several elections, having abandoned their traditional partisan loyalties.[10]

I prefer the term "angry middle" because the actual foot soldiers that I talked to who were at the core of the movement seemed more motivated by a gut-level anger and sense of betrayal than a truly radical questioning of American society. Most thought of themselves as patriots, seeking to "take America back," but few gave any thought to the bloody history of American nationalism (Manifest Destiny, the slaughter of Native Americans, slavery, imperialism) when they turned to potent symbols like the flag and the American eagle. Thus their "radicalism" was pretty shallow, or, to be kinder, myopic. And I think "middle" is less a valid description of their ideological leanings than it is of where they stood between the truly poor and the upper middle class. These were people of average income who largely received few special favors from government—neither welfare for the poor nor corporate welfare for the rich and well connected. As for ideology, while they may have insisted that they were not of the left or right, many of their populist prescriptions could easily be identified with proposals from both those camps.

Perhaps the best way to describe them is as a bloc of newly activated citizens who previously had not thought of themselves as political dissenters, and who saw all existing political institutions (the two parties, the business establishment, the mainstream media, and the established left and right) as part of the problem. These people were indeed worried, as Dionne writes, about the present and the future, both of their economic standing and of larger cultural changes happening in the country. But Gargan's troops were not just anxious. They were the most motivated edge of that larger body; the people whose anger had finally pulled them off their sofas and whose economic circumstances allowed them to devote a lot of volunteer time to political protest.

It was also important that Gargan was an authentic original, not a professional agitator who had been air-dropped into the scene by some Washington lobby. Members of the angry middle were distrustful of anything that smacked of political careerism, whether it came from old-time politicos or the new would-be leaders of the growing protest movement. At the same time, the very fact that this movement was self-made left it with huge weaknesses and blind spots. For example, to protect the privacy of the people who joined THRO, Gargan never made his 150,000-person mailing list available to anyone else. Local chapters formed around his cross-country jaunts, but not because Gargan organized his list by zip code and gave local organizers names of people in their area to contact.[11]

While Gargan prided himself on not being a politician, he was in favor of third-party politics. In the middle of the 1992 election he got involved with a group organized by Rochester, New York, pollster Gordon Black that was trying to ride the swell of enthusiasm around Perot's candidacy to create a new party, which they had dubbed the Independence Party. Black had done polling and focus groups for Perot in the spring of 1992, and had released an influential survey that in June titled "The Politics of American Discontent" showing strong support for a new party.[12] He had promises of a half-million dollars in initial funding from sources other than Perot, a plan to hire organizers, contacts with a number of the other fledgling third-parties starting up in Perot's wake, and a strategy aimed squarely at the millions of Americans alienated by big government and big business—people who he believed, would be inclined to support a more effective government if it were less corrupt and more responsive.

"From day one," Black told me in the fall of 1992, "our strategy has been to pull together the class of angry people," which he centered on the millions of "entrepreneurs running small and medium-size businesses." Their unifying targets would be "the runaway deficit [and] getting money out of politics," steps that were needed in and of themselves as well as to restore public trust in government.[13] In addition, the Independence Party's first statement of principles called for orienting government policy toward job creation by small and midsize businesses, reduction of welfare dependence, a "reduction of dependence on defense expenditures as a substitute for an aggressive industrial policy" (Black's poll showed a majority favoring a 50 percent cut in defense spending), less expensive and more widely available health care, increased spending on education, greater investment in treatment for drug and alcohol addiction and increased support for conservation.[14] (Compared to the party platform that would later be promulgated by Perot, this was a markedly progressive package of ideas.)

In the "1992 Election Edition" of the THRO newsletter, Gargan sent his 150,000 subscribers a questionnaire asking them if they would support this new third party, above and beyond their efforts to watchdog the next Congress. The party's draft statement of principles was included in the newsletter. Nearly all of the people who responded to his survey backed the Independence Party, and many—perhaps as many as "ten thousand or so" volunteered their names and addresses to get involved. "I went up to that first meeting in Rochester [in July 1992] and said, 'Look what I got'—a box full of names of people willing to take a leadership role,'" he said. "From that, we were able to get about twenty states going [with Independence Party efforts] and another twenty bumping along."[15]

At its peak, the movement had a quasi-religious fervor to it. Framed on the wall in Gargan's office in Cedar Key is one letter that captures the time: "Mr. Jack Gargan," it reads,

> "I'm excited about you.
> "God chooses a 'nobody' from time to time, stands them on the shoulders of the downtrodden, and gives them a slingshot.
> "I am a black woman, knowledgeable and mad.
> "I am praying for you."

When I asked Gargan about the letter, he took it down from the wall. It clearly brought back the days when as many as ten thousand letters a day poured into his office like a just-discovered Texas oil gusher. His eyes watered as his reflected on the letter's biblical imagery. "David and Goliath—you know how that turned out, don'tcha?" he asked.

But this David failed to slay Goliath. How does a movement that garnered 19 million votes in 1992 and spawned a mass membership organization of 1.5 million people end up a mere eight years later with less than a half-million votes for its presidential candidate, Pat Buchanan, with its one popularly elected official, Jesse Ventura, deserting it, and with an almost nonexistent degree of local organization?

The flip answer was once supplied by Eugene McCarthy, a former presidential candidate and a maverick in his own right. Interviewed by Carolyn Barta of the *Dallas Morning News*, he was asked about his suggestion that the aardvark be the symbol for the Perot movement or the Reform Party. McCarthy said, "The aardvark, according to natural history, didn't evolve from anything and it's not evolving into anything. It's kind of a one-time absolute animal, it has no metaphor. And I think that was the case with Perot, it was just, 'Here I am, and now I'm not here.'" Barta asked, "And not going anywhere?" "Yes," McCarthy answered.[16]

The full answer is a bit more complicated. The Perot movement was both a victim of its own success—the major parties co-opted the deficit issue—and destroyed by its own leader's authoritarianism and inability to capitalize effectively on the massive grass-roots upswelling he had tapped. And none of the movement's other leaders had the capacity to pull it together or set it on a fresh path.

The Democrats and Republicans Respond

No one expected Perot to get nearly 20 percent of the vote in 1992. Recall that he had shocked most of his followers by dropping out in July, citing vague threats to his family, and then, after reemerging and performing quite well in the presidential debates, seemingly torpedoed his candidacy with a paranoid appearance on *60 Minutes* the Sunday before the election. Exit polls even showed that he could have gotten 36 percent if voters thought he had a chance to win.[17] His public standing actually soared after the election. So both parties moved quickly to co-opt his message, particularly his zeal to eliminate the deficit.

Even though Clinton's "Putting People First" economic plan had originally contemplated an economic stimulus package of greater public spending that would increase the deficit anywhere between $20 billion to $60 billion, the Democrats quickly adopted Perot's emphasis on reducing the federal deficit as their own. In December 1992, Clinton ended his two-day economic conference in Little Rock—to which he had prominently invited former Perot economic adviser John White—by hedging on the issue, telling the press, "If you define stimulus as meaning am I going to deliberately increase the deficit in this budget year, the answer to that is I haven't made up my mind yet."[18] But his stimulus proposal was eventually trimmed to a mere $16 billion, which died in a Senate consumed by Perot-inspired deficit-cutting fervor. For the first half of his first year, Clinton's top priority was the passage of a five-year, $500 billion deficit reduction program. Even though Perot was taking potshots at his administration—saying that he wouldn't have hired Clinton for any job above middle management, for example—White House officials were under orders to speak no ill of him, *Time* magazine reported.[19]

Republican leaders took an equally friendly approach toward Perot, at least at first. In the heat of the battle over the Clinton budget proposal, for example, Bob Dole—then the Senate minority leader and the GOP's leading contender for the 1996 presidential nomination—took to the Senate floor to say that "Ross Perot has got the message. He's been out among real people."[20] And after Perot ran an informercial attacking the budget deficit, Dole called to offer his praise.[21] Republicans like Rep. Newt Gingrich of Georgia, Rep. John Doolittle of California and Senator Kay Bailey Hutchison of Texas all told the press that they had joined United We Stand America.[22] And he was invited to address the incoming class of freshmen House Republicans, a rare honor.

Both parties also tapped top pollsters from their ranks to study the Perot phenomenon and report back on how to capture his voters. Stanley Greenberg, Clinton's pollster, produced a report for the conservative-leaning Democratic Leadership Council titled "The Road to Realignment: The Democrats and the Perot Voters." Greenberg found that Perot voters were both antigovernment and antiestablishment, distrustful of almost all big institutions from Congress to big business and big labor. Their interest in the deficit, he discovered, was not a top priority in and of itself (they were more concerned about the economy, jobs, and health care), but as "a symbol of the mess in Washington [and] problems growing out of control." Thus, Democrats could win the support of Perot voters by reforming government and making it work for average people again. "The Democrats will win over Perot voters only when the Democrats are seen to represent the people and to oppose greed, privilege and special interests," Greenberg wrote. "To win over Perot voters, Clinton must emerge as a reformer— even as he seeks to govern successfully."[23]

Frank Luntz, who had actually done polling for Perot before returning to the GOP fold, told his fellow Republicans in an article for the right-wing Heritage Foundation's *Policy Review* that they needed to be careful in how they went about the business of opposing the Clinton administration if they wanted to win back the support of Perot voters, most of whom had voted for Presidents Reagan and Bush. Republicans were distrusted as much as Democrats by this swing group, he warned. "It has to be clear that opposition to the president is based on principle, not partisanship. It must be cloaked in plain talk, not inside political-speak," Luntz advised. But he projected that Republicans could succeed if they paid attention to the roots of Perot voters' frustration. "So much of the Perovian anger was generated by the perception that 'they're always shafting the middle class' and the pervasive attitude that 'I'm tired of the government taking [and then wasting] my money.' . . . If Republicans can show that Mr. Clinton's new spending programs will come from the pockets of the middle class, they will lay a path for bringing these voters to the GOP."[24]

Still, Perot continued to haunt the two parties, at times even leading in surveys asking voters who they would hypothetically prefer for president in 1996. In May of 1993, a *U.S. News and World Report* poll found that in a three-way race he would tie Clinton with 35 percent of the vote, with Dole trailing at 25 percent.[25] Asked that same month, "Do you think Ross Perot generally represents your views or not," 48 percent said yes.[26] Almost 40 percent of those polled by Gallup for CNN/USA *Today* in March of 1993 said they were a supporter of Perot's (nearly a quarter describing themselves as a "strong supporter"). Tougher measures were needed to defuse the Perot threat.

For the Democrats, the ideal opportunity to tackle Perot and damage his high standing in public opinion came in the fall of 1993, as Congress debated Clinton's proposal for a North American Free Trade Agreement (NAFTA). An unusual array of opponents to the treaty arose, ranging from Patrick Buchanan on the right and Perot in the middle to Jesse Jackson and Ralph Nader on the left. Congress was split, with most Democrats in the House expressing opposition and insisting on tougher protections for labor and the environment. The NAFTA opposition demanded a real debate with the Clinton adminstration.

It was an opportunity for a political master stroke by the White House. Instead of agreeing to debate Nader, who had the greatest support among labor unions and environmentalists, the Clinton administration chose to engage Perot, offering to send Vice President Al Gore to debate him on the *Larry King Show*, Perot's favorite venue.[27]

Gore, who had an undeserved reputation as wooden and boring, battered Perot merci-lessly, interrupting him at will, connecting him to the protectionists Smoot and Haw-ley, who had helped bring on the Great Depression; and declaring that Perot represented fear and the politics of the past while the administration represented hope and the future. Thus, instead of engaging the serious questions about NAFTA, Gore successfully caricatured its opponents as Perot-style kooks. After the debate was over, the percentage of people who said they would consider voting for Perot had dropped to 28 percent (from 45 percent in May 1993), according to a survey by Celinda Lake and Ed Goeas for *U.S. News and World Report*.[28]

Republicans also took a harder approach toward Perot once the shock of the '92 vote had subsided. On one hand, top leaders like Dole stopped treating him with kid gloves. After earlier suggesting that President Clinton put Perot in charge of his rein-venting government program, Dole trashed Perot as "a walking sound bite," "a great hit-and-run artist" who can make a splash and then "run back to Dallas on his private jet."[29] Dole also pointed out that Perot didn't deserve his standing as the leading candi-date in the polls against the Democrats. "He's actually got a pretty liberal record," Dole said on CNN's *Inside Politics* in late August 1993. "He was for more taxes than Clin-ton, he had a 50-cent gas tax. That would be a hard sell out in the Midwest and cer-tainly a hard sell up in New England," Dole added, suggesting that Perot would have a tough time as a future presidential candidate.

At the same time, GOP leaders in Congress modeled whole chunks of their "Con-tract With America" on the agenda laid out by Perot in his 1993 book *Not For Sale At Any Price*, including support for term limits, a line-item veto, a balanced budget amendment that would require a three-fifths vote to raise taxes, various internal reforms of Congress's workings, and requiring that Congress be governed by the same laws it imposed on the rest of the country. They even added a special Gargan-style clause to the version of the contract that they published in *TV Guide* reading, "If we break this contract, throw us out."[30]

Perot, who at this point was insisting that he did not want to run again for president and that America didn't need a third party, was obviously pleased by the attention. Appearing yet again on the *Larry King Show* on October 4, 1994, he called on "Mr. and Mrs. America" to give the Republicans a majority in the House and Senate. "Let them have a turn at bat," he said, promising that if they didn't deliver on their promises, "I will give you every ounce of everything I have, and we will create a third party that will deliver."[31] Two-thirds of the people voting in 1994 who had supported Perot two years earlier voted for Republicans for Congress.[32]

The cumulative effect of the Republican landslide of 1994, Clinton's 1993 deficit cutting, and Gore's Perot bashing was to cut the wind from Perot's sails, but not to totally destroy his prospects. Though it would be years before the budget was balanced, and despite the fact that little had been done to enact the sorts of far-reaching political reforms demanded by the anti-incumbent movement, public perceptions of Perot's viability as the leader of any serious third-party effort were in obvious decline. Among independent voters—a broader group than the core who had voted for Perot in 1992— the tiny Texan was viewed negatively by 52 percent, with 25 percent viewing him favorably, according to a survey done after the 1994 elections by Stanley Greenberg. Still, a Gallup poll released February 10, 1995, showed he still had some standing. In a hypothetical three-way race with Dole and Clinton, Perot garnered a healthy 18 percent, compared to 41 for Dole and 39 for Clinton.

Stomping on the Grass Roots

In retrospect, it's clear that the Perot movement didn't collapse solely because the two parties did their best to absorb its energies and marginalize its leader. Many of the movement's core activists were so alienated from the major parties that a few ameliorative actions were not going to be enough to draw them back into the two-party fold. If anything, action on the budget deficit and the passage of free trade agreements between 1993 and 1995 had the effect of shifting some of Perot's more affluent and educated backers out of his camp, while more younger and less well-off voters were drawn to him, according to polls.[33] Perot's own actions, and those of the people he hired to oversee United We Stand America, and later, the Reform Party itself, had a huge impact on the movement's fortunes.

There is a repetitive pattern to the history of Perot's movement. At several crucial moments, political activists struggling to build a new, independent political force collided with the interests of the man in Dallas. Amazingly, at the same time that one cohort of Perot followers were discovering that he was not the great man they thought he was, another wave of eager volunteers arose to fill their shoes. It was like the children's story *The 500 Hats of Bartholomew Cubbins*, in which the lead character keeps pulling off his hat only to find another one beneath it. Or, to use a more brutal metaphor, like the World War I battle of Gallipoli, in which each succeeding wave of infantry leaping out of the trenches imagined that it would survive the machine-gun fire that mowed down its predecessors. Somehow, when one group of dissidents would surface, making credible charges of Perot ignoring the wishes of the elected leaders of his so-called grass-roots organization and abusing the trust of literally thousands of hardworking volunteers, others either didn't hear or didn't want to listen. Either people really didn't have access to the many reports of trouble within the Perot movement, or they actively disbelieved them—seeing the mainstream press as yet one more face of a political establishment they had come to totally distrust. And so the whole cycle would be repeated again, with new true believers rising to leadership roles, experiencing the reality of Perot's management, and then dropping out in disillusionment.

Perot officially launched United We Stand America in February 1993, describing it as a citizens lobby that would watchdog the two major parties. "I am Ross; you are the boss," he told his supporters, promising that they would control the organization. Over the next several months, he spent nearly $10 million of his own money to build it (according to the organization's tax filings),[34] taking out ads in *TV Guide* and other newspapers, running half-hour infomercials on NBC-TV, and making speeches across the country. Surveys done for Perot by Gordon Black claimed that anywhere between 13 percent (in February) to 24 percent (in April) of the American public said they were planning to join the group.[35] Dues were $15 a year (later raised to $20). Perot declined to release the actual membership numbers, and various press outlets suggested that UWSA might have anywhere between 2 million and 5 million members. Reporting for *The Perot Periodical*, a quarterly newsletter I had started in 1993 to track Perot and his movement, my colleague Mark Spencer discovered that the group had mailed only 1,232,588 copies of its mid-September national newsletter. Other credible sources suggested a membership of 1.5 million. But that was still indicative of an impressive base of support, more contributors than either the Democrats or the Republicans could claim.[36] (By comparison, in 1990 the Sierra Club said it had 565,000 members meeting in 378 local groups, and the National Organization for Women reported some 280,000 members spread across 800 chapters in 1993.)[37]

What happened? The voices of the disillusioned tell the story best, as they tumbled out of the Perot movement in succeeding waves. Bob Erwin, a retired New York City high school teacher, had been active in the Perot campaign practically from the very beginning, in April 1992. A year later, he had joined UWSA, but published "A Volunteer's Lament," asking for more democracy within the group. Here is some of what he had to say:

> What promised to be vigorous democratic participation has increasingly become a personal tour de force by Ross, who's down on the court playing one-on-one with the media while his volunteers sit in the stands as his cheering section. We expected to suit up and train to become a world-class team. Instead small groups of us wander down to the local schoolyard for pickup games. On our own initiative, without guidance or encouragement from Perot headquarters in Dallas except for soliciting memberships ("the only game in town," we are told), we demonstrate against the North American Free Trade Agreement, present forums on issues, network with other civic-action groups and establish contacts with elected representatives. Important? Surely. But no substitute for standing united on the big issues and pursuing the big agenda.
>
> All political organizations are prone to factional conflicts. United We Stand America is no exception. Within it there are two factions that have been at odds from the

beginning: Dallas' hired hands and the volunteers. Those paid operatives in Dallas are out of their real professions and seem not to have a clue to the skills needed to direct the volunteers. Throughout the petition, election and membership campaigns, incompetence and conflict reigned. Our successes were almost all products of "creative chaos" initiated by the volunteers.

Since the November election, the volunteer contingents in many states have split into two general camps: controlists and activists. The former—whatever their motives—preach a do-nothing-'til-we-hear-from-Dallas sermon at every juncture. They have nigh-zero tolerance for dissent. They resent initiatives by volunteers. They run illegal credit checks on dissidents. They even excommunicate volunteers without due process. . . .

Of course, they have many wannabe activists who will stay loyal until they suffer an achey-breaky heart, usually just after Dallas appoints an executive director for their state. The directors, often from out of the state where they were sent to work, almost without exception launch thoroughgoing changes in the organizations without consulting the members who live there. Nearly every time that affliction strikes, the ranks of the dissidents grow.

The activists' main demands are:

- Empower the members to choose local leaders democratically. (Dallas controls the database and keeps it completely secret.)
- Charter the state organizations with democratic safeguards.
- Empower the states to nominate, and members to elect, the national leadership. (At the moment, ultimate power lies in the hands of a three-person board of directors in Dallas—a far cry from making The People the Boss.) [38]

These complaints about the lack of internal democracy were amplified by the fact that the state executive directors of UWSA, tapped by Perot to run the state chapters, were disproportionately hired out of the military. My colleague Tom Gogola and I ultimately determined that seventeen out of forty-nine of those hired by early 1994 came out of the armed forces, including the group's second national executive director, Vollney Corn. Corn told Gogola that Perot had specifically looked for recruits among retiring personnel at the Army War College. [39] For a long time, I thought this predilection for retired military came from Perot's interest in working with people comfortable commanding a large organization from above, like himself. (He prided himself on his Navy background, was a fierce hawk and defender of the war in Vietnam, and ran his company Electronic Data Systems according to a very strict and conservative code of conduct.) But Jack Gargan, speaking from years of close experience with the Perot movement, saw something else. "Perot hired mostly middle-level officers because they are used to taking orders and implementing them," he told me when I visited him in Cedar Key in 1998. "There were damn few of them who were higher in rank than major."[40]

Disunited We Fall

During UWSA's first two years, the group was wracked by internal disputes over state charters and bylaws that were ultimately a fight over how much of a top-down or bottom-up organization it would be. Unfortunately, "For the People," words emblazoned on the group's eagle banner, meant something very different from "By the People." The results were comical and ruinous. For example, congressional district coordinators were given master lists of their local members only if they first signed confidentiality agreements binding them as to their use. Dallas also kept the upper hand over fractious grass-roots chapters by literally setting up UWSA as a franchise operation.[41] This approach might work for a trade organization or guild, but it cut sharply against the grain of grass-roots organizing.

Problems began to break out all over the country. From day one, dissident members in New York state battled Perot over the used of the name United We Stand, and several went on national TV to condemn his practices. One, Joyce Shepard, even created a countergroup called DUPED, for "Disenchanted United People for Equality and Democracy in UWSA."[42] Florida, the first branch of UWSA to hold an official state convention (in July 1993) and elect a board of directors, was also the first to self-destruct. By February 1994, all three of the elected statewide officers had resigned, along with thirteen out of twenty-three of the group's elected congressional district coordinators.[43]

United We Stand projected a united image to the press when it held a three-day leadership conference in Dallas that same month. At Perot's behest, the group's paid state directors and elected volunteer state chairs met together to develop an action plan for UWSA's reform agenda. The meetings were closed to the press, however. And little information was provided about UWSA's actual membership or decision-making process. When Perot and the state leaders held a press conference at the end of the meeting, Perot insisted, "You've heard me say a hundred times, I'm incidental to this organization. This is their organization. They run it, they control it, they make decisions." So when Dan Balz of the *Washington Post* asked him, "How many members do you have?" he deferred to Debi Berberich of Kentucky, who said the state chairs had voted 42-8 not to disclose the number. She instead pointed to a huge poster beside her showing the $4 trillion national debt, saying that was the only number that they cared about.[44]

What wasn't reported at the time was how Perot used that February 1994 conference to cement his hold on UWSA. Kirk MacKenzie, the volunteer who was the elected chairman of UWSA–California, recalled that the decision was made to have an eleven-member board. "Few people realized what was happening. They [Perot's Dallas operatives] said, 'You get to pick five.' If this is a people's organization, why aren't all ten filled by volunteers? Five were all Perot's paid staff. People like Darcy Anderson [UWSA's first national director] and Sharon Holman [Perot's spokeswoman and longtime employee]. And they said, 'By the way, would you like to have Ross Perot on the board? Who the hell is not going to vote for Perot on the board?' It was manipulated to make it look like we wanted Perot on the board." His conclusion: "They wanted absolute control from the start. He's a very control-oriented individual."

As the elected chairman of a chapter that initially had 180,000 members, MacKenzie was shocked by how he was treated. "Dallas never contacted me and never once did Perot or anybody in Dallas ask for my opinion or to check members' opinions. We had members that wanted to do things, but basically we were stonewalled. His message was financial accountability for our government, quarterly reports, yet Ross Perot was the most secretive in the world about UWSA's money." The overall problem was "duplicity," MacKenzie said. "If he had said 'I'm Ross, I'm Boss, I know what I'm doing, follow me'—no big problem. The real problem is that he says 'I'm Ross, you're boss. I'm helping you build your own organization.' So people take time away from their families, children, spouses, and spend money they can't afford, to find out that this was not their organization either. I had a woman who was selling her blood in order to come to meetings. I stepped away from my company for a year, took no pay, tried to help my country, and I certainly expected a fight. But not from within UWSA."

MacKenzie took it upon himself to call around to other state chairmen to find out, "Jeez, is this just me?" His discovery was "about 70 percent had a problem, but not all at the same time. There was a four-step process to enlightenment. First you know something's wrong. You think it's the state director. Then you get to the regional director. Then you're convinced they're the problem. Then you contact Dallas and reach the national director, and you realize that they are just doing what they are supposed to do. Then you realize that it is Ross Perot. This process takes time. Florida and New York were ahead of me. I was contacted by New York people before I was elected, but I just wrote them off. Of those 70 percent, many didn't want to go public, many didn't want to go against a billionaire."[45]

By the summer of 1994, at least fourteen elected state chairs of UWSA had quit or been forced out of the organization for all sorts of reasons, including showing independent initiative and disagreeing with their Dallas-paid state director. Some also quit because they couldn't afford to keep volunteering so much of their time, and they were galled at the amount of money from membership dues that went to the paid UWSA staff instead of reimbursing their out-of-pocket costs.[46] In response, some grass-roots leaders of UWSA made efforts to try to fix the situation. One was led by Dave Morgan,

the volunteer who was elected chair of UWSA–Washington state, where Perot had gotten 24 percent of the vote in 1992 and where his anti-incumbent troops had played a
big role in the ousting of most of the state's congressional Democrats in 1994. With the
support of grass-roots leaders from eleven other western states, Morgan called for a
"Mid Course Correction" in a June 1994 memo that was widely circulated throughout
the movement. Morgan was blunt, saying "the wild flower of UWSA is being choked
out by the weeds of organization. We stepped out of the box in concept, but stepped
into the box in execution. As a result we have no clear direction, no clear mission, and
no clear plan." Morgan suggested phasing out the state UWSA franchises, organizing
teams by congressional districts that would work on whatever issues they wished, with
national headquarters acting as the hub and the paid staff assisting the members in
whatever ways they could.[47]

At first, Morgan got a friendly reception from Perot's lieutenants in Dallas. Some of
his recommendations were adopted, including the loosening of rules requiring the formal licensing of state chapters and the idea of working in teams. But then excerpts
from another critical report written by Morgan and other state chairs hit the Internet,
and the fur flew once again. According to Morgan, Perot was so incensed at the partial
release of this report that he insisted its authors recant their findings or lose their state
charters. "Perot went crazy over one recommendation, which got posted on the Internet, that the regional directors were not effective." These UWSA employees were
Perot's chief troubleshooters. Some state chairs did drop their criticism, Morgan said,
but their spirits were crushed. "We're all just ordinary people."[48]

By May of 1995, at the end of all the vituperation, Morgan told one Perot loyalist
who wrote him out of concern that he was "burn[ing] down UWSA" that the only person to blame for the group's failures was Perot. "I am offended by my leader, Ross
Perot, lying to me over and over again. He treats those who would only ask, 'What do
you want, Ross?' like we are traitors. I worked within the system that Ross told me to
build. I built it. Then he complains that the bylaws are killing us. He is the one who
told us to write them, for crying out loud. Now it seems he can't understand how or
why we chew each other up time and again. The reason is that Ross is like [a] father
that abandons his child. UWSA was fathered by Ross. We, his children, needed his
leadership and his guidance. (We still do.) We have gotten neither leadership nor guidance from Ross. In fact, [he] lies to us. Not a good thing to do to [sic] in front of the
children. He is the 'dead beat dad of UWSA.'"[49]

Morgan's fellow Washingtonian Skip Leuschner, a retired rear admiral and the former commanding officer of the USS *Enterprise*, had come to a strikingly similar conclusion. He too, was fed up with being treated like a child by Perot and his hired hands,
constantly being cajoled to get more dues-paying members but given no other meaningful role to play. "We are UWSA's Girl Scout Cookie salesman [sic], and like those

charming but unsophisticated children, we have been entirely excluded from organizational brainstorming and policy making," he wrote in a message circulated on a UWSA e-mail list-serve. Leuschner, one of the most prominent recruits to Perot's grassroots banner, threw in the towel. "The fact is, I am angry, truly angry, about a missed opportunity for UWSA to become a well organized, major political power in the USA. That opportunity is gone. Can't be recovered or revitalized because too many former enthusiasts share my anger. UWSA, Inc./Dallas has no credibility, and I can't think of any strategy to restore it. All because of simple, correctable (but to date, uncorrected) ineptness in leadership, administration, money management, intellectual and practical honesty, you name it, by a 'closed-to-member-input' hireling hierarchy in what we believed was to be a grassroots movement."

Leuschner's words could serve as UWSA's epitaph. "I have given 2 years of my life to UWSA, Inc. already, with no return on investment," he said. "All I got was a dime-store certificate of appreciation in a plastic frame with a facsimile of Ross' signature—quite suitable for a Girl Scout Cookie salesman, but to me, this cheap gimmick only served to reveal the infantile mentality of UWSA, Inc. 'leadership.' We would really like to have a UWSA, Inc. that was useful, helpful and needed, but there is no such thing yet. Enough."[50] Or, as Kirk MacKenzie put it, "We're not dissenters or defectors, we're disillusioned. The enlightened. We came, we saw, we left."[51]

Membership in the organization rapidly crashed. A survey of people who had called Perot's 800-number in 1992 to work on his petition drive found that only about 20 percent reported remaining active four years later.[52] The group's tax filings showed a precipitous drop in dues collection, from $18.3 million in 1993 to $4.4 million in 1994.[53] A state-by-state survey conducted independently of Dallas by leaders of the UWSA–Ohio chapter in the summer of 1995 discovered only a few states that claimed to be going strong. For example, Colorado went from twenty-eight thousand members in 1993 to fourteen thousand a year later, according to its former chairman. The chapter had boasted leaders in all sixty-three of the state's counties and an extensive communications network for contacting and activating members. But, after numerous tussles with Dallas—the state board went so far as to threaten to cancel a rally in Denver that Perot was scheduled to address if he refused to meet with the membership—UWSA–Colorado voted to disband in April 1995.[54]

Chapters in California that originally had hundreds of active members who sponsored debates, put out newsletters, and held issue forums "now consist of a dozen people who meet only irregularly," Michael Gunn, an activist trying to drum up support to put a political reform initiative on the state ballot, reported in May 1995.[55] South Dakota's membership plummeted from three thousand to five hundred.[56] Washington state imploded from fifty thousand members to no more than fifty, according to its state chair.[57] The chair of UWSA–Florida told the Ohio surveyers, "Many wonderful people have been, and still are being screwed, blued, and tattooed by Dallas!"[58] The entire board of the Massachusetts chapter voted to disband in January of 1995,[59] as did the board of directors of the Hawaii chapter in February 1995.[60] And when Marilou Stanley, the popular executive director of UWSA–Arizona, was fired by Dallas in June 1995, her board appointed her state director, and the chapter essentially broke away from Perot's control. In response, in the UWSA national newsletter, the phone number for people to call for information about Arizona issues and activities was changed to an 800-number that was routed to the UWSA–New Mexico office.[61] Not long after that, a self-organized group of state leaders and activists met in Las Vegas and symbolically "fired" Perot.[62]

If the Perot movement ever had a chance of developing into a truly viable third party, that possibility was probably destroyed by what happened within United We Stand America—well before Perot created the Reform Party in September 1995 and long before Patrick Buchanan took it over in 2000. After all, the millions of people who joined and supported UWSA were the activist core of the 19 million people who voted for Perot in 1992. And though each individual voter might well ask himself or herself, "Why bother? One person can't make a difference," this well-known paradox of collective action was nullified by the presence of so many fellow citizens identifying with UWSA, along with Perot's implied promise to spend more money on the costs of organizing. The leading activists inside UWSA were a cross section of middle America: medium-status professionals, small-business owners, sales representatives, self-employed entrepreneurs, and a few who made their living using their hands.[63] But as UWSA lost most of its best volunteers between 1993 and 1995, and Perot's public image suffered from the many credible reports of his high-handed and disastrous management of the group, it became less likely that the Perot movement would be able to grow beyond its narrowing base of loyal diehards.

Put another way, the Perot movement completely lost its moorings between 1993 and 1995. With the exception of a few states like Minnesota and Oregon, where the original anti-incumbent activists of 1992 had started third parties and made some inroads on their own initiative, most of the people still involved in the movement as it evolved, under Perot's command, from a nonpartisan watchdog role into an explicit third-party effort, were either "Perotbots" in thrall of the tiny Texan, budding politicos in his pay (and activists hoping to be paid by him), or devotees of some other charismatic leader seeking to take over from Perot. Here and there one still found hardworking and sensible volunteers who admitted Perot had serious flaws but valued his efforts to oppose international trade agreements and the like. But for the most part, by 1995, Perot and his remaining followers had lost whatever organic connection they originally had to the "angry middle." Instead, they steadily moved toward the fringes of American politics, a place where disaffected political activists often thrive, but do so by warring with each other at the expense of building an organization capable of winning mass support.

4

The Rise (and Fall)
of the Reform Party

The Last Refuge of Scoundrels

Though Perot got more votes in 1992 than any third-party or independent candidate for president in U.S. history, he did not want to start a third party—or at least that was what he claimed. "If I ever have to run in 1996, we have failed," Ross Perot told CNN's Larry King. "We don't have four years to wait. We want the two-party system to work."[1] On the day of the climactic vote on the North American Free Trade Agreement, which he had vociferously opposed, he told the *New York Times* that United We Stand America could evolve into a third party if the two parties did not change direction and become more responsive to average voters. "But that's up to the membership, not me," he insisted. "I have no personal goals. I would prefer a strong, responsive two-party system. That's my dream."[2]

Eventually, Perot went back on these words in a manner that sowed even more doubts about his political skills among the millions of people who had once supported him. But before he decided to plunge into forming the Reform Party, other people had the same idea. As noted in the previous chapter, a group associated with pollster Gordon Black had formed a Federation of Independent Parties organizing committee as early as the fall of 1992. While Perot focused publicly on building UWSA as a nonpartisan organization, these more venturesome pioneers continued to try to cobble together the various state efforts that were growing independently out of the first Perot campaign. They were joined by some preexisting formations like "A Connecticut

Party," the third party that had been Lowell Weicker's vehicle to the governor's office in 1990 (so named as to give the party the alphabetical advantage of being listed first on the state ballot).

After more than a year of internal negotiations, the Federation of Independent Parties was ready to hold its inaugural convention. "It is the intention of the delegates to create a new kind of political party which is centrist in its direction, which focuses on reform of the current political system to provide for the inclusion in all Americans [sic] in the democratic process, which promotes fiscal responsibility on the part of government and individual responsibility on the part of all Americans, and which seeks to end the rule of a class of career politicians by replacing them with citizen legislators from this party who will be more concerned with the problems of our country than with being reelected," said the April 12, 1994, press release from Nicholas Sabatine III, a small-town lawyer from Wind Gap, Pennsylvania, who had helped start a third party in his state. Representatives from twenty-four states were expected to attend.[3]

It was spring, and the cherry blossoms in Washington, D.C., were in bloom. The Stouffers Hotel in Arlington, Virginia, across the river from the Capitol, was a twelve-story concrete-and-glass tower along a stretch of corporate office buildings known as Crystal City. The new party's birthplace was not very auspicious, but probably a practical choice for the lower hotel rates. I walked in to the main hall, expecting to see lots of middle-aged white men and women, the core base of the Perot petition drive. Instead, amid the older couples and funny guys in tri-corner hats and red-white-and-blue sports coats were a large number of younger people—an interracial, cosmopolitan-looking group. Many of them circled like worker bees around a few people seated at the New York delegation's table. It took me a moment to recognize the attractive African-American woman seated at the table. Lenora Fulani was the perennial candidate of the sectlike New Alliance Party (NAP), having run for president in 1992 and for governor of New York before that. Her mentor and the party's intellectual guide, Fred Newman, an older white man with a graying beard and wild hair, sat next to her at the center of the hubbub.

This wasn't the coming together of the "angry middle." As the day unfolded, I watched as the leaders of several of the fledgling state parties that arose from the Perot campaign entered into an open embrace with the leaders of another cult of personality. The world of third parties has always had its hucksters, little grouplets with charismatic leaders that preyed on gullible individuals. My friend and colleague Bruce Shapiro laid it all out in a long cover story he wrote for The Nation in 1992 titled "Dr. Fulani's Traveling Snake Oil Show." Not only did the New Alliance Party have a controversial reputation for its practice of recruiting members through "social therapy" groups, and for its checkered past of neo-Marxist communalism and alliances with everyone from conspiracy theorist Lyndon Larouche to black nationalist Al Sharpton (during his most flamboyant and irresponsible years) and Nation of Islam leader Louis Farrakhan. The NAP also had a long and sordid record of latching onto and trying to take over stable organizations to move them into the Newman-Fulani orbit. Earlier targets included the New Jewish Agenda, a progressive peace-and-justice coalition; the California Peace and Freedom Party; the AIDS activist group ACT-UP; the All-African Unity Party; and the American Public Health Association. All had experienced similar takeover fights, in which their meetings would suddenly swell with a large number of well-organized outsiders.[4]

I later learned that the New Alliance Party's involvement with the Federation of Independent Parties had been a problem for many former Perot followers well in advance of the Arlington convention. Fledgling Perot-inspired parties from several states—including Georgia, Illinois, Kansas, Maryland, and South Carolina—had decided not to attend in reaction. (Some were also put off by Gordon Black's earlier association with Perot in 1992 and early 1993 as his pollster. Many of these people wanted nothing to do with Perot. Their reflexive distrust of politicians now extended to the antipolitician from Texas, whom they saw as a would-be dictator.) As a result, by this process of self-selection, nearly half the 110 delegates there were NAP members.[5] I watched as they voted as an organized bloc, and the other delegates, politically inexperienced and clearly impressed by the NAP members' skills and energy, pretty much let them stack the party's executive committee with Fulani followers, including Jim Mangia, a gay activist from Los Angeles, as secretary.[6] (Mangia would eventually come to serve in that same position in the Reform Party.)

The delegates voted with little dissent to call the new party the Patriot Party and to adopt a constitution and bylaws. And the supposed basis for cooperation between the largely white, suburban, middle-class Perotistas and the NAP members who claimed to speak for the black urban underclass? Ralph Copeland, co-founder of the Oregon American Party, a Perot '92 offshoot, told the convention, to great applause, "We are not the white, middle-class, disenfranchised Perot movement. We are not the black, ghetto-based, disenfranchised movement. We are all disenfranchised politically. But as Perot said, 'United we stand.'" This was a reflection of a theme that Fred Newman had been developing for some time: that a third party should be built solely around the issue of opening up democracy. Other ideological differences supposedly didn't matter.[7] Jacqui Salit, a vivacious, dark-haired woman who served as Fulani's spokeswoman, told me in a follow-up interview, "The Patriot Party is a new kind of political party, one that won't be tied down by pointless political differences."[8] The beauty of this approach is that not only did it elide all the policy conflicts one might expect to encounter in any serious effort to merge groups claiming support among white suburbanites and the urban minority poor, it also allowed the NAP to sweep its entire prior history in left-wing sectarian politics under the rug.[9] (This dodge would become even more important a few years later, when Fulani entered into a bizarre alliance with right-wing Patrick Buchanan as he sought the Reform Party's nomination.)

As it was, the embryonic Patriot Party was already a very odd beast. In addition to a few candidates for office who emphasized their support for traditional Christian values and several speakers who talked about their background in the Marines, praising the military, there was Colin Moore, an African-American lawyer from New York City who earned some notoriety as the defense attorney for one of four black men charged with assaulting and raping a Central Park jogger. During the trial, Moore charged that the police cared about the case only because the jogger was white and well-to-do, and he compared the defendants to Jewish victims of Nazi Germany. A few weeks after the Patriot convention, Moore was barred from practicing law for three years for unethical treatment of several clients.[10] Then there was James Edward Bess, an African-American man from Washington state dressed nattily in the manner of a member of the Nation of Islam, who was asked to give a benediction before the party began its election of officers. Bess was a supporter of Fulani's who worked with the NAP on several projects in the late 1980s.[11] He would be of little note, except that less than six weeks later he took a gun and fired several times at Nation of Islam firebrand Khalid Muhammed after a speech at the University of California in Riverside, hitting him in both legs.

As best as I could ascertain, there was no other connection between Bess, a defrocked Nation of Islam minister, and the New Alliance Party. All the Patriot Party officials I spoke to after the shooting expressed shock at the incident.[12] But some prominent members of the party did have a friendly relationship with Nation of Islam head Louis Farrakhan. (Farrakhan had suspended Muhammed, his senior aide, after Muhammed gave a speech describing Jews as "the bloodsuckers" of the black community and the pope as a "no-good cracker," racist statements that were too much even for Farrakhan, a notorious anti-Semite.)[13] Fulani and Newman's friendship with Farrakhan was no secret at the Patriot Party convention. Copies of the NAP's *National Alliance* newspaper were scattered all over the Arlington convention hall, with a prominent ad selling videos of "A *Real* Black-Jewish Dialogue," showing Farrakhan seated between Fulani and Newman (who is Jewish) for an interview on Fulani's cable TV show.

Since most of the speakers at the convention, Perotistas and Fulani followers alike, kept insisting that "we have more in common than what divides us," it seemed important to ask if that included support for Farrakhan. During a postconvention press conference, party chairman Sabatine told me, "I don't know that much about Mr. Farrakhan. I haven't had a chance to sit down at a table and talk to him. I have had a chance to sit down with Lenora Fulani. I know for a fact that she is not an anti-Semite or a racist." Later, he told me that the issue "is not relevant to what this party is about now." And he predicted that "as the Patriot Party starts growing, Lenora and I both know her associates will become more and more of a minority in the party."[14]

Other important backers of the new party effort did have concerns, however. Lowell Weicker's "A Connecticut Party" decided not to affiliate after attending the Arlington convention. Gordon Black, the pollster who had helped get the Patriot ball rolling, noted that some state parties were being split by the presence of the NAP faction. But he agreed with Sabatine in expecting that the party would grow rapidly as more people joined from the Perot movement, and "in that context, they're not a threat."[15] Theodore Lowi, the Cornell political scientist who had helped give the fledgling effort intellectual grounding, was far less sanguine. "You have expanded the party by incorporating racists from the New Alliance Party," he wrote in a memo he distributed to the Federation of Independent Parties mailing list. "A third party will always attract radicals, crazies, and other kinds of extremists. That's in the nature of the beast. We had taken care to avoid this in our original organizational efforts. The Patriot Party has put the effort at risk." In a concurrent letter that he sent to Fulani, he said, "I will not be part of any third party, however passionately I want to see a third party succeed, which carries party opportunity to such an extent that they will let the ugliest racism go by with a finesse."[16] And with that he submitted his resignation from the federation.

Perot: "It's My Party, and I'll Run It How I Want To . . ."

From this point onward, there were only three significant branches of the political movement that grew out of the Perot 1992 campaign: the nonpartisan group United We Stand America, which was in decline but still under Perot's firm command; the Patriot Party, which, partially as a result of the Fulani connection, did not grow much beyond its first convention; and a few intrepid state parties, most notably the Minnesota Independence Party, and a handful of independent candidates for office, like Jack Gargan. None of these efforts appeared likely to sweep the nation anytime soon.

That, of course, was not the impression conveyed by the announcement of Perot's national convention in Dallas in August 1995. The event had originally been billed as a special meeting—a "Declaration of Independents! Conference"—for United We Stand members who had, at Perot's behest, spent most of the first half of the year holding local forums on whether a new political party would be good for the country.[17] Presumably the third-party question would be decided there. One UWSA regional director, Ralph Perkins, told a newspaper in March that 60 to 65 percent of the people attending these forums believed a third party was needed; early reports from states like Texas also suggested that Perot's top aides were helping stir a groundswell in favor.[18] And then, without any consultation of UWSA's members, Perot revealed in early June that instead the event would be a national conference on "Preparing our Country for the 21st Century," and that he had asked the top leadership of the Democratic and

Republican parties to address the UWSA membership. If the Arlington meeting of the Patriot Party was weird, this promised to be bizarre.

Perot invited every current presidential candidate from both parties, the top parties' congressional leaders, and the parties' national chairmen and other top spokesmen (pointedly excluding Vice President Al Gore). With the exception of President Clinton, they all decided to attend. "I look forward to participating in what will be an important forum," said Senator Christopher Dodd, then the Democrats' national chairman. "The fact that so many prominent politicians are willing to travel to Dallas . . . is a vivid demonstration of how much influence Mr. Perot and his supporters still wield," noted the *New York Times*.[19] Only former Connecticut governor Lowell Weicker, then publicly considering an independent run for the presidency, dared to say what was on everyone's mind. "We all know what it's about, which is to wheel and deal a little in Dallas." He added, "The only blessing I need to run is my own."[20]

Despite (or perhaps because of) the attendance of all these luminaries, Perot had trouble filling the Dallas Convention Center. He had originally projected a crowd of eight thousand, but the final total was closer to just three thousand. This was despite the fact that most of UWSA's paid staff were mobilized for the months prior to the event to assure turnout. Members had to pay their own way, and many reported that they couldn't afford to go or were not interested in being props for Perot's dog-and-pony show. One wrote the UWSA list-serve:

> Here in Colorado Springs we are upset, confused, irritated, and downright angry. Several of our members were intending to go to the National Meeting to take part in the historic beginning of a third party, or if we were lucky, to hear Mr. Perot or some other high qualified leader take over the Democratic Party. Now on Friday Char Roberts forwarded the news that Russ Verney says "This conference will provide an educational opportunity to hear outstanding speakers discussing balanced budget" and related items. The outstanding speakers invited are such "greats" as Bill Clinton and Arlen Specter. We can get that drivel for the next nine months right off the TV and I can sit there with my zapper at the ready. We had hoped to be able to go there to Dallas, meet with like minded people and discuss our agreements and differences — not spend about $1,000 to hear political campaign speeches.[21]

Advance registration for the conference was so weak, at the last minute Perot decided to make the event free to all local firefighters, nurses, police, teachers, other civil servants, and senior citizens.[22] Still, the eight thousand-seat arena was never even half full.

All the big-name speakers did their best to rouse the nearly all-white crowd, but only a few, most notably right-wing firebrands Pat Buchanan and Alan Keyes, drew something more than polite applause. Buchanan in particular won a hearty response with a speech that was full of the harsh antigovernment and anti-elite rhetoric then popular with the militia movement. "When I raise my hand to take the oath of office, your New World Order comes crashing down," he roared, decrying the "surrender of our sovereignty to multinational institutions." The whole crowd was with him as he focused on America's economic ills and attacked NAFTA and GATT, and he kept them with him as he bashed illegal immigration, but he lost some as he shifted into an attack on liberal cultural values and abortion. "He hits all the hot buttons, but he's not my cup of tea—I'm into the politics of coalition, not division," said a mustached Texan seated next to me. An African-American member of UWSA from Illinois seated near us was silent and did not applaud. Still, a good number of people, maybe 10 percent of the audience, jumped out of their seats to shout, "Go Pat Go," when Buchanan finished with a call to help him win the Republican nomination.

Alas, that was the high point for the official proceedings. Later in the day, House Speaker Newt Gingrich got a tepid response when he admitted to the audience that his Republican majority had failed on one promise in the Contract With America, term limits. After someone in the audience shouted out, "Why should we trust you?" he got cheers when he said, "You shouldn't. Don't trust anyone you loan power to." Democratic Minority Leader Richard Gephardt got little response until he mentioned his opposition to NAFTA. Bob Dole, the Republicans' leading presidential candidate, was received politely, with the audience using his speech to send a subtle message. When he said "I guess everybody here is frustrated with the political process," someone shouted "YEAH!", provoking laughter and jeering. And when he ticked off a list of political reform measures that Republicans had helped pass, admitted that "we have one thing left—campaign finance reform," the audience responded with more jeers. Still, there was Perot, bouncing out after each speaker finished to wrap his arm around him and beam to the audience, "Now isn't that the greatest speech you ever heard in your life!"

In many ways, the event was a perfect crystallization of all that was wrong with Perot's operation, if building a vibrant political organization was ever the goal. Everything was top-down, with Perot available to his supporters only as the man with the microphone. His ad-libbed comments frequently showed that he was out of touch with their feelings. Workshops were held on various issues, but these were presentations from experts, not debates by participants. There was no real structure or process for participants to discuss or decide anything. People were given a booklet in which to write their comments on each speaker, to be turned in at the end of the weekend. But there was no seating by state, making it hard for people who might have a common interest by virtue of where they lived to even find each other. "They've managed to keep people from congregating, making them passive observers," noted Nick Sabatine, attending the event on behalf of the Patriot Party.

Needless to say, the third-party issue was scarcely touched by the big-name speakers from the major parties, and Perot avoided it in his remarks from the stage. The one workshop on "New Political Force: Party vs. Other Options," which did attract a large crowd to a side room at the convention center, was described by Dallas staffer Jeff Zucker, the outgoing editor of UWSA's national newsletter, primarily as an opportunity for participants to vent their feelings about the question.[23] Third-party advocates who wanted to use the conference to move forward were stiff-armed and ended up renting a suite in a hotel across the street, where about 120 people came to a meeting called by Sabatine.[24] Others who didn't want to annoy Perot by prematurely announcing a new national party stayed away, but tried to meet people of like mind. "You don't get Perot's ear," complained Richard Porter, an activist who headed UWSA–California's New Party Task Force. He was frustrated because he knew the deadline to collect the tens of thousands of signatures needed to put a new party on the ballot in his state — October 24, the earliest in the country and a full year before the next election — was rapidly approaching, and nothing had been decided.

As for Perot, he acted as though all these people didn't exist. My colleague Mark Spencer ran into Perot as he climbed into a golf cart after inspecting the booths and tables (while most of the participants were off attending workshops). Spencer asked him, "What is your response to all of the people who have come here to ask you to form a third party?" Perot's clipped answer was "They haven't talked to me about it."

Though Perot's conference resolved nothing about the future of his movement, it did offer one hint. The core of people still strongly loyal to Perot and capable of financing their own participation in his conference was tilting toward the populist right. That was made plain by the strong response to Pat Buchanan, above all the other speakers. But there was other evidence of a growing nativist tendency in Perot's movement, despite the Texan's own insistence that he didn't want the involvement of anyone who hated other people. Two southern California chapters of UWSA sponsored speeches by Jim Townsend, publisher-editor of a far-right magazine called the *National Educator* and the western bureau chief of *The Spotlight*, one of the most stridently anti-Semitic newspapers in the country.[25] Another chapter, in West Hills, California, published harsh anti-immigrant articles in its monthly newsletter, warning how "cosmopolitans" who "fashioned the Soviet Union" as their "dream" were polluting America's purity.[26]

UWSA's California chapters actually played a major role in collecting petition signatures to put Proposition 187 on the ballot in 1994. Known as the "Save Our State" initiative, Proposition 187 called for denying schooling and most medical services to California's undocumented immigrants and requiring state employees at all public health offices, police departments, schools, and welfare offices to report people without proof of legal residency to the Immigration and Naturalization Service.[27] At a rally in Buena Park in Orange County called by UWSA in the fall of 1994, the audience of three thousand gave one of the warm-up speakers, a retired INS official and leader in the Proposition 187 campaign, a standing ovation, a markedly stronger response than they gave Perot's speech that followed with its familiar emphasis on the deficit and trade.[28] Perot did little to deflect this tendency; indeed he fanned it with harsh criticism of President Clinton's foreign policy choices, particularly his decision to send troops to Haiti.

No one else had stepped forward and caught the public's eye with an alternative model of the movement's future during this period, as less committed and newly alienated Perotistas continued to melt back into the woodwork. Lowell Weicker's "A Connecticut Party" nominated his lieutenant governor, Eunice Groark, for governor, but with far less name recognition than the party's founder, she came in third in the election, with just 19 percent of the vote. One of the party's congressional candidates also managed to get 15 percent in the general election, but for all intents and purposes A Connecticut Party petered out, mainly because Weicker had decided to spend his political capital while in office on his legislative priorities rather than building the party. For Weicker, the party was just a vehicle for him to win office, little more.

During 1993–94, Jack Gargan put together an independent campaign for governor of Florida. Drawing on a deep well of support from his THRO days—a thousand people came to Tallahassee to hear his announcement speech—he marshaled a volunteer base that rapidly collected some fifty thousand petitions statewide to put him on the ballot. When that effort fell short of the nearly two hundred thousand signatures required—an almost insurmountable goal—he decided to take advantage of the fact that it was easier to enter the major-party primaries. As a Democrat challenging the incumbent governor, Lawton Chiles, he pulled 28 percent of the vote. That was a healthy total for a political newcomer, though Tom Fiedler, political editor for the *Miami Herald*, said later that it "was more a sign of conservative frustration with Governor Chiles and not so much a pro-Gargan vote."[29] Gargan ran first as a Perot-style government reformer promising to cut waste, paperwork, and taxes, but made his biggest splash for his harsh approach to crime. "I favor caning," he told the *Herald*, claiming such an approach to young, first-time offenders would deter much law-breaking. He also vowed to "fast-track" the 342 convicted murderers on Florida's Death Row.[30] His disciplinarian candidacy also promised "zero tolerance for drunk driving," "zero tolerance for rowdyism or truancy" by students, and said that "fathers will support their offspring or go to jail."[31] Gargan said his run for governor represented "a first step in a new direction," but the voters clearly didn't care for the direction. (It was significant that Perot declined to give Gargan any help, no doubt recalling Gargan's quiet criticism of him in 1992. Despite the fact that UWSA–Florida members leaned more toward Republican Jeb Bush in the governor's race, Perot endorsed Democrat Chiles, Gargan's opponent in the primary.[32])

So, by September of 1995, Perot and his movement seemed to be stuck in place and slowly sinking. Perot had blocked any internal resolution within UWSA about the third-party question, his indecision about the matter was draining energy from the stumbling third-party efforts already under way in and around the Patriot Party, and no one else had arisen from within the movement to point a new way forward. (Dean Barkley had run for Senate in Minnesota in 1994 and gotten 5.4 percent of the vote, making the Independence Party a major party and drawing Jesse Ventura's quiet interest. But the rise of Ventura's innovative campaign was still three years away.) All the little third-party shoots that had started growing in the fertile soil of 19 million Perot voters seemed to be failing.

Other Wild Cards Get Played

Aware that the public's hunger for more choices had not abated, the media began talking up the possible candidacy of Colin Powell, retired chairman of the Joint Chiefs of Staff. *Time* and *Newsweek* each put him twice on their covers, with the latter asking in September, "Can Colin Powell Save America?"[33] All this attention was used adroitly by Powell to sell his autobiography, *My American Journey*, but before he quelled the speculation of a possible independent candidacy or run for the Republican nomination, the polls suggested he would take the country by storm. For example, the *Times* poll taken in mid-September showed him beating President Clinton in a head-to-head match-up 50-40 percent and him running second as an independent in a three-way race with Dole, losing to Clinton 37 to 32 to 24 percent.[34]

There was also a lesser smattering of attention to politicians like Senator Bill Bradley, Democrat of New Jersey, who had announced his retirement from the Senate, and to Weicker. Bradley went on the *Charlie Rose* show on PBS in August, saying that he would not challenge President Clinton in 1996 but that he hadn't ruled out a run as an independent. "My instinct as a politician is that there's a yearning among the American people for some straight talk and some yearning for politicians to step up and begin to address what most people are concerned about," he told Rose.[35] He also told him he'd have a book, as yet untitled, coming out that winter. Weicker made similar noises to veteran *Washington Post* columnist David Broder, who wrote a column titled "Dark Horse May Make a Presidential Run." "If I feel I can contribute to the national debate," he told Broder, "I'll do it," promising a decision by the end of the year.[36] Like Powell, he timed this announcement to the publication of his autobiography, *Maverick*. If nothing else, the free publicity one could get from toying openly with a presidential bid could help sell books, one tangible effect of the public's desire for more options.

These dalliances ultimately matured into a more serious discussion among a group of seven prominent Democratic and independent political figures organized by former Governor Dick Lamm of Colorado. The group included former Massachusetts Senator Paul Tsongas, who ran for president as a Democrat in 1992; former Colorado Senator Gary Hart, who did the same in 1984 and 1988; Angus King, the newly elected independent governor of Maine; Tim Penny, a former House member from Minnesota; as well as Bradley and Weicker. As first reported by *Time* magazine, the Lamm group met over the fall of 1995 several Sundays by conference call, where participants "talked in detail about the need for a third voice to challenge the two-party system."[37] They shared position papers and agreed on the need for an independent approach that would be socially liberal, fiscally conservative, and pro–environmental protection, and for an overhaul of the corrupt campaign finance system.[38]

Lamm was probably the most important addition to the mix of names being thrown into the presidential speculation game. Hart had been damaged by scandal, Tsongas was fighting recurrent bouts of cancer, King had just entered office, and Penny, a conservative Democrat, was not very well known. Lamm, a controversial figure when he was governor for having once suggested that the elderly had "a duty to die," was often praised by mainstream pundits for his willingness to talk openly about supposedly taboo topics like reducing Social Security benefits. Even though news of Lamm's secret group only broke at the end of November, he had evidently been thinking about an independent run for some time, first for the U.S. Senate and now for the White House. "I've got a serious question whether either political party can put together the agenda that starts educating the public on the need to make some hard choices," he told his hometown paper at the end of August. "One of the options I really looked at was whether it's time for a third political party, or more particularly, whether it would be worth my time and effort to run as an independent."[39]

Lamm's willingness to speak what he saw as hard truths had not won him an enthusiastic response within his original party, the Democrats. So it was understandable for him to look elsewhere to promote his ideas for "compassionate austerity." The same was true of the other participants in the Lamm group. Penny, for example, favored the privatization of Social Security—another proposal that was then considered taboo— and had joined with the libertarian Cato Institute that summer in launching an effort to convince the public of the need for that extreme change.[40] Bradley was on a crusade that fall for "radical campaign finance reform," telling audiences around the country that "the single most important thing that we can do is to take money out of politics."[41] Hart, who had also thought about running for the same Colorado Senate seat that tempted Lamm, had given up on mainstream politics, saying both major parties had become a single ruling party, a "government party."[42]

These experienced politicians were all confronting the unpleasant reality that the two major parties preferred to avoid discussion of serious issues, blocked needed political reforms that would open the system more to the voices and concerns of average people, and suppressed electoral competition. It made sense for all of them to look toward a third-party or independent bid as a way of revitalizing politics and raising important issues. Their ruminations caught the eye of the political press and a few campaign consultants, and some in the small group of third-party activists who had helped start the Federation of Independent Parties. But ultimately, the Lamm group was a case of too many generals and no foot soldiers.

Perot Makes His Move

And meantime, the general with the professional field staff and the troops finally decided to use his army. On September 25, 1995, Perot went on *Larry King Live* to announce the creation of a new party "for the independent voters." In California, it was to be called the Reform Party, so as to not conflict with an existing party called the American Independent Party (an old holdover from George Wallace's third-party campaigns). Perot wanted the name in the rest of America to be the Independence Party, but swiftly dropped that when it became clear there would be too much confusion juggling two names. Perot claimed to not be financing the party, though ultimately he spent $9 million of his own money getting it off the ground. He likened his role to the grain of sand that irritates the oyster, with the pearl created "the American people once more [having] confidence in their government."

Though Perot acted as if this had been a reluctant decision, his close aides had actually been exploring the third-party option for quite some time. His move may have been prompted by a desire to get out in front of Colin Powell, who was then playing a very public game of footsie with the press over the prospect of his running for president possibly as an independent. Interviews with people close to Dallas, however, indicate that Perot moved because other independent third-party activists with their own financing had met with him and told him they would go forward if he did not.[43] Less than a week after that meeting, Perot made his announcement on King's CNN program.[44]

On the show, Perot described the new party as a collective enterprise: "We are announcing it tonight. . . . we will hit the streets next Monday. . . . we have got an organization in California. . . . we will wait until these other guys [the major parties] get through [with their presidential selection process], then we will start our presidential primary. . . . we will take care of all of this. . . . we will encourage the finest people in our country. . . . [the candidate] pledges that these reforms that we are proposing in our platform make sense. . . . then we raise the money for that candidate. And we have a candidate for the people." Unfortunately, at no point did Larry King ask Perot who the "we" really was.

A good number of volunteers did come forward. But the heavy lifting was paid for by Perot and carried out by the fifty state executive directors of UWSA, who converged on California (and Ohio and Maine, the other two states that had early qualification deadlines) to staff the petition drives to certify Perot's new party. Still, that wasn't enough. Needing to register eighty-nine thousand voters into the new party in California in less than thirty days, Russ Verney, a top Perot aide from UWSA who was the new executive director of the Reform Party, called Jim Mangia, the Los Angeles–based national secretary of the Patriot Party and a longtime Fulani follower, to ask for help. The Patriot Party quickly decided to call on its members in the state to reregister as Reformers. California "set the stage for continuous collaboration" between the two groups, recalled longtime Fulani aide Jacqui Salit, who listed another ten states as places where the Patriot Party was crucial to the fledgling Reform Party's ballot drive.[45]

Thus, Lenora Fulani and her loyalists got in on the creation of the Reform Party at the ground floor. At the Patriot Party's third annual convention, held at the World Trade Center the following April, the alliance was cemented further. The party's 110 delegates voted to join the Reform Party's push to nominate a presidential candidate (abandoning their own separate effort).[46] Capping the day was a love fest between Fulani—then the chair of the New York Patriot Party—and Verney. Fulani told of how Verney, a former chairman of the New Hampshire Democratic Party, had blocked her from entering a televised debate when she ran as a presidential candidate in 1992. "I like to think I won the second round," she exulted to the crowd in the Marriott Hotel's grand ballroom. She concluded her speech by introducing Verney as "an ally and a friend." Blushing, he stepped to the podium and returned the compliment.[47]

Perot said that he was starting a third political party, but he clipped its wings from the start. Starting with his comments on *Larry King Live*, it's clear that what he actually imagined was more an institutionalized vehicle for an individual candidacy for the presidency. Unlike a full-blown political party, where members and leaders would meet at a convention of duly selected delegates to hammer out common principles, the platform for his Reform Party sprung Athena-like from his wallet. A one-page "Principles of Reform" listing nine key planks was ready the night he went on the air, and Perot referred to it as the party's platform. He even said whoever stepped forward and received the party's banner would have to pledge their support to that platform.[48] And in contrast to a party that contests elections for offices across the board, Perot decreed in advance that the party would not run candidates for Congress. So much for real independence. This couldn't be worse news for the majority of the public that was interested in a new major party that would generate new leaders accountable to its adherents. Again, Perot's personal predilections were preventing the evolution of an organization with a strong grass-roots base. The Reform Party as created by Perot was to be like an extravagant beach house built on stilts—top-heavy, rickety, and in danger of being toppled or swept away because of its weak foundation.

Nevertheless, Perot's decision to go forward had the effect of at least temporarily quieting some of the dissenters within the broad anti-incumbent movement, as it appeared that he was at least moving in step with their wishes. "This is a redeeming act on his part," Phil Madsen, the founder of the Minnesota Independence Party, told *Time* magazine.[49] Gordon Black also applauded Perot's move, saying "It's not about Perot. It's really about the fact that we're going to have a party and we're going to have a presidential choice in 1996."[50]

The time, again, seemed ripe. The Republican Party appeared headed toward nominating an old party warhorse with no compelling vision of the future in Bob Dole, while the Democrats cruised comfortably toward renominating President Clinton, despite nagging questions about everything from his character to his handling of foreign policy. By the time Dole had sewed up his nomination, 45 percent of the public said they were dissatisfied with the Dole-Clinton choice and wanted a third-party alternative.[51] But the fledgling Reform Party rapidly ran into problems of its own creation.

First, there was confusion about how it would pick its nominee. According to Perot, by the summer of the election, anybody who participated in forming the party, whether by signing a petition or registering as a member, would be sent a ballot listing all the declared candidates. Contenders receiving more than 10 percent of that vote would then be certified as eligible for the party's nomination, which would be conducted by mail and over the Internet, with the results to be announced at the national convention. On the surface, this looked like an innovative way to open up the process to millions of average voters, which might have redeemed Perot's image and invigorated the party's base. But the details left many concerns.

For example, it was unclear who would be responsible for collecting the list of eligible voters and whether that list would be made available to all the contenders in advance of the vote. Nicholas Sabatine, who briefly considered tossing his own name into consideration, pointed out another problem. Perot's name was being used as a stand-in on petitions being carried by Reform Party organizers in as many as a dozen states, where local laws required a new party to list a candidate in order to qualify. People signing those petitions were inevitably going to be predisposed to support Perot, Sabatine argued. "I'd feel more comfortable if he'd drop the facade bullshit and come out and say that he is running and here's why," Sabatine told me.[52]

Second, Perot refused to make a Shermanesque statement that he wasn't going to run for president again, all the while insisting that "This isn't about me," and declaring that the whole Reform Party project could be short-circuited if its membership believed the Democrats or Republicans had come up with "George Washington the

Second." In that event, he said, "we will be the swing vote to make sure that candidate gets elected."[53] Still, he said the ultimate decision would be up to the party's members. And he bolstered speculation that he would indeed run after telling a Texas radio station, the same day that Bob Dole locked up the Republican nomination, that if the party's members wanted him to run, "then certainly I would give it everything I have."[54]

Third, there were loud complaints from the remaining activists who had joined UWSA (and not quit) because they still believed in the vision of a nonpartisan watchdog organization. They said, in effect, that UWSA was being improperly cannibalized in order to build the new party.[55] In addition to shifting almost all the paid staff of UWSA into the "Committee to Establish the Reform Party"—legally a different organization to keep within the law preventing nonprofit, tax-exempt groups from endorsing candidates, but with the same address and phone numbers as UWSA[56]—Perot's people insisted on taking UWSA's property as well. Fax machines, computers, and the organization's most prized asset, its membership lists, were transferred over. Given how much money Perot had pumped into the group, he could legitimately claim that it owed him these assets. Still, the board of UWSA-Ohio disagreed and filed a formal complaint with the FEC, arguing that Perot was improperly using a nonprofit organization to promote partisan political ends.[57] The FEC ultimately took no action, but the dispute stirred up more bad press for the fledgling party.

"The Reform Party is a Potemkin village," warned Mick Ringsak, a Vietnam veteran and shoe-store owner from Montana who had been on UWSA's national board from its inception through July 1995. "The public doesn't know what it's getting." Ringsak, like many former Perot activists, was unsure of the third-party route and had called his fellow United We Stand members and urged them not to carry petitions for the Reform Party. "Then I heard Perot on a local radio show claiming that 'right now we have volunteers busting their butts at the local mall and post office and Safeway store.' So I went down there and didn't find anybody except at the Safeway, where there were four state directors, the paid employees of Ross Perot."[58]

All these questions had the effect of stunting the party's development, both in causing some independent-minded politicians to stay away and in giving voters reasons to be skeptical about the party's real purpose. In an interview that spring, Dick Lamm told me, "Perot and his party are blocking, are filling up all the available space, at just the time that somebody like [Lowell] Weicker or somebody else could come along and have a chance up the middle. There's so much disillusionment out there."[59]

At the time, Weicker was involved in quiet conversations with multimillionaire businessman Tom Golisano of New York, who was willing to run as his vice president and put serious money into financing a campaign. If he was paying for his own candidacy, Golisano would face no personal spending limits. But the two men disagreed on a number of points, including whether to compete directly against Perot for the Reform nomination, or to run as pure independents.[60] Lamm said that Weicker had tried to get a commitment from Perot that he would not run, but couldn't. "Lowell was willing to roll big dice, but he can't roll them past Perot," he said. And Lamm smelled a rat. "It sounds seductive: [Perot's] not sure he's going to run, he's set up this party, he'd like someone else to do it." His reading of Perot's real intentions: "They'd like to give dignity to their process by having Perot beat somebody."[61]

Lamm to the Slaughter

Weicker ultimately decided to hold back. Not so Lamm, who announced his candidacy for the Reform nomination on July 9 after earlier receiving a favorable response speaking at the party's June 1 California state convention and earning a swath of admiring articles in the mainstream media, particularly from journalists who agreed with his willingness to make a frontal assault on government entitlement programs like Social Security and Medicare. "America needs a decade of reform and renewal," he declared in his announcement speech, attacking the major parties for "listen[ing] to money, not to people." He called for a focus on balancing the budget, closing the trade deficit, and promoting responsibility instead of indulgence. Lamm made his decision freely admitting that he didn't know whether Perot would run, but added, "This party has to declare its independence from Ross Perot."[62] Lamm knew he was taking a risk. "This could be historical," he said just before announcing his decision. "[Or] I could end up with egg all over my face. It could be I have completely misjudged the water."[63]

Lamm had his answer soon enough. One could almost hear Ross "This is Not About Me" Perot muttering that the former governor of Colorado has a "duty to get out of the way," echoing Lamm's infamous declaration that the elderly had a "duty to die." First Perot upstaged Lamm's campaign announcement with one of his own the following evening, again on Larry King's TV program. Then came stories of unexplained delays holding up the delivery of preference ballots listing Perot and Lamm to many of the party's members, especially those in New York, Minnesota, Colorado, Arizona, Hawaii, and Oregon—states where former Perot followers and party activists had shown real independence from Dallas.[64] (There were reports of people receiving multiple ballots as well.)[65] And finally, after promising to give Lamm the party's 1.3 million membership list, Perot reneged, citing dubious legal arguments about possibly violating campaign contribution laws.

Lamm's central problem was that the national coordinator of the fledgling party, Russ Verney, was also Perot's campaign manager.[66] This double role had all kinds of disturbing implications. For example, as party coordinator Verney insisted there was no legal way for the party to give its mailing list to Lamm's campaign, saying that would be an illegal campaign contribution. He did offer to mail out literature for Lamm, but said the letters would have to first be cleared by the party to make sure they were "professional and present a positive campaign." Verney insisted, "There will be no negative campaigning in the Reform Party." But to Lamm, this was a requirement to "send my literature down to Dallas and have it approved—in other words, censored by the people that I'm running against."[67]

All these machinations had a huge, unseen impact on the grass-roots activists involved in the broad third-party movement spawned in 1992. For many, the behavior of the Perot forces around the Reform Party's presidential nomination was the final straw. "No one I'm in touch with is going," said Kirk MacKenzie, the Californian who had been the elected chair of that state's UWSA branch. "It's doomed from the start. Most of the people who care about the issues don't believe in Perot or anything he touches anymore. They're just trying to make a living now."[68] Few of the people who had been sent a ballot decided to participate in the preference vote between Perot and Lamm. According to the accounting firm Ernst & Young, which oversaw the balloting, only 43,057 ballots were cast of 880,298 that were mailed out—a turnout of less than 5 percent. Perot was favored by 65 percent of those voting, with Lamm getting 29 percent.[69]

Others spent their free time exchanging phone calls and e-mails trying to figure out what was really going on between the Perot and Lamm camps, trading gossip about various players and where their loyalties lay. The pathologies of belonging to a tiny organization with a hugely inflated presence in the media were coming to the fore. Rather than organize to get more voters to join the movement or strategize effective ways to build an internal counterweight to Perot's power, these people imagined they were participating in third-party politics when all they really were doing was spectating, obsessively, about the direction of a vehicle they had no chance of driving. What had once been an outward-looking effort had now almost completely turned inward.

People starting grasping at straws. Members of the UWSA–New York chapter, for example, were simultaneously supporting Lamm and griping that he wasn't attacking Perot hard enough. "Lamm has to expose Perot and come out as the liberator of the grass roots," said Alex Rodriguez, a leader of the New York group.[70] He and his fellow dissidents spread word of a supposed floor demonstration against Perot that would happen during the first half of the party's national convention in Long Beach, California, where both Perot and Lamm would be speaking in advance of the final vote on the nomination. The convention had been split into two parts—the first in Long Beach, California, on August 11 (the day before the Republican National Convention started meeting in San Diego), and the second in Valley Forge, Pennsylvania, a week later.

But the only demonstration that took place in Long Beach was one organized by people who wanted to come out full force for Perot. Criticism of the party's skewed nominating process or its lack of internal democracy seemed to have inflamed most of

Perot's diehard followers. "We are tired of politicians," said Lorrie Ebert, an older woman in a red-white-and-blue straw hat from San Bernadino who had helped pull together a rump rally for Perot outside the Long Beach convention hall. "We're going to end all that," she added. It's time for a businessman to get in there." Furthermore, she shouted to the crowd of a hundred or so people, "Governor Lamm is a whiner and a complainer, and we real Reformers don't like his attacks on Ross Perot." A tape played Sousa marching music, and then Lenora Fulani, stood up to speak: "Some . . . criticize Mr. Perot's style, some don't like his allies, like the articles that have attacked him for having me in the party. The political establishment types hate it when people of different backgrounds come together. They don't seem to get that we are all Americans." Both women expressed the views that were binding the party's core members together at that point in its history: a blind faith in Perot's saving power and a mystical sense that "the people" could be one. "One People, One Leader" is a sentiment familiar to students of past authoritarian movements. These Perot loyalists apparently found it comforting to imagine themselves as victims of a media conspiracy rather than address the question of what kind of party they were actually building and why it was failing to attract more support.[71]

The Long Beach convention was like a Norman Rockwell simulacrum of what a happy, unified political gathering was supposed to look like—except that the real Norman Rockwell was much more open to dissent than Ross Perot. "Proper attire required," said the signs posted outside the hall. "No distribution of information allowed," the signs added. Inside, the "delegates"—an odd choice of words since these participants weren't representing anyone but themselves and weren't voting on anything of importance, such as a party platform, were treated to a syrupy display of patriotic reenactments and heart-thumping videos that would have made Walt Disney proud. Even the supporters of Lamm, whose cuckolded candidacy had given Perot exactly the fight he was looking for, didn't seem to mind that they had absolutely no say in the construction of the party's platform or the setting of its rules. No floor demonstration of the sort bruited by Alex Rodriguez and other Lamm backers took place. The gathering suggested that the single most important fact about the Reform Party was that Perot, a control freak who had his company treasurer measure employees' skirts to make sure they were the proper length, was comfortable with it.

A week later, the results of the vote between Perot and Lamm were announced, and to no one's surprise, Perot won. "In Perot We Trust," read the placards at Ross's coming-out rally in Valley Forge. Supporters filled the low-ceilinged hall, and though they were boisterous, there was a clammy air of desperation to the gathering. The evening began with a video trumpeting that "today we are eagerly assembled in Valley Forge to see democracy in action." Lamm gave a speech urging the party to the right on immigration, scaring the audience with nightmarish visions of an America overrun with more than a billion people, like India. Before Perot came out, the crowd was then treated to a series of videos prepared personally by him extolling his history of helping POWs, paraplegics, imprisoned Electronic Data Systems employees, and other Americans in need. It was a hint of how Perot hoped to overcome questions about the nasty side of his character—by showing off his patronage of the commoners. Nicely defusing the class issue, one of his beneficiaries, a Vietnamese he helped rescue after the war, asked, "How many rich people in Ross's position would do the same thing for us?" The crowd of white middle-class retirees and young people roared. Then, after a short bio-pic that neatly skipped over less flattering episodes in his past, like his failed attempts to "save" Wall Street and General Motors and his rise to riches off of government Medicare and Medicaid contracts,[72] the "man of action" himself appeared, promising to "get into the heads of every single American by November."

Perot had plenty of solid issues to run on, especially the failure of the two major parties to do anything serious about campaign finance reform, the trade deficit, or underfinanced government liabilities like pension funds and bank insurance funds—topics he often mentioned. But by this point in the developing Perot movement, support for the Texan wasn't really about actually solving these problems. Only one-fifth of the public viewed the Reform Party at this stage as a genuine party, the rest seeing it as primarily serving "as a platform for Perot to promote himself and his ideas."[73] And it was clear from his many choices in managing the party that Perot had little taste for participatory democracy. Devotion to Perot was now becoming a measure of how many Americans had given up on the democratic conversation altogether in favor of following a flawed but still charismatic leader.

Reforming the Reform Party?

A few savvy party activists read the writing on the wall. Led by Phil Madsen, along with Ron Barthel, the vice chair of the Oregon American Party, and Laureen Oliver, chair of the New York Independence Party—all supporters of Dick Lamm's presidential candidacy—they started exploring ways to ensure that, whatever happened on Election Day, the Reform Party might still become a democratically driven organization. This, they believed with good reason, could rescue their movement from marginality. Shrewdly, they sought to exploit a little-known feature of federal law pertaining to how the Federal Election Commission treats nationally organized political parties. The law distinguishes between state party committees and national party committees. Individual parties can exist in several states—or in just one state—without being recognized as a nationally organized party. In fact, the national Democratic and Republican parties are really federations of fifty state parties, with a national committee—known respectively as the Democratic National Committee and the Republican National Committee—responsible for conducting national party business, raising funds to support federal campaigns, organizing nominating conventions, and the like.

Not only did recognition from the FEC as a national committee convey a higher status, it had tangible benefits as well. While individual contributions to a political action committee were capped at $5,000 per year, an individual could give up to $20,000 per year to a national party committee. Parties are also allowed to spend more than PACs directly on behalf of their federal candidates. Furthermore—and this was the keystone—according to federal law governing the financing of presidential elections, if Perot got more than 5 percent of the vote in 1996, whoever was the presidential candidate of the party four years later in 2000 could receive somewhere between $10 million and $20 million in public funding for his campaign, and the party would also get a somewhat smaller amount to hold its national convention. (Indeed, the fact that Perot had gotten 19 percent of the vote in 1992 gave him access to $29 million for his 1996 general campaign. This is the only place in federal law where smaller parties get anything remotely like proportional representation—in this case their funding was based on how well their candidate did in the prior election compared to the vote received by the major candidates.) Whoever controlled the national party would be in charge of some very important party-building resources.

Madsen's "Reform Party Democracy Caucus" had one significant piece of leverage in this fight. In the eyes of the FEC, it is not enough to run one candidate for president in order for a party to claim national party status. The party has to be running candidates for all levels of office in several states, as well as demonstrate that it is engaging in ongoing activities like voter registration and education. Taken as a whole, the Perot Reform Committee (the formal name for Perot's party-building committee as well as his de facto campaign committee until he was actually nominated) plus the various new and old state parties that had decided to join in the Reform Party's process for picking a presidential candidate surely would qualify for national party status.

What Madsen and his confreres had discovered is that no formal application for that status had been made by the summer of 1996. In addition, several of the larger state parties formed prior to Perot's unilateral decision the previous fall were unhappy with his dictatorial ways and wanted a more democratic structure for the national party. Their plan was to recruit these parties into an interim national party committee clearly distinguished from the Perot Reform Committee, and then apply to the FEC for recognition as the proper authority to speak for the national party.

Their trump card was, they believed, the fact that a good deal of the lower-level party activities that were used by the FEC to judge whether a party had achieved national status were going on inside their affiliated state parties—as opposed to states where Perot had relied heavily on his paid, outsider staff. Many of these latter states had bylaws drafted by Dallas that vested all control in a tiny executive committee loyal to Perot, but little real base of grass-roots activists.[74] Madsen believed once the FEC recognized their national committee, that body would have the power to decide which state parties were included. And in his vision, this freestanding national party committee could require that those state parties include democratic principles in their constitution in order to be duly recognized as chapters of the national Reform Party.

What these pro-democracy activists within the Reform Party were hoping is that the FEC would, in effect, decide to help them fix their party's internal affairs. "If the state party organizations do not have the right to set up the national committee, who does?" asked Madsen. "The Perot Reform Committee does not equal the Reform Party," he asserted in a conversation we had just prior to the party's convention in Long Beach.[75] But this was expecting too much of the Federal Election Commission. After all, the six FEC commissioners—three Democrats, three Republicans, appointed by the president but in fact selected by their party's leaders—have never shown themselves to take an active interest in small-d democracy. Instead, over the years, they have hewed closely to their respective party's interests and, where necessary, acted in concert to block challenges to both parties. Incumbents have rarely been punished for violating federal campaign finance laws; investigations have been allowed to drag out for so long that by the time any fine has been levied, most voters have forgotten the cause of action. Even when the FEC's own lawyers have investigated a case and called for tough steps—as occurred after the 1996 election, when the agency's top counsel recommended hitting the Clinton and Dole campaigns with multimillion-dollar fines for violating the law regarding their use of so-called soft money to pay for electioneering TV ads—the agency's commissioners have shown no shyness in overruling them.[76]

Thus it was ultimately easy for the Perot loyalists to outmaneuver their internal foes. The democracy activists made the first open move, holding an organizing meeting at the end of September in Schaumburg, Illinois, a village northwest of Chicago. The geographic shorthand of people in the movement that had made "Dallas" synonymous with Perot's top-down, autocratic rule now adopted "Schaumburg" to refer to Dallas's opposition. Sixty Reform Party members from fifteen states came, led by a central group from the states of Delaware, Minnesota, North Dakota, Oregon, Rhode Island, and Virginia—all places not controlled by Perot loyalists.[77] The Schaumburg group created a "National Reform Party Steering Committee" representing their fifteen states and filed for recognition by the FEC as the national committee of a political party on November 3, 1996. They noted in their application that in addition to nominating Perot for president, at least thirty-two other candidates for federal office had qualified for the ballot in the states under their fold. Three of their affiliates, New York, Minnesota, and Oregon, had even achieved major-party status under state law.[78]

The rest of the Perot-led movement quickly responded with vitriol. Dozens of letters flooded the FEC from Reform Party operatives opposing recognition of the group's petition. Many of these complainants were not disinterested party representatives, however. Approximately half the letters were signed by employees of the Perot '96 campaign and its precursor, the Perot Reform Committee.[79] But they had, from the point of view of the FEC, valid arguments—the main one being that no small group of state parties could claim to stand for all nationally. "To approve their request [for recognition as a national committee] would be establishing precedent for a group of five states to take control of the national committees of the Democratic, Republican, and other political parties," wrote one Perot loyalist. Other letter writers argued that the Schaumburg group was acting precipitously, in a sort of power grab. In response, the FEC's general counsel asked the group's lawyer to provide signed statements of support from several of the candidates for federal office that it was claiming in its request for national committee status, including such a statement from Perot himself or his campaign treasurer. This was a requirement the Schaumburg group clearly could not fulfill.[80]

Madsen himself was bombarded with angry e-mail, telling him that he should have waited until every state in the country had a viable Reform Party organization up and running so that it could fairly participate in the national party, arguing that there was no rush unless he was trying to illegitimately seize control. The letter writers contended that the presidential campaign then under way ought to be his top priority and pointed out that he didn't have Perot's permission to do what he was doing. He answered with a pithy e-mail of his own:

> If I saw evidence of a good faith intent or effort toward establishing democratic party organizations in the new party states or unorganized states, I would be content to wait. . . . Instead, I see numerous party constitutions or bylaws popping up in the new party states that look like they were drafted in the former Soviet Union. . . . Week by week, state by state, where they can get away with it, small groups of people who have a greater loyalty to Dallas and Ross Perot than to the party members and democratic principles are establishing themselves as party leaders with no accountability, no democratic checks and balances, and no recourse for party members who will likely object to such power grabs after they learn of them. To advocate delay in democratic organizing while this is going on is like advocating no action until you hear tomorrow's weather report, while the floodwaters are rising in your basement right now.

As for acting without Perot's sanction, he responded, "We do not want permission from Perot, [Russ] Verney or Dallas to do what we're doing. Seeking their permission would undermine our purpose, which is to establish the national Reform Party as a freestanding, democratic, self-governing entity." He concluded his e-mail noting that the

Schaumburg group had been completely aboveboard in its dealings with Dallas, send-ing Verney copies of every document they produced and acknowledging Perot for get-ting the party off the ground.[81]

Such gestures at bridge building meant little to Dallas. The Perot camp struck back in force two weeks after Election Day, holding a conference call with a handpicked group of party members from forty-nine states and the District of Columbia. The par-ticipants quickly decided to appoint Perot, his running mate, Pat Choate, and cam-paign manager Verney to organize a January 24–25 meeting in Nashville to choose party officers and begin the process of filing for national committee status. The vote was 45 in favor, 2 against, and 3 abstentions. Perot's opponent Dick Lamm was also ini-tially appointed to this steering committee, but quickly decided to decline after hear-ing one party leader from Oregon kicked off the conference call for denouncing the way Perot and Verney were operating.[82] News of this phone meeting call was quickly communicated to the FEC by Verney as further evidence of who really held the reins of power with the party.[83] Later research by party dissidents revealed that thirty of the forty-seven state party representatives participating in the call were either on the pay-roll of one or more of Perot's various campaign entities or an active volunteer in the Perot Reform Committee.[84]

Still, the Schaumburg activists made one more stab at reforming the Reform Party from within, traveling to Nashville at the end of January to participate in the party's first formal national organizing meeting. Of the forty-two recognized state delegates, seventeen had been on the Perot '96 campaign staff, three had been appointed to their positions by Perot '96 staff, and two had close informal ties to the campaign. Six recog-nized delegates came from states that were part of the Schaumburg group. Despite this imbalance, at first it appeared that a compromise acceptable to both sides had been worked out, setting up a seven-person interim board of directors. But then the pro-Perot faction voted down that proposal in favor of a board of officers that put all operating authority in the hands of the party chairman, who clearly was going to be Perot's man, Russ Verney. This crossed the line for the Schaumburg group, which was "very worried," as Dean Barkley of the Minnesota Independence Party put it after-ward, "that the leadership elected at this meeting would be nothing more than Perot paid staff that would give the image that the Party was indeed 'Ross Perot's Reform Party.'" So, to jeers and applause from the remaining Perot loyalists, the Schaumburg group walked out.[85]

The split was a raw one. On one side there was Verney, a gruff, colorless man with a New Englander's accent and the instincts of a veteran pol (he had once been chair-man of the New Hampshire Democratic Party), spinning the split to the press. Among "the vast majority of members of this party," he claimed, "there is a great deal of pride in Ross Perot." The Schaumburg dissidents, he said, were a group of malcontents that was "circling the wagons and firing inward." On the other side were state-level leaders like Ralph Copeland of Virginia, a retired insurance executive, who called the Nashville meeting "a fork in the road [with] the Perot party . . . going down one path, and the democratic, third-party movement . . . going down another."[86] Perot, who briefly addressed the Nashville gathering surrounded by bodyguards, later told the press "the party is not in my shadow" and dismissed the Schaumburg mavericks as a "tiny, little dissident group."[87]

The Schaumburg dissidents tried to continue their battle for FEC recognition, but after it became clear that they had little chance of winning, they decided in early October 1997 to break away and form a new party, calling themselves the American Reform Party.[88] The ARP tried to position itself as a home for moderate independent voters, emphasizing many of the same issues talked about by the original Reform Party, but without Perot's baggage or any of the movement's neuroses. A few of its most active members ran for office, the party hammered out serious position papers on a few issues like immigration reform and put out a well-edited quarterly newsletter. But despite the hard work of a devoted band of perhaps a few hundred, the ARP never took off. After inconclusive conversations with Lowell Weicker and John Anderson about the 2000 presidential election, the ARP's leaders ended up endorsing the Green Party's Ralph Nader for president.

Meanwhile, the barely one-year-old Reform Party was already in decline. While Perot's second run for the presidency was more focused than his 1992 roller-coaster, his reputation preceded him everywhere he went. He was unable to lure a politician from either of the major parties to be his running mate (both Rep. Marcy Kaptur, an Ohio Democrat, and Rep. Linda Smith, a Washington Republican, reportedly turned him down), so he ultimately selected Pat Choate, a policy analyst known mainly for his criticism of free trade, who had coauthored Perot's 1993 anti-NAFTA book *Save Your Job, Save Our Country*. He decided to limit himself to the $29 million in public campaign funding from the FEC, with the perverse result that the Commission on Presidential Debates—a supposedly nonpartisan body set up and chaired by two former heads of the Democratic and Republican parties—decided to exclude him from participating in the fall TV debates. The commission argued that by limiting his spending, Perot had no serious chance of winning the election, and thus did not deserve to be included in the debate. Perot sued, but to no avail. It was a critical blow to his already shaky candidacy.

Perot tried to make three issues the central themes of his campaign: economic policy, trade, and campaign finance reform. He ran half-hour TV infomercials calling for the privatization of Social Security, the dismantling of the Internal Revenue Service, and major political reforms. But even with the late-breaking news of huge questionable campaign contributions to both major parties, including millions in soft money

from foreign sources, Perot's campaign never caught on. His penchant for quirky statements was never far from the surface, as when he suggested that Puerto Rico was not
part of the United States,[89] or when he deliberately mispronounced the names of some
Asians who had been named in the Clinton fund-raising scandals, caustically asking,
"wouldn't you like to have someone named O'Reilly out there [giving money],"[90] or
when he suggested that wife beaters be "marked with an X."[91] The improving economy also muffled the "giant sucking sound" of jobs going overseas, undermining his
attacks on free-trade policies. Signs of a shrinking budget deficit didn't help Perot either
on his signature issue.

Ultimately Perot got a little more than 8 million votes, a big drop from the 19.7 million he received in 1992. He had money, but nowhere near the $72 million he spent on
his first campaign. He also was denied the legitimacy that comes from inclusion in the
nationally televised debates, and his message was far less compelling. More than half of
Perot's 1996 voters told pollsters their vote was more an anti–Clinton/Dole statement
than pro-Perot. His 8 percent was enough to guarantee the party's next presidential candidate a pot of gold in 2000, estimated at $12 million to $15 million, which would keep
the party in play for at least one more four-year election cycle. His showing also qualified
the party for ballot status in thirty-three states, a major step forward that could reduce the
costs of getting on the ballot next time around. But Perot's top-down approach didn't do
much to strengthen the local and state efforts that are critical for a party to truly take
root. Several other Reform Party candidates running for lower-level offices publicly complained that Perot did little to nothing to help them with their races, even avoiding joint
appearances.[92] After the election was over, Perot told his state allies that they would have
to raise their own budgets. And though the national committee loyal to Perot eventually
won recognition from the FEC in March of 1998, this news did not produce much of a
boost at the local level, where the party had begun to atrophy.

5

Getting Past Perot

Nostalgia Is Not Enough

In the twentieth century, America has seen a number of charismatic presidential contenders run on a third-party line. Teddy Roosevelt, Robert LaFollette, George Wallace, John Anderson, and Perot all drew millions of votes. But none of these candidates succeeded in transforming their personal following into a durable political party capable of contesting for office at all levels and influencing policy. Now, in the wake of Perot's second failed run for the presidency and his withdrawal of financial support to state-by-state organizing efforts, the Reform Party was spiraling down the same path to oblivion. The party's national spokespeople would continue to appear in the news, well-known (and not so well-known) presidential pretenders would maneuver to get its $12.6 million in federal funding, and some diehard activists would go through the motions of holding state conventions. But the truth was there was very little there.

In just two years after the 1996 election, the party's declining local energies caused it to lose ballot status in fifteen states, according to Richard Winger, editor of *Ballot Access News*.[1] That's because minor parties aren't always guaranteed a line on the ballot—even when their presidential candidate does comparatively well. Many states require that they either run someone for statewide office and get a minimum percentage of the vote to get and keep a ballot line, or register a certain number or percentage of voters into their party. For example, in Maine, which was Perot's best state in both 1992 and 1996, the Reform Party failed to gather the two thousand signatures from party members needed to place a gubernatorial candidate on the 1998 ballot, guaranteeing their loss of major party status in the state. Local Reformers would thus have to push petitions up the hill all over again for the next presidential election. In Texas, Perot's home state, the party gave up its drive to collect forty-four thousand petition signatures (1 percent of the electorate) needed to keep its ballot line after reaching just half that goal.[2]

In the fall of 1997, Pat Choate, the party's 1996 vice presidential candidate, made an audacious promise to the press that Reform would spend $2 million running forty to fifty candidates against vulnerable Republicans in the 1998 off-year elections, to punish them for failing to pass electoral reforms and for supporting further expansion of free-trade agreements. "You broke your pledges, you broke faith with us, let's see how you like being a potted plant for two years," Choate said to the GOP. Those Reform spoiler candidates never materialized.[3] And the few who did run for high-level offices in 1998 got no significant material aid from the national Reform Party, other than modest help with ballot access and being featured on its website.[4]

One of those candidates was Jack Gargan, running to revive the movement he had launched eight years earlier. His reason for taking on incumbent Karen Thurman, a popular middle-of-the-road Democrat representing Florida's Fifth Congressional District: "The job is not done." A look at Gargan's difficulties made clear how hard it was to grow the Reform Party beyond its charismatic and flawed founder. Despite Gargan's rocky relationship with Perot over the years, by 1998 the party was touting him as its leading contender for Congress.[5] And his rationale for running yet another quixotic race—alarm about the direction of the nation's finances, disgust with the self-protective elite running Washington, and a fierce patriotism that veered toward xenophobia— obviously still motivated a bloc of devoted supporters. Older white couples and retirees and refugees from what they perceived as urban chaos especially seemed to respond to this message. But the trajectory of Gargan's congressional campaign showed how tough the path forward really was.

In general, the rules everywhere are unfairly stacked against new political parties— and they are often harder on state-level candidates than they are on presidential contenders. This is not accidental, according to ballot access expert Winger. State legislators that write the laws are more concerned about anything that would make it easier for third-party candidates to run and threaten the local duopoly; they don't mind as much if people get on the ballot for president. In Winger's view, third-party activists have been frequently more focused on presidential politics and so relieved to encounter easier ballot regulations for that office that they haven't protested the obvious disparities for lower-level races.[6] Since 1892, when states first started printing ballots and legislatures began regulating who could be on them, the thresholds for getting and staying on the ballot have risen, sometimes drastically. The median level required by states to maintain a line on the ballot quintupled, from 1 percent to 5 percent of the vote, between 1892 and 1976, Winger said. It improved to a median of 2 percent as of 2000. The median number of petition signatures required to get on in the first place has also risen since the early 1900s, and despite years of unsung and heroic lobbying by Winger and other third-party advocates, the rules haven't improved much.[7]

In Florida in 1998, the rules couldn't have been tougher. Perot's 9 percent showing in the state in 1996 legally meant nothing in terms of ballot access, unlike in many other states. Instead, Florida required minor parties wishing to run candidates to either get 5 percent of the state's voters to change their party registration by January 1 of the election year—a truly impossible task—or to collect petition signatures from 5 percent of the registered voters in whatever district their candidate was seeking office in by the middle of July. Major party candidates were only required to pay a simple filing fee.[8] For Gargan, this meant that even before he tried to engage Thurman, he needed to spend precious resources getting some 12,141 valid signatures.

Gargan did start his campaign with some encouraging indications. He had run a spirited primary challenge four years earlier against Democratic Governor Lawton Chiles and, significantly, in the rural counties that made up the western and coastal half of the Fifth Congressional District, he had done quite well. In his home county, Levy, he got 45 percent of the Democratic vote. In neighboring Citrus County, he took a solid third of the vote. When I interviewed him at his home in Cedar Key in early 1998, Gargan thought that this showed he had a shot at beating Thurman. "The truth is my support is probably much stronger among Republicans than it is among Democrats," he pointed out. "And we've got a lot of independents in this area, and that's the swing vote. If I can hold onto 40 percent of the Democratic vote and get 30 to 40 percent of the Republicans and all of those independents—hey, I've won."

In 1996, Perot did substantially better than his national average in Thurman's district, pulling 13 percent of the vote. Arguably, the thirty-five thousand people who voted for Perot there then should have given Gargan a healthy base to build upon. But Gargan insisted that he was "not a Perot candidate," adding, "I don't bring his name up at all in my campaigning—it's a two-edged sword. I would get a lot of votes because of him, and I would lose a lot. A shame, but that's the way it is."[9]

Gargan's chances were also helped by the apparent weakness of the Republican Party in the district. In 1994, the Republican candidate was drag racing champion Don "Big Daddy" Garlits, a local institution whose Museum of Drag Racing sits just off the interstate an hour south of Gainesville. He quickly achieved notoriety for claiming that "black people have more power than white people," and advocating the use of torture in prisons and public paddling of juvenile lawbreakers. Two years later, the GOP nominee tried to make crime the central issue, but was undone after the news broke that he had been arrested for carrying a concealed weapon without a permit. In 1998, the Republicans' sole announced candidate, a local businessman, dropped out of the race in May, leaving Gargan a clear shot at Thurman.

But these advantages amounted to little as Gargan's campaign unfolded. His problem was that he had scant idea how to demonstrate the same "mad as hell" freshness that made Perot attractive in the very first place (before his campaign cracked up in the summer of 1992). The Gargan campaign was more a walk down memory lane than the invention of a new politics. Though he ultimately drew 34 percent of the vote (67,147 actual votes), a record for a postwar third-party candidate for Congress, he showed little creativity in how he crafted his message.

For example, the hot issue in Thurman's district, according to people living in Gainesville, its most populous city, was out-of-control real estate development. A lively group of local activists, in fact, had run several dissident Democrats against pro-developer incumbents on the local county commission, winning some striking victories. Congresswoman Thurman, predictably, was comfortably aloof from the issue, as real estate interests and building trade unions contributed significant amounts to her campaign treasury. The League of Conservation Voters gave her a paltry 38 out of 100 rating. But when I asked Gargan about whether he planned to raise the topic in his race against Thurman, he demurred, saying that they probably agreed on most environmental questions. "Why do it when it's not going to get people excited?" he answered. "You'd really just be wasting your time." In Gargan's view, the whole of Alachua County, which included Gainesville, was Thurman's "liberal stronghold."

This was just one sign of the cultural distance between the Reform Party's older and more rural world of political disenchantment from the more cosmopolitan one engaged in the fight against pollution and sprawl. Gargan had perfect pitch in 1990, when he began his campaign against the incumbentocracy. But eight years later he was showing that he had developed his own ideological views and wasn't open to altering them. His choice of issues to run on—fiscal discipline, term limits, campaign reform, and immigration reform—was indicative. When he said "the job is not done," the main task he had in mind was taming federal spending, not reforming the political process itself so as to break the power of special interests over policy making.

At that time, the federal budget deficit had dropped to $22 billion, and some analysts were beginning to talk of a possible surplus on the horizon. But Gargan was unmoved by the pronouncements coming out of Washington, D.C., implying they were just more of the same bull. "There is no surplus," he snorted. "If we only had a $22 billion deficit last year, how come the national debt went up $150 billion?" Thus Gargan's number one reason for trying to unseat Thurman was her support for "reckless spending." This was perhaps a good issue to appeal to the conservative farmers and retirees living near his home in Cedar Key, but no way to reach the more populous section of the congressional district around Gainesville, where many people owed their jobs to government spending on the state university, medical center, and veterans hospital.

Gargan also got little traction from his attacks on Thurman for dithering on term limits, his signature issue and one backed by the vast majority of Florida's voters. And then there was immigration reform, an issue that Gargan highlighted even though he admitted it probably wasn't high on most of his prospective constituents' lists. "You drive through this district and you will not find a large immigrant population," he noted, "so it's not in people's minds directly." Nevertheless, he argued, "it is creeping across the country, and we will see it here, sooner than we expect." When he brought this up, Gargan sounded a lot like the white California United We Stand members who backed Proposition 187 in 1994, seeking to deny state services to illegal immigrants, ostensibly because they were a drain on the treasury. "Why shouldn't they sneak in if they know they can have that baby here and—boom—immediately be on our welfare rolls and get free medical assistance while we have American citizens who can't afford proper prenatal care?" he asked. His solution: impose heavy fines on businesses that rely on undocumented workers, and "put them all on a boat and send them back where they came from if they're here illegally."

Despite his difficulties, Gargan's spirits never sagged. In late June, as his campaign struggled to collect the thousands of signatures needed to get him on the ballot, he agonized, "One bad rainy weekend could do us in." Florida's weather was a real problem for his petitioners. "I'm just worried someone will have sunstroke—and a lot of my volunteers are elderly, you know."[10] A month later, having become the first third-party candidate to get on the ballot for Congress in Florida, he exulted. "We did it! Now watch me not only get the 30 percent you predicted but actually win," he wrote me. "It only makes it harder, not impossible, that I'm such an amateur 'politician.'"[11] A month before the election, he was touting polls suggesting that he was hovering between 44 percent and 48 percent of the vote, and looking forward to his one chance to debate his opponent, on a local FM radio station. "We're moving right along in spite of having no money," he said. "Be sure to call me when I move into my Capitol Hill office!!"[12] Gargan's reference to lacking money was a tip-off to the real state of his campaign. Thurman ending up outspending him $472,959 to $28,485, a ratio of nearly 17 to 1. The ingredients that made Jesse Ventura's victory possible—high name recognition, inclusion in televised debates, sufficient public financing to run broadcast ads, easy voter registration rules, and, most important, a fresh and compelling message— were only barely on the table for Gargan. Nostalgia for the glory days of the early 1990s when he rode high was not enough.

Gargan's troubles were mirrored all over the country, as the self-selected band of stalwarts calling themselves Reformers flailed and foundered. In California, none of the party's candidates managed to get more than 1.5 percent in the June 1998 open primary vote.[13] Reinforcing the party's image as detached from political reality, its Senate candidate decided to run without accepting any money from anyone.[14] In Illinois, the party tried to recruit millionaire Republican Morry Taylor, who had spent $8 million of his own money on a quixotic but energetic campaign for the presidency in 1996, to run as its candidate for governor, even putting him on its line without his permission. That attempt at short-circuiting the tough work of local party building was quickly aborted when Taylor pulled his name off the ballot.[15] In Arizona, a Reform candidate advocating English-only as his number one issue stepped forward to run against incumbent John McCain, who was probably the most reform-inclined Republican in the U.S. Senate.[16]

Some party diehards took to blaming the people instead of themselves, in an echo of the playwright Bertolt Brecht's jibe about the East German Communists who complained that the people were not enthusiastic enough about their brand of socialism. If the people have let down the regime, Brecht wrote, perhaps the government should "dissolve the people and elect another." Dawn Larson, a forty-ish Perot '96 staffer from Illinois who was one of the shrillest supporters of the Texan I ever encountered, posted this revealing message in early 1998:

Where ARE the Reformers? The 1998 mid term elections are upon us. I work with local, state and national candidates and their grassroots supporters who ARE trying to build something, who ARE giving 100% to the cause and who ARE making the sacrifices necessary to build this Party. But in the course of that work on a day-to-day basis, I have often asked that same question when meetings that should have reasonably had ten or twenty reformers produce only two skeptics with a laundry list of complaints. . . .

. . . Where are the volunteers who don't CARE who is in charge as long as the work is getting done? We all know where the critics are—where is everybody else?

Where are the volunteers, supporters, contributors and where are the Reform Party candidates for public office who will step up to the microphone and let the voice of reform be heard through them? Where is the outrage over the fact that our local, state and national Reform Party leaders have been literally locked out of the public debate by the media? Where is the outrage among rank & file Reformers that many of the ballot lines created through the 1996 candidacy of Ross Perot, will not be filled in November because potential candidates are not willing to run for those offices?

. . . Has the myth that "Dallas" runs the show been perpetuated for so long and among so many that absent an office, absent paid staff and absent the bells & whistles of a traditional organization that the anti-leadership rhetoric has finally taken it's toll? . . . Are some potential leaders afraid to lead for fear of being called "controlling" by the media, or the naysayers or even the "alleged" grassroots? Are some reformers afraid to follow their leaders, or get involved—for fear of being called sheep by their peers?

There are many opportunities to get involved. A political party is a free association of citizens—but they are also free not to associate and to go their own way. When reformers at the grassroots level choose not be involved, it leaves those who are doing the work short on patience, resources and manpower. When reformers at the grassroots level think ANYONE else "should" anything they have lost their vision and lost the essence of the movement. Those who think a "free association" means no structure, no rules, no starting point from which to grow, no infrastructure from which to build and no compromise to making it work—are terribly misguided souls. Those who put short term gain ahead of long term objectives and stand down when they should stand up— have lost the vision.

In 1992, Ross Perot said to the American people that if they wanted to place blame and determine whose fault it was—they should go look in the mirror.[17]

As for Perot, there were signs that he had lost interest in the day-to-day affairs of the party he founded. After taking a hands-off approach for many years to Perot Systems, the computer services business he started after selling Electronic Data Systems to General Motors, he retook the helm of the company in late 1997 and quickly began imposing his unique management style on his staff. Out was the looser Silicon Valley culture embodied by the company's previous chairman, Morton Meyerson, a longtime Perot associate. In were Perot's old-fashioned edicts: drug testing for job applicants and a reevaluation of the company's policy of giving health benefits to same-sex partners.[18] The only new political initiative he took during these years was to issue a call, at the party's annual national convention held in Atlanta in September 1998, for President Clinton to resign in the wake of the publication of the Starr Report. The national Reform Party apparatus was quick to swing behind Perot's summons, collecting the names of hundreds of thousands of people who supported it.[19] But there was nothing original to this position, as most of the country's Republican leadership and even a few gutsy Democrats had expressed the same view. Nothing in Perot's action suggested this was why his third party was needed—to raise an issue the major parties wouldn't touch.

The Ventura Effect

If it weren't for Jesse Ventura's establishment-shocking victory in the Minnesota governor's race on November 3, 1998, the Reform Party might well have been declared dead by the mainstream media well in advance of the 2000 election. Ventura was almost the political inverse of Perot. Ventura was sane, funny, self-deprecating, and grounded in the reality of working people's lives, not a secluded kooky billionaire surrounded by sycophants. He was a patriot like Perot, but not an antiforeigner demagogue. He was also a real libertarian who never tried to buy a politician or get a government subsidy, unlike Perot, who was a big donor to Richard Nixon and other Washington insiders. Thus there was nothing hollow or hypocritical about his insistence on political reform. And instead of preaching austerity and belt-tightening as Perot had, Ventura's tune was the good-time rock 'n' roll of a state enjoying a record budget surplus. Of course, despite all these differences, the party's leaders were quick to take credit for his come-from-nowhere upset. "This is a major victory for the Reform Party and all of the people who have worked so hard to build it," Perot crowed the day after the election. He of course added his personal congratulations to Ventura.[20]

The real relationship between Perot and Ventura, or lack thereof, was far from friendly. As with all the other true believers in third-party politics that ran under Reform's banner in 1997 and 1998, Perot had given Ventura no meaningful help. By October 1998, Ventura, who had floated around 10 percent in the early polls, had collected enough money in small donations to qualify for more than $300,000 in public funds. But the funds were payable after the election and then only if he topped 5 percent of the vote. A bridge loan was needed. The Ventura campaign sought assistance from Perot and the national party. Dean Barkley, Ventura's campaign chairman, wrote in his diary: "After weeks of begging from the national Reform Party for Jesse to speak at the National Reform Party Convention in Atlanta [in September 1998], we reluctantly agree to send Jesse with the promise that the national party would attempt to locate a bank that would provide us with the swing loan or to donate $20,000 to the state party to help in the campaign. We sent Jesse and the national party went back on both promises that were made. Why? You guess. They have done little of anything to help the campaign."[21]

The experience left Ventura quite bitter. He had voted for Perot in 1992 and in 1996, after first supporting Dick Lamm in the party's primary. "Ross was initially good, but in the last election he hurt the party," Ventura said when I interviewed him in Minneapolis in early October, four weeks before he was elected. "The national Reform Party hasn't supported me one bit. So why should I support them? In fact, I'm going to lead the charge when I win of changing our name [in Minnesota] back to the Independence Party. I want to break off from the national Reform Party. They're carrying an agenda I disagree with." Once again, Perot's leadership style was poisoning the party's chances for future growth. And he and Ventura clearly had very different ideas about how to build it up.

Ventura added, "I think the way you win and become a solidified party is by going out grass-roots and winning elections, at the local level and at the state level. They have only focused on Ross Perot and the national level. All their other elections are just cannon fodder. They flew me to Atlanta so they could parade me around down there to show the press, 'look what great candidates we've got.' I had to attend," he said, recalling the party's promise to help his campaign with its short-term financial problem. "I operate under a simple premise. Fool me once, shame on you. Fool me twice, shame on me. They hadn't fooled me yet."

Ventura operated under a code of honor that bonded him tightly to his friends and led him to never forget the people who had crossed him.[22] Thus there was good reason to expect payback, when the moment was ripe. But first Ventura's close associates tried to deflect attention from their past frustrations with Dallas. A month after the election, Dean Barkley, Ventura's campaign manager, said that Minnesota was still part of the national party and that Ventura's attitude toward quitting it had "evolved." "I don't think Jesse has any intention of going to war with Perot," he added. "He wants to see what Verney and Perot have in mind with the [presidential] nomination process [for 2000]. Hopefully, there will be a meeting with Verney and Perot so they can talk heart-to-heart about how to build the party. A viable third party is still the goal."[23] (No meeting between Ventura and Perot ever occurred.)

Phil Madsen had a more black-and-white view. The scrappy activist had gotten the Independence Party going in Minnesota in 1992, and while pushing for changes with the national Reform Party had also put a good deal of energy building his state party. In 1998 he had run the Ventura campaign's website, a job that he only half-jokingly referred to as "director of virtual field operations." Now, Madsen said, "Jesse Ventura has displaced Perot." I asked Madsen if his effort to revive the small-d democratic underpinnings of the Reform Party had gotten a second wind in the wake of Ventura's victory. At that point, a few weeks after his election, the answer was no. "We're not seeing a national uprising around Jesse Ventura," he admitted. "People are thinking, 'Is it safe to become hopeful again?' There was a lot of heartbreak last time."[24]

That mood was to change by the middle of 1999. After the initial shock wore off, the national press quickly dropped its condescending attitude toward Ventura and turned him into a bona fide international celebrity. Suddenly, there was intense speculation about the chances of Ventura being the "Ross Perot of 2000," the populist outsider who could steal the presidential election away from the Democrats and Republicans.[25] A poll done by Republican Frank Luntz discovered that nearly a third of registered voters would consider voting for him if he ran, and 15 percent said they would definitely vote for him.[26] Ventura enjoyed the attention and didn't mind stoking the press's fevered coverage with an occasional offhand remark about the White House. Some of the members of his campaign team did little to hide their own interest in getting him to run.

But a Ventura for President run in 2000 was not going to happen. Ventura and his advisers knew that first he had to demonstrate that he could govern effectively. He also had strong personal doubts about what the presidency does to a person and his family, and insiders said his wife, Terry, was opposed to the idea of his entering the presidential race. Thus, early in 1999, seeking to channel the public interest in his running in a more productive direction, his campaign staff set up a national organizing effort "to help recruit and support a viable third-party candidate for president in 2000." Interested citizens were invited to register on the Ventura campaign website and thereby demonstrate their support for a third-party candidate. The idea was to build a large national list, to "serve as an incentive for a viable third-party candidate to enter the race." His staff made clear that the list would not be used to support a Ventura candidacy. Tellingly, they also announced that "it will not be made available to Ross Perot."[27]

Attention within the party turned to its coming national convention, at which a new slate of officers would be elected and rules governing the party's process for nominating its next presidential candidate would be reviewed. With Ventura's election renewing interest in the Reform Party, and with a $12 million plum to hand to its nominee, the party suddenly seemed relevant again, a wild-card factor that had to be watched, and potentially the home for a post-Perot revival. The old struggle within the Perot movement between independent-minded bottom-up activists and Dallas flared up again.

The first skirmishes occurred over the seemingly simple question of where to hold the convention. Prior to Ventura's election, the party's executive committee had tentatively announced plans to meet in Minnesota in the summer of 1999. But after his leap to national stardom, they made a curious decision to move the gathering to Dearborn, Michigan. The party's public relations chair, Donna Donovan, told members in an e-mail that "Minnesota is a very conflicted state for the Reform Party," specifically citing Phil Madsen's presence there and his earlier role in the Schaumburg group. She also noted "there are a number of [Reform Party] members in Minnesota who have turned against Ross Perot" and insisted that "we owe it to him . . . and to ourselves . . . to have our convention in a place where we know he will be welcomed warmly and without reserve."[28]

Dale Welch Barlow, a member of the party's national committee from Oklahoma and briefly its interim vice chair in 1997, found Donovan's argument specious. "Just think, folks, if we DON'T have our convention in Minnesota, it will not only give Phil [Madsen] the great satisfaction that he has pulled off a major coup in our party, but also the fact that he will NOW be able to travel to our convention, outside his state, and claim that we have rejected his leader, Jesse Ventura. Is this the situation, you truly want?" she wrote in an e-mail response to Donovan, adding, "I contend that we, Reformers, are still the brave, forthright, benevolent souls that started out in 1995, to form a new independent political party composed of volunteers that would 'take our country back.'"[29] Barlow, who had personally collected more than four thousand petition signatures for Perot's 1996 campaign, lost this argument. But she represented a potentially important new wing of the party: state leaders and activists who had proved their loyalty to Perot—to the point of vocally opposing the Schaumburg group when it tried to refashion the party in 1997[30]—but who were now speaking up in favor of new blood, seeing Ventura's win as a chance to renovate the party's image and prospects.

Ventura also saw an opportunity for a bold move. On June 28, a month before the Dearborn convention was to begin, he sent an open letter to all the delegates, endorsing Jack Gargan as his candidate for national party chair. He didn't mince words:

> It's no secret that except for Minnesota and perhaps one or two other states, the National Reform Party has declined dramatically in recent years. We can turn that around. To do so, party members in all states must focus on supporting candidates and winning elections at all levels of government—everything from city hall to the White House, including county offices, state legislative seats and the U. S. Congress. . . . In Minnesota, we began by winning one or two here and there. They added up as our support base grew over the years. Then we scored big in 1998. The same thing can happen in other states, and ultimately nationwide, if our party leaders focus on supporting candidates and winning elections.
>
> Jack Gargan is such a leader. He is the candidate for national party chair I have full confidence in. Mr. Gargan's credentials as a true reformer predate those of most Reform Party members. Over the years he has built or helped build impressive organizations, and run exemplary campaigns for political reform. His reform credentials, organization building skills and candidate experience make him uniquely qualified to address the challenges the national party faces today.
>
> Mr. Gargan tells me that if elected as national party chair, he will immediately move the national party headquarters to Florida. Like me, he is deeply troubled by the current state of the party's rules. Mr. Gargan assures me that as soon as the party headquarters is established in Florida, he will next focus on reforming the party's rules and power structure. Like me, Mr. Gargan believes party rules should vest power at the grass-roots level, empower all members equally, hold party leaders accountable to the members, and create a fair and open playing field for any candidate who may seek the party's nomination for president.
>
> I trust Jack Gargan. As National Reform Party chair, he would be a leader we could all be proud of. With his experienced hand on the wheel and my public support, we can do much to re-inspire the millions of Americans who rose for political reform in 1992. Together, Jack Gargan and I can help make the Minnesota miracle happen in other states. With Jack Gargan as National Reform Party Chair, the party can become hopeful once again and prove worthy of its name.[31]

Ventura's endorsement of Gargan hit the Dallas camp like a thunderbolt. The party's new star was backing someone who had his own independent standing apart from

Perot, along with solid national media experience from his "Throw the Hypocritical Rascals Out" days. Some responded by immediately questioning whether Ventura really knew what his letter said, or if he had just signed something written for him by Phil Madsen, who was such a burr in Dallas's side.[32] In fact, Ventura had personally overseen three revisions of the letter.[33] And the governor made sure to back up his endorsement with political muscle. His letter concluded with a not-so-veiled threat. "If the convention delegates are not willing to elect and support the best person for the job, I'll remain reluctant to fully embrace the National Reform Party. I'll be pleased to keep my party activities within Minnesota's borders, leading by example as I have been doing. And I'll keep my national party options open."[34]

No one was hit harder by Ventura's ultimatum than Russ Verney, the party's founding chairman. At first he seemed non-plussed by the implicit criticism of his stewardship of the party, telling the New York Times, "I welcome as many candidates to go after the job as possible because competition is healthy. On the other hand, Jesse's letter sounded a little dictatorial itself, too much like an ultimatum. I prefer to think he's been badly served by his staff."[35] But within days, he admitted that he had been stung by the attack, adding, "The whole goal in leadership is to develop new leadership. As soon as I feel there's a potential for strong leadership in the party, I want to step aside. I've been at the head of this for seven years, and it's time for others to take over."[36] A day after saying that, Verney announced that he would not run again for party chairman. Though he denied that Ventura's endorsement of Gargan was the reason, he tellingly offered his support to either of the other two candidates for party chair, saying that both national vice chairman Patricia Benjamin of New Jersey and Pennsylvania chairman Thomas McLaughlin, had "the skills, experience and dedication necessary to lead this emerging party."[37]

Primed by the advance indications of a Ventura-Perot fight for control of the party, some two hundred members of the press traveled to Dearborn for the July 23–25 convention. That made more than one reporter for every two delegates. Only four states sent full delegations; several were missing entirely.[38] Despite a thunderstorm in Minnesota that kept Ventura from flying in, he addressed the delegates by phone on Friday night. Having already made his attitude known, he was magnanimous toward Perot, the party's founder. "We owe him a great debt," Ventura said, and thanked him "for a job well done," drawing loud applause from the crowd.[39]

Perot's turn came the next day. He managed to speak for nearly forty minutes without saying Ventura's name or referring to his position as the party's highest-ranking public official. He also slammed Dick Lamm, his 1996 opponent, for having been invited by the Clinton White House to sleep in the Lincoln Bedroom. Then, in the only reference to the Gargan challenge, said, "I've been told that the team that worked for this person [Lamm] is back again. Now, so there you are, OK?" Perot was obviously referring to Minnesotans Barkley and Madsen, who were in Dearborn to rally support for Gargan.[40] Like his right-hand man, Verney, Perot preferred to act as if the party didn't have any problems other than a bad press. "The last thing I want is all these things that I see in the paper day in and day out about catfights [in the party] and this and that and that have nothing to do with fact," Perot said. He ended his speech, which many delegates noted contained little new beyond his now-familiar boilerplate about solving the country's problems, with a weak nod toward the future. "The thing I want you to understand is that as long as I'm helpful to the organization I'm certainly happy to help participate in any constructive way."[41]

The stage was set for the culminating battle for the new party chairmanship. Early indications suggested that Pat Benjamin, the current vice chair, had the upper hand, as she quickly won the public endorsement of Pat Choate, Verney, and six executive committee members.[42] Gargan's supporters hadn't even been allowed to get their hands on the delegate list in advance of the convention.[43] There were also questions about which way the Fulani camp, now a sizable and organized minority within the party, would vote. But once the affable and ardent Floridian had a chance to meet with and speak to delegates, it was clear he had a strong chance of winning. He also charmed the press with a witty stump speech that had many reporters laughing along with the delegates.

"Some of the stuff you've heard about me is true," Gargan told the convention prior to the vote for party chair. "I ride a motorcycle. I shoot a pretty fair game of pool. I've been known to stay up all night playing poker. And I have an eye for the ladies. And those are my good qualities." Joking aside, Gargan also made clear that a vote for him was a vote for a new direction. "If you don't realize that Governor Ventura's victory is our ticket to party survival and build on that victory, then don't vote for me," Gargan told the delegates. "In one tremendous showcase victory, he has blown away that Republican and Democratic lie that says your votes don't count [when you vote] for a third party." Gargan won in a runoff with 213 votes to Benjamin's 135 after the third candidate was eliminated.[44]

Gargan's victory led many in the media to quickly conclude, as Doug Friedline, Ventura's 1998 campaign manager, put it, "The party's no longer just Ross Perot's party."[45] Phil Madsen's reading was the same. Was it now safe to be hopeful again, I asked Madsen, catching him on a cell phone as he drove home from Dearborn. "Certainly since Dearborn, there's increased interest in participation," he responded. "People are calling everyday. We're getting a lot of unsolicited calls from citizens nationwide, wanting to join the Reform Party and/or run for office." Madsen was referring callers to Gargan, and expressed some frustration with living in the eye of the Ventura hurricane. "Everyone wants Jesse to go out and build the party for them. He can't do it, he's a full-time governor. We built our state party without Ventura; others can do it too." Madsen was trying to do what any activist with a real party to nurture would do—get back to the real grunt work and out of the rumor mill of e-mails and phone calls discussing what would happen next with the national party. "Right now we're trying to put together our state fair booth, we've got a big push for a unicameral legislature to do. I'm tired of national party politics," he told me. "We went to work to get Gargan elected, but we have our own business to tend to here in this state."[46]

Over the phone a few days later Gargan was still on a high, telling me of all the projects he wanted to get moving on. "We've got umpteen details to look at, not the least of which is the presidential nomination process. We've got an ad campaign coming, plus a funding mailer that hasn't been approved yet. . . . We've got to get ballot access, get delegates, rebuild the base, get the College Reformers project going again. It's an endless list. And we have to heal all these damn rifts. When you kind of drift for a few years, and have a big tent, instead of concentrating on what it takes to win, you argue about what divides you. We were splintered six ways to Sunday. But something happened at the convention, and people became refocused. Even some members of the press described to me a pumped-up feeling."[47]

But outgoing chairman Verney knew better than many who thought the party had undergone a transformation. Responding to suggestions that a changing of the guard had occurred, he claimed, "It has never, ever been Ross Perot's party." Significantly, he added that it's also "not Jesse Ventura's party" either. "This party belongs to the elected members."[48] The truth was actually in between. A majority of delegates had expressed a preference for a genuinely different party chairman, one who was more free-wheeling and not beholden to Perot. But apart from electing a Gargan ally, Ronn Young, as the new party treasurer, there had not been a full-blown housecleaning. Verney, whose term in office would not officially expire until the end of the year, was not about to go quietly into the night. And even after that transition, the party's eleven-member executive committee, which actually had the power to unite against the party chairman, would remain dominated by allies of Verney and Perot, and they knew it.[49] Gargan knew this, too, though he hadn't advertised the fact to the press. "Until I'm actually chairman, I can't do a damn thing," he told me that August.

Enter the Buchanan Brigades

The next six months were a time of outright war between the Gargan/Ventura wing of the party and the Verney/Perot/Choate old guard, with the presidential race as the ultimate bellwether of the party's future. There were nasty arguments over who would control the $2.5 million in federal funding to hold the party's national nominating convention in 2000 and whether that convention would be held in Long Beach, California, as in 1996, or in Minnesota, to take advantage of Ventura's popularity.[50] People even tangled over who owned the "www.reformparty.org" domain name and controlled its e-mail list-serves. But the biggest questions were over the party's process for picking its nominee—and who that person might be.

Under the rules voted on in Dearborn, the party's candidate would be selected by a "national primary" mail-in ballot starting the following July and culminating at their August convention. Since the party had lost its line on the ballot in all but about twenty states, potential nominees were expected to get on the ballot in other states as independents. The party would include them in its national primary if they were working to get on as an independent candidate in enough states to win a hypothetical majority of electoral votes. Ballots would then be mailed to people who signed their petitions along with registered party members, as well as anyone else who requested one. The convention delegates could also overturn the results of the mail ballot, but only by a two-thirds vote.

This process in effect made Reform a party for rent. Anyone with a strong grassroots base and/or deep pockets could try to take it over. To many observers, it also appeared tailored to another Perot candidacy. To the Ventura-ites, all of them social liberals or libertarians, it left the party vulnerable to a possible takeover by the pro-life forces of Patrick Buchanan, who was then toying publicly with leaving the Republican presidential race for the Reform flag.

Gargan wanted desperately to revise this process, not to keep Buchanan from coming in, but because he worried that it could bankrupt the party, or result in a hostile takeover from any direction. "Either someone with a lot of money or a big following could stuff the ballot," he told me. "And that could break us. We have to send out millions of ballots. They could literally take over the party. We are not well enough established—they could walk in and take us over." In his view, the Democratic and Republican nominees could each flood the Reformers' "national primary" with mischief-making voters seeking to nominate whatever candidate might hurt their opponent most.[51] And someone was going to have to come up with millions of dollars to pay for the mail-in balloting process.

In response, Gargan wanted to make it impossible for people who were not members or who had not signed a Reform ballot petition to vote on the party's nominee. He also wanted to ensure that the convention could not overturn the result of the vote without a cause like the nominee's illness or incapacitation.[52] But the party's bylaws didn't allow changes to be made once the presidential election year began, and Gargan wouldn't become chair until then. Verney offered to step down early, but only if Gargan endorsed the existing process, as he interpreted changes to that process as emanating from Ventura's advisers and an improper intrusion on party protocol.[53] Gargan refused and the impasse continued.

As the incoming party chair, Gargan was officially neutral about a possible Buchanan entry. "My candid opinion: I like him as a person, but I think his positions on social issues wouldn't go down well with a lot of Reformers," he told me soon after his election in Dearborn. "He has as many supporters as detractors. We need someone with more supporters than detractors. But in the end it's going to be up to the delegates to choose."[54] Ventura had no such need for diplomacy. He just knew that Buchanan was too right-wing for him, and for the chances the Reform Party had of connecting to many independent-minded voters. "He carries too much of a religious agenda, and I'm a firm believer in separating church and state," Ventura said of the talk-show host and perennial presidential candidate, back in October 1998. Ventura did allow that Buchanan "had some good ideas, certainly, and he's a very bright man." But did he get swept up in his brigade? "Nooo," Ventura replied, drawing out the word for emphasis.

But Ventura, who insisted he wouldn't run himself, couldn't recruit anyone else to run either. For much of 1999 he tried talking to a variety of people, ranging from Republican Colin Powell[55] to former-Republican Lowell Weicker[56] and real estate mogul Donald Trump.[57] All of these men ultimately rejected Ventura's entreaties, though each of their encounters made for great copy. At one point, Ventura actually offered to break his pledge not to run for national office if he could be Powell's vice presidential nominee, but the African-American retired general had already hitched his wagon to Republican George W. Bush's campaign.[58] Trump, one of the least qualified people to carry the Reform banner after all his years of plying politicians with big contributions, played his dalliance with the Reform Party for all it was worth, generating untold column inches of tabloid speculation and presumably boosting sales of his latest book. But he cagily left himself an obvious out, saying that he wouldn't run unless he was sure he would win the presidency. The closest Weicker came to running was to give a windy speech before the October 1999 convention of the American Reform Party.[59] Former presidential candidate John Anderson even got into the act, urging Weicker to run and then floating his own name for a few weeks.[60] Anything to stop Buchanan. But no one would, or could, stop him.

Two days after the mid-August GOP presidential straw poll in Ames, Iowa—at which Buchanan delivered a bitter attack on the Republican establishment for selling out on everything from NAFTA and trade with China to Kosovo, abortion, and immigration—the conservative columnist and TV commentator convened a meeting of his top advisers to discuss his future. As my friend and colleague Doug Ireland reported with me in *The Nation,* those joining the discussion at Buchanan's McLean, Virginia, home included his sister, Bay, who was his campaign manager; campaign director Jay Townsend; treasurer Scott MacKenzie; and two wealthy Buchananites: former Reagan Customs Commissioner William von Raab and South Carolina–based textile baron

Roger Milliken (who participated by speaker phone).[61] With the exception of the candidate's wife, who kept her counsel, the recommendation was unanimous: Buchanan should seek the Reform nomination, as that path was wide open, while his chances of winning the Republican nomination looked terrible.

To that point in the GOP race, Buchanan's campaign had not caught fire, as both billionaire Steve Forbes and social conservative Gary Bauer were dividing the right-wing anti-Bush vote. Buchanan was reduced to single digits in the all-important New Hampshire polls, where he had won four years prior. By contrast, one national poll showed him drawing 16 percent of the vote in a three-way race, with Bush at 39 and Al Gore at 35.[62] If he stayed at that level, he would be almost certain to win a place in the televised debates, and from that difficult-to-reach plateau Buchanan imagined that he could reach the presidential summit. Three days after the powwow at Buchanan's home, the newly minted Reform Party Draft Committee for Buchanan, with von Raab as chairman, sent an e-mail out to Reformers soliciting support.

Not only did Buchanan's inner circle want him to switch parties, he was also being actively wooed by Pat Choate, who like Buchanan was an ardent economic nationalist. While Perot said nothing publicly, Choate hinted that Perot had also given his blessing to Buchanan.[63] The apparent hand-off made a certain sense. Perot clearly was not too pleased with Ventura's flamboyance, both for his feather-boa-wearing and pot-smoking past and for his public criticisms of the tiny Texan. While Perot and Buchanan differed on abortion, and Perot had in the past criticized Buchanan's harsh language about immigration,[64] on many other issues beyond trade policy—gay rights, feminism, pop culture, and the role of the military—they were much closer. Instinctively, both were opponents of Ventura's libertarianism.[65]

Opposition within the Reform Party to a Buchanan candidacy wasn't just confined to the Minnesota mafia around Ventura. In August, Michael Novosel, who was the party's Southeast regional representative and treasurer of the Georgia Reform Party, reacted to the rumors of Buchanan's impending conversion by saying, "Don't forget that it was the Republicans' move to the right on religion that pushed a lot of Reformers out of the GOP. If Buchanan came into our party, it would be the beginning of the end. He might bring in a lot of people, but half the current ones would leave. And any hope of positioning the party in the center would be over."[66] In New Hampshire, the Reform Party postponed its state convention out of fear that members of Buchanan's brigades were trying to take it over, weeks before his party switch was even official.[67] One Reform activist who was a former newspaper editor started a website aimed at blocking Buchanan, saying, "The American people continue to demonstrate they do not want Buchanan. For us to hold him up after he's been rejected again and say, 'here is your choice' is ridiculous."[68]

But Choate argued that the Reform Party could ignore Buchanan's fundamentalism. He wrote one Ventura supporter in the party an e-mail insisting there was nothing to fear. Speaking of Pat and Bay Buchanan as a team, he said:

> I appreciate your concern about the Buchanans. But their interest if they come to the Reform Party, as I suspect they will, is *not to take over the Party* to secure the nomination for President. Moreover, if they come, Pat has personally pledged to make a 5 year commitment to build the Party—nationally, state and locally. In their efforts, what Pat and Bay want are delegates not the positions of State Chairs, National Chairs, etc— that is, the positions that control the Party.

He also said that Buchanan was not going to remake the party in his image. "While I disagree with Buchanan on his position on abortion, his positions on most other issues and our platform are almost identical. Moreover, *he has pledged to campaign on our platform.*" [Emphases added.][69]

Choate was making the same arguments publicly. "[Our party] should be [a] particularly comfortable [home] for Buchanan because of its emphasis on issues," he wrote in a public appeal to Buchanan in August. "While his position on social issues neither qualifies nor disqualifies him for the nomination, Buchanan's platform is similar to that of the party on campaign reform, trade, national security, education and federal debt, among other issues."[70] This was actually quite a stretch, as Buchanan's positions on trade were far more explicitly protectionist than the party's, and his calls for vastly increasing the military budget, eliminating many of America's overseas bases, and abolishing the Department of Education went far beyond anything discussed by the Reformers in their highly sketchy platform.

Amazing many observers, Choate was soon joined by Lenora Fulani, who rapidly came out as a full-bore Buchanan backer, especially after he took her to lunch in late September at the Essex House Hotel in New York City to talk about the logistics of mounting a third-party run. The move propelled her into the first ranks of the cable TV talk shows, truly an impressive accomplishment even for one of America's most versatile political chameleons.[71] Asked a few days later about Buchanan on CNN's *Inside Politics*, for example, she averred, "He definitely is a good selection." She admitted that Buchanan's conservative ideology might lead to conflict within the party, but in a striking echo of her and Fred Newman's earlier argument for getting "beyond politics" in the Patriot Party, she said that in the Reform Party, "we know how to put issues of ideology, either mine or Pat Buchanan's, on the back burner and fight for a more open process that's inclusive of all kinds of people."[72] The jarring contrast between Choate arguing that Buchanan belonged with Reform because of their harmony on issues, and Fulani arguing he should join because the party was putting ideological issues to the side, didn't bother either Choate or Fulani, who soon emerged as co-chairs of Buchanan's Reform campaign!

Russ Verney also expressed support for Buchanan's entering the Reform fold, though he tried to couch his feelings in more general terms. For example, he defended him during the controversy over Buchanan's book *A Republic, Not an Empire*, saying that "a vigorous debate of foreign policy" would be healthy for the country. He also insisted that Buchanan was not an anti-Semite. "What happens when you leave the Republican and Democratic party in this country is you instantly become a leper within the colony of Washington," Verney argued. Adopting a public posture of neutrality, Verney said that he was open to any serious candidate seeking the Reform nomination, as long as they made "an investment and a commitment to building this new political party."[73] But this was an empty position, as the only other person making noises about running during the months when Buchanan let on that he was really preparing to switch parties was Donald Trump, and few took his candidacy seriously.

All that was left was for Buchanan to make the switch for real. On October 25, he did so with a flourish, giving a rousing speech that was full of his familiar oratorical flair. "Sometimes party loyalty asks too much," he said, quoting President John F. Kennedy. "And today it asks too much of us." Speaking at the Doubletree Hotel in Falls Church, Virginia, before an audience of three hundred that included many of his long-time supporters along with a good number of Reform Party officials, he went on:

> Today, candor compels us to admit that our vaunted two-party system is a snare and a delusion, a fraud upon the nation. Our two parties have become nothing but two wings of the same bird of prey. On foreign and trade policy, open borders and centralized power, our Beltway parties have become identical twins. Both supported NAFTA and GATT and the surrender of our national sovereignty to the WTO. Both supported the extension of nuclear war guarantees to the borders of Russia. Both supported the illegal war on Serbia. Both support IMF bailout of corrupt regimes. Both vote for MFN trade privileges for a Communist Chinese regime that today targets missiles on American cities. The appeasement of Beijing is a bipartisan disgrace, and we will not be a part of it.
>
> Neither party speaks for the forgotten Americans whose jobs were sent overseas to finance the boom market of the 1990s that the rest of us enjoy. Both parties are addicted to soft money. Both write laws with lobbyists looking over their shoulders. Both embrace the unprincipled politics of triangulation. And neither fights today with conviction and courage to rescue God's country from the cultural and moral pit into which she has fallen.

The day of the outsider is over in the Beltway parties; the money men have seen to that. Never again will our political establishment permit a dissident to come as close to capturing a nomination as we did in 1996. They have rearranged the primary schedule and rigged the game to protect the party favorites. Candidates of ideas need not apply, as both parties seek out the hollow men, the malleable men, willing to read from teleprompters speeches scripted by consultants and pollsters for whom the latest print-out from the focus group is sacred text.[74]

He also pledged to withdraw American troops from their far-flung overseas commitments, to phase out foreign aid, to kick the United Nations out of the United States, to put a halt to legal immigration, to abolish the Department of Education, to appoint a new Supreme Court that would undo the *Roe v. Wade* ruling, and to raise tariffs on foreign goods. So much for putting ideology on a back burner and working solely for a more inclusive political system. Buchanan was planning to shift the Reform Party from the center to the right, and the party was too weak to stop him.

Reform Cracks Up

The stage was now set for the final dizzying downward spiral of the Reform Party. The trajectory of its self-destruction was replete with irony. First, the party's old guard, led by Russ Verney and Pat Choate, working in alliance with Pat Buchanan, combined to pummel Jesse Ventura to distraction and to throw Jack Gargan and his allies out of power. They succeeded beyond their wildest expectations when Ventura not only gave up his effort to coax someone to run against Buchanan for the party's nomination but decided to leave the party altogether. Ironically, in neutralizing Ventura and smashing Gargan, the old guard also obliterated those independent forces inside the party that might have rallied people against Buchanan's effort to remake the party in his image.

Soon, it became clear that whatever nice words the Buchanan camp offered the old guard about unifying the party around political reform issues and putting social issues to the side, were just that—words. For while the party regulars concerned themselves with purging the Ventura/Gargan forces, Buchanan's brigades were busy methodically collecting delegates for the party's nominating convention. The old guard "understood" that the Buchanan campaign might want to assure itself of having at least one-third of the delegates under its control to prevent the convention from voiding his presumed victory in the party's "national primary." By the time it became clear that Buchanan was after two-thirds or more of the delegates—a number that would give him total control of the convention and the ability to rewrite the party's bylaws, it was too late to do much to stop him. And so Reform Party hacks like Verney found themselves on the receiving end of the same kind of manipulative tactics that they had used in the past to outmaneuver and smother the party's independent "democratic reform" forces. Only this time, they were being employed by Buchanan and in the very way that Gargan had warned could occur. In the end, all that was left of the party's hollow shell broke in two pieces, with the old guard huddled bizarrely around another minor party's candidate for president, the Natural Law Party's John Hagelin, and the Buchananites holding Reform's reins.

The party's final crack-up started with Verney's counterattack on Ventura, mounted in the wake of the Minnesota governor's interview with *Playboy* magazine, which came out at the end of September 1999. Ventura was his usual provocative and entertaining self, taking digs at various politicians, touting his version of the Reform Party's appeal ("I'm fiscally conservative, but I'm socially liberal"), opposing gun control *and* the death penalty, defending flag burning and gays in the military, suggesting the decriminalization of drugs and prostitution, endorsing welfare but opposing arguments that government should provide people with jobs, and stating his belief that the U.S. military-industrial complex killed JFK. But three statements got all the attention. The first suggested that America wasn't really the land of the free because of the power of religion:

> Organized religion is a sham and a crutch for weak-minded people who need strength in numbers. It tells people to go out and stick their noses in other people's business. I live by the golden rule: Treat others as you'd want them to treat you. The religious right wants to tell people how to live.

Later in the interview, after talking about his own experiences with prostitutes as a young man in the Navy, Ventura was asked about the sexual harassment charges brought against the Navy in the Tailhook episode. He answered:

> I don't condone what happened, but I understand it. These are people who live on the razor's edge and defy death and do things where people die. They're not going to consider grabbing a woman's breast or buttock a major situation. That's much ado about nothing.

Pressed further by the interviewer, who noted that such harassment was "not trivial for the woman who is being grabbed," Ventura likened the situation to the scene in the movie *A Few Good Men* where Jack Nicholson, the sadistic commander who runs the U.S. Guantanamo base in Cuba, says, "You can't handle the truth."

> What he's saying is: You create me, you live by the very freedom that I provide for you, then you question the manner in which I provide it? . . . You created this Frankenstein, then all of a sudden you're appalled.[75]

Unfortunately for Ventura, these statements were quickly taken out of context. The Associated Press, for example, summarized his interview by reporting that "Among other things, Ventura said organized religion is for 'weak-minded people' and that the Navy's Tailhook sexual harassment scandal was 'much ado about nothing.'"[76] Though the governor quickly clarified his statements, saying his remarks about religion referred to extremists and that he didn't condone the actions at Tailhook, the damage to his public image was done.

Outgoing party chairman Verney did his best to add to the scandal by rushing to the TV talk shows with a quick call for Ventura to resign his membership in the Reform Party. His open letter to the governor said, "Your comments in the November 1999 *Playboy* article about religion, sexual assault, overweight people, drugs, prostitution, women's undergarments and many other subjects do not represent the values, principles or ethics upon which this party was built. . . . Members of the Reform Party from coast to coast are outraged about your comments. In just one interview you have managed to severely damage the credibility and integrity of thousands of Reform Party members." He called on Ventura to "stop the cascading damage to the reputation of the members of the Reform Party by accepting personal responsibility for your actions and the attendant consequences" by quitting the party whose fortunes he had so recently revived.[77]

Did Verney act at the behest of Perot—who was still paying his salary, after all? One can only speculate. Needless to say, his hyperbolic action stirred up a storm within what remained of the party. Anne Merkl, a member of its executive committee, criticized Verney for acting on his own and going to the media before and also for overreacting. She suggested that a simple letter of rebuke to Ventura, rather than a call for his resignation, would have been sufficient to distance the party from the controversy.[78] Rick McCluhan, the party's Minnesota chairman, shot back at Verney to resign. And Jack Gargan wondered publicly why Verney had not made similar remarks about Pat Buchanan, who was then enmeshed in a storm of controversy for suggesting that Adolf Hitler was not a direct threat to the United States after 1940, a year before the United States entered World War II. "How come we don't hear this righteous indignation that he [Buchanan] should be thrown out," Gargan asked. (Verney cagily replied on *Meet the Press*, "First, he's not a member of this party. And second, if he's a member of this party and he's embodied as the leadership of this party in the public's mind, he will be held—everyone will be held—to the same standard.")[79] One Reform Party leader who supported Verney's call was Texas party chair Jeanne Doogs, who later surfaced as a supporter of the Buchanan candidacy.[80] And another was Pat Choate, speaking as one of Buchanan's co-chairs.[81]

The episode left Phil Madsen upset and anxious. "Verney didn't just call for Governor Ventura's resignation from the party," he said in an e-mail. "He went on talk show after talk show running the Governor into the ground." Madsen was also furious that Verney was grandstanding and doing nothing to build up the party. "When appearing in front of numerous national audiences, Verney did not once offer a reason why citizens should join the Reform Party. He rarely if ever mentioned that Ventura is a good and capable Governor. . . . And to what end? Was the party well served by Verney's actions? Did we raise more funds because of Verney's interviews? Did we recruit more members? Did Verney add to the party's credibility by doing what he did?" Madsen held out hope that things would soon change. "There is little need to take action against Verney," he wrote. "He will be out of the national party chair on January 1. . . . Russ Verney has no mandate. Jack Gargan does. Verney is on his way out. Gargan is on his way in. While Verney is technically a party spokesperson by virtue of the office he now holds, Jack Gargan is the authentic spokesperson based on the Dearborn delegate vote. . . . For the life and growth of the party, January 1, 2000 cannot come soon enough," Madsen concluded.[82]

Gargan, however, was slowly sinking under the weight of all the work he was already doing without a staff, secretary, or paycheck. An e-mail he sent to Reform Party members that fall made clear he was running at an inhuman pace. "I'm still putting in 15 and 20 hour days, 7 days a week trying to stay up with all the hundreds of e-mails, letters, phone calls and media requests which flood this place daily! It has not let up one bit since the convention!" Ever the optimist, he said, "That's good—shows there is an extremely high interest nationwide in the Reform Party. I have also attended RP rallies in Cocoa, Florida and Jackson, Mississippi; done dozens of radio and TV talk shows, spoken at several political meetings such as the Tiger Bay Club in St. Petersburg, and responded to several dozen newspaper and magazine interviews."[83]

And while all this went on, the Buchanan campaign was on the march. One shrewd observer accurately predicted, "Once Buchanan dispatches his orders, his Buchaneers will descend pirate-like upon the party. They will stuff more envelopes, stay longer at meetings. They will make the party their own. This will be more than a nomination; it will be a coup from within.[84] Sure enough, news of Buchananites infiltrating state parties started to spread, first Connecticut on September 25, then Massachusetts on October 6, Iowa on October 15, Rhode Island at the end of the month, New Mexico on November 13, and Arkansas on December 12. In each case the reports were similar. The local Reform Party would experience a sudden influx of new members, former Buchanan Republicans who had switched their party affiliation en masse. These would then flood the state convention and vote to either take control of the party's central committee or to install friendly Reformers in exchange for delegate slots.[85] Most of these state party meetings were attended by fairly small numbers of people, anywhere from fifty to two hundred, according to local reports. If Buchanan had twenty-five thousand devoted followers—and that was a conservative estimate of his donor base—

then he had an average of five hundred people in each of the fifty states. Just 10 percent or 20 percent of that hard core would be enough to dominate most Reform Party state chapters.

The Buchanan assault wasn't really a secret. Linda Muller, a devoted volunteer who ran her own "Internet Brigade" for Buchanan, circulated the following instructions on November 15:

> In order to assure that Pat wins the Reform Party nomination at the national convention, it is imperative that all Buchanan supporters attend their local Reform Party county and state conventions. Even though Pat wins the Reform Party popular vote, Buchanan supporters must represent OVER 1/3 of the national delegates (200) at the Reform Party national convention next year (August 2000) in order to prevent the ANTI- Buchanan Reformers from using a party rule allowing them to nominate another candidate at the convention with a 2/3 majority vote. Naturally, we want to block any attempts of an anti-Buchanan coup, but to also show our strength to the nation. First, we must be elected as state delegates at the county conventions and later as national delegates at the state conventions. Loyal Buchanan Reform Party insiders tell us it is very important for Buchanan supporters to win the county chairman positions, as well as all delegate positions. In some states national delegates are appointed by committees, not elected.[86]

A few days later, Bay Buchanan, her brother's campaign manager and field general, issued a statement disavowing Muller's message. "While Linda certainly is well-intentioned, she does not speak for our campaign, either officially or unofficially. Linda Muller is a strong supporter of Pat's, but because she has no association with the campaign, she lacks any knowledge of our strategy." She went on to say that "we have been welcomed to participate at every level [of the party]."[87] It was a face-saving gesture, but the Buchanan onslaught continued regardless.

Meanwhile, Gargan prepared to take over the party's reins and do some urgent housecleaning. In mid-December he sent out an e-mail message to the members promising "a 'bottom-up' organization after 1/1/2000." And he sent two missiles over the bow of Verney and crew. The first insisted that any state party wishing to attend the national convention in August would have to "pass the test of having a truly democratic process govern their election of delegates and leadership offices." And the second promised that he would call a national committee meeting to allow members to decide where the convention should be. "While I personally prefer the central location and lower prices of Minnesota, I will give 100% backing to whatever site is voted by the members."[88] Both of these moves were clearly unacceptable to the party's old guard and its rising Buchanan faction, for they would threaten the standing of all the delegates Buchanan was amassing and potentially place the convention in Jesse Ventura's home state. Two weeks later Gargan confirmed their worst fears by making Phil Madsen his new Rules Committee Chairman, with a mandate to determine the level of democratic practice and grass-roots power in each state Reform Party. It was the equivalent of signing his own death warrant.

Acting without Gargan's approval, the party's vice chairman Gerry Moan got a majority of the party's national executive committee to vote to hold a meeting of the party's national committee (made up of three delegates from each state, plus the national and regional officers) in Nashville in mid-February. The top agenda item was to recall the party chairman.[89] In response, Gargan called for an emergency national convention of all the party's delegates for sometime in March. The long knives were finally out. While the rest of the country was tuning into the early presidential primaries in Iowa and New Hampshire, and many independent voters were thrilling to John McCain's surprising strength, the Reform Party was bogged down in increasingly vitriolic and arcane arguments over who was in charge, where their convention should be, whether this meeting or that meeting was legal, even which website—www.rpusa.org or www.reformparty.org—was the official one. [90]

The day before the climactic national committee meeting in Nashville, Governor Ventura called a press conference to announce that he was leaving the national Reform Party. Standing on the front steps of the governor's mansion, joined by his Lieutenant Governor Mae Schunk and the men and women who ran his successful campaign and built the third-party movement in Minnesota, Ventura delivered a deadly sound bite. "The national Reform Party is hopelessly dysfunctional," he declared acidly. He mentioned several factors in his decision. First there was his distaste for the party's likely presidential nominee: "I can't stay in a party that will have Pat Buchanan as its nominee and is getting David Duke's support." Then there was the effect that the Reform Party turmoil was having on his efforts to build the Minnesota party: "Seeing qualified people avoiding our party, like [moderate Democrat] Tim Penny didn't help." And finally, it was "seeing that Jack Gargan wasn't getting his due" after January 1, when he took over the party reins. "Last year, Gargan was elected in a totally fair election," Ventura said. "Tomorrow, they're trying to pull him out illegally. I feel bad for Jack."

"I'm an Angus King independent now," Ventura declared, aligning himself with Maine's governor, who belongs to no party. He announced plans to change the Minnesota party's name back to Independence, and urged that like-minded people form similar parties in other states. Phil Madsen was happy. "There's an opening now for people in other states—not for us to do the work for them, but for them to emulate what we've done here in building a viable third party and then come and affiliate with us." He envisioned the steady growth of centrist parties modeled on Minnesota, "now that we've taken out the garbage." But he admitted, "our thinking isn't national at all."[91]

The End of the Party

On the eve of the Nashville meeting, knots of serious, anxious people gathered in hall-ways and at the bar of the Marriott Hotel. I ran into Russ Verney in the lobby. He had his game face on. His response to Ventura's quitting the party was "I wish him well. It will have minimal impact on the Reform Party." Was the party hopelessly dysfunc-tional? "Our political obituary has been written so many times since 1992, but we're the Energizer bunny. We keep going and going." Off to the side, a circle of about fif-teen or twenty dissident members caucused, pondering whether to quit the party alto-gether and listening to Mary Clare Wohlford and Bill Wohlford, an older couple from Virginia, who were trying to organize a Quaker-style meeting to start the next day off to allow for a heart-to-heart talk that might prevent the party from imploding. A Perot supporter who was obviously drunk wandered into their midst and loudly interrupted their discussion. People's faces showed shock and dismay.

Late into the night, the credentials committee—a group appointed by the anti-Gargan executive committee and dominated by the old guard—heard testimony from different state delegations and reviewed competing claims to seat national committee members. The crowd in the room was all white, and the average age was over fifty. A number of people held video cameras, recording the proceedings not so much to document his-tory as to collect ammunition for the next round of arguments. The scene reminded me of what I had heard about meetings of various old sectarian parties of the left. He who argues the longest and stays the latest usually wins the vote. The Reform Party had evolved its own weird form of Stalinism.

The next morning I visited early with Jack Gargan in his hotel room. Dark clouds were gathering outside, and Gargan, dressed neatly in a dark blue suit, joked about the weather school of journalism. He was exhausted and depressed. "This is tearing the hell out of our candidates all over the country. I would rather this be a meeting to mend the party rather than its total destruction," he said. But he wasn't optimistic. "I'm going to chair the meeting and put everyone on notice that it's a nonmeet-ing," explaining that he was operating on the advice of his lawyer. The rebel-lious party executive committee had already made clear that if Gargan tried to do that, they would take the gavel from his hands. A nasty storm was indeed going to break.

Knowing that this was Jack's swan song and aware of the incredible strain he had been under for the last six months, I asked him why he didn't just give up. "Do you think I like this?" he answered mournfully. "We are on the edge of an incredible oppor-tunity," he insisted. "We could come out as a major force in American politics, or we could self-destruct with all this crap." He figured that it was worth one more shot, reminding me, "I'm entering my eleventh year in this. It'll be me or them. It's a long shot, but if we come out with me [still in charge] all we lose is twenty *yappers*," his word for his opponents within the party.

The morning started with the Pledge of Allegiance and a moment of silence for the victims of an Alaska Airlines plane crash that had just occurred. A couple of hundred people packed into the hotel's main meeting room, delegates to the front, press and observers to the rear. TV cameras were stationed along the walls on either side. Gargan stood at a nondescript podium in front and attempted to begin. The crowd allowed him a few words. Reminding them that it was coincidentally Abraham Lincoln's birthday, who started in politics as a candidate of a third party, he said, "We are standing at the cross-roads, folks. It's all hanging on us," he said quietly. "If we don't get all together and move in the direction that Ross Perot started us on. . . . This is a now-or-never situation." He paused, and a delegate asked for a prayer for unity. Everyone stood, and for a moment there was an odd calm in the room.

Then Gargan tried to do some housekeeping related to credentials, asking if there was a quorum. Suddenly, Verney stood at the mike in the middle of the room and asked the chair, Gargan, to call the meeting to order and ask the secretary to call the roll. Gargan's lawyer, up on the stage with him, said the request was out of order since this was not a legally called meeting. The crowd started to growl, "point of order, point of order," and then Jim Mangia—the party's secretary (and longtime Fulani follower) strode aggressively to the center mike. "We will meet today, we will meet today," he chanted, and much of the crowd joined in what was clearly a planned intervention. Up on stage, Gargan was at the mike saying, "There is a thirty-day requirement for a meeting to be legally called . . . there is no vote because there is no meeting," but his voice could barely be heard.

With Gargan insisting that the meeting was illegal and Mangia hovering next to him on stage, Verney took the floor mike and asked for the party's vice chair, Gerry Moan, to call the meeting to order. People started walking out, led by Michael Novosel of Georgia. One shouted, "If this is democracy, then I'm leaving." Shoving matches started breaking out up near the front of the stage. I looked back at one point during this and saw Verney calmly chatting with one of the bouncers at the door, looking like the cat who ate the canary. A delegate from Maine made a motion calling for Gargan's removal as party chairman, and suddenly people starting chanting in unison, "Roll call, roll call." Mangia, sharply dressed for television in a gray suit, electric blue shirt, and dark tie, began to call the roll of states. Meanwhile, the pushing and shoving up front was getting nastier, and the party's vice chair announced that the hotel security staff had warned that they would terminate the meeting if it didn't calm down. At this point, Gargan tried again with the crowd, telling them that he couldn't call the meeting to order and reminding them that in his view the proper venue for dealing with the party's internal matters was the emergency convention he had called for the following month. "We will not have mob rule in this party!" he declared, but only six or seven people stood to cheer with him. A floor motion was made to make Gargan step aside, since he wouldn't call it to order. One or two Gargan allies objected, but within minutes Mangia had taken a vote. By 95 to 14 the delegates whose credentials were unchallenged had voted to give the gavel to Moan, the party's vice chair.

Dale Welch Barlow, the impassioned Oklahoman who had been the party's first vice chair, decided she'd had enough. Summoning all the moral authority she had from years of loyally volunteering for the cause, she took the floor mike to tell the crowd that the hotel manager had told her that one of Verney's lieutenants, Dror Bar-Sadeh, was instructing the hotel sound technician on his earpiece when to lower the volume on Gargan's microphone and raise it for the floor mike. "Now we know that this is controlled. You just don't see it. These people are unethical, they are corrupt. This is a high-tech lynching," she shouted. And then the sound was turned down on her, as Moan blandly told her from the podium, "Thank you for your concern." (Barlow resigned from the party a month later, saying she had gotten "a master's degree in how not to build a political party.)[92]

Having taken over physical and then organizational control of the gathering, the assembled national committee members spent the rest of the day voting to recall Gargan and Ronn Young, his party treasurer; to hold the party's convention in Long Beach instead of Jesse Ventura's Minnesota; and to seat several new state delegations tilted to Patrick Buchanan. Topping the proceedings off, they elected Pat Choate as the party's new chairman. What was truly amazing was the delegates seemed to be willfully ignoring political reality. Just a day after Ventura announced his disaffiliation from the national Reform Party, not a word was spoken from the meeting floor about the party's loss of its most charismatic and only successful high elected official. Nor did anyone devote any time to exploring the party's underlying problems—its loss of ballot status in about a dozen states since 1996, the difficulties most state chapters had in holding onto registered members, attracting strong candidates and building any kind of institutional base, and finally the negative image of party founder Perot.

But renovation was not on the mind of the majority of national committee members who came to Nashville, restoration was. When the time for the final vote on Gargan's fate came, the crowd grew uncharacteristically still. But the outcome was anticlimactic: a whopping 109–31 for Gargan's removal, with one abstention.[93] And the mood of the moment was harsh. David Goldman, chairman of the Florida Reform Party, had tried to put forward a compromise resolution that would have made Gargan the honorary chair of the party, while stripping him of real power, and called for balancing roles for each faction of the party in the distribution of the other top offices. But as the anti-Gargan juggernaut rolled on, he barely got a hearing. "I feel like a peacenik at a Veterans of Foreign Wars event," he told me.

Afterward, Verney serenely prowled the hotel lobby. "It's a very healthy day for the party," he told me while smoking a cigarette, denying that Reform had just given itself another black eye. Lenora Fulani, who had seen Verney's forces shove aside her allies in the New York state delegation, was less sanguine. "In my opinion, the entire leadership we elected last year in Dearborn has failed in their mandate to share power," she said, arguing that they all should be replaced. "Right now, Americans everywhere are demonstrating that they want political reform—and the fastest-rising group are the independents. Instead of focusing on capturing that, we've been involved in a top-down struggle over control of the party."

In retrospect, Gargan's election was never fully the cleansing act that he and others portrayed it as. Day-to-day control of the party was vested in the eleven member national executive committee, and the old guard held a reliable majority of votes on most important issues. At the same time, Gargan probably overplayed a weak hand, speaking with unusual candor to the media about the party's problems in ways that may have given some voters hope that Reform was reforming itself, but ultimately inflaming a potent and ultimately lethal backlash against him among party regulars— even those who might have been disturbed by the rising role of Buchanan in the party.

As the day wound down, some of the dissident delegates made clear that they had had enough, and were going back to their state parties to urge that they disaffiliate from Reform and link up with Ventura's fledgling Independence drive. Many were still absurdly pinning their hopes on Donald Trump, who, they excitedly told each other, was supposedly spending the weekend deciding whether to join Ventura and run for president under a new Independence banner. "There are Reform groups in twenty-two states that could announce their support for Trump if he runs," said Mary Clare Wohlford.[94] This just seemed like more pie in the sky. One TV reporter who had been tracking Trump closely, smirked. "This is just him stretching it out some more," the reporter said privately. "He's selling his hotels and casinos." (Indeed, early the next week Trump closed the door on any presidential run.)

The meeting ended with Pat Choate, the party's new chair. Choate, who announced his resignation from the Buchanan campaign immediately on being elected party chairman, gave a rousing speech promising the assembled group that, "because of us, this year there will be a real debate over trade, over globalism, over illegal immigration, over our foreign entanglements, and over real political reform." It sounded just like a Buchanan campaign speech. The crowd gave him a series of standing ovations. The fact that Buchanan's latest foray into the news mix included his outspoken support for Austria's far right leader Jorge Haider didn't seem to faze them. To the remaining Reform diehards, the fantasy of having restored party control to rightful hands was obviously more comforting than dealing with political reality.

For a brief, imperfect moment in late 1998 through perhaps the fall of 1999, it seemed possible that the Reform Party movement was poised for rejuvenation and that it might begin to embrace the Minnesota model of party building. The biggest third-party effort of the 1990s had been given a second chance. That moment was now clearly over. All that was left now was farce.

Breaking Up Isn't Hard to Do

Having worked together to push the Ventura/Gargan forces out of the Reform Party, the Perot and Buchanan wings of the party soon discovered they had a taste for pushing each other around too. Perot's lieutenant Verney gave the first hint of this split right after the Nashville smackdown, when he called conservative columnist Robert Novak to tell him that Republican maverick John McCain had clearly picked up Perot's reformist banner, and that he saw "a real chance" for McCain to become the nominee of both the Republican and Reform parties.[95] Rumors also started to spread of a "Draft Perot" movement among some party members, led by party secretary Jim Mangia, a gay man who opposed Buchanan's racist and sexist views. Then the conflict broke into the open in June, when Buchanan's handpicked state chairman in Delaware called for Mangia's resignation, using plainly homophobic language. The "Reform Leadership Council"—a self-selected group of party leaders connected to Verney—complained loudly, and the floodgates were opened.[96]

"Here is somebody you invite over to your house," Verney complained, "and the first thing they do is start evicting you." Another top party official called Buchanan's efforts to take over the party state-by-state "a Viking raiding party."[97] But all the Buchanan campaign was doing was playing by Reform's rules, bringing new people into the party's underpopulated state structures and taking the spoils that followed. When Perot finally made clear that he would not accept any kind of draft, at the end of June, most of the remaining original Reform activists swung behind John Hagelin, an astrophysicist who had run for president in the past as the candidate of the Natural Law Party, and was now trying to cobble together a kind of Reform–Natural Law fusion bid. Even Lenora Fulani, who for much of the spring was still backing Buchanan and promoting their "left-right alliance,"[98] finally dropped that charade and swung behind Hagelin. (Though she gave an ideological explanation for her switch, Buchanan suggested it was because he rejected her request to be made the party chairman at his nominating convention.)[99]

Hagelin, whom the *New York Times* aptly christened "the Presidential Candidate From Maharishi U." for his close ties to the Maharishi Mahesh Yogi and his university in Iowa, now had his fifteen minutes of fame.[100] Newspapers dutifully ran short profiles, noting his support for preventive medicine and the benefits of transcendental meditation. An unfailingly polite and formal man who always traveled with a retinue of equally serious and well-dressed aides, Hagelin had gotten .12 percent of the vote for president in 1996. This time around, he had decided to try to unite several third parties around his candidacy (the Greens rebuffed him), and he had retooled his platform to try to make it more to the liking of Perot followers, highlighting his support for fair trade and tax cuts. But Hagelin's base, rooted in alternative health practitioners and religious devotees, was truly tiny. It was extremely unlikely that he could displace Buchanan.

Still, the Buchanan campaign left nothing to chance. Taking full advantage of the party's open presidential primary—which Jack Gargan had presciently warned was made for mischief—Buchanan staffers sent Michael Farris, the chairman of the party's nominating committee, a list of more than five hundred thousand supporters to mail ballots to. Since the rules called for ballots to be sent to anyone who signed a petition to put a candidate on the ballot, registered as a party member, or requested one directly from the party, the Buchanan campaign was within its rights to claim that all these people had sought ballots through its offices. The Hagelin-Verney camp quickly challenged that assertion, claiming that many of the names were longtime Buchanan supporters from his days as a Republican who had no intention of joining or building the Reform Party. Ironically, Verney and crew were engaged in a replay of the battle they fought in 1996, only instead of holding the high cards, as they did then against Dick Lamm, they were up against a better-organized and more ruthless adversary this time.

Everything came to a head two days before the Long Beach convention was to open, at a meeting of the Reform national committee that had been called at the behest of a group of committee members supporting Buchanan. Both sides sought to control the credentialing of delegates for the convention, and when the people opposing Buchanan lost, they walked out. For the rest of the week, there were two competing Reform Party conventions running cheek-by-jowl at the facilities of the Long Beach convention center. The Buchanan supporters had more than two-thirds of the delegates at the larger convention hall and a boisterous crowd of several thousand true believers for his acceptance speech. They also had Gerry Moan, the Reform Party's national chairman (he had inherited that role after Pat Choate stepped down due to illness) on their podium, giving their proceedings the further stamp of legitimacy they wanted. The Hagelin supporters were a city block away in a much smaller hall that they never managed to fill with more than a few hundred.

The high point of absurdity finally came as the two sides duked it out over the results of the party's national primary. Hagelin and his supporters said that Buchanan's vote should be voided because he improperly sent out more than five hundred thousand ballots to non-Reformers. Buchanan's supporters obviously disagreed. But when it came time on Saturday afternoon to announce the results, each side switched positions. Michael Farris, the chair of the nominating committee that had overseen the summerlong ballot process, held a press conference to announce that the results would be made public at the Hagelin/Reform convention. While he was doing that in one room, the Buchanan/Reform convention delegates voted overwhelmingly to set aside the primary entirely. Moan told the audience there, "In true democracy, voting wins—you will decide our nominee!" That is, the 500 or so delegates sitting in the room would decide, rather than 880,000 who had been sent ballots. Buchanan's victory in that room was a given. "What are you going to do, Jim?" Moan asked like a schoolyard bully, taunting his former colleague Jim Mangia, who had taken the lead in the anti-Buchanan fight.

Then, over in the Hagelin/Reform hall, Farris unveiled a Powerpoint projection of the state-by-state results. Only 78,068 people had even bothered to vote, and of those, Buchanan won 63.4 percent. The only states carried by Hagelin were Hawaii, Colorado, and North Carolina. A funereal silence hung over the room as the reality of the numbers sunk in. Then Mangia took the stage and said that Buchanan had won only because of ballots fraudulently submitted. He quickly proposed a motion disqualifying Buchanan from receiving any verifiable votes, and lo and behold, John Hagelin was anointed as the party's nominee. The audience erupted in cheers, as if the bad dream were over. It of course wasn't, but it was still amazing to see how easily party diehards could disregard reality, even as it was punching them right in the face.

A few weeks after Reform's split convention, the FEC ruled in Pat Buchanan's favor and gave him $12.6 million in public financing. Buchanan had gone into the hospital for gall bladder surgery a few days after leaving Long Beach, and between that, the ugly fracas over his nomination, and the delay in getting the funding, his campaign never recovered. That's assuming it even had a chance. It certainly wasn't helped by his selection of Ezola Foster as his running mate. Little-known outside of her hometown of Los Angeles, where she and her husband had been active in the anti-immigrant movement that gave rise to Proposition 187, Foster, an African-American woman, warmly embraced Buchanan's position on the Confederate flag during her inaugural press conference. "That war was more about states' rights than anything else," she said, smoothly equating the heritage of slave owners and slaves in a manner reminiscent of Ronald Reagan's infamous Bitburg tribute to Nazi S.S. men, a speech written by Buchanan. Later, it was reported that Foster was a leader of the California branch of the John Birch Society, one of the country's oldest ultraconservative organizations.

Considering that Buchanan had once toyed seriously with finding an anti-NAFTA Democrat to balance his right-wing prejudices on the ticket, the Foster pick and his ferociously nativist speechifying were clear proof that Buchanan had decided to focus on disaffected Republicans and other denizens of the far right as his strategy to lift his poll numbers out of the very low single digits. Buchanan was a skilled campaigner and television pugilist, and it was tough not to be impressed by his gumption and professionalism. But it was also hard to see how his harping on abortion, illegal immigration, and the New World Order would win him many friends beyond the fever swamps of the right. During his acceptance speech in Long Beach, he appropriately referred to his adopted home as a "New Reform Party"; indeed, he had completely transformed it into an entirely different vehicle than originally envisioned by Perot or projected by Ventura. It certainly seemed prophetic to me that the yacht he and Foster strode off to ride for a two-hour harbor cruise after their beautifully staged press conference was called the "FantaSea One."

And sure enough, Buchanan ended up with just 442,368 votes nationwide (.43 percent). John Hagelin got 89,236 (.09 percent). Neither was anywhere close to the 5 percent needed to keep a finger in the public funding pot made available to major presidential candidates. For all intents and purposes, the Reform Party experiment was dead. The fears of Jesse Ventura, Phil Madsen, and Jack Gargan and many others had come true.

Immediately after the announcement of the Reform Party's national primary results in Long Beach, I bumped into Pat Choate walking from one convention to the other. He rubbed his salt-and-pepper beard and said, mournfully, "I actually always agreed with Jack Gargan on this. The process was too open, too loosey-goosey, too open to mischief." Choate's mention of Gargan prompted me to give Jack a call. He was home in Cedar Key, but he had been watching the proceedings on C-Span.

"This is the demise of the Reform Party," said Gargan, the man who more than any other had started it all. "I think any shred of credibility has been lost. Every damn thing I said would happen has happened — hijacking the party, stuffing the ballot, strong-arming the delegates." He had watched, hoping despite himself that perhaps the grass-roots wing of the party would somehow revive itself. But he noted that both the Hagelin and Buchanan crowds seemed to be full of new people, that nearly all the longtime Reform activists were gone, with the exception of the leaders who had orchestrated his own departure.

So, I asked him, what's next for you? "I'm going to support Ralph Nader. We're friends," he answered. "I'm thinking of calling him tomorrow and asking him how I can help him. There is a very strong movement among old grass-roots Reform members to try to support Nader. I was just waiting to see what happened in Long Beach. Now I know."[101]

Organizing the Left

The Greens and Ralph Nader

6

Compost Rotten Politics

Between one-third and one-half of the land surface has been transformed by human action; the carbon dioxide concentration in the atmosphere has increased by nearly 30 percent since the beginning of the Industrial Revolution; more atmospheric nitrogen is fixed by humanity than by all natural terrestrial sources combined; more than half of all accessible surface fresh water is put to use by humanity; about one-quarter of the bird species on Earth have been driven to extinction; and approximately two-thirds of major marine fisheries are fully exploited, overexploited, or depleted.

The conclusions from this overview are inescapable: during the last few decades, humans have emerged as a new force of nature. We are modifying physical, chemical, and biological systems in new ways, at faster rates, and over larger spatial scales than ever recorded on Earth. Humans have unwittingly embarked upon a grand experiment with our planet. The outcome of this experiment is unknown.

— Jane Lubchenko

The Green Challenge

Opening the April 1998 national conference in Santa Fe of the Association of State Green Parties, Green Party activist Patrick Mazza invoked these words from Jane Lubchenko, one of the original signatories of the Scientists Statement on Global Climatic Disruption and a past president and chair of the American Association for the Advancement of Science. Mazza, an environmental writer from Portland, Oregon, with a resonant, deep voice, paused to let the scope of Lubchenko's warning sink in. The circle of twenty-eight delegates from nearly twenty states, along with fifty observers, young and old alike, nodded gravely.

"We're an asteroid striking the earth," he concluded, invoking an image of cataclysmic disaster that was then riding high in the popular culture in the form of two Hollywood movies, *Armageddon* and *Deep Impact*.

But Mazza's analogy also unwittingly described America's Greens. To be sure, the Greens are sincerely motivated by a desire to defend the earth from environmental cata-

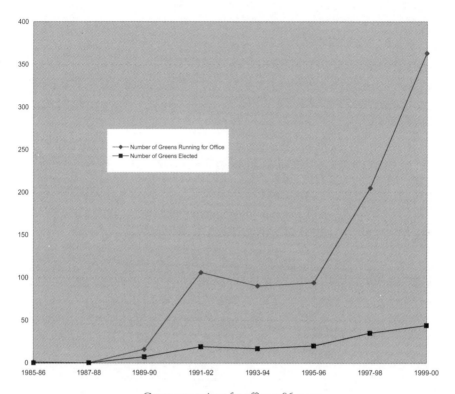

Green campaigns for office 1986–2000

strophe, along with a passion for economic justice and political reform. Their emergence in the United States in the wake of more robust Green parties in Europe and elsewhere suggests a hopeful future. But until the 2000 election their efforts to alter the course of human recklessness here in the land of the free had little concrete impact, like shooting stars bouncing off the earth's atmosphere or burning up before hitting the ground.

Since 1990, several hundred Greens have run for local, state, and federal office. As of 2001, the party can boast of a record number of ninety-one elected officials spread over twenty-one states. Of course, winning elections isn't the only measure of third-party success, and the Greens can also credibly claim to have shifted the trajectory of many races, injecting important issues into local debates and affecting the broader consciousness of millions of voters. In a few states—New Mexico, Maine, Connecticut, and Hawaii—they have been genuine players in statewide and congressional politics. And in those and several others (primarily California, Oregon, Washington, Alaska, Minnesota, Colorado, Pennsylvania, New York, and Washington, D.C.) they have achieved some real successes in local and municipal races, electing a number of mayors, city council members, and county commissioners. After running candidates in fourteen states in 1991–92, and eighteen states in 1995–96, the party's reach took a big jump in 1999–2000, with office seekers in a total of thirty-four states.[1]

Their critics would be more savage, saying yes indeed, the Greens are like an asteroid hitting the earth, but that the only thing they have struck so far is the center-left of American politics, blowing up Democratic majorities and getting antienvironmental Republicans elected. In the wake of Ralph Nader's second Green campaign for the presidency, this charge has only gotten more explosive. GREEN just stands for "Get Republicans Elected Everywhere in November," many Democrats bitterly complain, pointing to the 96,837 votes Nader got in Florida as proof that he cost Al Gore the 2000 election. Greens respond that Gore was the architect of his own defeat, or, as Nader put it in one postelection interview, that "Gore slipped on fifteen different banana peels and they've just chosen to focus on one."[2] Nevertheless, the acrimony between Democrats and Greens is real, while Republicans are no doubt quietly gratified by the split.

Thus the emergence of the Greens presents many challenges for progressive supporters of third-party efforts. Is there a way out of the "spoiler" trap? Or is the two-party duopoly so badly spoiled that the best thing people of conscience can do is strike out on their own, despite the potential short-term danger of hurting Democrats and helping Republicans? Can the Greens make good on their promise to break open the political duopoly? Against the obstacles facing all third parties in America, which strategy makes the most sense for Greens to follow—running local candidates with a real chance of winning or running high-visibility candidates in high-level races as a way of reaching and educating more voters?

Having spent a good chunk of the last few four years talking to and observing Greens up close in places ranging from New Mexico and California to Maine, New York, New Jersey, and Washington, D.C., I can say one thing for certain: They are fired by the same rebellious spirit that has propelled every other third party in American history to stake its claim on the national stage. And even after getting just 3 percent of the presidential vote in 2000, and sparking widespread recriminations from Democratic liberals, that spirit has not dimmed. The Greens are not going away—especially as long as the duopoly keeps avoiding serious issues like unbridled corporate power, environmental degradation, economic inequality, and political corruption, alienating millions of voters in the process. The question is whether the party can grow bigger—develop its state and local organizations, broaden its base, and throw some weight around on the national stage—or if it will tread water until some cataclysmic wave carries it to higher ground.

Early Seeds

To understand where the Greens are headed, it makes sense to first briefly look at their origins. Unlike the Reform Party, which was largely built from the top-down and thus had a rickety frame easily toppled by an outsider, the Greens were built from the bottom up. No mogul financed their early growth or paid for their national conventions and public relations. This was a party that, until very recently, subsisted solely on the labor and energy of volunteers—with all the good and bad effects that flow from being rooted in the minds and muscles of political beginners. Even now it is led by volunteers, though some have gained real campaign experience over the last few years. It has likewise been a party with an almost reflexive allergy to hierarchy or charismatic leaders. Also unlike the Reform Party, which had no clear ideological core beyond what its founder tried to implant in it and which seesawed all over the political map once that founder left the stage, the Greens early on collectively agreed on some common principles to focus their work. But it took them a long time to gather themselves into a force for electoral action, a process that was undoubtedly a result of the conditions of the party's birth.

If the Reform Party was the first political party in America to be born in response to a televised appeal (Ross Perot's appearances on *Larry King Live*), the Greens started in large part as a response to a book. In 1984, Charlene Spretnak and Fritjof Capra published *Green Politics: The Global Promise*, a study of the rise of the Green Party of West Germany and a call to establish a Green movement in the United States. The book struck a nerve among ecological, antiwar, and feminist activists, many of whom were searching for a way to knit together their work into a larger holistic movement for fundamental social change. At Spretnak's invitation, sixty-two people came to a national meeting in St. Paul, Minnesota, in August 1984. They were "independent peace activists, community organizers, organic farmers, religious people, bioregionalists, feminists, several academics, and a couple of union members who sought to create a new, values-based, multi-issue movement and political party in this country," in the words of one participant.[3]

As befits book readers, these fledgling Greens took words seriously. To their credit, they listened to Spretnak's advice and worked hard in St. Paul to hammer out a clear set of guiding principles as one of their founding acts. These have come to be known as the "Ten Key Values" of the Greens:

1. ecological wisdom;
2. personal and social responsibility;
3. grass-roots democracy;
4. nonviolence;
5. respect for diversity;
6. postpatriarchal values;
7. decentralization;
8. community economics;
9. global responsibility;
10. future focus.

From the very start, these Green pioneers were as much interested in movement building as they were in party organizing, probably even more so. Spretnak's own blueprint for "the Green alternative" offered several different approaches for discussion, only one of which was a full-fledged political party. Indeed, she questioned whether a Green Party in America was really viable, arguing that it would take an enormous amount of money to sustain. She also warned that unlike West Germany's system of proportional representation, which guaranteed some seats to minor parties, the American winner-take-all system would produce "inevitably early losses [that] could be demoralizing to party members." When the Greens of West Germany moved into electoral politics, she noted, they suffered all kinds of stresses, including the demands of campaigning, critical press coverage, a need to develop detailed policy positions on almost every topic, problems managing their legislative strategy, and internal conflicts between members and officeholders and among officeholders. As a practical matter, she counseled caution and patience before leaping into the electoral arena.[4]

The early American Greens were self-selecting individuals attracted to a holistic vision of politics, movement-style activists nervous about building a traditional party structure, and hyperintellectual types with either the free time to spend on intensive reading and introspective debate or the passion to make that time despite the demands of day-to-day life. Thus, at first they did not produce anything like a typical political party, either at the national level or in their individual states. Many formed local groups, joined regional groupings, and loosely participated in an "Interregional" (the Green word for "national") Committee and in a "Green Committees of Correspondence" (a conscious remembrance of the original Committees of Correspondence that brought together the founders of the United States in the years before the Revolutionary War). The idea was to be strongly grounded in local units, whose numbers slowly grew from twenty-five in 1984 to nearly three hundred in the fall of 1990. However, efforts to come together in any kind of representative national body were weak. No one really had the power to make it happen. Delegates were supposed to come from dues-paying locals, but their participation was episodic. The Interregional Committee had little authority to act in lieu of a national gathering, which was deliberate. Meanwhile, the simple act of hosting a national gathering tended to burn out local activists.

And when they did come together, these Greens loved to argue with each other! Here's a description of their first national gathering, in Amherst, Massachusetts, over the July 4 weekend in 1987:

A chicken barbecue . . . touched off a protest from animal rights crusaders. Some women at the conference were incensed about what they felt was an overwhelming male tone to the proceedings. And an intense argument about the role of population growth in environmental destruction erupted during several workshops. Still, this diverse crowd of activists—socialists and entrepreneurs, Goddess worshippers and solar engineers, old hippies and clean-cut college kids—found a wide swath of common ground. They all fear[ed] the direction that corporate-dominated industrial society was taking us and felt that traditional liberal and leftists solutions were not enough to avert an increasingly grim future.[5]

That common ground kept a core group of activists going, despite their lack of resources and evident disagreements. But an honest appraisal of their progress, written by John Rensenbrink, a professor of political science from Maine who has been involved with the Greens from the birth of the movement was not encouraging.

"Seven years after [the] initial national organizing meeting in St. Paul," he wrote in his valuable book *The Greens and the Politics of Transformation,*

the Greens (USA) were still a small and insignificant group of mostly middle-class whites, with a sprinkling of other people of color, scattered in small groups around the country. They had not yet fully developed a fund-raising arm, they had consumed much energy in a seemingly arcane dispute over whether to be more "social" or "deep" in their understanding of ecology, and their regional and interregional . . . organization was weak even by standards of confederation. And, most trying to all of those Greens who saw the vacuum of vision and direction in the upper regions of mainstream politics, the Greens seemed so tied up in awkward structures of their own making, and so hesitant in their gestures toward political engagement, that the prospects for a successful Green politics seemed to be fading away.[6]

Reports on this period of the Greens' political development read like a paper produced by the Rand Corporation or some government bureaucracy. The Green Party Organizing Committee fought with the Left Green Network at Interregional Committee meetings over what kind of national structure to form; arguments flew over Strategy and Policy Approaches in Key Areas (SPAKAs), a precursor to a Green platform; and tiny numbers of delegates struggled to create new coordinating bodies like a Green Council or a Green Congress. All this took place without the benefit of e-mail, by the way.

Meetings of Greens also tended to be obsessed with process, out of a well-intentioned desire to break down inherited modes of behavior that oppressed many people, especially women, and the belief that their means had to be as pure as their ends. Drawing heavily on practices prevalent in the feminist, peace, and antinuclear movements of the 1970s, the Greens preferred facilitators to leaders, tried to make decisions by consensus, and placed great importance on democratic discussions. Meetings even had "vibe watchers" to alert the group to unresolved or unexpressed emotional issues. To express approval, participants were encouraged to "twinkle"—to wave their open hands over their heads—instead of clapping, a practice imported from the deaf community that to the Greens was supposedly less domineering. This insistence on hyperdemocracy may have satisfied those Greens who believed, as Rensenbrink put it, that "the way you organize yourselves should be in a manner that prefigures the kind of society you say you want to bring into being."[7] But while this set of cultural choices made sense to the people who were creating Green politics from scratch, it tended to produce a small and insular world, not one likely to draw many less politically conscious newcomers to it.

This emphasis on purity of process is often a phenomenon of middle-class activism. Instead of being based concretely on interests, this style of politicking is primarily an expression of personal values. As David Croteau pointed out in his study of the gap between middle-class and working-class politics, "when activists use values as the basis of their politics, they can justify their political actions despite their inability to connect with a broader citizenry." Most working-class people, Croteau argued, tend to see such cultural and political "statements" as "expressions of fringe elements who can be readily dismissed, and they see those engaging in futile political acts as privileged and naïve actors." But Greens were just reproducing the culture they came out of, not realizing how their common devotion to political folk music, vegetarian cooking, and other markers of the "alternative lifestyle" set them apart from many of the people they wanted to stand with.[8]

People who wanted to take Green ideas to large numbers of voters by contesting elections also found their hyper sensitive process unrealistic and stultifying. Frustration about how long it was taking to move toward concrete electoral activity finally bubbled up and found expression in the wake of the Greens' fourth national gathering in Elkins, West Virginia, in August 1991. By that time, formal Green parties had begun to coalesce on their own initiative in a few states, most notably Alaska, where a 1990 gubernatorial candidate had gotten 3.2 percent of the vote, giving the party a formal line on the ballot, and in a handful of other states where activists were registering party members in order to obtain ballot status. A group of Greens that included Rensenbrink saw these fledgling parties as the building blocks of a larger national party, but they were up against opposition from others who thought that contesting elections was not sufficiently revolutionary and that elected officials couldn't produce real change.

This difference in vision led to an open split in the Green movement between those who wanted to concentrate on movement building, with electoral politics playing a secondary role, and those who wanted to play in the political arena while continuing to emphasize activism around issues. The first tendency found its expression when the Green Committees of Correspondence were replaced by a new organization, called the Greens/Green Party USA (G/GPUSA), which aimed to guide both party- and movement-building efforts. It was to be governed by dues-paying activists organized in movement locals, with no representation for state parties. And it was dominated by a group of leftist ideologues who took on their opponents with harsh and sometimes personal attacks. In response, a more electorally oriented group broke away and formed the Green Politics Network in the spring of 1992.

This latter group set in motion the events that led to Ralph Nader's 1996 presidential campaign and the formation of the multistate Association of State Green Parties. But it would be a mistake to assume that the ASGP are the realists and the G/GPUSA the fundamentalists, categories that some have used to explain arguments among the German Greens, as if the first group were pragmatists and the second one extremists. Much of the difference between the two is more about how best to structure the Green movement in a manner that is democratic and accountable to its base (though the G/GPUSA's platform is definitely more leftist than the ASGP's). Leaders of the ASGP also think that anyone serious about changing the direction of the country has to contest for formal power. As Rensenbrink told me during a June 1995 conference on third-party unity efforts held in Washington, D.C., "What's happening now is a new approach that in a subtle and profound way sees electoral politics as direct action. Our gubernatorial candidate in Maine in 1994, Jonathan Carter, emphasized confronting the establishment in their center of power. You know, damn it, I think the left analysis has been good, but it has seen politics as superstructure and not as, itself, the generic factor in history and thus a generic terrain for action."[9] Translation: Elections matter.

Though the split between these two branches of the American Greens has not fully healed, as of this writing twenty-nine of the thirty-nine existing state parties have affiliated with the ASGP, while the G/GPUSA membership has dwindled in most states outside of Missouri and New York.[10] In addition, both bodies were working out a compromise proposal for an eventual merger that would lead to the creation of one national party structured as a federation of state parties.[11] Thus, in the last ten years, a state-based model of party building gradually won out over the primarily movement-oriented model. But the tension between supporters of internal hyperdemocracy and those who wanted to move and not "waste time" on process remained, a legacy of the Greens' roots.

Flowering in New Mexico

All this deep history would be of little importance if the Greens had remained the sort of visionary debating society Rensenbrink described in 1991. But starting in the early 1990s, Greens in at least fourteen different states began entering the electoral arena in daring ways, not only winning local offices but challenging the major parties in some high-level races as well. New Mexico was their flagship, and an ideal place to glimpse all their potential and problems. Nowhere else has the party played out as many scenarios for Greens in state politics. In Maine, for example, Greens have twice run strong candidates for governor, but they have never elected anyone to a significant local office in a major city or county.[12] Greens have thirty-five local officeholders in California, including nineteen city council members and a half-dozen mayors,[13] but they've never had a consequential showing in a statewide race. Hawaii's Greens have made a big splash too, getting 14 percent for their U.S. Senate candidate, Linda Martin, in 1992, and three times electing women to the County Council of the Big Island of Hawaii. But the Hawaii Greens have yet to swing a congressional race, and the state's unusual racial composition (majority Asian-American, one-third white) makes their experience somewhat exceptional.

In New Mexico Greens have three times drawn double digits in U.S. House races (acting as "spoilers," in the view of the Democrats who lost), along with running regular statewide candidates and electing and reelecting local officeholders. Not only have Greens in New Mexico struggled with the divisive issue of spoiling, they have had to deal with charges that they are not diverse enough. These issues plague Greens across America. So while it may have just been coincidence that the Greens first made a national splash in New Mexico, the state has been an ideal petri dish for testing the prospects of Greens nationwide.

The New Mexico Greens' breakthrough came in 1994, with Roberto Mondragon's run for governor. Until then, the Greens had essentially been invisible to mainstream public consciousness. All that changed in July of that year, when the *New York Times* published a lengthy story titled "Rebellion of Greens Is Brewing in the West."[14] Mondragon, a fifty-four-year-old former Democratic lieutenant governor who was also a Spanish-language radio broadcaster, had been first elected to the state legislature at the age of twenty-five. Now, after a failed run for Congress in 1982, he had decided to reenter politics as a Green, dispelling the image of the Greens as total amateurs. Not only that, he was a Hispanic native of the state, bringing high-level diversity to a movement that was primarily led by well-educated whites.[15]

Challenging Governor Bruce King, a wealthy, conservative, seventy-year-old Democrat close to the state's business elite of ranchers and oilmen, and Gary Johnson, an energetic Republican newcomer who was also a millionaire, Mondragon had a strong appeal to many of the state's Hispanics and other moderate-income voters. A modest man with a grizzled face and a white beard, he was a well-known and much-liked local personality who had a small part in Robert Redford's movie *The Milagro Beanfield War*, a story dear to his heart for its advocacy of the common people against the state's big landowners and resource hogs. He and Steve Schmidt, his candidate for lieutenant governor, ran on a platform fashioned by Schmidt that melded environmental and economic concerns ("We absolutely refuse to cater to holier-than-thou Range Rover environmentalists," Schmidt said), and blended in issues of high concern to Perot voters, including term limits, campaign finance reform, and deficit reduction. At its core, the Mondragon-Schmidt Green platform upheld the populist traditions of the Democratic Party—calling for universal health care coverage, a "living wage" instead of a minimum wage, deep cuts in military spending and corporate welfare, and increased spending on public schools. But it was far from a doctrinaire "left" document, including explicit support for small business and property tax reform rather than pie-in-the-sky proclamations of nationalizing industries or abolishing the military.[16]

Significantly, Mondragon and Schmidt weren't running alone, but as part of a slate of candidates vying for a wide range of state and local offices. And while Republicans triumphed across the country in 1994, gaining a majority of the U.S. House for the first time in many years, the New Mexico Greens demonstrated there was substantial public support for a new politics in their state. Their candidate for state treasurer, Lorenzo Garcia, a Vietnam veteran and federal bank examiner, got 33 percent of the vote. Fran Gallegos, another veteran and former Republican with innovative ideas about alternatives to incarceration, got 43 percent in her bid to become a Santa Fe municipal judge (setting up her eventual victory two years later). And Mondragon and Schmidt got 10 percent statewide, despite having raised just $100,000. Most promising, they won the vote among eighteen- to twenty-nine-year olds.[17] (Schmidt was also appointed to a seat on the state board of education as a result.) Suddenly, the Greens were on the map.

Three things were coming together for the Greens of New Mexico during this period: their own focus on local-level organizing around a progressive platform, growing disaffection with the national Democratic Party's move to the right, and a spate of electoral opportunities created by lousy Democratic candidacies in the state itself. First, at roughly the same time that the Green Politics Network was breaking away from the Greens/GPUSA to push for more state-level party building, a few New Mexico Greens saw an opportunity to enter directly into local races. In Santa Fe, they started slowly, seeking to build up political capital doing grass-roots organizing against some local development projects and pushing for a living wage. They helped found Citizens for Property Tax Justice, gaining the trust of many of the city's old Hispanic families, and played a role in authoring a bill that would have given tax relief to people threatened by gentrification. Not insignificantly, the bill passed both houses of the state legislature only to be vetoed by the conservative Democratic governor Bruce King, an ally of the real estate lobby. The Santa Fe group also busied themselves organizing a local currency modeled on the "Ithaca Hours" bartering system that helped support local businesses and build community bonds.

In Taos, the Greens were less patient. Not only that, they showed a knack for the nuts and bolts of creating a serious campaign. They were led by Abraham Gutmann, an owner of a small business and former world traveler who had settled in this enclave of the counterculture high in the Sangre de Christo Mountains in the northern part of the state. In 1992, he took what had been essentially a local Green discussion group and built a modest but effective political machine. Running one-on-one against a Democratic candidate for state representative, Gutmann got nearly 40 percent of the vote. A fellow Green, Andres Vargas, ran for district attorney and scored 42 percent.

These almost successful forays in 1992 helped convince Greens in Santa Fe to run in the next election cycle. Cris Moore, a bright young physicist, had just moved there after getting his Ph.D. from Cornell. While in college he had been active with the Student Environmental Action Coalition, a network of hundreds of campus chapters. From there he flowed naturally into the Greens, and at the tender age of twenty-five, he decided to run for city council. The election was held in the spring of 1994. Moore, who had no prior experience campaigning for office, was blessed by a strong circle of supporters. Xubi Wilson, a local baker, had been a student organizer in New York and had worked on Democrat Ann Richards's gubernatorial campaign in Texas. Melissa MacDonald had worked in Arkansas with ACORN (the Association of Community Organizations for Reform Now, one of the country's strongest grass-roots groups). Nate Downey had volunteered on Gary Hart's presidential bids. Mitch Busczek had solid training running school board campaigns.

"Mitch got us into doing voter identification calls and made us write a turnout plan, precinct by precinct," Wilson recalled.[18] These skills were critical. As Moore told fellow Greens from around the country during a discussion of party-building strategies at the ASGP's Santa Fe conference, "We had one experienced guy join our first campaign, and we learned from there."[19] MacDonald, Downey, and Wilson also worked hard to bring in volunteers and create solid systems for collecting data, following up, and divvying out tasks. Ultimately they built a base of about one hundred volunteers. And instead of running as some kind of utopian radical, Moore focused on bread-and-butter issues of concern to average working people in Santa Fe, like defending people who were being pushed out of their homes by rising property values due to gentrification and talking about closing the gap between wages and the cost of living. He also opposed development on Atalaya Mountain near Santa Fe. Moore's candidacy was endorsed by the Sierra Club, the American Federation of Teachers, AFSCME (the state employees union), the Communications Workers, and the Hospital/Health Care Workers Local 1199. In a seven-way nonpartisan race, he received 33 percent, beating his nearest competitor by 8 percent.

Looking back on his first victory, Moore felt several things made it possible. "Some Green campaigns I've seen have been handicapped by an unrealistic desire to have a consensus process throughout the campaign." Instead, he said, "We had a more traditional model, and I as a candidate was thrilled to be told what to do and where to go— unlike the typical Green ideal of hyperdemocracy." He pointed to the Greens' early coalition work as vital. "We also were able to put together a good alliance of different constituencies, raising money from wealthy liberals, getting young volunteers, and having Hispanic support among some of Santa Fe's oldest families. This was an outgrowth of having worked on a number of key issues, including property tax reform and preserving the local mountains. This work was collective but I was often the spokesperson, so it fed into my campaign."[20]

He also didn't take a casual view as to how easy it is to run a viable campaign for office. Moore said, "My advice to candidates: if you don't have at least twenty people who are *not* Greens who know you and really care about you winning, it's too early to run." He also cautioned people against quixotic forays into local politics. "If you can't get at least 10 percent in a race in a small district, it's too early to run. I can support 'educational campaigns' at a national or state level, or in a large city, but in a small town there's no excuse to run and get single digits. If anything, that low of a turnout probably hurts your future chances of organizing more than it helps, by labeling you as a gadfly."[21]

Democratic Refugees

Moore's victory gave the Greens of Santa Fe the confidence to think bigger, but they would never have gotten veteran politicians like Mondragon to rally to their banner that summer were it not for the larger trends within the local and national Democratic Party. Bill Clinton's election in 1992 was also a resounding victory for conservatives in the Democratic Party, who blamed party liberals for the losses of George McGovern, Walter Mondale, and Michael Dukakis. Clinton, a southern governor who catered carefully to his state's business establishment after one unsuccessful term in office as a semiliberal, had been one of the founders of the Democratic Leadership Council, an elite body that looked to corporate America for support and pushed the party to the right on issues like crime, welfare, and foreign policy. During the primaries, his leading opponent was former California governor Jerry Brown, who ran a progressive campaign focused on political reform, universal health care, respect for human rights, and radical tax reform. One of the authors of Brown's "Take Back America" platform was none other than Steve Schmidt, who had earlier worked on Michael Dukakis's 1988 run.

Unlike past years, when losing candidates for the Democratic nomination were allowed to speak to the national convention and make their dissenting views into a "minority report" to the party's platform, in 1992 no such accommodation was made for Brown and his supporters. Schmidt recalls that the turning point came when the party's platform committee came to Santa Fe to hold a regional hearing. "Our issues had taken us from dark horse to second place in the primaries. So Jerry [Brown] asked me to meet with Ron Brown [the Democratic national chair], to put forward our proposal that electoral reform and campaign finance reform be the focus of the first 100 days of the Clinton administration. Start by pushing money back from the trough that was corrupting Washington, and then go with health care reform. And Ron Brown said, 'Get lost.' " In Schmidt's view, that was the moment that many progressives stepped away from the Democratic Party.[22] Among the people listening during the platform committee's hearing was Roberto Mondragon, who had supported Democratic liberals like Robert Kennedy, George McGovern, and Ted Kennedy, and had last been involved in party politics supporting Jesse Jackson's presidential bids in 1984 and 1988. Afterward, Schmidt recalled, "Roberto came to me and said he'd run with me if I'd run with him."[23]

At the urging of Abraham Gutmann and other Greens, Schmidt soon decided to switch parties and bring the "Take Back America" platform that he had helped craft for Jerry Brown and turn it into the New Mexico Greens' platform. Gutmann was also working on converting Mondragon, who later said he was impressed with the party's positions. "The Green Party stands for what the state Democratic Party ought to stand for," he told the *New York Times*. Voicing his outrage at how the party who had nurtured him had changed, he added, "There used to be room for liberals in the Democratic Party here. But there isn't room anymore. If you look at the contributors for the Democratic Party today, it's the same people that you'll find on the list of contributors for the Republican Party."[24] (Mondragon's last bid for public office had been in 1982, when he faced Democrat Bill Richardson in a contest for the First Congressional District seat; Richardson's war chest of $400,000 was ten times what Mondragon could raise.)

Ultimately, Mondragon's decision to switch parties was triggered by the results of the 1994 Democratic primary in New Mexico, in which the incumbent governor, King, defeated his lieutenant governor, Casey Luna, thanks to the late entry of Jim Baca, an environmentalist who had just been fired from his position as head of the federal Bureau of Land Management. Baca split the anti-King vote with Luna, enabling King to win with a bare plurality. Luna, in Mondragon's view, "would have been a move away from the good 'ol boy system," while Governor King just represented the interests of ranchers, including his own King Brothers Ranch.[25] According to Mondragon's campaign treasurer, Norm Shatkin, "Middle-class Hispanics were outraged over Casey Luna's defeat. They felt that King had stolen the primary by inducing Jim Baca to run, thereby taking away enough votes from Luna to give King a plurality."[26]

Though Mondragon ran to win, not just to teach King a lesson, he never fully joined the Greens despite being their candidate. Part of this was due to an internal misunderstanding. Mondragon had somehow gotten the impression that the Greens had wealthy sponsors across the country who would help raise something like $700,000 for him, which would have made for a very strong campaign. This money did not exist; nor did movie star director Robert Redford pony up any money to help.[27] About

$100,000 was raised, half by the Greens and half by Mondragon's own political net-work.[28] Money problems aside, Mondragon turned out to be more concerned than his fellow Greens about the risk of tilting the governor's office to the Republicans.

Late in the race, some labor unionists with the same worry brokered a meeting between the Democratic and Green candidates at the governor's mansion. By then, Mondragon knew he wasn't going to win and thought that the Green Party's role should be to influence the Democratic agenda. "There were twenty-four items on the list that we brought with us to the governor. Most should have been Democratic issues anyway, like increased education funding and more support for labor rights," Mondragon recalled later.[29] But the biggest item required a revolution in Green thinking—power sharing with the Democrats. "We wanted to be able to recommend one out of every five members of state commissions," Mondragon said. "That's ultimately what the Green Party can do, if all it's going to be able to get is 15 or 17 percent in elections."

The Greens' campaign froze all activities as the news leaked that their candidate was thinking of dropping out in exchange for this deal with Governor King. "We went back to Norm Shatkin's house to discuss it with the Greens," Mondragon recalled, "and they just said no. They told me I'd be seen as a sellout." At that point in the race, Mondragon had barely any money left, and he was upset at the Greens for not doing more to bolster him. "'Come on, get real,' I tried to say to them. But it was too soon. They weren't ready to talk coalition politics." In the end, the deal fell through, partly because King refused Mondragon's request to call Casey Luna to reconcile, and because Steve Schmidt told his running mate that it would happen only over his dead body.

Democrat King ended up losing to the Republican newcomer Gary Johnson, 50 percent to 40 percent, with the remainder taken by Mondragon. Many Democrats concluded that the Greens had swung the result to the GOP, but a postelection poll by the University of New Mexico found that had Mondragon not run, his voters would have split almost evenly between the other two candidates.[30] But the race did expose many fault lines beneath the surface of the Greens' electoral ambitions. One was the division between white progressives and Hispanics. Both had good reason to be frus-trated with the Democratic Party, but the whites, who tended to be better educated and relatively well-off, had more latitude to leave the fold, and Hispanics, who tended to be poorer and more dependent on state services, had more reason to be wary.

A second tension was between environmentalists and social justice advocates. According to Norm Shatkin, Mondragon's treasurer, the activists who worked hard to put environmentalist Jim Baca on the ballot in the Democratic primary did little to help Mondragon, despite his Green label. This was partly because he was a vocal sup-porter of allowing logging on public lands that had been owned for centuries by the state's Hispanics but illegally confiscated after the United States annexed the region from Mexico. For him, this was an issue of community justice, for them it was an environmental crime. Finally, the Mondragon campaign highlighted the difficulty the Greens—like any other political party—could have with a leader who was his or her own person.

Feet on the Ground

Had the Greens gone after only high-level offices like governor, where they had little hope of an upset, the party might not have gotten very far. But in New Mexico the Greens have been grounded by their local electoral victories. By electing Cris Moore to the Santa Fe City Council in 1994 and Fran Gallegos as a municipal judge two years later, they not only validated their efforts and gave their supporters a sense of accomplishment. They gained something to lose, providing ballast for the rough seas of intraparty politics. Like the Reform Party, Greens have certainly had their splits. In 1995, open conflict broke out over the forest logging issue, for example. (Significantly, it was Moore who hammered out a party consensus statement on that issue.) In 1996, the New Mexicans experienced a tough if civil primary battle between Abraham Gutmann and Sam Hitt, the leader of a determined environmental group called the Forest Guardians. Guttman won, but the conflict weakened his Senate campaign and exhausted many core Greens.

No political party can avoid such schisms. Democrats and Republicans also have strong disagreements within their ranks—think of the conservative Democratic "Blue Dogs" in Congress and their nemeses in the Progressive Caucus, or the vicious public name-calling that erupted a few years ago between New Jersey Democratic Senators Bob Torricelli and Frank Lautenberg. But major parties hold together despite their internal conflicts because both sides have more to lose from openly splitting their party—threatening their privileged position as partners in the two-party duopoly—than they have to gain. Intraparty fights among Democrats and Republicans also tend to take place between officeholders who are often from different parts of the country, where regional differences explain some political variations. And fewer incumbents are party animals these days, running candidate-centered campaigns with their own fund-raising bases. Thus it is very rare to see open conflict expressed among people with different philosophies within one of the major parties. It's far better, from the individual politician's point of view, to go along to get along.

Third parties are much more vulnerable to internal splits. For starters, they are made up of strong-willed people with an intense identification to something, either a charismatic leader or a set of ideas. And, particularly when they haven't managed to elect any of their own to office and when they haven't habituated voters to identify with their line, they have almost nothing to lose. Often, some of their members come

to define victory not in electoral terms, but in terms of ideological or personal con-
quests over their foes within the party. Instead of figuring out how to end their marginality, they come to take it as a given or even a mark of pride. Forward motion is defined
in the context of a tiny fishbowl, stocked only by the hard-core party faithful. A circle
facing inward, rather than outward.

By comparison, said Cris Moore, "Having someone in office has done a lot to
mature the local Greens as an organization." By this he doesn't mean lowering their
sights, but doing the nitty-gritty work needed to sell their ideas to a majority of voters or
legislators. "Sometimes progressives will get someone elected and then say, 'Will you
please introduce this resolution against the Gulf War, or this resolution for the land-
mine ban, or to declare Santa Fe a safe zone for undocumented immigrants'—all
things we've actually had to deal with here," Moore recalled. "Now I tell activists,
'Lobby the other councilors, and when you get five votes, call me.' If you want to win
you have to do your homework and get a bunch of other councilors on board. I learned
a lot from sponsoring a resolution endorsing the land-mine ban. I thought it was a
slam dunk, and I only got two votes out of eight. My attitude now is I need to do my
homework and the activists need to do theirs, too."

Focusing on winning local races also forced the Santa Fe Greens to prioritize issues
that would help build their base rather than take up every single topic in the leftist
smorgasbord. Said Moore, "I applaud people who are working to prevent the Cassini
[plutonium-powered space] probe from being launched, but does that really help build
a movement? Do other people in the community really care about it? When people
with a single-issue focus like that come to our local meetings, I try to turn them away—
or tell them that first they need to show that a lot of the people in the community care
about it before we can take it on."[31]

In 1997, Chris Roybal, a Democratic city councilman in Espanola City whose family has lived in Santa Fe since the time it was a Spanish possession, wrote an open letter attacking the Greens as "wealthy Anglo carpetbaggers." Speaking from the Hispanic
heart of the state Democratic Party, he wrote: "We do not have the benefit of trust
funds or the luxury of taking on causes that benefit the salvation of the whales far away
at the expense of our own economic development and well-being here at home. We
are here forever, as were our ancestors before us, loving and protecting our lands—not
just having a summer condo to live in during the good weather periods." Cris Moore's
reply was an eloquent statement of his vision of the Green Party:

> The co-chairs of the Santa Fe County Green Party are Peggy Prince, a fourth-genera-
> tion New Mexican, and Miguel Chavez, a 13th-generation native and a leader of the
> effort to establish a Hispano Cultural Center in Santa Fe. Municipal Judge Fran Galle-
> gos is a Green who grew up in Villanueva. Tesuque Tribal Councilor Michael Vigil is
> a Green too. . . .

Chris Roybal says we have trust funds. We could use the money! The Greens I know are landscapers, waiters, teachers, small-business owners, and State and City workers. He accuses us of racism because we ran an Anglo candidate, but the same people accuse us of tokenism when we run Hispanics.

He also says he doesn't have time to "save the whales." Funny, neither do we. The Greens have been spending our time on fighting for property tax relief for low-income families, higher wages for hotel workers, and affordable health care, as well as opposing development of our mountains and protecting the Rio Grande from a copper mine. Why aren't the other parties involved in these issues?

Let's face facts. Clinton joined with the Republicans in destroying welfare and abandoning low-income people. Neither old party takes campaign finance reform seriously, because both are in bed with big corporations. If Chris Roybal and others want to join a party that still stands for something, the door is open. In the meantime, please don't tell lies about us.[32]

Gunning for Congress

While Cris Moore has been the New Mexico Greens' political anchor, he is by no means a moderate when it comes to challenging the two-party duopoly. "Building a progressive third-party movement right now is a lot more important than sending one more Democrat to Congress," said Moore. "Even people who want to move the Democratic Party to the left ought to recognize that it's just not going to happen inside their party," added Moore. "It's like Frederick Douglass said: 'Power concedes nothing without a demand.'"[33] Thus, when President Clinton appointed New Mexico's Democratic Rep. Bill Richardson to become the U.S. ambassador to the United Nations in December of 1996, Moore threatened publicly to run for Congress if the Democrats didn't nominate someone to replace Richardson in the House who would "stand up to Bill Clinton and his slide to the right."[34] The Green Party's interest in entering the high-level race to fill the open seat only increased after the Democrat-led state legislature ignored their lobbying that winter for electoral reform (they wanted the ability to cross-endorse candidates, such as progressive Democrats), meaningful property tax relief, or a mere bottle recycling bill.

And the final straw came after the major parties picked their candidates. The Republicans nominated Bill Redmond, a Christian minister from Los Alamos who was close to the fundamentalist right. The Democrats went with Eric Serna, a Hispanic member of the State Corporation Commission who had no special qualifications for the position other than his family's long association with the party establishment. Worse, he was dogged by ethical questions about his past behavior, ranging from his having asked employees under his supervision to shop at his family's jewelry store, and using a car loaned to him by car dealers regulated by the commission, to failing to recuse himself from cases where he may have had a personal conflict.[35] Many liberal Democrats in the district were unhappy with the choice. To make matters worse, Serna was nominated at a closed-door meeting of the party's central committee rather than a more open forum.

Instead of asking Moore to risk his increasingly secure seat on the Santa Fe City Council, the Greens turned to 51-year-old Carol Miller, a longtime community health care advocate who lived in the poor mountain village of Ojo Sarco, an hour outside of Santa Fe. Miller, a Jewish rabble-rouser with flowing white-gray hair who seemed most at home in the pueblo health clinics of the Native American community, had worked for years in public health policy and was the immediate past president of the state's Public Health Association. Her strong advocacy for a Canadian-style single-payer system, as well as her support for far-reaching campaign finance reform, eliminating corporate welfare, and promoting education and women's rights, won her many plaudits, including the endorsement of both of the state's leading newspapers.[36] A number of Democratic activists endorsed her, including several members of the party's central committees in Santa Fe and Los Alamos. (On the other hand, Roberto Mondragon switched back to the Democratic party to endorse Serna, saying that he felt it was important that at least one of New Mexico's three congressional seats be held by a Hispanic.) Miller mobilized hundreds of volunteers over the course of the eight-week campaign with only a fraction of Redmond and Serna's war chests. Like Jesse Ventura, she also benefited from the "pox-on-both-your-houses" syndrome, as Redmond and Serna ran many negative ads attacking each other—though unlike Ventura she had only a scant $7,000 to spend on her own broadcast ads.[37]

Miller ended up with a stunning 17 percent of the vote, including majorities in several Santa Fe precincts—the highest percentage of the vote garnered by a third-party candidate in a three-way congressional race since 1950.[38] Not even a last-minute blizzard of radio ads personally recorded by President Clinton calling on the district's Democrats to come out for Serna could save the day. Her 17 percent of the vote was reminiscent of Ross Perot's 19 percent in 1992. But while Perot fractured George Bush's Republican base by making political reform and a balanced budget his central issues, Miller cracked the Democrats' solid 2-1 base in New Mexico's Third Congressional District by making campaign finance reform and a more humane budget her priorities. This suggested that as President Clinton moved his party to the right on budgetary issues and into the pockets of big money on campaign finance matters, incumbent Democrats who stood with him had become vulnerable to a challenge from the progressive-populist direction.

Miller's showing set off a chain of events that thrust the Green Party for the first time into the heart of national politics. Serna lost the race 43 percent to 40 percent, putting Republican Redmond into an office long held by the Democrats. Interparty recriminations flew, with Democrats attacking Greens for spoiling and the Greens saying that it was Serna who was the spoiled candidate—pointing out that he had managed to get only 22 percent of the registered Democrats in the district to vote for him. Less than a year later, Albuquerque Republican congressman Steve Schiff died of cancer, and the Greens decided to run a candidate in the June 1998 special election to fill his seat. There too, the Democrats had nominated a weak candidate, millionaire Phil Maloof, a state senator with close ties to liquor and gambling interests who was the scion of one of New Mexico's richest families. And there too, the Greens' candidate, fifty-three-year-old Bob Anderson, a part-time university teacher, union organizer, and Vietnam vet, ran a strong campaign.

After Anderson was included in a three-way televised debate his poll numbers jumped into the double digits. His easygoing manner charmed many viewers, and his intelligent answers convinced many that the Greens were not kooks. Afterward, so many people came by Anderson's campaign office to request literature he actually ran out of fliers. Aware of the threat the Greens posed, President Clinton flew into the state a few days before the election to attend a Democratic fund-raiser in Albuquerque, where he pleaded: "I would ask that people in New Mexico who have voted in the past for whatever reason for the Green Party but who honestly care about [the] environment to take another look at the consequences of their votes."[39]

Clinton's overture did little to help Maloof, whose sloppy campaign convinced many observers that he was simply not ready for Congress. (Asked at one debate about the Endangered Species Act, he appeared confused and answered that he enjoyed camping.) He took some distinctly right-of-center positions—backing Newt Gingrich's call for a further cut in the capital gains tax rate, and suggesting that part of the Social Security and Medicare trust funds be invested in the stock market. In contrast, Anderson was the only one of the three candidates to oppose any privatization of Social Security, and he campaigned hard for a living wage, universal health care, and more drug treatment programs. As with the earlier Serna-Redmond-Miller battle, the two major party candidates in this race also spent millions of dollars on ads attacking each other harshly, driving many undecided voters toward the Green, who ran a positive campaign.[40] "Any time the Greens are in the race and it goes negative, people can say, 'I'm tired of this,' and they look to Greens as an alternative," warned Democratic House Speaker Raymond Sanchez, a Maloof backer.[41] In the end, Anderson racked up 15 percent of the vote, tilting the race to the Republican, Heather Wilson, who won 45 percent of the vote to Maloof's 40 percent.

Spoiling for Success

Anderson's showing proved that the Greens were not a flash-in-the-pan phenomenon. But both he and Miller were banging their heads against the proverbial wall called winner-take-all elections. In New Mexico, races for low-level offices like city council don't have party labels attached to them. In fact, when Cris Moore ran for city council, his campaign literature played down the fact that he was a Green. (The local media, on the other hand, always reported his party ties.) Not so for positions in the state legislature or Congress. And thus every time the Greens ran for higher office, they had to address head-on the "spoiler" issue and the argument that people were just "wasting their votes."

By the fall of 1998, both Greens were running again, this time in regular elections for the two congressional seats. And they were stirring up a fury of activity by national Democrats and their allies. At one point, House Minority Leader Richard Gephardt, in line to become Speaker if his party gained just twelve more seats, called Anderson at home to ask him to drop out of the race, surprising him while he was taking a bath.[42] "I had been out campaigning and decided to sit in the tub and relax and read the paper," said Anderson. "I was screening my calls." Then a caller said he was Dick Gephardt, and Anderson realized that it was the House Democratic leader. "I jumped up out of the tub," Anderson said. "I was standing in the middle of the hallway, dripping wet and talking to one of the most powerful leaders in the country."[43] Anderson politely turned Gephardt down.

While Anderson was again running against Democrat Maloof and Republican Wilson, who was now the congresswoman, Carol Miller had a tougher race. Instead of opposing an ethically impaired Democrat like Eric Serna, she was contending with Democrat Tom Udall—the state attorney general and son of Stewart Udall, the former secretary of the interior, who was still revered in the state. Unlike Serna, the worst that could be said of Udall was that he hadn't cracked down hard on local corruption, which had grown with the spread of tribal casinos, and his economic program amounted to the usual Democratic pieties about improving education. Plus he campaigned like the seat was already his, thanks to his family's illustrious past. But Udall understood the need to recapture the disaffected Democrats who had voted for Miller a year earlier. He made much of his family's environmental record and subtly shifted to the left on some other issues, coming out in favor of universal health care, for example. An early September poll showed him leading Representative Redmond 42 to 35 percent, with just 8 percent supporting Miller. It looked as if she was headed for a big drop from the 17 percent she had gotten one year earlier.[44]

Not only were many liberals coming back to the Democrats in the Miller-Udall-Redmond race, some Greens even broke with their party over Miller's second run. "On the rare occasions when Democrats do put up progressive candidates, in the sense of having clean records and taking progressive positions, either we should endorse or take no position," party co-founder Abraham Gutmann told me in April of 1998, well before Udall had won the Democratic nomination.[45] Later that summer, he said, "We have a lot in common with Udall. [And] Like it or not, if we're successful we're going to be in coalition with the Democrats. Punishing them when they do the wrong thing, but working in government with them. I don't see us in coalition with the Republicans, and I don't see us gaining a clear majority of anything in the near future." He contrasted Miller's run against Udall to Cris Moore's steady growth in office, saying, "It's the difference between people who rock the vote violently, and people who can get on board and do something. Of course I'd prefer Carol to Tom Udall in the Congress. But the reality is if Redmond gets in there for a full term it will be very difficult to dislodge him. We'll be looking at nearly a fully Republican delegation from New Mexico."[46]

Miller was unrepentant. Even before Udall was picked as the Democratic candidate (Serna ran again in the primary and lost), she was publicly committed to running again. "Only a white person tells you that it's interesting to them that Udall is coming into the race," she told me that spring during a long conversation as we walked the dirt road that runs past her modest house in Ojo Sarco. "On the other hand, a lot of Hispanics say if he's in, they're coming to me." Her point was that the Greens could broaden their support among the district's Hispanics if they didn't assume that a candidate's environmental credentials were all that it took to define them as a progressive. "In fact," she said, "people feel that the Greens will be killing themselves if they don't run against Udall. That would destine us to always being a white Santa Fe–based party." Miller, who had originally moved to New Mexico from California to support the third-party efforts of La Raza Unida, a Chicano movement that briefly surged in the 1970s, had always been critical of the Greens' lack of diversity. "It's the only majority-Anglo thing I do in my life, and I think that's something that we really need to remedy."

Thus when Udall beat Serna in the Democratic primary, Miller was unfazed at the thought of opposing someone with better credentials. To her both represented opposite sides of the same devalued Democratic coin. "They both come from political families and just feel like the office is owed to them." If anything, Udall's victory gave her some relief, as the racial tension of being an Anglo running against a local Hispanic would not be repeated. And she was furious at the behavior of Greens like Abraham Gutmann for suggesting that she drop out of the race so as to not hurt Udall's chances. "He's one of those 'wheeler-dealer' Greens," she said with derision. "He has no elected office in the party, and he puts himself above it with this personal strategy of his, recruiting candidates on his own and talking to Democrats." In fact, Gutmann had indeed spoken to some liberal New Mexico lawmakers about getting both Miller and Anderson to drop out of their races in exchange for a cabinet seat in the state. "My question is how are you in a feminist party and you get your strongest candidate and all the men run around undercutting your campaign," Miller asked in response. (Jokingly, she said the only job she would take was ambassador to France.)

Miller's uncompromising stance was backed by the New Mexico Green Council, the party's governing body, but won her few friends among established political groups. The only unions to support her were a small hospital workers local and a theater and stage local. The Sierra Club, which had backed Serna in the earlier race despite his lack of an environmental record, was certainly not going to go anywhere close to her this time. Nor did women's groups or pro-choice groups, even though Udall was waffling on the late-term-abortion issue. The stance of these groups left Miller angry. "These so-called nonpartisan PACs all have this 'electability' argument. But they always support a bad Democrat over a worse Republican. They don't care about issues or honesty. Look at [former Illinois Congressman] Dan Rostenkowski. How many years did people cover up for his corrupt behavior? How many tax breaks did he write into law for special interests? He actually helped companies pollute the environment, and they had us pay to clean it up." It was clear that she saw little value in saving one Democratic seat in Congress, against the larger goal of building a new party. "This is the kind of thing that gets me really angry. Things couldn't have gotten so bad in this country without a lot of bad Democrats."

Miller almost physically recoiled from the "spoiler" question. "Since Clinton came to power," she said, "the GOP holds eighteen more governorships, over five hundred seats in legislatures have changed from Ds to Rs, and four hundred elected officials have changed registration from Democrat to Republican." In her view, Clinton's move to the right had succeeded only in turning off many Democratic voters, leading to more Republican victories. Having worked in Washington first in the Public Health Service under the Reagan administration and then in the Clinton administration on Hillary Clinton's Health Care Task Force, Miller said she saw too little difference between the two parties. And, she was disgusted by the gap between Democratic rhetoric and action. "I was there in 1993," she said. "We had a Democratic president, a Democratic Senate and a Democratic House. And we still couldn't do anything. I'm running against the failure of the Democratic Party."[47]

Interestingly, however, Cris Moore and Xubi Wilson and some of the other Santa Fe Greens decided to hold back from the Miller-Udall-Redmond fight as the campaign unfolded, putting more of their efforts into some local races where Green prospects were brighter.[48] One candidate they were enthusiastic about was Cliff Bain, a self-employed contractor who was running for a newly created position on the Public Regulation Commission. It was a two-way race against a Democratic incumbent who the Greens felt was overly friendly to lobbyists (a progressive Democrat had lost the primary). Bain emphasized the need to end the politics and patronage that had characterized the commission's work, charging that cronyism had produced high energy prices, lousy phone service, and the like. All the state's major newspapers and weeklies had endorsed him. In addition, Bain's campaign was doing a fair amount of outreach to Republicans since they didn't have anyone in the race, and his issues—increasing competition and lowering prices for utilities, could be pitched as pro-business. His prospects looked good, but party strategist Wilson was worried about the backlash from Miller's tough campaign. "A lot of people are so angry about Carol's running," he told me. "It's hurting Cliff's race, hurting our fund-raising and our volunteering. And it's exactly our strongest areas where people are angriest about her running again."[49]

Both congressional races looked tight going into the final days before the election. But while Udall's campaign was clearly benefiting from his district's predominantly Democratic tilt, Maloof, who was running in more of a swing district, was struggling to dispel perceptions created by his earlier loss. Editorials in the state and local papers suggested to voters that it was time to correct the accident of electing far-right Rep. Redmond because of the three-way split caused by Miller's first run, while they also praised Rep. Wilson and heaped scorn on Maloof's lack of political maturity. Maloof, like Udall, was trying to win back voters that he had lost to the Greens. But unlike Udall, who could call in celebrity Robert Redford to remind voters of his family's progressive past, Maloof had fewer assets. To reach progressives, he hired some local peace activists to work on his campaign. He also flip-flopped on a controversial local issue, coming out against development in a Native American monument called the Petroglyphs. His progressive Democratic supporters also played hardball, sending out mailings attacking Anderson's claims to have been a union organizer and spreading rumors about his service in Vietnam. President Clinton tried to help as well, cutting a deal for the federal government to buy the Baca Ranch, a huge holding in the Jemez Mountains, to the applause of local environmentalists.

In the end, Udall won his race with 53 percent of the vote; Redmond got 43 percent, and Miller, 4 percent.[50] Undecided voters were clearly affected by last-minute headlines suggesting that the race was a "dead heat," and swung to Udall to ensure his victory. On the other hand, Wilson won her race over Maloof with 48 percent of the vote to his 42 percent, one point more than her victory over him in the June special election. Anderson's vote dropped, but he retained a respectable 10 percent.[51] Other Green candidates for state offices had mixed results as well. Damacio Lopez, a hardworking campaign finance reform advocate running for secretary of state, got just 6 percent statewide. Sam Hitt, the well-known local environmentalist who had earlier lost the 1996 Green primary for U.S. Senate, ran this time for Commissioner of Public Lands and drew a solid 16 percent. Cliff Bain got 30 percent of the vote in his race for a seat on the Public Regulation Commission. And one Green candidate for the state legislature got enough votes to swing the office from a Democrat to a Republican.

All of these contests produced much tension between Greens and local Democrats angry at losses to Republicans. Greens had two responses. First, that Democrats should stop taking progressives for granted and pay more attention to their concerns. Second, that Democrats should support the enactment of instant-runoff voting to end the problem of vote splitting. Under such a system, voters would indicate their first, second, third, and so on choices on the ballot, and those whose candidate got the least number of first choices would have their votes transferred to their second choice, until one candidate achieved a majority. As a result of the Green challenge, New Mexico has become one of a handful of states where such legislation has shown real prospects (the others are Alaska, where the "Republican Moderate" party has siphoned votes from the Republicans at the same time that Greens have threatened Democrats; Vermont, where the Progressive Party has a solid presence and a third of the state Senate has cosponsored a bill; and Washington state).[52] Indeed, after losing his second bid for Congress, Phil Maloof returned to the state Senate and became a lead sponsor of the instant-runoff bill.[53] But so far, the reform has not passed, and Greens and Democrats remain at loggerheads.

Some Democrats think the New Mexico Greens are bound to dwindle as it becomes clear to their voters that they can't win high-level partisan races and only act as spoilers in a state where Republicans are on the rise. Jerry Bradley, the president of New Mexico Progressive Action, said, "These are people who are not plugged into New Mexico politics. The people who have a stake in the economic and political reality have not fallen for this—Hispanics and the organized working class," he argued.[54] Others questioned whether they could ever win a big race. Cisco McSorley, a Democratic state senator who represents the Albuquerque university district that has been a hotbed of Green votes, said, "There's a world of difference between getting 20 percent and being able to elect somebody."[55] Toney Anaya, a former Democratic governor of the state with close ties to the progressive community, saw both a bright side and a dark side to the Greens' staying power. "The Greens have an excellent future if they focus on nonpartisan races," he said during an interview in his Santa Fe law office. "But unless we change our laws to permit fusion or instant-runoff voting, it's going to be very tough for Greens to win, and we're going to end up with more Republicans getting elected."[56]

On the other hand, Cris Moore argued, by continuing to run and do well in a variety of races, the Greens had changed the dynamics of New Mexico state politics. "I think we've shown there's a solid Green vote out there," he said as the 1998 election came to a close. "Even if we were somehow whittled back down to 5 percent—and I don't think that's going to happen—that would still have an effect on certain races. I just don't see the two-party system recovering. Too many people have taken that step and voted for a candidate they really want instead of the lesser of two evils."[57] And Steve Schmidt, the party's 1994 lieutenant governor candidate and platform crafter, was sure the Green challenge has already produced results. He cited new attention to the Hispanic land-grant controversy, improved positions taken by Democratic officeholders and candidates, and pro-environmental moves made by Clinton. "Many environmental groups had been lobbying for [the Baca Ranch purchase] unsuccessfully," he pointed out, "but what turned it around was Clinton's perception of Green Party voting strength."[58] Moore summed it up succinctly, saying, "Campaigning to Green voters is now part of the game."[59]

Whither the Greens?

So far, despite all the turbulence, Moore's prediction has held up. Not only was he reelected to the Santa Fe City Council by an absolute majority of 58 percent in the spring of 1998, other Greens were winning local races as well. Sherry Tippett was elected to a local school board seat in 1999, and Gary Claus was reelected to the Silver City City Council. In 2000, incumbent Santa Fe municipal judge Fran Gallegos returned to office with 49 percent of the vote, and the local Greens gained another city councilor in Miguel Chavez, who won with 40 percent in a four-way race. Two other local Green activists, Melissa MacDonald and Xubi Wilson, lost their races for different county commissioner seats, but MacDonald came very close with 46 percent. Cliff Bain also improved on his 1998 run, getting 33 percent of the vote in his bid for a seat on the Public Regulation Commission. Finally, a new Green candidate, Marvin Gladstone, drew 10 percent of the vote statewide in a race for the Court of Appeals. Overall, the number of people registered as Greens is still a tiny fraction of the state total. But it is noteworthy that the total has risen consistently, from four thousand in June 1992 to five thousand in June 1996, nearly seven thousand in April 1998, and almost twelve thousand as of February 2001.

The Greens of New Mexico have continued to thrive for a number of reasons. Third parties often do well among newcomers who lack attachments to the old political establishment, and New Mexico has been a magnet for thousands of young people and other outsiders attracted to its physical beauty. Many of these people have also been impressed by the party's platform, which has given the Greens philosophical grounding at precisely the time that national Democrats wandered the political horizon, led by a president who happily "triangulated" his differences with Republicans and trampled most traditional Democratic positions in the process.

The Greens were also prospering because of how badly New Mexico did during the so-called Clinton boom. After eight years of national economic expansion, New Mexico still had the highest national percentage of residents without health insurance. With much of its large Native American and Hispanic populations trapped in persistent poverty, the gap between rich and poor only worsened in recent years. Astutely, Greens focused their political efforts around real social needs, like property tax relief for low-income families, higher wages for hotel workers, and affordable health care. At the same time, many state Democratic leaders shifted to the right, doing the bidding of wealthy special interests in the legislature and trying to keep the support of Hispanic Democrats through patronage—a process that turned off many voters.

State law in New Mexico has also been relatively hospitable to minor political parties, requiring a new party to collect petitions from one-half of 1 percent of the number of people who voted in the previous election in order to qualify for the ballot. (Candidates also have to collect their own petitions, an unnecessary redundancy.) That's not to say that the Democrats who dominated the state legislature didn't try at first to stamp out the nuisance rather than learn to coexist with the Greens. After Mondragon's 1994 run, reported ballot access expert Richard Winger, they changed the law to prevent someone from being a candidate unless they had been a registered member of the party for four months prior. Mondragon had switched from Democrat to Green the day he announced his candidacy. And they doubled the number of petitions needed for a party to get on the ballot—a change that did not affect the Greens since they had already cleared the state's 5 percent threshold for being considered a major party.[60]

Having achieved major party status, the Greens' candidates and platform were given near-equal coverage by the mainstream media. The value of this achievement can't be underestimated. Green candidates were regularly included in debates, and in some races were even given free broadcast time by local TV stations along with the other two parties' candidates. In April 1998, to take another unusual example, the *Albuquerque Tribune*, the state's leading newspaper, published an extensive summary of each party's platform and actually gave the Greens more space than the Democrats or Republicans.[61]

But however helpful local conditions may have been, the New Mexico Greens' biggest asset has been their relatively close-knit circle of hardworking organizers and strategists. This group, which has numbered about two or three dozen people over the years, has different tendencies, with some people more inclined to concentrate on local races, others to national politics, and real variations on how hard a line they take on protecting the environment or how willing they are to sometimes support Democrats. But they have all been committed to building the party, and they have evolved a kind of "work democracy" where those people who put in real and effective effort on a party project are accorded greater respect and voice in decision making. Such a strong core group is a prerequisite for any successful third-party project, and it is no accident that it developed in a small state where extensive face-to-face interaction between organizers was easy to accomplish because they mostly live in the same two or three cities (Santa Fe, Albuquerque, and Taos).[62]

The same thing has happened with the Greens in small states like Hawaii and Maine, as well as with the Progressive Party of Vermont (where the core coalesced around socialist Bernie Sanders's years as mayor of Burlington, elected several Progressive

Party legislators from the city, and has now gone statewide thanks in part to the availability of public funding for the gubernatorial race). Greens in larger, more populous states like California and New York have had successes in local races but much greater difficulty uniting around a statewide strategy. Not only have they lacked, up until now, the resources to pull off a significant statewide campaign, they haven't even had the capacity to meet regularly to develop the trust needed to unite their local core groups around a common goal.

Thus, for several years Greens in New York had several competing factions dispersed among an upstate group, a Long Island group, and various New York City groups, for example. In California, some of the Greens' most talented organizers, who tend to gravitate toward the candidates with the strongest prospects, are resented by other party members who see them as budding professional politicos more interested in making a name for themselves than building the party. While the Internet has certainly made it easier for people to communicate intensively with each other—playing a vital role, for example, in the extensive consultative process that drafters of the ASGP party platform employed to expand and revise that document—e-mail is a poor substitute for regular, shoulder-to-shoulder interaction. If anything, the reliance on e-mail heightens the speed by which gossip and misunderstanding can spread within a community, damaging relationships in the process.

So far, U.S. Greens have had the bulk of their successes winning nonpartisan races in places like Arcata, Santa Monica, and Sebastopol, California; Boulder, Colorado; Flagstaff, Arizona; Chapel Hill, North Carolina; Woodstock, New York; Dane County, Wisconsin; and of course Santa Fe. With a few interesting exceptions—like the working-class city of Duluth, Minnesota, and the Republican-leaning suburban town of Modesto, California, where they have elected city councilors, or Hartford, Connecticut, and Washington, D.C., where they have elected several people of color—the Greens are mostly developing in progressive college towns and some tiny rural counties. Even though Green officeholders are gaining notice as practical, solution-oriented politicians with innovative ideas, for the most part these are not places where most Americans live—or more crucially, these are not where those people who are least connected to the two-party system, the poor and the working class, live. The Greens' openness is both a blessing and a curse—they have lots of people, especially young people, coming to them with plenty of political energy. But the resulting base is not the broadest one to build on.

The Greens also have had difficulties developing significant institutional backing—a problem that will linger as long as the winner-take-all electoral system forces them into the spoiler role. Here and there individual Green candidates have been supported by local unionists, or endorsed by a national issue organization like the National Organization for Women, or the Human Rights Campaign Fund, or even the reflexively pro-Democrat Sierra Club. But until now they have had little to fall back on beyond devoted volunteers, some of whom know what they're doing and some of whom do not. Which means in practice their state parties are primarily candidate driven, leaving them terribly vulnerable to dramatic swings in energy. High-level candidacies can definitely draw attention to the party and attract new volunteers, but serious campaigns cost money, and many states are just too big to be done on the cheap. And sometimes individual officeholders just get tired and need a break.

That's what happened with Keiko Bonk-Abramson, who was the sole Green on the Big Island of Hawaii's County Council and served as mayor when the rest of the council split evenly between Republicans and Democrats in the mid-1990s. Something similar happened in Arcata, California, a radical college town in the northern part of the state. Greens won a majority of the city council and the mayor's office in 1996, but two years later had great difficulty finding people who wanted to run for those positions again, since they involved overseeing such mundane aspects of town life as traffic lights, pothole repairs, and what to do about panhandlers. "The reality is that we are a political party of people who don't want to do politics," Melanie Williams, a founder of the party and a political science instructor at Humboldt State University, told the *Los Angeles Times*. Somehow, all the global attention the Arcata Greens got for taking over the town didn't inspire more people to come forward. "The town hall stuff is pretty boring. We did a lot of arm-twisting," she said, "but nobody wanted to do it."[63] One of the unspoken facts of party politics is that it's hard to recruit people to run for office in the first place, and often the ego investment involved impels folks to want to run for high-visibility offices rather than start with modest but essential positions on school boards and the like.

Some of the Greens' high-level officeholders may also experience a special kind of isolation. That's what seems to have happened to Audie Bock, a filmmaker who shocked California Democrats by winning a runoff for a partisan seat in the state assembly from the Oakland area in 1999. Bock's victory was built by area Greens who had been organizing locally since 1991, running eight different races in nearby Berkeley and North Oakland, and who saw an opportunity in the special election to replace the outgoing assemblyman. Since no candidate got more than 50 percent in the first round, Bock made it into a runoff against outgoing Oakland Mayor Elihu Harris despite getting just 9 percent. Harris then made a series of mistakes (including offering a free chicken dinner to low-income voters if they had voted in the primary, which became a major scandal), and the Greens managed to raise enough money to hire a full-time campaign manager and coordinate extensive phone banking, tabling and door-to-door precinct walking. By positioning Bock as a credible alternative to Harris, the Greens benefited from a big vote against politics as usual. Of course, the fact that there was no Republican in the running made a major difference as well.[64]

But once Bock got to Sacramento, the lone Green in the state legislature, something changed. Within six months of getting elected, Bock fired her original staff, including Michael Twombly, a Green who had been her chief of staff, and started relying on aides loaned to her from Democratic members of the assembly. One former aide said, "Audie seems to have gotten caught up with the Capitol culture. She's a changed person." Bock also changed her party registration from Green to "decline to state," claiming she wanted to avoid the cost of running in a party primary. "She has spent an unusual amount of time (for her) raising campaign money," the former aide said. "She's obsessed with the idea." The Greens who had put together her win said they understood her desire to focus her resources on the general election and agreed that they would have had a hard time raising the quarter- to half-million dollars needed to run a serious campaign.[65] But behind the scenes, they said that getting elected had gone to her head and she had lost touch with the base that had brought her there. One California Green strategist said the problem was rooted in the fact that the Greens had never expected to win the race and so did not vet Bock as carefully as they should have before nominating her. Sure enough, Bock went down to a resounding defeat in 2000, having cut herself off from the only sure source of support that she had.

The Green path is not an easy one. Factor in how third parties are discriminated against in many states in terms of their ability to get on the ballot and on the public airwaves, and they are in a fairly tenuous situation. This is in essence what has happened to the Maine Green Party, which was just a few years ago among their strongest states.[66] In 1998 the party was knocked off the ballot and forced, essentially, to start over. Two years later, the Maine Greens managed only to muster four candidates for the state legislature, and this was under the new system of "Clean Elections"—full public financing for candidates who could collect a modest number of $5 contributions from voters in their districts. One Maine Green who qualified for such funding was knocked off the ballot because no one voted for him during the party primaries, and he forgot to vote for himself!

But the Green story is far from over. Leaving the Association of State Green Parties conference in Santa Fe in 1998, I spotted a bumper sticker on a car in the parking lot. "Compost Rotten Politics," it read. One thing the Greens have going for them, despite all the obstacles, is an aging two-party political system that keeps turning off masses of voters and, in effect, generating more manure for their garden. And we've only begun to see what kinds of fruits can be grown in the changing climate.

It's tempting to say that New Mexico is a special case—full of newcomers in search of new politics, exceptionally poor, a small state with relatively easy access to the ballot and the media, where the Democrats have been particularly inept and the Greens have been blessed with a critical mass of gifted organizers. I'm more inclined to say that the New Mexico Greens' organizing model is worth emulating—build a local foundation through electoral work connected to community-based issue activism; choose selected higher-level races to run in, preferably where the party already has a base; push for electoral reforms to allow people to vote for the best candidate and not the "least worst"; use the power to "spoil" very carefully, not indiscriminately, and highlight the party's ten key values—especially if organizers can involve more people of color and working-class people from the start. Such a model may well be exportable to other states.

It was with such a goal in mind that a small group led by New Mexican Steve Schmidt and Californians Greg Jan and Mike Feinstein (a Green member of the Santa Monica city council), set out in late 1994 with a proposal for a "40 State Green Organizing Effort." In Schmidt's words, "The 'serious, credible, platform-based' model we had been using became the basis for a national organizing effort." The next summer the New Mexico Green Party, led by Cris Moore, invited Greens from around the country for a national gathering that brought together activists from all wings of the movement. At this event, Schmidt and the others laid out their argument that the time was ripe for the Greens to run a presidential campaign that would foster the development of Green state parties in the same way that high-level state races could nurture local Green organizing.

"On the 'short list' of candidates we presented—accompanying a national survey of Greens expressing broad support for a presidential campaign that would build the Green Party— were the names of [farmworkers organizer] Delores Huerta, [Texas populist] Jim Hightower and Ralph Nader," Schmidt recalled.[67] One candidate—Nader— was open to a possible run. In the fall of 1995 he made that interest concrete by allowing the Greens to put his name on their ballot line in California. A new experiment in third-party politics was under way.

7

Nader's Gamble

Ralph's Rules

Illustrating the principle of the lever, the Greek mathematician Archimedes is said to have once exclaimed, "Give me a place to stand, and I will move the world." Over nearly four decades in public life, Ralph Nader has embodied Archimedes's principle, working hard to leverage his efforts into all kinds of society-shifting social changes. Trailed by a private investigator hired by General Motors into the very halls of Congress in 1966 after he started exposing the criminal dangers of shoddy auto design, Nader won national publicity and universal admiration. After he successfully sued GM for invasion of privacy, he promptly plowed the proceeds into founding the first of his dozens of public interest organizations. His creativity and drive attracted literally thousands of idealistic activists and lawyers who flocked to work under him in the 1960s and 1970s, and together with a sympathetic press and friendly Congress they leveraged the creation of federal regulatory agencies including the Occupational Safety and Health Administration (OSHA), the Environment Protection Agency (EPA), and the Consumer Product Safety Administration. Nader's organizations have been responsible for such laws as the Safe Drinking Water Act and the Freedom of Information Act. Public Citizen, the consumer advocacy group he founded in 1971, works on everything from monitoring Congress and watchdogging health care and energy policy, to leading the fight for fair trade and against corporate globalization worldwide.

But starting in the 1980s, Nader began to see that the efforts of the public interest community he had helped spawn were regularly being blocked and trumped by an equally well-organized and much better funded mobilization of big business. It's getting harder and harder to get anything done, he would tell audiences. Congress was in thrall to big money; the media were doing fewer investigative reports, those that they did do weren't reverberating into legislative action the way they used to; and the White House was a "corporate prison," subservient to powerful special interests no matter who was president. Some of Nader's friends and associates tried to get him to enter electoral politics himself, in the hopes of transforming his high public standing—*Life* magazine called him one of the hundred most influential people of the twentieth century—into millions of votes. In 1992, he resisted an organized "Draft Nader for President" push led by several close allies in the public interest community, but traveled up to New Hampshire and asked voters to write in his name as a stand-in for "none of the above" and to demand a new set of enhanced citizen powers, which he called a "democracy tool kit." Two percent of the voters in each major party primary, Democrats and Republicans alike, wrote in Nader's name. It was a disappointing showing to his supporters, but Nader saw a silver lining in how some of the other candidates, particularly Democrat Jerry Brown, adopted whole chunks of his reform platform.

By the time the 1996 election rolled around, Nader was ready to experiment with a slightly bigger lever. Angered by many of President Clinton's rightward moves—the push to pass the North American Free Trade Agreement and the General Agreement on Tariffs and Trade, the sellout to corporate managed care instead of universal health care, and finally a decision to rescind the federal highway speed limit—Nader agreed to a request from Greens Steve Schmidt, Mike Feinstein, and Greg Jan along with other progressive activists[1] to put his name on the California Greens March 1996 primary ballot for president. Ultimately he got on the ballot in twenty-one states, plus the District of Columbia. But he insisted on not raising or spending more than $5,000 for the race—the triggering threshold that would have forced him to file an extensive financial disclosure statement with the FEC. His aim was not to hide his assets (as he willingly divulged those four years later), but to force Greens to do their own heavy lifting. "I intend to stand with others around the country as a catalyst for the creation of a new model of electoral politics, not to run any campaign," he said in a November 25, 1995, press release. "The campaign will be run by the people themselves and will be just as serious as citizens choose to make it."[2]

The result was not quite what Schmidt, Feinstein, and Jan had in mind when they originally proposed a Green presidential bid to their colleagues back in 1994–95. Nader's willingness to go on the ballot gave Greens a huge new asset to generate voter interest in their work, and new Green parties were spawned in several states as a direct result. But his stubborn refusal to take any money created huge legal headaches for those Greens who decided they wanted to advance his cause. Nader traveled to Los Angeles to accept the Greens' nomination in August 1996 and he welcomed many invitations to speak over the course of the year, which local Greens were able to convert into de facto campaign events. Nader hoped his unusual self-denial would prompt an outpouring of bottom-up citizen energy rather than the usual celebrity candidate–centered campaign, but that's not quite what evolved. Two different Nader for President campaign committees—a "clearinghouse" based in Washington, D.C., coordinated by Linda Martin, a Green who made a serious splash in Hawaii politics with her 14 percent showing in the 1992 Senate race, and a California committee run by Jan and Feinstein—raised money, distributed information, and connected volunteers with local organizers. But it was a Kafkaesque experience, as Martin makes clear in her passionate and entertaining campaign memoir, *Driving Mr. Nader.*

"Nader's refusal to declare himself a candidate and thereby avoid disclosing his personal finances made it impossible for us to raise serious campaign funds, prevented us from coordinating his travel, public appearances and media statements, and even prevented us, under the strictest interpretation of the FEC regulations, from any direct contact with the candidate or his associates," Martin wrote.[3] These "Nader Rules," she added, were a source of constant frustration and made for much bewilderment on the part of Greens and others. Nader even declined an offer from progressive investment guru Peter Camejo to raise several million dollars for him through his socially responsible investor clientele, Martin reported.[4] To the chagrin of one hardworking Green volunteer who was putting together a thick packet of materials for a petition seeking to get Nader into the presidential debates, Nader wouldn't even let his staff release a list of his past speaking engagements for fear of creating any shred of coordination between himself and the Greens.[5]

Nader explained his decision in an article in *The Nation*, writing "I've been criticized by some for choosing to go about matters in this way, but my goal is to encourage a campaign dependent on self-reliant citizen muscle at the grass-roots, not some guy on a horse. This is a test, certainly of people in the Green party and other progressives, of whether they are going to step up their mobilization. In some states, the Greens are already forming parties as a result."[6] He didn't want to run as a charismatic hero, which would allow people to lean on his celebrity rather than develop their own power and organization. In doing this, he was implicitly responding to those progressives who argued that presidential campaigns were a waste of time, and making his own critique of campaigners such as the Rev. Jesse Jackson, who got millions of votes on the force of personal charisma and effort, but did little to build enduring grass-roots organizations in his wake. Asked to comment on Nader's statement in *The Nation*, political commentator Kevin Phillips said drily, "Nader's desire to rely on grass-roots activists to make everything happen may be too idealistic. Sometimes you don't get grass without fertilizer and hands-on lawn care." Steve Cobble, a political consultant who was then serving as political director of Jesse Jackson's Rainbow Coalition, was even blunter, telling Nader, "If you're not going to do it seriously, don't do it."[7]

In the end, Nader disregarded his critics. The result, from the perspective of Green activists, was not all that awful. The "Nader Rules," wrote Martin, "imposed a commit-tee of equals' process on the Greens that evolved, almost organically, into a federation of independent Greens—the Association of State Green Parties," which came into for-mal existence a few weeks after the 1996 presidential election was over, at a meeting in Middleburg, Virginia.[8] The Greens had doubled their ballot standing—going from hav-ing just five state parties with an official line on the ballot to ten. But to the rest of the world, Nader's behavior seemed bizarre proof that he was "not serious" about running for president. The lack of a real campaign structure also meant that little was done to fan the sparks of public support that his name alone prompted. After cruising as high as 10 percent in some state polls, such as in California and Connecticut, his home state, he ended up with just 680,000 votes nationwide, or .7 percent overall.

The Power to Dream

Nader's 2000 campaign effort was a different story entirely. For the first time, Nader really ran for elective office. Working with Greens across the country, he and his staff built a national organization that got him and his running mate, Winona LaDuke, a Native American environmental justice advocate, on the ballot in 44 states. They raised far more money than anyone expected, went up on television with their own ads, and mobilized a small army of 150,000 volunteers. Despite these achievements, it's worth keeping one simple fact in mind: his whole operation was a flea-bitten mouse compared to the multimillion-dollar white elephants that were the Bush and Gore campaigns. Bare-bones is too charitable a term. No one in the central campaign team apart from the national field director had any serious prior electoral experience. Theresa Amato, Nader's campaign manager, came from Illinois where she had previ-ously worked as a public interest lawyer. One of Nader's top press aides was a junior taking a break from college. His paid field coordinators in the states ranged from sea-soned Green veterans of numerous local campaigns to incompetents who refused to wear a watch! Nader visited all fifty states in little more than a rental car (and some-times his sister Laura's beat-up old Volvo). Tarek Milleron, Nader's taciturn and hard-working thirty-three-year-old nephew, took a break from getting his Ph.D. in ecology from Utah State to juggle driving, logistics, and keeping track of Nader's overflowing folder of clippings and speech notes. Only in September did the campaign deploy two advance men, George Farah and Andy Goldman, energetic go-getters in their twenties who had no prior campaign experience but figured out what to do pretty quickly. (A third advance man who briefly worked for the team was known as "the retreat man" for his less-than-impressive performance.) Traveling on and off with Nader during the final weeks of the campaign, I couldn't help but marvel how this ball of chewing gum, baling wire, and spit had managed to jolt the well-oiled gears of America's duopolized presidential selection process.

The campaign's most successful venture, its "super-rallies," came not from the D.C. headquarters nor from the far-flung field staff, but from a couple of Nader zealots from Portland, Oregon, who didn't know any better. Greg Kafoury and Mark McDougal, two baby-boomer trial lawyers, came up with the idea to try to fill the Portland Memorial Coliseum after being asked by Nader to pull together a campaign event for him in late August. "We were thinking that it would give people something to do and not just talk about getting 1 to 2 percent of the vote," McDougal recalled. They ran into a lot of resistance. "The local Greens were against the super-rally idea because they thought it was 'too corporate,'" he said.[9] And the D.C. staff thought Nader was risking "major humiliation and financial disaster," Kafoury added.[10] Nothing could be worse than dropping tens of thousands of scarce dollars on a half-filled arena to produce a flop that the press would pounce on.

Instead, the first Portland super-rally, on August 26, was a stunning success. Despite the fact that the only entertainment was the candidate himself, plus a few warmup speeches by local Green figures, 10,500 people paid $7 to pack the hall. At that point in the presidential campaign, it was the largest crowd that *any* candidate had drawn—and no one thought Bush or Gore could have dared charge admission to one of their speeches. Soon, Kafoury and McDougal, along with Kafoury's twenty-two-year-old son Jason, and Charlie Cray (a Naderite on leave from the publication *Multinational Monitor*) were off to Minneapolis, Chicago, Madison, Milwaukee, Boston, Seattle, New York, Oakland, Los Angeles, and D.C. to put together similar gatherings of anywhere from five thousand to fifteen thousand. Pop stars Eddie Vedder, Patti Smith, Bonnie Raitt, Jackson Browne, Willie Nelson, Chuck D, Adam Yauch, Ani Difranco, and Ben Harper sang; politically engaged celebrities Susan Sarandon, Tim Robbins, Danny Glover, and Bill Murray appeared; activists including Michael Moore, Jim Hightower, John Anderson, Cornel West, Barbara Ehrenreich, Howard Zinn, Randall Robinson, Jello Biafra, and Tom Tomorrow spoke; and TV talk-show host Phil Donahue emceed. For a moment, all the loose threads of Nader's humble campaign were woven together.

Madison Square Garden on October 13 was the high point. Imagine the spirit of John Lennon channeled through C-SPAN. Fifteen thousand mostly white twenty- and thirty-somethings plus a number of gray-haired people paid $20 each to be there. No doubt, as Danny Goldberg, a progressive record company executive told me backstage, "most of them came to hear Eddie Vedder," the lead singer of Pearl Jam, an alternative rock band that has sold millions of records. Many young women in the crowd were also there to catch Ani Difranco, an independent folk-rock singer with a devoted following who had defied intense pressure from women's groups concerned about Nader's potential to tip the election to Bush. But Nader himself was the top bill, and the crowd sat and cheered through a vintage hour of his scathing and visionary critique of American politics.

Ironically, neither Nader nor most of his core entourage of lawyerly young and not-so-young men and women knew anything about Vedder, Difranco, or the other musicians performing that night. His circle of veteran supporters were, like Nader, ascetic abstainers from the counterculture. But for the college kids and twentyish slackers who were by then thronging Nader's volunteer ranks, there was no generation gap. The same thing that made them love Vedder's soulful singing and Pearl Jam's war on Ticketmaster's jacked-up prices and led them to memorize Difranco's growling spoken-word poems and swirling feminist anthems attracted them to Nader's iconoclastic campaign. They each embodied independence from all the hucksterism, dishonesty, greed, short-sightedness, and inauthenticity of American mainstream culture, which is to say corporate culture.

Nader's inspiration of tens of thousands of young people was the single biggest achievement of his campaign. Starting out, his top advisers all knew that he retained a high level of name recognition among older voters, who remembered and respected his courageous battle against the auto companies and his successful efforts to enact a raft of environmental and consumer protection legislation some thirty years ago. But despite his regular visits to college campuses over the years, beyond a small core of devoted younger activists who gravitated to his far-flung public interest projects, the younger generation had little idea who he was. A March 2000 survey found that 52 percent of people ages eighteen to twenty-nine either had never heard of him or didn't know enough about him to venture an opinion, twice the level of people over the age of fifty. "We have real challenges here," said lawyer Carl Mayer, a longtime Naderite with a deadpan manner and a quick smile who was the campaign's treasurer. "You've got a generation that doesn't know him at all. But then they hear him talking and say, 'Christ, this guy is the only one who's saying anything at all.'"[11] Mayer was right. By the fall Nader was practically a rock star himself.

Lennon came to mind as Nader leaned into the opening cadences of his hourlong speech at Madison Square Garden, one of the best I heard him give on the campaign trail. "Welcome to the politics of joy and justice," he started, a familiar hopeful beginning that on other campaign stops often turned into an overwhelming and discouraging recital of all the betrayals Nader saw perpetrated by the Clinton-Gore administration. But that night Nader was in a more visionary, uplifting mode, reminding the audience that the last time he had spoken in the Garden, it was the October

1979 "No Nukes" rally, and "since that rally, not one new nuclear plant has been ordered in the U.S.A."

We can win, he was telling the crowd. Reminding everyone of all the things they had lost control over—their privacy, the ability to raise their children free of corporate commercialism, their right to choose a doctor or know what's in their food and air, the great commonwealth of public lands, the airwaves, trillions in pension funds—he asked the throng, "Isn't it time for the American people to take control of what they already own?" They roared YES in response. Then I really heard echoes of Lennon:

"Imagine if we had our own TV and radio stations, instead of the corporate, homogenized media we now have," Nader asked. "Imagine if they began to pay rent to us, the owners of those airwaves, for a change." He went on. "Imagine if we could use the airwaves not just to transmit information, but to connect people to people to be creative and dynamic participants in the creation of our own civic culture, rather than a nation of spectators and purchasers, which is what big business wants," he continued. "Imagine if workers controlled their own pension funds, so when they invest in those giant corporations they could force changes in their behavior."

It wasn't quite the poetry of Lennon's "Imagine there's no heaven, it's easy if you try." Nader is probably more comfortable testifying before a congressional committee on C-SPAN than he is inspiring a mass audience with flowing rhetoric. (Once he told me that he deliberately chose to tone his speaking style down, saying with his characteristic mangling of verbs and adverbs, "You don't want to overstir inspirationally so they forget the necessity of their role perspirationally.")[12] Still, that Friday night he tried valiantly and succeeded in conveying, with the words if not the lyricism, his vision of a renewed civic society.

He reminded the young people of all the struggle and sacrifices of the abolitionists, the suffragettes, the trade unionists, the dirt-poor farmers of East Texas who built the Populist movement of the 1880s and 1890s, the five young black men who sat in at a lunch counter and ultimately forced the Supreme Court to outlaw "separate but equal," the women's equal rights drive, the environmental movement, the gay and lesbian civil rights movement. Imploring the crowd, he said: "Think of the courage, think of the determination, think of how badly they wanted justice—and take motivation from it." The crowd of thousands listened closely—you could see them all because, in a nice democratic touch, the Garden's house lights had been turned up.

Nader continued with a litany of attacks on those he called "frightened liberals"— people who were supporting Al Gore even though they knew better, in his view. He reminded his audience that the number of people without health insurance had increased by 10 million during the Clinton-Gore years, that the Democrats had trashed civil liberties, that 20 percent of the country's children still lived in poverty and that, most critically, Clinton and Gore had caved in time and again to corporate power.

"There's a disconnect," he argued, citing the widening gap between rich and poor. "There's an apartheid economy here." Turning to the presidential debates then under way, he reminded his listeners of many of the ways Gore and Bush had agreed with each other, calling their joint appearance not a debate but "a massive TV exercise in platitudinous dittoes." LET RALPH DEBATE! LET RALPH DEBATE! the crowd chanted.[13] "Never again will this crooked debate commission hold the key to our democracy," Nader declared, vowing to replace the bipartisan group with a more impartial body. "They threw out the wrong guy this time!" he shouted, and the audience responded with a standing ovation.

Winding down, Nader asked his listeners the central question of his campaign: "For whom is it such a great economy?" Then, after recalling for them how tough daily life is for most Americans, the unnecessary traffic snarls, the scramble to pay the bills, the bombardment of commercials everywhere, the invasions of privacy, the lack of time to devote to community, he went deeper, asking, "Who designed this economy anyway? It's time it was designed as if people mattered." But his was never a message of despair. Against entrenched interests, Nader quietly reminded the crowd, "the American people have periodically risen up and said yes—we're going to have the power." The crowd roared its approval. And then the all-star bill of speakers and performers—Robbins, Sarandon, Murray, Donahue, Moore, Vedder, Harper, and Difranco—thronged the stage to join Patti Smith in an unexpectedly rousing rendition of her populist anthem "People Have the Power," from the album "Dream of Life." Vedder strummed an acoustic guitar while Smith, in a black jacket and black pants, her long dark hair flying and arms waving, led the crowd in her incantation:

> The people have the power
> The people have the power
> The people have the power
> The people have the power
>
> The power to dream / to rule
>   to wrestle the world from fools
>   it's decreed the people rule
>   it's decreed the people rule
>   LISTEN
> I believe everything we dream
> can come to pass through our union
> we can turn the world around
> we can turn the earth's revolution
>   we have the power
> People have the power . . .

Nader was clapping and swaying to the music, standing to the back as if this was a rally for someone else, until Ani Difranco gently grabbed his arm and pulled him up to a mike to sing along. Soon, the sixty-six-year-old was leaning into the refrain, singing as heartily as Sarandon and Robbins, who were grooving to the moment like the days of bread and roses had never passed. By the end of the song, Nader was flushed and a bit teary, even overwhelmed. The man who preferred perspiration to inspiration was getting it. "We are rewriting history," Smith shouted to the crowd. "We are going to reclaim our political process. Don't forget this night."

Setting the Stage

Madison Square Garden in mid-October was a long way from Nader's February 21 announcement speech in Washington, D.C., which the TV networks didn't even cover and the *New York Times* scanted with a seven-paragraph story.[14] And this dearth of attention was not just because he was a third-party candidate. Not only was he up against all the usual obstacles—discriminatory ballot access, condescension from the media, inadequate funding—he was dealing with a problem of his own making, the residue of his "noncampaign" of 1996. He knew he had to convince people that he was serious this time, but it's illuminating to see what he thought that meant, originally. Speaking at a meeting of the Association of State Green Parties in Connecticut in June of 1999, he promised that if he ran, he wouldn't limit his fund-raising as severely as in 1996 and that he would make at least three major appearances in every state where he was on the ballot before the summer was through, with more selective targeting of key states in the fall.

But at that point, despite the urging of many Greens who understood the pressures of organizing a full-blown campaign, he refused to make an absolute commitment to run. In an interview with me in mid-November of that year, when he was much closer to going ahead, he bristled at my suggestion that fund-raising would be an obvious measure of his seriousness, saying "I want to see hour-raisers, not just money-raisers. We do want to raise a million bucks, minimum. But we don't want to become a fund-raising machine with the press focusing on how much money you raised today." He promised that he would release a detailed financial disclosure statement, as required by law, but insisted he would not release his tax returns, citing privacy concerns. He also refused to make any commitment to a budget for television ads, preferring to envision a campaign that would be built around grass-roots organizing.[15] Building a bigger lever, and expecting citizen-activists to take an equal part in the heavy lifting, were still top priorities for him.

There were reasons to be optimistic about Nader's prospects as America celebrated the false millennium of January 1, 2000. Three converging forces—the public's continuing dissatisfaction with the major parties, the growing power of disaffected citizens to band together quickly via of the Internet, and the twenty-four-hour-a-day need of our tabloidized media system for fresh stories to tell—were combining to boost third-party politics closer to the political mainstream. That, plus the unexpected election of Jesse Ventura, had made anything seem possible. Polls then showed that anywhere from one-third to one-half of the public favored having more options on the ballot than just George W. Bush and Al Gore. And all the reporting on Pat Buchanan and Donald Trump's Reform Party moves suggested that Nader would also draw a good deal of free media attention as well.

In addition, Buchanan's decision to switch to the Reform Party suggested a real opening for Nader. "The Reform Party's nomination of Buchanan [may] open up more space for a polar opposite, like Ralph, to get engaged," said Steve Cobble, who was now quietly volunteering strategic advice to the Nader camp.[16] Buchanan as the Reform nominee would presumably siphon hard-right votes away from the Republican candidate, taking some of the edge off the argument that Nader would merely "spoil" the Democrats' presidential hopes. It also might give him a clear shot at the millions in the angry middle who had voted for Perot; most of these people weren't going to endorse Buchanan's religious fundamentalism.

Second, an aggressive Nader-Green campaign could offer a clear-headed alternative to Buchanan's xenophobic populism. Without Nader in the race, there was a real danger that many working-class people would be attracted to Buchanan's aggressive attacks on the global elite, since Democrats and Republicans alike were orienting their campaigns at well-off suburban "swing voters." Not only could Nader inject critically needed arguments into the national debate, his candidacy could also exert a useful counterpressure on the Democrats' instinctive centrism. He might also draw some otherwise discouraged voters back into the polling booths, where they would likely vote for other progressives down-ballot, a prospect that was not lost on the Democratic leaders of the House and Senate, who thought majority status was within their grasp.

Finally, there was a new factor that no one could have predicted: the Seattle Movement. Fifty thousand protesters had converged at the end of November 1999 on the World Trade Organization's meeting in Seattle and effectively shut it down. Burly steelworkers marched side-by-side with young people dressed as endangered sea turtles, thousands of radicals blocked the city streets around the convention center, and the WTO delegates were prevented from leaving their hotels. "We don't want you! We didn't elect you! And we don't want your rules!" the demonstrators chanted. While the news media zoomed in on the violent actions of a few anarchists, the real news was the emergence of an unprecedented degree of cooperation among the varied constituencies opposed to corporate-dominated "free trade."[17] And at the center of the protests, along with the AFL-CIO and many leading environmental groups, was Ralph Nader and Public Citizen. Seattle was a shot in the arm for progressive activists everywhere, and the Nader campaign knew that the alliance of young people, environmentalists, and labor rank-and-file activists could be its secret weapon.

It looked as if the chickens were coming home to roost on eight years of the Clinton-Gore administration's tilt to the right. In addition to political independents attracted to his honesty and students energized by his idealism, Nader seemed well positioned to rally many of those people who had tasted one too many betrayals from their supposed Democratic defenders. Trade unionists were fed up with free trade sell-outs, family farmers were fighting corporate agribusiness, organic food activists were disappointed in the administration's failure to even require product labeling, community organizers were dismayed at the continued toll of police brutality and incarceration of nonviolent drug offenders, welfare rights activists were outraged by the elimination of guaranteed benefits to poor women and children, and campaign finance reformers had had enough of the administration's corruption. There were too many issues on which Gore and Bush, their parties' eventual nominees, agreed whole-heartedly (as outlined in the introduction to this book, including note 13). Leading progressive rabble-rousers like Jim Hightower and Michael Moore, who had expressed support for the Democrats in 1996 and 1998 elections, were now out in force for Nader.

This did not mean all would be smooth sailing. Unlike in 1996, when Nader's lack of intensity was mirrored by the inevitability of Clinton's reelection, in 2000 the strength of the Green challenger was matched by a zeal rarely seen among liberal Democrats for their party's nominee. The passion among liberals rose in inverse proportion to Gore's evident weaknesses as a campaigner, as these Democrats transferred their anxieties about Gore—which they rarely expressed—into anger at Nader. Some of this was simple political pragmatism, of course, among liberal Democrats who had decided to back the lesser of two evils. But the fervor with which the liberals pursued their anti-Nader campaign was unexpected. Nader and the Greens were challenging their raison d'etre. How can you remain with a party that has so sold out its soul, they were asking. The liberals' response was to exaggerate the Bush threat. America, they claimed, stood on the verge of a takeover by the combined forces of religious fundamentalists and big business. The only thing that stood in the way of this was a Democrat in the White House, they argued, ignoring the evidence of eight years of Clinton-Gore backsliding on everything from corporate welfare to the role of religion in public life. And so, while the Clinton-Gore years fed the current pushing Nader's candidacy forward, they also turned liberal Democrats (with a few exceptions) into rabid partisans. The result, when things got tighter than anyone expected in the fall, would be ugly.

Chewing Gum and Baling Wire

Nader started out with a simple plan. His goal was to get at least 5 percent of the vote, which would qualify the Greens' 2004 presidential candidate for millions in federal funding—though he quickly learned not to make that fact explicit, as it tended to downplay his potential. The first phase of his campaign was focused on getting on the ballot in as many states as possible and overcoming the "he's not serious" residue of 1996, primarily by visiting all fifty states and raising money. The second phase was to be more issue driven, while the infrastructure for getting out the vote was put into place. And the final phase would be aimed at producing that vote, with millions of letters mailed, calls made, and grass-roots shoe leather deployed. Nader was insistent about sticking closely to his anticorporate agenda, with the hope of drawing together a "blue-green" alliance of labor rank and file, students, progressives, and nonvoters. He was also reluctant to play with the tools of pop culture, eschewing most media gimmicks, photo opportunities, celebrity appearances, and the like.

The campaign got off to a clumsy start. Amato, the campaign manager, didn't come on board until March 1. "We had one cell phone, no lease, one fund-raiser, one scheduler, and a webmaster," she recalled. "The field director [Todd Main] arrived March 5th."[18] Amato's late arrival came after Nader first tried to hire Cobble, who had extensive electoral experience in progressive Democratic politics, and after the failure of a deal to bring on Mike Dolan, the brilliant organizer from Public Citizen who had masterminded much of the Seattle protest. John Richard, a quiet, affable man in his midforties who had been with Nader since 1978 as his de facto chief of staff, was also offered the job but turned it down, citing family obligations. Despite that, he played an important behind-the-scenes role in the campaign's key decisions, as did Russell Mokhiber, another longtime Nader lieutenant, and Carl Mayer, the campaign's treasurer. Nader cast about for several months to find a press secretary, first hiring Steve Conn, who came out of the Public Interest Research Group of Alaska, and then tapping Jake Lewis, who had worked for many years for Democratic Representative Henry Gonzalez.

Marnie Glickman, a twenty-nine-year-old dynamo fund-raiser who had previously been the deputy development director of EMILY'S List (a PAC that raises millions every year for female candidates), was hired in January to be finance director. Having worked on eight federal campaigns prior to coming on board with Nader, she had the most electoral experience of anyone on the staff. Unfortunately, she quit in mid-April, quietly telling associates that although Nader was serious about running, his senior staff hadn't even written a campaign plan.[19] After Glickman left, her deputy, Darci Andresen, gamely took up the task of coordinating fund-raising. But she had no prior experience in the field.

Nader's problems finding experienced staff was part of the background noise of the campaign. Privately, he said, "we didn't get the A team." Considering Nader's decades of work in the trenches of the public interest world and the literally thousands of talented people he had trained and mentored, this was more than a bit unsettling. Many people had urged him to run for president over the years, and promised to drop whatever they were doing when he did. But now they weren't all coming out of the wood-work. Some, Nader said, had grown older, started families, and were understandably no longer able to uproot from settled lives. Others felt too tied to Democratic politics to burn their bridges. Many of his steadfast allies were ambivalent, drawn to his cause but put off by his leadership style. As one said, "you don't work with Ralph, you work for him."

On the other hand, there's no question that Nader's friends at various nonprofits could have done more to assist the campaign. "Instead of asking their lawyers, what can we do to help him legally, they're blaming the law for tying their hands," said one top Nader aide. Thus, when Nader keynoted a rally on April 16 in Washington at the height of the anti–World Bank protests, he was forbidden by the event's sponsors, which included several unions that had endorsed Gore, to even mention his candidacy and was told to stick to issues. (His staff did sign up several thousand volunteers by circu-lating through the crowds, however.)[20] Instead of using Nader's run as a new source of power and leverage for their own fights within the Democratic Party, these forces apparently saw him mainly as a threat to be contained. Much later, after the election, Nader would be vilified by top labor leaders for having split the Seattle coalition of unions, environmentalists, and youth. But the truth was the coalition was weakened first by the AFL-CIO's early and unconditional embrace of Gore, an avid supporter of Clinton's free trade policies.

The campaign's late and slow start produced a cascading series of problems, which were compounded by Nader's decision to spend most of the first three months of his campaign—from mid-March to mid-June—flying around the country keeping his promise to the Greens to campaign in all fifty states. One unfortunate result was that Nader ended up missing getting on the ballot in a few states. Later, though Nader won some of his lawsuits against unfairly early deadlines, a judge failed to place him on the ballot in South Dakota because his volunteers had collected so few petitions there as it was. In Illinois, they kept petitioning despite missing the deadline, and eventually won their fight to get on the ballot.[21]

Nader's marathon push to visit all fifty states before the Greens' national conven-tion in June exposed other weaknesses. One was how difficult it was to coordinate activities with the far-flung and loose-knit network of local Greens. The problems flowed from the top down and the bottom up. Nader often changed his schedule, rarely giving local organizers enough time to pull together their plans. This was typical of the major-party campaigns too, except that Gore and Bush had scores of paid orga-nizers to deal with every shift in their itineraries. By contrast, the Nader campaign tried to make do without an advance team on the ground, which in some cases resulted in events with embarrassingly small turnouts—ten people in an auditorium in North Dakota,[22] five at a press conference in Concord, New Hampshire.[23] Local Greens were also often overwhelmed by the sudden demands coming out of D.C. "It's not like there were Green Parties well developed on the ground with lists in hand everywhere we went," campaign manager Amato later recalled.[24]

The collision of inexperience, time pressure, and sloppy communication produced an infamous incident that Nader's nephew Tarek Milleron, who traveled with him everywhere, was still talking about months later. On the Nader-Greens campaign list-serve, it was known as the "Feed Ralph" episode. Dean Myerson, a leading Green activist from Colorado who had been hired by the campaign in early spring to coordinate with local Greens, set off the discussion with a message reporting, "When I met Ralph at the [Denver] airport yesterday, he looked flat-out exhausted. It was 4 pm and he hadn't had a bite to eat all day. Everyone wants to pack his schedule and never leaves time to eat. And we had 5 hours in the car to and from the Laramie [Wyoming] event to look forward to. Campaign HQ called him on the cell and asked to go over one of the policy statements with him on the phone, but he was too tired to do it."[25]

The response from an embarrassed Dave Rowland, the co-chair of the Utah Greens who oversaw the visit to Salt Lake City where Nader was not fed, spoke volumes about what was going on within the campaign. "Perhaps a straight account of what we had to deal with will lend perspective, because working out the logistics of Nader's visit, which everyone here, incidentally, considered to be a resounding success, were far from simple," he wrote, chagrined but determined to let it all hang out. "What we, and I believe, most states find ourselves faced with is the contradiction of trying to plan meaningful events for the candidate without knowing, specifically, minor (That's a joke) details such as the time of the candidate's arrival and departure. In our case, we found out what we were dealing with less than a week before Nader was actually here." He went on:

> We had believed, early on, that we would have Nader for a full day. Then it became a half day. Then it was whittled to four and a half hours. Add to this mix, the early edicts of what was expected when the candidate was actually here: speaking events, preferably, to some degree, in a campus setting; a press conference; editorial board meetings with the daily papers and other important local media. We had confirmed appointments with both for editorial board meetings, one at 10:00 A.M. and one at 3:00 P.M. We ended up having to dump them both. Not good, but there was nothing we could do about it. Nader's stay simply did not extend to those hours, although, again, we didn't know that for sure until the last minute. Individual local media personalities had lined up to do one on one interviews with Nader. We had to scrap those on the spot, so we could get Nader to the airport. I'm sure he never knew, and no one ever told him. Our events went overtime in every instance. An ill-will fallout? Probably. [As for] a fund raiser—we had one scheduled. Again, no, it didn't come off as planned: no candidate!

As for failing to feed Nader, Rowland explained that when he finally got the final schedule from Myerson, he told him of their plans to treat the candidate to lunch at a local vegan restaurant owned by Greens. Myerson casually said to forget about it, that the tightness of the visit would not probably allow for it. So Rowland innocently assumed other arrangements for feeding Nader had been made. His e-mail prompted responses from organizers in New Jersey and Minnesota, who described similarly frustrating experiences getting confirmation of Nader's schedule too late to mail fliers, or last-minute changes upsetting carefully stacked itineraries.[26] Months later, Milleron, Nader's hardworking aide-de-camp, had a sardonic view of the whole feeding snafu. "The Greens must think we photosynthesize," he said.

These sorts of problems crop up in all kinds of seat-of-the-pants campaigns, and though painful, they aren't fatal. But foul-ups like these led Nader to lapse into micromanaging everything. For example, the D.C. headquarters was forbidden to put out press releases without his explicit approval. In May, the Texas Greens called to ask for a quote from Nader to put in their press release announcing their success at collecting nearly seventy-five thousand petition signatures in forty-five days, qualifying the party for the ballot. They were told that the headquarters couldn't give them anything and that Nader was on the road and unreachable. Two days later, the Texans put out their release after pasting in a bland quote from Nader off the campaign's website. His office called two hours later with an approved quote. "Day-to-day mistakes by the campaign caused Ralph to clamp down entirely," said one aide. "Press releases with spelling errors. Incompetent field staff."

In this aide's view, much of the problem flowed from Amato's inexperience. "She didn't make a strong case for what to do in the campaign. She never said, 'We have to do X.' And Ralph would have relaxed if he felt there was a strong guiding hand in D.C." But this was not a campaign with a James Carville or Lee Atwater, strategic masterminds, in the driver's seat. A "kitchen cabinet" of about a half-dozen Nader advisers and intimates discussed strategy with Amato and her top staff all the time, with Nader the first among equals. The process of running a presidential campaign run by committee produced intense jockeying among senior staff and advisers, with the candidate holding onto the final decision-making power. Amato also jealously guarded her access to Nader and reacted to most proposals with caution, resulting in friction with go-getters like Kafoury and McDougal, the super-rally organizers. But Nader liked her—not only because she was a solid chief executive, but also because she didn't threaten his ultimate management of the campaign.

The campaign's difficulties also resulted from decisions—or indecision—that occurred prior to Amato's involvement. "Tactically, we were at a disadvantage starting late," she admitted after the campaign was over. She had to build a staff from scratch while dealing with the critical and complicated task of getting on the ballot in as many states as possible. Meanwhile, thousands of volunteers were flocking to the campaign, basic materials had to be produced, there were a million details to manage. The biggest impact was on fund-raising. It wasn't until late June that the campaign sent out its big direct mail appeal for funds, as various packages had to be tested first. Thus, it wasn't until late July that the funds really started pouring in, enabling Amato to triple the staff to more than one hundred by the end of August, including hiring field coordinators in many states. It was, in effect, as if the Nader campaign didn't really get out of first gear until Labor Day.

Strategically, the campaign was also hampered by Nader's unwillingness to insert himself into the news if the number one story of the day didn't relate directly to his central issue: corporate power and the democracy gap. "At times it felt like he was running to be president of the Consumer Federation of America," said John Bonifaz, a young lawyer who is the founder and director of the Boston-based National Voting Rights Institute. Recounting an informal strategy discussion held on a Sunday in Washington in April, Bonifaz said that Nader refused then to go to Miami to criticize Gore's and Bush's positions in the Elian Gonzalez asylum case. "He said, 'No, it's like moths to a light. There's no way they will pay attention to my message.'" Later that spring, Bonifaz called Amato to suggest that Nader go to Austin, Texas, to protest Bush's decision to execute Gary Graham, a prisoner on death row. With Gore also in favor of the death penalty, Nader was the sole candidate who opposed capital punishment. "She says, 'Who?'" Bonifaz recalled. "Then, a few days later, the *New York Times* editorialized on it. I called Theresa again, but she says, simply, 'The answer is no.'" Bonifaz tried one last time in June to urge Nader to broaden his campaign message, play off of opportunities presented in the news, and loosen up his face-to-face campaigning. He didn't get a response.[27]

Nader was committed to run the campaign his way, with several speeches a day, usually before a college audience. Only on a few very rare occasions did he do outdoor events, preferring the safety of an indoor setting. Suggestions that he mingle with demonstrators who had come to Washington for the "A16" protests against the World Bank meeting in mid-April were dismissed by the campaign, though he did walk picket lines with striking workers at several points, and marched in a few "living wage" rallies as well. He was also aggressively self-effacing. This was a candidate who almost couldn't bear to speak in the first person. Nader never mentioned his own stirring biography, how he was the son of immigrant parents who were devoted community activists. I rarely heard him talk of his own courageous battle against General Motors, how he almost single-handedly took on the country's most powerful corporation over safety issues, how they put private investigators on him, and how he ultimately triumphed. When he did, it was in a backhanded context—to show listeners how much America had changed for the worse. He knew that he didn't beat GM on his own. Back then—

the mid-1960s— the political system often produced real changes in public policy. The media took their job to expose corporate wrongdoing more seriously, congressmen weren't afraid to hold tough hearings in response, and the president (Lyndon Johnson) genuinely cared about domestic reform.[28]

Later, as the campaign gained momentum, Nader bent many of his own rules. He started to talk more about issues far from his central concern. Racial profiling, the Middle East, gay and lesbian rights, ending the drug war—he took forthright positions on all these topics. In some cases, like gay marriage, he expressed his support with a bit of a defensive annoyance, as he thought his 1996 remark about "not [being] interested in gonadal politics" had always been twisted out of context to make him sound homophobic when he was simply not prepared to campaign on that issue.[29] Not only did Nader make clear his progressive views on most subjects far afield from corporate power questions, he allowed himself to become a better campaigner in conventional terms. His speeches were full of jokes and applause lines. His sound-bites during TV interviews got so smooth that ABC's George Will asked when Nader got to be such a good candidate. This was something, considering that Nader hated how broadcast news had shrunk the length of a sound-bite down to an average of just seven seconds, causing him to joke derisively that someday soon he would be reduced to a mere "sound-bark." Most amazing to his closest circle, by the end of the race he even was saying to audiences, "I want your vote."

Without any notes beyond a single scrap of paper listing his key points (that Tarek Milleron or one of his other aides often had to scramble to find at the last minute) and an accordion manila folder bulging with reports and news-clippings, Nader managed to deliver a remarkably effective stump speech. That is, especially when he had less than an hour to talk. (Once, when Nader was drifting past the ninety-minute mark and threatening, yet again, to throw off the rest of the day's schedule, Milleron took off his watch and taped it to a note that he handed to his uncle. Fifteen minutes later Nader still hadn't stopped. Nor, in this case, had the audience's attention flagged.) Often he was as good as a professional stand-up comedian. To illustrate a serious point about how bad local TV news broadcasts had gotten and how little real news they delivered while using the public's airwaves to collect millions in advertising revenue, he gave an extended depiction of a typical news show. In a couple of minutes he went from the opening crime stories ("if it bleeds, it leads"), to the obligatory animal story and sports coverage, but centered on a bottomless obsession with the weather.

"Everybody's got the Storm-Track Doppler-Radar Team," he'd say. "And first they hit you with the weather 'teaser': 'There's a big front out over the Aleutian Islands, coming down over the Rockies, headed our way!'" The audience would start to titter knowingly. "Just tell me if it's going to rain tomorrow," he'd declare, in an Everyman voice. "No, they've got to give you four minutes of extended forecasts. Plus, they tell you, 'today it was 65 degrees in Long Beach, it was 67 in Orange, and it was 66 in Laguna!" Pointing up at an imaginary screen, he'd pantomime like a TV weatherman. "And if they didn't use up enough time with that nonsense," he'd add, "sometimes they'll tell you, 'and twenty years ago today it was 72 in Torrance'! Meanwhile, some citizen's group has issued a report or held a press conference and just prayed for thirty seconds of coverage. There's a Chimpanzee Channel. Isn't it time we had our own Citizens Channel?" By this time, regardless of which part of the country he was in, Nader's audience was roaring with laughter and shared anger.

Only once did I hear a personal edge in Nader's outrage. It came during a generally low-key speech he gave at Stanford University on October 23. He had been quietly chiding the two thousand-plus students in attendance to recognize how privileged they already were and to devote their lives to something more than personal financial success. He had drifted onto the topic of the media, and how Bush and Gore never talked about the effects of greater corporate concentration in that sector of the economy. Suddenly, he lowered his voice. "I haven't told this story before," he said. Then he recounted how he had tried to get some national attention to Cesar Chavez, the longtime head of the United Farm Workers, during his last hunger strike. "He had been fasting for twenty-eight days, and still no national TV coverage," Nader recalled. "So I called up one news producer I knew and implored him to do the story. He asked me how long Cesar had been fasting, and then he said, 'Why don't you call me back on the thirty-sixth day? That's when it gets *real* dangerous.'" The growl in Nader's voice was uncharacteristic. But it was the inversion of human values that made his voice tremble with fury. Call us back when the great man is truly on his deathbed, the TV newsman was saying. If it bleeds, it leads. Nader and the Greens wanted to stand for the opposite principle, that society should be led by the values of the heart, not the wallet.

The Campaign Unfolds

Despite being largely ignored by the mainstream news media, the Nader campaign was not discouraged by his rocky start. Indeed, it got a nice boost in early April, when the Zogby Poll announced that he had vaulted past Pat Buchanan into third place, drawing 6 percent of the vote to Buchanan's 4 (Bush had 43 to Gore's 39 percent). Zogby told reporters that Nader was strongest in the West, drawing as high as 9 percent in California.[30] He was also showing surprising strength elsewhere. Prior to his first campaign visit to Oregon, a mid-April poll found him at 7 percent, with a personal approval rating above that of Bush and Gore.[31] An Ohio poll pegged him at 4 percent, but with the best net favorable rating (positives minus negatives) of anyone in the race.[32]

Nader was also working hard behind the scenes to woo those pieces of organized labor that hadn't joined in the AFL-CIO's early endorsement of Gore, as part of his strategy to build the "blue-green" coalition that had surfaced with such force in Seattle. Upset at the administration's record on trade issues and unsatisfied by Gore's promises to make improvements on existing accords once in office, the United Auto Workers, United Steel Workers, and Teamsters unions were all sitting on the fence. With Congress due to vote on giving China permanent normal trade relations, these unions were also hoping to maximize their leverage over Gore. Two days before the critical vote in the House of Representatives on May 24, when it was clear that Gore would stand with business-oriented Democrats and Republicans in supporting the China deal, UAW President Stephen Yokich announced that his union was fed up with Gore's "holding hands with the profiteers of the world" and said that he would look elsewhere for leadership. "We have no choice but to actively explore alternatives to the two major political parties," said Yokich. "It's time to forget about party labels and instead focus on supporting candidates, such as Ralph Nader, who will take a stand based on what is right, not what big money dictates."[33] A month later, Nader won a standing ovation from the executive board of the Teamsters. "There is no distinction between Al Gore and George W. Bush when it comes to trade," said James Hoffa, the union's president. He told reporters that Gore was "wrong on trade," adding "we agree wholeheartedly with what Mr. Nader has said."[34] Hoffa, like Yokich before him, did not endorse Nader, but explicitly called for him to be included in the presidential debates.

The Greens started getting serious and respectful attention from the press. It wasn't at the same level of daily, saturation coverage devoted to the major candidates, but it was real. I caught a glimpse of this new attitude in the middle of May, when Nader came to New York City to do some press interviews and fund-raisers. Along with Tarek Milleron and Carl Mayer, we paid a courtesy call on Jim Roberts, the political editor of the *New York Times*. The *Times* was a constant source of concern to Nader, perhaps too much so. But he knew that the "paper of record" was the single most important agenda setter for the rest of the press. News editors and television producers across the country took their lead from the *Times*. If something was front-page news there in the morning, it usually showed up on the network news that night. If the *Times* decided someone deserved daily coverage, every other outlet would immediately take notice. Thus, Nader's conversation with Roberts, while informal, was of great importance.

Roberts was not the stereotypical *Times* man. In cowboy boots, a tailored shirt, and an expensive-looking shag haircut, he looked like he would have been just as comfortable in a Hollywood agent's office. Sitting in a bland editorial meeting room on the third floor, he immediately addressed Nader as an intimate, as if he talked to presidential candidates every day and didn't mind giving them a little friendly advice of his own. Which was probably true. Roberts asked a simple question about Nader's plans for the Green Party convention in June and got his assurance that he was comfortable running on the Green ticket. Then he zeroed in on Nader's plans for California, "where you have the potential to do the most damage," he noted, chuckling appreciatively. He was obviously referring to Gore. Nader patiently described his years of work in California on consumer issues, and then launched into a thumbnail portrait of the campaign's goals and strategy. "Democracy's being closed down," Nader lamented. "Here's the test. Nothing happens anymore after a front-page story in the *New York Times* on a corporate abuse. No calls for hearings, nothing." Roberts responded, "It's true." Moments later, after Nader lambasted Clinton and Gore for failing to strengthen enforcement of health and safety standards in the poultry industry, Roberts helpfully suggested, "You've got a campaign finance connection here, too," referring to the fact that Tyson Foods was a big contributor to Clinton-Gore.

This seemed like one very sympathetic editor. After listening to Nader describe his contacts with labor and his plans to get into the debates, Roberts leaned back in his chair and said, "The mind-set of an editor [about you] is this is an interesting sidelight. You convinced us it was serious. And you have the potential to do damage. Now you have to not be a novelty, to take the next step." Nader hunched forward and asked, "How?" Roberts quickly replied, "You start drawing big crowds, we'll pay attention." Then he added, "I could be interested in covering you in California—when will you be there next?" Nader turned to Milleron, who told him either the following week or the end of June. And indeed, the *Times* later sent reporter Sam Howe Verhovek to travel with Nader, and he filed a lengthy story on July 1.[35]

The respectful press coverage continued all the way through the Greens' convention in Denver, on June 23–25. A week before it began, the *Washington Post* ran on page one a feature story on the candidate in the field. It wasn't a seven-part, twenty thousand word depiction of every stage of his life, which the *Post* offered its readers on Bush and Gore. And it was published on a Saturday, the day when the fewest readers pick up the paper. But it was a straightforward account of Nader's evolving campaign, with a decent summary of the issues he was raising.[36] The day the convention opened, the *Times* carried a lengthy story by its top political reporter, Richard Berke, titled, "Once Seen as Odd Man Out, Nader Is Rocking Gore's Boat." Like many other reporters, Berke mainly covered Nader from the perspective of how he might affect the Gore-Bush horse race, rather than on his own terms. But for Nader, these stories represented real progress.

More than two hundred press outlets registered to cover the Denver convention, and for Greens like Mike Feinstein and Steve Schmidt, who had done so much to set in motion the Green-Nader marriage, it was a moment to savor. The irrepressible Feinstein, who was happiest when roller-blading the Santa Monica boardwalk in a pair of skimpy shorts, had put on a spiffy jacket and tie and tucked his ponytail under his collar.

"This is giving us a practical national electoral project to work on together that is challenging us to become professional and mature in order to be successful," he told me as we sat together outside the main convention hall at the Renaissance Hotel. "We're not theorizing anymore. We've got real timelines to execute. And it's not internal either. We have to speak to our nation as a whole." As the editor of the ASGP's *Green Pages* newsletter, Feinstein knew, perhaps better than anyone, the real state of local Green work around the country. And he was thrilled at how the Nader campaign was spurring the expansion of the Green Party into more states and expanding its reach beyond the progressive enclaves that it had already begun to tap with the strategy of running people for low-level offices.[37] Schmidt, the refugee from the Jerry Brown campaign who had run with Roberto Mondragon in New Mexico in 1994, was now presiding over the Greens' emerging national platform. "I'm getting calls from *Time*, CNN, the *Wall Street Journal*," he reported happily. "They're taking us seriously now."[38]

Perhaps the Greens' biggest success story was Texas. The story started with David Cobb, a thirty-four-year-old firebrand who was an insurance defense lawyer for Farmers Insurance Co. in Houston until Nader's 1996 campaign reawakened his interest in electoral politics. He volunteered for Jesse Jackson's 1988 presidential run when he was a student and tried to help Jerry Brown in 1992. But he had quit in disgust at the huge sums of money needed to be a viable candidate. "In 1996, I didn't even know there was a Green Party effort," he recalled as we talked over breakfast at the convention. "One day, I was lying on my futon, listening to Jerry Brown's radio show, when on came Nader giving his acceptance speech at the Green convention in Los Angeles. And as I listened, I literally started to lean forward, until soon I was doing a Rocky dance, literally crying." Cobb had felt a touch of the civic revival that Nader sought to ignite in all his listeners.

So back in 1996, Cobb set out to build the Green Party in Texas, a state most inhospitable to third parties. "To get traction, we decided to work on local issues that resonated with us and then go to the organizations already working on them to offer our help," Cobb recalls. "We went to ACORN to help on its minimum wage campaign. We went to the AFL-CIO to ask where to put Greens to join a Teamsters picket line. We worked with local Latino groups on their police brutality protests. 'Your issue is our issue,' we said. By the time we had our founding convention in March of 1999, it was held at the Harris AFL-CIO County Hall, I'm proud to say. 'This hall is your hall,' the local AFL head said to us." Getting ballot status in Texas was a crucial hurdle for the Greens and the Nader campaign, since an early failure there would have taken a lot of air out of their growing national bubble. Petitioners have just seventy-five days to collect 37,381 valid signatures, the deadline is May 30—way before most people are even thinking about the presidential election—and petitions can be signed only by people who didn't vote in the major party primaries. Well aware of the stakes, activists in three other states that were among the party's strongest branches—California, New Mexico, and Pennsylvania—raised $20,000 to send a couple dozen volunteers to help with the Texas drive. This added to $20,000 raised in-state, and a base of some two thousand people who came to rallies in Austin, Houston, and Dallas when Nader barn-stormed the state in March. "Those seventy-five days were like riding in a marathon bicycle race," Cobb told me, "building the bike while you race." Ultimately, the Greens collected 74,100 signatures.[39]

The Texas story was the biggest, but not the only, sign of the Greens' growing insti-tutional maturity at the state level, where any new political party ultimately has to be built and sustained. Two measures of organizing seriousness were their increasing comfort with fund-raising and hiring paid staff to maintain and build their chapters. Four years earlier, there wasn't much to report—Greens seemed to have a genetic pre-disposition against anything that smacked of power or organizational hierarchy. But by 2000, in California, the Greens' Senate candidate Medea Benjamin—the founder of Global Exchange—had six paid staff, a total budget goal of $600,000, and plans to do some radio and print ads. The Southern California Americans for Democratic Action had endorsed her, as did the *LA Weekly*.[40] In Oregon, an offshoot of the local Pacific Green Party created a political action committee and hired two and a half paid Nader organizers—which perhaps explains how Nader hit 7 percent in the state before he had even campaigned there. "Back in the old days of the Pacific Party," said Blair Bobier, one of the Oregon party's founders, "if I wasn't doing everything myself, I knew everyone. Now Greens come up to me and hand me literature without even knowing who I am."[41] The Maine Greens claimed 136 people committed to donating a dime a day to the party, enough to hire a part-time organizer to register new voters.[42] The Pennsylvania Greens were running a dozen candidates for local office; their Lancaster chapter had about one hundred members who paid $25 a year in local dues. The Texas Greens were raising enough money to pay Cobb one thousand dollars a month.

Not everyone at the Greens' convention thought everything was looking up. Over breakfast, Tom Linzey, a burly, sandy-haired young lawyer from Shippensburg, Pennsyl-vania, expressed a more nuanced view. Linzey spoke from experience, having spent the previous several years giving local Greens free legal advice through his Green Ballot Clearinghouse. Like Feinstein, he was one of the few people at the convention who intimately knew what was actually happening with Greens all over the country. "I think we have deepened our parties in some places," he began, citing states like Texas and Delaware as fast-growing newcomers. "But with Nader starting so late, we've been basi-cally forced to run a whole campaign in three months." Linzey feared this would burn out many new volunteers and not leave time for people to really deepen their organiz-ing skills. And he noted that when it came to recruiting candidates and prioritizing races, there was still no real party infrastructure. "Right now it's all ad hoc. People come forward on their own, and we have no idea if the district makes sense. That's why I wrote a plan for the clearinghouse to do district-level research and targeting." But the money to implement his plan didn't exist, and he didn't think it would appear until after the election, when the ASGP would presumably be able to get access to Nader's donor lists. "Our real challenge is to get the state parties on a stable funding base. Most state parties operate on a budget of five thousand dollars or less," Linzey added.[43]

Linzey's analysis was sobering, and none of the other veteran Green activists that I spoke to in Denver disagreed with its essence. Still, this weekend was their chance to party, in more ways than one. As Jim Hightower gave one of his classic rabble-rousing speeches to a packed room of more than a thousand participants and observers, I spotted Carol Miller, Carl Mayer, Steve Schmidt, Dave Cobb, Mike Feinstein, Dean Myerson, Tom Linzey, and Steve Cobble all standing together in the rear of the hall, along with Harvey Rosenfield, Nader's closest ally in California, and Ronnie Dugger, the founder of the Alliance for Democracy and a newly minted Green. They were all smiling and savoring the moment. The convention culminated with the traditional delegate roll call, and then, before Nader stepped forward to give his acceptance speech, his campaign unveiled a five-minute video produced by Bill Hillsman, the Minnesota adman who had been so crucial to Jesse Ventura's and Paul Wellstone's winning campaigns. It was "Ralph does MTV," but despite the incongruity, it worked. Set to a pounding drum track, the video showed a quick montage from Nader's storied past: his appearance with John Lennon and Yoko Ono on a TV talk show, his testimony before Congress, his goofy appearances on *Saturday Night Live* and *Mr. Rogers' Neighborhood*. The audience roared as the words "STOP CORPORATE WELFARE" blazed across the screen and images from the Seattle protests reminded them of their core concern.

After the video, Nader came out and gave one of his trademark stem-winders, running one hour and forty-five minutes and covering well more than the twelve single-spaced-page advance draft given to the press. It was a far rougher performance than those that came later in the campaign, as he was largely reading from his prepared text and muffed many of his planned applause lines. Still, for people perhaps hearing his full-blown civic philosophy for perhaps the first time, thanks to C-SPAN's live coverage, it was a strong introduction to the campaign's themes. "The Green Party stands for a nation and a world that consciously advances the practice of deep democracy," Nader said. He went on:

A deep democracy facilitates people's best efforts to achieve social justice, a sustainable and bountiful environment and an end to systemic bigotry and discrimination against law-abiding people merely because they are different. Green goals place community and self-reliance over dependency on ever larger absentee corporations and their media, their technology, their capital, and their politicians. Green goals aim at preserving the commonwealth of assets that the people of the United States already own so that the people, not big business, control what they own, and using these vast resources of the public lands, the public airwaves and trillions of worker pension dollars to achieve healthier environments, healthier communities and healthier people.

Afterward, Nader expressed satisfaction with how the speech went. "I see such energy in that audience," he marveled. And he reiterated the underlying goal of all his efforts. "We have to raise our expectations of what we can achieve. Expectation levels are everything."[44]

8

The Duopoly
Strikes Back

"Uncluttering" the Playing Field

Just as the media and Nader himself were raising the bar at the Greens national convention in Denver in June 2000, the Democrats and Al Gore took their first moves to lower the boom on the troublesome maverick. For the most part, Gore's supporters had said little about him through much of the spring,[1] with the exception of liberal Massachusetts congressman Barney Frank, who set to work early at corralling progressives for the vice president.[2] But as the polls showed Nader on the rise, the Gore team responded with a two-pronged strategy reminiscent of their treatment of Perot in 1993. First, Gore tacked left. For example, on the same day of Nader's acceptance speech in Denver, the Gore campaign went after "Big Oil," promising to go after its "stranglehold" on the economy by promoting more clean energy sources and greater efficiency. Sounding like a Nader acolyte, Gore spokesman Chris Lehane said, "The entrenched interests want to protect the status quo, and the apologists for these interests say that we simply cannot have a clean environment and affordable energy at the same time. They say we can't do this. Al Gore says we can."[3]

A few days later, Gore expanded his neopopulist rhetoric to take on the big pharmaceutical companies as well. His new line, repeated again and again in stump speeches, was "The question is whether you're for the people or for the powerful." Enlarging this theme, he went after the Republican Congress for blocking needed reforms like prescription drug benefits or a patients' bill of rights at the behest of wealthy special interests, and said those same interests were bankrolling George Bush's campaign.[4] Republican commentator William Kristol observed, "Ralph Nader may well have made Al Gore a better presidential candidate. He has forced Al Gore to be more populist." Kristol added, "The response to Nader has energized the Gore camp. The last ten days have been the first time since the primaries that you watch the evening news and think, 'Hey, Gore is on the offensive.'"[5] Indeed, Gore's poll numbers rose each time he turned on the "populist" juice. His problem was that, thanks to his own conservatism and his need to succor his financial sponsors, he always pulled back and avoided talking about any kind of systemic changes.[6]

Gore and his allies also went on a different kind of offensive, seeking to discredit Nader. At the end of June, news broke that he had recruited Toby Moffett, a former member of Congress from Connecticut who had once been close to Nader, to help line up progressives against the Green candidate. Moffett and Nader were both of Lebanese extraction, their fathers were friends, and in 1971 Moffett had founded the Connecticut Citizen Action Group with Nader's support. Moffett, now a lobbyist for Monsanto, the agriculture multinational, advised not attacking Nader directly. But that didn't stop Gore loyalist Harry Reid, Democratic senator of Nevada, from going to the press to charge that "Ralph Nader is a very selfish person, and he's on an ego trip." Reid added, "He has no respect for the process."[7] Whether or not this line was inspired by the Gore campaign, it was soon adopted and spread in a big way by the editorialists at the *New York Times*, who unloaded with the first of several frontal attacks on Nader and his campaign.

Called "Mr. Nader's Misguided Crusade," the paper's lead editorial on June 30 charged him with "engaging in a self-indulgent exercise that will distract voters from the clear-cut choice represented by the major-party candidates, Vice President Al Gore and Gov. George W. Bush." Picking up on Senator Reid's remarks, the *Times*'s editors blamed Nader's run on "ego."(Considering that Nader could barely bring himself to speak in the first person while on the stump, traveled economy class, and lived on a pittance, this was a bizarre accusation.) While admitting that Nader might "enliven" the public debate on many issues, the paper contradicted itself, arguing that the Nader candidacy could only "cloud" the "main election choices." "[G]iven the major differences between the prospective Democratic and Republican nominees, there is no driving logic for a third-party candidacy this year, and the public deserves to see the major-party candidates compete on an uncluttered playing field." Though the paper did say that it respected Nader's right to run, its real message was just the opposite. Social critic and *Nation* columnist Christopher Hitchens put his finger on it later, calling the *Times*'s position the exact reverse of Voltaire's: "I respect what you have to say, but I will fight to the death to prevent you from saying it." Nader's response to the *Times*'s censorious editorial was captured by *Harper's* editor Lewis Lapham, who happened to be visiting him that day for a magazine profile. "You've got to love these people," he said to Lapham. "They think the American electoral process is a gated community."[8] But soon everyone was taking potshots at Nader.[9]

Between Gore stealing his thunder and liberals pooh-poohing his candidacy, for the rest of the summer Nader's rise in the polls was blunted. In a bid not to be completely swamped by the hoopla of the Republican and Democratic conventions, his campaign launched its first TV ad in early August. A spoof on the Mastercard "Priceless" ads, the Nader ad (produced by Bill Hillsman) portrayed Bush and Gore as bought and paid for by special interests, and showed the Green candidate doggedly working at his desk, ferreting out "the truth." It also made the point that if Nader were not included in the presidential debates, truth would be the casualty. The campaign spent $800,000 on the ad, a huge portion of its budget. And its timing wasn't bad, as Gore's selection of Connecticut's Senator Joe Lieberman as his running mate, one of the two or three most conservative Democrats in the Senate, had effectively nullified most of his bashing of big business. (Gore's claim to be fighting for the people against the powerful rang hollow after his operatives overwhelmingly rejected proposals for the party platform supporting universal health care, a moratorium on the death penalty, penalties for corporations that pay low wages, tougher rules for international trade, and increased spending for the poor.) But after another populist blast from Gore in his acceptance speech, Nader's poll numbers dropped from 6 to 3 percent. His staff argued to him that the money had been well-spent and had kept him on the playing field.[10] But all Nader noticed was that for $800,000, his poll numbers had been halved. That experience soured him on spending much more money on paid advertising.

The campaign did get a second breath of life in September, as the super-rallies began to take off and all the new staff that had been hired over the summer finally got into gear. Regular e-mail alerts started to appear that gave supporters a host of volunteer tasks to perform and even suggested a message of the week. "Corporate Clean-Up" vans fanned out across the South seeking to drum up support where the Greens were weakest. And hundreds of student chapters formed. At Boston University, for example, two sophomores founded a Green Party chapter in mid-September; six weeks later they had at least forty hardworking members who managed to pull together a Nader rally on two days' notice. I had a chance to speak with this group of activists as they waited to take a group photo with the candidate and was struck by one thing: all of them were freshmen or sophomores. Unlike many campus political groups, which take time to grow and are usually led by upper classmen, this was a fresh outpouring of new energy.

The focus of this energy was the presidential debates, the last choke point protecting the two-party duopoly from serious competition. In January, the Commission on Presidential Debates—a private body set up and controlled by the two major parties—decided that a candidate had to have at least an average of 15 percent support across five national polls in late September in order to be invited to participate. The commission claimed this standard would ensure that the public would hear only from those candidates with a serious chance of winning the presidency, but this was a transparently silly excuse. For one, it was not impossible with a candidate with a lower standing in the polls to win: Ventura was hovering around 10 percent when he joined Skip Humphrey and Norm Coleman in their debates, and in 1992 Russ Feingold—the eventual senator from Wisconsin—won a three-way primary three weeks after polling at just 10 percent.[11]

The debate commission had perpetrated, as the League of Women Voters had warned when it disassociated itself from the commission in 1988, "a fraud on the American voter."[12] If 15 percent had been the threshold, Jesse Ventura, Ross Perot, and John Anderson would have all been excluded from debates that they participated in the years they ran for high office. Besides, if having a serious chance to win the presidency was the most important criterion, why did the commission invite Bob Dole in 1996, even though he had never led in the polls and most knowledgeable observers wrote off his chances? The claim that having more than two candidates would confuse voters was also ridiculous. The public had tolerated—nay, it had enjoyed[13]—the participation of a half-dozen or more candidates in the Republican presidential primaries of 1999–2000, as well as similar encounters of Republicans and Democrats in 1996 and 1992. More voices meant more views and, ultimately, greater voter participation.

Jamin Raskin, a professor at American University and the lawyer who led Perot's 1996 and Nader's 2000 legal challenges to the commission's authority, put his finger on the problem. "The question the commission uses to determine who debates shouldn't be 'Who do you plan to vote for?' The question should be, 'Who would you like to see in the debates?'"[14] In fact, more than half the public supported Nader's (and Buchanan's) inclusion in the debates.[15] As Raskin wrote in a seminal essay he titled "The Debate Gerrymander," "The whole point of a political campaign period is to allow candidates— through popular appeals, organizing and debates—to change public opinion."[16] Control over access to the debates really was a form of mass mind control. But these arguments had no impact on the commission, which had never really had an open mind about the issue.[17] The Nader campaign filed a lawsuit seeking to block corporations from donating money to the commission under the argument that this was an illegal corporate contribution to the Bush and Gore campaigns. Beer giant Anheuser-Busch was the sole sponsor of the final debate in St. Louis, for example, and critics also noted that the commission's corporate sponsors were all predisposed to favor free trade, a topic on which there would be no debate if Nader (and Buchanan) were excluded, since Bush and Gore marched in lockstep on that issue. But the lawsuit also made no headway.[18]

So there was nothing left to do but turn to the streets. Nader followers turned to nonviolent civil disobedience, occupying the offices of the debates commission in

Washington, D.C., and the state Democratic Party headquarters in Madison, Wisconsin. But the main action was in Boston, where twelve thousand Nader supporters paid $10 each to rally at the Fleet Center two days before the first debate. This was just a warm-up. Many more came out the night of the debate at the University of Massachusetts/Boston campus to voice their dismay. They were met by members of an Iron Workers Union local who had been mobilized by state union leaders backing Gore. Many ugly confrontations ensued, with Greens spat upon, cursed, and roughed up, all in full view of the police, who did nothing. One Green who tried to defend her comrades from verbal and physical abuse was incensed by the cops' lackadaisical attitude. That night, she e-mailed an angry message to her friends. "The police protect their own cronies, and the system protects its own as well," she wrote. "I don't want to sound like a nut, but if you want to feel powerless, try having a voice against the established power structure and see how quickly people turn on you and label you an Enemy (or a commie dyke, if you're lucky). You will not be who you know yourself to be; you will become a threat, a criminal, and you will not be protected. When huge men knock down women while the police turn a blind eye and riot police mace skinny kids for waving a sign on the wrong side of a fence, your perspective changes pretty dramatically."[19] As a barely organized party with no real power, the Greens had little pull with local authorities; nor did they have much ability to coordinate their own loosely connected troops in any self-protective manner.

And while Greens were getting their own bitter taste of power realities outside the debate, inside at the entrance to the viewing hall Nader was being insulted as well. A college student had given him his ticket, which entitled the holder to a seat not in the main auditorium, but in a side viewing area. Despite this and the fact that he had been invited onto the premises by Fox News in order to participate in a live postdebate commentary, Nader was blocked from entering the area by a private security consultant working for the debates commission, backed up by three state troopers. According to Nader, the consultant "told me that he was 'instructed by the commission' to advise me that 'it's already been decided that, whether or not you have a ticket, you are not invited.'" Nader backed off, not wishing to risk arrest, but quickly moved to make the most of the sordid encounter. He charged the debate commission with violating his civil rights and, after an offer to settle was ignored, sued in federal court in Boston. The case will go to trial sometime in 2002.[20]

Media watchdog groups like Fairness and Accuracy in Reporting (FAIR) were outraged by Nader's exclusion. But few, if any, of the many journalists and pundits who were so upset a few months later at how the "sanctity" of democracy was violated in Florida ventured more than a shrug of perfunctory protest at the commission's behavior. A rare exception in a mainstream outlet came from iconoclast Philip Weiss in the New York Observer, who admitted that his support for Nader was making him an unpopular figure at Manhattan dinner parties. "Eight years ago, Ross Perot believed that Republican operatives had invaded his daughter's wedding," Weiss noted, "and he got to be in the debates. Ralph Nader is one of the most powerful minds in America — and he can't even get into the spin room."[21]

Crunch Time

While Nader's exclusion from the bipartisan-sponsored debates was a foregone conclusion, the impact was not. Pollster John Zogby detected a modest "surge" in his public support in the immediate aftermath of the Boston debate, undoubtedly a product of all the publicity from the protests as well as a sign that some voters were disappointed enough with Bush's and Gore's lackluster performances to look elsewhere.[22] Nader sidestepped the second debate, but attempted to view the third debate in St. Louis, where he was again physically excluded, despite holding a press pass to enter the debate compound to be interviewed.

Something was beginning to go right for the campaign. Just weeks before the election, despite being locked out of the presidential debates, with 1 percent of the money and 1 percent of the media attention, Nader experienced a notable rise in the polls. He was at 6 percent in California,[23] 7 percent in Wisconsin,[24] 8 percent in Minnesota,[25] 8 percent in New Jersey,[26] 8 percent in Rhode Island,[27] and 10 percent in Oregon.[28] A mid-September poll put him at 17 percent in Alaska.[29] Not only that, donations were pouring in at a faster rate than anyone had expected. One in seven voters was still undecided, a sign of ambivalence about Bush and Gore and an indication that Nader could rise further.[30]

But with the race between Gore and Bush still as tight as ever, the attacks on Nader and his supporters were becoming more passionate and widespread. The heat started with feminist leaders like Patricia Ireland, of the National Organization for Women, and David Smith, spokesman for the Human Rights Campaign, the nation's largest gay rights organization, charging that he was indifferent to the threat of a Bush victory.[31] (Ironically, Ireland had herself been a supporter of NOW's initiative to create a progressive third party back in the early 1990s, as an alternative to the Democrats' rightward drift. And in 1996, after President Clinton signed the "welfare reform" bill, Ireland was one of several activists who went on a hunger strike in protest. Now she was corralling voters for the very man, Gore, who bragged about his role in pushing Clinton to sign that bill.) Gloria Steinem, another Gore supporter, took to visiting campuses and reading her "Top Ten Reasons Why I'm Not Voting for Ralph Nader (Any One of Which Would Be Enough)."[32] And a group of about a dozen former Nader's Raiders went public with a call to their former boss to pull out of the race.[33]

But this was nothing compared to the fear campaign whipped up by Gore and his allies as the election came to a close. Everything that Carol Miller had seen in her congressional campaigns in New Mexico was repeated, only on a much larger scale. The National Abortion Rights Action League spent at least $1.5 million on TV ads declaring that a woman's right to choose was endangered and warning that a vote for Nader equaled a vote for Bush. NARAL's ad said: "If you're thinking of voting for Ralph Nader, please consider this. This year, a five-to-four Supreme Court decision narrowly protected *Roe vs. Wade*. As president, George W. Bush would reverse the court, with antichoice justices Scalia and Thomas in control." NARAL concluded, "Voting for Ralph Nader helps elect" Bush, so "before voting Nader, consider your vote. . . . It's your choice." On the screen, photos of Nader and Bush subtly inched toward each other with a photo of the court in the background.[34]

The Sierra Club and the League of Conservation Voters piled on with ads of their own stating the differences between Gore and Bush that avoided naming Nader but implied that a vote for the Green would lead to more despoiling of the environment. And the liberal organization People for the American Way ran an ad playing off of Nader's parody of Mastercard: The ad opened with an announcer saying, "Nine black robes: $945. One wooden gavel: $14. Forty years of influence over our freedoms: Price-less." The announcer went on to discuss Bush as a candidate who opposed "choice, gun control, and strong environmental protections," and then described Gore as a candidate who "favors justices who are pro-choice, support gun safety laws and environmental protection." The ad ended with a veiled question for Nader voters — "with our freedoms at stake, shouldn't you cast a vote that really counts?"[35]

Some Nader supporters tried to make a nuanced response. Steve Cobble, an adviser to the campaign, wrote a widely circulated article arguing that in the great majority of states, people could vote their conscience. The reason: electoral votes are cast by state, and it's winner-take-all in each state (except Maine and Nebraska). "Thus, a Nader vote has no chance of 'spoiling' the outcome for Al Gore," Cobble wrote, "unless it potentially changes the outcome within that state." Cobble pointed out that in about thirty-five states, either Bush or Gore was so far ahead that the other wasn't bothering to campaign there. (He was right. According to the *National Journal*, neither Bush nor Gore visited Idaho, Utah, Montana, North Dakota, South Dakota, Nebraska, Kansas, Oklahoma, Mississippi, South Carolina, Hawaii, Delaware, or Vermont between April 1 and the election. In addition, there were a grand total of six presidential TV ads run in four of the nation's top eight media markets — Boston, Dallas, New York City, and Washington, D.C. — while more than sixty-five hundred presidential ads aired in just eight media markets in so-called "battleground" states.)[36] Those thirty-five were "safe" states in Cobble's view. In others, he suggested following columnist Molly Ivins's advice, which was to check the polls just before Election Day, and if it was close, to vote for Gore to keep Bush away from the Supreme Court, but otherwise, to vote for Nader.[37]

Nader himself endorsed this approach, contrary to the widespread impression that he didn't care who won the election or even favored Bush's victory. Of course, he never directly said, "vote for Gore instead of me," and he was quite vociferous in arguing that no candidate could assume any vote was "his," that they all had to earn their votes, and that as someone seeking to build a new party he was obviously in the business of trying to win every vote he could get. But he often told questioners that he wasn't bothered by so-called tactical voting. "If a Sierra Clubber wants to engage in tactical voting," he told an audience at Chico State University in California on October 23, "then wait till one or two days before, check the polls, and if Gore is 10 or 15 points ahead, then vote for the Green Party to create a powerful new watchdog party with a far better record on the environment." The day before, he gave a very similar answer at a press conference in Oakland.

Nevertheless, many attackers paid no attention to what Nader was actually saying. The editorial writers at the New York Times unloaded on him not once but twice in the two weeks before the election. First they charged him with "willful prankishness" for continuing to run, claiming that they would see his insolence "as a disservice to the electorate no matter whose campaign he was hurting." This seemingly nonpartisan and dispassionate statement was followed by a lengthy description of Gore's virtues, and how much better he would supposedly be on a few issues of concern to Nader voters. "[Nader] calls his wrecking-ball candidacy a matter of principle, but it looks from here like ego run amok," they concluded.[38] Barely a week later, the Times led its editorial with a direct personal assault on talk-show host Phil Donahue, and praised his wife, Marlo Thomas, for scolding him for backing Nader. "It is past time for everyone, including Mr. Gore, to get tougher on Mr. Nader," they editorialized. Citing no evidence, they added, "He is being more open these days about his willingness to throw the election to Mr. Bush and his desire to damage the Democratic Party."[39] Considering that the Times editorial board never extended Nader the courtesy of inviting him in for a formal meeting, it seemed as if the paper's editors didn't want to bother with finding out directly if their own rhetoric about Nader was true.

Neither did a prominent group of academics and writers, who announced they were "appalled" at Nader's "wrecking-ball campaign" and charged that he "will do anything and say anything" to reach his goal of 5 percent. Their statement, published in the online journal Salon, claimed falsely that given a choice of Bush or Gore, Nader had said he would vote for Bush, and incorrectly charged him with favoring the ending of all U.S. aid to Israel.[40] These Gore supporters were of course entitled to their views. But as self-proclaimed "Concerned Scholars, Writers and Activists," they were awfully quick to charge Nader with "Orwellian utterances" that dissolved under the slightest inspection. For example, in mid-August, after Robert F. Kennedy Jr. wrote in an op-ed for the *New York Times* that Nader had said he would vote for Bush,[41] the paper published a letter from Nader saying "I have never said that I would vote for George W. Bush, whom I have strongly criticized across the country, if forced to choose between him and Al Gore. Indeed, I have never stated for whom I have ever voted or expect to vote since the 1960s, though it can be assumed that I will vote for the Green Party candidates this year."[42] And while the Association of State Green Parties issued a release October 24 endorsing a United Nations resolution condemning Israel's handling of the Palestinian protests and calling for an end to U.S. aid to Israel until the country agreed to withdraw from the occupied territories and recognize the Palestinians' right of return, this statement went beyond Nader's own position on the conflict.[43] Nader was against any immediate aid cutoff, arguing that it would reduce U.S. influence and only embolden the Israeli right. At most, he talked about eventually phasing down economic aid to the country, citing former Prime Minister Benjamin Netanyahu's support for the notion.

If Nader really wanted to try to deny Gore any chance of election, then the best evidence for that incendiary charge would be found in his campaign itinerary. Some Nader critics charged both during the election and afterward that the proof of Nader's malice was his concentration on battleground states in the race's final weeks. For example, a reporter for the *American Prospect*, a liberal magazine, claimed that "in the final week, Nader is campaigning exclusively in those states in which his candidacy has a realistic chance of flipping the state from Gore to Bush."[44] Actually, he spent the last seven days of the campaign in Wisconsin, Colorado, California, Florida, D.C., New York, Massachusetts, New Hampshire, and Maine. Of those nine, all but Wisconsin, Florida, and New Hampshire were considered safe Gore states by most experts.

In fact, in the final weeks of the election, Nader and his top advisers were torn about where precisely to focus their energies, not because they wanted to defeat Gore but because they wanted to maximize their own vote. Steve Cobble, the strategist with the most experience in past elections (he had run Jesse Jackson's delegate operation in 1988 and had worked on Carol Moseley-Braun's and Toney Anaya's successful campaigns in Illinois and New Mexico), sensed earlier than most that Nader was in real danger of falling short of his bottom-line goal of getting 5 percent of the vote. "They're ignoring him to death," he said in late September, bemoaning the media's spotty coverage of the campaign. And he knew that Gore's populist posturing was still robbing Nader of support. "Prescription drugs and 'I'm for working families' shouldn't have worked so well for Gore," he noted, "but there was no way to answer in the 499 out of 500 places a day where Ralph wasn't."[45] Nader, of course, was running no paid advertising during most of this period. And as many as half of his supporters were telling pollsters that they might switch their vote.[46] Cobble was well aware how the fear of a

Bush victory could cost Nader support. "When the conversation is about spoiling it increases the nervousness of half our vote," he said. Former Perot supporters didn't care, nor did young people, he reasoned. But liberals were another matter. So Cobble urged that Nader focus on safe states. "A liberal in Austin [Texas] is worth more to us than a liberal in Madison [Wisconsin]."[47]

But others in the campaign thought that Nader couldn't stop visiting the battle-ground states, for two reasons. One was pragmatic. They feared if he went where the national media weren't, he would drop totally off the news. And the media were focused almost entirely on what was happening in the dozen or so swing states in the final weeks. The second reason was that they had a real base in many of those states, and it was under attack. Not only were Nader voters in states like Oregon, Washington, Minnesota, Wisconsin, and Michigan being hit by a deluge of left-leaning Democratic surrogates including Rev. Jesse Jackson, Senator Paul Wellstone, and Representatives Barney Frank, Maxine Waters, John Conyers, Nancy Pelosi, George Miller, Tammy Baldwin, Jesse Jackson Jr., Jan Schakowsky, and John Tierney,[48] they were under a hailstorm of negative ads designed to scare them into backing Gore.[49] Some were also dealing with a daily barrage of physical intimidation. Nader needed to go into those states not just to defend his base, but to stand by the people who were standing by him.

Late night in a dressing room backstage after his Oakland super-rally on October 21, Nader debated these options with a circle of trusted aides, including Greg Kafoury and Mark McDougal, the super-rally organizers; Ross Mirkarimi, a savvy Green from San Francisco who was his California campaign director; and Tarek Milleron, his nephew. Nader had written out a draft plan for the last two weeks that he called his "ideal itin-erary." Starting on October 25, when he would be back in D.C. after finishing the remainder of his trek through California (plus a stopover in Arizona), it continued as follows (the notes after each date are Nader's):

October 26: Ohio
October 27: Iowa (5000 rally in Iowa City)
October 28: New York/New Jersey (Cooper Union, 5000 rally in NJ)
October 29: DC (rest)
October 30: DC (calls)
October 31: Michigan/Minnesota (Dearborn, Nightline in St. Paul)
November 1: Wisconsin (10K rally in Milwaukee)
November 2: California (15K L.A. super-rally)
November 3: California (rest)
November 4: Colorado (Boulder 5000 rally)
November 5: DC (MCI Center super-rally)

November 6: Florida (Tallahassee)
November 7: DC

Nader's draft was shaped by several variables. He needed to be in D.C. at his campaign headquarters to deal with all kinds of last-minute decisions. On October 30, the staff had also scheduled a bloc of long-distance conference calls with various constituencies and interviews with the international press. *Nightline* had arranged for a town hall meeting with Nader and Minnesota Governor Jesse Ventura on October 31. Though Nader had snubbed Ventura earlier in the fall by not appearing at an "all-candidates" debate that the third-party governor had hosted at the end of September, there was no way he would miss this one-on-one encounter. The D.C. super-rally was also critical, even though the campaign's top staff were terrified that it would be a bust. Nader needed to rest, and he preferred to stop either in D.C. or at his sister's in the Bay Area. And Florida was on the schedule, even though Nader had never broken above 5 percent in state polls, because it was rich in votes. Nader's aides had noticed that after one trip to the state earlier in October, their numbers had doubled from 2 to 4 percent statewide. In the country's fourth-largest state, that was a lot of voters.

But this wasn't the final word. A number of Nader advisers argued that his plan left out visits to strongholds in the Northeast like Connecticut, Vermont, and Massachusetts. They prodded him to make at least one stop somewhere in the Pacific Northwest, another place where his polls had been strong. They argued that he had to give up on the rest days. And they urged him to skip Florida—especially on the day before the election, arguing that it was too late, he would be swamped by the closeness of the Gore-Bush fight there, and no one would pay attention. (They also pushed him to get his running mate, Winona LaDuke, out to Alaska, Hawaii, and Indian reservations across the mountain states. But LaDuke, who had had her third child early in the year, was a part-time campaigner at best.)[50]

Ultimately, Nader spent the last two weeks of the election campaigning (in this order) in D.C., Ohio, Iowa, Pennsylvania, New Jersey, New York, back to D.C. (two days), Michigan, Minnesota, Illinois, Wisconsin, Washington, Colorado, California, Florida, back to D.C. and New York, then Massachusetts, New Hampshire, and Maine. He finished on Election Day with a brief stop in front of the Liberty Bell in Philadelphia. Compared to the draft he had proposed in Oakland, he had cut out a rest day, and added stops in Illinois, Pennsylvania, Washington, Colorado, New York, Massachusetts, New Hampshire, and Maine. Florida was still on the schedule, but moved back from the day before the election. Half of these states were still in play between Bush and Gore, and the rest were not.[51] In terms of actual time in each state, Nader spent roughly about 40 percent of his precious final two weeks campaigning in battleground states. Had he simply wanted to deny Gore the election, he could have campaigned solely in the Rust Belt states of the Midwest and Pacific Northwest. Instead, he tried to go where the most votes were and where the media were, and let the chips fall where they may.[52]

The Aftermath

In the end, Nader's support crashed, just as he had worried. Most of his supporters were cowed by the Democrats' scare campaign, big-time. Fear won out over hope. And this was true not only in battleground states like Oregon (where he got 5 percent), Minnesota (5 percent), Washington (4 percent), New Mexico (4 percent), and Wisconsin (4 percent). The Nader vote also withered in safe states like California (4 percent), New York (4 percent), and Connecticut (4 percent), which Gore won by 11, 25, and 17 points, respectively. Only in a handful of states did Nader beat his 5 percent goal: Republican-dominated Alaska (10 percent); Vermont (7 percent), where Anthony Pollina's strong third-party candidacy helped; heavily Democratic Massachusetts and Rhode Island (each 6 percent); and independent Maine (6 percent). In Texas, another safe state because of Bush's insurmountable lead (he won it by 21 points), Nader got just 2 percent. The Democratic chestnut, that Gore was less evil than Bush, won out. And among independents and young voters, the two groups least susceptible to that argument, Nader did not do well enough to make up the difference he needed to get to 5 percent.

The Voter News Service exit polls suggest that most of Nader's votes came from young people and students, with a smattering of older independents and progressives. He got 5 percent of the eighteen- to twenty-nine-year-old vote, 6 percent of the independent vote, and 6 percent of the self-identified liberal vote. By comparison, very few self-described conservatives (1 percent) or moderates (2 percent) tilted his way. Another indication of the leftist skew of his base: of the 9 percent of the electorate that thought Gore's positions were too conservative, Nader got one in ten votes. This was a dramatic shift for Nader from 1992, when he campaigned in the New Hampshire primary, asking voters to write his name in "as a stand-in for 'none-of-the-above'" and as a protest vote for political reform. That year, he received 2 percent of the Democratic vote and 2 percent of the Republican vote.[53] Of all subgroups, people who voted for Perot in 1996 were most likely to vote for Nader; he received 7 percent of their votes. In doing so, he undoubtedly took some votes that otherwise would have gone to Bush, who won most Perot '96 voters.

While Nader did slightly better than his overall 3 percent showing with voters making less than $15,000 a year, his 4 percent tally with this group was undoubtedly a reflection of his base among college students rather than any connection to the urban poor. Nationwide, he only got 1 percent of the African-American vote, a sign both of this group's strong Democratic loyalties and Nader's late and weak attempts to reach them. He got only 1 percent of the African-American vote in D.C., for example, while getting 5 percent overall there. (Gore won the district with 86 percent of the vote.) And in states with large university populations, he did markedly better with voters under the age of twenty-nine, accounting for 16 percent of the votes in Massachusetts, 10 percent in Wisconsin, and 8 percent in California.

Perhaps the toughest indictment of Nader's campaign came from Eric Alterman, a Gore supporter who was a columnist at *The Nation* magazine. He wrote: "This nascent leftist movement has virtually no support among African-Americans, Latinos or Asian-Americans. It has no support among organized feminist groups, organized gay rights groups or mainstream environmental groups. To top it all off, it has no support in the national union movement. So Nader and company are building a nonblack, non-Latino, non-Asian, nonfeminist, nonenvironmentalist, nongay, non-working people's left: Now that really would be quite an achievement."[54] But Alterman's heated charge overshot the mark. While it was true that Nader did worst among African-Americans and Latinos (2 percent), his Asian-American support equaled his white support at 3 percent. Gay voters did not abandon Nader either, giving him 4 percent of their vote nationwide and significantly more than that in some states (in Oregon, he got 12 percent of the gay/lesbian vote). A few national unions—the United Electrical Workers and the California Nurses Association—endorsed Nader, contrary to Alterman's claim. And he got 3 percent of the vote of union members, the same as his national average.[55]

The geography of Nader's support shows he mainly did best in the cultural enclaves that already defined the Greens' base for local races: progressive university towns like Gainesville, Florida; Athens, Georgia; Austin, Texas; Madison, Wisconsin; Chico, California; Lawrence, Kansas; Columbia, Missouri; Iowa City, Iowa; and Lexington, Kentucky.[56] This is not to say that Nader only did well in outposts of the counterculture. In the Minnesota Iron Range, an old labor stronghold, he got between 6 and 10 percent, though the Democrats' scare tactics pushed his numbers down in Flint, Michigan. In a number of states—Minnesota, Wisconsin, Kansas, Colorado, Montana, as well as the Pacific Northwest and New York and New England—his base was evenly spread across urban, suburban, and rural centers. Overall, however, Nader's support was concentrated in just one-quarter of the nation's counties.[57] (For a four-color map showing Nader's county-by-county vote, go to www.spoilingforafight.com.)

For leaders of the Green Party, Nader's showing still contained many positives. As a result of the campaign, new Green parties were taking root in conservative states like Nebraska, Kansas, Utah, Montana, and Mississippi and growing at healthy rates in Texas, Wisconsin, Connecticut, Minnesota, Iowa, and Pennsylvania. In Wyoming, Idaho, and Indiana, three states where Nader failed to get on the ballot, his write-in total broke national records; in a few counties in Wyoming, he actually got more than

7 percent of the vote in write-ins.[58] A record number of eighty Greens held elective offices, and a few Democratic officeholders decided to switch parties.[59] The California Green Party's registration level was up by a third. Nader's 6 percent showing in Rhode Island and 5 percent in Minnesota were high enough to qualify the state party for public matching funds for its local candidates. In San Francisco, a Democrat running for supervisor, Matt Gonzalez, announced his party switch and still won a resounding two-thirds majority of the vote in a runoff race against a candidate backed by incumbent Mayor Willie Brown. The Association of State Green Parties was close to having active affiliates in thirty-nine states, and they had official lines on the ballot in a total of twenty-three, up from ten after the 1996 election.[60] Green parties in other countries also benefited as in many cases there was more coverage of the Nader campaign in their local press than there had been of their own candidates. These were important consolations. But questions about the wisdom of putting so much energy into presidential politics still remained.

Was the Moment Ripe?

Nader's own explanation for his poor showing was fairly simple. "There's this psychology among voters not to stray [from the major parties]," he said with a sigh in an hour-long phone conversation a few weeks after the election. "The most disappointing thing to me was the way the polls shrank. They gave every indication to me of holding, going into the last weekend before Election Day, even surging in some places." But the "Molly Ivins" strategy of tactical voting was "a complete failure," in his words. "People don't think about the Electoral College at all," he lamented. (Of course, that was before the Gore-Bush collision in Florida!) He expressed doubts that paid media might have helped him get that message out at the end. "We had that big media buy during the conventions, and we went down," he said. "Anyway, the clutter of ads at the end was staggering. The Democrats spent $8 million in Michigan alone!" Nader admitted that he had been wrong to start so late. But he wasn't sure that much could have been otherwise. "If we had started in November [1999], it would have been better, but I'm not sure the intensity could have been kept up with some people," he said, adding that it would have been hard to get out the campaign's radical message so early in the political season—especially during the primaries, when many of the mainstream candidates were touting their reformer credentials. "Too many people were giving [campaign contributions] to [Bill] Bradley and [John] McCain. That opened up substantially after March."

The conventional wisdom of political professionals is that an attack on TV has to be answered on TV, and in the final weeks of the election Nader was being bashed unmercifully with scarcely a peep of a response. After a lengthy internal debate over the wisdom of running a second ad produced by Bill Hillsman, Nader let it fly. But there was only about $200,000 in the campaign kitty to pay for it, and, according to Hillsman, the only city where Nader's advertising even got close to minimal visibility was Portland, Oregon. Hillsman mourned the missed opportunity. "I think 5 percent was within our grasp. But he needed to put more money into media. This was a campaign where we never reached critical mass with TV and radio. Ralph wasn't talking to rank-and-file voters, or reaching liberal independent suburbanites, because he wasn't on the air. Our message never got out to the Anoka's," he said, recalling the Minnesota county that was the epicenter of the Jesse Ventura vote. "Basically, it ended at the city limits. College campuses and urban centers."[61]

Nader never accepted this analysis. "I don't believe in that approach," he said. "I believe we need to find a million people willing to give one hundred hours a year and $100 a year. And I'd spend that money heavily on person-to-person organizing. We did our best in Massachusetts, where we had two organizers going door-to-door for six months." Indeed, Nader had gotten 33 percent of the vote in Sheffield and 14 percent in Great Barrington, two progressive towns in the Berkshires.[62]

Nader's invocation of his "million, hundred, hundred" scenario for building a new progressive reform movement was not new. I had heard him use the exact same formulation in 1992, when he put his pinky toe in the water of presidential politics by allowing some of his associates to run a write-in Nader campaign in that year's New Hampshire primary. Some of the same people involved in his 2000 campaign were there in 1992, like Carl Mayer and Greg Kafoury, and they had hoped a strong write-in showing might actually induce Nader to become a real candidate. "If we build it, he will come," Kafoury had said back then. Their instincts had been good, as the Perot phenomenon later that year showed that America was ready for an explosion of anti-incumbent sentiment. But Nader, committed to his philosophy of civic advocacy, was not prepared to enter partisan politics. He obviously changed his mind in 2000. Somewhere in California in mid-October, as we got back into his rental car after another sold-out event, he turned to me and said, "You know, I should have done this in 1992. But I wasn't ready."

Nader's personal insight raised a different question. Compared to 1992, when America was seemingly seething with "throw-the-bums-out" fervor compounded by various congressional scandals (the savings and loan bailout, the House bank check bouncing) and the lingering effects of economic recession, was the fat, happy, America of 2000, with less than 4 percent unemployment, really as ripe for a populist outsider campaign? In the fall of 1999, a California political analyst named Bill Bradley (not the senator), wrote a perceptive column. He started by noting how neither Bush nor Gore, the putative nominees of their parties, had ignited much genuine excitement. "So most of the attention in national politics has passed, at least for the moment, to unconventional contenders and potential third-party candidates," Bradley wrote. "But the anger needed to sustain such candidacies as decisive challenges to status quo politics isn't there yet. People have lowered their expectations about politicians, who currently rank just above used car salesmen and journalists in public esteem." He attributed this decline of expectations in part to President Clinton, who made a virtue of small government initiatives, though he also thought that part of the reason Clinton had survived impeachment was due to the public's low expectation of politicians in the first place. Bradley continued:

> Add to that the widespread sense that Watergate is par for the course in U.S. politics . . . and a lengthy economic recovery relentlessly reinforced by media reports and you have an absence of widespread anger. Of course, the economy isn't nearly as good for most Americans as the media makes it out to be, but times are really bad for only a few and, if you view politics as an essentially rigged system, as most Americans now do, who cares? The cynicism is unearned, and for many, especially the youngest voters, a product of knowing but not knowledgeable media-derived attitudes, but it is no less real for its tinniness. So what we have is not an alienation factor, but a disdain factor. Which is probably not enough to sustain any but the most extraordinary unconventional candidacies.

Nader, in Bradley's view, was unlikely to fit that bill.[63]

I think there is something to Bradley's analysis that helps explain Nader's disappointing finish, though the strength of John McCain's 2000 run suggests that the popular desire for an across-the-board housecleaning in Washington never disappeared as much as Bradley surmised. In fact, in the spring of that year, a quarter of the public said they would vote for McCain as a third-party candidate against Gore and Bush.[64] But Bradley is right to point his finger at the public's declining expectations for politics. To this I would add an especially distressing problem for third-party organizers: the background noise of Perot's Big Bang. By this I mean not just his explosion in 1992, which was a moment of rising hope for many Americans, but his implosion in the years following. Nearly 20 million Americans took a chance on Perot in 1992, pinning their hopes for dramatic reform on his quirky candidacy. Eight million people—some the same voters from before and others younger and less well educated, took another chance with him in 1996. And all they got was dashed hopes and shattered dreams.

To be sure, a significant number of Perot voters migrated over to Nader. But many others—particularly those who helped put the "angry middle" on the map in the early 1990s—may well have been exhausted by their dalliance with Perot. Their withdrawal from politics wasn't proof that Americans were suddenly more content with their dysfunctional government. But maybe many were more resigned to the seeming immobility of the status quo and intimidated by the personal sacrifices that they knew, from bitter experience with Perot, it would take to organize an outsiders' movement again. Nader, quite astutely, always zeroed in on this problem of expectations. But in addition to all the other factors hindering his rise, I think the Perot implosion added an invisible undertow.

As it was, the Nader campaign tended to focus its energies more at students, young people, and progressives than at political independents. A number of Reform Party leaders endorsed him, including Jack Gargan in Florida and several party activists in Texas, as well as the splinter American Reform Party, but the campaign didn't maximize the impact of this news. Nader met with Ventura, who declared that he should be included in the debates. But the popular governor never made any endorsement, only saying that he wasn't voting for a major-party candidate. Despite the opportunity created by Buchanan's hijacking of the Reform Party, Nader never made a concerted bid for former Perot voters.

Dan Johnson-Weinberger, a campaign staffer working out of its Chicago office, was delegated the "Perot voter" portfolio. But he felt that Nader was more focused on building a "Labor-Green" coalition than an "Independent-Green" coalition. He told me that the head of the Minnesota Independence Party, Rick McLuhan, was ready to make a public endorsement of Nader but couldn't after he skipped Ventura's "all-candidates" debate. "I think he burned a bridge there," Johnson-Weinberger said. "I think he could have gotten an endorsement from Ventura if he had focused on it; there was a 30 percent chance, at least." Johnson-Weinberger saw plenty of grass-roots support for Nader from former Perot voters. "In the Chicago office, all the people walking in say they voted for Perot in '92. They all use the same rhetoric — 'I like Nader because he has integrity. I trust him.'" But the campaign did little with this potential. Instead, it fell into the well-worn groove of courting (and arguing with) progressives.[65]

There were other external conditions beyond the campaign's control. Certainly, no one could have predicted that Patrick Buchanan would put in such a weak performance — especially after polls in 1999 showed him drawing into the low double digits as a third-party candidate. Had there been a genuine four-way race, with or without a four-way debate, it would have been much less likely for Nader to be caught in such an ugly endgame with the Democrats. And certainly, no one thought that the race between Gore and Bush would be so close — another factor that ultimately depressed Nader's vote totals.

But there were some things the Nader campaign could have done differently. It could have chosen a more active vice presidential candidate than longtime environmental justice activist Winona LaDuke. Her presence on the ticket was obviously reassuring to hard-core Greens who were concerned that Nader would neglect their broader platform in his efforts to focus on corporate power and democracy issues. But LaDuke was nowhere near as visible on the campaign trail as Nader, and he stood by the platform pretty reliably. Her absence sometimes angered and confused women who came to rallies expecting to see her speak. The campaign also could have started earlier, and it could have tried to set aside money for last-minute response ads.

But these are quibbles against some larger questions. One is whether anyone can claim to be building a people's movement when big chunks of "the people" aren't with you. The second is whether Nader confused people with a seemingly contradictory message—sometimes saying his third-party bid was aimed at teaching the Democrats a lesson and forcing them in a more progressive direction and other times saying he didn't care what happened to the Democrats, he was building a new party regardless. And the third is whether he ran too much as a progressive prophet scolding the right-drifting Democrats and not enough as a maverick independent challenging both parties.

Writers such as Vanessa Daniel, in the Oakland-based magazine *Colorlines*, and Salim Muwakkil in the *Chicago Tribune*, drew a bead on the overwhelming whiteness of Nader's supporters. The candidate tended not to handle the criticism well, sometimes even blaming African-Americans who asked him about the problem for not bringing more friends with them to his rallies! It was true that many of Nader's progressive positions were of express value to people of color. He was the only candidate supporting a Marshall Plan for the cities as restitution for slavery, and the only committed opponent of the drug war and the death penalty. As Muwakkil wrote, "He speaks to problems that have their most damaging effects in African-American and Latino communities."[66] But Nader was primarily interested in talking about America's unresolved problems in class terms, not racial ones.[67] He rarely campaigned in black churches or historically black colleges. Considering that so many of the vast army of discouraged voters that he had hoped to reach were likely to be people of color, this was a real shortcoming.

Nader also alienated some observers with his occasionally contradictory rhetoric. Many times he said there was no meaningful difference between Bush and Gore, or "the only difference was the velocity with which their knees hit the floor when corporations knock on the door." But he also frequently lamented the rightward drift of the Democratic Party and held out his candidacy as the way to move it in a more progressive direction. This, he said, could be accomplished if Democrats realized they couldn't take progressive voters for granted anymore, that they had somewhere else to go. Sometimes he said he would support running more Green candidates for Congress, even if it meant that more Democrats, even possibly those with good records, would lose their races in the short run.[68] But at the same time that he admitted his willingness to drench Gore's Democrats in a "cold shower" of being out of power, he also suggested that his candidacy would be a boon to congressional Democrats by bringing more voters to the polls who would tilt their way. He wanted Democrats punished for their right-wing betrayals and rewarded for being more progressive than the Republicans running Congress.

Pushed to clarify, Nader would say that he never intended people to think that there were no differences between the two major parties, just that there were "few major differences" when examined in terms of their relationship to corporate power.[69] And he said that he never contemplated knocking out Democratic progressives like Paul Wellstone or Russ Feingold—indeed after the election, he properly claimed some credit for helping Democrats Maria Cantwell and Debbie Stabenow win their close Senate races, bringing the Democratic Party to parity with Senate Republicans.[70] "Conservative Democrats have a sense of political entitlement to progressive votes that is, frankly, insulting. They expect progressives to roll over and back the Democratic nominee—no matter how bad," he told journalist John Nichols a few days before the election. "We are creating a Green Party alternative that says to the Al Gores and the Joe Liebermans that there is going to be a penalty paid from now on for rebuking and rejecting the soul of the Democratic Party historically—the progressive wing."

But given that many Greens and potential supporters lived in progressive strongholds (like Santa Fe or Madison), support for Green candidacies in those areas could well mean undermining decent Democrats in the process. It was a seemingly unresolved contradiction for Nader and the Greens. Nader resolved it by saying that he saw the party moving through two phases—an early one in which its candidates in some places would challenge both parties but draw more votes from former Democrats and in others where its presence on the ballot might actually assist some Democrats, as he believed he had done for some congressional Democrats. In a later, more mature phase that he saw taking eight to twelve years, the Green Party would be close to a major party itself.[71]

Whether the Greens will ever reach that stage remains to be seen, though the odds for success are long. Which brings me to the final question about the strategy that Nader and the Greens have taken for challenging the two-party duopoly at the national level. After years of hard work as a nonpartisan citizen advocate, in 2000 Nader came out as a full-blown left-winger, taking strong positions on the death penalty, the military budget, health care, gay rights, labor organizing, racial profiling, reparations for slavery, hemp, sanctions against Iraq, Palestinian rights—you name it. And while he focused on a set of issues surrounding corporate power and democracy that could appeal to an independent skeptic, he saddled himself with the mantle of a fledgling social democratic party whose core activists are primarily white progressives with a crunchy granola flavor. (Ironically, for someone who wanted to focus on class, he managed to adopt many positions on other issues without gaining much ground with progressives concerned with "identity politics." At the same time, his embrace of so many leftist causes may well have hurt him with nonprogressives who might have responded to his class-based message.)

For all the times Greens said they were "neither left nor right but out in front" of America's tired political dichotomy, most of the time in most of the places where they are active, Greens are of the left. And many Americans have a reflexive allergic reaction to leftists. Some of this is a residue of the Cold War and McCarthyism and years of ingrained propaganda against socialism, communism, and even liberalism. Some is due to the media's conservative bias, which has turned genuine left-progressive voices into an endangered species on the tube. But while majorities of Americans agree with the left about a host of major issues (taking care of the poor and the elderly, making health care affordable to all, making the minimum wage into a real living wage, protecting the environment, civil rights, and equality for women and minorities, defending human rights at home and abroad), they often turn away from joining actual leftists, for two reasons.

One is the undeniable panoply of narrow issues that many leftists espouse. Phil Madsen of the Minnesota Independence Party once told me of how, early in his life in politics, he went to a caucus meeting of the Democratic-Farmer-Labor Party and was shocked at how much time was spent discussing the conflict in El Salvador. It wasn't that he didn't care about the issue, it was just too far from his own life and interests. And he didn't have the time to spare. Many leftists also make an unconsciously elitist assumption that other Americans have—or ought to have—the free time to spend fighting the good fight to free someone wrongly sentenced to death row or to stop a spacecraft filled with plutonium from being launched. But they don't. Politics, to most Americans, is at best a "necessary evil" that they only engage in when they have to. That is to say, when their own interests are at stake.

Frame issues in terms that relate to people's own lives, and they will listen. That is why Nader's long-standing consumerism and defense of "the little guy" against predatory corporations made him a genuine American hero to people who had never heard of such brilliant cultural critics as Noam Chomsky or Barbara Ehrenreich. But something changed when he decided to run seriously as the Green Party's candidate for president. "I always framed things as an appeal to traditional values," Nader insisted afterward. "I would define the corporatists as the extremists, pointing out their exploitation of children and commercialization of childhood, for example. I was always careful to appeal to conservatives."[72] This is true. But he also talked constantly about how Democrats had betrayed their progressive roots. And what Nader didn't see after he left the stages of his many rallies was the carnival around his campaign: earnest young men and women, some in dreadlocks and sandals; older white academics; hippies and former hippies, slackers and a few hip-hoppers; tables laden with literature discussing the plight of Mumia Abu-Jamal or the dangers of electrical power lines or animal rights; even newspaper clippings documenting the efforts of "Nudists for Nader" (after all, the Greens had nothing to hide).[73] It was celebratory, it was exuberant, and it was— in too many places—in a self-indulgent cultural cul de sac.

Even worse, many Greens seemed to wallow happily in their own marginality. They took their own failure to break through with the general public not as a sign of their own failed approaches to organizing, but as proof of their righteous martyrdom. Their weakness, they said, was the fault of the corporate media, or of the two-party duopoly, or of the role of big money in politics—and indeed, all of these things have made it very hard for political dissidents of the left to make much headway in American politics. But the isolation of the left took on the comfort of a persecuted sect. People withdrew to cultural enclaves like Madison or Santa Fe because they felt supported there, yes, but also because these places were an escape from the messy, corrupt, hopelessly dysfunctional rest of the country. Some Greens I met in northern California and on the upper west side of Manhattan exemplified this for me. Their passions were entirely focused on issues like the conflict over the future of Pacifica radio, or the legalization of hemp, or human rights in Tibet. These were all valid concerns, but they weren't anywhere near the needs or interests of most Americans.

"Vote Your Conscience," read the placards handed out at Nader's super-rallies. It was a noble position, and the core motivation for many if not all of his supporters. There *was* a joy connected to voting *for* someone among Nader's fans, a feeling of liberation after years of swallowing compromises. As a force for motivating people to take unusual steps in their lives, this sense of morality empowered cannot be underestimated. It may yet be that like the abolitionists of more than a century ago, the people who flocked to Nader's Green banner may well have crossed a psychological threshold that places them in solid opposition to the established order but frees them to push harder for fundamental changes. Now, as outsiders to the two-party system, they may knit together their visions into a compelling argument other Americans will find hard to ignore. But until that happens, hard truths still have to be faced. The main one is that Nader and the Greens didn't reach all Americans. According to exit polls, Nader's support came almost entirely from the left side of the spectrum; obviously, conservatives, moderates, and even most independents weren't hearing him.

Ultimately, there may be a hard lesson here for anyone seeking a way out of the two-party duopoly. Yes, the mythic party of nonvoters outnumbers that of the Democrats and Republicans and is potentially more progressive in its leanings. But there are also many independent voters who are open to new choices beyond Tweedledom, and these people vote more regularly than typical "nonvoters." Thus it may make more sense to build a third-party campaign as an independent-populist play rooted in the "angry middle" than as a holier-than-thou purely progressive bid. It may also make sense to stop expecting ideological purity from candidates, if the goal is to win a plurality of the vote, rather than to just be a prophetic minority. This is, of course, assuming that the goal of a progressive third party is to speak to a majority of Americans and shift the country in a different direction, rather than just to create a refuge for exiles from one of major parties.

Jesse Ventura, who may be a political genius or just an unusually good self-promoter, understood the instinctive political attitudes of most Americans very well. In *Do I*

Stand Alone?, his second book written since entering politics, he made explicit his identification with average working people against the career politicians who serve the interests of the two major parties. As he put it, "My point of view is that of a working family
man, not a political 'favorite son.' And as a member of the Minnesota Independence
Party, I'm an outsider to the good-old-boy networks that the two traditional parties have
carefully woven into every aspect of our government." Ventura then condemned the
reflexive positions of both "rightists" and "leftists," insisting that he approaches every
issue on the merits. But for him "the only special interest" he represented was "the interest of the working man and woman." As he surveyed the many issues confronting America, he came down on the progressive side of the equation on almost every one: he was
for fair taxation, equal rights for women and gays, choice, unions, freedom of speech,
public financing of campaigns, religious freedom, reining in the power of huge corporations when they harm individuals, affordable housing, expanded drug-treatment programs, and an end to the war on drugs. He was against racism and the religious right.
But he reached these conclusions without any of the baggage carried by the left.[74] Maybe
that explains why Ventura was able to do so well with the angry middle.

While Ventura showed how a third-party original could break the two-party lock on
politics, he has since shied away from providing coherent leadership that could carry
people forward into a new political paradigm, preferring a safer form of personal politics that was quintessentially in tune with the media age. But the essential kernel
remains. Political labels do not mean a lot to most Americans, except as a shorthand
way to pigeonhole distant politicians. What matters is not how a would-be maverick
positions him- or herself on some right-to-left checklist, but how well he or she con-
nects to where people are and sees how to carry them forward. Put another way, "progressive" really should have only one meaning in politics: the effort to connect to the
concerns of average people for a better life. Jim Hightower, a progressive Democrat
who broke with his own party in 2000 to keynote the Greens' Denver convention and
speak at many Nader super-rallies, understood the wisdom of this approach when he
said, "The real political spectrum in America is top versus bottom, not right versus left.
And we need not just the beansprout eaters, but the snuff-dippers, too."

Such a strategy doesn't have to mean jettisoning progressive principles—indeed most
of these speak to the majority of Americans when they are framed as appeals to fairness,
justice, and democratic empowerment. But it does mean taking very seriously the need
to speak to Americans where they are, without expecting them to come all the way over
to the progressive side of the box on their own. Nader's gamble was that his thirty-seven
years as a citizen advocate, his convincing fight for the "little guy," and his defense of civic
values over corporate values would transform the Greens into a new kind of populist/
social-democratic party. Clearly that didn't happen—or at best, it is only beginning to
happen. Instead, in the 2000 campaign, Nader became a "Green"—and despite his
best efforts, that term by itself still doesn't mean much to most Americans.

Organizing from the Bottom Up

The New Party and
the Working Families Exception

A Safe Way
Out of the Box?

The shorthand strategy for accomplishing all this is to get the Bruce Springsteen, Lauryn Hill, and Pete Seeger vote united in one party.

—*Daniel Cantor*

Bad Endings

Al Gore lost the 2000 election for a lot of reasons. Some were political. He was hurt by his long association with President Clinton. There were too many versions of Gore—the man of the people, the candidate of small government, the arrogant preacher, and the meek me-too-er. He backed off of using quasi-populist themes that had clearly boosted his standing when he plugged them hard.[1] He blew the debates. He alienated liberals with a final TV ad that boasted of his role in welfare reform. He lost his home state of Tennessee to George W. Bush by 51 to 48 percent and President Clinton's home state of Arkansas by 51 to 45 percent. He turned off young voters with the selection of Joe Lieberman as his running mate and their condescending attacks on popular entertainment, producing a huge drop-off in Democratic voting among those twenty-nine and younger, costing the ticket almost 3 million votes compared to 1996.[2] Pat Buchanan's gallbladder operation in late summer defanged his right-wing threat to Bush. Ten times as many Florida Democrats voted for Bush than swung to Nader. Senior citizens, the supposed core of Gore's base in that crucial state, split their vote evenly between the two major candidates.

And some of the reasons for Gore's loss were ostensibly procedural. The television networks' premature announcement of Bush's "victory" and the vice president's aborted concession speech on Election Night created a psychological dynamic that made it nearly impossible for Gore to push for a full recount in Florida. Bush's allies in Florida and on the Supreme Court also prevented a proper recount there, while tens of thousands of former felons living in the state—people who had paid their debt to society—were illegally denied their right to vote by Republican registrars. Outdated vote-counting technology produced disproportionate undercounts in districts with high minority populations.[3] The "butterfly ballot," designed and approved by Democratic election officials, confused older voters in Palm Beach County, costing Gore thousands of likely votes. And while the Republicans went all-out to defend their ill-gained Florida win, even sending young Hill staffers to verbally and physically harass local election officials, the Gore campaign told labor organizers, minority-rights activists, and other Democratic partisans to sheath their swords and avoid similar confrontations.[4] Maintaining the appearance of political stability in America was, in the end, more important to Gore than fighting for the principle of "one-person, one-vote."

But in the days and weeks after Election Day, these points were rarely heard. Instead, only one message was voiced by politicos and editorialists alike: Ralph Nader spoiled Al Gore's chances for victory. NARAL president Kate Michelman declared, "He cost Al Gore the race. Not only by what happened in Florida, but by making these other states a threat to Al Gore." Democratic Senator Joe Biden concurred, "Nader cost us the election." AFL-CIO President John Sweeney called the Nader campaign "reprehensible." He added, "As a rule, we really reject the role that Nader played in the political process this time around." Amy Isaacs, director of the liberal Americans for Democratic Action, said, "People basically view him as having been on a narcissistic, self-serving Sancho Panza, windmill-tilting excursion."[5] Watching the election returns at a party with the Clintons in New York City, and listening to the president tick off the states where Nader was hurting Gore, publisher Harold Evans declared, "I want to kill him." To which Hillary Clinton, newly elected senator from New York, responded, "That's not a bad idea."[6] Former Democratic presidential candidate Michael Dukakis made a similar comment that night, saying if Nader tipped the race to Bush, "I'll strangle the guy with my bare hands."[7] Editorial writers and columnists competed to come up with their worst put-down for the Green candidate. USA Today opined that Bush owed Nader a Supreme Court appointment.[8] Thomas Friedman, a New York Times neoliberal, suggested making Nader ambassador to North Korea.[9] Anthony Lewis, another more venerable Times columnist, proposed naming a clear-cut national forest after him. The New Yorker ran a sneering back-page of cartoon "thank-you cards" for Nader that praised him for turning Yosemite into a shopping mall and Alaska into an amusement park.[10]

Ironically, Reform Party candidate Pat Buchanan actually "cost" George Bush more states and more electoral votes than Nader did Gore, if one assumes for argument's sake that every vote Buchanan and Nader got would have instead gone to the major-party candidate closest to them on the political spectrum.[11] And Nader's presence in the election arguably helped Gore in two significant ways. First, by impelling Gore to strengthen his own appeal to the lower half of the electorate with neopopulist rhetoric about taking on the drug companies, the oil companies, and HMOs, Nader indirectly shifted the tilt of the Democrat's message in a way that clearly improved Gore's polling. And second, by standing to Gore's left, Nader made it extremely hard for the Republicans to paint Gore as "hopelessly liberal"—the tactic they had used with great success in their presidential victories in 1980, 1984, and 1988.

Some observers saw beyond the anti-Nader vitriol. "The passions aroused by the Nader campaign have much in common with those elicited by John McCain and Bill Bradley in their primaries," wrote Robert Reich, former Clinton labor secretary, a few weeks after the vote. "We are witnessing the birth pangs of a reform movement in America intent on ending the corruption of our democratic system by money." Reich urged that "this is the hour for reform, not recrimination."[12] Political historian Kevin Phillips noted in the *Los Angeles Times* that the combined vote for Al Gore and Ralph Nader was 52 percent, the highest center-left total since Lyndon Johnson's 1964 landslide. "Nader and his voters may now be what George C. Wallace was after in 1968: a pivotal force to be courted," wrote Phillips.[13] Democratic Minority Leader Richard Gephardt evidently agreed with Phillips, inviting Nader to his office early in 2001 and complimenting him on running "a terrific campaign." Gephardt took admiring note of Nader's ability to draw paying crowds to his rallies, admitting that the Democrats couldn't get people to pay to listen to them talk policy.[14]

But most Democrats simply wanted revenge. "We're not going to touch him with a ten-foot pole," said Congressman Robert Wexler of Florida. "Who's going to work with him now?" echoed Representative John Conyers of Michigan, a longtime Nader ally.[15] James Carville, the hot-tongued Clinton loyalist, declared that he wouldn't even breathe Nader's name. When Senate Democrats briefly held committee chairmanships at the beginning of January 2001, they ignored written requests from Nader to testify against the nominations of John Ashcroft as attorney general and Gale Norton as interior secretary. And Nader-affiliated groups such as Public Citizen and the Aviation Consumer Action Project lost at least $100,000 in funding, as a handful of wealthy contributors withdrew their support in anger at Nader's supposed impact on the election.[16]

It seemed as if the worst of all worlds had happened. Nader had failed to win the 5 percent the Greens needed to get federal funding for the 2004 presidential campaign *and* he was perceived, rightfully or wrongfully, as the number one reason Democrats lost the election. Fifty-two percent of the electorate may well have voted for a center-left candidate, but that still didn't change the bitter reality of Bush in the White House. Some activists saw the perverse result as providing new impetus for a set of electoral reforms that would guarantee a fairer counting of all votes cast, and more crucially, ensure that whoever won the election had a real majority, through the institution of "instant-runoff voting." And, indeed, such a movement has been gaining ground since the election.

But others quietly shook their heads, even as they recognized the potential silver lining in the new constellation of forces seeking far-reaching electoral changes. These activists—people with their roots in the very same progressive causes that had built the Nader effort, environmentalists, labor organizers, community organizers, and academics—had taken a hard look at the realities of American electoral politics, understood the hurdles erected by the two major parties, and been honest with themselves about the resources it would take to mount a frontal attack on the duopoly. They had decided such a challenge at the presidential level was just not feasible. The problem of "spoiling" in the winner-takes-all process was just too much of a deterrent to the kind of organizing they wanted to do. So they went another way.

Back in 1980, some of these people had tried to do something very similar to what Nader and the Greens did, and they had learned an important lesson. That was when a collection of environmentalists, antinuclear activists, feminists, civil rights veterans, and antiwar activists formed the Citizens Party and ran well-respected ecologist Barry Commoner for president. The party was in many ways a precursor to the Greens in ideological terms, but it was much more top-down. And it was a near-total failure. Its founding convention was a nationally televised fiasco, with rancorous interventions by various sectarian groups. Republican John Anderson's decision to drop out of his party's presidential primaries and run as an independent undercut the Citizens Party's efforts to raise money and get into the news.[17] And with almost no money and little media attention, Commoner got only 234,294 votes, or .27 percent of the total cast. The Citizens Party had a few modest local victories, but after Commoner became a supporter of Jesse Jackson's 1984 Democratic campaign for president, the party ran an even less well-known feminist activist, Sonia Johnson, as its candidate in 1984. Then it quietly disbanded.[18]

Restarting Fusion

Daniel Cantor and Joel Rogers set out to avoid precisely these kinds of pitfalls when they conceived the New Party in the fall of 1989. The two were a powerful pairing of brains and wits. Cantor, then a thirty-four-year-old activist who had just played a key role in Jesse Jackson's 1988 effort to reach out to labor unions, was the party's "tummler"—a master organizer, fund-raiser, networker, cheerleader, and strategist. His range of contacts from years with ACORN (the Association of Community Organizations for Reform Now), work in the United Labor Unions, an ACORN organizing arm in Detroit and New Orleans that later merged with the Service Employees International Union, the Veatch/Unitarian Universalist Foundation, a progressive outfit on Long

Island where he was a program officer, and the Jackson campaign, was formidable. Everyone liked "Danny" for his self-deprecating sense of humor, his honesty, and his constant efforts to bring people together. Rogers, then a thirty-seven-year-old professor at the University of Wisconsin Law School, had raced through college in record time (he earned his B.A. in economics, political science, and philosophy from Yale at the age of 20, and later earned a degree in law from Yale and a Ph.D. in political science from Princeton). While sustaining an impressive output of academic writing on a variety of subjects ranging from labor law to economic development, Rogers was a key figure among progressives around the country in strategizing ways to open up the political system. A brilliant thinker with a dry wit and a humanist's heart, Rogers could talk faster than an auctioneer at Sotheby's, packing more complicated ideas into a single paragraph than most academics put into an entire lecture.

Neither man wanted to repeat the failures of past third-party experiments, but at the same time they both felt a real frustration with the limits of the two-party duopoly.[19] And so they set out to revive an old political practice that had been prevalent in America since the dawn of the Republic until the 1890s: fusion. Also known as cross-endorsement, fusion had given minor parties a substantial role in winner-takes-all elections all through the nineteenth century. Under this system, a candidate could be endorsed by more than one party, with the votes for that person counted separately under each party's name and then tallied together. Rather than asking supporters to "waste their votes" on candidates with little chance of winning, fusion allowed minor parties to maintain a separate identity while contributing to a major party candidate's victory. But it existed because it served the needs of at least one of the major parties, who often initiated fusions to shore up a weak position vis-à-vis the other major party. According to historian Peter Argersinger,

> If fusion sometimes helped destroy individual third parties, it helped maintain a significant third party tradition by guaranteeing that dissenters' votes could be more than symbolic protest, that their leaders could gain office, and that their demands might be heard. Most of the election victories normally attributed to the Grangers, Independents, or Greenbackers in the 1870s and 1880s were a result of fusion between those third party groups and Democrats. That some politicians regarded fusion as a mechanism for proportional representation is not surprising.[20]

Argesinger added that minor parties regularly "received at least 20 percent in one or more elections from 1874 to 1892 in more than half the southern states," thanks to fusion. And between 1878 and 1892, they held the balance of power at least once in every state but Vermont, "culminating in 1892 when neither major party secured a majority of the electorate in nearly three-quarters of the states."[21]

Unfortunately for third-party supporters, the fusion laws worked too well for the comfort of the major parties. Starting after the 1892 election, when the Populist "People's Party" made extensive use of fusion with Democrats, threatening to become a major party in its own right, Republican-dominated state legislatures moved to ban the practice. One Republican Minnesota state senator made clear exactly what his party was doing, saying, "We don't propose to allow the Democrats to make allies of the Populists, Prohibitionists, or any other party, and get up combination tickets against us. We can whip them single-handed, but don't intend to fight all creation."[22]

The fusion bans and ballot access restrictions that followed effectively smothered the existing third parties. At the same time, the major parties also were imposing a myriad of new voter registration rules (literacy tests, poll taxes) that effectively shut out millions of blacks, the rural poor, and working class city-dwellers and immigrants.[23] Voter turnout among people of lower incomes—which used to be as high as any other social group, thanks to political parties (major and minor) that were rooted in their neighborhoods and articulated their concerns—dropped significantly, never to recover.

For the next century most third-party efforts in America were centered more on charismatic candidates than on ongoing organizations. The reason was simple: it's very hard to persuade people who want to vote according to their values to support minor candidates who are very likely to lose, or even worse, to "spoil" a race and cause the person they like least to get elected. Without the ability to cross-endorse, fledgling parties had a much harder time attracting support both from individuals and from institutions since most of the time all they could do was run marginal or spoiler candidates. It was a Catch-22: new parties needed strong candidates and institutional support if they were to become big enough to reach large numbers of voters, but those kinds of major players wouldn't join them if all they could do was get 1 or 2 or 3 percent of the vote. And so minor party organizations rarely managed to grow.

There were a few exceptions, like the Farmer-Labor Party of Minnesota and the LaFollette Progressives of Wisconsin, which thrived during the Depression years, and the Socialist Party, which had a concentrated base in a few areas like New York City and Milwaukee and managed to elect a few members of Congress. ("Sewer socialism," devoted to municipal reform, honest government, and a degree of public ownership, also thrived in a surprising number of cities; Milwaukee's last Socialist major left office in 1960.) These exceptions only proved the rule, that in a winner-take-all system, stable, substantial third parties were only viable during times of extraordinary social stresses or in locales where their members were close to a numerical majority.

While fusion was still legal in eight states in 1990, in practice it was only a live factor in one: New York. There, cross-endorsement by minor parties like the Liberal Party, the Conservative Party, and the American Labor Party had made the difference in many races, including those of Mayors Fiorella LaGuardia, John Lindsay, and Rudy Giuliani of New York City; Governors Herbert Lehman, Averill Harriman, and George Pataki; and Senators Robert Wagner, Lehman, and Al D'Amato. Even the presidential vote was affected: Franklin Roosevelt, John F. Kennedy, and Ronald Reagan would have lost New York state if not for substantial fusion votes.[24] But New York's third parties were scarcely vehicles for mass participation or social change. The leaders of the Liberal and Conservative parties had both let their grass roots wither, content to trade their line on the ballot for patronage favors from the major-party candidates they endorsed. The American Labor Party, undermined by McCarthyism and internal disputes, closed down in 1956. And the Right to Life Party, a new entrant in 1970, was a marginal factor due to its single-issue dogmatism.

Appropriately enough, it was the action of New York's Liberal Party, which endorsed Republican prosecutor Rudy Giuliani in his first 1989 race against black Democrat David Dinkins, that got the New Party ball rolling. Dinkins won that race narrowly, but the turncoat move by the Liberals—a shell of the party they started out as in the 1940s—prompted then Democratic Governor Mario Cuomo to tell Jan Pierce, then the head of the powerful Communications Workers of America union local, that he might be willing to ditch the Liberals and accept the nomination of a new, progressive party when he ran for reelection in 1990. That remark traveled from Pierce to Bob Master, one of his deputies, to Cantor, a childhood friend of Master's. Cantor contacted Rogers, whom he had gotten to know when they collaborated a few years earlier on a book that Cantor had coauthored on the breakdown of Cold War attitudes among American labor unions as they grappled with U.S. foreign policy toward Central America in the 1980s.[25]

"Danny called me up and said, 'You're the political scientist. If we were to start a party, what would it look like?'" Rogers recalled many years later. "I wrote him a fifteen-page memo, and soon we got together in New York, and eventually that memo became 'Party Time.'" Initially Cantor and Rogers were trying to respond to Cuomo's offer to accept a new party's endorsement. In New York, the only way for an upstart party to get a regular line on the ballot is to draw at least fifty thousand votes for its candidate for governor. Cuomo's interest in getting revenge on the Liberal Party seemed like a golden opportunity for a newcomer, since he was then still highly popular in the state. Rogers continued with his recollection: "We went to all these meetings, and people kept asking for more paper—what's the strategy, what are its principles, how are you going to clear the legal hurdles, where will you get the money." So they expanded their memo, ultimately reaching forty-four single-spaced pages. "I disappear back to Wisconsin, thinking this is one more wasted political project. Danny goes to the Xerox machine at Veatch [the foundation where he was then working] and sends out hundreds of copies. A little while later he calls me and says, 'You know, there's a lot of interest in this.'"[26]

What Cantor and Rogers produced was in some ways analogous to the Port Huron Statement, a 1962 manifesto written by Tom Hayden that launched the Students for a Democratic Society and a good chunk of the New Left. Only instead of crystallizing the consciousness of an entire generation, what these two co-conspirators were hoping to do was channel a kindred sensibility into a focused, and potentially quite powerful new political party that would stand to the left of the Democrats but manage to reach beyond stereotypical "limousine liberals" to rank-and-file unionists, underserved minorities, disaffected independents, and idealistic young people. And unlike the Port Huron Statement, which unselfconsciously expressed the views of privileged, middle-class radical students, the New Party's founders wanted their effort to be rooted in low-income communities.

"We propose a cross between the 'party within the party' strategy favored by some Democratic Party activists and the 'plague on both your houses' stance adopted by some critics of both major parties," they began. For convenience, and because they believed it was important that the party seem "fresh, simple, and, above all, not weighted down with ideological baggage and labels," they proposed to call their new experiment the "New Party." Their intended audience were progressives, defined as "people who are committed to democracy" as opposed to liberals, who they wrote, "don't believe working people have much capacity to govern their own affairs."[27] They envisioned a vehicle that would empower working people, that respected and supported unions, and that disdained liberals who just sought to decide what was best for others and administer their lives in a more compassionate fashion.[28] And they declared a commitment to using that vehicle to shift public policy in a better direction:

> We are tired and outraged by the corruptions of U.S. party politics and the public policies they produce. We are fed up with declining living standards, rising poverty and inequality, bad jobs and bad wages, racial and gender injustice, and the denial of a fulfilling life to too many working Americans and their children. We are fed up with exporting violence abroad, lying to citizens at home, and leaving political power to the rich and infamous.
>
> What do we want? We want to invest in ourselves: in health, education, housing, retraining, and physical infrastructure. We want an economy that is competitive, trade that is not ruinous to our standards of living, and an ordering of economic relations that doesn't wreck the environment on which we all depend. We want to reward hard work: with better wages, working conditions, and a say in the running of the economy. We want accountable government that works, and a political process that's not completely corrupted by big money interests. We want fair taxes, based on the ability to pay. We want to build a pluralist society where skin color doesn't determine life chances, gender doesn't determine labor market position, sexual preference doesn't lead to

ostracism, every child is housed and fed and decently educated, and the parents of each child are respected for doing the hardest work of all—raising and nurturing the children who will be our future. We want, in short, to take this country back. Government of the people, by the people, and for the people. It's that simple."[29]

In their plan, the New Party would be a membership organization, with dues ($36/year, $12 for people making less than $12,000, $2.40/year when part of an affiliating institution like a labor local), organized on a state-by-state basis, with local chapters, and with a dual focus on elections and on efforts to mobilize people around issues. Chapters would be chartered based on reaching specific membership targets, at which point the national office would repatriate 60 percent of the dues collected. Representation on decision-making bodies would be based proportionally on each chapter's size. The party would endorse progressives, either Democrats or those running on its own line, and it would also provide grass-roots muscle and training to the best ones.

There was no intention of trying to create the party by starting with a presidential campaign, or, as Rogers drily put it, referring to the Citizens Party fiasco, "we certainly didn't want to run a noncharismatic, well-meaning professor for president again to build a mass formation."[30] Nor was it to arise a la Reform, with a charismatic booster appearing on nationwide TV, or the Green way, with self-selecting individuals appointing themselves as party leaders. The New Party was built by design. Cantor and Rogers projected that the party would start small, aiming at the many nonpartisan races for low-level offices like school board, park commission, city council. Noting that most of the tens of thousands of elections held every two years in the United States were officially nonpartisan, they argued that the party didn't need a ballot line to start organizing an independent electoral force.

Ultimately, they hoped to become a factor in higher-level battles for state and congressional office through the astute use of their own line on the ballot—either to reward good Democrats and signal public support for progressive policies, or to communicate disapproval to bad Democrats who had gone too far to the right. Progressives, they argued, were trapped in an abusive relationship to the Democratic Party, giving it their votes, money, and time and getting little or nothing in return. The only way to change an abusive relationship, they said, was to be able to make a credible threat to leave it. And that's why a New Party was needed.

It all depended on fusion—or at least in their view it did. And so one of the first steps they took, with the critical help of Rogers's wife, Sarah Siskind, a class action litigator based in Madison, Wisconsin, was to go to court to try to pry open the nearly century-old ban on fusion in most states. Siskind had to find a minor party with ballot status that would nominate another party's candidate. That candidate, at the same time, had to be willing to accept the nomination. "There were so few parties with ballot status," Siskind recalled, "and those that had it, such as the Libertarians, would have been happy to have major parties fuse with them, but they were not interested in ever nominating a nonmember. It was tough."[31] She found her first case in her home state, when a minor party called the Labor-Farm Party tried to back Secretary of State Doug LaFollette, who was already a candidate in the Democratic primary. After the state board of elections refused to put LaFollette on Labor-Farm's line, the party sued, with Siskind's help. In *Swamp v. Kennedy*, they argued that the party's First Amendment right of free association had been violated, and that the state ban on fusion unfairly burdened minor parties.

There were good reasons to expect that the ban might fall. In 1986, the Supreme Court had held, in *Tashjian v. Republican Party of Connecticut*, that the state could not interfere with the right of a political party's members to freely associate with non-members, without a "compelling" state interest in doing so. The issue at stake was a Connecticut law that prevented nonmembers from voting in party primaries, but the principle went deeper. "Were the State . . . to provide that only Party members might be selected as the Party's chosen nominees for public office, such a prohibition of potential association would clearly infringe upon the rights of the Party's members under the First Amendment to organize with like-minded citizens in support of common political goals," wrote the majority of Justices Marshall, Blackmun, Brennan, Powell, and White. Even Justice Scalia, who dissented in that case, agreed that "The ability of the members of [a political p]arty to select their own candidate . . . unquestionably implicates an associational freedom." Three years later, in *Eu v. San Francisco County Democratic Central Committee*, the Court unanimously struck down a California law that prevented parties from making endorsements of candidates in advance of their primaries. "Freedom of association also encompasses a political party's decisions about the identity of, and the process for electing, its leaders," the opinion said.[32]

Language like this gave the New Party's founders hope as they went about getting their effort off the ground. Starting out in the spring of 1990, they focused on trying to bootstrap together a coalition in New York that could quickly gather twenty thousand signatures needed to put the party on the ballot, in order to take Governor Cuomo up on his offer to accept the party's cross-endorsement. In addition to Jan Pierce of the Communications Workers of America (CWA), they hoped to enlist progressive union leaders Dennis Rivera of Local 1199 (the hospital and health care workers union) and Stanley Hill of AFSCME's District 37 (the government workers union).[33] They also wanted prominent activists from African-American and Latino communities, as well as leading feminists and environmentalists. "We want something that will signal to several different sorts of progressive communities," they wrote in an early planning memo, "that this thing has backing, is 'for real,' and that they're not excluded from it."[34]

Things didn't jell as quickly as Cantor and Rogers hoped, however. While the theory of the New Party looked good on paper, it was far harder to get the actual players in the various movements they had targeted to agree to work together. In New York, it proved impossible to put the pieces of the puzzle together in time for the November 1990 election. "Many of these institutions are so big they have real power in the existing framework of affairs," said Bob Master, Cantor's friend at the CWA. "So they feel they don't need to work in coalitions where they will have to share power." Several years later, Master would play a big role in the New Party's greatest success, helping to launch and lead the Working Families Party. But in 1990, he was a skeptic. A decade earlier, at the age of twenty-five, Master had supported Barry Commoner's Citizens Party, as a response to Jimmy Carter's support for deregulation and his failure to pass labor law reform. But in 1980, when he joined with other labor firebrands like William Winpisinger of the Machinists union in walking out of the Democratic Convention, few people followed. "I remember saying, 'Carter or Reagan, what's the difference?' Then came the PATCO [Professional Air Traffic Controllers Organization] firings," in which President Reagan summarily fired thousands of air traffic controllers for going on strike. Master added, "It was also plain that African Americans were clearly wedded to the Democrats," another blow to the Citizens Party project. So when the New Party proposal surfaced a decade later, Master said, "I advocated baby steps."[35] Not only did key unions balk, Cuomo lost interest in the idea. Instead, he took the Liberal endorsement along with the Democrats, and went on to crush his two opponents (a Republican and a Conservative) by a huge margin. The New Party's New York launch was shelved.

Money was also a critical issue. Cantor's rough budget to get the party off the ground with an office, an executive director, administrative support, and two organizers came to $250,000. Any number of unions could have ponied up a good chunk of that amount from their own treasuries, but Cantor found no takers. So he came up with an ingenious method to convince individuals to invest in a project that had no track record and no clear prospects. "You know how penguins all line up at the water's edge?" Cantor would say, a sly grin on his face. "Then they wait until one slips in and shows that the water's fine. Well, we did the same thing with donors."[36] Cantor sought pledges from an array of people willing to become "penguins"—to put up $5,000 or more, but to not be obligated to donate that money until he had tallied at least $300,000 in waiting.

Ultimately, it took more than a year to raise that money, which came from a group of about five hundred donors. In January 1992 (a month before Ross Perot would explode on the national stage and Ralph Nader would fold up his "none-of-the-above" tents in New Hampshire), the train was finally leaving the station. The New Party opened an office in Bloomfield, New Jersey, and hired Sandy Morales Pope to be one of its national organizers, along with Cantor. Pope had previously been the executive director of the Coalition of Labor Union Women and was also a veteran activist in Teamsters for a Democratic Union. Elaine Bernard, a leader of Canada's New Democratic Party who was running the Harvard Trade Union Program, pitched in to hammer out a party constitution that would balance the voices of individual members and institutional affiliates.

A significant array of experienced organizers voiced their support for the project, including Gary Delgado, founder of the Center for Third World Organizing; Marie Wilson, executive director of the Ms. Foundation for Women; James Steele, a veteran organizer in New York's African-American community; Amy Newell, general secretary-treasurer of the United Electrical Workers; Mark Ritchie of the Institute for Agriculture and Trade Policy, a leader in the rising movement against corporate-managed trade; Denise O'Brien of the Iowa Farm Unity Coalition; Madeline Talbott and Wade Rathke, top organizers with ACORN; John O'Connor of the National Toxics Campaign; Barbara Dudley of Greenpeace; Steve Cobble, political director of the Rainbow Coalition; and Harriet Barlow, a founding co-chair of the Citizens Party. Prominent academics signed up, including Frances Fox Piven (a key leader of the voter registration movement that led to the passage of motor-voter), economist Juliet Schor, African-American scholar Manning Marable, historian Howard Zinn, and linguist Noam Chomsky. So did writers/activists Gloria Steinem, Jim Hightower, Todd Gitlin, and Barbara Ehrenreich. Philanthropist David Hunter, who had supported the Citizens Party experiment in 1980, opened doors to many potential funders that he knew from his days with the Stern Family Fund.

Eight years later, these people would divide, some quite vocally, over the Nader 2000 presidential campaign. But in 1992, the prospect of building an independent, progressive political party that wouldn't waste people's votes or act as a spoiler brought them together with a heady sense of possibility that maybe small-d democrats, labor organizers, environmentalists, feminists, family farmers, poor people, and students could somehow create something greater than the sum of their parts. That optimism about the New Party's prospects continued even after they lost their Wisconsin case in district court and in the Seventh Circuit Court of Appeals in 1991. The circuit court had refused to take the case, but New Party supporters were buoyed by the dissenting language of three conservative judges (Kenneth Ripple, Richard Posner, and Frank Easterbrook) on the panel, who wrote:

> The Supreme Court has recognized that the right of a party to nominate a candidate of its choice is a vital aspect of the party's role in our political structure. . . . When a minor-party nominates a candidate also nominated by a major party, it does not necessarily "leech onto" the larger party for support. Rather it may—and often does—offer the voters a very real and important choice and sends an important message to the candidate.

If a person standing as the candidate of a major party prevails only because of the votes cast for him or her as the candidate of a minor party, an important message has been sent by the voters to both the candidate and to the major party.

They added a final warning, with a degree of prescience that indicated what the New Party was really up against: "A state's interest in political stability does not give it the right to frustrate freely made political alliances simply to protect artificially the political status quo."[37]

Cantor and Rogers, ever the visionaries, was not deterred by the loss of the *Swamp* case. In an August 1992 memo to the party's "penguins," Cantor used a parable that Rogers frequently told, the story of the optimistic child. "At the optimist's birthday party, the birthday girl is shown into a large room in the center of which is a large pile of horse manure," he wrote. "The parents are worried, but the kid is beside herself with glee. 'Wow,' she exclaims, 'there's got to be a pony in here somewhere.'" He likened the High Court's rejection of the party's appeal as "essentially manure," but noted that the "pony" of the case was that it had garnered national attention and significant legal support from groups ranging from Ralph Nader's Public Citizen to the Liberal and Conservative parties of New York. Ultimately, he argued, the high court would take up the fusion issue if two or more circuit courts of appeal decided the issue different ways. And so, Sarah Siskind, the New Party's volunteer counsel, set about finding another ripe challenge to a state's ban on fusion.[38]

Getting Off the Ground

In the meantime the hard work of organizing was under way. The New Party was radically different from the Greens in that it generally supported Democrats or independent progressives (in nonpartisan races); it was extremely reluctant to "spoil" races. It was also a very sophisticated political operation. Though, anyone could join the party, and its leaders made a concerted effort to create a "brand" that people around the country would be attracted to, the party's organizers had no intention of spurring New Party chapters to crop up everywhere the same way Greens or Reform Party activists had tried to expand. Said Sandy Pope, one of the party's first national organizers, "We looked for groups that had some kind of a base in the community already and had some kind of infrastructure support, whether that was an office or staff people who could give a little time. Something to anchor the group. In some areas, it might have been an ACORN effort that already had an office and some leaders. In other places it was a union local."[39] This approach was eminently pragmatic. As Tom Hucker, an organizer who came on board in 1995 and eventually became one of its field directors, said, "Going from zero to one hundred members is very difficult anywhere, unless you have an organization that will turn its list over and have its president aggressively recruit members."[40]

The New Party brand would prove useful in attracting paying members among white, middle-class baby boomers with a social conscience, many of whom were impressed by the favorable notices the party received in outlets like *The Nation, In These Times*, the *Utne Reader* and National Public Radio. At the same time, a more integrated mix of lower-income working-class people were being drawn into the party's local chapters through door-to-door canvassing and house parties. Total membership grew from about two thousand in 1992,[41] to nearly five thousand in April of 1995,[42] to seventy-five hundred in March of 1996.[43] By October of 1997, that number hit 11,500, and two-thirds were current in their dues.[44] About one-fifth of the members were sustainers, people who gave $5 or more per month, usually by setting up an automatic monthly contribution on their credit card. This steadily growing pool allowed the party to hire full-time staff and interns, and to subsidize salaries for local organizers. "We may not have Perot's cash," Cantor said in explaining the party's efforts to grow, "but our ideas have greater appeal. If that means financing our own expansion, then that's what we're going to do."[45] By 1997, the party's annual budget was about $1 million.[46]

There was little that was random or self-selecting about where the New Party started to take root. In Little Rock, Arkansas, and Chicago, chapters were launched by organizers connected to ACORN; that group's one hundred thousand member households had decided they needed a way to engage in electoral politics that was larger than their own political action committees. Wade Rathke, ACORN's lead national organizer, was in on the founding discussions that led to the New Party, and the group's political director, Zach Polett, also came to play a big role in guiding New Party field organizing for the party in both of those cities. In the working-class city of Missoula, Montana, and the majority-black D.C. suburbs of Montgomery County, Maryland, local labor leaders took the lead.[47] In some cases, the party's national organizers bonded with already existing or emerging local progressive coalitions. In Wisconsin, for example, their model matched the goals of a group called Progressive Milwaukee, made up of activists from labor, the African-American community, women's groups, and students and environmental organizations, which had just come together to support five independent candidates for the county board, four of whom won their races.[48]

For the most part, the party strove to build itself with a multiracial, working-class base and labor union support from the start.[49] As Peter Shapiro, its first Maryland organizer, put it, "we knew if the New Party started in Takoma Park," a Washington, D.C., suburb filled with white progressives that was known for its nuclear-free zone and other leftist pieties, "it would end there."[50] They believed, with the evidence of experience, that groups that start out with an all-white, middle-class base almost never integrate themselves. Only rarely did a New Party chapter get formed around a primary base of middle-class whites and progressive academics, as occurred in the suburbs of Nassau County, Long Island. And even there the group's leaders made sure to focus their efforts on the majority-black town of Hempstead. "It's hard to get invited to dinner when the first course has already been served," said Becky Glass, an early supporter who is now the director of the Midwest States Center, a regional center that works to advance the growth and effectiveness of multi-issue coalitions.[51]

In Dane County, Wisconsin, the home of the progressive university town of Madison, the party couldn't resist the chance to unite local units of the Rainbow Coalition, the National Organization for Women, the Labor-Farm Party, and the Greens. Cantor later said that Dane was far from the model they wanted others to copy. "It's like saying Arcata," an isolated northern California college town where the Green Party controlled city hall from 1996 to 1998, "tells you how to organize the Greens elsewhere."[52] That may have been true, from the point of view of the party's national leadership. But the New Party *idea* was potent enough to draw in its own true believers—people who fervently wanted to build a sensible, progressive counterforce that would start local, choose its battles with care, and in one or two decades stand poised to run and elect its own candidates for high office. Though Cantor and Rogers believed legalizing fusion was the only way the party could ever reach that stage, many of the people they attracted believed that "building a new majority from the ground up"—one of the party's slogans—was the real goal, regardless of what happened in the courts.

Even though the New Party arose at the same time as the early third-party organizing among activists in the Perot movement, there was almost no crossover between the two efforts. Cantor did attend one of the first planning meetings of the Federation of Independent Parties in Kansas City in 1993, but he was put off by signs that the emerging Patriot Party would be Lenora Fulani's new home. "We were very clear that if [Fulani's] New Alliance Party was involved, we weren't," he told me in the spring of 1994. He and Rogers later made a quiet trip to Dallas to meet with Perot, Russ Verney, and Clay Mulford, whom they hoped to persuade to support their effort to revive fusion. But they got little interest. Verney did tease Rogers, praising him for the New Party's political program and taunting him at the same time. "You've got the analysis," Verney told Rogers. "The problem, Joel, is that I have a couple of billion dollars and you don't have a dime." Not only did the New Party and Perot movement fail to click at the leadership level, their activists and members came from different social classes and age groups and had very little interaction at the grass roots. Occasionally, Cantor would muse about trying to take over a Reform Party chapter somewhere. But he and his colleagues always saw more pitfalls than potential in such a conceptual leap.[53]

Right from the start, New Party chapters began fielding or endorsing candidates for office. By the spring of 1993, twenty of twenty-eight people they backed in three states

(Arkansas, Missouri, and Wisconsin) had won their races for city council, county commission, county judge, and the like. Two early losses in freeholder races in Essex County, New Jersey, where the district was almost as big as that of a member of Congress, taught them to stick to smaller jurisdictions. "We shot too high there," said Pope.[54] Cantor concurred, saying, "We could never get institutional support or geographic focus in New Jersey. In a sense [the freeholder races were] our most Green-style effort (organizing-wise, not base-wise, as both our candidates were black), and was one of the experiences that galvanized our views on how to build something durable."[55] Their explicit model was the Christian Coalition, which had also built itself by quietly concentrating on local races rather than being tempted by flashy runs for higher office. Cantor could point to organizing committees in a dozen states, and highlighted prospects in places ranging from the Little Rock, Arkansas, school board and the Missoula, Montana, city council, to a potential fusion ticket with Democrat David Dinkins, mayor of New York City. "Mistakes will be (and have been) made," he told supporters, "but the overall feeling is one of steady progress."[56]

One place where the party stumbled early was, again, New York. Here, despite their own insistence on growing slowly, developing a genuine base and acting in a way accountable to that membership, the party's leaders tried to move too fast. Attracted by the possibility of making a big splash, they entered into an alliance in early 1993 with the remnants of the Majority Coalition for a New New York, a labor-community effort primarily backed by Dennis Rivera's powerful Local 1199 union, a close ally of Mayor Dinkins. Dinkins had presided over years of budget austerity and an expansion of the city's police and jails program. His Republican opponent, Rudy Giuliani, augured worse. But to many new members of the New Party in New York, the whole project contradicted the party's social democratic goals *and* its promise to be driven from the bottom up. Tom Leighton, then a dues-paying member of both the Majority Coalition and the New Party, reported that there was no consultation with members prior to the merger.[57]

Though the New Party's contemplated cross-endorsement of Dinkins never occurred, the episode also earned the party a mixed reputation among some local activists and a scolding from local progressive writer Doug Henwood in his *Left Business Observer* newsletter.[58] In retrospect, Cantor admitted, "It definitely caused an internal conflict here and there." But he argued that the party needed to be open to opportunities to work with local players with a real base. "It's pretty hard to build a party without institutional support, even if that brings preexisting ties and political baggage." As for not consulting local members, Cantor said, "There wasn't much of an organized base then in New York, except a little bit in Brooklyn. There were members, but there wasn't a structure for making decisions."[59] Clearly it was going to be difficult to build a party uniting individual progressives, who tended to be well educated, independent, and argumentative, with institutional players like unions who tended to play politics in a more pragmatic and less open manner.

But overall, their targeting worked well. By the spring of 1994, New Party–backed candidates had racked up 10 more wins (out of 17 races);[60] a year later they had won an additional 47 out of 70 for a total batting average of 77 out of 115.[61] By the fall of 1995, they had picked up six more, out of seven, winning a working majority on the Missoula and Madison city councils, a similar majority on the Little Rock school board, and electing their first mayor, African-American David Harrington, in Bladensburg, Maryland. They also had their first state-certified ballot line in Wisconsin's New Progressive Party.[62] Perhaps their biggest win was in Chicago, where a New Party coalition powered by the local ACORN chapter and members of the Service Employees Local 880 (itself an offshoot of ACORN's United Labor Unions) went up against the Democratic Party machine of Mayor Richard Daley and beat an entrenched incumbent.

These places were all showing what an independent political organization with a real dues-paying membership base and engaged institutional allies could achieve in local politics under certain conditions. Either elections had to be nonpartisan, where there were no party labels on the ballot and candidates simply qualified by petitioning or paying a fee. Or, the locale had to be under de facto one-party domination. Either way, "spoiling" was not a problem in these settings, though New Party activists were still up against an entrenched power structure. In Little Rock, they blocked efforts to privatize public services, defeated an initiative to raise sales taxes to build jails, fought sprawl, and passed a campaign finance reform measure; in St. Paul they galvanized opposition to public subsidies for a sports stadium; in Chicago, Milwaukee, Missoula, Dane County, and the Twin Cities, they helped spearhead successful campaigns to raise the minimum wage to a living wage for employees of companies receiving large public contracts. Indeed, as a result of these campaigns the New Party can claim a share of the credit for injecting the term "living wage" into the national discourse.

Some of their success was rooted in a shrewd understanding of how easy it might be to win local races in a time of lowered political expectations and minuscule voter turnouts. Cantor called it his "1-percent rule": 'Can you sign up 1 percent of the registered voters in a district?" One hundred members out of ten thousand voters usually yielded a core group of about thirty activists, with the rest being more or less passive supporters and sources of money. "We've found each activist can usually deliver around thirty votes, through their own networks and efforts. That gets you about one thousand votes. In a setting where only 20 percent vote, that's close to enough to win," he said. In effect, this was the mirror image (in miniature) of the Christian Coalition's strategy for building a local power base, except the New Party was aiming to knit together minorities, working-class whites, young people, women, and progressive suburbanites in defense of public programs and a broader definition of the common good.

This is not to say that the New Party model was a perfect blend of issue work and electoral campaigns. Compared to the Greens, who were perhaps too loose in their style and open to almost anyone, the New Party was a tightly wound watch. Even in the chapters that had no ACORN presence, there was pressure from the national office to conform to that group's intensive system of neighborhood organizing, with door-to-door canvassers who were expected to raise a good part of their own salaries. The national office also asked a great deal of its organizers, who were often very young. They were expected to do many difficult things at once: to go to colleges and middle-class areas and get people there to join, preferably as sustainers, and at the same time to do the real organizing of a base in poorer black and brown neighborhoods, and to go to labor unions to get money to do living wage campaigns, and to also recruit and support candidates for local office.

Mixed Results in Milwaukee

Tammy Johnson, a twenty-four-year-old African-American organizer who was hired in 1994 by Progressive Milwaukee after it affiliated with the New Party, initially appreciated the challenge of doing both social justice organizing and electoral work. "What attracted me to the New Party was you weren't just working the regular voter list," she recalled. "With the issue work, you were trying to reach out and mobilize new people. The Democrats weren't doing that." But Johnson, now a national organizer with the Applied Research Center in Oakland, experienced some of the toughest ups and downs of any New Party organizer. At its height, the Milwaukee New Party had three hundred dues-paying members, including one hundred sustainers, and a total of one thousand people on its mailing list. In 1995, the chapter mobilized hard behind Rose Daitsman, a homegrown candidate for school board who promised to fight city hall's plans for privatizing public education. The mayor put his entire machine behind her opponent, the Chamber of Commerce and local editorialists weighed in, and still Daitsman nearly pulled off an upset, losing with 49 percent of the vote to her opponent's 51 percent, fewer than two thousand votes citywide. The Milwaukee New Party had raised $30,000 in support of Daitsman and fielded about 130 volunteers on Election Day. Even though they lost, the feisty group taught the local power structure they were a new force to contend with. The chapter went on to elect two state senators and an assemblyman, and to successfully pressure the city council to pass one of the first "living wage" ordnances, a modest measure requiring all city contractors to pay their employees at least $6.05 an hour.

But the Milwaukee New Party disbanded three years later. The reasons given by Johnson, who was there from the beginning to the end, are revealing. First, it was hard to hold together their coalition of labor activists, black and Latino neighborhood organizers, gays and lesbians, and white progressives. "Progressive Milwaukee came out of some labor leaders, but not labor institutionally," Johnson said. Bruce Colburn [the secretary-treasurer of the Milwaukee County Labor Council] and John Goldstein [the head of the Amalgamated Transit Union local] gave their names and personal clout, but we never got a lot of institutional buy-in from labor. We could go into a labor council and talk to the head, but that didn't mean we walked out with anything." At the same time, other parts of the community, like black and Latino leadership, were never fully knitted into the coalition. "There were black and Latino leaders involved in the founding of Progressive Milwaukee," she said. "But I think the politics changed. The mayor's office was quite successful in co-opting people from those communities, and as new leaders came up they wanted to stand on their own rather than join a coalition." When Colburn, a son of the working class who played a big role in motivating and holding together the chapter's differing constituencies, stepped aside to become deputy director of the AFL-CIO's Midwest region, the chapter lost its dominant personality and a lot of its glue. Progressive Milwaukee "never really developed a solid organizational infrastructure," concluded Johnson.[63]

The ACORN style of intensive door-to-door canvassing to sign up members also wasn't appropriate to Milwaukee culture, said Johnson. "At that time in Milwaukee, people had gotten very cynical about folks going door to door selling their wares," she recalled. "ACORN hadn't succeeded much there after years of trying. There had been too many groups saying, 'If you give us $5, we'll save the world.' People were cynical about that." In general, she found it exceedingly difficult to develop a supportive base of volunteer labor, something she attributed in part to the fact that the local university was made up primarily of working students, who didn't have the extra spare time one might find among students at a more elite institution of higher education. "Our volunteer base got energized around elections and sometimes issues. We never figured out how to make that an ongoing part of the organization. We never found someone to be the treasurer, for example. So, I found myself doing a lot of administrative work on top of everything else. This is not the 1960s with a lot of stay-at-home moms who can volunteer their time," she said, referring to how hard it was to sustain her own organization. "And college students are working two jobs so they don't have time either. We never got over that hurdle."

Johnson found herself in growing conflict with the national New Party office, which pushed its organizers hard to produce results and was trying to expand the party rapidly in the mid-1990s. "New Party leaders wanted us very much to use the ACORN model to build the base, where the question was 'Did you meet your quota today?' And we said that wouldn't work." Money was a related battleground. "National was saying, 'You can't use national as a bank,'" Johnson recalled. Some union locals gave money to the chapter to do living wage organizing and for support with other labor actions. But it was never enough to hire a second organizer.

"The real core issue with the [national] staff was that they wanted to expand," said Johnson. "They looked at their database and saw that they had 200 members in Denver and said we should start a chapter there." Indeed, the New Party launched new units in Denver and St. Louis in 1996, though the reason for targeting those cities was more complicated. Both had ACORN chapters and SEIU (Service Employees International Union) locals that were interested in backing a New Party effort, and the party had raised some money from donors that was specifically earmarked for expansion. In any event, neither of these New Party branches still exist. "Meanwhile in Missoula," recalled Johnson, "the chapter once took out a loan to pay its organizer. I remember one Christmas not getting my paycheck. They would kick it back to the locals and say they weren't pulling their full weight. What got to me was that they were adding all this new staff, starting five to ten new chapters, and the existing chapters weren't being taken care of. Like being one child in ten, and Momma wants to have ten more, and you're not eating three squares a day."[64]

Johnson talked with fellow New Party organizers around the country and started agitating for better working conditions. "In 1995–96, I was the head of an effort to try to unionize the New Party organizers. It was about respect, not being respected. It was about not getting paid some paychecks, or getting paid late. It was about not being heard when we said this is what's happening in our chapter and what our leaders are saying, and you're not hearing and putting me in an uncomfortable position. I said we're not going to run a living wage campaign unless our organizer is getting paid a living wage. And the unions that were part of my chapter stood up for me." Johnson started at $20,000 a year and was being paid $24,000 when she left three years later. Most other organizers were paid less, $15,000 to $17,000. In general, the national office subsidized its local organizers to the tune of $1,000 per month, poverty wages that were typical pay for ACORN or other groups doing grass-roots organizing. Any salary above that, or benefits, came from the local chapter. Unfortunately, the party couldn't pay a good enough salary to retain people for the long term, even if that was preferable to churning through youthful, idealistic recruits. And most of the organizers apparently accepted that reality. Johnson's effort eventually died a quiet death.[65]

Despite the difficulties, Johnson still thought the New Party effort made a valuable contribution to Milwaukee that went beyond its electoral victories and living-wage fight. "There are not many places to cut your teeth doing progressive electoral work. The New Party created that and did a big service in doing so," she said. "We showed a lot of people how to get some political power, who learned some tricks of the trade of running elections. It was a good training ground for people, including me."[66]

Challenging the Machine in Chicago

Even when a chapter had a solid infrastructure, there was also an ebb and flow to New Party organizing. In Chicago, home of one of the last great corrupt political machines, the party celebrated a half-dozen important victories and mourned an equal number of tough defeats over a five-year period.[67] The chapter there was kicked off in the fall of 1994 by Mahaley Somerville, a septuagenarian ACORN organizer, who rallied residents of Lawndale, a poor neighborhood on Chicago's west side. Plantation politics was the rule, where the white-dominated Democratic party machine ruled through patronage and voter intimidation. Lawndale was pocked by dozens of empty lots that had been turned into illegal dump sites by city contractors, which the area's representative on the city council, alderman Jesse Miller, was doing little to fix. At a "Dump the dumps" meeting organized by ACORN, Miller walked in, and Somerville quickly got residents chanting, "Dump Miller, Dump Miller." The connection between issue-based work—cleaning up the vacant lots—and electoral action was made clear to hundreds of onlookers. "Lady, you better sit down before you have a stroke," Miller told Somerville. "Not until I unseat you," she shot back. And that became the first New Party campaign in the city. Their candidate, a former social worker named Michael Chandler, was the only one to beat an incumbent in the city's aldermanic elections the next spring. Suddenly the New Party was on the map.

Fresh from this victory, some New Party chapter members, led by Ted Thomas, an African American who was the president of Chicago ACORN, went to a meeting of the Twenty-ninth Ward People's Assembly, the local Democratic Party organization tied to Danny Davis. Davis was a county commissioner who had been on the city council when Harold Washington was mayor, during that brief period when the regular Democratic machine had been upended. Now, Davis saw kindred spirits in the New Party and joined up. A few days later, Representative Cardiss Collins announced she was retiring. Davis quickly announced his candidacy, and when the Democratic primary was held, he did better in the Twenty-fourth Ward, where the New Party had already built a base, than anywhere else in the city. Soon, Davis was on his way to Congress (and, reflecting their close ties, the Davis organization and the New Party started sharing membership lists and fund-raising efforts).

That year, the Chicago New Party also got involved in supporting a progressive running for state representative on the northwest side of the city, Willie Delgado. His district was of interest not only because it connected Puerto Rican and Mexican-American communities with an integrated neighborhood called Logan Square, where the party already gained some members from among sympathetic activist types. Delgado was also chief of staff to state Senator Miguel del Valle, one of the most dynamic progressives in the state legislature and someone the party wanted to align itself with. The district was part of U.S. Representative Luis Gutierrez's base, another important Latino progressive. Delgado lost by four hundred votes, in part because the Democratic machine put another person named Delgado on the ballot in the primary to confuse voters. But the chapter gained members from supporting his race, and they learned valuable get-out-the-vote skills that would come in handy.

Chicago's incestuous machine politics provided the New Party with many opportunities to advance its efforts. "We don't need term limits here," joked Jonathan Green, the party's young but savvy chief organizer, "since everyone seems to get indicted within ten years of getting elected. It's almost automatic." An FBI sting operation created an opening on the city council in early 1997, but the party learned a tough lesson in that race. "We got clobbered," said Green. "There were only two races in the whole city, and the mayor put everything he had into ours. Anyone who was black who worked for the city was in our district that day." More than four hundred "regular Democrats" were out on Election Day in support of Daley's candidate, and the New Party's man got just 17 percent.

The party was also clashing with Mayor Daley on what was becoming one of its signature issues, the living wage. Daley came out against the proposal in the spring of 1996, which for the New Party organizers was almost manna from heaven in terms of the opportunities that created for mobilizing people. "Going to city council meetings and hearings and holding accountability sessions with aldermen really became part of our culture," Green recalled. And after their members were literally locked out of the council chambers on July 30, 1997, when it voted down the living-wage measure— "you've got to picture all these older black women stuck in the hallways while guys in suits get carded in," Green said—the New Party had a new slogan and campaign: "Payback Time in '99."

What was intriguing about the work the New Party was doing in Chicago was that it didn't require the use of fusion at all. It did take a lot of shoe leather and strategic thinking about issues and attentiveness to local community needs and careful balancing of local coalition supporters. But because Chicago was a one-party town where all the significant political battles happened inside the Democratic Party primaries, party labels mattered far less than real organization. For many of the players who got involved there—ACORN, Local 880, Representatives Davis and Gutierrez, state Senator Del Valle, the New Party was a vehicle that allowed them to join together in something that was larger than themselves in fighting battles against a common and much bigger adversary. This was a model that would continue to bear fruit for the party in Chicago and elsewhere. But if the New Party was going to truly shake up America, and "rock the Congress," as its co-founder Joel Rogers once projected, its top leaders and funders still felt it was going to need the ability to run in higher-level races using its fusion strategy. This is because they wanted to draw in real muscle from the union movement, and the only way most major unions would even consider a third-party option was if it wasn't going to spoil races.

Their Day in Court

New Party hopes for an end to the ban on fusion leaped upward after the U.S. Court of Appeals for the Eighth Circuit ruled in the party's favor on January 5, 1996. Two years earlier, incumbent state Representative Andy Dawkins of Minnesota had accepted the endorsement of the Twin Cities Area New Party as its candidate for the November 1994 election. He was already the candidate of the Democratic-Farmer-Labor Party, but that party did not object to the New Party's cross-endorsement. As expected, the secretary of state's office rejected the New Party's nomination papers. The party lost its initial lawsuit in district court, but won a solid victory on appeal. The justices on the appeals court were impressed by the U.S. Supreme Court's earlier rulings in *Eu v. San Francisco* and *Tashjian v. Republican Party of Connecticut*, and they understood precisely how a ban on fusion burdened the New Party's core associational rights. "By foreclosing a consensual multiple party nomination, Minnesota's statutes force the New Party to make a no-win choice," they wrote. "New Party members must either cast their votes for candidates with no realistic chance of winning; defect from their party and vote for a major party candidate who does; or decline to vote at all." The state of Minnesota had argued that the ban was needed to prevent splintering of the major parties, but the appeal court was not swayed. "Rather than jeopardizing the integrity of the election system, consensual multiple party nomination may invigorate it by fostering more competition, participation and representation in American politics," they responded.[68]

Minnesota appealed, and within just a few months, the Supreme Court agreed to take the case. The New Party had hoped to use the court of appeals ruling to buttress similar lawsuits in other states, in order to gain greater support for its position and take short-term advantage of the immediate unbanning of fusion in the seven states covered by the Eighth Circuit. Instead, events were moving somewhat faster than expected. But even as they prepared for oral arguments, scheduled for December of 1996, the party's leaders were anticipating a national victory. Coupled with encouraging signs coming from an AFL-CIO invigorated by the new leadership of John Sweeney, they allowed themselves to dream how quickly things could begin to move. Their newsletter told members, "Imagine a scenario in which sensible progressive parties, rooted in but not limited to Central Labor Councils, are cross-endorsing candidates in the 1998 state legislative and Congressional races on a platform of 'living wages,' starting-gate equality for children, and radical campaign finance reform." Central Labor Councils were the hub of municipal labor power in dozens of cities, and New Party leaders were working hard to convince the AFL to graft the party's model of community-labor electoral coalitions onto that base, far more substantial than anything they had attained on their own. "Would [such a scenario] be earthshaking?" they asked their members. "No. Would it be a huge improvement over the current debased political debate? Of course."[69]

"I've been saying to labor, women's groups and civil rights groups for the last several months, 'You don't have to be a third party freak to think this is a good thing,'" Rogers told the *National Law Journal* a week before the case was heard in Washington. "We could all get together, have a simple program and create electoral formations in a couple dozen states almost overnight. We would say we're going to endorse people based on certain values. Overnight, it would establish a new political discussion."[70] Actually things weren't quite that simple, since third parties seeking to take advantage of fusion would still have to deal with restrictive ballot-access laws. They also needed to make sure that states counted their votes separately, as was the practice in New York, to ensure they got as much credit as possible for their efforts.[71] Still, the New Party train was picking up speed. Cantor had two dozen people on staff, and some $12,000 a month was coming in from sustainers. "Any night of the week," he boasted, "there's a New Party meeting going on somewhere in the country. No other third party can say that."[72]

Some of the nation's sharpest political journalists were beginning to pick up the scent of a major story. A good number of mainstream papers sent reporters to a press briefing the party held the day before oral arguments. Their prize attraction was Harvard law professor Laurence Tribe, a liberal powerhouse who had an unsurpassed batting average in his many appearances before the high court. David Broder, a top reporter and columnist at the *Washington Post*, had many questions. What's the value of enhancing the power of organized minorities? What if this stimulates the creation of a Christian Coalition party in fusion with the Republicans? Professor Tribe replied that more democracy was a good thing. Was there any evidence that fusion led to increased turnout? Broder asked. No, Tribe answered, but there was plenty of evidence that turnout dropped dramatically in the Midwest when fusion was banned. Indeed, voter turnout throughout the nineteenth century was much higher than anytime in the twentieth century.

The morning of oral arguments was sunny but cold. A brisk wind blew across the steps of the Supreme Court building. Inside the court's chambers it was warm and quiet, though the room was packed. The high ceilings, plush red velvet curtains, and marble pillars all communicated order and seriousness, an aura enhanced by the justices' long-standing refusal to allow the use of any recording devices or TV cameras inside their lair. The need for mystery became disconcertingly clear to me as I listened to nine very human and fallible individuals pontificate, some with learned and barbed questions, and others whose remarks suggested they had not bothered to read the two sides' briefs beforehand. Justice Clarence Thomas never said a word. It was a very odd feeling, to see so much power concentrated in a few people who were essentially accountable to no one but history.

Minnesota's assistant solicitor general, Richard Slowes, went first.[73] Seconds into his opening remarks about the state's interest in preventing voter confusion, he was interrupted by several justices asking their own questions, as is their prerogative. Most of their queries were technical, dealing with the mechanics of counting two lines of votes for the same candidate. Early on Justices Stevens, Ginsburg, and Souter all made clear that they thought Minnesota's argument had little merit. "You'd have to be pretty dense to be confused on this one," Justice Stevens said. Justice Ginsburg added, in a reference to her own native New York, "Are we supposed to erase from our minds that there is at least one state that has had a lot of experience with fusion candidates? There's no large confusion, there's no major problem." ("New Yorkers are smarter," Justice Scalia interrupted, to general laughter.)

When Justice Stevens pressed Slowes to explain what the state's "preeminent interest" was, the lawyer had little to add beyond avoiding voter confusion. Justice Ginsburg then interjected, "Is that not offset by voter information? When voters see someone not only on the line of a major party but also a minor party line, that is telling voters more about that candidate. Is that irrelevant?" Slowes meekly answered, "It's not irrelevant, but that kind of communicative use of the ballot is not constitutionally compelled." And when he suggested that fusion would create a situation ripe for ballot manipulation, where candidates could set up bogus minor parties to get their name on the ballot more than once, as the "No New Taxes" candidate or the "Tough on Crime" candidate, Justice Stevens responded that such parties would have to meet all the rules for getting on the ballot, and they would be splintering their own base. "Has this ever happened?" he asked, sure that Slowes's argument made little sense.

The hearing seemed to be going well for the New Party. And it only got better when Justice Souter, a nominee of President Bush, addressed Slowes after he argued that a ban on fusion would prevent "excessive factionalism," another interest the state might have in preventing the practice. "Without the benefit of history, I could listen to your arguments," Souter told him. "The trouble that I have in giving any kind of deference that way, however, is the history." Souter had obviously read the amici curiae from the Republican National Committee;[74] the Conservative and Liberal Parties of New York; the Reform Party; the ACLU; Brennan Center for Justice; and People for the American Way; and a group of twelve university professors, all in support of the New Party. "The reason we have these antifusion laws in so many states was basically a very widespread effort simply to maintain the relative hegemony of the two parties, the Democrats and Republicans. They weren't worried about voter confusion. They didn't want new parties," Souter declared. "Is it unfair to bear that history in mind?"[75] Slowes was taken aback. "With respect," he began slowly, "yes, I think it is unfair for you to look back that many years, particularly because this court has said that a legitimate constitutional state statute will not be struck down on allegations of improper motive. There's nothing in the record to suggest what the Minnesota legislature was thinking . . ." Suddenly Justice Scalia, the court's leading conservative, jumped in, obviously tired of listening to Slowes muff the case.

"You would concede the major point, would you, that there is something wrong about the state establishing its electoral machinery in such fashion as to facilitate and encourage a two-party system as opposed to proportional voting, for example?" Scalia growled. "Is there anything wrong with that, as long as you don't ban third parties? If that were the value it would not necessarily be constitutional." This was a bad sign for the New Party. At no point in its history had the High Court ever claimed that, nor did the Constitution ever even refer to political parties. According to Richard Winger, the editor of *Ballot Access News*, who was sitting beside me during the hearing, the term "two-party system" had never been used in any Supreme Court decision dealing with ballot access. Indeed, the very idea that the two major parties could rig the ballot-access laws to protect a two-party system had been rejected in *William v. Rhodes*, a 1968 ruling prompted by George Wallace's third-party presidential bid that overturned Ohio's ridiculously difficult ballot-access law.[76]

Worse yet, Justice Breyer then chimed in to second Scalia. "What am I supposed to do legally if I think that is the whole point [of banning fusion]—a two-party system and the advantages it entails? I think this represents a judgment of the legislature." Slowes answered by saying that states could do that, as long as they didn't close the door to other parties. He finished by depicting a slippery slope. "Our position is that the argument the respondent is making would really take you into all of those areas . . . of calling for multimember districts, proportional representation, which would certainly help minor parties, even nonpartisan ballots. What it comes down are these are issues of political engineering," he warned, citing an arena that the Supreme Court has traditionally tried to leave to the legislative branch. Justice Stevens made one last remark meant to push the argument in a better direction. "I don't know why [states] couldn't ban third parties altogether, by this logic," he suggested, implying that Scalia was taking the Court in a direction fundamentally at odds with the First Amendment. But in just a half-hour, it had become clear that the New Party's case was no slam dunk.

Then it was Professor Tribe's turn. Deferring to his standing as one of the nation's top constitutional scholars, the justices gave him about two minutes to speak before diving in. He opened by saying that the case wasn't about political engineering, and joking that New Yorkers clearly weren't confused by their multiparty system, nor were they smarter than Minnesotans. (Rehnquist interjected that "New Yorkers like confusion.") He then tried to ground his argument in core First Amendment values. "The ban on consensual fusion literally infringes on the right of people to get together and pick their standard-bearer and get him on the ballot." He argued that Minnesota misunderstood this interest by arguing that new parties were supposed to only introduce new faces, not support major-party figures—even if that was crucial to their ability to build support for their concerns. He also pointed out that the state was also objecting to minor parties that might stand for single issues, like cutting taxes, another infringement on free speech. He was trying to warn them that the state should stay neutral in how it regulated politics. But the court's conservative justices did not seem very impressed with that concern.

"It's not possible to have a politically neutral electoral system, it seems to me. You're always making judgments that are either going to favor larger parties or smaller parties." Justice Scalia asked, a few minutes into Tribe's turn. "Why is it necessary for the state to draw up a balloting system that does not disfavor small parties? I think they can do it," he added. Tribe said states couldn't constitutionally go out of their way to hurt third parties and that the state had to have "plain vanilla" reasons, politically neutral ones, for coming up with a system that hurt smaller parties. Justice Scalia came back at him a minute later, saying, "I think it's pretty plain vanilla to say I like the two-party system and this fosters the two-party system." Justice Breyer seemed to concur, noting that there were lots of other electoral rules, like the winner-take-all system and single-member districts, that were also unfair to third parties. "There are good arguments for and against such things. Proportional representation in many parties allows parties to grow more quickly and is a better representation of people's views. On the other hand, two parties, which is a much worse [form of] representation, and interferes with people's ability to choose what they want, has the advantage that we know whom to hold responsible for good or bad government. . . . How can I say that the state has no right in these kinds of things to decide between either of those two models of democratic representation?"

Tribe then tried to separate fusion from other electoral reforms, arguing with a somewhat tortured analogy. "I would urge a distinction between the basic architecture of the system—the decision to have single-member rather than multimember districts, ruling out proportional representation . . . deciding where to draw district lines, how a candidate gets on the ballot, [and decisions made] once the building has been designed, the basic architecture has been set." At that point, Tribe was intimating, the state should not take aim at the content of political alliances. He hadn't finished his disquisition before Justice Scalia stopped him. "Why can't you design the building to favor a two-party system?" He disparaged New York, claiming, inaccurately, that it had a full-fledged three-party system thanks to fusion. In fact, the third-largest party in New York, the Conservatives, had only 1.5 percent of the total of registered voters in the state. He and Tribe were locked in conflict. "The state cannot simply force herd everybody onto the left or right side of the road," Tribe replied. Clearly Scalia disagreed. "The New Party is entitled to have a candidate, just not any particular candidate," he stated, not caring that this infringed on the party's right of association.

Justice Breyer, a potential swing vote, was still searching for a principle around which to organize his response to the case. In his view, the right to fuse with another party's candidate was not that important, in the larger scheme of other elements of electoral design, in affecting the strength or weakness of both major and minor parties. "What is the touchstone here?" he interjected. Tribe's answer returned to the First Amendment. "This [the fusion ban] tells people what the substance of their consensual political alliance can be" and is a violation of the First Amendment, he urged.

The tipping point came when Chief Justice Rehnquist broke in. Some of his earlier questions had to do with how unbanning fusion might affect states that had open primaries, and similar arcana. Now he noted that states that prohibited write-in voting would also be affected if fusion was allowed, since a new party might want to rally support for a candidate it cross-endorsed through that method, too. "If we rule for you," Rehnquist declared, "it would result in quite sweeping changes in a lot of states." (Imagine Chief Justice Earl Warren saying that when faced with the *Brown v. Board of Education* school desegregation case.) Tribe immediately tried to downplay that concern, suggesting that there were pluses and minuses to taking the nomination of a minor party. But by his tone alone, Rehnquist—a onetime supporter and adviser to right-wing Republican presidential candidate Barry Goldwater, and a man who had tried to intimidate minority voters physically when they went to the polls in Arizona in the late 1960s—was hinting where the Court was headed. Four justices—Rehnquist, Scalia, O'Connor, and Thomas—were undoubtedly lined up against the New Party. Only Souter, Ginsburg, and Stevens seemed strongly on the party's side. Breyer and Kennedy were in the middle, and both had indicated sympathy with both the state's argument about voter confusion and Scalia and Rehnquist's interest in propping up the two-party system. It didn't look good.

Afterward, on the courthouse steps, New Party co-founders Cantor and Rogers embraced Harriet Barlow, one of their earliest and most dogged backers. Other party leaders from nearby Maryland were there too. And everyone looked shaken. Professor Jamin Raskin, of American University Law School, who was a fan of Tribe's and himself a rising expert in the field of election law, said he would have taken a different tack. "The Court led him down the road of political science. I would have taken the two-party system on directly and insisted that the Constitution does not allow the establishment of a two-party system, much less two specific parties." Raskin also worried that the argument had been too abstract. "When you take on the rights of third parties, there should be a sense of indignation and injustice," he told me. Richard Winger noted that Tribe came prepared to rebut the state of Minnesota's brief, regarding the dangers of voter confusion, but the judges weren't really interested in that. Instead, they pressed him to explain why a state couldn't simply squelch smaller parties, a topic that he seemed ill prepared for.

An hour later, at an informal lunch in Tribe's suite at the Watergate, no one was openly second-guessing. Tribe padded through the apartment in slippers, telling people that he never jumped to conclusions based on the justices' comments during oral argument. This was sage advice. But Rogers and Cantor were both glum. Rogers was in a very cynical frame of mind. "Why don't they just simplify things and pass two laws," he asked me bitterly, "that there only be two parties, the Democrats and the Republicans, and that money should speak louder than votes?"[77] Even Cantor's eternal optimism was blunted. "If this is defeated, there will never be a serious, durable third party in America," he declared.[78]

Entrenching the Duopoly

The Supreme Court handed down its decision in *Timmons v. Twin Cities Area New Party* on April 28, 1997, ruling 6–3 that Minnesota's ban on fusion did not violate the Constitution. The opinion was written by Chief Justice Rehnquist, and joined by Justices Scalia, O'Connor, Thomas, Breyer, and Kennedy. Not only did the court strike a deadly blow at the New Party's hopes to become a national force, it was the first time that the High Court said that the state had a legitimate interest in favoring the existing two-party system. Half of Joel Rogers's worst fear had come true. Tossing aside past rulings where the court had rejected attempts by the existing major parties to artificially prevent others from effectively competing with them, the Rehnquist decision conjured this state interest from whole cloth. Only the court's more recent ruling in *Bush v. Gore* is more breathtaking in its usurpation of democratic values. (And the same core majority of conservative justices, minus Justice Breyer, was dominant there.)

Rehnquist started by acknowledging the First Amendment right of citizens to associate together in political parties in order to advance common goals and ideas. This he juxtaposed against the state's interest in enacting "reasonable regulations of parties, elections, and ballots to reduce election- and campaign-related disorder." He then proceeded to run blithely over a party's core interest in presenting its candidates to voters by appearing on the ballot, while exaggerating the disarray that might be caused by allowing one party to fuse with another by cross-endorsing its candidate. "That a particular individual may not appear on the ballot as a particular party's candidate does not severely burden that party's association rights," he wrote. "Minnesota has not directly precluded minor parties from developing and organizing."

Note the insertion of the weasel word "directly." In that section of his opinion, Rehnquist had just dismissed the Eighth Circuit Court of Appeals' argument that the ban on fusion forced members of the New Party to make a "no-win" choice between voting for a candidate who couldn't win, defecting from their party, or not voting at all. What he was implicitly endorsing was the *indirect* suppression of minor party hopes. "The New Party remains free to endorse whom it likes, to ally itself with others, to nominate candidates for office, and to spread its message to all who will listen," he added, soothingly. This reasoning was reminiscent of the comment by French writer Anatole France that "the law, in its majestic equality, forbids the rich as well as the poor to sleep under bridges, to beg in the streets, and to steal bread." Of course, the law doesn't stop the poor from being poor, any more than saying that the New Party's freedom of expression was not infringed by the ban on fusion, even though the state was allowed to take away the single biggest reason that anyone might want to listen to it.

Most Americans would be surprised by Rehnquist's next assertion. Denying the New Party's claim that its ability to nominate the candidate of its choice was a core form of political speech, he wrote, "Ballots serve primarily to elect candidates, not as fora for political expression." This statement drew a direct riposte from Justice Stevens in his dissent, which was joined by Justice Ginsburg and Justice Souter (in this part).[79] "The right to be on the election ballot is precisely what separates a political party from any other interest group," Stevens wrote. And party labels next to candidates' names were inescapably a form of speech that many voters used, quite properly, as a shorthand way of informing themselves about candidates on the ballot.

While downplaying the impact on the New Party of banning fusion, Rehnquist dwelled at length on the supposed danger of voter confusion resulting from an overcrowded ballot filled with spurious minor parties abusing fusion. The newly formed "No New Taxes" party would be countered with a "Fiscal Responsibility" party, the "Conserve Our Environment" party would be matched by a "Healthy Planet" party, and so on, each cross-endorsing an opposing major candidate and turning the ballot into "a billboard for political advertising," he predicted.[80] Why this couldn't be more easily addressed by reasonable ballot-access laws preventing such abuses, rather than violating the New Party's associational rights, went unaddressed.

Finally, Rehnquist took a major leap from the general state interest in political stability to a particular interest in enacting "reasonable election regulation that may, in practice, favor the traditional two-party system . . . and . . . temper the destabilizing effects of party-splintering and excessive factionalism." He and the other concurring justices, like many people, could only imagine a third party as a divisive force. It fell to Justice Stevens to note that "the parade of horribles that the majority appears to believe might visit Minnesota should fusion candidacies be allowed is fantastical, given the evidence from New York's experience with fusion. . . . Indeed, the activity banned by

Minnesota's law is the formation of coalitions, not the division and dissension of 'splintered parties and unrestrained factionalism.' "[81]

Constitutional scholar Richard Hasen saw grim tidings in the decision. "Beyond ballot access cases, *Timmons* will make it easier for states to entrench the two-party duopoly through campaign finance laws, policies regulating access to public television, patronage cases, partisan gerrymandering, and potentially a wide variety of other measures," he wrote a year later in the University of Chicago's *Supreme Court Review*. (Indeed, as Hasen pointed out, the same year as the *Timmons* decision, the High Court rejected an appeal from the Florida Libertarian Party seeking to overturn a Florida law that provided for subsidized filing fees solely for the candidates of the two major parties.) What most concerned Hasen was the fact that the Supreme Court never actually examined its underlying premises that the two-party system was worthy of protection, or whether such protection was actually necessary.[82]

Richard Winger of *Ballot Access News* was horrified. "Never before had the Court used the term 'two-party system' to justify discrimination against minor parties," he wrote in his newsletter. And he pointed out that the three Supreme Court opinions that Rehnquist used to support his conclusion had nothing to do with minor parties. "One was a reapportionment case, and the other two concerned patronage. In each case, the context was that the state should strive to keep each of the two major parties competitive with each other." Winger remonstrated that this was often precisely what minor parties did—keep the two-party system healthy by helping to break one party's "lock" on the presidency, for example. "Why did the Court choose this case, at this time, to say (for the first time ever) that the 'two-party system' must be 'protected' against minor and new parties?" Winger speculated that it came precisely as public interest in third-party candidacies was on the rise, and that the Court wanted to prevent such behavior. After all, he noted, in the last decision on this subject, *Burdick v. Takushi* (1992), upholding Hawaii's ban on write-in votes, the Court had said "there is no constitutional right for a voter to vote for anyone he or she wishes." [83]

No Shortcuts

In the wake of losing their bid to legalize fusion politics, the New Party's leaders put on a brave face. Secky Fascione, a labor organizer with the Hotel Employees and Restaurant Employees local in Missoula, Montana, and a rising figure within the party's ranks, said that fusion was not the be-all and end-all. "Here in Missoula we've always seen fusion as one political tactic—albeit one that could be very useful in 'top of the ticket' partisan races. The heart of our strategy has not been fusion but the unglamorous work of building local labor- and community-based organizations and precinct networks, recruiting our own candidates for office, and then pounding on door after door on Election Day."[84]

But quietly, the party's founders mourned what could have been. In February, a few months before the *Timmons* hammer fell, they had been invited to address the AFL-CIO's executive council meeting on the topic of fusion and independent politics. It was the first time in the history of organized labor that a new party had been invited into the inner sanctum of the trade union movement. And while the meeting was just an opening, Cantor had already fielded healthy indications of interest from top officials like Andy Stern of the SEIU and Steve Rosenthal, the AFL-CIO political director, who wanted to demonstrate some muscle against a conservative Democrat. Had the party won *Timmons*, Rogers and Cantor both believed, the leaders of organized labor—who had always been somewhat wary of the New Party because they feared it would inevitably turn in the direction of spoiling races—would have gotten involved in a much more serious way.[85]

Instead, Cantor wrote a memo for a September leadership meeting in Chicago that he titled "No Shortcuts." A lot of tensions spilled out at that session. Joel Rogers, the party's national chairman and its most visible spokesman, had made clear to his colleagues that he would leave the New Party if the Supreme Court ruling went the wrong way, since he believed it meant no durable, national third party could be built under the current electoral rules. "We never intended to be a national party," said Secky Fascione, putting a different spin on what Cantor and Rogers had started. "This was always about building progressive parties at the local and state level that would be issue and value oriented. We very much borrowed those issues and ideas from the Christian Coalition, which did that very effectively with school boards and the like. We always knew this required favorable rules. We though the Supreme Court might jump-start that with the *Timmons* case. But we should not be surprised that the court did not open up that process."[86] Wade Rathke, the veteran ACORN organizer, argued that the New Party could continue as a sort of "intentional community"—calling itself a party even if it couldn't have its own ballot line. But Rogers just thought that view was unrealistic.

The meeting in Chicago forced a real clarification in the New Party's self-definition. Until the *Timmons* decision, its leaders had managed a tricky balancing act: projecting the New Party as a full-blown third-party effort to sympathetic progressive activists and philanthropists, as a nonspoiler to national labor and constituency group leaders, as a modest network for resource pooling to savvy local organizers who agreed to affiliate with the New Party in exchange for some organizing subsidies, as an independent political machine capable of winning a modicum of power to local labor and community organizations. Now it was impossible to be all those things at once. "We raised national money around winning our legal strategy," Cantor said later.[87] That money was drying up. But many local activists had joined the effort because they bought into the larger vision. And they didn't think the fusion loss stopped them from proceeding. As Tammy Johnson put it, "Revolutions don't happen overnight." In effect, the party's founders had succeeded beyond their expectations, nurturing an internal culture that had taken on a life of its own.

To Cantor, who was more in the middle between Rogers's view that the game was over and those who just wanted to keep going as if nothing had changed, apart from a sense of "dismay" at how bluntly Rogers framed the matter, the real important debate was "How important is a ballot line to being a party?" Some people felt there was value in using the term as a kind of shorthand that made it easier to explain what the group was doing, rather than "intelligent, independent, municipal-level community-labor electoral organizing." On the other hand, he said, the use of a "party" label might be overly polarizing. A general consensus did emerge out of the New Party's post-*Timmons* gathering in Chicago. As Cantor put it in a letter to one supporter,

> We see no choice but to start local and avoid the idiocy of Presidential politics. We need to build real grassroots organizations. Run people for offices where we can win. Not spoil or ask people to waste their votes, time or money. Recruit candidates out of local unions and community organizations. Create a farm team of candidates who can move up to higher level office over time. Take advantage of fusion in the states where it still exists. Work to change ballot rules in states where it does not. Run people on the Democratic Party ballot line where that makes the most sense, but do so from an independent base. Frame issues as top-bottom, not liberal-conservative. Experiment with progressive ballot initiatives. Invest heavily in training our own members and leaders. Create precinct level organization in target districts. And all the while promote a values-centered politics that comes out of and is accountable to a real grassroots base.[88]

This in fact is what the New Party continued to do in Little Rock, Arkansas; Missoula, Montana; Dane County, Wisconsin; the Twin Cities, Minnesota; Portland, Oregon; Montgomery County, Maryland; and Chicago, Illinois—all places where strong local chapters were established and where the party decided to concentrate its declining national resources after the *Timmons* boom was lowered.[89] In these places, the larger project of building a national party was always secondary to creating an independent political organization capable of effecting local changes.

For example, in Chicago the party built a "people's machine" that has continued to win some significant victories against Mayor Daley's regular Democrats. Their candidate for state representative in the Thirty-fifth Ward, Willie Delgado, ran again in 1998 after the incumbent was indicted in another one of the city's never-ending corruption scandals. Against Daley's regulars and the local alderman's business-backed operation, the New Party built a sophisticated campaign. Working in close cooperation with progressive

Democrats up-ballot, they registered thousands of new voters, scoured voting records to prevent fraud, sent targeted mailings to Hispanics, seniors, and parents of school-age children (alerting them that the incumbent had voted against a tax increase that would have helped local schools), and meticulously constructed a computerized voter file tracking likely supporters. On Election Day itself, they fielded dozens of volunteer poll watchers, passers (people who handed out palm cards and spoke to voters on their way into the polls), and runners (who, alerted by their poll watchers, ran to the homes of people identified as supporters who hadn't voted yet). The Daley machine had plenty of men on the streets for its candidate, but Delgado was ultimately triumphant. He won with 52 percent of the vote in the two-candidate race, an average margin of just four votes per precinct. But in the areas where the New Party focused its efforts, he had an average margin of twenty votes—the cushion that assured his victory.[90]

A few months later, the party mobilized quickly, along with ACORN and SEIU Local 880, to protest the city council's move to vote itself a pay increase from $75,000 to $95,000 for their part-time jobs. With the TV cameras rolling, they effectively shamed the council into passing the living-wage ordinance that it had rejected just a year earlier. In early 1999, all the party's coalition work on this and other issues paid off when another seat on the city council opened up. This time, Ted Thomas, the party's state chair and president of Chicago ACORN, announced his candidacy—the first time the party ran someone generated from its own ranks.[91] And though Mayor Daley had his own candidate, a broad array of local unions came out for Thomas with troops and money. He won the twelve-way primary with 22 percent of the vote and racked up a strong victory a few months later. The Chicago City Council had gained another one of its rare independents. Thomas planned to stay close to his roots, setting up an advisory council made up of local neighborhood representatives and holding big town meetings to hammer out an agenda for the ward.[92] Long-term grass-roots organizing was producing a new model of representative leader—rather than an officeholder who was the sole decision maker, Thomas was committed to be an alderman who was a community mobilizer.

In other cities where nonpartisan elections made the New Party municipal strategy workable, victories kept rolling in.[93] In Little Rock, the New Party, through its elected officials and organizational base, led an antisprawl campaign that has made unrestrained development the major issue in local politics. In Maryland, the chapter decided to turn inward, merging with two other activist groups and reinventing itself as a statewide organization. In Oregon, the Missoula New Party persuaded the city council to pass a living wage ordinance in early 2001, after facing a backlash from business and narrowly losing an initiative on the issue two years earlier. The Missoula chapter claimed 560 dues-paying members at the end of 2000, which, in a locality of about eighty thousand people, was an influential body.[94] In St. Paul, Minnesota, the party kept the heat on the mayor's unpopular efforts to use public funds to subsidize a sports stadium. Overall in the Twin Cities, it had two thousand dues-paying members, several large union affiliates, deep ties with community and church groups, and a big hand in the passage of five laws, including a charter amendment that put the local police department under the jurisdiction of a civil rights ordinance. They had also played a big role in electing two dozen people. All this on a budget of $100,000 a year. "If you look at what many foundations spend their money on," said Tom Hucker, the party's national field director, "they'll say something like this can't be done. Instead they'll spend $2 million on a 'visioning project,'" he added, wryly.[95]

Convinced that the fusion loss had effectively stymied the party's chances to go national, the Maryland and Minnesota chapters both eventually voted to disaffiliate and focus their resources solely on local organizing. Compared to the party's other chapters, where ACORN organizers played a larger role, acting like a political party rather than an independent pressure group was seen by leaders in these two states as no longer helpful. But that didn't change their commitment to keep organizing. And while municipal New Party ventures and their offspring kept chipping away at their local power structures, in New York the New Party model finally struck gold. "After *Timmons*, those of us who continued to think that building a party was still the way to go felt, 'Hey, we may have lost elsewhere but we didn't lose in New York,'" said Zach Polett, ACORN's political director and a longtime New Party field director. Of course, fusion politics had never gone out of fashion there. "And that's why we reached out again in New York to try to make it happen."[96]

This time, the stars were in alignment.

10

The Little Third Party
That Could

Every Vote Really *Counts*

There almost wasn't a Working Families Party in New York. On Election Night, November 3, 1998, the party's organizers gathered in the Two Boots restaurant in Manhattan's East Village and cried their hearts out. They needed fifty thousand votes on their line for Peter Vallone, the Democratic candidate for governor whom they had cross-endorsed, and as of 11:00 P.M., with 80 percent of the precincts reporting, the board of elections told them they had tallied only about thirty-five thousand. Bob Master, the political director of the Communications Workers of America (CWA) Area One local and one of the party's chief spark plugs, got up and gave a fiery concession speech thanking everyone for how hard they had worked. And then the multiracial crowd, burly members of the Mason Tenders union, top officials of the auto and communications workers, gray-suited elected officials, youthful community organizers from ACORN, bus drivers from Staten Island, activists from the South Bronx, downtown hipsters, gays, lesbians, and straights, writers and artists, downed their beers and went home to nurse their sore feet.

The ambitious attempt by a coalition of unions, community organizations, and public interest groups to create a new progressive-populist force that could supplant New York's decrepit Liberal Party and counter the state's rightward drift had seemingly foundered on the most annoying of obstacles. For starters, a lot of people hadn't even bothered to vote, since the reelection of incumbent Republican Governor

George Pataki had been a foregone conclusion for most of the campaign. Vallone, a Democratic Party hack from Queens, was disliked by many liberal-leaning voters for his role in bottling up legislation as Speaker of the New York City Council, and for his support for Mayor Giuliani's brutal police tactics. The WFP had endorsed him for tactical reasons, but few voters were used to thinking in those terms. Thus the fledgling party literally had to identify, contact, and convince nearly every voter they got.

Anyone seeking to cast a "pure" protest vote could go for "Grandpa" Al Lewis, an eighty-eight-year-old semicelebrity actor from the TV show *The Munsters*, who ran for governor on the Green Party line and soaked up nearly all the media attention that went to New York's third parties in the 1998 cycle. (Indeed, with far less of a grass-roots field operation than the WFP, Lewis tallied more than fifty thousand votes, giving the Greens their own line on the ballot for the next four years.) Most depressing to WFP activists—they knew from direct personal contact with hundreds of voters that many people *wanted* to use their line, but simply couldn't find it on the ballot and gave up! In New York City, the party was on Line 1L. On Long Island, Westchester, and upstate, it was 2H. In Albany, it was 3G.

But that same cockamamie voting system was ultimately the party's salvation. The morning after the election, they discovered they had reached forty-five thousand votes when all the precincts reported. There might be a few more coming when absentee ballots were counted, but they still assumed they had fallen short. Karen Scharf, a leader of Citizen Action who was on the WFP board, was on the train back up to Albany sitting next to Mark Dunlea, a lawyer and top New York Green Party activist. "You've won," Dunlea told Scharf. "What do you mean?" she asked, astonished. Dunlea explained that the WFP would undoubtedly gain enough votes once all the voting machines were "recanvassed," a painstaking process in which every paper tally was rechecked against the machine totals. In 1996, he told her, Ralph Nader had sixty-five thousand votes statewide on Election Day, and gained eleven thousand more from the recanvass. Not only that, WFP leaders also discovered that in Manhattan, the computer program used by the elections board and the police to tally the night's total could only accommodate the results from one machine per election district. But many districts used two machines to accommodate heavy turnout. Sixty thousand votes in Manhattan weren't counted at all on Election Night. Out of a total of 6 million cast, that was an inconsequential number. But to the WFP, which had a lot of early support on the liberal West Side and in Greenwich Village, this news came like a thunderbolt. "There really ought to be a sign in some of those districts," Master joked later. "If you want your vote counted tonight, vote here. If you want it counted three weeks from now, vote here."[1]

Two weeks after Election Day, an e-mail went out from the New Party titled, "Hello Copy, Get Me Rewrite . . ." Ultimately, the WFP was certified as having received 51,325 votes. It was a squeaker, but now the party had its line on the ballot (at least until 2002, the next gubernatorial election). Soon, hundreds of incumbent officeholders would be calling its offices, seeking its support and worrying, as politicians tend to do, about what might happen if they didn't get it. The press also started paying more attention. Thousands of people began getting accustomed to voting, and identifying, with the WFP label. In the weeks after that awful Election Night, Bob Master and some of the party's other instigators had talked about soldiering on without the line, petitioning to get its candidates on the ballot in races where it wanted to try to play a role, and making a difference in the state elections of 2000 and the New York City mayoral and city council battles of 2001. But the truth was that the coalition that built the party would have probably fallen apart, or, if its leaders were lucky, barely treaded water. After all, the six-month push to gather enough signatures to be placed on the 1998 ballot, to print and mail hundreds of thousands of pieces of literature, and to make tens of thousands of get-out-the-vote calls had left the fledgling party organization more than $100,000 in debt. Instead of asking its constituent institutions to invest in a winner with an invaluable asset, a line-less WFP would have likely been begging donors just to keep its doors open.

Instead, the party started 1999 with close to $200,000 in dues pledged or on their way, including $25,000 from the United Auto Workers (regions 9 and 9A, representing sixty-two thousand workers) and $20,000 each from the CWA (representing seventy thousand members), ACORN (whose twenty-thousand-member base was concentrated in New York City) and the Mason Tenders District Council (a thirteen-thousand-member union primarily representing construction workers and asbestos and hazardous materials handlers). Other substantial commitments came from UNITE, the textile workers union; several Teamsters locals; a few AFSCME locals including District Council 1707, representing twenty-five thousand employees of nonprofit caregivers; and the Buffalo Teachers Federation. About fifteen smaller union locals also affiliated right from the start as well, including units representing painters, nurses, mail-handlers, lithographers, and bus drivers. In addition to ACORN, the largest and most powerful community organization involved with the WFP, Citizen Action of New York, the Long Island Progressive Coalition, and the New Party of Long Island were also founding affiliates.

After helping get the WFP rolling, Cantor had decided to step down as the New Party's executive director and move back to New York in order to become the WFP's interim state coordinator. And he was relishing the challenge. "We have to figure out how to be a party, something more than a coalition, combining institutions and individuals. Some people think of this as a smarter version of the Liberal Party, while the bulk of us have a larger vision." There was already an emerging consensus among the party's affiliates to start off with a major push to increase the state minimum wage, then just $5.15 an hour, to the highest level in the country. "The focus is to brand ourselves ideologically [with such a campaign] and to build up our base," Cantor explained.

One big task was engaging the rank-and-file membership of the unions that were joining the WFP as institutions. Another related job was getting people registered as WFP voters, which in many cases meant tricky calculations about urging people to switch their Democratic Party affiliation. In many local districts, the real fight for power was in the Democratic primary, while in other places the WFP could be more of a swing vote. At the same time, they needed to actively register their own voters because under state law only WFP registrants could vote on selecting the party's state committee. (There never was any intention to call the party the New York New Party, by the way. Even though the New Yorkers launching the effort drew much from the New Party model, they did not see themselves as part of a national effort. During their early planning the party's founders had polled on various other names, including Citizens Party, Common Sense Party, and Progressive Party. "Working Families" came out on top, doing particularly well with union members and people of color.) A third big test was nurturing the creation of local chapters and clubs, and figuring out how to balance their natural desire for local autonomy with the need for a unified voice. But Cantor knew he and his comrades were working with far more initial support than any New Party chapter ever had. And as far as dealing with elected officials, "We're having no problem getting our calls returned," he reported. "Every day I get a letter from someone asking for our line." There was an impish glee in his voice.[2]

An early strategy memo written by Master and Cantor gave a clear sense of how they hoped to use the party's electoral leverage to shift policy in a new direction.

We should see Row H [their ballot placement] as a "carrot and stick" that can reinforce a legislative program designed to move the political debate in Albany and elsewhere in the direction of meeting the needs of our constituencies. The carrot is to reward legislators who genuinely support and fight for our program with an additional line. And the stick is to hold out the threat that those who don't support our program will a) not get the line and b) may find someone else running on our line. Right now we believe the threat, even given the lopsided nature [of most contests for state legislative offices], is sufficient to have an impact. At some point, we actually have to exercise the threat to make sure the major parties take us seriously. We only have to run an independent in a close race once for the party leaderships to develop a healthy and genuine fear of us.[3]

At a late January retreat, about fifty of the WFP's leaders gathered to hammer out the core components of the party's legislative program. They wanted to focus on an economic populist approach that would build maximum unity among their diverse supporters; they wanted to push the edge of the debate beyond where the major party leaderships wanted to go, and they wanted goals that had some chance of success. Beyond raising the minimum wage, there was clear consensus on supporting campaign finance reform (public financing of elections), expanding child care funding, education reform (smaller classes, opposition to privatization, greater support for the state's public universities), and fiscal responsibility (which for them meant only revenue-neutral tax code changes, not risky tax cuts).

At the same time, some internal differences emerged. For some of the smaller, specialized trade unions, whose members already made upward of $20 an hour, raising the minimum wage meant little. Defense of abortion and gay rights, two lesser planks in the WFP program, troubled leaders of some unions with heavily Catholic memberships. ACORN members, who generally did not belong to unions, had little interest in raising New York's absurdly low workman's compensation rates. And some WFP leaders worried that they needed to do more to appeal to independent voters, perhaps by exploring property tax relief, or going after corporate welfare subsidies in the state budget. Not only would fusion raise complicated questions about how to relate to the major parties, it was clear that the WFP would have to evolve its own internal form of fusion.

But this was nothing new. If every political party is a complex balancing act of constituencies, personalities, powerbrokers, and interests, the only thing unusual about the WFP was how transparent some of this was. The party's very birth was a brilliant and precarious act of political alchemy. While the impetus came from veteran organizer Jon Kest of ACORN holding meetings with various principals, it would never have gotten off the ground without the early commitment of the CWA and UAW.[4] "I think the shock that people felt in terms of union support on this drove it to the next stage," said Richard Schrader, then the New York City director of Citizen Action. "Add to that the sheer enmity that David Dinkins and [his deputy mayor] Bill Lynch feel toward the Liberal Party and a momentary interest in Peter Vallone's gubernatorial candidacy, and all of these somewhat conflicting interests came together and started talking it through."[5] Ironically, Dinkins and Lynch had been at loggerheads with Vallone in the early 1990s, when the then-mayor was frustrated by Vallone's control of the city council and his deputy led the effort to unseat some pro-Vallone incumbents.[6] But now being at the same losing end of politics turned them into momentary allies.

"You have to look at changes within the labor movement to understand the rise of the Working Families Party," said the CWA's Bob Master, one of the party co-chairs. "From John Sweeney on down, there's a real willingness to at least look at new strategies and new allies." He also noted that it was no coincidence that the impetus came from unions like his and the UAW, along with Teamsters locals, rather than the big teachers unions, who were known for their close ties to the Democrats, or the state employees' unions. "The private-sector unions don't have the same day-to-day institutional needs that require them to enter into permanent relationships with elected officials," he said. "Our union is comfortable going to war. We were out on strike in 1986, 1989, 1998 and likely will be in 2000. We understand you get things from your adversaries [only] with power."[7] Several WFP labor leaders in New York City had worked together in 1997 on the populist campaign of city councilor Sal Albanese. And then there was the spur of Republicans in power in Albany and New York City, and the sight of some of the city's biggest labor heavyweights, including Stanley Hill of AFSCME District Council 37 and Brian McLaughlin of the Central Labor Council, endorsing incumbent Republican Giuliani for reelection.

Many local progressives had also changed their attitude toward the question of making political compromises and alliances after watching Governor Pataki and Mayor Giuliani roll over state and local Democrats. Neither ACORN nor Citizen Action had much great enthusiasm for endorsing Vallone. However, each organization recognized that Vallone's weak gubernatorial campaign gave them an opportunity to create a new ballot line without really worrying that they would elect him, and at the same time they used the new line to get something significant from him in exchange for the endorsement. For Citizen Action that was an improved public financing system for New York City elections; for ACORN it was a new grievance procedure for handling workfare complaints.

It helped as well that no one player in the WFP was so big that it could overwhelm all the others. Had a union like 1199 been involved from the start, it's doubtful others would have come on as full partners. Finally, there was the painful example of the Liberal Party, which, the common joke went, was neither liberal nor a party. "People look at [Ray] Harding, see a guy with no organization and no troops but with tremendous political clout, and they ask, 'Why aren't we doing this? Why don't we have this kind of clout for our kind of politics?'" Master declared.[8]

But though the WFP's deep institutional support gave it muscle, it also constrained its room to maneuver. As Master candidly said to me one morning over coffee and muffins near the CWA's offices near Wall Street, "Our ability to operate independently increases the lower on the ballot you go." For the WFP's founders, there was never any serious question but that the party would endorse Democrats for high-level races, whether that was Al Gore for president or Hillary Clinton for U.S. Senate. Indeed, in my very first conversation about this with Cantor in early 1999, a full year before the presidential election, he admitted that those moves were inevitable—barring an unexpected progressive challenge from within Democratic Party ranks. Master acknowledged, "We don't have a huge amount of leverage right now, and we just don't have the track record and political power to begin dictating whether this candidate is acceptable or not."[9] Unstated in that honest assessment was the fact that Master's boss was Morton Bahr, a close supporter of the Clinton administration and not someone who would allow one of his locals to wander off the reservation.

To WFP co-chair Jim Duncan of the United Auto Workers too, being an independent political party did not necessarily mean independent of the Democrats. "Being independent means being independent of big special interest money," he said in a speech at the party's first state convention. "It means not taking money from large corporations like the other political parties do, and so not owing them your soul. It means being independent of any one person's private agenda. . . . We support politicians when they support our issues, and we're thankful to those politicians who support us. But this is not an old-style political machine. There's no 'boss' at the top. There's no politicians or candidate or wanna-be candidate calling the shots. . . . Above all, what building an independent party means is that this is a political party formed by, run by and funded by working people."[10]

Thus, from the start, the WFP was a hybrid: tactically shrewd, committed to maximize its leverage for winnable goals, but not purist; beholden to working people but willing to make deals with others who were not; based in a diverse array of institutions but needing solid grass-roots involvement. Whether this would be a successful and sustainable blend would depend on the choices its leaders made and the opportunities that presented themselves.

Going to Work

In March of 1999, just a few months after getting its ballot line certified by the state, the WFP made its first major foray in local elections, supporting two Democrats running against incumbent Republican members of the Hempstead village board of trustees. Even though two-thirds of the town's forty-seven thousand residents were black, a Democrat hadn't won a municipal race in more than twenty years. "If we screw up, no one will notice," Cantor said beforehand. Instead Hezekiah Brown, a former labor relations teacher and school board member, and Wayne Hall, the president of the town's Little League, pulled off surprising upsets. Moreover, they gave all the credit for their wins to the WFP's grass-roots organizing, which had involved making about ten thousand voter contacts, most of them door-to-door. "In the end, it was big shock, even to us," Cantor related later. "What it showed was in lower-turnout races, our stuff goes a long way."[11]

Over the next year, the party racked up an impressive record. Of 225 candidates running with its line, more than half won. In New York City, it helped education activist Eva Moscowitz take a city council seat that had been previously in Republican hands; the WFP was responsible for securing 10 percent of her total vote and as much as 20 percent in a few targeted election districts. On conservative Staten Island, the WFP outpolled both the Liberal and Independence parties. In Brooklyn, the party chose one race to fuse with the Greens, drawing 14 percent against a conservative Democratic city council member from Sheepshead Bay who had voted in favor of a landlord-favored bill loosening lead paint standards. In Nassau County, WFP members boosted the Democratic tidal wave that ended one hundred years of uninterrupted Republican control of the county legislature.

North of the city, they suffered narrow losses in the Poughkeepsie mayoral race and in a Westchester County legislative seat but knocked off incumbents in Schenectady and Albany county races. Two African-American women they backed won village trustee seats in Spring Valley, an outer suburb of New York City, while they sent a strong message to Rockland County Democrats by cross-endorsing a local Green and getting 17 percent of the vote. Upstate, in the Erie County race for county executive, the party's candidate got just under six thousand votes on the WFP line. Finally, joining with an array of Democratic politicians, unions, and community groups, they ran a successful campaign to defeat Mayor Giuliani's proposed changes to the city charter. In all, the party's local candidates totaled twice as many votes as a year earlier, despite the lower turnout of an off-year election.

The party's local chapter development was also starting to take off. In Rockland, the party aimed high early on, getting involved in a special election for an open state senate seat in May of 1999. The party endorsed the Democratic candidate, a member of the county legislature named Ken Zebrowski, and with five veteran organizers working full time managed in just five weeks to pull eighteen hundred votes for him on their line, almost 5 percent of the total cast. "This showed us there was a market for the WFP in Rockland," says Ericka Bozzi Gomez, the twenty-seven-year-old organizer who was assigned to build the chapter. (The WFP also got a bit of a black eye in the Zebrowski race, as he came out late in the election for a repeal of the commuter tax. His move was meant to appeal to suburban independents but only resulted in the loss of substantial revenue for New York City services after Republicans in Albany leapt on the Democratic concession. Zebrowski lost by a narrow margin.)

A critical early move was pushed by the Rockland chapter's firebrand, Irv Feiner. A veteran of left politics, Feiner was old enough to recall the old American Labor Party, a New York party that had died out in the 1950s. "All the energy we used in the late 1940s in support of third parties, had it gone into the Democratic Party we could have taken them over," he mused. Yet, he saw a lot of promise in the WFP. "There are three directions this party can go. It can be a pain in the ass. It can stay relevant by being where most of the people are. Or it can be a combination of the first two. I opt for that." At his urging, and with the reluctant support of the party's state executive committee, the WFP in Rockland joined with the local Liberal party in cross-endorsing a Green county legislative candidate. "That was a district where we knew a Republican couldn't win," says Feiner, "and we felt it was important to take a stand. You can't be a populist party if you support people who raise their salaries $7,000 and throw in a dental plan when so many people lack health care."[12] Though the Democratic incumbent won with 53 percent, the Green-WFP-Liberal lines combined got 17 percent. "Afterwards," recalled Gomez, "Paul Adler, the chairman of the Democratic Party in the county, told us that this three-party coalition could tip a lot of elections. He noticed that we got more votes than the Conservative Party did. 'This could help push the Democrats back to the left,' he told us."[13]

Gomez and the Rockland WFP chapter put much of their energy into building a living wage coalition, signing up twenty-three local organizations and building a database of six thousand people interested in the party's work. Aware of the votes the WFP had pulled for him earlier, Zebrowski acted as the lead sponsor of the party's bill. But even though Democrats controlled the county legislature 11-6, getting the bill passed was far from simple. Zebrowski needed constant reminders from the chapter to stay on course, and local business opposition nearly prevented a vote from even happening. "This bill was almost killed five separate times in the legislature—the only thing that saved it was that we refused to go away," Gomez said. Members of the party picketed regular legislative meetings, demonstrated in front of the county executive's home at 8:00 in the morning on a Saturday, and most important, turned up the heat in lawmakers' districts. That's how two crucial conservative Democrats were tilted into the yes column. "We did a postcard campaign in one of these guys' districts," recalled Tom Stoner, a forty-nine-year-old graphics designer who was the chapter co-chair. "When you get several hundred postcards from people in the poor, Latino section of your district that's been organized by the WFP, and where you aren't particularly strong, you'll pick up the signal."[14]

Across the Hudson River in nearby Westchester County, the WFP was also looking to build a living-wage coalition. But first the chapter saw an opportunity that it couldn't pass up. In the normally staid village of Pelham, a bedroom suburb in the southern part of the county, residents were dividing along class lines over a proposal to allow a developer to build a 150-apartment assisted living complex in the center of town. Five of the village's six trustees, including three Democrats up for reelection in the spring of 2000, were supporting the plan because they saw it bringing in critically needed tax revenue. But the town's wealthier residents, clustered on Pelham's south side, were worried that the project would depress their property values. They also fanned fears that it would fail to draw in enough retired seniors capable of paying high rents and would turn into low-income housing. When the Democratic Party held its local caucus to endorse its slate, this group of more affluent homeowners packed the meeting and voted to endorse not the party's incumbents, but their Republican challengers. Suddenly, thanks to the quirks of New York's fusion law, the rich had, in effect, taken over both the Republican and Democratic parties in Pelham.

Mike Boland, the WFP's twenty-three-year-old Westchester organizer, recalled what happened next. "One of our major affiliates, the Westchester Coalition of Professional Firefighters, called me up. They were interested in the issue because the project would mean a lot of jobs." On very short notice, the WFP's local chapter and state committee quickly decided to jump into the race, giving their line to the three Democrats who had just been knocked off the Democratic line by the project's opponents. In a quirky way, it was the WFP versus the two major parties. The party put about twenty-five people into the field in the days before the election, local firefighters, volunteers from nearby Sarah Lawrence College, staff, and party members. They identified about twelve hundred likely supporters, made hundreds of reminder phone calls, and knocked on doors extensively throughout the town's working-class northern section. Ultimately, they fell short, with 36 percent of the vote. But against many voters' ingrained habits to stick to familiar party labels, and the undeniable strength of the other side's subtly racist message, this was not a bad showing. The night of the election, Boland and many of the WFP's younger volunteers were staring morosely at the floor as the results came in. But Cantor, the party's director, was there to congratulate them for their hard work. "This has been a really good staff training exercise," he told me. "The skills people learned here will be put to good use."

Indeed they were. That same spring, in a special state senate election in Far Rockaway, a working-class corner of Queens dominated by the local Democratic machine, the WFP got 58 percent of the vote in five election districts. Turnout in those areas was as high as 11.2 percent, which doesn't seem like much except for the fact that turnout was at just 3.6 percent in the rest of the district. And in a crucial Nassau County legislative race, the WFP got 5 percent of the vote for Craig Johnson and 20 percent in the white, working-class community of Manor Haven, where it focused its resources on neighbor-to-neighbor campaigning. Like the Greens of New Mexico, who had done particularly well in two special election races for Congress in 1997 and 1998, and the Greens of Oakland, who had mobilized many of their most experienced organizers to get Audie Bock elected in her 1999 bid for the California state assembly, the WFP was at its most potent in special election battles.

But unlike the Greens, who so far have elected only a few officials who are African American or Latino, and whose reach into the lower income brackets has largely been confined to students and other people who are poor by choice, the WFP could genuinely boast of the multiracial and working-class base it was building. Gloria Waldron, a middle-aged African-American woman with her own home-based architecture business in Brooklyn, got into the party through her involvement with ACORN in fights over housing and redlining. At a meeting of WFP members at the party's modest headquarters in downtown Brooklyn, it became clear that she had a very basic and compelling understanding of the party's raison d'etre. "We tend to lean more to the

Democrats than the Republicans because we find they listen more," she said in a lilting Caribbean accent. "But they are both big parties, rich man's parties. We need a party for the little people." By voting on the WFP line, she said, the Democrats would know how many of those people supported them. "The world has two types," she added, "sharks and sardines. Sharks have power by virtue of their size. The sardines have power only in their numbers." Her table-mates, veteran neighborhood organizers who had come up through ACORN's ranks, nodded in agreement. No college-educated, middle-class white person, no matter how well intentioned, could have made this point with the same credibility as Waldron.

The same could be said about Bertha Lewis, a WFP co-chair (along with Bob Master of the CWA and Jim Duncan of the UAW). Lewis started her career in theater, but soon discovered she had a talent for organizing and moved to the political stage. As ACORN's director, she was a fierce champion of her members' interests; as a WFP co-chair she often took the podium to fire up rallies, drawing reticent white unionists into call-and-response chanting with black party members more used to the church tradition. Her vision of the WFP's role in New York politics was a little bolder than those of her union allies—perhaps because they were already major players and ACORN really represented many of the most disadvantaged and disenfranchised. Sitting with Gloria Waldron and other WFP activists from ACORN, she laid it all out.

"If we can identify 8 to 12 seats on the City Council, where these people are absolutely aware that a large part of their election came from the Working Families Party, that know us and understand who we are, we will have done something. We'll have people we can go to for help with neighborhood problems. And we have to put together an agenda for them, since a lot of them don't know what they want to do. We could be the difference in primaries, between a good Democrat and a bad Democrat, that 10 to 12 percent that actually gives someone a spine. We could be the fear factor, telling someone that 'I've got to do this, because I don't want these people to run against me next time.'"

Lewis grew more expansive. "In four years, you can begin to grow folks for real, outside of the Democratic machinery. Rather than coming out of the Democratic clubs, this could be another school that people could come out of. I dream of a pure, unadulterated, born-and-bred WFP-er, someone who has never even thought of being a Democrat. I dream of the day when the kids who graduate from the ACORN high school here in Brooklyn actually come back and want to be a politician running on the WFP line. I dream of the day where you'll be able to see WFP on the map all over the state, where every four years we won't have to worry about getting fifty thousand votes on our line. That's what keeps me going every day. To give black and Latino lawmakers an agenda and have them define it in the face of the power brokers in Albany. To take back the state. We can do that because for the first time ever in a political party a grass-roots organization has a base. This is in our blood. This is what we do. It would be wonderful to have ACORN members in office. And it would be wonderful to have a situation where people fear us."

"Sharks," Gloria Waldron added, and her teeth glinted in a smile.[15] She ended our meeting by asking everyone to hold hands and bow our heads as she led an informal prayer.

Wagging the Dog?

By the summer of 2000, the WFP was really beginning to make waves. Its annual budget was up to $800,000, supporting a paid permanent staff of sixteen. A dozen chapters had been established around the state. Some bigger unions, like Local 1199, UNITE, and the National Education Association, had decided to affiliate, though still in a modest way. And for the first time in years, the political center of gravity in New York was shifting. "Feeling Vulnerable, Albany Republicans Nudge Senate to the Left," read the headline in the New York Times, reporting on how the GOP majority was loosening its stranglehold on the state legislature in response to worries from some of its more marginal members that they might face a more vigorous opposition on Election Day than in the past.[16] To protect themselves, they passed a hate crimes bill covering gays and lesbians (after blocking the same for more than a decade), acceded to a new gun control measure, and agreed to expand health care coverage for the working poor (a deal that was primarily leveraged by Dennis Rivera's powerful 1199 union). Most telling, they opened the door to a sizable increase in the state minimum wage, negotiating seriously over that issue with Assembly Democrats who themselves had started to show some initiative after years of letting the Republicans shape the state agenda around low taxes, budget cuts, and tough-on-crime posturing.

This impulse did not come from regular Democrats, who have long had a cozy relationship with the Republicans. And it certainly did not come from the Liberal Party, which was essentially now a family law firm with a ballot line to barter for patronage jobs. Despite the fact that registered Democrats outnumbered Republicans in New York by almost two to one, and national Democratic candidates ranging from Michael Dukakis to Bill Clinton had taken the state in presidential elections, state Democratic leaders had done little to upset the balance of power. New York had the most highly unionized workforce in the country, and yet it was also number one in income inequality.

Even with fusion as an option for third parties, New York had evolved its own version of duopoly politics. Most infamously, when he was governor, Mario Cuomo conspicuously refrained from helping Democratic candidates for the state Senate unseat Republican incumbents. Critics were never able to figure out if this was because the liberal governor cut a deal with his Republican opponents, or if he liked having a Republican majority in the state senate that he could blame for blocking initiatives that his base would give him credit for—even if he really didn't want them to pass. (The late Walter Karp, the country's best dissector of duopoly politics, wrote a whole book about this game of propping up "indispensable enemies.")[17] Each party has controlled one house in the legislature for many years, and they have a well-known understanding not to use their respective fund-raising arms to aid candidates of their own party when they run against incumbents in the chamber that the other party controls. Such attacks would most likely be futile, as the parties also cooperate in the drawing of legislative district boundaries so as to ensure the maximum number of safe seats for their members—picking their voters before the voters pick them. At the same time, both party committees happily rake in huge donations from special interest groups and lobbyists, and collude in blocking any campaign finance reform legislation that might clean up that swamp and make it possible for challengers to compete with them on a level playing field.[18]

While the Working Families Party was nowhere as oppositional as the Greens, its demonstrated ability to mobilize both base voters (black and brown) and occasional voters (white working stiffs and suburban independents) around an economic populist agenda and the vision of political independence had given it some real muscle in state politics. Less than a year after the party kicked off its push to raise the minimum wage all the way up to $6.75 an hour and index it to inflation—which would make it the highest in America—there was real movement on the issue. The Democrat-controlled Assembly rushed to pass the WFP's bill, and then, in a real sign of the party's growing influence, all of the vulnerable Senate Republicans from Long Island, New York City, and Westchester County were practically begging for the WFP's endorsement, offering their support for the WFP's minimum wage increase in exchange. The moment presented the WFP's leaders with a difficult quandary: cut a deal with Republicans that would help nearly nine hundred thousand of the working poor, or try to reduce the size of the Republican Senate majority in order to pass this bill and others down the road. A deal nearly happened, despite heavy pressure from state Democrats on the WFP not to endorse any of their opponents. What killed it was a last-minute lobbying campaign by the state's business community.[19]

At the same time, it should be noted that the WFP's minimum wage bill included its own modest deal with the devil. Earlier in the year, the state minimum was about to rise from $4.25 to $5.15, a move aimed at helping migrant workers and others not covered by the federal minimum. As a result, some 111,000 waitresses, busboys, and bartenders—whose wages were pegged at just two-thirds of the state minimum since they also get tips—were about to see their hourly minimum rise from $2.90 to $3.50. That is, until the restaurant industry weighed in and got its Democratic allies like Assembly Speaker Sheldon Silver to agree to roll that raise back to $3.30 an hour. Even worse, this last-minute change also delinked the waiters' wage from the general minimum. Future increases in their wages would no longer come if the overall state floor was lifted. Organized labor had made a big push to help the migrant workers, even though they are not allowed to unionize. But the restaurant workers were left hanging. The WFP's own bill did nothing about this, out of a pragmatic calculation that they weren't powerful enough to take on the restaurant association. And they gladly stood with Speaker Silver at a press conference touting their own minimum wage bill, giving him political cover after he sold out the restaurant workers. Unlike other, more ideological third-parties, the WFP's leaders understood that it meant little to make demands on the political system that they had no ability to enforce. Their power to dictate terms would be defined by how well they did in elections.[20]

"One of our biggest problems is we have to figure out how to wag the dog and not just be the tail that gets wagged," Cantor said to me several months into the party's first year of existence. How not to be a mere adjunct of the Democratic Party, especially in the top-of-the-ballot races that draw most public attention, is a complicated problem for the WFP that is rooted in the forces that birthed the party and not an issue that is about to go away. Certainly the party's early and enthusiastic endorsement of Hillary Clinton in the 2000 U.S. Senate race put the matter front and center. This, after all, was a first lady who once said, "There is no left in the Clinton White House,"[21] and whose trail of deceit and expediency left little to the imagination. But the WFP's leaders knew that they weren't strong enough to do anything different that wouldn't blow up their coalition, and that they had to patiently build for the day that they could act more independently.

That's not to say that Hillary Clinton got the WFP line for free. Each of the party's major constituent organizations had lengthy interviews with her, and some managed to extract a useful promise or two in exchange. She told Citizen Action that she would support the group's comprehensive "Clean Money/Clean Elections" full public financing approach to campaign finance reform. (A year later, to her credit, she joined as a co-sponsor of Senator Wellstone's bill with the same title.) Bob Master pointed out that "in the process of our interviewing her for the endorsement she heard from UAW people on how her position on trade is no good, and there's been some impact on her speaking out for the right to organize and the need to raise the minimum wage."[22] She also came out against a bill that would cap damages paid to workers injured by asbestos—though it was sponsored by her colleague-to-be, Senator Chuck Schumer.

Still, the Hillary pill did not go down easily with all the WFP's members. More than a few of them hissed when Clinton mentioned her support of welfare reform during a speech she gave at a WFP fund-raiser at the Sheraton hotel in Manhattan in mid-February 2000. An African American at the event who was one of the party's rising stars told me that the endorsement was just for "political expediency." One of the party's full-time staffers was blunter. "One-third of our members think she's a hero," this person said, referring especially to its African-American and Latino members in places like

Brooklyn and Queens. "One-third are just 'eh' on her, but agree she's better than [Republican nominee Rick] Lazio. And one third probably think she's a dyke, and I don't mean that in the positive sense," referring to many of the party's unionized white suburbanites and outer borough dwellers. Ericka Bozzi Gomez, the Rockland County organizer, agreed with this picture. As she worked on the party's big get-out-the-vote effort that fall, she told me, "I definitely have a separate column for my 'yes' votes for Zebrowski and for Hillary. But I tell the one-third that don't like her to put the 880,000 minimum wage earners in the state ahead of whatever they think of her personally."[23]

For Jim Duncan, party co-chair, this was a no-brainer. "If we draw 150,000 to 200,000 votes that help elect Hillary Clinton, every politician in the state is going to stand up, take notice, and want those votes in the future," he told the thousand WFP delegates who came to the party's first state convention in March 2000. (Total New York turnout in a presidential election year was expected to be about 7 million.) "And I can promise that we will deliver those votes only to those candidates and elected officials who deliver for us—on raising wages, improving workers comp benefits, funding health care, child care, and education." And, indeed, there was no open grumbling among the party's core activists at the convention, though Irv Feiner, the rumpled old leftist from Rockland, was worried about the future. "If Hillary gets that many votes on our line, the dynamics of New York state will be tremendously changed," he said. "It'll be tough. There will be competing interests within this organization. You can't allow the loony left to go crazy, but you also can't allow labor to ignore certain things either."

Feiner was putting his finger on one of the WFP's major fault lines, the divergent impulses of organized labor and middle-class progressives. "You can't have a serious third party without labor," he said. "And I understand the difficulties some of them have with their own members." Many of the WFP's unions included relatively well-off suburban whites—people who had populist attitudes about economics, but were often conservative on many social issues and wary of paying higher taxes to help troubled inner-city dwellers. "You certainly can't force labor leadership past where their members are," Feiner added. But he knew that someday the WFP would face a reckoning. "Somewhere along the line, if the Democratic Party doesn't straighten out, there will be a split," he predicted.[24] The role of organized labor in the party was also important because it was unions who were providing the lion's share of the party's funds, rather than individual members. As long as that was the case, the WFP would tilt toward the more cautious, close-to-the-vest tactics of union political directors, and the independent development of local chapters would be restrained by labor's pragmatism.

The WFP's other big fault line was, not surprisingly, race. While this surfaced along a whole array of issues—tax policy, education funding, welfare reform—none was hotter than crime and the police. At first, the party's founders swept the problem under the carpet. They said nothing publicly even after Peter Vallone, their cross-endorsed nominee for governor in 1998, spoke out in support of Mayor Giuliani's police after they stormed a Harlem youth rally.[25] But two years later, when Patrick Dorismond, a twenty-six-year-old Haitian-American security guard was shot to death after he angrily rebuffed an undercover cop who asked him if he knew where to buy drugs, the issue could wait no longer. The party's executive committee drafted a statement on Dorismond's shooting, which was delivered with great passion by Bob Master at the height of the party's first convention. "The Executive Committee of the Working Families Party has decided that we could not let this evening pass without expressing our concerns about the profound problems of racial disunity and police violence now taking place in New York City," he began, speaking to a packed room at the Desmond Hotel and conference center in Albany. In the back of his mind, he told me later, he was worrying about the many white members of his own union who themselves had relatives or friends who were cops. Yet he plowed ahead:

> From our very inception, the Working Families Party has held as one of its essential values that the concerns that unite us far outweigh those that divide us. We recognize, respect, and celebrate our diversity; but we also deeply believe that all working families, regardless of color, care more than anything about having a decent job, providing for the health, safety, and well-being of their families, and giving their children the opportunity to achieve their highest aspirations, whatever they may be.
>
> . . . we all know how difficult it can sometimes be to hear one another, to understand one another, across the racial disharmony that has so often tragically divided us throughout American history. Few of us truly understand the experiences and perspectives of those of a different race.
>
> . . . Bridging these differences in experience, perception and emotion is especially difficult when it comes to the problem of police violence. This is a complicated, highly charged issue. . . . We know that the vast majority of police officers are trying to do a difficult job, protecting the public, under difficult circumstances, to the best of their ability. Most have no hatred in their hearts, and seek only to serve the public. Many would probably look at me and say "what do you know, you live in a relatively safe neighborhood, how can you possibly know the decisions we have to make every day on the street?"
>
> That may well be true. But I do know a few things for sure. For me, as for many of you in the room, my children are the center of my life. I have two wonderful kids, a daughter who will be 8 next month and a son who will be 11 in June. I know that a few years from now, when Ben is a teenager out on his own, I'll have a lot to worry about: where he's going, who he's hanging out with, whether or not he's started fooling around with drugs or alcohol. As any of you who have older children know, these are the worries that plague any parent of a teenager. And when he gets a few years older than that, I'll have to worry about his common sense behind the wheel of a car, the decisions he makes as a new driver.

But what I will not have to worry about is that an overzealous cop is going to throw him up against the wall and frisk him, just because his hair is red; or worse, draw a gun on him because he fits the "profile" of the most recent criminal suspect. I know that I won't have to teach him to stick his hands out the window of the car if he's ever pulled over by the police, in order to reassure a nervous, poorly trained, or overanxious police officer. I won't have to worry about these things because I'm white, and for the most part, white parents are spared this terrible additional heartache of parenting a teenager.

This is just plain wrong, and it is inconceivable why the mayor cannot comprehend these things. . . . Something is wrong and something needs to be changed—police tactics, police training, police management. We can and must do better. Racial disunity, racial fear, racial killings must not be the price of safety on the street.

In New York City, in New York state, we all must find ways of coming together, not pulling apart. We need leaders who can bring us together. We need leaders who can foster understanding and appreciation of the ways in which we are unique and different, but especially of the values and concerns that unite all the state's working families. Hopefully, in November, we will elect this kind of leadership.

Master finished his remarks by asking for a moment of silence. And then a thousand black, white, and brown New Yorkers, inner-city dwellers and comfortable suburbanites, spontaneously linked arms to sing "We Shall Overcome," the old civil rights hymn. A few members of Master's own union walked out during the speech, which Master later likened to sticking his finger "in an electric socket," but the vast majority of those in attendance stood in solidarity with their black and brown comrades.[26]

"That speech summed up for me who this party is, why this party is, and what this party is," Bertha Lewis of ACORN told me later. "This is not some fairytale land. You've got poor people, middle-class people, white people, black people all in a room together. What do you think you're going to get? That was our founding convention. Bob could have shied away from the issue and said nothing, which is what the other parties usually do. But if this is not going to be just a labor party, or just a community organization party— if this is going to be something dynamic, you are going to have conversations where race matters, and more so than race, where class matters and where gender matters. Sure, some of our state committee meetings are contentious, but I say, good for us."[27]

Building a Base

The future of the WFP is wide open. Everyone involved knows that what they are doing will take many years of constant struggle and hard work, that even the little victories will not come easily. The 2001 mayoral battle in New York City was sure to strain the party's internal alliances. The party also was hoping to affect a number of city council races. And the hard work of building local chapters and screening local candidates will never end. As Cantor said in his memo to the New Party's stalwarts after their Supreme Court loss, there are no shortcuts.

The WFP's Rockland chapter learned this lesson at the end of 2000, as its careful base-building work to pass a countywide living-wage bill fell short by one vote. The betrayal came not from the one Republican whose support they had managed to obtain, but from a Democratic legislator from Ramapo who had given them his word and then double-crossed them. Ryan Karben, the turncoat, was said to have higher ambitions to someday run for county executive and then Congress, and decided he needed the support of the local business community more than its activist heart. "A young Al Gore," Tom Stoner, the chapter co-chair called him bitterly, and promised revenge. (Cantor speculated that if Karben didn't come back around on the living-wage issue, the WFP might try to beat him in the primaries or run an independent against him in the next general election.)[28]

But the Rockland living-wage push paid off in other ways. "I'm getting tons of calls from Haitians, blacks, and Latino folks who have always been hard-core Democrats," Ericka Bozzi Gomez said afterward. The chapter's ranks had grown from 30 dues-paying members to 136 by the November 2000 election.[29] And the WFP's organizing cadre had learned important lessons that they would use as they set up living-wage coalitions in Suffolk, Westchester, and Albany counties. Gomez admitted that in some ways, the Rockland effort had been built backwards. "It was a breach birth. We started with 30 members off the Zebrowski special [election] and went right into the living wage push, instead of building our base first."

By the spring of 2001, the Rockland WFP had reached a plateau. "Right after the election, everyone was tired," said Tom Stoner. "We had just gotten our butts kicked on the living wage." The chapter had also lost the support of Bozzi, their full-time organizer, who was now assigned to organizing living-wage efforts in the rest of the state. But they were holding their own, without the help of any paid staff, which was very good news in the eyes of the WFP's leaders.[30] Affirming that they had a real base, they had gotten close to sixteen hundred votes for Hillary Clinton on their line countywide. Most members were renewing. A newsletter was going out regularly to of more than fifteen hundred people. "Suburban organizing is interesting," said Stoner, with a rueful chuckle. "But slow growth is better than fast growth based on unreal expectations," he added. "We've got a committed core of twenty-five people who have been with us for eighteen months and they're not flagging."[31] The chapter was kicking off a six-month effort to carefully construct a broad-based committee to address the problem of affordable housing in a comprehensive, homegrown manner.

Statewide, the WFP had much to crow about for its overall growth. The party had tallied 102,360 votes for Hillary Clinton on its line, 2.7 percent of her total and 1.5 percent of the overall vote. This was almost exactly double the number of votes the WFP got for Peter Vallone in 1998. "How Sweet It Is!" Cantor exulted in an e-mail to party supporters, in which he boasted with just a little too much spin that the WFP was now the state's fourth-largest party, just behind the Conservatives and ahead of the Liberal and Independence parties.[32] In fact, according to the number of votes each party got for the candidate it endorsed for president, the WFP was fifth, as the Greens had gotten 244,030 for Nader.[33] And while the WFP's 88,395 votes for Gore were more than the 51,325 it got in 1998, this increase was in line with the overall increase in turnout expected in a presidential election year.

But the party had put all its focus on producing a big boost for Hillary Clinton on its line, mobilizing thousands of volunteers and building an extensive grass-roots network that contacted voters in a variety of ways.[34] Here, it had striking successes, particularly in districts that were strongly Democratic in leaning but historically low in voter participation. The party also demonstrated that it could appeal to so-called swing voters—the "forgotten majority" of white working-class men and women living in the outer boroughs of New York City or economically troubled upstate counties. And it had done these things against an overall statewide trend that saw the vote for Senate on other third-party lines drop substantially.[35]

Many black and brown voters were excited about Hillary Clinton's Senate run (even after Rudy Giuliani, their nemesis, dropped out of the race), and turnout in inner-city neighborhoods was understandably strong. But the WFP surpassed expectations in the districts where it, along with ACORN, worked hard to contact occasional voters, people who had voted only once in the last four elections. In some assembly districts in Bushwick, Bedford-Stuyvesant, and East New York—the poorest parts of Brooklyn— the WFP's total jumped more than 600 percent.[36] And white working-class voters and suburban union members—people who often felt some hostility toward the Democrats and Hillary Clinton for their perceived elitism and supposed coddling of minorities—proved open to the argument that a vote on the WFP's line would send politicians a message in support of "quality public schools, affordable health care, and good jobs that pay living wages."[37] Those were the words the party's organizers used in their script for volunteers doing phone banking.

The only places where the WFP's local presence didn't translate into increased votes were the New York City suburbs. Its vote in Rockland County did triple compared to 1998, but otherwise its showing in Nassau, Suffolk, and Westchester was disappointing. The party also saw little increase in its support in the city's liberal and progressive neighborhoods, but its leaders didn't appear too disturbed by this. In fact, they were pleased to note that their total was far less dependent on progressive districts than in 1998.[38] A year earlier, Daniel Cantor had said to me that his "nightmare headline" for the WFP would be "Tired Liberals Regroup under New Banner." His hopeful preference: "Unexpected Cross-Racial Alliance Emphasizes Class Issues and Makes Headway." Well, he wasn't much of a headline craftsman, but he was getting his wish.[39]

The Future

11

The Prospects for America's Third Parties

The Democratic Muscle

The three-volume *Encyclopedia of Third Parties in America*, published in 2000, has entries for 117 parties, covering almost every substantial national- and state-level effort from A to W, from the Afro-American Party of the 1960s to the Workingmen's Party of the 1830s. This is out of a larger pool of perhaps 200 third parties that have formed and disappeared since the early 1800s. Today there are at least 38 third parties active at various levels of meaningful organization. Twenty exist in one state only.[1] Thirteen others are primarily doctrinal sects or cults of personality with little hope of reaching pluralities, if not majorities, of voters.[2]

That would leave five with national prospects, but for all intents and purposes, the Reform Party died after the 2000 election. In April 2001, Russ Verney, its original chairman, left his job as Ross Perot's right-hand man to work for a public interest group, Judicial Watch. "There aren't many remnants of [the party] left," Verney acknowledged as he made the move. The only thing that could revive Reform would be another presidential run by Patrick Buchanan. The right-wing columnist raised about $15 million in 2000 (apart from the $16.6 million he received in public funds during the primaries and for the general race). Much of that came from small individual donors. So, at least the potential base for a Buchanan candidacy remains. But it doesn't seem likely.[3]

That leaves four parties—the Greens, the Libertarians, the New Party, and the Labor Party—with serious aspirations of reaching the broader citizenry. But it makes little sense to include the Labor Party in that number until it actually starts running candidates in elections. To the remaining group of three, I would add three of the existing single-state parties—Minnesota's Independence Party, Vermont's Progressive Party, and New York's Working Families Party—as models that have something to say to the rest of the country.

Do third parties have a future in American politics? Specifically, do they have a future beyond nipping at the heels of the major parties? Unless or until states actually outlaw their existence, third parties will show up periodically on the ballot. That's the "easy" part. Enough Americans believe in fair play to give party activists that first leg up, a signature on a petition form.[4] And some of these parties are making the petitioning process less onerous, both by suing state elections officials and by carefully planning their ballot drives.[5] Third-party bids will keep on coming. But will they ever get strong enough to force the major parties to make changes in policy, or elect enough of their own to govern in a different direction? Specifically, do these six third parties have that kind of future?

The signs ahead are both good and bad. While the terrorist attacks of September 11, 2001, produced an immediate public outpouring of support for the government and all its institutions, this moment cannot last unless it is accompanied by a far-reaching set of changes in how mainstream politics is now conducted in America. Without such changes, political alienation, the breeding ground for third-party hopes, could easily reignite. Consider all the cources of the gap between the rulers and the ruled in America seems to grow greater. Candidates campaign with highly staged appearances at locations where the hosts have good reason to behave, like public schools and senior centers; when citizens organize to "act up," politicians are usually nowhere to be found. Real, unscripted, interchange in public between politicians and their subjects is a rarity. During the 2000 New York Senate race, Hillary Clinton actually dared to charge admission fees at some of the stops on her vaunted "listening tours."[6] Even the rare "town hall" style meetings held by the occasional senator or representative involve the public primarily as spectators; the politician holds the microphone and sets the agenda, the audience hoots, whistles, applauds, or waits in line for a brief moment of self-expression.

Accountability, in the sense of organized people marshaling their collective memory against the record of the action, or inaction, of the politician representing them is practically non-existent. Instead, we have partisan name-calling, in which tiny but influential groups of Democratic and Republican loyalists and pundits accuse the other side of all manner of ethical and legal violations, while ignoring or justifying the exact same behavior by their own. (Or worse—they both agree to sweep certain scandals under the rug.) This is not accountability, but a kind of mutually assured protection racket. Step back from the details of the day-to-day political struggles in Washington, and what do you see? Both the Democrats and Republicans are in a kind of slow-motion collapse, where the main thing keeping them standing up is the fact that they are falling into each other, like two drunks holding each other up as they stumble down the street.

This lack of accountability combined with the reality that most seats in Congress are safe for life has produced a culture of near impunity. U.S. representatives use their websites to advertise everything but their actual voting record. Politicians who once promised to limit their own term in office renege, telling their constituents they know better now. The number of millionaires in Congress vastly outpaces their presence in the general population, reinforcing a dramatic distance from the lives of most people. In one congressional district in the Northeast, the same House member who once marched in his hometown's July 4th parade beside the firefighters has now developed a taste for expensive hand-tailored suits and cufflinks. One U.S. senator (now under investigation for corruption) takes a private chartered jet to fly fifty miles from one local town to another. The traffic jams his constituents must live with every day are not for him.

Other, more formal, entry points to the political discourse for the voices of ordinary people are blocked as well. Only one-eighth of 1 percent of all Americans old enough to vote gave a federal candidate for office a $1,000 contribution in the 2000 elections. Most people instinctively understand that under the terms of our campaign finance system they are priced out of real access and influence as effectively as if Congress enacted a new poll tax, charging people for their right to vote. Instead, under the guise of "campaign finance reform," in the spring of 2001 the Senate voted to double the individual contribution limit to $2,000 — a boon to incumbents and wealthy donors but a mockery of real reform. And, because of the lack of public financing, even the good people in Congress are forced to spend most of their time chasing checks from the rich. Is it any wonder there's more interest on Capitol Hill in cutting tax rates for the wealthy, deregulating the financial sector, and making bankruptcy law friendlier to credit card companies than there is in expanding health care coverage to the uninsured or rebuilding crumbling public schools? Even in the heat of the post-September 11 crisis, some members of Congress were pressing to reward their backers in the energy industry with a rush to open the Alaskan wilderness to oil rigs, while others bickered over extending unemployment benefits to people displaced by the attacks.

Signs of voter unhappiness with the electoral process that intensified after the Bush–Gore fight over the recount, have been met with modest improvements in some places and back-room backsliding in others. In general, the Florida crisis prompted state legislatures to produce mostly technical fixes to their voting systems.[7] Despite hundreds of bills introduced and lawsuits filed, little has been done to address the underlying inequalities exposed by the vote count in Florida. As of May 2001, two states had moved seriously to restore the right to vote to former felons who had paid their debt to society — New Mexico and Connecticut. In Florida, where investigative reporting showed that tens of thousands of people had been unjustly deprived of the franchise, nothing was done about this scandal. (Not only did the state legislature reject a proposal to restore former felons' voting rights, it eliminated some public matching funds for campaigns as part of its "electoral reform" package.)[8] Elsewhere, state Republican Party leaders contemplated quiet steps to restrict their primaries to party members only, disturbed by the surprising strength of maverick Senator John McCain among independent voters. In California, Democratic Governor Gray Davis squelched legislative proposals for Election Day voter registration à la Minnesota, fearful that such a change would produce more Jesse Venturas.[9]

The democratic impulse is a muscle that must be exercised regularly; when people grow up in a political culture that devalues their participation and treats them as passive objects to be manipulated, that muscle atrophies. Nothing illustrates this better than the generally quiescent response to the destruction of public space where democratic interaction can take place. Americans take it for granted now that most of the locations where they casually encounter fellow citizens are legally closed to civic affairs. Instead, they see politics as at best something to be watched on TV or read about in the newspaper. Shopping malls and supermarkets are deemed private property, where no petitioning or other forms of political gathering can be legally prohibited, even though these places have effectively destroyed the old "Main Street" village thoroughfare. Life in retirement villages and gated communities is often governed by restrictive bylaws that suppress on-site political activity by their residents, or require them to stick to nonpartisan affairs. But few people seem to mind. Thus, when the U.S. Postal Service announced that it would no longer permit petitioning on the property of post offices, there were a few protests but no sustained outcry. With the major political parties and incumbent politicians more and more in thrall to the demands of big money fund-raising, and much valuable work of public interest conducted by nonprofit, nonpartisan groups that are legally obligated to avoid direct involvement in elections, often the only places where the citizenry's democratic muscles are still being developed to their fullest are the nation's third parties.

The future of America's leading third parties—the Greens, the Libertarians, the New Party, the Minnesota Independence Party, the New York Working Families Party, and the Vermont Progressives—depends entirely on their ability to build those muscles. Can they? To take Daniel Cantor's sage observation about the New Party and extend it, the only answer is, there are no shortcuts. While public interest in third-party alternatives remains high in the abstract, the actual level of tangible resources available to these projects to tap and channel that interest is fairly low. Three factors are critical: money, organizers, and public awareness. Money can come from public sources, rich individuals, affiliated institutions, and members. Organizers—the people who actually do the work of building the party—can be either paid or volunteer. And public awareness of specific third parties and their candidates—the most precious and intangible of political commodities—can come from their own efforts to project themselves into the public eye (high-level races, celebrity candidates, cutting-edge issue campaigns) as well as from sympathetic media coverage.

Each of these six parties have some of these assets in hand or in reach. Take money, politics' mother's milk. Nader raised $8.8 million in 2000 from a pool of some eighty thousand individual donors. The Libertarians' presidential candidate, Harry Browne, raised just over $2 million, and the national party raised and spent $3.3 million on top of that. Membership dues cover New Party chapters' local operating costs. The Working Families Party had a statewide budget of about $800,000 in 2000. Jesse Ventura's campaign committee raised about $200,000 in 1999, most of that from selling campaign memorabilia like action dolls; his party also tapped $20,000 in contributions under the state's tax refund program. And Vermont's Progressives drew on the state's innovative Clean Elections full public financing program, raising more than $35,000 from more than sixteen hundred small contributors in order to obtain some $260,000 in public funding for their 2000 gubernatorial candidate, Anthony Pollina. All of these totals show the parties in question have developed real funding bases that they should be able to continue to tap for the near future.

In some cases, this money is already enough to pay for staffing. The Libertarians have a national staff of about a dozen. Nader is keeping on eight people from his campaign and he has started a nonprofit, Citizen Works, to help build the Greens. The WFP has a full-time staff of sixteen. Officeholders ranging from Governor Ventura on down provide their own in-kind contributions of time and effort. Elsewhere, the money is thinner but keeps a core of one or two key campaign organizers going. Communications technologies like e-mail and the World Wide Web are also lowering the cost of organizing and advertising. Of course, money isn't everything in third-party organizing. Enthusiasm and devotion keep hundreds of volunteers active in all these parties. Nor do third parties need financial parity before they can break through to voters. The strong showings of Green congressional candidates in New Mexico—who were vastly outspent by their opponents—along with Ventura's victory, suggest that if a third-party candidate has a strong message and enough resources to be heard by voters, disgust with the major-party choices can translate into a rapid rise for the alternative candidate.

Changing the Media Mind

But if America's leading third parties are to thrive, there will have to be an alteration in the media's attitude toward the phenomenon. Despite their current and historic contributions to the democratic process, third-party candidates are generally treated as nuts, nuisances, or nonpersons. The night that Jesse Ventura won in Minnesota, on-air correspondent John Hockenberry of MSNBC openly sneered.[10] NBC's Tom Brokaw asked Ventura if he should be addressed as "Governor Jesse Ventura, or Governor Jesse 'The Body' Ventura." You could almost hear the snickers from the control room. The New York Times front-page story on his win couldn't resist poking fun at his roots in the professional wrestling business. Robert Scheer, a liberal columnist for the *Los Angeles Times*, said on his radio show on KCRW, "The people of Minnesota should be spanked for letting this happen."[11]

Press coverage of the Reform Party shenanigans was equally telling. Granted, some of the oddballs who presented themselves at the party's meetings deserved criticism. But opinion magazines of the center-left and center-right, including the *New Republic* and the *Weekly Standard*—places where so-called opinion leaders go to get their dose of conventional wisdom, took remarkably similar approaches. Along with extensive investigative features reporting on Perot, Buchanan, and Fulani's involvement in the party—much of it quite good—these magazines reveled in the opportunity to make fun of the average Americans who were attracted to the party. Their reports on its 1999 convention in Dearborn, Michigan, where support for Jesse Ventura produced a resounding rebuke of the Perot-Verney leadership of the party and set off Jack Gargan's ill-fated chairmanship, were full of derision. Their reporters seemed to be more interested in their own ability to write a colorful put-down than address any serious questions about the party's future.[12] To my knowledge, only three mainstream outlets— ABC News, *USA Today*, and the Fort-Worth *Star-Telegram*, delegated a full-time reporter to the third-party beat in 2001. And even though these reporters did their jobs with much gusto, they often had to fight to get their stories aired or published.

Few journalists wore as many of their biases on their sleeves as Tucker Carlson, a young Republican who made his mark at the *Weekly Standard* and then vaulted, with his bow tie, to CNN's *Crossfire*, where he played the conservative to Bill Press's liberal. An interview he did in mid-July 1999 with third-party advocate and former independent Governor Lowell Weicker was quite revealing of the mainstream view of such efforts. "Why burden Americans with another name on the ballot?" Carlson asked Weicker. "It seems to me that third-party candidacies aren't going anywhere. Protest candidacies as yours, I think we'd both agree, make people cynical. They see a name on the ballot. They think, he's not going to get elected. You know, this is why American politics is pointless, because people who can't win run." Carlson seemed to be saying that he would prefer it if there was just one candidate on the ballot at a time.[13]

But this notion of democracy as a burden and third-party candidates as bothersome wasn't just held by up-and-coming right-wingers like Carlson. The very same attitude imbued the *New York Times*'s editorial attacks on Nader's campaign. His was "a self-indulgent exercise that will distract voters from the clear-cut choice represented by the major-party candidates. . . . The public deserves to see the major-party candidates compete on an uncluttered playing field."[14] Contorting themselves in knots, the paper's editorialists were at pains to explain why they had criticized the Commission on Presidential Debates for excluding Perot in 1996 but agreed with its decision to exclude Nader and Buchanan in 2000:

We argued that since Mr. Perot had run a strong race in 1992 and still had a broad national standing four years later, he had the right to debate President Clinton and Senator Bob Dole. This year, however, neither Ralph Nader nor Patrick Buchanan has yet reached the status of a candidate with demonstrated national support. Should that change as the campaign progresses, the commission can respond accordingly. For now, the public deserves to see Mr. Bush and Mr. Gore lay out the substantial differences between them, without interference from third- or fourth-party candidates who have not built solid constituencies.[15]

Actually, in 1996, Perot was at 8 percent in the polls when the commission arbitrarily decided to exclude him; four years later polls showed Nader at anywhere between 4 and 6 percent when the commission snuffed his debate bid. In both cases those numbers showed "solid constituencies" in support of their candidacies. The *Times* also paid no heed to polls showing a majority of Americans wanting Nader and Buchanan included in the debates.

The *Times*'s editorial attacks on Nader's candidacy, and by extension all unsanctioned third-party behavior, were truly startling when read against other statements made by the paper on the issue of democracy. Not only were the paper's editorialists strong advocates of reducing money's role in politics, they had several times in the not too distant past stood up and roared against attempts to close the ballot to unwanted candidates. In January of 2000, the paper of record lambasted George W. Bush "and his New York henchmen—Gov. George Pataki and the Republican Party chairman, William Powers" for indulging "in a shameful display of Soviet-style politics." Their crime? Rigging the state's Republican primary so that Bush would be the only candidate on the ballot. This was explicitly an editorial in favor of a multicandidate election, since the *Times* was advocating on behalf of Steve Forbes's and John McCain's efforts to get onto state ballots. The paper even ran a map showing New York's "democracy-free zones"—congressional districts where those candidates had their petitions challenged "and voters may therefore have their choices narrowed because of an unfair and outdated system."[16] A little more than two-and-a-half years earlier, the *Times* congratulated Governor Tom Ridge of Pennsylvania for vetoing a new set of ballot access rules that would have drastically increased the number of petition signatures needed for third-party candidates to get on the ballot there and shortened the period during which they could be collected. Noting that third parties were on the rise nationally, the *Times* scolded the state legislature for trying to monopolize its hold on power. "The legislators might keep in mind that it was the Liberty Party of 1840 that prompted people to think about the idea of abolishing slavery, and an upstart Republican Party that introduced a politician named Abraham Lincoln," the *Times* concluded.[17]

As public opinion leaders at the nation's most prestigious newspapers and journals justified closing their minds to vigorous public debate and political competition, the country's public broadcasters were given the same message by the Supreme Court. Once upon a time, twenty-odd years ago, the High Court ruled that a "central tenet of the First Amendment [was] that the government must remain neutral in the market-place of ideas." But then came *Forbes v. Arkansas Educational Television Commission*. On May 18, 1998, the court turned its back on its own First Amendment doctrine, ruling that a state-owned public television station, the Arkansas Educational Television Commission (AETC), could legally restrict a 1992 congressional candidates debate it organized to just the Democratic and Republican nominees, even though it shut out a ballot-qualified independent candidate named Ralph Forbes. The *Forbes* decision was bad news for minor parties and maverick candidates and another stake in the heart of democratic civic culture.

In a manner eerily reminiscent of its earlier ruling in the New Party's *Timmons* case, the Court's 6–3 majority blithely skirted the essential facts of the case. (In fact, it was the same majority of six in the *Timmons* decision.) In his opinion, Justice Anthony Kennedy wrote, "Forbes was a perennial candidate who had sought, without success, a number of elected offices in Arkansas." (The same was true of Abraham Lincoln in Illinois before he was elected president.) In fact, Forbes had twice been a serious contender for the Republican nomination for lieutenant governor of Arkansas, receiving 47 percent of the statewide vote in 1990 and carrying fifteen of the sixteen counties within the Third Congressional District—where he next sought office—by absolute majorities. In 1992, he decided to declare for Congress as an independent, and managed to collect more than six thousand signatures to qualify for the ballot. But even though he was on the ballot, the AETC staff excluded him from their debate because they deemed him not viable. They noted his lack of a paid staff or a formal campaign headquarters (he was running his campaign from his home) as well as the fact that the local media weren't planning to report his vote totals in their Election Night coverage as proof that he wasn't a serious candidate.

It did not trouble the Supreme Court majority that the AETC had included similarly weak candidates—including one who raised less money than Forbes—in debates it sponsored in Arkansas's other congressional districts, solely because they were Democrats or Republicans. Instead the justices seemed satisfied AETC's decision to exclude Forbes was "a reasonable, viewpoint-neutral exercise of its journalistic discretion." But there is nothing neutral about suppressing the speech of unpopular candidates. Even worse, AETC was allowed to do this even though it was a government agency running five public television stations, paid for by state taxpayers, with a board appointed by the governor. Most Americans would object if the government started printing the words "not viable" next to the names of some candidates on the ballot. But that, essentially, is what the Supreme Court allowed the AETC to do in the *Forbes* decision.[18]

The Prospects for America's Leading Third Parties

There are no shortcuts. And in addition to fairer coverage, today's third parties need tangible evidence that they are making progress if they are to keep their adherents' support and thus keep generating financial and volunteer support. I can see several paths forward. One is to use the existing openings at the level of nonpartisan races to elect local officials and produce modest innovations at the policy level. The second is to work hard to change the rules of elections, by enacting reforms like instant-runoff voting, fusion, public financing, same-day voter registration, nonpartisan redistricting, and free TV time for candidates (if not a Citizens Channel). The third is to run head-on at vulnerable major-party incumbents, deliberately spoiling for a fight. And the last is to somehow reorient politics by making an issue so salient voters decide to abandon the old liberal-conservative paradigm for something new. As of early 2001, America's leading third parties were working on all these strategies, with different priorities and prospects.

First, the state-specific parties:

Minnesota Independence Party (www.eindependence.org) — Thanks to Governor Ventura, the party has a real presence in state and, to some degree, national politics. Assuming he runs for reelection in 2002, that presence will be reaffirmed. So far, all he has said on that front is that he will wait until the state deadline in July 2002 to formally file, since he believes campaigns are too long. And if he runs, he says, he won't actively raise any money. Whether he will stick to that promise remains to be seen, though Ventura is probably the only politician currently alive in America who could run for reelection that way and win.

Beneath Ventura, the Independence Party is growing, though not necessarily fast enough to avoid the fate of "A Connecticut Party," which was also built around the popularity and success of an independent governor, Lowell Weicker, but didn't outlast his exit from politics. Unlike Weicker, however, Ventura has made a real effort to support lower-level candidates of his fledgling party. In 2000, the Independence Party fielded several congressional candidates who had significant effects on their races. One, Tom Foley, got 20.6 percent of the vote running in a three-way race for the seat vacated by Democrat Bruce Vento. Its Senate candidate, James Gibson, got 6 percent — enough to help tip the seat to the Democrats. Ten of the party's candidates for state legislative seats got 10 percent of the vote or more — one even hit 23 percent. And at least a dozen others drew in the high single digits. These showings are serious. Redistricting in 2002 may loosen the hold of some incumbents and create fresh opportunities in some legislative seats. Said Dean Barkley, one of the party's longtime leaders and now director of the Minnesota Planning Agency for Ventura, "The fact that we have had eight years of party building, six of which predated Ventura, gives us a stronger base. That gives us a better chance of surviving Jesse's exit from politics if that happens, but it doesn't mean we will. It just gives us a better chance."

Whether or not Ventura runs again (a likely but not definite prospect), he is working to create a real legacy of changes in the state from his tenure. After starting out with a modest agenda of returning the tax surplus to Minnesota's voters and increasing funding for public education—goals that were accomplished in his first year—Ventura decided to push for a few more ambitious reform items in his second year in office. He threw his support behind a drive to shift Minnesota to a unicameral legislature, called for a return to a single session of the legislature once every two years, backed some campaign finance reform measures, and proposed creating a citizen-driven redistricting process to take it out of the hands of the two-party duopoly. He also called for revamping the state's tax system to put less emphasis on property taxes and more on sales taxes, and took on the education establishment, insisting on tougher measures to judge schools' performance and an end to giving teachers automatic raises solely on the basis of each year they work. After allowing his commissioner for public safety (a former tough-on-crime Republican) to undermine his original support for the medical use of marijuana, he revived the issue and at least got a serious study of it rolling. Of course, calling for change and making it happen isn't the same thing—and Ventura has few allies in the legislature.

In 2001, Ventura pushed the legislature's warring halves to the verge of a government shutdown and ended up producing a budget that tilted to the Republicans on fiscal issues and to the Democrats on social issues. The budget did shift some of the burden for funding education off of property taxes and onto the state income tax—a more equitable approach—but its sharp cuts in the income tax and paltry increases for public education drew much Democratic ire. At the same time, Ventura expanded health insurance for children in poor families, eased back some welfare cutoffs, and forced the Republicans to back down on measures to restrict abortions. His unicameral legislature proposal and campaign finance bill made little headway.

Still, Ventura's model retains its relevance to third-party organizers in other states. He has shown that a "middle coalition" of independents, young people, folks of moderate income, inner-ring suburbanites, and reformers of all stripes can be constructed and driven right through the heart of the two-party duopoly. That example still has the power of a "demonstration project." But while the Minnesota model still stands, it won't spread unless its leaders take concrete steps to help fellow travelers in other states. And as of early 2001, there were few signs that this was going to happen. Ventura campaign manager Doug Friedline was trying to make a living as a full-time political consultant specializing in unconventional candidates. First, he courted two professional wrestlers who briefly considered a political bid (Jerry Lawlor and Ric Flair). He was hired to run John Hagelin's fall 2000 presidential campaign. Then he briefly went to work for a Libertarian candidate in New Jersey's 2001 gubernatorial race. When a maverick Republican state senator, Bill Schluter, decided to run in that race as an independent, Friedline switched houses. Adman Bill Hillsman had finished his stint with Nader, was looking into working for candidates in the New York City and Detroit mayoral races, and waiting to see what developed in Minnesota in 2002.

Dean Barkley and Phil Madsen, the party's veteran organizers, were focused on keeping the home fires burning. Barkley was busy recruiting a new party chairman and trying to find a strong Senate candidate to run in 2002 against incumbent Democrat Paul Wellstone and likely Republican nominee Norm Coleman. "That race will be a fair test to see if we can duplicate Jesse's win in 1998," Barkley commented. "But I do believe it's winnable if we can attract the right kind of candidate." He also projected that the party, which currently has one member in the legislature (a former Republican who switched parties), could elect some of its own. "If we have the governor at the head of the ticket, with a good Senate candidate, we should be able to recruit some good people for the legislature. Having a good candidate at the top helps, but it doesn't get you there. But if we can't make it stick here, maybe it's not going to work. I hope it will work."

Madsen was still the party's webmaster and treasurer of the Jesse Ventura Volunteer Committee, though no longer on a paid basis. In his view, the Independence Party had grown enormously from the day he stood up at a Perot petitioning meeting in the summer of 1992 and announced that he wanted to start a third party. But he still saw growing pains. Enthusiasm among party volunteers was often hard to sustain. The party's state committee had been distracted by a sexual harassment lawsuit against its chairman, and its fund-raising efforts were hampered by the perception that money raised would go to help defend against that suit rather than build the party. But Madsen believed those problems would blow over, pointing proudly to the fact that party members agreed on the rules for dealing with internal disputes and nothing had provoked a crisis of the kind seen when the Reform Party split apart because its last few members couldn't even agree on how to make decisions. In the meantime, he said, the Independence Party's chapters were still initiating their own projects, particularly in the fourth and sixth congressional districts where its voter base was strongest. "We could grow a lot faster if we took PAC money," he joked. But he was proud of the many subtle changes under way in the state thanks to the Independence Party's existence.

Most impressive was the party's intervention in the all-important process of drawing new election district lines after the 2000 census. "Traditionally redistricting has been a two-party conversation, where the incumbents pick safe seats for themselves," Madsen observed. "This time there's a third party involved." Governor Ventura had appointed a citizens commission with people from all three parties as well as some public interest groups, with Barkley at the head. They were focusing on creating truly competitive districts. "Take the Bloomington area," Madsen said. "One side is Republican, on the west. Eastside tends to be Democratic. Traditional redistricting would divide them between east and west to create two safe districts, one for each party. Our idea is to divide them into north and south to make them competitive. This will draw more people to run, and these candidates will have to try to get Republican and Democratic votes, which will hopefully drive them toward the center. It will also help third parties if the district isn't safe for one party or the other. And more competition means more people will come out to vote, and hopefully a better discussion of issues that matter."

He also thought that even though the party had yet to elect more officeholders, it was winning other kinds of victories that would keep its activists involved. "The treasurer of our congressional district committee just finished a term on a state compensation board," Madsen told me. "I've got another guy on our committee who sits on the Metro Council," which oversees Twin Cities development issues. "And he's proud as a peacock about some water policies they've changed and money they've saved. There are three people on the state campaign finance board. There's one woman on the state arts board, who's real happy about the support she's been able to bring into the arts community from the Ventura administration. By getting involved in the governing process and making a difference, people can see that we matter. It's not just an exercise in futility."

As for helping other activists in other states build their own versions of the Independence Party, Barkley said, "I've been as supportive as I can. The best thing I can do is make this administration the best as it can be, to show that a third way can work. Anyway, they've got to have a base of support. You can't base it solely on a single personality. Weicker showed that. You've got to do that first before you go into a national party mold." He also discouraged anyone who expected Governor Ventura to go on a national proselytizing tour to drum up support for third parties in other states. "If a state would ask, 'We've got this organizing committee, would you come down?'—sure we would. But we can't make it happen. We can be icing on the cake, but they've got to make their own cake."[19]

Madsen concurred. "The whole goddamn world would love it if Jesse Ventura would come door-knock in their neighborhood. And it's not going to happen. If we want a national party that's authentically bottom up, it has to start that way. We do make our rules available on the website, and we do chat with people and offer advice. We basically say, go ahead and do what we did in Minnesota. The dream is a bunch of states would surface, a couple dozen say, and then they would form a national organization. If Minnesota steps forward to do that, we're right back to a top-down organization." He continued, "Take this fantasy—Jesse Ventura goes to California, hosts a rock concert for one hundred thousand people. The cost of a ticket includes a $5 membership in the party and people filling out a form changing their party registration. In theory you could do that overnight and have one hundred thousand people, which gives you a ballot line in California, and $500,000. But the reality is that most of those people would be there for the concert. You can use the Ventura mystique to attract a crowd, but the quality of the crowd is what matters. You'd do better knocking on a hundred doors."

"One slogan we had early on," Madsen added, remembering the building of the Minnesota party, "was 'the first thousand was the worst thousand.' We always reminded ourselves that it would get easier after that. You've got to get a thousand people to say yes to you and hang on. And for every five people that you recruit, you're going to lose three in six months. If you're lucky one of the two remaining will be active. And to succeed, you have to be happy to take that deal all day long. I have friends who call and say 'I know ten people who quit the party because of you.' And I say 'I know fifteen who have come in.' I'll take that deal every day."[20]

Vermont Progressive Party (www.progressiveparty.org)—An outgrowth of twenty years of patient organizing, this party might stand as a beacon for Green Party efforts in other states—especially after it endorsed the Nader-LaDuke ticket and produced its second-highest total anywhere in 2000. The Vermont Progressives grew up in the shadow of socialist Bernie Sanders's successful independent campaigns, first for mayor of Burlington, the state's largest city, in 1980, and then later for the U.S. House of Representatives. Their effort was similar to Greens elsewhere in that it drew energy from the thousands of baby boomers who moved to the state in the 1960s and afterward, attracted to the state's beauty and small-town communities. But it was different in one crucial way—from the beginning it was built around a Vermont-centered vision of uplifting the lives of working people. Thus Sanders succeeded first in Burlington's poorest wards, and later always did well with working-class voters elsewhere in the state.[21] The Progressives proved they were a durable phenomenon when they elected Sanders's successor, Peter Clavelle, as mayor, as well as several state legislators from the Burlington area. Indeed, they have effectively replaced the Democrats as Burlington's second party and have held the mayor's office to this day (minus one term which the Republicans won). But while they built a sophisticated political operation that delivered a solid vote for Sanders every two years and took the lead on a number of local issues, such as saving family farms and expanding health care coverage, they didn't become a full-fledged state party until the 2000 election. Instead, for many years, they operated as the Progressive Coalition, deliberately avoiding any bid for statewide party status.[22]

The reason for that was threefold. First, the coalition's leaders worried if they became a formal party, they wouldn't be able to prevent interlopers from jumping onto their ballot line and muddying their message. This was because Vermont does not use party registration, and instead has an open primary process that allows every-one to vote in whatever party primary they prefer. This allows all kinds of mischief, such as voters supporting someone who they think would be the worst candidate for a party they dislike. And it produces a system that is very candidate centered, which the Progressives feared would dilute their party's identity. Second, Sanders was always wor-ried about creating a statewide party and then being linked to a handful of self-appointed leftists who might have no connection to working-class Vermonters. Since he controlled the money raised for his congressional campaigns, he held the ace card in how his get-out-the-vote network could be used. The third reason the Progressives held back is they simply didn't have the resources to go to the next level and do so in an organized manner. So despite having elected and reelected Congress's sole genuine independent, it seemed that Vermont's Progressives would never go the next step of concretizing that support into a solid third party. But they knew they had to keep try-ing, since the majority vote Sanders got every two years showed that potential voter support was there for other candidates as well.

"When it became clear that Bernie could raise his own money and campaign appa-ratus, then we were totally beholden to him," said Ellen David Friedman, a veteran organizer with the state National Education Association who has been long involved in Vermont progressive politics. "The question was always, 'When would Bernie be ready to start a third party?' And he would never be ready." But all that changed with the passage in 1997 of Vermont's new campaign finance law, which provided for full public financing of statewide candidates if they first qualified by raising at least $35,000 in amounts less than $50 from at least fifteen hundred people. With nearly $300,000 in campaign funds, the Progressives' gubernatorial candidate, Anthony Pollina, a long-time community organizer who was previously the director of Vermont Public Interest Research Group, was able to build a substantial campaign. Indeed, said David-Friedman, the Progressives' founding vice chair, "A lot of Bernie's apparatus moved over to Pollina's campaign."[23]

During the campaign, Pollina was also included in all the statewide debates, in which he forcefully argued for living wage jobs, support for affordable housing, univer-sal health care and tried to push the political envelope, raising rarely discussed issues of corporate power and economic democracy. According to Terry Bouricius, another Progressive Party activist who just stepped down from his seat in the state legislature,[24] public financing made a huge difference to Pollina's credibility. "In the last campaign, Anthony Pollina was treated 100 percent fairly in the media, and it was all because he had access to money—that was much more important than his poll figures. The fact that he had money meant the press would cover him." Pollina ended up with just 10 percent of the vote, but also with universal acknowledgment as the winner of the debates and a fresh voice to be listened to.

Like Sanders, Pollina did best in the rural counties that make up Vermont's Northeast Kingdom, the most conservative and rural part of the state. And while his activist base was progressive to the core, his campaign made fascinating inroads with Republicans, particularly sportsmen concerned about protecting the state's natural environment. For example, James Ehlers, the publisher of *Vermont Outdoors* magazine, a gun enthusiast who also runs the Lake Champlain international fishing derby, the region's biggest sporting event, came out for Pollina. "He was convinced that if these folks could understand that the Republicans were so pro-development that they wouldn't act in defense of the habitat, they would support Anthony," said David-Friedman. Of the half-million people living in Vermont, ninety thousand hold hunting licenses, she pointed out. Thus this was a vital group to reach.

David-Friedman admitted that Pollina's breakthrough to this constituency came late, though she argued that he clearly took votes from the Republican candidate, Ruth Dwyer. "Some of the people we met with liked Anthony but didn't want to risk reelecting [Democratic governor] Howard Dean—it was the reverse of liberals who worried that a vote for Anthony would elect Dwyer," she laughed. She also acknowledged that it would be harder for progressives in other states to be greeted in the same way among white conservative men because Vermont has such a tiny minority population. A Progressive Party elsewhere would have to deal with more of a racial backlash, assuming that it included defense of social programs that primarily help poor people, who are disproportionately black or Hispanic, as part of its platform. "It all depends which issues you lead with," she said. "We are talking about progressive forms of taxation, universal health care, environmental sanctity (which in other places is more of a left-right issue, I admit), but with the sportsmen base, you just replace the word 'environment' with 'habitat,' and we're right in tune with each other." Since the election, Ehlers has been taking Pollina to wild game suppers and fish and game clubs, where he is always recognized and welcomed warmly.[25]

Vermont's Progressives are now at a new plateau. Their future prospects depend in part on the continuation of the state's public financing system, which is under some attack in the legislature and the courts. They are also making a strong push to pass instant-runoff voting (IRV) for all federal and statewide races. The Democrats in the state, including Governor Dean, are supportive, as are some Republicans who have signed on as co-sponsors. But according to Bouricius, who was working full time on the effort as a field representative for the Center for Voting and Democracy, "There are a bunch of Republicans who like plurality elections since they see the Progressives as a bigger factor [hurting Democrats] than the Libertarians are in hurting them." Republicans now control Vermont's house, thanks to a strong backlash from the passage of the state's groundbreaking civil union law.

"Even if we lose both public financing and IRV," Bouricius said, "the Progressive Party is in a very good position to be a significant factor." He noted that in addition to four state representatives from the Burlington area, the party had elected local officials to nonpartisan offices in Rutland and Brattleboro. And he predicted that redistricting in 2002 would produce more open seats or weak incumbents where the party might have a shot of electing more legislators. "Money isn't everything in those races, since so many of the districts here are so tiny," he added. "We also have a full-time staff person with an office in Montpelier, based on massive fund-raising on our part—using lists we have been compiling for decades, asking people for money by phone. In a little state like Vermont, that's pretty amazing." While they weren't organized with dues-paying members (which is against state law for political parties), the Progressives' activist base was well within Daniel Cantor's 1 percent rule. In Washington County in the central part of the state, for example, the party had three hundred volunteers who worked on the Pollina campaign, out of a total voting population of around thirty thousand. The party still had to deal with the state's open primary system, and Bouricius didn't rule out the possibility that Democrats could try to keep Pollina from running for governor again, as is expected, by putting a cat's-paw up against him in the Progressives' 2002 primary.[26] Nor did anyone know whether Bernie Sanders would agree to run on the party's line for Congress that year or stick to his independent status.

Whatever happens to Vermont's Progressives in the next few years, their model ought to especially inspire Greens elsewhere. This is a progressive third party rooted in the world of average working people. Its top officers are organizers connected to the local United Electrical Workers and National Education Association unions. It has a real base, both in terms of voters and financial supporters. Pollina did best among young people and voters with low incomes. The party's platform emphasizes democratic decision making about economic development, focusing on battling corporate agribusiness, alternatives to imprisonment, support for unions, more equitable funding of public education, land-use planning to prevent sprawl, affordable day care, opposition to electricity deregulation, and support for public utilities. At the same time, the party has not shied away from taking a forthright position in favor of social justice for gays and lesbians—backing the state's new civil union law in the face of a vociferous conservative backlash. It has a solid and sensible core of veteran activists who have worked long and hard with each other and avoided many of the self-marginalizing habits of other progressive third-party efforts. In Pollina, it has a responsible and passionate leader who is committed to building the party further. With him running again, along with further recruitment of legislative candidates, the Progressives seem poised to continue their steady growth.

The Working Families Party (*www.workingfamiliesparty.org*)—Days after Al Gore ended his effort to re-count the votes in Florida and George W. Bush was recognized as the country's next president, the three co-chairs of the WFP did an unusual thing. Refusing to accept Bush as legitimately elected, they issued a cry to arms. "With the end of the election has come the inevitable call from the punditocracy for bipartisanship, compromise, and conciliation. The dominant view is that all Americans should fall in behind the president-elect and help him succeed. We firmly reject this view. We believe it is the responsibility of Democrats and progressives to do everything possible to ensure that George Bush, his right-wing Congressional allies, and his policies, fail," they insisted in a press release. "The Supreme Court may have made George Bush the President, but that does not mean that we accept him as legitimately elected," they added.[27]

It was the first time the party's leaders had ever made a pronouncement beyond the provincial arena of New York politics. Asked about this statement some months later, party co-chair Bob Master said that it arose out of his own personal anger about the election, which was shared by co-chairs Bertha Lewis and Jim Duncan. It was not something demanded from below by the WFP's chapters or membership, though no one objected to it. Two things were clear from this. First, that influencing national politics really wasn't part of the WFP's raison d'être. And second, that its members didn't think (or weren't yet thinking) of using the party for expressive or symbolic purposes.

Such interests may yet develop as the party matures. But for now it is safe to say that the WFP is another useful "demonstration project," though one with a different potential audience than the political independents who might want to duplicate Ventura's Independence Party in their state. "What we're showing the labor movement is that you can recruit rank-and-file members to an organization that will challenge the Democrats from a progressive direction," said Master, the political director of the Communications Workers of America regional local. What's more, he noted, this organization was "more populist and diverse than the labor movement itself." Hopefully, Master added, labor unions in other states would decide that it made sense to join with community organizations to build a larger vehicle for electoral action, and that they should push for changes in state laws to allow similar fusion parties to develop elsewhere.

At the same time, he admitted that the labor-community alliance at the heart of the Working Families Party was still fragile. "The unions find the community organizations irritating because they have a broader perspective," he noted, citing the example of an issue that recently came up in Suffolk County, where the county executive vetoed the creation of a hiring hall for undocumented workers. The WFP's member unions were understanding, because they didn't want the county government undercutting demand for unionized workers. But the community groups insisted that something needed to be done to help the county's exploited immigrant labor force.[28]

The party's role in New York City mayoral and council elections of 2001 brought to light other aspects of its potential and limitations. Early in the year, the WFP demonstrated its grass-roots pull by turning out more than one thousand members and supporters to a mayoral candidates forum on economic development. In an otherwise desultory election, that was proof of real street muscle. The WFP was backing more than a dozen exciting progressive candidates for city council seats, and it had launched a major push to enact a living wage covering workers in the city. At the same time, party organizers admitted that they should have started earlier in recruiting candidates for the many council seats opened up by term limits. One early supporter of the WFP, journalist Doug Ireland (my friend and sometime co-author), chided the party for not doing more. And he attacked it for endorsing an African-American candidate for city comptroller, Bill Thompson, who had previously become Mayor Giuliani's chosen Board of Education president by opposing safe-sex education and the teaching of toler-ance for gays and lesbians. "Some kids of 'working families' thus deprived of life-saving education will die as a result," Ireland wrote in the July 2, 2001, issue of *The Nation*. "Right now the WFP is a ballot line, not a full-fledged political party, and it is domi-nated by the labor leaders who pay the bills, not a broad 'community-labor-religious coalition,'" he added.

In my view, Ireland's judgment is a bit too harsh. Yes, there is the danger of the party developing merely into a progressive version of New York's Liberal Party—where a politically wired group of labor leaders and a handful of supporting community orga-nizations deploy the WFP ballot line to win concessions from politicians that benefit their members, and sometimes the larger community, but no larger mobilizing of the public around a different kind of politics takes place. At the same time, the WFP's local chapters and individual members have the potential to push the party in a more broadminded direction—and many of its top leaders share that vision. Several of the party's early endorsements, of Peter Vallone, Hillary Clinton, and now Bill Thompson, suggest that expediency rules over vision when it comes to the party's high-level choices. But the party is still just a mere toddler. Its chapters are just beginning to grow and assert themselves. Over time, it will become clearer if the WFP is to become strong enough to act more independently. Right now, the potential is still there.

Though the WFP was inspired in large degree by the New Party model and vision, it has not affiliated with the national New Party network. "The people who formed the WFP did not want to be part of a national effort, even as they drew on NP staff resources and experiences," Cantor said. From a very practical point of view, there is no need for the WFP to do so, as it already has a fusion-friendly environment to work in and more than enough to do in its own backyard. Paying dues to a national organi-zation that it doesn't need doesn't make any sense. So beyond helping with an intrigu-ing New Party effort to use existing law in the neighboring state of Connecticut to build a WFP-style party, the New Yorkers aren't doing much beyond their own bor-ders. If the WFP is to have a national impact, it will either be because others decide to emulate it, or because it decides to use its unique leverage in New York to influence a congressional or presidential election.

Three National Projects

The New Party (www.newparty.org) — For the New Party's current leaders and activists, what the Working Families Party is doing stands as vindication of their original emphasis on fusion and a model for them to use in trying to revive fusion in other states. Of course, that effort suffered a huge setback in the *Timmons* decision. But the Supreme Court didn't say that states had to outlaw cross-endorsement, only that they weren't constitutionally required to allow it. Standing in this narrow crack, New Party leaders, particularly its long-distance runners in ACORN, are hoping to pry open the political process in a few more states in the coming years.

One state to watch in the short run is Connecticut, where cross-endorsement is legal but rarely practiced. "The problem there is the way you qualify for the ballot is each office individually," said Zach Polett, ACORN's political director. "And the first time you run, you can't fuse under the current law." What this means is a WFP-style project in Connecticut there has to be built literally district by district. Polett continued, "So the strategy there is to identify legislative seats where you can get 1 percent of the vote, without spoiling, around an issue agenda, to build a line to use for community-labor purposes." Many of Connecticut's city councils and school boards also have a minority representation rule that prevents any party from holding more than two-thirds of the seats. It is this rule that helped the Greens elect an African-American woman, Elizabeth Horton-Sheff, to the Hartford City Council. According to Polett, several Connecticut unions have met with ACORN staffers recently in the hopes of launching a WFP-style effort soon.[29]

But the WFP's Bob Master, whose Communications Workers of America local includes seven thousand workers in Connecticut, was not sure if the moment was right yet, even as he took part in Polett's meetings. "Up there, the big problem is that the most aggressive force in labor is Local 1199. And they're entirely focused on dumping [incumbent Republican Governor John] Rowland." Since the state's fusion law requires that the first time a new party runs for an office it has to stand on its own and get at least 1 percent of the vote, that apparently ruled out a run for governor in 2002, Master said. Also the most sympathetic players in the state—ACORN, his CWA local, and the United Auto Workers local (another key piece of the WFP coalition)—were all much smaller in Connecticut than in New York.

Elsewhere, Polett said, "There is an interest and ability to build successful local progressive political parties where the rules are favorable. Both the Little Rock New Party and the Missoula New Party are good examples of this. Both have elected slates of progressive, independent New Party candidates to local office around a clearly identified program. Both include labor, community, and issue organizations as well as interested individuals in their membership and leadership. Both these local parties work well, at least in part, because elections are nonpartisan so the local New Party affiliates don't need a ballot line, since no one else has one either, and don't face the problem of spoiling elections for Democrats."[30] But what the New Party's experience in nonpartisan races or one-party regimes like Chicago also showed is that it was hard to build and sustain these chapters without one or two committed local institutions like a labor local or an ACORN chapter to anchor the base. Otherwise the sheer costs of keeping the party going on volunteer energy alone were too high. And many independent progressive activists were more attracted to the Greens, with their clearer emphasis on opposing the two-party duopoly.

Jim Fleischmann, the party's new national director, said that beyond working within the existing web of state election laws, the party hoped to use ballot initiatives to legalize fusion in a few more states soon. "In Montana and Oregon, we have local organizations that are beginning the process of building the coalitions to go to the ballot to overturn the fusion bans," he told me in March of 2001. "Key people from unions and community organizations that have a vision are strategically lining up opportunities in those states and Connecticut."[31] But Fleischmann acknowledged that the New Party's national engine has been all but shut off and would take some effort to restart.[32] The fund-raising and expressions of support that rolled in when there was a possibility of winning a sudden shift in state electoral rules as a result of its Supreme Court lawsuit have all dwindled away. And the disaffiliation of its Maryland and Minnesota branches meant the loss of many dues-paying members. "Part of our problem is the desertion of a lot of political talent when it wasn't clear that we'd be able to bust out," he said. "The attention span of foundations and pundits is just a little bit longer than the electorate. For some folks, we were the hot new flavor."

"When you had a sexy notion of the Supreme Court case, it was easy to get people to lay down a check," said Secky Fascione, the party's national co-chair and another long-distance runner. "Organizing is hard work, moving warm bodies and green dollars. *Timmons* gave us a chance to raise money, but when it went back to the hard work of moving low-income people, some folks got less interested in sending checks." She added, "As an organizer, I'm not surprised that it's hard to make changes in America."[33]

The Libertarian Party (www.lp.org)—The Libertarian Party says it ran more than 1,430 candidates for all levels of office in the 2000 elections, including candidates for 255 of the 435 seats in the U.S. House as well as 25 of the 33 Senate seats up for election. This is certainly an impressive accomplishment—the first time in eighty years that any third party has run for enough seats in Congress to win a hypothetical majority. But although those House candidates received 1.7 million votes, their support was spread thin. Nearly all of the party's contenders drew in the 1 to 2 percent range, which was occasionally enough to affect the results of a major-party battle, but not a sign that a real base was being built. A glance at the county-by-county returns for Libertarian presidential candidates in 1992 and 1996 showed the same thing—nowhere in the country were they able to garner more than about 2.6 percent of the vote. The Libertarians' problem was that their "party of principle," with its platform devoted to "individual liberty and personal responsibility, a free-market economy of abundance and prosperity, and a foreign policy of non-intervention, peace, and free trade," was too diffuse to build up substantial support anywhere in America's geographically bound system of electoral representation. While the party was also using the same opportunity to run and elect candidates in local, nonpartisan elections that was giving Greens and New Party candidates a modest boost, it hadn't figured out how to make a big enough splash in some high-level race to force the electorate to sit up and take notice.

One solution promoted by L. Neil Smith, the publisher of the *Libertarian Enterprise*, was to stop wasting time on the presidential election and on running candidates for as many offices as possible—the party's perennial priorities—and instead target vulnerable Republicans for defeat. "He who can destroy a thing controls a thing," Smith argued, quoting Frank Herbert's science fiction novel *Dune*. "The strategy is simple: identify Republican office-holders who won their last election by a margin of five percent or less," he said in a June 1997 article. "Ignore every other position on the ballot. Run Libertarians against these Republican five-percenters, the object being to *deny* them their five percent and put Democrats in office in their place." [Emphasis in the original.] He argued that even though the Democrats were the more "big government" party, Republicans had given the country many authoritarian laws, like the RICO statute, the war on drugs, the Brady gun control bill, and a national ID card plan. His strategy would either accelerate the proliferation of antiliberty laws under the Democrats, producing an "inevitable reaction," or it would force the Republicans to genuinely change and come out as fierce defenders of the Bill of Rights. "Libertarians will know it's time to stop taking the GOP's five percent away because they won't be able to," Smith concluded.[34]

Judging from the last two congressional elections, some Libertarians are following Smith's advice. In 1998, one Libertarian Senate candidate took enough votes to tilt the race to the Democrat. In 2000, two of the party's House candidates and another Senate contender did similarly well. Even though these Libertarians hadn't managed to get anywhere close to 5 percent of the vote in these races, they did get the attention of some Republicans. Chuck Muth of the Republican Liberty Caucus, a GOP group, was seriously upset. "Libertarians need to understand that they're nothing but spoilers," he told *National Review*, a conservative flagship. "And Republicans need to learn how to earn their votes."[35]

It is possible that Libertarians can carve out a role for themselves with this kind of explicit spoiler strategy, though it's far from clear that their voters will stick with them if they fear electing the "worst of two evils" as a result. Smith's alternative strategy also doesn't address the Libertarians' core problem: they are too doctrinaire to ever garner a large share of the vote. A majority of the public certainly has a "live-and-let-live" attitude that often translates into support for liberal-to-libertarian stands on social issues, especially those relating to personal privacy. But the public is nowhere close to the Libertarians' "live-and-let-die" absolutism. Not only do Libertarians oppose taking public campaign financing as a form of "welfare for politicians" (a noble position that means they will often be handicapped in their bids to reach voters), they often voice support for some far-out proposals. For example, their last presidential candidate, Harry Browne, called for eliminating the income tax and getting the government out of the education business. "Let people buy education for their children the same way they buy the other products and services they need," Browne declared.[36] Over the last few years, the party has come out against expanding Medicare (one of the country's most popular programs), called for a boycott of New York City until its mayor ended its policy of seizing the cars of people arrested for drunken driving, and even demanded that the government not ban human cloning.[37]

The Libertarian Party's taste for self-marginalization was in full bloom in the months after Jesse Ventura got elected in Minnesota. During the campaign, Ventura took many libertarian positions—opposing gun control, the death penalty, and the criminalization of drug use, and calling for lower taxes, tolerance of gays and lesbians, and less coddling of people on welfare or students on financial aid. He even questioned the laws against prostitution. When he was asked for a one-word description of his political philosophy, he often said libertarian, noting that he had scored 100 on the "World's Smallest Political Quiz" created by the party's co-founder, David Nolan.[38] But instead of embracing him once he was elected, Libertarian Party activists quickly turned sour. The editor of their North Dakota state newsletter wrote an article for the party's national website that attacked Ventura for wanting, among other things, to "make government more efficient, create jobs, reduce the student/teacher ratio, provide Internet access to schools, put monitors on school buses, provide shots for children [and] manage recycling programs better."[39]

Early in Ventura's tenure, he was invited by the libertarian Cato Institute to be its featured speaker at a local seminar, along with the institute's president, Edward Crane, and Eric O'Keefe, a former director of the party. By now it had become clear that while Ventura was libertarian on many social issues, he also believed that government had a positive role to play in modern life in such areas as education, public health, research and development, transportation planning and infrastructure. This displeased Minnesota Libertarians immensely. Several at the Cato event heckled him when he brought up his proposal to develop light rail for the Twin Cities to relieve auto congestion. They argued that government had no role to play in transportation. Annoyed by the heckling, Ventura told the Libertarians that their candidates were losers.[40] Not long after that, he told Minnesota Public Radio that he was renouncing Libertarianism. "I used to say I was libertarian—never again. Because I believe there is a role for government to play. I believe there is a role of common good for the average citizen that government needs to have, and they don't quite see it that way."[41] Until the Libertarians decide that they need to move at least halfway to where voters are, and not reject would-be champions to their cause because they are impure, they will remain a fascinating but marginal party.

The Green Party (www.green-party.org)—In 2000, the decentralized network of state Green parties produced more candidates, got more votes, elected more people, registered more Greens, and achieved ballot status in more states than ever before. But this increase in energy and local activity came at a price. Like it or not, a cloud continues to hang around their heads—is President Bush their fault? Did Nader's run only make things worse? On top of all the structural obstacles to third-party growth, Greens now also face the enmity of some people who otherwise might be natural allies or sympathizers, especially among organized labor and in minority communities. More than anyone else, the Greens need to succeed somewhere with their efforts to enact instant-runoff voting. Such a breakthrough would allow voters to rank their choices at the ballot box and not worry about "wasting" their vote or spoiling. With such a system, Greens could get a true measure of their support. It would also help defuse the charge that they are a destructive force. And even if it passed in only one state, such a model would help immensely in persuading people to support it elsewhere.

But while the Greens' head-on runs in some high-visibility races have given them the leverage to press for IRV in places like New Mexico and Alaska, their upstart tactics haven't won them universal acclaim from the power brokers who can make or break that reform. When their IRV bill came up for a vote in the Democrat-controlled New Mexico state legislature in 1998, not one Democrat voted against it. "But not all Democrats support it as much as others," said state Senator Cisco McSorley, a progressive Democrat who was the bill's lead sponsor that year. "We have to convince a lot of centrist Democrats to get it through all the committees it needs to go through to get it passed." That year, the bill died on a tie vote in one committee with two Democrats absent. "Every single Republican went to the committee and two other Democrats were involved in critical budget matters, and we couldn't get them to the vote," McSorley recalled. The state legislature meets for only a thirty-day session, so bills often die in the snarl of competing measures. But McSorley saw a deeper problem. "When the Greens cost us another seat, how will we convince centrist Democrats that this is a group that we can work with? For a centrist Democrat, why enhance the power and visibility of another party?" he asked.[42]

The next few years will be the Greens' proving ground. Even without the passage of IRV, there are many places where they can expand their efforts, ranging from low-level nonpartisan races to high-profile House and Senate bids. Nader has promised to field candidates in one out of every five congressional races, but it's doubtful that many of them will be strong contenders. That is because the Greens' greatest strength, and weakness, is their openness and passion. The truth of third-party politics in America is getting a line on the ballot is, relatively speaking, the easy part. Using it wisely is much harder. Just controlling the use of the party's ballot line is not a simple thing. For example, in 2000 the New Mexico Green Party didn't want to field anyone in the race to unseat Republican Rep. Heather Wilson, having made their point in 1998 with Bob Anderson's strong showings. "We need to pick and choose our races in places where we feel we can challenge, as well as places where there haven't been challenges before yet there's a desire for change," Cris Moore explained. But a Green candidate, Dan Kerlinsky, a forty-seven-year-old child psychiatrist, surfaced on his own, and despite the efforts of the party's leaders, qualified for the ballot under state law. Contrary to the New Mexico Greens' careful emphasis on local bread-and-butter concerns, Kerlinsky ran as a visionary who wanted to parachute ten thousand therapists into the world's trouble spots, ban homework for schoolchildren, and fight dictatorships with thousands of camcorders. Ultimately, he got 6 percent of the vote, while Wilson topped her Democratic opponent, 50 to 43.[43]

"To be in a third party you have to be intentionally outside the box—legally, culturally, historically, socially," said David Cobb, the Texas Green who was also the Association of State Green Parties' legal adviser. "You have to be comfortable with that. And there are two types of people who are—visionaries and kooks."[44] As the two-party duopoly continues to spin off new dissenters, the Greens will keep attracting both types of volunteers—independent thinkers and wing-nuts. In some places, their local efforts and victories will ground their work, as has happened in Santa Fe. In others, their chapters will stay bogged down as they struggle with transitory volunteers, earnest utopians, ideological zealots, and unproductive inward-focused debates. That pattern of internal confusion and ineffectiveness could be broken with solid leadership and professional training of local organizers. This is something the New Party has done for years with its most promising activists, through an annual Community Action School at the James MacGregor Burns Academy of Leadership at the University of Maryland at College Park. But despite the desire of many leading Green organizers to set up similar training programs, so far the resources have never been there to make them happen.

The way forward will also be complicated by the relationship between Nader and the party. The ASGP is a confederation of state parties without a strong center. Even reconstituted as a national Green Party, it will still be highly decentralized. And it is linked indelibly in the public mind to a national leader, Nader, who isn't even a party member. Nader says he wants to build the party, but will have no direct relationship to its structures. He's not a Perot, using his money and access to the media to drive a party from the top down. But neither is he a Cris Moore, part of a de facto collective of equals who share the hard work of strategizing and door knocking. Nader is a lone wolf who takes advice from many people but ultimately listens only to his own counsel. No one in the Greens is his equal. On the positive side, his efforts to bring the Greens closer to his longtime philosophy of civic empowerment and away from their reflexive leftism may yet produce more inroads into the angry middle tapped by a Jesse Ventura or the sportsmen environmentalists that an Anthony Pollina is reaching. But at the same time, Nader's reluctance to inject himself into current events may cause the Greens to miss crucial opportunities, while his deliberate self-restraint may just confuse and disappoint supporters rather than nurture new leaders, as is his intention.

Nader's seeming disappearance in the immediate aftermath of the 2000 election left many Green voters hanging. Refusing the urging of many, including his closest advisers, he avoided going to Florida during the vote count fiasco and took no part in anti-Bush demonstrations around the president's inauguration in January. Senate Democrats Pat Leahy of Vermont and Jeff Bingaman of New Mexico snubbed his written requests to testify against the appointments of John Ashcroft and Dale Norton. But instead of reminding those senators that he had gotten nearly 3 million votes, including many in their own states, by rallying his supporters in some concerted fashion, Nader did little more than complain on talk radio. When the Democrats selected Clinton fund-raiser Terry McAuliffe to be their new party chair, despite the fact that it was he who persuaded Clinton to turn the White House into a Motel Six for wealthy donors, Nader could have issued a one-line press release saying "I told you so."[45] Instead, precisely at the moment that Democrats were ganging up on Green voters for their supposed naivete, Nader was nowhere to be seen—not even projecting a counter-message on his own website.

In his defense, Nader said, "I didn't keep a low profile. The press just disappeared." He cited more than a dozen press conferences he had held around the country between December 2000 and April 2001 that garnered little attention. "People don't see anything, and then they say, 'where's he been'?" In his view, the problem lay in a press that covered him only when the story was how he could affect the presidential horse race. Without that frame, he was no longer news. But he also insisted that he wouldn't start "grandstanding"—going to where the press was to get coverage for the Greens by virtue of his celebrity. "Going to Florida would be like Jesse Jackson. Running to the cameras." Besides, he said, California Green Senate candidate Medea Benjamin went there and did a fine job of representing the party.[46] While Nader may have been right about not building the Greens around media stunts and wanting to allow other party leaders to emerge, his relative silence during the Florida vote did nothing to counter the charge that he was insensitive to the historic grievances of the nation's minorities. Eventually he came out with a strong statement condemning the systemic disenfranchisement of many black voters. But it was late.

"Ralph's tactics need to change," said Steve Cobble, one of his Washington advisers. "He's not a public interest lawyer anymore. He's got a base of three to five million people now who will listen to him if he goes out and tells them what to think."[47] Matters were also not helped by the inability of Nader and the ASGP to move quickly after the election to set up any kind of joint coordinating apparatus. In part, this was the continuation of an ongoing problem. Candidate campaign organizations and party committees always move to different rhythms and respond to different needs, but in the case of Nader and the Greens the disjunction was particularly troublesome. Not only had Nader started his campaign too late, in the view of many Greens, he now was taking his time setting up a postcampaign vehicle to fulfill his promises to build the party, watchdog the major parties, and recruit more candidates. On the other hand, the leaders of the ASGP didn't have any proposals of their own as to how to proceed. "When we get questions from reporters about what's happening with the Green Party," said Tom Sevigny, one of the ASGP's three co-chairs, "we try to defer everything to the state level." When the ASGP's steering committee met with Nader for several hours on a weekend in mid-November 2000, nothing solid was accomplished, according to several participants. "We don't want this to just be Ralph Nader's party, with us parading him out but having nothing underneath," Sevigny said, making the best of an awkward reality. "We have no control over Ralph," he added. "We take what we can get."[48]

Tom Linzey, a lawyer who had been the ASGP's legal adviser for most of the mid-1990s, had a harsher view of the relationship. "It's inevitable that we'll become part and parcel of the Ralph Nader Party," he said. Why? "There's no money. Without it, and without us getting the 5 percent that we needed to get federal funds for 2004, Ralph is probably the only person who will be willing to step forward to run then." Linzey zeroed in on the imbalance in power between Nader and the Greens. "Ralph is bigger than the party. If he was really interested in helping the Greens raise serious money, rather than these $5,000 to $10,000 stops here and there that he's been doing, he would transfer his funding lists to us." The ASGP had been seeking access to Nader's list of campaign donors, but the most he had shared so far were lists of people who had contacted the campaign expressing interest in joining local party efforts, not contributors. "If Nader doesn't respond to questions about this it's because he doesn't have to," Linzey added, noting again that the Greens had no power to compel Nader to do anything.[49]

Having just spent nine months traveling the country glimpsing the real state of local Green politics as he campaigned, Nader and his circle weren't about to blindly bind themselves to the party, however. "If I became a Green, then I'd have an official capacity, and I'd be asked to take sides," Nader insisted. "I wouldn't be able to appeal to a broader audience. I'd be pigeonholed, and everything the Greens say would be attributed to me."

He also didn't want to take a central leadership role. "I don't like to tell people within a party, do this and do that. I'm not that kind of kingmaker." Nader also was still thinking about how best to get the party's activists to develop their own democratic muscles. "I'm now the nation's expert on the weakness of the Greens' funding base," he said, half-joking. "Wherever I go, I tell them that they have to face up to it, they're not correlating their concern for the world with their contributions. Same with the Campus Greens—they're having a big discussion about whether they should have membership dues. There's a lot of money out there, but they don't like to ask for money or ask each other for money."[50]

"There are three types of Green state parties," said Carl Mayer, a Nader confidant from Princeton, New Jersey, who was the campaign's treasurer and who ran for Congress as a Green in 2000, nearly costing the Democrats a House seat. "In New York and Missouri, it's crazyland, where people who aren't seriously interested in electoral politics are in control." Mayer was referring to leaders of the Greens/Green Party USA, who had bases in both states. "In California, New Mexico, Oregon, and maybe Washington, there are sophisticated, credible parties. But in the vast majority, they're well-intentioned people with little clue how to move forward." Mayer's goal was to ramp up those volunteers by "parachuting in organizers who would show local Greens how to develop their own leaders." But he agreed with Nader's reluctance to get drawn under the ASGP's shaky umbrella. "Why should Ralph submit himself to the Green Party?" he asked. "Why shouldn't he try to shape it?"[51]

Throughout the winter and spring of 2001, Nader and his inner circle deliberated how to move ahead. One proposal, advanced by his campaign manager Theresa Amato and top lieutenant John Richard, was essentially for a holding action. Their idea was basically to sidestep the Greens' internal affairs and instead to create a nonprofit group that would continue to put on super-rallies, nurture some new local leaders, and collect names. Greg Kafoury and Mark McDougal, who had pulled off all the super-rallies of the campaign, felt this was too limited. "We can't wait and see what's happening a year from now," McDougal said. "We have to maintain and build our ballot access, for one." This was not an insignificant issue, especially if Nader wanted to run again in 2004. He also feared that Amato and Richard's idea was too standoffish and would just alienate the Greens.[52]

Fearful that vital momentum was being lost, Kafoury and McDougal flew to Washington at their own expense the first weekend in March to meet with Nader and the rest of his closest advisers. Afterward, Kafoury was euphoric. "We said to him, this is a unique opportunity to make a move. Bush is showing his true colors. Clinton is disgraced. The Democrats are without leaders. No one is setting a progressive agenda. He's the only one who can do it." Five hours of intense conversation ensued. The result, Kafoury said, was that "Nader is ready to throw himself fully and wholeheartedly into a political effort that will last for years. The thrust will be to create a big strong active Green Party along with broader groups that don't necessarily buy into the whole Green agenda." As for dealing with the Greens' internal needs, Kafoury said the solution was to grow and to give people things to do, rather than just things to talk about.[53]

Conscious that no third party in twentieth century America has survived without a prominent national leader, but wary of doing all the heavy lifting himself, Nader promised that he would not step out in front of the Greens' own level of ability, no matter the demands or expectations placed on him. "There are 24 hours in a day, and I'm one person, that's the last thing I remember. They've got to start getting their own leaders and energy levels." His comments paralleled Jesse Ventura's similar reluctance to run around the country building Independence parties. "One of the first things I said to the Greens in 1996 is you show me time and energy and I'll show you time and energy. Dimension one is I will show them more time and energy than any one of them will, and that's not just the ability to get on the media. I'm still looking for them to match that. Dimension two—you want more than that, you're going to have to show me more. It takes two to tango. You can't push a string forward."[54]

Even though he was critical of Nader's distance from the ASGP's structures and process, David Cobb sketched out a similar vision of Nader's role. "Nader can act in a constructive way by being the elder statesperson for the party, a position he has earned, continuing to provide leadership on issues and as a spokesperson, and to identify those folks who have demonstrated organizational capacity and help them out, but not to control it. At the end of the day it's our party to build and control. This cannot be the Nader party. It has to be a party of citizen activists who have rolled up their sleeves and are saying, 'Damn it, democracy is at stake in this country, and we have to save it.'" Cobb was pointing toward a larger role for the Greens than just being an outlet for progressives upset with the rightward drift of the Democratic Party. "This isn't just about trying to force the Dems to the left. I don't believe that can be done, given how corrupted the party has become. It ought to be the political arm that reflects and helps to develop a larger people's movement. In Austin, we had over one thousand people marching in the street to protest the Fortune 500 meeting here. The last time that happened was a generation ago, during the nuclear freeze movement. This is a historically pregnant moment. Something is about to happen."

Toward Democracy in America

Is something about to happen? There is one scenario that some Greens with a sense of history talk about: that their emergence may mark the beginning of the end of the current two-party system and its replacement by a new one. John Berg, a political science professor at Suffolk University in Boston, has drawn a specific analogy to the rise of antislavery parties in the 1840s, the collapse of one of the two major parties, the Whigs, a few years later, and the birth of the Republicans. In 1840, the American Antislavery Society split, with one half supportive of running a candidate, James Birney, for president, and the other half more interested in taking direct action to help free slaves. Birney, the candidate of the newly formed Liberty Party, hardly ran a campaign, and was actually out of the country for most of the year. Four years later, the party nominated him again, and this time he ran for real and took 2.3 percent, enough to constitute the margin of victory in Ohio, Michigan, and New York, and more important, to tip the election from the Whig candidate, Henry Clay, to the Democrat, James Polk. Both major-party candidates were slaveholders, Berg noted, "but Polk was committed to the annexation of Texas and other proslavery causes, while Clay was more inclined to compromise. Texas was admitted in 1845 . . . adding a new slave state. Antislavery Whigs blamed the Liberty party; Liberty supporters retorted that the Whigs should have offered a better candidate. Whether condemned or praised, Birney's 2.3 percent proved that the issue of slavery could no longer be compromised or ignored."[55]

The members of the Liberty Party were so committed to abolishing slavery that they refused to even work with antislavery members of the Democrats or Whigs, arguing that their participation in pro-slavery parties was immoral. Liberty's dogmatism precluded the party's expansion, but in the meantime another abolitionist party formed that wasn't quite as hard-line, the Free Soil Party. The Free Soilers were created after abolitionist Democrats and Whigs (known as "Barnburners" and "Conscience Whigs") walked out of their party conventions in early 1848. The new party got 10 percent of the popular vote in that election, but foundered after the Compromise of 1850, which temporarily quieted the nation's growing division over the slavery question. Two years later, when that compromise fell apart with the passage of the Kansas-Nebraska Act, which allowed the expansion of slavery, the resulting uproar led to the formation of the Republican Party, which combined Free Soilers with other antislavery Whigs and Democrats. The Whigs' collapse was also hastened by the brief rise of the Know-Nothing Party, which fed on anti-immigrant sentiment.

Could Nader and the Greens spark a similar political reformation with the issue of combating plutocracy as their moral crusade? It is likely that the activist passions inspired by the issue of corporate power will continue to grow. The protests in Seattle and elsewhere, after all, were just one manifestation of this global movement. But there's also no question that the American political system is nowhere near as flexible or open to new parties as it was in the 1840s and 1850s. Back then, a party formed when a critical mass of people came together and called themselves a party, nominated candidates, printed their own ballots, and persuaded people to take those ballots and vote for them. Cross-nomination, or fusion candidacies, were common. American mass society was just being created and the cost of communicating to one's fellow citizens was much lower than it is today, even with the Internet. And people's political consciousness was higher. The slavery issue confronted Americans with a daily moral dilemma. By comparison, the victims of corporate greed today are often hidden or far away. In addition, if the Greens or other dissenters allow their opposition to the depredations of multinational capital to become in anyway linked to support or sympathy with the people behind the terrorist attacks of September 11, they will find their way forward completely blocked, And some opponents of the anti-globalizer will no doubt play that card against them.

Still, despite the obstacles presented by living in a modern postindustrial society with a million news outlets and a million diversions, real change can happen when individuals decide, one by one by one, to organize themselves and others to make it happen. "In order to do third-party politics, you've got to have true believers," said David Cobb, who during 2000 was Nader's Texas campaign coordinator. "We live in a two-bedroom cottage here, a little bungalow, and we turned our whole house into a campaign headquarters. The breakfast nook was an office, the garage was storage space, we had four computers networked through the house. We had a copy machine donated. It was crazy." But Cobb, who had taken a big pay cut to throw himself into organizing, was in it for the long haul. "You've got to have the kinds of people who believe in the principles and the values to throw themselves off the cliff," he said, reflecting on his own motivations. "I think third-party activists and organizers, something spoke to them in civics class in junior high. I can make myself all weepy eyed about 'We the People' and stuff like that. I really can."

In order to form a more perfect union, we the people need to support these kinds of challenges to the status quo. As Justice William O. Douglas of the Supreme Court once wrote,

> All political ideas cannot and should not be channeled into the programs of our two major parties. History has amply proved the virtue of political activity by minority, dissident groups, which innumerable times have been in the vanguard of democratic thought and whose programs were ultimately accepted.

Douglas added that "the absence of such voices would be a symptom of grave illness in our society."[56] We need to support these voices, with our own dollars and time, as well as with the public guarantee of a level-playing field. That means—for all political parties and their candidates—fair treatment by the media, equal access to the ballot, full public funding as an option to replace dependence on wealthy special interests, inclusion in and expansion of debates and other public forums. We need to take seriously the problem of minority representation, and try some experiments with instant-runoff voting, multiple-member districts, and other forms of proportional representation. In a word, we need to apply antitrust thinking to the two-party duopoly.

Many of America's ills are related directly to the lack of genuine competition in the political arena. More competition would mean more mobilization of neglected voters, more voicing of disparate views, and greater attention to the solution of the nation's problems. Democracy, after all, is the greatest system ever invented for identifying and solving problems—when it is allowed to work. The great wonder of American democracy is that it has been open to changes in direction. With one exception—the Civil War—we have been able to resolve our differences through democratic means. When women demanded the right to vote, when workers demanded the right to organize, when blacks and gays and lesbians demanded equal civil rights—it is true that in each of these cases protest began on the streets, outside the electoral system, and many lives were sacrificed in these struggles. But ultimately the political system responded and expanded and changed direction.

In recent years American democracy has been losing its flexibility and, on some issues, becoming quite brittle and unresponsive. Today, at a time of rapid economic, social, and technological change, there are some fundamental questions about the direction of the country that are simply not being asked. People who are trying to ask them have been shunted to the margins of the major parties by the power of big money, and sometimes even gassed and shot at by water cannon in the streets of our major cities. Travel the country and you encounter not so much cynicism as disillusionment, a sense of betrayal, of being let down. Even as the country rallied together to face an external foe, these feelings lurked not far from the surface. People are angry about politics, but they have also been resigned to its failure.

This is not the way it ought to be. Politics encompasses everything that we can and must do *together*. It includes how we educate our children, design our communities and neighborhoods, feed ourselves and dispose of our wastes, how we care for the sick and elderly and the poor, how we relate to the natural world, how we entertain and enlighten ourselves, how we defend ourselves and what values we seek to defend, what roles are chosen for us by virtue of our identity and what roles we create for ourselves. Politics, at least in the small-d sense of the word democratic, also means being able to ask—as a community, not just as isolated individuals—fundamental questions about where we're going as a country, what the future should be for the generations that follow. We need to be able to ask those questions and deliberate their solutions, loud and long. And to do so, we need third parties.

Notes

Introduction

1. In fact, the actual vote in Dixville Notch, New Hampshire, was 21 for Bush, 5 for Gore, and 1 for Nader. This was nowhere near as bad as the 1-out-of-80 vote that Nader thought he had heard on the news that morning, but at 3.7 percent it was a fairly accurate indication of his overall total. The town's voter registration is skewed with 16 Republicans, 9 independents, and just 2 Democrats.

In 1992, when Nader experimented with presidential politicking, asking people voting in the New Hampshire primary to write in his name as a stand-in for "none of the above" and as a protest vote for a renewal of democracy, he went up to Dixville Notch. "Only in New Hampshire do you travel four hours to meet eight voters," he reminisced later. Andre Marrou, the Libertarian candidate for president that year, worked the tiny hamlet even harder. The result then was Marrou 11, George Bush 9, Pat Buchanan 3, Nader 3, Clinton 3, and Paul Tsongas 2. Jim Cole, "Tiny N.H. Towns Cast Nation's First Votes," Associated Press, November 7, 2000.

2. ABC News press release, "Election Outcome: A Nation Divided," November 8, 2000. "Nationally [Nader's] supporters said that if it had been just a Gore-Bush race, 47 percent would've picked Gore, 21 percent Bush; the rest would have sat it out."

3. Theodore Lowi, "The Party Crasher," *New York Times Magazine*, August 23, 1992.

4. "Monopoly Politics Redux: Lopsided Congressional Races," Center on Voting and Democracy, www. igc.apc.org/cvd/op_eds/cong2000.htm.

5. John Whitesides, "Most Races for Congress Over Before They Start," Reuters, October 30, 2000. "Ten members of Congress have died since November 1992," Whitesides reported, "while only eight have lost in primary challenges."

6. Rob Richie, Center for Voting and Democracy, Update on Fair Elections, December 21, 1998, e-mail.

7. Center for Responsive Politics, www.crp.org. In 1998, 143 House candidates—the highest number in a decade—were financially unopposed, which means their opponents spent less than $5,000 on their campaigns.

8. Center for Voting and Democracy, "Monopoly Politics 2000," http://www.igc.org/cvd/2000/results.htm.

9. Richard Winger, *Ballot Access News*, December 5, 2000, issue. In 1998, Winger reported, the frequency of one-party state legislative elections was even higher—41.1 percent.

10. Wayne Barrett, "The Albany Glacier," *Village Voice*, December 5, 2000.

11. Kevin Sack, "Statehouse Journal; On the Bipartisan Bayou, a Brouhaha," *New York Times*, February 5, 1999.

12. Jane Mayer, "How the Democrats Learned to Love Tom DeLay," *New Yorker*, December 6, 1999. Jo Ann Matranga, the 2000 candidate against DeLay, got 36 percent of the vote.

13. A full list of Gush and Bore's "suffocating consensus" would also include their agreeing that:
- tens of billions of dollars in corporate welfare should go untouched;
- tax cuts on income should not include any change in the payroll tax, the tax that most affects the majority of working Americans;
- some form of ballistic missile defense should be built;
- health care reform is best governed by the private market;
- no moratorium on the death penalty is warranted, despite the danger of executing innocent people;
- jails should continue to fill with nonviolent drug offenders under "mandatory minimum" sentencing laws and those caught in "three strikes, you're out" laws;
- civil liberties come second to the fight against "terrorism";
- free trade comes before the interests of workers or the environment;
- gays should not be allowed to marry and should continue to be denied spousal Social Security, pension, and tax benefits, immigration rights, visitation rights, and so on;
- clean needle exchange should not be embraced as public health policy (though the medical community agrees that this is an effective AIDS-fighting tool);
- the federal minimum wage does not need to be enough to lift a family of four above the federal poverty level;
- there's nothing wrong with genetically modified foods;
- monetary policy is best made by an unaccountable Federal Reserve Board partially appointed by private bankers;
- Depression-era rules preventing banks, securities firms, and insurance houses from owning each other were properly repealed by Congress;
- the United States should continue to spend $100 billion a year defending Europe and East Asia, even though our European and Japanese allies can afford to defend themselves;
- NATO should be used as a unilateral interventionist force in places like Yugoslavia;
- the United States was right to invade small countries like Grenada and Panama when our interests appeared threatened, but it was right not to intervene to end genocide in Rwanda;
- sanctions on Iraq and Cuba should be continued, despite their effects on civilians, while no similar conditions should be placed on China;
- the United States should oppose the empowerment of War Crimes Tribunals capable of bringing human rights violators to justice;
- U.S. energy policy should be founded on military support for the dictators of Saudi Arabia and the other oil kingdoms;
- relying on a narrow elite of wealthy, special interest donors is a fine way to finance election campaigns.

14. To be fair, an author more sympathetic to the right than this one could construct a parallel condemnation of Bush and Gore, only with more of a critique from the right than the left. From that perspective, the two men were indistinguishable because they said nothing about such issues as abolishing the Internal Revenue Service or the federal Department of Education, shutting down legalized gambling, ending diplomatic relations with China and Vietnam, or stopping the practice of abortion apart from so-called partial-birth abortions. And significant chunks of the public support these positions as well.

15. I will use the term "third party" in this book even though it is a misnomer. It implies that a two-party system is a natural fact of life, rather than an artificial construction propped up by state regulation. It also leaves out fourth and fifth and sixth parties, and so on. And it incorrectly fuels the impression that most Americans live in a two-party setting that is occasionally disturbed by a third-party challenge, when in fact for most elections most of us live in districts that are dominated by one party. Often, the third-party challenger is really the second party in the race!

16. J. David Gillespie, *Politics at the Periphery: Third Parties in Two-Party America* (Columbia: University of South Carolina Press, 1993); Immanuel Ness and James Ciment, *The Encyclopedia of Third Parties in America*, Volumes 1–3 (Armonk, NY: M. E. Sharpe, 2000).

17. These points are made in further detail by Theodore Lowi in "What's Wrong with the Two-Party System? Damn Near Everything, in Practice, Theory, and Ideology," paper presented at the opening plenary session of Independent Politics in a Global World, a conference held at CUNY Graduate Center, New York City, October 6–7, 2000.

18. In Maine, Massachusetts, Arizona, and Vermont, candidates who voluntarily agree to raise little to no private money can qualify for full public financing for their election campaigns. Depending on the office they are running for, they qualify by collecting a threshold number of small (e.g., $5) contributions. They are then liber-

ated from the private money chase and free to spend all their time meeting constituents and discussing issues. One-third of Maine's legislators and nearly one-fifth of Arizona's are currently "clean" incumbents. For more information, visit Public Campaign's website at www.publicampaign.org.

19. In 1998, Democrat Harry Reid beat Republican John Ensign for the U.S. Senate seat from Nevada by just 428 votes; Libertarian Michael Cloud got 8,044 votes in that race, or about 2 percent. In 2000, Libertarian Jeff Jared got 64,734 votes in the Washington Senate race, or about 3 percent, arguably helping Democrat Maria Cantwell beat Republican Slade Gorton by 2,228 votes. John J. Miller and Ramesh Ponnuru, "The GOP's Libertarian Problem," *NationalReview.com*, March 19, 2001.

20. Gillespie, *Politics at the Periphery*, p. 10.

21. Until June 1998, citizens were allowed to gather signatures in front of all post offices, so long as the petitioners were not disruptive to postal business. The new policy prohibits "soliciting signatures on petitions, polls, or surveys" in front of any post office. The Initiative and Referendum Institute, ACLU, and a coalition of citizen groups, sued the U.S. Postal Service in June 2000, charging that this policy violates the First Amendment. The case was in the discovery phase as of July 2001, with the plaintiffs hoping for a summary judgment in their favor.

22. Those states are Arizona, Arkansas, District of Columbia, Hawaii, Maine, Massachusetts, Minnesota, New Jersey, Oregon, Rhode Island, Vermont, Wisconsin. It is very likely that third-party activity will expand in the four current Clean Elections states; already the availability of full public financing has produced more serious third-party candidacies in Vermont, Maine, and Arizona.

Chapter One

1. "Minnesota Poll," *Minneapolis Star-Tribune*, March 1, 1998.

2. "Minnesota Poll," *Minneapolis Star-Tribune*, June 4, 1998.

3. Clark H. Bensen, "Polidata Election Reports, Presidential Election 1996 and 1992." Unless otherwise noted, all county election data cited come from Bensen's invaluable database.

4. "On July 26, 1992, I founded the party. The opposition was intense. A majority in Minnesotans for Perot opposed me. I got death threats, harassing calls. Most just wanted to stick with Perot. The nature of the controversy was that I hadn't gotten Perot's approval. But he didn't ask us for permission to quit, so I said we didn't need his permission to start a third party." Phone interview with Phil Madsen, founder of the Minnesota Independence Party, November 30, 1998.

5. "For Congress/Sixth District: Barkley over Sikorski, Grams," *Minneapolis Star-Tribune*, October 19, 1992.

6. Barkley first met Ventura during his 1994 Senate campaign, when Ventura was a talk-radio host on KSTP-AM and invited him on his show several times. In an excerpt from his political diary, published in the *Minneapolis Star-Tribune* on November 8, 1998, Barkley wrote: "He allowed me a great deal of time to talk about my campaign on his show and he seemed very interested in the 3rd party movement. He often referred to the Democrats and Republicans as the DemoCrypts and the ReBloodicans [a reference to the rival street gangs, the Crips and the Bloods]." In our conversation, Barkley credited his appearances on Ventura's show as well as Ventura's on-air references to his campaign as having propelled his Senate candidacy over the 5 percent threshold, a crucial boost. Interview with Dean Barkley, January 6, 1999, at his office in the state Capitol.

7. See chapters 4 and 5 for the fuller story.

8. Ventura was the honorary chair of Barkley's 1996 Senate campaign. On July 4 of that year, he marched with him in a parade in Annandale, a town northwest of the Twin Cities. "During that parade I noticed that Jesse was receiving most of the applause and cheers from the crowd even though this was my hometown," Barkley wrote in his diary. "I made the comment to Jesse during that parade that you should be the candidate, not me, and that next time it was his turn. He laughed at me at that time." Ventura's recollection is similar. "From the beginning of the campaign, Dean kept sidling up to me and whispering, 'You know, Jesse. This campaign is great, but we have the wrong candidate. I think you should be running instead of me. You have the name. You can do it.' I said, 'Dean, I don't wanna go to Washington; I wanna live in Minnesota; I don't wanna live out there inside the Beltway—who wants to do that?'" In Annandale, hearing the cheers of the crowd, Ventura insisted again that he didn't want to run for the U.S. Senate. "Then as a joke," he writes in his autobiography, "I said, 'I'll tell you what. I'll run for governor.' That was what started it. It snowballed from there." Barkley diary; Jesse Ventura, *I Ain't Got Time to Bleed* (New York: Villard, 1999), pp. 155–6.

9. Christian Collet, "The Polls—Trends: Third Parties and the Two-Party System," *Public Opinion Quarterly* 60 (1996): 431–49. At its peak, Powell fever crested with an ABC/*Washington Post* poll showing him as a hypothetical independent presidential candidate leading with 36 percent to Clinton's 28 percent and Dole's 23 percent.

10. *Minneapolis Star-Tribune*, September 23, 1998.

11. Patricia Lopez Baden, "Ventura Borrows the Mike and Steals the Show," *Minneapolis Star-Tribune*, September 19, 1998.

12. Dane Smith, "Second Debate Takes Candidates to New Terrain," *Minneapolis Star-Tribune*, October 3, 1998; Conrad deFiebre, "Ventura Wins Crowd's Cheers Debating in Usual DFL Territory," *Minneapolis Star-Tribune*, October 7, 1998.

13. While it is true that Lincoln won the presidency in 1860 by winning just 40 percent of the popular vote in a genuinely four-way race, and his Republican Party was only six years old at the time, it is an exaggeration to refer to his victory as a "third-party victory," given the way we now think of third-party challengers. America's stable two-party system of Democrats and Whigs began disintegrating in the 1840s, as the slavery issue spawned the abolitionist Liberty and Free Soil parties and anti-immigrant sentiment fueled the nativist Know-Nothing Party. In 1854, the year of the Republican Party's birth, it won nearly half the seats in the U.S. House of Representatives, consolidating supporters from the Liberty and Free Soil efforts. At the same time, the Know-Nothings momentarily surged and the Whigs collapsed. By 1860, when Lincoln ran, the Republicans were already the nation's second major party, dominant in the Northeast and Midwest.

14. Ventura, *I Ain't Got Time to Bleed*, pp. 165–66.

15. Amy Kuebelbeck, "Minnesota Candidate Makes Sexy Pitch," Associated Press, October 21, 1998. Dane Smith, "Rivals Assail Ventura's Remarks on Prostitution; Consider Legalizing It to Control It, He Says," *Minneapolis Star-Tribune*, October 22, 1998.

16. Sam Howe Verhovek, "Angry Voters Aren't Sure Where to Place the Blame," *New York Times*, October 11, 1998.

17. From the Jesse Ventura website, www.jesseventura.org, October 11, 1998.

18. Phil Madsen, the campaign's virtual field director, said Ventura's opponents tried to deflate his campaign with the prostitution controversy, but that quick use of the campaign's three thousand-member e-mail list, known as the JesseNet, forced the press to correct the story. "Their supporters and their operatives around the state were all talking about how Jesse now favors legalized prostitution. 'You gonna vote for somebody like that?' We got a press release up quickly, we sent a message out to the Jesse Net giving them the actual quotes. They then had it in their hands from an authoritative source exactly what had happened, they had the facts. And within a day or two that story had died completely. You know, the whisper campaign and the rumor mongering didn't work because we had enough supporters out there who knew what the truth was. But the best part of the deal was that Jesse did not have to go back to the press and demand a correction, he didn't have to beg for one. The people let the press know what was going on, and the media, to basically, I guess, to get the egg off their face, did feature articles on that incident and on the misquote. And so it wasn't one little thing in the corrections page, but there was some serious backpedaling that went on in the media. And we never talked to them once about it. We told our supporters about it and on their own they went after them." Transcript, Politics Online Conference at George Washington University's Graduate School of Political Management in Washington, D.C., December 7, 1998.

19. Barkley diary.

20. Ventura, *I Ain't Got Time to Bleed*, p. 162.

21. Barkley diary.

22. Realplayer versions of ads from the 1998 race can be found at http://www.ktca.org/election98/adwatch.htm.

23. Hillsman made the interesting argument that working on a limited budget would force more campaign consultants to be creative and unconventional in their communications strategies. Since consultants are paid a percentage of their total advertising "buy," he argued, they have no incentive to make quality ads that might prove more effective than the pablum they now rely on. Fast work and volume purchases of advertising time make them more money, with the result that much political advertising appears familiar and tired. Steven Schier, "Jesse's Victory: It Was No Fluke," *Washington Monthly*, January/February 1999.

24. Phone interview with Bill Hillsman, December 8, 1998.

25. Phone interview with Ed Gross, December 7, 1998.

26. Brian Sweeney, "An Insider's Account of the Coleman Campaign," *Minneapolis Star-Tribune*, November 15, 1998.

27. A body double was actually used for some of the shots.

28. Wy Spano, "On Course in the Best-Governed State in America," *Minneapolis Star-Tribune*, December 10, 1998.

29. MN-politics.com, October 29, 1998.

30. Andrea Stone, "Alternative Parties Can't Get Out of Minor League," *USA Today*, October 30, 1998.

31. Editorial, "It's Been Fun, but the Election's Near," *Minneapolis Star-Tribune*, October 30, 1998.

32. Hillary Clinton apologized to Ventura for the remark after he was elected. Jesse Ventura, *Do I Stand Alone* (New York: Pocket Books, 2000), p. 2.

33. Interview with Dan Erhardt, chairman of the Anoka county commission, in Anoka, January 5, 1999.

34. Interview with Adam Glickman, New Party communications director, in New York City, January 15, 1999.

35. Phone interview with Doug Williams, December 8, 1998.

36. Interview with Al Garcia, in Anoka, January 5, 1999.

37. Interview with Donna Handel, in Anoka, January 5, 1999.

38. Debbie Howlett, "'Body' Bulldozcs into Politics, a New Arena for Ex-Wrestler," *USA Today*, November 5, 1998.

39. David Peterson, "Even Pollsters Say They Were Surprised by Ventura Win," *Minneapolis Star-Tribune*, November 6, 1998.

40. "How Minnesotans Voted," *Star-Tribune*/VNS Exit Poll, November 4, 1998.

41. Dane Smith and Robert Whereatt, "Ventura Elected Governor," *Minneapolis Star-Tribune*, November 4, 1998. A month after the election, Coleman was still pooh-poohing Ventura's accomplishment. His victory was a fluke, he told Republicans at a postmortem gathering. "If somebody hits a 3-point shot from behind the half-court line, do you change the game plan?" he asked. Rochelle Olson, "DFLers, GOP Seek Road Maps in Era of Ventura," Associated Press, December 6, 1998.

42. James Lileks, Newhouse News Service, November 5, 1998.

43. Phone interview with Myron Orfield, December 8, 1998.

44. Phone interview with Dean Barkley, December 3, 1998.

45. Phone interview with Dave Mann, November 30, 1998.

46. Phone interview with Mike Kaszuba, December 23, 1998.

47. Ventura's willingness to explicitly identify himself with average working people against powerful special interests is made clear in his second book, *Do I Stand Alone?* "My point of view is that of a working family man," he writes in the book's introduction. "I've actually come under criticism for representing the common people. Kris Berggren, a writer for the *National Catholic Reporter*, said in February 1999 that I 'clearly respect Joe and Jane Sixpack.' Other reporters have run with that notion and used it to insult me, as though I should be ashamed to speak for the ordinary people who don't have million-dollar bank accounts or ten different diplomas on their walls" (pp. xx–xxi).

48. A month after his inauguration, Ventura unveiled his first biennial state budget. For weeks, local pundits and political professionals had been speculating about whether he would be up to the complex task of understanding and managing the state's $22 billion budget. And many raised questions about whether he would be able to follow through on his two major promises to the voters: to return the state's burgeoning surplus back to the taxpayers, and to reduce public school class sizes in grades K–12.

Early in the weeks after the election, the leaders of the state Republican Party had been quick to seize on Ventura's win as a vindication of their antitax, small-government philosophy. And they moved right away to propose an immediate income tax rebate in the face of predictions of at least another billion-dollar surplus for the 1999 tax year. Somewhat sourly, Democrats in the state legislature—where the party had just lost its majority while holding onto the Senate—had endorsed Ventura's call for a tax rebate as well. But there was an air of despair among Democrats. After all, their candidate had just come in third. And Ventura, whom many remembered from his days as a blustering talk-radio host, didn't seem likely to embrace many of their pro-government priorities.

Ventura's budget proposal thus came as a bit of a shock to both major parties. In a rebuff to the Republicans, he suggested that the state return about $1.1 billion of the coming year's surplus to the taxpayers not in the form of an income-tax cut, their favored vehicle, but as a sales-tax rebate. One big difference: none of the rebated money would be subject to federal income tax. But more important, instead of favoring those taxpayers in the top brackets, Ventura's plan channeled most of the money directly at the middle class, people making between $30,000 and $90,000 a year, and capped what high-income taxpayers could receive. And while the Republican proposal gave nothing to low-income taxpayers, Ventura proposed a modest, permanent reduction in their income tax burden.

"It was rewarding those who brought us here," admitted Dean Barkley a few days later, "people making between $30,000 and $100,000 a year. The middle class needs a break. If this was also good politics, so be it. I think we've already won the legislative fight, though the Republicans just haven't figured it out yet," he added. Ventura told the *Star-Tribune* the same thing, saying "My closest friends, truly my friends, are much more middle-class Minnesotans," he said. "They have incomes between $30,000 and $90,000, and that's my basis and where my roots come from. The Democrats tend to help the poor and the downtrodden, or believe they do, and the Republicans naturally look to the more affluent. It stands to reason that a centrist will work more on the middle incomes." Barkley phone interview with author, February 10, 1999; Patricia Lopez Baden, "Ventura Says He'll Propose Rebate Based on Sales Tax," *Minneapolis Star-Tribune*, January 12, 1999; Patricia Lopez Baden and

Dane Smith, "Momentum Builds for Sales Tax Rebate," *Minneapolis Star-Tribune*, January 13, 1999; Dane Smith, "Rebate Debate: Base It on Income Tax or on Sales Tax?" *Minneapolis Star-Tribune*, January 19, 1999; Mike Meyers, "Figuring Who Gets What from a Sales Tax Rebate Won't Be Easy," *Minneapolis Star-Tribune*, January 20, 1999.

49. Ventura's later writings on his role in politics make clear his strong identification with working people. See chapter 8 for further discussion.

50. Walter Karp, *Indispensable Enemies: The Politics of Misrule in America* (New York: Franklin Square Press, 1993), pp. 110–11.

51. "If there is a dominant value orientation of the United States people, if there is a civil religion, it is achievement. Winning is god, and adherents of the religion worship at a pyramidal altar where striving is endless because every success becomes a failure for not having done better. In the United States the true temple is the stadium, and people gather there by the thousands to watch in rapt and roaring tribute to the winner." Tex Sample, *Blue-Collar Ministry: Facing Economic and Social Realities of Working People* (Valley Forge, PA: Judson Press, 1984), p. 23.

52. Arianna Huffington, "Ventura Highway: The High Road to Winning," syndicated column, November 12, 1998.

53. Senator Paul Wellstone, "'98 Voters Were Standing Up for the Little Guy Against Big Money," *Boston Globe*, November 11, 1998.

54. CNN, *Late Edition with Wolf Blitzer*, November 24, 1998.

55. "Respondent's Social Class, Self-Identification 1956–1994," National Election Studies, http://www.umich.edu/~nes/nesguide/toptable/tab1a_8.htm. See chapter 2 for further discussion.

56. Interview with Dean Barkley in his office in the Minnesota Capitol, January 6, 1999.

Chapter Two

1. "Who Will Be a Third-Party Candidate in 2000?" *Crossfire*, July 13, 1999.

2. "Pat Buchanan Answers Questions about Third-Party Run," *Inside Politics*, June 23, 1999.

3. A syndicated column written by Arianna Huffington floating the idea of a Beatty candidacy drew more than five thousand e-mail responses, including many spontaneous offers of campaign contributions. Beatty was sufficiently intrigued by the notion to consult with a number of people about it. In the interests of full disclosure, I should note that, through a common acquaintance, he asked me for a memo on Perot's entry into politics, focusing on how he used 800-numbers and other technology to build his independent base of supporters, which I freely provided.

4. According to one survey sponsored by *The Hotline*, in hypothetical three-way matchups with Bush and Gore, Ross Perot would get 14 percent, John McCain 13 percent, Jesse Ventura 13 percent, Pat Buchanan 10 percent, Warren Beatty 7 percent, Heather Locklear 5 percent, Donald Trump 5 percent, and Lowell Weicker 5 percent. Western Wats Opinion Research Center/*Hotline* poll conducted August 24–31, 1999, surveyed one thousand likely voters; margin of error +/- 3.1%.

5. CNN/Gallup/*USA Today* poll conducted July 16–18, 1999; surveyed 1,031 adults; margin of error +/- 3%. Fifty-one percent said they would be satisfied with the choice of Bush or Gore.

6. By 67 to 28 percent, the public favored "having a third political party that would run candidates for President, Congress, and state offices against the Republican and Democratic candidates," according to a CNN/Gallup/*USA Today* poll conducted July 16–18, 1999. (The poll surveyed all adults, not just registered voters; it carried a margin of error +/-5 percent.) In that same poll, nearly half—46 percent—said they would not be satisfied if George W. Bush and Al Gore were the only two candidates on the ballot for president and said they would want to see a third-party candidate on the ballot as well. A similar survey of registered voters, who are a slightly more conservative group than the public at large, conducted June 23–24, 1999, by Fox News/Opinion Dynamics, found that 54 percent thought "it would be a good idea if a third national political party was formed which would run candidates for president, Congress, and state offices against the Republican and Democratic candidates." Thirty-two percent thought it was a bad idea. The poll followed that up, asking respondents: "Which of the following statements comes closer to your opinion? Statement 1: 'Voting for a third party candidate sends an important message that the political system needs to change.' Statement 2: 'Voting for a third party candidate is a wasted vote.'" The first statement received 55 percent support; the second one, 36 percent. The third-party question was not asked as frequently in 2000, but one poll, done in March 2000 for *Newsweek* by International Communications Research, found people supporting the proposition "We should have a third major political party in this country in addition to the Democrats and the Republicans" by 58 to 33 percent. The Pew Research

Center also asked this question in mid-June 2000, finding the spread had narrowed to 52-42 percent. Still, a majority favored the idea of having a third major party.

7. They are David Zuckerman, Steve Hingtgen, Carina Driscoll, and Bob Kiss, state representatives from the Progressive Party in Vermont, all from the Burlington area; New Hampshire state Rep. Steve Vaillancourt of the Libertarian Party; Bob Lessard of the Minnesota Independence Party (he is an ex-Democratic incumbent who was elected as an independent in 2000 and switched party affiliations afterward); Julie Jacobson, a Green member of the Island of Hawaii County Council; Art Goodtimes, a Green member of the San Miguel County Board of Supervisors in Colorado (he was a Democratic incumbent who switched to Green and was then reelected in 2000); Elizabeth Horton-Sheff, a Green member of the Hartford City Council in Connecticut (where local law limits the number of seats the majority party may hold, making room for a minor party like the Greens to gain a seat) and John Halle, a Green who was elected to New Haven's Board of Alderman in 2001. There are also six independent members of state legislatures in Georgia (2), Maine (2), Pennsylvania, and Vermont, though only three of these are "true" independents in the sense of never having been elected previously as a Republican or Democrat. *Ballot Access News*, April 1, 2001.

8. E-mail from Steve Schmidt to author, August 20, 1998.

9. E-mail correspondence with Char Roberts, spring 1995.

10. E-mail correspondence with David Wiesner, spring 1995.

11. Steven Rosenstone, Roy Behr, and Edward Lazarus, *Third Parties in America* (Princeton, N.J.: Princeton University Press, 1996), p. 162.

12. For example, the percentage of Americans who think "you can trust the government in Washington to do what is right just about always [or] most of the time" dropped from 73 percent in 1958 to 40 percent in 1998. Those thinking that government can be trusted "only some of the time" rose from 23 percent to 58 percent. This skeptical attitude is shared uniformly across varying levels of education, income, occupation, race, age, and political ideology. Though there has been a significant lessening of public distrust between 1994 and 1998, the last time a majority said they trusted the federal government was in 1972, before Watergate. Similarly, the percentage of Americans who say "the government is pretty much run by a few big interests looking out for themselves" as opposed to being run "for the benefit of all the people" has risen from 29 percent in 1964 (when the question was first asked in the NES survey) to 64 percent in 1998. Again, there is little variation among Americans on the basis of socioeconomic background. Since 1970, a majority — across the board — has believed that a few big interests dominate government. All references to NES data can be found at http://www.umich.edu/~nes.

13. For example, according to the NES, the percentage agreeing that "people like me don't have any say about what the government does" rose from 31 percent in 1952 to a high of 56 percent in 1994, improving somewhat to 42 percent in 1998. "People like me don't have any say" is a strong statement of alienation. And it's significant that Americans are more likely to agree with it if they are black instead of white, poor instead of well-off, have just a high school education or less compared to a college diploma or post-graduate degree, or work in blue-collar jobs rather than white-collar or professional fields.

14. By comparison, the percentage of registered Democrats dropped from 41 percent in 1970 to 33.1 percent in 1990 to an estimated 29.5 percent in 1998. And the proportion of registered Republicans has shown a similar pattern of decline, going from 25 percent in 1970 to 23.1 percent in 1990 to an estimated 22 percent in 1998. Committee for the Study of the American Electorate, "Final Post Election Report," February 9, 1999, http://www.gspm.org/csae/cgans5.html.

15. These totals are derived using the NES party identification seven-point scale and combining the separate categories of "independent independent," "independent Democrats," and "independent Republicans." In *The Myth of the Independent Voter* (Berkeley: University of California Press, 1992) political scientists Bruce E. Keith, David B. Magleby, Candice J. Nelson, Elizabeth Orr, Mark C. Westlye, and Raymond E. Wolfinger, make the argument that most of these independent voters are actually "covert partisans" who nearly always vote with the party they lean toward. Thus, they would count "independent Democrats" and "independent Republicans" in their respective party columns. They have a point, insofar as most of the time voters do not have a viable independent or third-party choice on the ballot, whether for president, Congress, or governor. However, as we shall see below, when such a candidate is included, independents are twice as likely to give their vote to that candidate than are strong Democrats or Republicans. Just because the two-party system keeps independent voters bottled up most of the time doesn't mean that their increase is a "myth" or a nonfactor in today's politics; quite the contrary.

16. "Independents Gaining," *San Francisco Examiner*, June 4, 1995.

17. Al Cross, "Motor-Voter Registrations Have Surprise Twist: Nearly One-Third Have No Party Preference," *The Cincinnati Enquirer*, March 9, 1995.

18. Florida Department of State, Elections Online, http://election.dos.state.fl.us/voterreg/vrhist.htm.

19. Anderson got 12 percent of the 22-to-37-year-olds and 19 percent of the 18-to-22-year-olds, compared to 6 percent overall. In 1992, Perot got 25 percent of the 18-to-33-year-olds, compared to 19 percent overall. And in 1996, he got 10 percent of the 28-to-43-year-olds, compared to 8 percent overall. Nader got 5 percent of the 18-to-29-year-old vote in 2000, compared to 3 percent overall. Younger voters also tend to register and vote at much lower rates than their elders, so any third-party effort centered on galvanizing young people also has to focus on these basics of civic participation. National Election Studies, "President Vote 2 Major Parties and Wallace/Anderson/Perot 1968–1996," http://www.umich.edu/~nes/nesguide/2ndtables/t9a_2_3.htm; Voter News Service 2000 exit poll, available at http://www.cnn.com/ELECTION/2000/results.

20. "How Minnesotans Voted," *Star-Tribune*/VNS exit poll, November 4, 1998.

21. Gallup News Service, poll releases, April 9, 1999, http://www.gallup.com/poll/releases.pr990409c.asp.

22. In 1998 in Rhode Island, Cool Moose Party candidate Robert Healey got 7 percent of the overall vote, but 11 percent of the independents. In New York, Reform Party candidate Tom Golisano got 7 percent overall, but 13 percent of the independents. In Pennsylvania, Constitutional Party candidate Peg Luksik (affiliated with U.S. Taxpayers Party) got 10 percent, but 20 percent of the independents. In Minnesota, Jesse Ventura won with 37 percent overall, but got 52 percent of independents. And in the California gubernatorial primary of 1998, independent voters in the county of San Bernardino gave 17.2 percent of their votes to third-party candidates, compared to just 8 percent of the Democratic voters and 6 percent of the Republicans.

Two years later, the Progressive Party candidate for governor, Anthony Pollina, got 10 percent of the vote, but 15 percent of the independents. Mary Brown, an independent who ran for governor of New Hampshire, got 6 percent overall but 8 percent among independents. James Gibson, a member of Jesse Ventura's Independence Party who ran for U.S. Senate in Minnesota, also got 6 percent total, but drew 9 percent among independents. Denise Giardina, a novelist who ran for governor as the candidate of the Mountain Party in West Virginia, got just 2 percent of the vote, but 4 percent of the independents. Thus, as the number of registered voters who are not Democrats or Republicans continues to grow, it is reasonable to expect better showings by third-party and independent candidates.

23. The modest 1.7 percent increase in turnout between 1996 and 2000 can be explained by the unusual closeness of the Gore-Bush race in many states, along with Nader's presence. About one-third of Nader's voters said they wouldn't have participated in the election if he hadn't been on the ballot, which translates into nearly 1 million voters or almost 1 percent of the total. Despite the fact that Nader was excluded from the presidential debates and had far less money to spend than Perot, his campaign can be credited with producing at least half the overall boost in turnout in 2000, again proving the value of third-party challenges to enhanced voter participation.

24. According to the Voter News Service exit poll, 53 percent of all the votes cast in 2000 were from people making $50,000 and up. According to the U.S. Census Bureau, 41 percent of all households had a family income of more than $50,000; http://www.census.gov/hhes/www/income99.html.

25. Frances Fox Piven and Richard Cloward, *Why Americans Still Don't Vote* (Boston: Beacon Press, 2000), p. 42.

26. Paul Kleppner, *Who Voted? The Dynamics of Electoral Turnout, 1870–1980* (New York: Harcourt Brace Jovanovich, 1982), p. 143.

27. Piven and Cloward, *Why Americans Still Don't Vote*, p. 43.

28. Peter Argesinger, "A Place on the Ballot: Fusion Politics and Antifusion Laws," *American Historical Review* 287 (1980), p. 300.

29. The major parties continued to take steps to deter third-party competitors from arising by further restricting access to the ballot. For example, in 1924, U.S. Senator Robert LaFollette needed only fifty thousand signatures to get on the ballot in all forty-eight states as the candidate of the new Progressive Party. In 1996, that same campaign would have needed 1.6 million signatures. E. Joshua Rosenkranz, *Voter Choice '96: A 50-State Report Card on the Presidential Elections* (New York: Brennan Center for Justice, 1996), pp. 13–14.

30. David Croteau, *Politics and the Class Divide: Working People and the Middle-Class Left* (Philadelphia: Temple University Press, 1995), p. 102.

31. It's worth noting that Croteau's eye-opening fieldwork and interviews with dozens of workers and middle-class political activists took place in late 1990 and early 1991, a period of economic recession. This was also at the end of a generation of business-oriented unionism at the AFL-CIO. Since John Sweeney and his reformers took the helm of that organization, America's unions have begun a concerted effort to expand their organizing efforts and reenergize their base. A new study by Croteau or someone following in his footsteps might well find some changes in the attitudes of workers toward political activism.

32. Richard Berke, "Nonvoters Are No More Alienated Than Voters, a Survey Shows," *New York Times*, May 30, 1996.

33. When asked why they didn't vote in the 1980 presidential election, 36 percent of the nonvoters gave a political rather than personal reason. "None of the candidates appealed to me" (13 percent), "[I] wasn't especially interested in that election" (14 percent), "my vote would have made no difference" (5 percent), or "politicians are all crooked" (4 percent). The Fitzpatrick poll had similar findings for the 1996 election. Thirty-eight percent didn't vote for essentially political reasons: they "did not care for any of the candidates" (16 percent), they were "fed up with the political system" (15 percent), or they "did not feel like candidates were interested in people like me" (7 percent).

34. In the *ABC News* poll, 60 percent of the nonvoters who said they had voted in 1980 recalled choosing either Jimmy Carter or John Anderson; only 30 percent said they had voted for Ronald Reagan. Considering that after an election, voters tend to "recall" voting for the winner, this is a telling finding. Sixty-seven percent of nonvoters said they had voted for the Democratic candidate for the House of Representatives, compared to 52 percent of regular voters.

35. In the Fitzpatrick study, nonregular voters were more likely than regular voters to favor a "none of the above" (NOTA) option on the ballot that would force new elections in the event NOTA got more votes than the candidates standing for election.

36. "Americans Who Say They Will Vote on Tuesday Share Many of the Same Attitudes as Likely Non-Voters," The Vanishing Voter Project, November 4, 2000, http://www.vanishingvoter.org

37. In an interview at the Minnesota statehouse the day Ventura was inaugurated, Koskinen, an older woman, expressed outright horror at Ventura's huge turnout. "He drew the tattooed, T-shirted guys in my district, the young beer-drinking types who don't think about public policy as much as the image of Jesse the bruiser. You know, 'My governor can beat up your governor.' They were coming out of the bars, inebriated, to vote for him. Frankly, that scares me." She admitted that she half hoped and half believed that Ventura was an anomaly. But she wasn't completely disdainful. "The good piece about the T-shirted, tattooed guys who came to the polls is they now have a reason to watch what government does and take an active part in their communities. My hope is this anomaly of voters doesn't remain an anomaly but becomes part of the rest of us." Koskinen may well have seen a lot of youthful beer drinkers at the polls, but the biggest surge in Ventura's vote came from people in the 30-to-44-year-old group.

38. Interview with Al Garcia in Anoka, Minnesota, January 5, 1999.

39. Jackie Calmes, "The Underdog Strategy," *Wall Street Journal*, March 31, 1999.

40. Phone interview with Frances Fox Piven, November 1, 1999.

41. Phone interview with Stanley Greenberg, October 1, 1999.

42. Interview with Rep. Jesse Jackson Jr., October 1, 1999. In the 1998 movie *Bulworth*, Warren Beatty played a despairing U.S. senator who decided to take out a contract on his own life to cash on a lucrative insurance policy. Thus liberated, he starts telling the truth about the corruption of American politics. The public falls in love with his candor, disenchanted voters flock to him, and his popularity zooms.

43. For example, in 1996 Buchanan got 8,604 votes in Racine, a blue-collar industrial city south of Milwaukee, compared to just 2,654 in 1992.

44. In 1992 and 1996, Perot did somewhat better with people making less than $50,000 than with those making more than that amount, according to the Voter News Service exit polls. The same was true for his support among union households. But the tilt was modest, on the scale of just 1 or 2 percent. As for Senator John McCain, whose insurgent campaign for the Republican nomination in 2000 attracted much support among independents and even Democratic crossover voters, there's little hard evidence that McCain reached very far into the deep well of public disaffection that defines the attitudes of most American citizens. Only in Michigan, where he was boosted by a very large number of crossover Democrats, did McCain score somewhat better among the less well-off and less educated than the upper brackets. In general, a profile of his voters would look like an inverted pyramid: heavier support from people as they move up the status ladder. Why the hole in McCain's base? The answer, it seems, is that his brand of patriotic populism lacked a real economic edge. Apart from some attacks on Bush's tax cut for favoring the rich, there was little in McCain's message that was really aimed at the needs of working-class Americans (and many of those voters remained closer to the Democrats than the Republicans). Thus, his was more an insurgency of regular voters, compared to the new voters who propelled Jesse Ventura to his 1998 win in Minnesota. If anything, the exit polls from 1996 show a larger proportion of younger, poorer, and less educated voters in the Republican electorate then than in 2000—the effect, perhaps, of Buchanan's volatile mix of xenophobia, right-wing Catholicism, corporation bashing, and talk of a living wage. Micah L. Sifry, "The McCain Vote," *The Nation*, April 17, 2000. Buchanan's billboards were described to the author over the phone by journalist John Nichols, February 12, 1996.

45. Sanders never hid the fact that he was a socialist, but he also never ran as the candidate of any party.

46. Orleans gave George Bush a solid majority in 1988, and its independent-minded citizens rewarded Ross Perot with 27.2 percent of the vote in 1992, substantially higher than his state average. Its median household

income in 1990 was $22,800, about $7,000 less than the state average. Only 14.2 percent of Orleans's residents were college graduates. The standard of living was low, with homes worth on average just $66,500—compared to $95,600 statewide. Nearly 15 percent of Orleans residents were living under the official poverty line, 4 percent more than in the rest of the state.

47. Sanders was also indirectly helped in 1990 by the National Rifle Association, which campaigned against the incumbent, Peter Smith, because he had softened his position in support of gun ownership. One can argue that this artificially boosted Sanders's showing in Vermont's more conservative corners, except that he has continued to do better than his state average in counties like Orleans in more recent elections, despite himself having become the target of the NRA.

48. For example, in the industrial town of Bristol, the Republican gubernatorial vote from 1986 held steady in 1990, while the Democratic column dropped by 7,000 and Weicker drew 9,500. Conversely, in the wealthy enclave of Ridgefield, the Republican candidate got 61 percent of the vote, while Weicker got just 30 percent.

49. Phone interview with Patrick Caddell, November 5, 1998.

Chapter Three

1. Gargan's initial selection of six newspapers was not accidental, however. Three of them, the *Tulsa World* of Oklahoma, the *Denver Post* of Colorado, and the *San Diego Tribune* of California, were in states that had just passed ballot proposals imposing term limits on members of Congress, an idea that was just starting to sweep the country.

2. All emphases and typographical errors are from the original ad, as supplied by Gargan to the author.

3. Interview with Jack Gargan in his home in Cedar Key, Florida, February 12, 1998.

4. Ibid.

5. Letter to Ross Perot from Jack Gargan, June 26, 1992, quoted in Gerald Posner, *Citizen Perot* (New York: Random House, 1996), p. 252.

6. Interview with Jack Gargan, February 12, 1998.

7. Though this book is exclusively concerned with popular support for independent and third-party politics, it is highly unlikely that any such effort can succeed in transforming America without breaking off some similarly minded segments of the business world. If history is the story of organized people struggling against organized money, there is no question that forward movement has often occurred when the business class has fractured and accommodated demands for change. For a fascinating discussion of how Perot's 1992 bid for support from maverick elements of the Republican and Democratic business communities fell apart, see Thomas Ferguson, "The Lost Crusade of Ross Perot," *The Nation*, August 17–24, 1992.

8. Ever the political purist, Gargan complained at the time that his bandwagon was attracting self-interested opportunists along with genuine patriots. "All these damn political hacks are jumping in too, muddying the waters," he told me in early July 1992, the first time I spoke to him. But whatever the cause, principle or opportunism, the effect was extraordinary. In 1992, there were 458 independent or minor-party candidates for U.S. House seats, nearly triple the number who ran two years earlier, according to data collected by Suffolk University professor John Berg, using election returns reported by *Congressional Quarterly*. Eighty-three of these candidates got more than 5 percent of the vote, and twenty-eight received more than the margin of victory between the major candidates. Berg's analysis shows that 1992 was the high-water mark for third-party congressional efforts, and that the entire period from 1988 to the present has seen substantially more such efforts than any time since World War II. John Berg, "Cracks in the U.S. Two-Party System," paper presented at the annual meeting of the New England Political Science Association, Springfield, Mass., May 3–4, 1996. A more recent analysis by Richard Winger confirmed Berg's finding, with one additional update. In 1992, minor-party and independent candidates cumulatively drew over 4 percent of the votes for Congress, more than any year since 1938. Since Berg wrote his paper in 1996, the non-major-party congressional vote climbed again, hitting 4.17 percent in 2000. *Ballot Access News*, May 1, 2001.

9. Joe Klein, "Stalking the Radical Middle," *Newsweek*, Sept. 25, 1995, pp. 32–36.

10. E. J. Dionne, *They Only Look Dead* (New York: Touchstone, 1996), p. 67.

11. In 1993, when Gargan decided to disband THRO, convinced that it has served its purpose and sparked other useful efforts, he destroyed his mailing list and burned the tens of thousands of letters he had received. "I let my whole organization go," he told me, "because I'm not a politician." Interview with Jack Gargan, February 12, 1998.

12. Gordon Black had an impressive group of backers, including former independent 1980 presidential candidate John Anderson, independent Governor Lowell Weicker of Connecticut and his campaign manager, Tom

D'Amore, a former GOP state chair; Cecil Heftel, a wealthy former member of Congress from Hawaii; Tom Golisano, a successful businessman and philanthropist from upstate New York; Lionel Kuntz of the Coalition to End the Permanent Congress (a group of failed and frustrated congressional candidates); Dean Barkley, a top leader of the Minnesota Independence Party; and Theodore Lowi, a political science professor at Cornell University who was a vocal and prominent supporter of third-party efforts.

13. Phone interview with Gordon Black, October 20, 1992.

14. "The Independence Party: A Statement of Principles," THRO newsletter, 1992 election edition, pp. 6–8.

15. Interview with Jack Gargan, February 12, 1998.

16. Carolyn Barta, "Interview with Eugene McCarthy," *Dallas Morning News*, August 9, 1998.

17. Gordon Black and Benjamin Black, "Perot Wins! The Election That Could Have Been," *Public Perspective*, January/February 1993, pp. 15–18.

18. *President Clinton's New Beginning: The Complete Text of the Historic Clinton-Gore Economic Conference in Little Rock, Arkansas, December 14–15, 1992* (New York: Donald Fine, 1992), p. 413.

19. "A Bride, A Corpse . . ." *Time*, June 7, 1993.

20. Laurence Barrett, "A Marriage of Convenience: Perot's Dalliance with the G.O.P. Gives Clinton Grief, but in the End It May Hurt Republicans Too," *Time*, July 5, 1993.

21. Kenneth Walsh, "Establishment Jitters: The Magnificent Obsession," *U.S. News and World Report*, May 17, 1993.

22. Howard Fineman, "Ross Perot's New Army," *Newsweek*, June 7, 1993, p. 24, and Barrett, "A Marriage of Convenience," p. 37.

23. Stanley Greenberg and Al From, "The Road to Realignment: The Democrats and the Perot Voters," Democratic Leadership Council, July 1, 1993.

24. Frank Luntz, "Perovian Civilization: Who Supported Ross, and Why," *Policy Review*, spring 1993, p. 23.

25. Gloria Borger and Jerry Buckley, "Perot Keeps Going and Going . . ." *U.S. News and World Report*, May 17, 1993.

26. *Washington Post*–ABC News poll, May 22, 1993.

27. Bill Turque, author of *Inventing Al Gore* (New York: Houghton Mifflin, 2000), wrote (pp. 282–83) that "Throughout most of the [NAFTA] debate, the administration avoided confronting Perot directly, for fear of offending his supporters. But a slip in his poll numbers that fall led to a change of plan at the White House. Positioning Perot, now a depreciating political asset, as the public face of NAFTA opposition might make it easier for House members with heavy Perot blocs in their district to vote yes. The time had come to take him on, and Jack Quinn [Gore's chief of staff] thought the vice president should be the point man."

28. Gloria Borger and Jerry Buckley, "A Giant New Sucking Sound," *U.S. News and World Report*, December 20, 1993.

29. James Barnes, "Still on the Trail," *National Journal*, April 10, 1993, p. 860.

30. Elizabeth Drew, *Showdown: The Struggle between the Gingrich Congress and the Clinton White House*, (New York: Touchstone, 1996), p. 30.

31. Katharine Seelye, "Perot Urges Voters to Fill Congress with Republicans," *New York Times*, October 5, 1994.

32. Stanley Greenberg's study of the Perot voters found that a majority had voted for Reagan and Bush in previous elections. So the 1994 "swing" of Perot voters to the GOP was more likely a return home than a result of Perot's call.

33. Mark Shields, "The Democrats and the Perils of Perot," *Washington Post*, March 25, 1996, citing a Peter Hart poll of two thousand Americans for the *Wall Street Journal*/NBC News that found that 60 percent of Perot's 1996 supporters were people who had not voted for him in 1992.

34. Curtis Wilkie, "For Perot, a Low Profile: After GOP Victory, Texan's Thunder Seen Stolen," *Boston Globe*, March 29, 1995.

35. Gordon Black and Benjamin Black, *The Politics of American Discontent* (New York: John Wiley, 1994), p. 192.

36. Perot never released the official total, claiming that UWSA's elected state leaders had voted to keep the number secret. But my colleague Mark Spencer was able to deduce UWSA's membership based on the fact that the Postal Service's bulk mail center in Dallas sent out that number of copies of the UWSA national newsletter in September 1993 according to publicly available records. Since the group's $15 annual dues were based on a family membership, it seems safe to allow a slightly higher number for their total membership. For more details, see "How Many Perotians Are There?" *Perot Periodical*, spring 1994. UWSA's 990 Form filed with the Internal Revenue Service for 1993 shows a total of $18.3 million collected in membership dues and assessments, which interpolates to a membership of about 1.2 million. The 1.5 million number comes from Mick Ringsak, a Vietnam vet and small-business owner from Butte, Montana, who was on UWSA's national board from its inception

to mid-1995. "We signed a contract saying that we'd never reveal that number," he said in a phone interview on March 20, 1996.

37. Theda Skocpol, "Associations Without Members," *American Prospect*, July 1–August 1, 1999.

38. Bob Erwin, "Wanted: Democracy for United We Stand," *Perot Periodical*, fall 1993, pp. 7–8.

39. Tom Gogola, "Perot's Troopers," *Perot Periodical*, winter 1994, p. 3; Micah L. Sifry, "Perot's Brass Roots," *Perot Periodical*, spring 1994. Our first report was picked up by *Newsweek*'s Periscope column, which then received a letter from Vollney Corn claiming that he had been misquoted. He said that United We Stand "never requested resumes from 300 colonels at the Army War college," only that "a job opening was posted there so the 30 or so retiring personnel would contact UWSA if they were interested in discussing opportunities with the organization." He also declared that "less than 20 percent of UWSA's national staff has served in the military."

40. Interview with Jack Gargan, February 12, 1998. One early UWSA state director, Marie George of Utah, reported that she had told Perot to divide her salary among the state's twenty-nine counties to help them be more effective, since she and her husband had their own business and she didn't need the money. Perot's reply, according to George, was that he could control her if he paid her salary but not the people in twenty-nine counties. She resigned her post in July 1993. UWSA Survey–Utah, Anne Saucier and Deb Taylor, "Survey of the States," August 1995.

41. This franchise approach had an odd result: by October 1993 the group's giant California chapter technically had only one recognized member, Jim Campbell, its paid state director. As a licensee of the United We Stand America, Inc. tradename and service mark, UWSA Inc. of California was legally obliged to comply with Dallas's guidelines and policies. Memo from Jim Campbell to all CDCs [congressional district coordinators], dated October 14, 1993.

42. The very first statement of dissent among UWSA members was published on May 10, 1993, and was written with a distinctly high-minded tenor. "WHEN IN THE COURSE OF HUMAN EVENTS, it becomes necessary for one People to declare their grievances against an unjust and dictatorial Political Association which have connected them with another, a decent Respect to the opinions of Mankind requires that they should declare the reasons which impel them to said Declaration," it began. This "Declaration of Self-Determination" went on to condemn the "appointed unelected" interim leaders of UWSA as puppets not representing its rank and file, to attack dictates from Dallas preventing UWSA members from taking stands on issues, and to complain that membership dues were being used solely for national expenses like infomercials rather than to help build local chapters. It was signed by Dr. Thomas Robert Stevens and Joyce Shepard, two UWSA founding members from New York. Kirk MacKenzie of UWSA–California unearthed it in 1996 and circulated copies, saying, "The problems were apparent even then [May 1993]. Unfortunately, I was a believer at the time, and discounted this document. In retrospect, I could have saved myself a lot of wasted time if I had listened."

43. "Most of us are leaving because the organization we thought we joined is not the one we've experienced these last eight months," Kathy Watterson, the group's state secretary wrote in a memo to the UWSA Florida state board. "Many good people have been termed 'obstructionists' or 'renegades' or 'malcontents' because they're standing up against things they believe are wrong. *To do so is not 'obstructionist' or 'militancy' but to manifest that character and integrity so often lacking in our elected officials.*" [Emphasis in the original.] Memo from Kathy Watterson, state secretary of UWSA–Florida, Inc. and a member of the board of directors, to the chairman and members of the board, UWSA–Florida, Inc., February 24, 1994.

44. Mark Spencer, "With the Branch Perotians in Dallas," *Perot Periodical*, spring 1994, p. 4.

45. Phone interview with Kirk MacKenzie, April 22, 1996.

46. Mark Spencer, "Riding Herd: How Perot and His Hired Hands Stomp on Their Grass Roots," *Perot Periodical*, summer 1994.

47. Dave Morgan, "Mid Course Correction Memo," June 1994, as reported in the *Perot Periodical*, winter/spring 1995.

48. Phone interview with Dave Morgan, March 20, 1996.

49. E-mail from Dave Morgan to Tony Hernandez, May 7, 1995, posted on the UWSA@shell.portal.com listserve.

50. E-mail from Skip Leuschner to UWSA@shell.portal.com, May 8, 1995. I interviewed Leuschner at length that spring, and discovered that he had played a central role in a successful Internet-organized effort to help unseat Democratic House Speaker Tom Foley in 1994 that was called "De-Foley-Ate Congress '94." He credited Perot for getting him involved in political activism following his retirement from the Navy after thirty-three years of active duty, but he said that he would not vote for Perot again after seeing how he failed to lead UWSA effectively. He was harshly critical of President Clinton, calling him "morally and ethically unqualified to be president," and pronounced himself "delighted" that "the Democratic monopoly on power" had been broken with

the 1994 elections. At the same time, he said he had "no enthusiasm for a Republican majority per se" and insisted that campaign finance reform was essential if Congress's corrupt, unethical behavior was ever to be changed. At bottom, he saw himself as a hard-core independent, unwilling to "sell my soul to the political establishment . . . to Democrats or Republicans or anyone else." The full interview appeared in the winter/spring 1995 issue of the *Perot Periodical*, in "Beyond Perot: Listening to the Independent Vote."

51. Phone interview with Kirk MacKenzie, April 22, 1996.

52. Ronald B. Rapoport and Walter J. Stone, "1996 Party Leadership and Presidential Selection Survey Results, The Reform Party in 1996: A Report to Respondents," available at http://faculty.wm.edu/rbrapo/reports/Index.htm.

53. Ernest Tollerson, "Perot Group Falls Far Short of Original Political Vision," *New York Times*, May 11, 1996.

54. UWSA Survey – Colorado, as reported by Dennis Weyl, former state chair, to Anne Saucier and Deborah Taylor, "Survey of the States," August 1995 (unpublished copy in author's possession).

55. E-mail from Michael Gunn to UWSA@shell.portal.com, May 29, 1995, subject: "What Killed UWSA."

56. UWSA Survey – South Dakota, as reported by Kathleen Christopherson, state chair, to Anne Saucier and Deborah Taylor, "Survey of the States," August 1995.

57. Phone interview with Dave Morgan, March 20, 1996.

58. UWSA Survey – Florida, as reported by Cherry Anderson, state chair/president, to Anne Saucier and Deborah Taylor, "Survey of the States," August 1995.

59. Phone interview with David Flagg, former Masschusetts congressional district coordinator, January 19, 1995.

60. E-mail from Dennise Kaiser Smith, former vice president of UWSA–Hawaii, to UWSA@shell.portal.com, July 13, 1995.

61. John De Lasaux, "Deserted in Arizona: Facing Dallas' Stone Wall," *Perot Periodical*, summer 1995, pp. 5–6. De Lasaux was president of UWSA–Arizona.

62. Press release, UWSA "Meeting of the States," October 29, 1995.

63. The UWSA activists who responded to Saucier and Taylor's August 1995 "Survey of the States" (plus the dissident leaders I interviewed) gave varying degrees of information about how they made their livings. In addition to a half-dozen who said they were retirees and fourteen other people who listed no occupation, they self-identified as follows:

- Professionals: a doctor, a former school administrator, a computer engineer for Cessna Aircraft, a manager of a "resort" in the French Quarter of New Orleans, a mortgage broker, a trainer of computer operators, someone with a full-time job in the medical field and a side business of her own, a forty-nine-year-old engineer, a worker for McDonnel Douglas, someone who retired from a fertilizer company, a stockbroker, a writer for outdoor magazines, a television graphics editor, a lawyer (Harvard Law graduate), a management recruiter, a software designer, a small-town lawyer serving people starting and running small businesses, a dentist who was retired military, a heart transplant nurse and former Air Force flight nurse, a photographer for Union Carbide, and an academic teaching political science in Madison, Wisconsin.

- Business owners: two generic "businessmen," an owner of a used car lot and other rental property, a part owner of a civil engineering and land surveying company, co-owner/operator of a small real estate business, a former owner of a Houston geophysical exploration company, an owner of a business in restructuring bankrupt companies, a shoe store owner, a retired businessman, a thirty-seven-year-old businessman, a real estate developer, an owner of a successful construction business, and a woman who owned a business with her husband.

- Sales: a medical software salesman, someone who had retired from computer systems sales and management, a dental equipment salesman, a former military man now in real estate, and a manufacturer's representative marketing various products.

- Self-employed: an Amway distributor, a computer programmer, a professional gambler, a real estate broker, a private investor, and a woman who assisted her husband in an advertising and public relations home business.

- Working class: two who worked in marine services, a retired railroad conductor, a tab puller in a bar, a worker for a home alarm company, an electrical construction worker, a retired gear lab technician for Dana Corporation, and a transportation dispatcher for public schools.

- Homemakers: a woman whose husband was in the hotel business and a woman whose husband owned a textile factory.

Chapter Four

1. Perot on CNN's *Larry King Live*, June 9, 1993.
2. Perot quoted in the *New York Times*, November 18, 1993.
3. Before deciding to cover the convention, I called Sabatine to find out more. Sabatine, a mild-mannered man with a slight Philadelphia accent, said that he had been on the state committee of UWSA–Pennsylvania, which had grown out of the Pennsylvanians for Perot petition effort, but explained his interest in forming a third party by saying, "We think United We Stand doesn't have a big enough hammer." In other words, it wasn't enough to lobby members of Congress or try to mobilize a swing vote for the good ones or against the bad ones. Sabatine claimed that three-quarters of the fledgling party's supporters were current or former Perot followers, but said, "Mr. Perot is not participating at this point, though I think he'll get involved sooner or later." Phone interview with Nicholas Sabatine, April 12, 1994.
4. Bruce Shapiro, "Dr. Fulani's Traveling Snake-Oil Show," *The Nation*, May 4, 1992. See also David Grann, "Coming Soon to a Presidential Campaign Near You," *New Republic*, December 13, 1999.
5. Party chairman Sabatine acknowledged this in a phone interview, April 27, 1994.
6. Fulani herself was nominated for party vice chair, but withdrew her name in a graceful maneuver that she said demonstrated her concern for real party unity. "Some people have expressed concern about my taking this role," she admitted as she stepped aside. "I never capitulate, [but] I do cooperate."
7. "We are building a major third party around the issue of democracy," Fred Newman told Bruce Shapiro back in early 1992. See Shapiro, "Dr. Fulani's Traveling Snake-Oil Show."
8. Phone interview with Jacqui Salit, May 2, 1994. Salit added, "The intent of the New Alliance Party is that by 1996 there will no longer be a New Alliance Party, there will be a national Patriot Party."
9. Fulani described her efforts in the January 27, 1994, issue of *National Alliance*, the NAP's broadsheet, in the following terms: "I have spent the last 12 years working night and day to build a Black-led, multi-racial, pro-gay and pro-socialist independent political party, and now I am working to unite the base of that movement with the mostly white 'radical center' of the Perot base because I think that we have a real shot at bringing a national third party into existence—a new kind of party that defines itself not in terms of programmatics but by its capacity to open up the political process."
10. Emily Sachar, "Jogger Case Lawyer: It's All Racial," *Newsday*, November 29, 1990, and Patricia Hurtado, "'I Was Set Up,' Says Suspended Lawyer," *Newsday*, May 26, 1994.
11. Phone interview with Jacqui Salit, June 10, 1994.
12. Bess was sentenced to life in prison for the assault.
13. "Muslim Shooting Suspect Killed His Brother in 1970s, Reports Say," Associated Press, May 31, 1994.
14. Phone interview with Nicholas Sabatine, April 27, 1994.
15. Phone interview with Gordon Black, April 27, 1994.
16. Theodore Lowi letter to Dr. Lenora Fulani, dated May 6, 1994, provided to the author.
17. UWSA's April 1995 national newsletter announced the meeting with the following headline: "1995 UWSA National Conference—Focus: 'Is a New Political Party Good for Our Country?'"
18. Fred Lindecke, "Area Perot Backers Meet on 1996," *St. Louis Post-Dispatch*, March 19, 1995, p. 5D; and Mark Spencer, "Feeling a Draft? The Evidence from Texas," *Perot Periodical*, summer 1995, p. 11. At a Houston meeting of the UWSA–Texas chapter, the organization's national executive director Russ Verney cited a Times-Mirror poll showing that 60 percent of the public favored a third party. According to Spencer's firsthand report, Verney then said the candidate to lead such a party would have to be a man with "integrity, ethical values, high moral standards, incorruptibility and convictions. . . . We don't want the lesser of two evils, we want the greatest statesman." As Spencer drily noted, "Verney didn't mention anyone by name; didn't have to."
19. Richard Berke, "Perot Calls Meeting for '96 Contenders to Address Issues," *New York Times*, June 3, 1995, p. 1.
20. Ibid.
21. E-mail from "LuckyDAD1@aol.com" to UWSA@shell.portal.com, May 29, 1995.
22. Cara DeGette, "Splitting Ranks: At Ross Perot's United We Stand Conference, Dissension Reigned Supreme," *L.A. Village View*, August 25–31, 1995.
23. Mark Spencer, "Third Party Dodge: Saying No in Dallas," on the *Perot Periodical* website at www.brainlink.com/~nota.
24. Speakers at the Patriot Party–sponsored meeting included Ralph Copeland, formerly from Oregon and now with the Virginia Patriot Party; Tom Pecarero, Erie County chair of the New York Independence Party; Sharon Forn of the far-right Colorado Constitutional Party; Skip Cook, a term-limits leader from Arkansas; Howard Johnson of the Florida Independence Party; Frank Conrad, representing a group of former UWSA–New Jersey activists who had linked up with the state's Conservative Party; Dean Barkley of the Minnesota Indepen-

dence Party; Louis Herrink of the Virginia Independence Party; Howard Phillips of the pro-life U.S. Taxpayers Party; C. W. Miller, of the Iowa United Citizens Party, a direct offshoot of the state's UWSA chapter; and the ubiquitous Lenora Fulani.

25. See "The Far Right Gets a Foothold: Southern California Uber Alles?" *Perot Periodical*, winter 1994, pp. 6–7.

26. Marc Cooper, "The Nativist Sons: Is This Your Friendly United We Stand Group?" *Perot Periodical*, winter 1994, pp. 5–6.

27. Dale Maharidge, "UWSA's New Scapegoat: Tired? Poor? Get Out!" *Perot Periodical*, fall 1994, pp 5–7.

28. Reported in the *Washington Post*, September 29, 1994.

29. Phone interview with Tom Fiedler, February 1998.

30. *Herald* staff, "Where Candidate Jack Gargan Stands on State Issues," *Miami Herald*, August 14, 1994.

31. Jack Gargan, Announcement of Candidacy for Governor, July 4, 1993.

32. Mark Spencer, "Remember November? Perot vs. UWSA (Or Was It Bush?)," *Perot Periodical*, winter/spring 1995.

33. Howard Kurtz, "Pressing for Powell: A General Trend," *Washington Post*, September 13, 1995.

34. John Broder, "The Times Poll: Powell's Centrist Views Find Favor among Republicans," *Los Angeles Times*, September 20, 1995. A late June poll done for *Time* by Yankelovich Partners found 55 percent of the public favoring an independent run for president and 29 percent giving Powell their support in a three-way race, with Clinton winning at 33 percent and Dole at 27 percent. Powell's favorable-unfavorable rating was a stunning 56-10 percent, while Perot's was a desultory 32-54 percent. John Stacks, "The Powell Factor," *Time*, July 10, 1995.

35. Transcript, *Charlie Rose Show*, August 17, 1995.

36. David Broder, "Dark Horse May Make a Presidential Run," *Washington Post*, May 29, 1995.

37. Jeffrey Birnbaum, "A Plot to Liven Up the Race," *Time*, December 4, 1995.

38. Richard Berke, "Centrist Democrats Discuss a Candidate of Their Own," *New York Times*, November 27, 1995.

39. Peter Blake, "Lamm Took Look at Independence," *Rocky Mountain News*, August 30, 1995.

40. Robert Rosenblatt, "Ex-Chief of Social Security Calls for Privatizing Fund," *Los Angeles Times*, August 15, 1995.

41. Martin Nolan, "Sen. Bradley Urges Political Fund Shifts: Seeks Constitutional Amendment," *Boston Globe*, October 25, 1995.

42. Fred Brown, "Spend Less, Get Better Campaigns," *Denver Post*, November 8, 1995.

43. According to Richard Winger, the editor of an invaluable newsletter called *Ballot Access News* and the country's leading expert on the hurdles that third parties have to clear to get on the ballot, Perot's son-in-law Clay Mulford, a lawyer, had called him nine months earlier, in December of 1994, to ask for all of his information on starting a new party. And Gordon Black had been invited to address Perot and his top staff in Dallas back in February 1995 with the arguments he made in his book *The Politics of American Discontent*, on behalf of a new party. Afterward, Black said, he was encouraged by Perot's aides to speak to UWSA chapters around the country, but by the summer he had still not gotten any indication from Perot as to his plans and was not invited to address the group's national conference in Dallas. In the meantime, he had discovered that he could put together a convention of thirty to thirty-five state parties at fairly little cost, building on existing parties that hadn't joined in the Patriot Party project and adding ballot lines in other states where the cost of qualifying was low. "For under $300,000, we could have thirty states," he recalled. His friend and associate Tom Golisano, an earlier backer of his third-party research, had already stepped forward in New York and spent $6 million to $7 million dollars on a gubernatorial campaign in 1994 that got the Independence Party on the ballot there. And Golisano was ready to put up the money needed to get a national party off the ground. "I told Clay Mulford, if Perot doesn't go, we are going to go in that direction," Black said. "We had reached a parting of the ways." Black and Golisano were hoping to create a centrist party dedicated to political reform, fiscal restraint, and social tolerance. "And we didn't have to do it with Fulani, the Patriot Party, and all that baggage," he added. This news apparently got Perot's attention, and the Texan asked for a meeting on September 20. "It was a very cordial conversation. In effect, we said, 'If you're not going to use your army, can we borrow it?'" Phone interview with Richard Winger, September 25, 1995; phone interview with Gordon Black, September 27, 1995.

44. In California, members of the UWSA chapter's New Party Task Force complained that they were not asked about Perot's decision, just informed a few days before the announcement of what his national staff was about to do. Sharon Lesk, executive director of the state chapter until she was fired in May 1995, said active volunteers in the organization were scared of being quoted. "They're afraid of Perot. They're afraid of what he can do. Nobody was told, nobody was consulted on whether it was a good idea or not." Micah L. Sifry, "Perot and the Independence Party ('It's My Party and I'll Invite you If I Want To.')," *The Perot Periodical*, http://www.brainlink.com/~nota/issue2/perot/perot3rd.htm.

45. Phone interview with Jacqui Salit, July 26, 1996. Salit, who was then a member of the Patriot Party's national executive committee and the editor of its national newsletter, *The Patriot*, listed Michigan, Wisconsin, New Jersey, Georgia, South Carolina, Alaska, North Carolina, Texas, Massachusetts, and Pennsylvania as states where the Patriot Party worked closely with the Reform Party's ballot drive.

46. The Patriot Party formally voted to dissolve itself and merge into the Reform Party on August 21, 1997. *Ballot Access News*, September 6, 1997.

47. Micah L. Sifry, "Tom (Remember Me?) Golisano Fights Lenora Fulani in Third-Party Brawl," *New York Observer*, August 5, 1996.

48. From the transcript of the *Larry King Show*, September 25, 1995:

King: I want [the party's] nomination. How do I get it?

Perot: We make sure that that person is very visible to our organization, so they know what that person stands for. That person pledges that these reforms that we are proposing make sense. And then—

King: He or she has to endorse your platform?

Perot: Well, they have to—Yes, because this is the Reform platform.

King: Okay.

Perot: If they don't agree—

King: When do they get to see the platform?

Perot: They can see it tonight, if they want to.

King: All right.

Perot: You can see it tonight. CNN has copies. And it is—

King: Of the platform?

Perot: Yes sir.

Perot went on the describe the key planks, which were, verbatim, 1) Set the highest ethical standards for the White House and Congress, 2) Balance the budget, 3) Campaign reform, 4) Term limits, 5) Create a new tax system, 6) Carefully put together plans to deal with Medicare, Medicaid, and Social Security, 7) Lobbying restrictions, 8) Foreign lobbying, and 9) Domestic lobbying.

49. Dan Goodgame, "This Time, Perot Wants a Party," *Time*, October 9, 1995, p. 53.

50. Associated Press, "New Party's on Line in NY," September 27, 1995.

51. CBS News poll of 1,265 adults surveyed March 10–11, 1996, margin of error +/- 3%. Sixty-five percent also said the current method of nominating presidential candidates generally does not produce the best candidates.

52. Phone interview with Nicholas Sabatine, March 20, 1996.

53. Transcript, NBC *Meet the Press*, November 19, 1995.

54. Dan Balz, "Dole Wins Midwest; Perot Talks of Run," *Washington Post*, March 20, 1996.

55. Ernest Tollerson, "Ex-Perot Volunteers Say Reform Party Is Using Old Tactics to Change the System," *New York Times*, August 10, 1996.

56. For example, a press release dated January 24, 1996, from the Citizens to Establish a Reform Party noted that its staff, "most of whom are former United We Stand America (UWSA) staff, met in Dallas, TX over the weekend to develop a strategic plan to get the party on the ballot in all fifty states."

57. The UWSA–Ohio board even claimed that when Perot's paid staffers were unable to persuade the duly elected volunteer board to support the creation of a "third" party, "they convened a meeting of a 'bogus' Board of Directors handpicked by them (including two members of the legitimate board), had this board elect new officers, and declared it to be the new board of UWSA–OH, Inc." United We Stand America–Ohio, Inc. vs. H. Ross Perot, FEC MUR 4284.

58. Phone interview with Mick Ringsak, March 20, 1996.

59. Phone interview with Dick Lamm, April 11, 1996.

60. Phone interview with Tom D'Amore, Lamm's campaign manager, July 25, 1996.

61. Phone interview with Dick Lamm, April 11, 1996.

62. Tom Kenworthy, "Lamm Seeks Reform Party Nomination," *Washington Post*, July 10, 1996. Lamm finally decided that Perot was testing him and wanted to see if he could rally Reformers to his banner. He told *Time* magazine that Perot had promised him that he wouldn't spend money promoting his own prospects—the two men were listed on the party's preference ballot as "most frequently mentioned" possible candidates and voters were encouraged to write in other names. Perot also assured Lamm that he would appeal to party members to donate to his campaign, were he its nominee. Laurence Barrett, "A Real Candidate or Perot's Sacrificial Lamm," *Time*, July 15, 1996.

63. Douglas Looney, "Pondering Presidency, Lamm Hears Hoofbeats of History," *Christian Science Monitor*," July 5, 1996.

64. Ernest Tollerson, "Reform Party's Crucial Surveying Runs Into Problems," *New York Times*, July 18, 1996; Lori Stahl and Richard Whittle, "Reform Party Leaders Agree to Make More Information Public," *Dallas Morning News*, July 19, 1996; Ernest Tollerson, "Perot Aide Now Says Party List Was Never Filed in Colorado," *New York Times*, July 21, 1996.

65. I personally received three ballots after making two separate requests.

66. Verney was the director of the Perot Reform Committee, the successor to the Committee to Establish the Reform Party. This committee was classified by the FEC as a candidate campaign committee, though Perot said it was a party-building organization.

67. "Cost of Reform Party List Comes between Candidates," CNN *Inside Politics*, July 24, 1996.

68. Phone interview with Kirk MacKenzie, August 8, 1996.

69. Donald Baker, "Nearly Two-Thirds in Reform Party Survey Back Perot," *Washington Post*, July 31, 1996.

70. Phone interview with Alex Rodriguez, July 23, 1996.

71. Other speakers at the "Red, White and Blue Friends/Grassroots Support Rally for Ross Perot for President" on August 11, 1996, included pollster Gordon Black; C. W. Miller, leader of the Iowa Citizens Party offshoot from UWSA; and Dale Welch Barlow, a fiery young woman from Oklahoma (who would later break with the Dallas old guard when it moved to depose Jack Gargan from his role as party chairman in February 2000).

72. See Todd Mason, *Perot: An Unauthorized Biography* (Homewood, Ill.: Business One Irwin Books, 1990); Daniel Gross, "Ross Perot's $100-Million Disaster," *Audacity*, summer 1994; Robert Fitch, "H. Ross Perot: America's First Welfare Billionaire," *Ramparts*, November 1971.

73. *Time*/CNN poll of 2,435 registered voters taken July 26–30, 1996, by Yankelovich Partners.

74. For example, Ted Muga, a dissident member of the Reform Party board in California, wrote the FEC saying, "Since the inception of our organization, we have been under the direct control and influence of the Dallas-based camp of Ross Perot and/or his paid staff, with little if any 'grass roots' participation." Letter from Ted Muga to Office of the General Counsel, Federal Election Commission, November 21, 1996, FEC AOR 1996-47.

75. Phone interview with Phil Madsen, August 8, 1996.

76. Serious reform of the FEC should start with taking control of the agency out of the hands of the two major parties, by requiring an equal number of commissioners who are genuine political independents or members of other parties.

77. Donald Baker, "Illinois Gathering Seeks Reduction of Perot's Influence within Reform Party," *Washington Post*, September 29, 1996.

78. Letter to the Office of the General Counsel, Federal Election Commission, from Burnham Philbrook, Re: The National Reform Party Steering Committee Advisory Opinion Request, November 3, 1996. FEC AOR 1996-47.

79. In one case, the same person, Bob Belcher of Trussville, Alabama, wrote the FEC speaking as the interim chairman of the Reform Party of both Alabama and Mississippi.

80. Letter from FEC General Counsel Lawrence Noble to Burnham Philbrook, December 2, 1996, in FEC AOR 1996-47.

81. E-mail from Phil Madsen to UWSA@shell.portal.com, September 6, 1996, titled "Point/Counterpoint Regarding the Reform Party National Caucus."

82. Katie Fairbank, "Reform Party Picks Committee," Associated Press, November 21, 1996; and Ernest Tollerson, "Perot's Breather for Reform Party Is Giving Way to Discord," *New York Times*, November 24, 1996. In a letter explaining his reasons for dropping off the party's steering committee, Lamm said that "I cannot participate in or recommend to any other elected official a Reform Party which is not inclusive, open and democratically organized. I fear no one, or few, will want to participate under your current plans. It keeps control in a small faction instead of being representative of all those who truly are interested in reform."

83. Letter from Russell Verney, national coordinator of Perot '96, Inc. and the Perot Reform Committee, Inc. to the Federal Election Commission, November 22, 1996; FEC AOR 1996-47.

84. Lee Stork, "History of the American Reform Party," provided to the author.

85. Memo from Dean Barkley to Reform Party of Minnesota Executive Committee, February 3, 1997.

86. Dan Balz, "Perot Forces Keep Dissidents at Bay," *Washington Post*, January 27, 1997.

87. Dan Balz, "Leaders at Convention Argue Role of Perot, *Washington Post*, January 26, 1997.

88. Bill Dedman, "Perot Dissidents Form a New National Party," *New York Times*, October 5, 1997.

89. "Assume that we continue to ship entire industries overseas to other countries, and then a major war breaks out ten years from now. We go to Puerto Rico and ask them politely if they will give us medicines and pharmaceuticals for our troops who are wounded in combat. Obviously, we have to manufacture these goods within our borders to defend this great country." Perot quoted in James Brooke, "Perot Sees Politics as Motivating Clinton's Raid on Iraq," *New York Times*, September 5, 1996.

90. Donald Baker, "Reform Party Candidates Grumble: Where's Ross?" *Washington Post*, November 3, 1996.

91. John Aloysius Farrell, "Campaign Comes Back to Perot," *Boston Globe*, October 19, 1996.

92. Baker, "Reform Party Candidates Grumble."

Chapter Five

1. Phone interview with Richard Winger, August 5, 1999.

2. Party chair Russ Verney explained this weakness by saying, "It's a matter of being realistic. We've decided we're not going to go for ballot access everywhere and we're not going to field candidates at every level unless we can see reasonable results down the road for all that effort and money. Texas and the other states had to face that reality." B. Drummond Ayres Jr., "Best Signature of All? Perot's on a Check," *New York Times*, June 17, 1998.

3. Though Verney acknowledged meeting with Democratic House Minority Leader Richard Gephardt in February 1998, he told the Associated Press that the plan to mobilize against Republicans fizzled because of grass-roots disenchantment with President Clinton's scandalous relationship with Monica Lewinsky. There were other indications prior to the Lewinsky scandal suggesting that few Reformers were sold on the idea of swinging the House to the Democrats. As it was, only three of the twenty candidates listed on the party's website in May 1998 were running against vulnerable Republicans. Erika Niedowski, "Reform Party Vows Congress Races against 40–50 Weakest Republicans," *The Hill*, November 5, 1997.

4. One of the few candidates who did get a big push of support from the national party apparatus was Juanita Norwood of Philadelphia, an African-American businesswoman and NAACP leader who tried to run in a special election to fill an open congressional seat that was the only predominately black district in the country without an African-American representative. Her chief opponent was the white Democratic Party leader of Philadelphia, Bob Brady, who did not live in the district. The Reform Party's volunteer public relations chair, Donna Donovan, sent a blast e-mail seeking financial support for Norwood (titled "CALLING ALL CARS! MUST READ!") and Verney flew in to assist her campaign. Interestingly enough, Norwood was recruited to run by Lenora Fulani, who grew up in her congressional district. Unfortunately, Norwood suffered a brain aneurysm late in the campaign and was hospitalized in its final days. Still, she managed to come in third with a respectable 11 percent of the vote. William Bunch, "Reform Party Taps NAACP Official to Oppose Brady," *Philadelphia Daily News*, March 26, 1998.

5. Phone interview with Reform Party public relations chair, Donna Donovan, February 5, 1998.

6. For example, in 2000 an independent candidate for president needed only .2 percent of registered voters in the state to sign petitions to get on the ballot in Alabama; an independent candidate for the state House needed 1.61 percent—or eight times as many. In New York, the presidential candidate of a new party needed .14 percent of registered voters while a candidate for the state House needed 2.13 percent. These estimates were compiled by Richard Winger of *Ballot Access News* based on state laws as of July 15, 1999.

7. The states discriminate against minor parties in a host of other subtle ways. On Election Day in Arizona, the two largest parties get a free list of the names of people who voted before noon, which helps them with final get-out-the-vote efforts; no other parties are given it. In New Hampshire, only members of the two largest parties can be ballot clerks. In many states, major party candidates always get the best positioning on ballots, while new parties are tucked in obscure rows or corners. Richard Winger, *Ballot Access News*, January 12, 1997, and September 6, 1997.

8. This discriminatory law has since been dropped by a constitutional revision supported by the voters in November 1998. A coalition of Florida's third parties played the key role in advocating for that change.

9. Interview with Jack Gargan in Cedar Key, Florida, February 12, 1998.

10. Phone interview with Jack Gargan, June 22, 1998.

11. Letter from Jack Gargan to author, July 7, 1998.

12. E-mail from Jack Gargan to author, October 9, 1998.

13. At the same time, the California Reform Party's board of directors wrestled internally with the strategic question of whether it should endorse candidates who were not running on the party's line. Michael Farris, a member of the California party's board, wrote an e-mail in January 1998 e-mail to the reform-california@uwsa.com list-serve titled "Why cross-endorsement in '98 helps the Reform Party." Given a base of less than 1 percent of the total number of registered voters in the state, he said the party's chances to win any races were nil, apologizing if this "came across as a splash of cold water." But he argued, sensibly, that "for the Reform Party to be influential in public policy, our party must be influential in the outcome of the elections. . . . Our endorsement should be a seal of approval the voters can count on, and we should use our endorsement to swing the best person for the job into office if that is its most effective use." He acknowledged this approach wouldn't

get voters in the habit of pulling the Reform lever, but said "although I would rather have these candidates switch parties now, political realities don't allow this as a possibility now." One response to his e-mail was titled "Aaaaarrrrrgggggghhhhh!!" and asked, "What real good could come out this strategy? . . . If a candidate is elected as a Democrat, or as a Republican, their loyalty is going to be to the party who put them into office."

14. "He is attempting to spend the least amount of money possible in a serious campaign," said an e-mail circulated by the Tim Erich campaign, "and hopes that independently minded California voters will recognize this great opportunity to support someone who doesn't just talk about reforming the democratic process in our country, but is actually doing it!" Unfortunately a no-money pledge means a no-vote result. "Vote For Common Sense Reform: Tim Erich for U.S. Senate in California," e-mail to reform-california@uwsa.com posted on January 28, 1998. The June 1998 returns for Reform Party candidates running statewide in California were: Jim Mangia (for lieutenant governor) received 0.7 percent of the vote; Valli Sharpe-Geisler (for secretary of state) received 1.2 percent of the vote; Tim Erich (for Senate) received 0.8 percent of the vote; and Denise Jackson (for controller) received 1.5 percent of the vote.

15. Scott Fornek, "Candidate Off Ballot—But He Wasn't Running," *Chicago Sun Times*, January 15, 1998.

16. Bill Muller, "'Official English' Backer Runs for McCain's Seat," *Arizona Republic*, February 3, 1998.

17. E-mail from Dawn Larson posted on uwsa@uwsa.com, titled "Re: Not surprising— Reform dead," February 12, 1998.

18. Alan Goldstein, "Perot Reshaping Namesake Company," *Dallas Morning News*, January 10, 1998.

19. "Should Clinton Resign? More Than 93% Say 'Yes'," Reform Party press release, October 7, 1998, http://www.reformparty.org/news/pr10_7_98.html.

20. "Reform Party Energized by Ventura Win in Minnesota," Reform Party press release, November 4, 1998, http://www.reformparty.org/news/pr11_4_98.html.

21. Barkley diary, *Minneapolis Star-Tribune*, November 8, 1998.

22. "I believe in the [Navy] Seal team code: We don't get mad, we get even." Ventura quoted in his interview with *Playboy* magazine, November 1999.

23. Phone interview with Dean Barkley, December 3, 1998.

24. Phone interview with Phil Madsen, November 30, 1998.

25. Dane Smith, "Ventura Still Not Talking 2000—But Others Are," *Minneapolis Star-Tribune*, June 17, 1998.

26. Tom Hamburger, "Pollster's Advice to GOP: Watch Ventura," *Minneapolis Star-Tribune*, March 18, 1999.

27. February 7, 1999, e-mail from jesse@jesseventura.org to all members of his volunteer network. According to Phil Madsen, who managed the site, three thousand people signed up in the first few months of 1999.

28. E-mail from Donna Donovan, posted on uwsa@uwsa.com, March 9, 1999.

29. E-mail from Dale Welch Barlow, posted on uwsa@uwsa.com, March 9, 1999.

30. "There are exactly fifteen Schaumburg people," Dale Welch Barlow told a reporter just prior to the Schaumburg meeting, when she was the Reform Party's interim vice chair. "They have absolutely no following whatsoever. I think they're paid hit men from one of the [major] parties." R. G. Ratcliffe, "Reform Party Faction Plans to Distance Itself from Perot," *Houston Chronicle*, October 2, 1997.

31. Letter from Gov. Jesse Ventura to national Reform Party delegates, June 28, 1999.

32. Cedric Scofield, a delegate from Minnesota and the national party's Midwest Regional Representative, quickly wrote an e-mail with a long list of questions about Ventura's letter. June 29, 1999, e-mail to venturaactive@egroups.com.

33. Madsen said, "I drafted the letter for Jesse initially, but he didn't like the draft. It went through three drafts, and he was directly involved in it." Phone interview with Phil Madsen, July 26, 1999.

34. Ventura's letter also implied that he would do more for the party with Gargan as chair than he actually intended to do. The truth was that Gargan, who had been drafted to run for party chair by some dissatisfied members, had approached Ventura seeking his support, not the other way around. The two men had met the prior year at the party's Atlanta convention and hit it off right away. Ventura actually told me in October 1998 that after meeting Gargan he thought the Floridian ought to be the party chairman. "I'd like to see him in charge," he said then. But the initiative came from Gargan's end, not Ventura. Interview with Jesse Ventura in Minneapolis, October 8, 1998.

35. B. Drummond Ayres Jr., "An Ex-Wrestler Goes to the Mat for Reform," *New York Times*, June 30, 1999.

36. Hugh Aynesworth, "Reform Party Chairman May Relinquish Post," *Washington Times*, July 7, 1999.

37. Verney's view of Phil Madsen was also telling: "He's a brilliant man whose whole goal in life is to create havoc." Thomas B. Edsall, "Ventura vs. Perot: Minnesota Governor Is Facing Long Odds Again In His Move to Revitalize Texan's Reform Party," *Washington Post*, July 13, 1999.

38. Mark Pazniokas, "Reform Party Snubs Perot's First Choice," *Hartford Courant*, July 26, 1999. He reported, "Only four states—Arizona, Connecticut, Minnesota and Rhode Island, plus the District of Columbia—could

find enough people to fill all their [delegate] slots, which are apportioned by population. Alaska, Idaho, Wyoming and Utah sent no one. Even Texas, Perot's base, sent only 17 delegates out of a possible 33. In all, only 356 of the 600 slots were filled."

39. Thomas Ferraro, "Reformed Reform Party Could Win In U.S.—Ventura," Reuters New Service, July 24, 1999.

40. James Bennet, "The Cable Guys," *New York Times Magazine*, October 24, 1999.

41. Thomas Ferraro, "Perot Preaches Unity to Reform Party Meeting," Reuters News Service, July 25, 1999.

42. Thomas Ferraro, "Ventura Nominee Named to Lead Perot's Reform Party," Reuters News Service, July 26, 1999.

43. Phone interview with Phil Madsen, July 26, 1999.

44. Many observers noted that Gargan was helped by a sizable bloc of votes commanded by Lenora Fulani, an indication still of how thin the party's base in the "angry middle" continued to be. Fulani herself narrowly lost her own bid to become the party's vice chair by 180 to 145, losing her runoff after initially winning 45 percent of the delegates in a three-way split. Thomas B. Edsall, "Reform Party Shifts Gears: New Chairman Favors Ventura's Style over Founder Perot's," *Washington Post*, July 26, 1999.

45. Carolyn Barta, "Ventura Supporters Wrest Control of Reform Party from Perot Team; New Direction, Relocation Of Headquarters Planned," *Dallas Morning News*, July 26, 1999.

46. Phone interview with Phil Madsen, August 10, 1999.

47. Phone interview with Jack Gargan, August 12, 1999.

48. Barta, "Ventura Supporters Wrest Control."

49. A few days after the Dearborn convention, on August 3, 1999, the party's incoming vice chairman Gerry Moan wrote an e-mail to several party list-serves titled "I Am Puzzled" where he expressed concerns at press reports suggesting that "Ventura strategists" were now directing the party. He wrote, "I intend to work very hard in support of the TEAM that was duly elected in Dearborn but I am getting a very queasy feeling about the usurpation of our electoral process We can't have a party moving in two different directions. If the media believes that the control of the party has moved to Minnesota (aka Jesse's Volunteer Committee) what will potential candidates think?"

In response, Cedric Scofield, a pro-Perot Minnesotan who was the party's Midwest regional representative, wrote a revealing message on August 5, 1999, to the statechair@reformparty.org list-serv. After bemoaning all the ways that Phil Madsen was supposedly the power behind Jack Gargan, he wrote, "Some good news is that, on the 11 person RPUSA EC [Reform Party national Executive Committee], it looks like we have, Fulani faction 1, Unknown 1, the rest of us 9. After the new officers take office in January it looks like, anti Perot fraction 1, Fulani faction 1, Unknown 2, the rest of us 7. Unfortunately, the EC does not have control over the appointment of Standing Committee Chairs. We can expect that, that will further usurp the EC, National Committee and State Parties, but *the majority we have on the EC is still a plus.*" [Emphasis added.]

50. Carolyn Barta, "Reform Party Leaders to Pick Convention Site; Minnesota No Shoo-In," *Dallas Morning News*, September 1, 1999. In an early sign that the party's old guard was holding on, its executive committee voted that day to keep the convention in Long Beach, California.

51. Letter from Jack Gargan to Reform Party members, August 27, 1999, and phone interview with author, September 23, 1999. In September, Gargan had done a survey of all the Reform Party's state affiliates, and only five—Pennsylvania, Connecticut, New Jersey, New Hampshire, and Florida—said they thought they were prepared for all the logistical problems that would arise once the balloting process began.

52. Phone interview with Jack Gargan, February 9, 2000.

53. Letters exchanged between Jack Gargan and Russ Verney on August 30 and 31, 1999, respectively.

54. Phone interview with Jack Gargan, August 12, 1999.

55. Dane Smith, "Ventura Muses on 2000 Dream Team; He Says a Presidential Ticket Headed by Colin Powell, with Him as No. 2, Could Win, But He's 'Not At All' Actively Seeking the Role," *Minneapolis Star-Tribune*, May 19, 1999.

56. Dean Barkley, Ventura's campaign chairman, said in phone interview in early July 1999, "We've been trying to recruit Lowell Weicker, and it's going well—he hasn't said no. He's the person I'd prefer. He's got an honest, refreshing approach; he doesn't do polling or focus groups, he just speaks his mind. The separation of church and state is firmly embedded in his thinking. He's got guts, charisma, and the fire in the belly. He was one of the first to leave the two parties, and he's a centrist." Asked if Ventura would back Weicker, Barkley said, "The governors met and they got along. In my opinion, he'd back him." Weicker's longtime aide and campaign manager Tom D'Amore said then that Weicker was far from a decision to run. "He said he wouldn't rule it out, but he's just as interested as Jesse in recruiting someone else to run."

57. "Why am I now considering a presidential bid? First, Minnesota Gov. Jesse Ventura has strongly encouraged me to seek the nomination, and I highly respect Jesse as the embodiment of the political qualities America needs and voters reward." Donald Trump, "America Needs a President Like Me," *Wall Street Journal*, September 30, 1999.

58. On April 22, 1999, Powell wrote a check for $1,000 to Bush's presidential campaign, according to FEC records. On the *Montel Williams* show in June, Ventura said he would take the vice presidential nomination, "but only for General (Colin) Powell." Carla Marinucci, "President Ventura? It Could Happen," *San Francisco Chronicle*, June 16, 1999.

59. Micah L. Sifry, "Weicker Stumps," *Salon.com*, October 4, 1999, http://www.salon.com/news/feature/1999/10/04/trump, p. 2.

60. Mike Allen, "John Anderson Mulls Challenge to Buchanan," *Washington Post*, November 14, 1999.

61. Doug Ireland and Micah L. Sifry, "Buchanan Breaks Ranks," *The Nation*, September 20, 1999.

62. Schroth and Associates poll of a thousand voters taken August 15–17, 1999, margin of error +/- 3%.

63. Asked by right-wing columnist Robert Novak what Perot thought of Buchanan becoming his party's standard-bearer, Choate said, "Ross Perot is staying neutral in this," but then he added, "He likes Pat Buchanan. He thinks he is a man of integrity. Pat Buchanan has come to his positions honestly. He doesn't run out and do a poll to determine what he thinks on issues. That's the kind of a person that a Perot can respect and the Reform Party can respect." Pat Choate interviewed on CNN's *Crossfire*, September 1, 1999.

64. In March of 1996, while Perot was building the Reform Party, he distanced himself from Buchanan, who was then running a strong campaign for president as a Republican. Referring to Buchanan's attacks on free trade and legal immigration from Mexico, Perot said, "His message is not mine. The last thing we should do is bang around on [America's trading partners]. We don't want to build a wall around America." Dan Balz, "Perot Decries Negative Tactics in GOP Race, Touts Third Party," *Washington Post*, March 8, 1996.

65. In his public statements about leaving the Republican Party, Buchanan made clear that one thing that delayed his final decision was his hope to meet with Perot in advance. No such meeting ever occurred, apparently out of Perot's desire to be seen as playing favorites. Buchanan's staff also wanted to make sure that he could continue to raise matching funds if he switched parties, and that the money he had already raised would count toward that end. But he was clearly convinced by the arguments of his advisers. Speaking with Brit Hume on the Fox News Channel on September 20, 1999, he said, "With Forbes with a hundred million dollars and Bush with a hundred million dollars you've got to say, 'Look. Be realistic. I can't raise the money from my folks.' . . . All of a sudden, lo and behold, there is this nomination that's wide open. They agree with me on trade policy. The former vice president[ial nominee] of the party comes and says, 'Hey, we've got a deal for you.' All these other folks say, 'Pat, we love you over here. I know they don't like you there. Come on home, fella.'"

66. Phone interview with Michael Novosel, August 1999.

67. Press release issued by the Reform Party of New Hampshire, September 23, 1999, announcing the postponement of its September 25 state convention.

68. Michael McGuire, editor of www.ReformNews.net, e-mail to grassrootsreform@egroups.com on September 17, 1999.

69. E-mail from Pat Choate to Mary Clare Wohlford, September 27, 1999, provided to the author.

70. Pat Choate, "Why Pat Buchanan Should Join the Reform Party," www.intellectualcapital.com, August 19, 1999.

71. Fred Newman boasted after Fulani's endorsement of Buchanan, "She's now getting media attention she's never gotten and she can speak for these issues," referring to her political reform agenda. Amy Waldman, "Strange Can't Begin to Describe It: Fulani and Buchanan See an Upside to Political Marriage," *New York Times*, November 26, 1999.

72. Lenora Fulani interviewed on CNN's *Inside Politics*, September 20, 1999. Jacqui Salit, the longtime Fulani aide, was also at the lunch with Buchanan (who was there with his wife, Shelley, and sister, Bay, his campaign manager) and came away thrilled. "This party is about being a nonideological force for political change." Buchanan's extremism was a perfect way to "make a point about the nonideological nature of the party," she claimed. Tucker Carlson, "Buchanan and His Friends," *Weekly Standard*, September 27, 1999.

73. Russell Verney interviewed on CNN's *Inside Politics*, September 21, 1999.

74. Pat Buchanan speech, "The New Patriotism," October 25, 1999.

75. Ventura *Playboy* interview.

76. Associated Press, "Reform Party Factions Spar," October 11, 1999.

77. Letter from Russell Verney to Governor Jesse Ventura, October 1, 1999.

78. E-mail from Anne Merkl to grassrootsreform@egroups.com. It read in part: "Even though, there would have been those who would have disagreed with Russ in sending out a letter of rebuke on his own relative to

Jesse's statements in *Playboy*, I believe that most Reformers would have had agreed with the action. A letter that would have simply stated that Jesse's remarks in *Playboy* did not represent the majority of the members of the Reform Party could have been sent out and the common sense public would have understood the meaning loud and clear. However, this was not the case. There is a big difference in a letter of rebuke than in one asking for an individual to resign. It is not the same.

"The unfortunate down side is this. Although Russ felt the need to make a stronger statement than a letter of rebuke on this matter, he acted entirely on his own, without gathering input from the Executive Committee — via Regional Rep's. BEFORE going to the media. . . . The "resignation vote" taken by the Executive Committee was a 'damage control' tool for Russ. He needed the support of the Committee to sanction his action of acting on his own in contacting the media relative to Jesse's resignation. However, the Executive Committee is not authorized to make a decision such as this. This was a monumental decision and my next question is this. Who will be next?? What will be the criteria used in determining who should be asked to resign? Will the membership be by-passed as in this particular case?" Merkl also pointed out that there were no provisions in the party constitution for the removal of a member.

79. Associated Press, "Reform Party Factions Spar."

80. Josh Romonek, "Buchanan Meets the Texas Reform Party," Associated Press, December 4, 1999, reported that Doogs had stepped down as Texas's chair to run Buchanan's campaign in the state.

81. "Jesse destroyed a major part of his base, both in Minnesota and nationally, with his interview. And in the process of doing that he destroyed a major portion of his influence within the Reform Party. His comments on religion and his seemingly condoning the Tailhook scandal, though he's equivocal in that part of the interview. But many people have interpreted that as being down on women. Those two things are killers." Pat Choate interviewed by *Salon.com* magazine, November 11, 1999, http://www.salon.com/news/feature/1999/11/11/choate.

82. E-mail from Phil Madsen to grassrootsreform@egroups.com on October 8, 1999. Madsen also tried to convince his former colleagues in the Schaumburg group who had left Reform and created the American Reform Party that this was the time for them to set aside their differences and reunite so as to strengthen the Gargan chairmanship of the party. Unfortunately for him, American Reform Party members were more entranced with the ethereal prospect of Lowell Weicker or John Anderson running under their banner. They were also unequivocally opposed to any involvement with a party edging toward Pat Buchanan as its nominee.

83. E-mail from Jack Gargan to grassrootsreform@egroups.com on September 23, 1999.

84. David Corn, "Loyal Opposition," *New York Press*, September 22, 1999.

85. Robert K. Pavlick and Kenneth B. Jones, e-mail to grassrootsreform@egroups.com, "EMERGENCY ALERT! The Trojan Horse Has Arrived!" September 27, 1999; George Bergeron, former national committee member, e-mail to grassrootsreform@egroups.com, October 6, 1999; *Des Moines Register*, October 16, 1999; Jim Sheehan, e-mail to grassrootsreform@egroups.com, October 28, 1999; Richard Damerow, former vice chair, New Mexico Reform Party, e-mail to grassrootsreform@egroups.com, November 21, 1999; Julia Silverman, "Buchanan Says He's Best Hope for Reform Party," *Arkansas Democrat-Gazette*, December 12, 1999.

86. E-mail from Linda Muller to grassrootsreform@egroups.com, titled "Duty Roster: Reform Party," November 15, 1999.

87. "Dear Friend [from Bay Buchanan]," e-mail to grassrootsreform@egroups.com, November 24, 1999.

88. "Dear Reformers," e-mail message from Jack Gargan to grassrootsreform@egroups.com, December 16, 1999.

89. Reform Party of the United States of America, Executive Committee minutes, January 25, 2000.

90. The party's new national treasurer, Ronn Young, was even filing suit against the outgoing leadership for failing to turn over the assets of the party, including its books, records, voter lists, press lists, and web domain, to the new officers elected with Gargan or appointed by him. "They want to rule or ruin," Young said of the "Dallas gang," and "they have been very successful in their attempts to cripple the party." Interview with Ronn Young in Nashville, February 12, 2000.

91. Governor Jesse Ventura press conference, February 11, 2000; interview with Phil Madsen at the governor's mansion, same day.

92. Barlow was ultimately removed from the hall by security guards. She had this to say about her Nashville experience: "Members who had posed, for years, as purportedly being 'fair and principled', ripped off their masks only to unveil the hateful and prejudicial bunch they had truly become. They didn't care if they tossed aside years of hard work members had to execute, in order to build viable parties, in their respective states. No, — it appeared their only concern was whether or not a state's membership would oust Jack Gargan, — that apparently was their ONLY criteria on whether or not to grant 'provisional' status to particular state party entities.

"The Nashville meeting turned into a well-orchestrated lynch job. They controlled the microphones, turning the volume up and down, as they pleased. They hired security guards to remove and threaten some of us who fought back. (They didn't succeed in shutting us all up.) And, they used Robert's Rules of Order, and the huge gaps in the party's constitution, to eventually vote Jack Gargan right out of his party chairmanship.

"They 'won' the lawsuit in Lynchburg. They won control of the Reform Party. And, they even convinced a federal judge they did it legally. But,—they didn't convince or brainwash the rest of us, in believing they did it justly. We didn't toss our ethics aside, like they did. We didn't fight unprincipled, like they did. But they did succeed in convincing us to no longer support the Reform Party Hoax . . .

"Within the Reform Party, we've met thousands of courageous, highly-principled and concerned citizens, who've been willing to make the personal sacrifice, of using their own time and money, to try and build a truly independent political party. And now, several hundred of us have become close, life-long friends . . .

"We've earned our master's degrees on how not to build a political party. We'll hopefully succeed the next time around to build the party of our dreams." Dale Welch Barlow, e-mail to grassrootsreform@e-groups.com, "Resigning from the Reform Party Hoax," March 28, 2000.

93. "Good thing this vote didn't count," Gargan told the meeting after he was deposed. He took his case to court, but ultimately gave up after losing his lawsuit in Lynchburg, Virginia, at the end of March.

94. Wohlford listed state parties or factions in Iowa, Mississippi, New Jersey, Virginia, Wisconsin as likely to join up if that happened, and pointed to possible followers in California, Indiana, Maryland, and New Hampshire.

95. Robert Novak, "McCain May Carry 2 Banners," *Chicago Sun-Times*, February 16, 2000.

96. Delaware party chair William Shields wrote an e-mail suggesting that Mangia should be removed from his position and ejected from the national convention "along with any trash or dangerous biological waste that may have found it's [sic] way onto the convention floor." Carolyn Barta, "Perot Faithful Blast Buchanan, Ally Urged to Quit for Anti-Gay Remarks," *Dallas Morning News*, June 2, 2000.

97. John Judis, "Buchanan 1, Reform Party 0: Unhostile Takeover," *New Republic*, June 26, 2000.

98. Lenora Fulani, "Fear in the Wings," Worldnet Daily, April 4, 2000.

99. Letter from Lenora Fulani to Patrick Buchanan, June 18, 2000. In it, she cast her proposal to be made party chair in terms of proving Buchanan's commitment to their "left-right alliance." He wrote in response, "On your insistence in New York last week that our campaign support you for Chair of the Party, as Bay told you, we do not believe that would be in the interests of our campaign or the Party. This is not because you lack the talent or ability; you have far more than enough. However, I do not believe you could unify the party at Long Beach; and any attempt by us to push your nomination through a defiant party would backfire, fail, and divide us for the fall, and for the future." Letter from Patrick Buchanan to Lenora Fulani, June 19, 2000.

100. Amy Waldman, "The Presidential Candidate from Maharishi U.," *New York Times*, July 7, 2000.

101. Phone interview with Jack Gargan, August 12, 2000.

Chapter Six

1. Data compiled by Mike Feinstein, editor of *Green Pages*, posted at http://www.greens.org/elections.

2. Ralph Nader interview with Brian Lehrer, WNYC-AM "On the Line," January 23, 2001.

3. Steve Chase, "Green Stormtroopers in the Streets of Berlin?" Z *Papers*, October 1999, http://www.zmag.org/zmag/articles/oct1999chase.htm.

4. Charlene Spretnak, "The Green Alternative: An Ecologically Based Political Movement Is Starting to Emerge in America," *Governance*, autumn 1984. Spretnak's other options included forming a "Green Network" that would link together like-minded people in information sharing but little else (she deemed this insufficient); a "Green Movement" that would be a national membership organization with paid organizers that would develop proposals, lobby the Democratic and Republican parties, endorse politicians but not run its own candidates for office; and two different variations that she described as "caucuses"—one within the larger Green movement that would work with the major parties, or a more formal Green Caucus that would exist within the major parties as a membership organization, again trying to influence the behavior of those parties from within.

5. Jay Walljasper, foreword to John Rensenbrink, *The Greens and the Politics of Transformation* (San Pedro: R. & E. Miles, 1992), p. xi.

6. Rensenbrink, p. 108. In a more recent book, *Against All Odds: The Green Transformation of American Politics* (Raymond, Maine: Leopold Press, 1999), Rensenbrink charitably describes these early years more as "the incubation period of the Green movement in the United States," during which fundamental debates over the soul of the movement were inevitable, necessary, and ultimately healthy (p. 169).

7. Ibid., p. 103.

8. David Croteau, *Politics and the Class Divide*, pp. 121–23.

9. Interview with John Rensenbrink in Washington, D.C., June 2, 1995.

10. After reaching a peak of perhaps six thousand members, the G/GPUSA was down to twelve hundred members in the spring of 1998, according to Howie Hawkins, a member of its three-person coordinating committee. The Nader 2000 campaign produced a modest rebound in the G/GPUSA's membership, to 2,350 as of January 2001. Interview with Howie Hawkins in Santa Fe, April 26, 1998; Starlene Rankin, "G/GPUSA Secretary's Report," June 2000–January 2001.

11. That compromise was rejected by the G/GPUSA at its national meeting in July 2001, so the ASGP filed for national party status without its participation.

12. Jonathan Carter got 6 percent of the vote in 1994 running for governor (the same year that Angus King got elected as an independent), and Pat Lamarche got 7 percent four years later in the same race.

13. California's Green mayors were, as of 2000, Kerry Arnett (Nevada City), Larry Barnett (Sonoma), Mike Feinstein (Santa Monica), Tim Fitzmaurice (Santa Cruz), Suza Francina (Ojai), and Larry Robinson (Sebastopol).

14. Dirk Johnson, "Rebellion of Greens Is Brewing in the West," New York Times, July 24, 1994.

15. In fact, several of the New Mexico Greens' earliest candidates were Hispanics, but the party's leaders did not deny that their base was primarily white.

16. Marc Cooper, "The Greens Climb in New Mexico," The Nation, October 24, 1994.

17. Sarah Horton, "Greens Get Wired at Zuma's Prior to National Convention," Santa Fe Reporter, August 14–20, 1996.

18. Interview with Xubi Wilson in Santa Fe, October 27, 1998.

19. Interview with Cris Moore in Santa Fe, April 26, 1998.

20. E-mail from Cris Moore to author, February 1, 2001.

21. Cris Moore e-mail exchange with Jason Kirkpatrick, then the Green mayor of Arcata, California, "When to Run for Office," January 18, 1998, posted to grns.usa.forum@conf.igc.apc.org.

22. Party co-founder Abraham Gutmann agreed with Schmidt, citing his own experience campaigning for Jerry Brown as well. "The bigger reason for the existence of the Greens is the move to the right of the national Democratic Party. . . . it's a wake-up call all the way to President Clinton. Look at the Social Security debate, all they're talking about is Republican solutions. No one is talking about lifting the cap over $65,000 on income being taxed. They're all talking about putting it into the stock market. The Greens force them to look over their left shoulder." Phone interview with Abraham Gutmann, July 29, 1998.

23. E-mail from Steve Schmidt to author, August 20, 1998.

24. Dirk Johnson, "Rebellion of Greens Is Brewing."

25. Interview with Roberto Mondragon in Santa Fe, April 27, 1998.

26. Interview with Norm Shatkin in New York City, April 15, 1998.

27. Redford, a longtime environmentalist, has always backed Democrats, coming to New Mexico in 1998 to help Tom Udall in his congressional race against Republican Bill Redmond and Green Carol Miller.

28. Interview with Norm Shatkin, April 15, 1998.

29. Interview with Roberto Mondragon, April 27, 1998.

30. Mark Oswald, "No Flash in the Pan," Santa Fe New Mexican, September 13, 1998.

31. Interview with Cris Moore in Santa Fe, April 27, 1998.

32. E-mail from Cris Moore to author, October 13, 1997.

33. John Nichols, "Spoiling for Success: In New Mexico, the Green Party Costs the Democrats a Congressional Seat," The Progressive, August 1997.

34. Cris Moore, press release, "Statement on My Intentions to Run for Congress," January 13, 1997. The district had given 23 percent of its vote to Mondragon in his 1994 gubernatorial bid, so the Greens knew they had a potentially strong base of support. Moore's gambit was designed to put pressure on the Democrats in the state legislature to take seriously the Greens' desire for electoral reforms that would end the "spoiler" problem.

35. Campaign profile of Eric Serna, Albuquerque Journal, May 12, 1997.

36. Albuquerque Tribune, the more liberal of the two state papers, attacked Serna in its May 9, 1997, endorsement editorial, saying that Congress was "the wrong job for him" and reminding readers that "he may have used his position [on the State Corporation Commission] to extract campaign contributions inappropriately, perhaps even illegally, from employees and people he regulated." Miller, the paper said, "strikes us as thoughtful, level-headed . . . fastidiously ethical about campaign financing [and with] many good progressive ideas on other issues as well." It recommended giving her a chance to fill out the remainder of Bill Richardson's term rather than hand the seat to Serna, the Democrat, potentially for a lifetime.

Two days later, the Albuquerque Journal's endorsement described Miller as the "only bright spot . . . in one of the more depressing political races in recent memory." It noted that "former Democrat and Republican loyalists are gravitating to the only candidacy that inspires the kind of organization fueled by grass-roots enthusiasm instead of special-interest campaign bucks" and said that "Miller has a shrewd, results-oriented understanding of the congressional ropes and of working both sides of the aisle."

37. Serna's ads portrayed Redmond as a "radical right-wing preacher who wants to impose his extreme values and social agenda on all of us," and taking him to task for opposing abortion, opposing gun control, and favoring school vouchers. In response, Redmond charged that Serna had a "seamy past" and called him a "corrupt politician."

38. *Ballot Access News*, June 2, 1997.

39. Tim Archuleta, "President Helps Pump Green Into Chavez Bid," *Albuquerque Tribune*, July 28, 1998.

40. "After these ads, and hearing about Heather Wilson, I don't think I'd vote for her for dogcatcher," Albuquerque retiree William Meilkle told a reporter. "And the more I see of Phil Maloof, the more I'm interested in finding out what the Green candidate is doing." Cindy Glover, "High Stakes Seat Spurs Attack Ads: Commercials Rub Voters Wrong Way," *Albuquerque Journal*, June 13, 1998.

41. Karen Peterson, "Wilson Wins House Race," *Santa Fe New Mexican*, June 24, 1998.

42. John J. Lumpkin, "Gephardt Asks N.M. Green to Quit 1st District Race," *Albuquerque Journal*, September 2, 1998.

43. Rachel Smolkin, "N.M. Rides Crest of National Green Wave," *Albuquerque Tribune*, October 24, 1998.

44. Cindy Glover, "AG May Win Back Democrats," *Albuquerque Journal*, September 15, 1998.

45. Phone interview with Abraham Gutmann, April 1, 1998.

46. Phone interview with Abraham Gutmann, July 29, 1998.

47. Interview with Carol Miller in Ojo Sarco, April 27, 1998.

48. Mark Oswald, "Miller's Run Finds Ambivalence," *Santa Fe New Mexican*, September 13, 1998.

49. Interview with Xubi Wilson in Santa Fe, October 27, 1998.

50. Udall spent $1.5 million and Redmond spent $1.4 million to Miller's $24,000. This is not counting additional expenditures by party committees and independent groups on behalf of Udall and Miller. Udall and Redmond spent $16.44 and $18.85 per vote, compared to Miller's $3.91 per vote. Center for Responsive Politics, www.opensecrets.org.

51. Maloof spent $3.9 million; Wilson $1.1 million, and Anderson $17,000, again not counting additional expenditures by other groups. That came to $51.97 for each Maloof vote, $12.67 for each Wilson vote, and 99 cents per Anderson vote. Center for Responsive Politics, www.opensecrets.org.

52. Similar bills to institute instant-runoff voting were also introduced in 2001 in California, Maine, Hawaii, Maryland, Massachusetts, Illinois, Oregon, New Jersey, and Minnesota. Alaska's voters will decide the question in a 2002 referendum. E-mail from Rob Richie, "Fair Elections update," April 6, 2001; *Ballot Access News*, March 1, 2001.

53. Other endorsers of instant-runoff voting in New Mexico include Common Cause, Public Interest Research Group, Democratic senator Jeff Bingaman, 1998 Democratic gubernatorial candidate Marty Chavez, former Democratic governors Toney Anaya and David Cargo, and state Democratic Party chair Ray Sena. Tabitha Hall, "Campaign for Instant Runoff Voting in New Mexico," *Green Pages*, spring 1998.

54. Phone interview with Jerry Bradley, April 14, 1998.

55. Interview with Rep. Cisco McSorley in Albuquerque, October 28, 1998.

56. Interview with former Governor Toney Anaya in Santa Fe, April 27, 1998.

57. Oswald, "Miller's Run Finds Ambivalence."

58. Interview with Steve Schmidt in Santa Fe, October 28, 1998.

59. Oswald, "Miller's Run Finds Ambivalence."

60. The New Mexico Greens did lose their major party status after the 2000 election due to Ralph Nader's failure to get more than 5 percent of the votes in the state. But this development came solely because of a decision by the secretary of state, a partisan Democrat, to count only presidential votes toward ballot status, unlike past elections when the Greens' showing in any statewide race was considered sufficient. The relevant section of the law reads: "'Major political party' means any qualified political party, any of whose candidates received as many as 5 percent of the total votes cast at the last preceding general election for the office of governor, or president of the U.S., as the case may be." In 2000, the Greens' candidate for Appellate Court Judge, Marvin Gladstone, received 10 percent of the vote statewide. The New Mexico Greens are suing to restore their major party status, a case that Richard Winger, ballot-access legal expert, said they are sure to win if they get a fair-minded judge. Interview with Richard Winger at "Third Parties '96" conference in Washington D.C., June 1995; E-mail from Winger to author, April 18, 2001.

61. "We the Parties: What New Mexico's Major Political Parties Stand For," *Albuquerque Tribune*, April 15, 1998. The Democrats got 21 column inches, the Republicans 13 inches, and the Greens 33 inches.

62. Xubi Wilson, one of the Santa Fe Greens' key strategists, also said that it is important that many party members are active in other local institutions. "The president of the NAACP chapter is a Green, as is the head

of the rape-crisis center," he told me, "which means that people have experience with us outside the ballot box." Interview with Xubi Wilson, October 27, 1998.

63. Mary Curtius, "How the Greens Got the Blues," *Los Angeles Times*, October 9, 1998. To be fair, Green Councilman Jason Kirkpatrick said he was stepping down solely because he couldn't live on the job's $277 per month salary. But conflicts among the three Greens on the Arcata council suggest that they did not have the kind of cohesive group or process for dealing with internal division that has helped the Santa Fe Greens.

64. Greg Jan, "Audie Bock Campaign Report: How We Beat the Democrats," *Green Pages*, spring 1999.

65. Chip Johnson, "Switching Party Colors in Mid-Term: Assemblywoman Bock Is Green No More," *San Francisco Chronicle*, October 12, 1999. "Bock Skips Primary, Dumps Key Staff," *Oakland Tribune*, October 11, 1999.

66. Through June 1997, the Maine Greens actually received more in taxpayer checkoff donations than did the state Republicans, and nearly as much as the Democrats—the Democrats got $10,468, the Greens $8,306, and the Republicans $6,446. *Ballot Access News*, August 4, 1997. In the first half of 2001, the party rebounded from its temporary loss of ballot status and collected nearly as much as the Democrats in tax checkoffs—$6,138 to $6,864. Nancy Allen, the party's media coordinator, credited Nader's 2000 run for the boost.

67. E-mail from Steve Schmidt to author, August 20, 1998.

Chapter Seven

1. The signers of a November 10, 1995, open letter urging Nader to go on the California primary ballot in March 1996 included Medea Benjamin, executive director of Global Exchange; David Brower, a longtime leader of the Sierra Club and president of the Earth Island Institute; Patrick Caddell, a Democratic political strategist; Peter Camejo, CEO of Progressive Asset Management; Randy Hayes, executive director of the Rainforest Action Network; Jay Levin, the founder of the *Los Angeles Weekly*; and Ramona Ripston, president of the Southern California branch of the ACLU.

2. "I will not seek nor accept any campaign contributions," Nader wrote, "but I welcome civic energy to build democracy so as to strengthen and make more usable our democratic processes for a just, productive and sustainable society."

3. Linda Martin, *Driving Mr. Nader* (Raymond, Maine: Leopold Press, 2000), p. 32.

4. Ibid., p. 100.

5. E-mail from Paul Smith to the author, September 25, 1996.

6. Ralph Nader, "A Choice, Not an Echo," *The Nation*, July 8, 1996. "Candidates aren't the only ones who should face tests in a campaign," he told me in a June 12, 1996, phone interview. "Citizens have to meet tests too. Are they up to it? People who say [to me] 'run all the way' I ask, 'Would you leave what you are doing now?' It's important to test the mettle of progressives. . . . When you have no dependency possibility, you have to depend on yourselves."

7. These comments are drawn from a symposium on Nader's campaign that appeared in the July 8, 1996, *Nation*, in response to Nader's essay in the same issue.

8. Martin, *Driving Mr. Nader*, p. 32.

9. Phone interview with Mark McDougal and Greg Kafoury, November 13, 2000.

10. Matt Welch, "Behind Nader's 'Mad Dash': How a Candidate Known as a Grim Droner Sold Out Arenas Like a Rock Star," Newsforchange.com, November 7, 2000.

11. Phone interview with Carl Mayer, April 12, 2000.

12. Interview with Ralph Nader, traveling from Newburyport, Massachusetts, to Manchester, New Hampshire, November 30, 1991.

13. The New York crowd also made up its own version of the hockey fan's singsong chant: "Boom-boom-buh-buh-buh, Let's Go Na-der!" instead of "Let's Go Ran-gers!"

14. Lizette Alvarez, "Vowing to Restore Confidence, Nader Joins Race," *New York Times*, February 22, 2000. Nader later blamed the lack of substantial coverage by the mainstream media on its obsession with the horse race between the two major candidates, but his choice of timing and venue for his announcement speech didn't help his chances. As Doug Ireland pointed out, "It came on Presidents' Day, the same day as the Gore/Bradley debate in Harlem and the day before the Michigan primary, where the Bush/McCain contest was absorbing the national media's attention." Doug Ireland, "Ralph Really Runs," *In These Times*, April 3, 2000. Though his announcement speech got almost no serious attention, Adam Clymer, the Washington correspondent of *New York Times*, later praised it as "the best speech announcing a presidential candidacy of this campaign." Contradicting the view of his paper's editorial page, he added that Nader's speech "presented a stark and provocative

contrast to those of the Republican and Democratic candidates, who sounded as if they had the same pollsters." Adam Clymer, "Green Horse Candidate," *New York Times Book Review*, October 15, 2000.

15. Nader did finally allow that he would "break through seven figures" in his fund-raising, a remark that I used, without attribution, in my December 20, 1999, *Nation* article, "Public Citizen No. 1: Is Ralph Nader on a Drive to the White House?" A year later, on the final night of the campaign, I reminded him that he had originally projected raising only $1 million, and only after some discussion allowed me to characterize his goal as several million. Did he ever think he would have hit $7 million, the total he had raised by the end of October, I asked. "Actually, that's the literal meaning of the word 'several.'" Even at 3:00 in the morning, Nader's droll sense of humor never left him.

16. E-mail from Steve Cobble to author, October 8, 1999.

17. Marc Cooper, "Street Fight in Seattle," *The Nation*, December 20, 1999.

18. Phone interview with Theresa Amato, November 14, 2000.

19. Phone interview with Marnie Glickman, March 1, 2001. The only campaign plan I ever saw was a one-page handwritten drawing done by Nader that laid out all the obvious elements of the campaign. But campaign manager Amato says while no formal plan was ever laid out, all the components were outlined early on and fleshed out as the campaign proceeded.

20. Interview with Dean Myerson in Washington, D.C., April 16, 2000.

21. The lesson to be learned by third-party organizers of all stripes: never stop collecting petitions, even after a deadline passes. Arbitrarily early deadlines can often be defeated in court, but you won't get on the ballot even if you win unless you've collected the necessary number of signatures.

22. Phone interview with Theresa Amato, November 14, 2000.

23. Ruth Conniff, "On the Road with Ralph Nader," *The Nation*, July 17, 2000.

24. Phone interview with Theresa Amato, November 14, 2000.

25. Message from Dean Myerson to gpty-rn-m@greens.org, April 26, 2000.

26. Rob Rafn of Minnesota wrote, in part, "We'd have meetings—and it should be communicated to Ralph that pulling together irregular (ie non-weekly) meetings of 25-35 people isn't easy, making sure everyone who showed up for the last one is clear where and when the next one is—and we'd have to tell eager volunteers that we still didn't have any confirmation on anything. And we'd have to watch the disappointment on their faces as they realized that they had shown up for another meeting for nothing. And we'd have to try and convince them that we'd hopefully have something to move on at the next meeting. And some wouldn't come back.

"Finally the day of our deadline [came] to reserve a space for Ralph's big evening fundraiser, when we were thinking 'OK, we don't have it confirmed yet, but we have to move, let's just assume we're doing it at this location and pay the $500 to reserve the space,' we were finally told that Ralph would only be in MN for the afternoon, and would not be able to do the big evening fundraiser that most of our planning had revolved around.

"So we had to shift gears yet again, knowing that an enormous amount of our energy had been expended unnecessarily working to pull together a nonexistent evening fundraiser, and we had to watch the disappointment on the volunteers' faces yet again at yet another meeting. And we had to watch as more volunteers dropped away for the following meeting.

"Another thing Ralph doesn't seem clear on is that without confirmation of time and location, you can't promote the event. You can't go around telling people that Ralph will be at X location at X time and then have that not happen. When we finally got confirmation the Monday afternoon before the event, we had to call together a spur of the moment meeting so that people could pick up stacks of flyers, the design for which had been all ready to go pending Ralph's confirmation. Due to the last minute nature of things, there was no time to get them professionally printed, which would have not only looked nicer but more importantly would have saved us money—we had to go to Kinko's instead." E-mail messages from Dave Rowland and Rob Rafn to gpty-rn-m@greens.org, both titled "Re: Feed Ralph," April 28, 2000.

27. Interview with John Bonifaz in Boston, November 14, 2000.

28. During Nader's last rally of the campaign, 1:30 in the morning of Election Day at the University of South Portland, he recounted how "when I went to Washington in 1964 and I took on the auto companies, people told me, 'You'll never win.' Well, we built a movement, and we went up to Capitol Hill, and there were people who listened to us, and they were called Democrats. And we had a press that covered that six-month struggle in 1966 as a daily story. And we had a president named Lyndon Johnson who would sign the law. Don't we deserve these three things? Well, we can't do this today. Thanks to campaign finance, the real government in Washington is the corporate government. George Bush and Al Gore don't matter that much. They write checks, and they buy and rent politicians. The White House has become a corporate prison."

29. William Safire, "The Nader Factor," *New York Times*, March 21, 1996. To clear the air with the gay community, Nader gave an early and extensive interview to my colleague Doug Ireland, a columnist for *POZ* magazine. In

it, he made clear that he favored equal rights, citing the recent decision by the Vermont Supreme Court that held that denying the benefits of marriage to same-sex couples was discriminatory. The Vermont decision, he said, "was right, a humane and touching decision with a very searching rationale—it's not only a matter of affinity, but of economics on health care and other issues, which makes it all the more needed." Nader also told Ireland he supported clean needle exchange, medical use of marijuana, strict medical privacy, and universal health care—all issues of great concern to people with HIV. His work, with Jamie Love of the Nader-founded Consumer Project on Technology, was in the forefront of the fight to cut the cost of AIDS drugs both at home and abroad, Ireland noted. These were all reasons for gays to support Nader, and indeed, the exit poll from the March 2000 California open primary showed him receiving 5 percent of the state's gay vote, while only getting 2 percent overall. Doug Ireland, "President Nader!" *POZ*, May 2000.

30. Zogby International, April 1–4, 2000, poll of 842 likely voters, margin of error +/- 3.5%. The poll also found that one in five voters said they would consider voting for a third-party candidate. In addition, a majority of the public favored the inclusion of both Nader and Buchanan in the presidential debates.

31. Jeff Mapes, "Bush, Gore Neck and Neck in State: An Oregon Poll Also Shows Veteran Consumer Activist Ralph Nader Well Ahead of Other Minor-Party Candidates," *The Oregonian*, April 24, 2000. The poll was conducted April 10–17 by Davis and Hibbitts Inc. and surveyed 504 likely voters; its margin of error was +/- 4.4%. Forty-four percent of the public expressed approval for Nader, compared to 38 percent for Gore and 39 percent for Bush.

32. The Ohio Poll, April 26, 2000, press release. Nader's net favorability rating was 24 percent, compared to Bush's 22 percent and Gore's –3 percent (more people viewed Gore unfavorably than favorably).

33. "Statement by UAW President Stephen P. Yokich: UAW Will Explore Alternatives to Major Party Presidential Candidates," press release, May 23, 2000, http://www.uaw.org/publications/releases/2000/0523.html.

34. Richard Berke, "Once Seen as Odd Man Out, Nader Is Rocking Gore's Boat," *New York Times*, June 23, 2000.

35. Sam Howe Verhovek, "Unlike '96, Nader Runs Hard in '00," *New York Times*, July 1, 2000. On the other hand, the newspaper of record took no note of the huge, paying crowds Nader started attracting in late summer with his super-rallies. Its "daily briefing" wrapup of the candidates' schedules did not mention his Madison Square Garden event—even though (or perhaps because) it was in the *Times*'s hometown. And at first, the paper ran only a short wire service story on that rally, following it a day later with a fuller report by its own correspondent. The only media outlets that took third parties seriously enough to assign a full-time reporter to the beat were ABC News, *USA Today*, and the Fort-Worth *Star-Telegram*. Their respective correspondents—Rebecca Bershadker, Tom Squitieri, and Maria Recio—did yeoman's work and greatly enjoyed the assignment. They also confided that, as the election drew near, it became harder to get their stories broadcast or published.

36. William Booth, "On the Campaign Trail, Nader Means Business," *Washington Post*, June 17, 2000.

37. Interview with Mike Feinstein in Denver, June 23, 2000.

38. Interview with Steve Schmidt in Denver, June 23, 2000.

39. Interview with David Cobb in Denver, June 24, 2000. No other third party had gotten on the Texas ballot with an all-volunteer effort in almost twenty years. (In 2000, Pat Buchanan used paid petitioners in Texas, and he also chose to qualify as an independent, not a new party candidate.)

40. Interview with Medea Benjamin in Denver, June 25, 2000. Ultimately, Benjamin raised just over $250,000.

41. Interview with Blair Bobier in Denver, June 24, 2000.

42. Interview with Tom Fusco in Denver, June 24, 2000.

43. Interview with Tom Linzey in Denver, June 24, 2000.

44. Interview with Ralph Nader in Denver, June 25, 2000.

Chapter Eight

1. The official Gore line on Nader for most of the year was well articulated by spokesman Doug Hattaway. Asked if he was worried about Gore losing support to Nader among labor and environmentalists, Hattaway said, "We are not taking their support for granted, but, at the same time, we are not quaking in our boots about Ralph Nader. The real choice in the election is between Al Gore and George Bush, and Al Gore is clearly the better choice." Thomas Edsall, "Nader Bid Complicates Gore's Task," *Washington Post*, May 25, 2000.

2. "I get all of Ralph's reports, and not once have I ever seen him lend his support to hate-crime legislation, to efforts to protect abortion rights or affirmative action. Not once!" Rep. Barney Frank told Pacifica Network News at the end of April. Furthermore, he added, "I work closely with all of the leading progressive groups in my state, and not one of them excited about a Nader candidacy."

3. Susan Page, "Gore Targets Oil Industry," *USA Today*, June 26, 2000. Two days later, UPI reported that the Gore energy plan "had been developed with the assistance of a Gore adviser who also works for large power companies that could get millions in taxpayer subsidies under the plan." "Gore Energy Plan: Just What the Industry Ordered . . . Literally," United Press International, June 28, 2000.

4. For example, Gore said this on NBC's *Today* show on July 11, 2000: "The Republican leadership in the Congress is responding to wealthy special interests. . . . They control the Republican leadership's decisions. It is the same group that has been financing Governor Bush's $100 million campaign. . . . The Republican leadership [needs] to start listening to their own people and their own moderate rank-and-file members and stop letting the special interests call the tune there. . . . The same group that is blocking the progress in the Congress is bankrolling [Bush's] campaign. They are all in it together."

5. "Special Report," Fox News Channel, July 5, 2000.

6. If Gore had been a real progressive populist, journalist Mickey Kaus quipped to David Corn, he would have started by shouting at his rallies, "I'm going to fight for us!" not "I'm going to fight for you!" Gore's careful attacks on corporate targets did not scare them from donating millions to the Democratic Party. The vice president's inner circle included many top lobbyists for major multinationals, and no one in the business community was truly threatened by his speechifying. Indeed, the *New York Times*'s Money & Business section reported that for all Gore's populist tub-thumping, "no sharp policy shifts are expected if he should move to the larger office down the hall at the West Wing." David Corn, "Let the Blame Games Begin," *TomPaine.com*, October 27, 2000; Jim Drinkard, "Dems Take Money from Groups Gore Bashes," *USA Today*, October 27, 2000; Stephen Labaton, "Business Awaits Its Regulator-in-Chief," *New York Times*, October 8, 2000.

7. Berke, "Nader is Rocking Gore's Boat," *New York Times*, June 23, 2000.

8. Lewis Lapham, "A Citizen in Full: Ralph Nader Campaigns for President with a Course in Civics," *Harper's*, September 2000.

9. To take, as an example, just the *New York Times*: First there was a sloppy attack on Nader by Anthony Lewis, a longtime liberal columnist. Lewis charged Nader with misrepresenting the real differences between Gore and Bush on the environment and the Supreme Court, and then perversely took him to task for not paying attention to the one area where Lewis thought Clinton-Gore and the Republicans had marched in lockstep, protection of civil liberties. Three weeks later Lewis felt obliged to issue a retraction, noting that Nader had indeed called Clinton's record on that topic "abysmal." The same day Lewis's original column ran, Michael Janofsky, one of the *Times* reporters on the third-party beat, delivered an old chestnut—the quadrennial story on all the obscure people running for president. Profiling the oddballs and zealots who had filed under all sorts of bizarre parties or as independents, his report had the effect of reminding readers there really were only two serious candidates in the race. And two weeks later, economic columnist Paul Krugman unburdened himself of an essay describing Nader as an "extremist" who wanted to "reeducate" Alan Greenspan—implying some kind of Maoist intention when all the candidate had said is that he wanted Greenspan to apply more humane criteria to his economic models. Anthony Lewis, "Dear Ralph," *New York Times*, July 8, 2000; Michael Janofsky, "Forget Third Party, These Presidential Hopefuls Offer Array of Choices," *New York Times*, July 8, 2000; Paul Krugman, "Saints and Profits," *New York Times*, July 23, 2000.

10. Phone interview with Theresa Amato, November 14, 2000.

11. David Umhoefer and Mike Nichols, "Moody and Checota in Close Race for Senate Nomination," *Milwaukee Journal*, August 16, 1992.

12. Until the early 1980s, the League of Women Voters had sponsored debates, but after the league invited independent candidate John Anderson to participate in 1980, the Democratic and Republican parties took it upon themselves to run the show. In 1985, Paul Kirk and Frank Fahrenkopf, then the respective national chairmen of the two parties, created the Commission on Presidential Debates, made themselves co-chairs and stocked its board with partisan allies. League of Women Voters president Nancy Newman condemned the new commission on October 3, 1988, saying it was withdrawing its sponsorship "because the demands of the two campaign organizations would perpetrate a fraud on the American voter. It has become clear to us that the candidates' organizations aim to add debate to their list of campaign-trail charades devoid of substance, spontaneity, and answers to tough questions. The league has no intention of becoming an accessory to the hoodwinking of the American public." For this quote and much of the rest of this analysis, I am indebted to Jamin Raskin's excellent article, "The Debate Gerrymander," from the *Texas Law Review*, June 1999.

13. According to Harvard's Vanishing Voter Project, voter interest in the presidential campaign tripled after a weeklong series of multicandidate primary debates in January 2000. Citing this, *Washington Post* columnist E. J. Dionne wrote on January 17, "The lesson is that multiple debates work, and we should have them this fall." Cited in *Ballot Access News*, February 1, 2000.

14. Interview with Jamin Raskin in Denver, June 24, 2000.

15. A September 13 Zogby International poll showed that 58.7 percent wanted Nader to participate in the presidential debates. Senators Russ Feingold, Paul Wellstone, and Barbara Boxer, former Senator Howard Baker, Representative Jesse Jackson Jr., Governors Jesse Ventura and Gary Johnson, former Governor Mario Cuomo, former third-party presidential candidates John Anderson and Barry Commoner, and media figures Brian Lamm, John McLaughlin, Don Imus, Phil Donahue, and William F. Buckley all voiced support for Nader's inclusion. Many newspapers also editorialized in favor of including Ralph Nader in at least one presidential debate, including the *Washington Post*, the *Seattle Times*, the *Houston Chronicle*, the *Los Angeles Times*, the *San Francisco Chronicle*, the *(St. Paul) Pioneer Press*, the *Christian Science Monitor*, and the *Worcester Telegram & Gazette*. Nader 2000 press release, "Public Opposes Nader Debate Lock-out," October 3, 2000.

16. Raskin, *Texas Law Review*, p. 1963.

17. An inside source with access to the planning for the first debate told me it was clear well in advance of the event that the commission had no intention of inviting more than two candidates since the security arrangements backstage called for only two bathrooms!

18. On September 1, a U.S. District Court judge agreed that the Nader campaign had standing to sue the FEC for allowing corporate contributions to the Commission on Presidential Debates, but refused to issue an injunction against the FEC failure to act against the debate commission. On November 1, the First Circuit affirmed that ruling, and said the FEC was acting within the law. On April 30, 2001, the Supreme Court declined to take Nader's appeal. Acting Solicitor General Barbara Underwood, writing for the federal government, urged the High Court to stay out of the Nader case. "Although the Supreme Court has upheld some restrictions on corporate campaign spending, the FEC has latitude and is not required to adopt the most restrictive interpretation possible regarding corporate financial assistance to nonprofit, nonpartisan debate-sponsoring organizations," she wrote. Apparently, the Court agreed that the Commission on Presidential Debates, despite its pedigree, was a nonpartisan organization, as opposed to a bipartisan one. Anne Gearan, "Supreme Court Rejects Nader Debates Suit," Associated Press, May 1, 2001.

19. E-mail on the "Boston protest" to gpusa-talk@greens.org, October 4, 2000.

20. Nader 2000 press release, "Nader Demands Apology from Debate Commission for Unlawful Exclusion From Viewing Room," October 5, 2000; e-mail from Theresa Amato to author, March 7, 2001.

21. Philip Weiss, "The Snooty Snub Nader, But I Think He's Great," the *New York Observer*, September 25, 2000. He also pithily described how the anti-Nader drumbeat was taking hold. "All this social nyah-nyahing has had a dramatic effect. Once said to number close to 9 or 10 percent, we Naderites have been whittled down to 2 or 3 or 4. A month ago we were Vermonters who didn't comb our hair. Now we're lunatics."

22. According to Zogby, Nader's support rose from 5 to 7 percent in the days after the October 3 debate, and he was drawing 17 percent among self-identified progressives and 18 percent among independents. Carol Giacomo, Reuters News Service, October 5, 2000.

23. Public Policy Institute of California poll, conducted October 11–18, surveyed 1,096 likely voters; margin of error +/- 3.5 %.

24. Zogby tracking poll, conducted October 26–28 for Reuters/MSNBC, surveyed 599 likely Wisconsin voters; margin of error +/- 4 %.

25. Mason-Dixon poll, conducted October 26–27 for the *St. Paul Pioneer Press*; margin of error +/- 4 %.

26. *New York Times* poll, conducted October 12–15, surveyed 908 registered New Jersey voters; margin of error +/- 3 %.

27. Brown University poll, conducted October 21–22 for the *Providence Journal*, surveyed 370 likely Rhode Island voters; margin of error +/- 5 %.

28. American Research Group poll, conducted October 20–24, surveyed 600 likely Oregon voters; margin of error +/- 4 %.

29. American Research Group poll, conducted September 11–17, surveyed 600 likely Alaska voters; margin of error +/- 4 %.

30. Press release, "One in Seven Likely Voters Still Undecided on a Presidential Candidate," Vanishing Voter Project, October 18, 2000.

31. Carla Marinucci, "Women, Gays Say Nader Not Defending Their Rights; Groups Maintain That Vote for Him Is Vote for Bush," *San Francisco Chronicle*, September 14, 2000.

32. Gloria Steinem took Nader to task for trying to get 5 percent of the vote to build the Green Party, for reminding people of Gore's original pro-life position on abortion when he was a congressman, for supposedly ridiculing the use of the word "patriarchy," for having chosen a Native American as his vice presidential candidate, and for the danger that a Bush Supreme Court would turn back the clock on women, gays, and the environment. My personal favorite Steinem "reason" was number nine: "He was able to take all those perfect

progressive positions of the past because he never had to build an electoral coalition, earn a majority vote, or otherwise submit to democracy." Somehow, Steinem didn't see entering the presidential campaign with a vigorous campaign as "democracy"—or maybe she thought majority rule meant minority voices had to "submit" by shutting up. Nader responded to the "patriarchy" charge by saying, mildly, that he preferred to use less academic-sounding terms like "equal rights."

33. Unlike most other democratic critics of Nader, this group made a respectful, but obviously unsuccessful, appeal to his conscience and legacy. Gary Sellers, et al., "An Open Letter to Ralph Nader," www.naidersraidersforgore.com.

34. NARAL's anti-Nader TV ad ran in Oregon, Minnesota, Wisconsin, Washington, Maine, Vermont, and New Mexico. Ronald Brownstein, "Liberals Beat Drum for Gore, Hope Nader Backers Listen," *Los Angeles Times*, November 1, 2000.

35. The League of Conservation Voters radio ads aired in Santa Fe and Albuquerque, N.M.; Portland, Maine; Tallahassee and Gainesville, Fla.; Madison, Wis.; Eugene, Ore.; and Seattle, Wash., according to the group. The Sierra Club focused on Oregon, Washington, Wisconsin, Minnesota, and Maine, and even placed ads in alternative newspapers popular on college campuses in Oregon and Wisconsin. The People for the American Way ad also ran in Oregon and Wisconsin. See Brownstein, "Liberals Beat Drum for Gore."

36. E-mail from Rob Richie, Center for Voting and Democracy, November 20, 2000.

37. Steve Cobble, "Your Vote Doesn't Matter: It's the Electoral College That Picks the President," *TomPaine.com*, September 29, 2000. Drawing indirectly on Cobble's advice, New York philanthropist Greg MacArthur announced that he was spending $320,000 of his own money to pay for ads in the national edition of the *New York Times*, along with regional papers and weeklies in New York, Massachusetts, California, Texas, and Colorado explaining that "in this state, a vote for Nader is not a vote for Bush." MacArthur was hoping to help Nader get over the 5 percent threshold nationwide, "and since he was shut out of the debates and shut out of everything else, this is the best I can do." After a poll showed that Gore's lead in California had shrunk to just 5 percent, MacArthur announced that he wouldn't run his "Citizens for Strategic Voting" ads there. Jennifer Bleyer, "Nader's Angel Pulls Ads, Defends Legality," Newsforchange.com, October 25, 2000.

38. Editorial, "Mr. Nader's Electoral Mischief," *New York Times*, October 26, 2000.

39. Editorial, "Al Gore in the Home Stretch," *New York Times*, November 3, 2000.

40. "Concerned Scholars, Writers and Activists 2000," *Salon.com*, November 1, 2000. The signers were, as listed: Benjamin Barber, Rutgers University; Paul Berman, writer and critic; Marco Calavita, film critic; Ellen Chesler, writer and critic; Mitchell Cohen, City University of New York, *Dissent*; Bogdan Denitch, City University of New York; Ronald Dworkin, New York University; Dagoberto Gilb, writer; Todd Gitlin, New York University; Francisco Goldman, writer; Mary Gordon, novelist and critic; Hendrik Hertzberg, the *New Yorker*; John B. Judis, the *New Republic*; David Kusnet, writer and critic; Jeremy Larner, writer and critic; Wendy Lesser, the *Threepenny Review*; Harold Meyerson, *Los Angeles Weekly*; Toni Morrison, Nobel laureate, novelist, and critic; Jo-Ann Mort, Open Society Fund; Brian Morton, novelist and critic; David Osborne, writer; George Packer, novelist and critic; Jayne Anne Phillips, novelist; Gloria Steinem, writer and activist; James Shapiro, Columbia University; Ruy Teixeira, Century Foundation; Siva Vaidhyanathan, New York University; Judith B. Walzer, formerly New School University; Michael Walzer, Institute for Advanced Study, *Dissent*; Jim Weinstein, *In These Times*; Sean Wilentz, Princeton University.

This group also accused Nader of saying that "the repeal of *Roe v. Wade* would be of little consequence," and said he was "never a champion of women's rights." In fact, Nader said that he did not believe that the GOP would support the repeal of *Roe v. Wade*, since that would split the party and threaten it with permanent minority status. He did make an unfortunate remark to the effect that if that Supreme Court ruling was overturned, the abortion issue would just revert to the states. Barbara Ehrenreich, a leading feminist supporting Nader, tried to address this conflict by pointing out that feminism included more than abortion rights. "While we retained abortion rights under the Clinton-Gore administration," she wrote, "we lost welfare—a blow not only to the about 4 million women who depended on it in 1996, but to uncounted others who would have turned to it as an escape from a violent relationship. For this and other reasons, political scientist Gwendolyn Mink has called welfare reform 'the most aggressive invasion of women's rights in this century.' The extent of the damage—in increased hunger, homeless, and possibly infant mortality—is just beginning to emerge. In the meantime, Gore boasts of welfare reform and even claimed, in his acceptance speech at the Democratic Convention, to have been the major force behind it. There are, in other words, feminist reasons to reject Gore and to fear a Gore administration." Nader 2000 press release, "In Open Letter to Women, Leading Feminist Supports Nader," November 3, 2000.

41. Robert F. Kennedy Jr., "Nader's Threat to the Environment," *New York Times*, August 10, 2000.

42. Ralph Nader, Letter to the Editor, *New York Times*, August 12, 2000.

43. The ASGP's statement was big news in the Jewish press and was quickly added to anti-Nader propaganda being circulated by Democrats. The Jewish Anti-Defamation League was also quick to condemn Nader for allegedly wanting to cut off aid to Israel. The result? According to the Voter News Service exit poll, Nader received only 1 percent of the vote of a very liberal minority that had earlier disproportionately supported his candidacy. Nacha Cattan, "Nader's Green Party Calls for Halt of Aid to Israel," *The Forward*, October 27, 2000; James Besser, "Nader Blasts Israel," *New York Jewish Week*, October 27, 2000; U.S. Newswire press release, "Israel Not to Blame for Middle East Violence, Says Anti-Defamation League to Ralph Nader," October 25, 1999.

44. Joshua Micah Marshall, "Long Knives for the Naderites," *The American Prospect*, www.prospect.org, November 3, 2000. The "Concerned Scholars, Writers and Activists 2000" group also claimed that Nader was "aggressively" focusing on votes "in vital toss-up states."

45. Phone interview with Steve Cobble, September 27, 2000.

46. ABC News press release, "Half of Nader's Supporters May Bail," October 26, 2000. The ABC News tracking poll found that 56 percent of Nader's supporters said that they might change their minds; only 44 percent were definitely for him. Of the waverers, six in ten said there was a good chance they would switch.

47. Phone interview with Steve Cobble, October 22, 2000.

48. Ethan Wallison, "Democrats Hit the Road to Stop Nader," *Roll Call*, October 30, 2000. Senator Wellstone distinguished himself by keeping his argument with Nader on a high plane. "I disagree with those who accuse Nader of embarking on a self-indulgent crusade or a wrecking-ball candidacy. By raising vital issues such as the domination of our politics by corporate money, increasing economic inequality, and the impact of our trade policies on global living standards, the environment and human rights, Ralph Nader has made an enormously valuable contribution to this campaign," he wrote in an op-ed piece. As a progressive Democrat, Wellstone was sharply critical of his party's performance on the issues of trade and welfare reform. But he insisted the differences between Gore and Bush outweighed the similarities. Paul Wellstone, "A Bush Victory Would Be Too High a Price to Pay for Nader Vote," *Minneapolis Star-Tribune*, November 3, 2000.

49. Celebrities like Martin Sheen, Rob Reiner, and Melissa Etheridge also helped with the anti-Nader call.

50. This reconstruction of the Nader campaign's strategic decision making in the final weeks of the campaign is based on several reporting trips I took with the candidate during that period as well as conversations with several of his top aides and advisers. In the interests of full disclosure, I should note that at times during the campaign, Nader and some of his aides asked for my informal advice on various matters, including this question of his final itinerary, and I freely offered my thoughts.

51. Ohio, Iowa, Pennsylvania, Michigan, Minnesota, Wisconsin, Florida, New Hampshire, and Maine were all toss-ups in late October, according to a poll summary published in the *Hotline* on October 27, 2000. New Jersey, New York, Illinois, Colorado, California, Washington, Massachusetts, and D.C. were not.

52. Here is Nader's campaign itinerary for the last month before Election Day, as supplied by Jeanna Penn, Nader 2000's scheduler. It is clear that he spent more time in "safe" states than he did in "toss-ups."

    10/7/00 New York City
    10/8/00 New York City
    10/9/00 Washington, D.C.
    10/10/00 Michigan/Illinois
    10/11/00 Kentucky
    10/12/00 Florida
    10/13/00 Florida/NYC
    10/14/00 NYC
    10/15/00 New Jersey
    10/16/00 Washington, D.C.
    10/17/00 Missouri
    10/18/00 Texas
    10/19/00 Texas
    10/20/00 So. California
    10/21/00 Central California
    10/22/00 No. California
    10/23/00 No. California
    10/24/00 Arizona
    10/25/00 Washington, D.C.
    10/26/00 Ohio
    10/27/00 Iowa

10/28/00 Pennsylvania/New Jersey/NYC
10/29/00 Washington, D.C.
10/30/00 Washington, D.C.
10/31/00 Michigan/Minnesota
11/01/00 Illinois/Wisconsin
11/02/00 Washington/Colorado
11/03/00 California (Long Beach super-rally)
11/04/00 Florida
11/05/00 Washington, D.C. (MCI super rally)
11/06/00 NYC/Massachusetts/New Hampshire/Maine
11/07/00 Pennsylvania

53. Nader's somewhat surprising appeal across party lines in New Hampshire in 1992 was reflected in the large crowds who came to his rallies, ranging from middle-aged men with gun racks on their pickups to young professionals bothered by high real estate prices to the familiar ponytailed Birkenstockers. He had recently led a successful populist uprising against Congress's attempt to vote itself a pay raise and his stock was high on talk radio dials across America.

54. Eric Alterman, "Not One Vote," *The Nation*, November 13, 2000.

55. While Nader didn't get many other organizational endorsements, he received the support of prominent blacks, feminists, and environmentalists, including Randall Robinson of TransAfrica, black intellectuals Cornel West and Manning Marable, writers Barbara Ehrenreich and Meredith Tax, and activists David Brower, Randy Hayes of the Rainforest Action Network, and Tim Hermach of the Native Forest Council.

56. In some wards in Madison, Nader got more than 20 percent of the vote. He also got 14 percent in Cambridge, Massachusetts, and 12 percent in Boulder, Colorado.

57. Voter News Service exit polls from www.cnn.com and Election Data Services postelection map and analysis published by *Roll Call* and the Associated Press. Out of 3,153 counties nationwide, Nader drew more than 2.65 percent in just 832 of them.

58. In Wyoming, according to Richard Winger, Nader polled 7.3 percent in Teton County, and 7 percent in Albany County on write-ins alone. His write-in tallies statewide were 2.1 percent there, 2.5 percent in Idaho and .8 percent in Indiana. The previous record for a presidential write-in was .7 percent for independent candidate Eugene McCarthy in California in 1976. *Ballot Access News*, January 1, 2001.

59. "In 2000, three sitting city councilmembers switched to the Green Party—Larry Barnett, Mayor, Sonoma, CA, Brian Laverty, Borough Council, Blossburg, PA and Katie Scheib, Borough Council, Lewisburg, PA. Two more switched in the midst of their campaigns, before they were elected—Anna Braun, City Council, Salem, OR and Matt Gonzalez, Board of Supervisors, San Francisco, CA. Still one more switched to Green after being elected, but before being sworn in—Marc Sanchez, Board of Education, San Francisco." *Green Pages*, winter-spring 2001.

60. E-mail from David Cobb, ASGP legal adviser, to author, February 27, 2001. Nearly all of those states required that local Greens either conduct registration drives or draw a minimum percentage of the vote for a statewide candidate by 2002 in order to maintain their ballot status.

61. Phone interview with author, November 13, 2000. According to Hillsman, the campaign's second TV ad (depicting kids contemplating their future—a parody of a Monster.com ad—which evoked the campaign's essentially humanistic and uplifting purpose) ran in Washington, California, Oregon, New Mexico, Minnesota, Wisconsin, Massachusetts, Maine, Vermont, Iowa, and Colorado in the last four days before the election.

62. Phone interview with Ralph Nader, November 22, 2000.

63. Bill Bradley, "New West Notes," September 22, 1999.

64. NBC/*Wall Street Journal* poll, conducted March 2–5, 2000 by Hart/Teeter; 1,213 adults surveyed; margin of error +/-2.9%. The poll put Bush at 34 percent, Gore at 33 and McCain at 24.

65. According to Dan Johnson-Weinberger, Nader also had a chance to get the endorsement of New York's Independence Party. But state Green Party activists fought this, arguing that it would undermine their local candidates. Though more than one party could endorse a candidate under New York's fusion law, as the larger party the Independence line would appear first on the ballot. If Nader took the Independence line, New York Greens feared people would vote for Nader and never spot the other Greens running. Bowing to their concerns, Nader downplayed the opportunity and skipped going to the Independence Party convention. John Hagelin of the Natural Law Party and anti-Buchanan faction of the Reform Party made the trip and personally promised his support for Independence's other state candidates. And that was all it took to get the party's endorsement. One Nader aide estimated that this misjudgment cost him as many as two hundred thousand votes in New York. This

strikes me as high, as Hagelin got less than twenty-five thousand votes from his Independence Party line there. Phone interview with Dan Johnson-Weinberger, October 1, 2000.

66. Vanessa Daniel, "Ralph Nader's Racial Blindspot," *Colorlines*, fall 2000; Salim Muwakkil, "Nader's Curious Lack of Black Support," *Chicago Tribune*, October 16, 2000.

67. "Although the most emotionally outrageous things come from racial issues, we have to connect them to the larger picture of class," Nader told a group of minority leaders in Milwaukee. "It would be a mistake if we concentrate just on race and not class." Laura Flanders, "Ralph's People Problem," *In These Times*, October 16, 2000.

68. "I hate to use military analogies, but this is war on the two parties," Nader told David Moberg of *In These Times* magazine. "After November we're going to go after the Congress in a very detailed way, district by district. We're going to beat them in every possible way. If [Democrats are] winning 51 to 49 percent, we're going to go in and beat them with Green votes. They've got to lose people, whether they're good or bad. They've got to lose people to be put under the intense choice of changing the party or watching it dwindle." From this, Moberg reported that Nader was willing to "sacrifice" progressives like Russ Feingold or Paul Wellstone. David Moberg, "Ralph's Way: Will His Strategy Work?" *In These Times*, October 30, 2000.

69. Ralph Nader, "Letter to the Editor," *New York Times*, August 12, 2000.

70. Phone interview with Ralph Nader, November 22, 2000.

71. Greens on the ground in those progressive hotbeds had their own way of dealing with the dilemma. In Madison, they reached an accommodation with progressive Democratic Representative Tammy Baldwin that had hundreds of local Greens carrying "Nader-Baldwin" palm cards to voters and Baldwin publicly expressing respect for Nader. In Santa Fe, leading Greens, city council member Cris Moore, deliberately downplayed their support for Nader in an effort to drum up more support for local candidates who they thought had a real chance to win. Melissa McDonald got 46 percent in her bid to become a county commissioner. Says Moore, "If I could avoid conflict with a potential voter by not bringing up the presidential race, I did. I suspect other Greens did the same . . . and Melissa got lots of crossover votes from Gore-ites. This shows a tricky conflict: in the places where we're most organized, we actually have something to lose in terms of local candidates and officeholders. While progressives often support our local candidates, we risk conflict with them on the high-level races. In places where the Greens were new, they could afford to go full-bore on the Presidential race, since they didn't need progressives' support for local races." John Nichols, "The Online Beat," *The Nation* website www.thenation.com, November 4, 2000; e-mail from Cris Moore to author, November 28, 2000.

72. Phone interview with Ralph Nader, November 22, 2000.

73. The group of Butte County Green Party members were actually wearing flesh-colored tights and "Nader for President" sashes when they rushed onto a concert stage in the Chico city plaza before a crowd of college students gathered for a show. The stunt got them on the front page of the local paper and was proudly displayed on a table outside a Nader rally there in October. Chris Martin, "Nude for Nader," (Chico) *Enterprise Record*, September 29, 2000.

74. Ventura is also for gun rights, tort reform that would restrict compensation of victims, and free trade on corporate America's terms. He also did color commentary for the now defunct XFL, the Xtreme Football League. Well, you can't be perfect—and he has a point when he says that tickets to NFL games have gotten too expensive for average families. Jesse Ventura, *Do I Stand Alone?* (New York: Pocket Books, 2000), pp. xx–xxi, 88–176.

Chapter Nine

1. Sifting the polling, political scientist Ruy Teixeira argued convincingly that "Gore's best period in the campaign by far was the month after his speech at the Democratic convention, when his populist profile was sharpest and freshest." Teixeira, "Lessons for Next Time," *American Prospect*, December 18, 2000.

2. Danny Goldberg, "Papa, Don't Preach: How Moralists Lost the Youth Vote," *American Prospect*, January 1–15, 2001.

3. Gregory Palast, "Florida's 'Disappeared Voters': Disfranchised by the GOP," *The Nation*, February 5, 2001; John Lantigua, "How the GOP Gamed the System in Florida," *The Nation*, April 30, 2001.

4. Amy Bach, "Wasted Labor," *Salon.com*, December 7, 2000, http://www.salon.com/politics/feature/2000/12/07/labor/index.html.

5. *The Hotline*, compilation of quotes from various outlets, November 10, 2000.

6. Frank DiGiacomo, "Ring-a-Ding-Ding! Bill and Hill's 'Crat Pack' Swings In," *New York Observer*, December 25, 2000.

7. Paul Starr, "The Morning After," *American Prospect*, December 4, 2000.

8. "Bush Owes Nader, Big Time," *USA Today*, November 9, 2000.

9. Thomas Friedman, op-ed column, *New York Times*, November 10, 2000.

10. Roz Chast, "Thank-You Cards for Ralph Nader," *New Yorker*, December 4, 2000.

11. Buchanan's vote in Iowa, New Mexico, Oregon, and Wisconsin was modest, but large enough to deprive Bush of victory in those states, while Nader's totals in Florida and New Hampshire appear to have tipped those states out of Gore's hands. It's not clear, however, that every Nader or Buchanan voter would have supported the major-party candidates, nor would they have flowed directly to the candidate "closest" to their own. Nader's total in New Hampshire was not big enough to alter the outcome there, based on exit polls saying that if he were not running 47 percent of his voters would have supported Gore and 21 percent Bush.

12. Robert Reich, "Taking Back Democracy," *American Prospect*, December 4, 2000.

13. Kevin Phillips, "Gridlock Central," *Los Angeles Times*, November 12, 2000.

14. This phenomenon was much on the mind of both major-party campaigns, apparently. Nader field director Todd Main reported that top advisers from both sides peppered him with questions about the super-rallies at a postelection conference of campaign staff held at Harvard University in December 2000. William Greider, "Nader and the Politics of Fear," *The Nation*, March 12, 2001; phone interview with Todd Main, April 12, 2001.

15. Tom Squitieri, "Democrats Close Capitol Hill Doors on Nader," *USA Today*, January 30, 2001.

16. Tatiana Boncompagni, "Nader Facing Trial Lawyer Backlash," *Legal Times*, February 12, 2001.

17. Phone interview with Harriet Barlow, February 7, 1992.

18. Among the Citizens Party's founders were Adam Hochschild, publisher of *Mother Jones* magazine; Maggie Kuhn of the Gray Panthers; Harriet Barlow of the Institute for Local Self-Reliance; author Studs Terkel; and, yes, Ralph Nader. Vernon Mogensen, "Citizens Party: 1979–1984," in *The Encyclopedia of Third Parties in America*, ed. Immanuel Ness and James Ciment (Armonk, N.Y.: M. E. Sharpe, 2000), Volume 1, pp. 201–205.

19. They weren't the only ones. The Democrats' shift to the right during the Reagan years had produced another burst of third party organizing among a group of noted progressives as the 1980s came to a close. This time, the impetus came from Eleanor Smeal and Molly Yard, the leaders of the National Organization for Women, who were angered when the congressional Democratic-leadership endorsed a Republican rider opposing federal funding for abortions in the District of Columbia. That insult came on top of the failure of several Democrat-controlled state legislatures to ratify the Equal Rights Amendment, and the inability of the Democratic-controlled Congress to override a presidential veto of Medicaid funding for abortions in cases of rape or incest. At their urging, NOW voted at its 1989 national convention to establish a "Commission for Responsive Democracy" to study the creation of a new party. The commission was formed a year later and held public hearings attended by many well-known liberals around the country through much of 1991. NOW's national delegates endorsed the formation of a "21st Century Party" at their 1992 convention. But nothing ever came of the project beyond a founding convention in August of that year. Most feminist political energy was instead channeled in the "Year of the Woman" efforts to elect more women to the Congress, an outgrowth of the outrage sparked by the Clarence Thomas–Anita Hill hearings.

"The founding convention of the 21st Century Party took place in Washington, D.C. [August 28–30, 1992] with more than 230 members from 30 states in attendance to adopt a constitution and platform. Its founding principles called for women as 52 percent of the Party's candidates and officers who must reflect the racial and ethnic diversity of the nation; and also called for an expanded Bill of Rights for the 21st century. Dolores Huerta, co-founder and Vice President Emerita of the United Farm Workers of America, was elected National Chair. Eleanor Smeal, president of the Feminist Majority, was elected National Secretary and Paula Craver, chief executive officer of Craver, Mathews, Smith and Company, was elected National Treasurer. Four of the original conveners of the Party were elected Vice Chairs: Patricia Ireland, president of NOW; Mel King, MIT professor and co-founder of the Rainbow Coalition; Sara Nelson, executive director of the Christic Institute; and Monica Faith Stewart, Black Women's Network, Chicago, IL." From "The Feminist Chronicles," a project of the Feminist Majority Foundation, http://www.feminist.org/research/chronicles/fc1992.html; Eleanor Smeal, "Why I Support a New Party," *Ms. Magazine*, January/February 1991.

At the same time that NOW was exploring its third-party options, Tony Mazzochi, a veteran labor organizer with the Oil, Chemical, and Atomic Workers union, launched an effort to organize a Labor Party. His group, Labor Party Advocates, toiled quietly for many years until holding its founding convention in 1996. The Labor Party began with the support of several major unions, including OCAW, the American Federation of Government Employees, the California Nurses Association, the United Electrical Workers, and the Longshoremen and Warehousemen's Union, representing more than 1 million members. The United Mine Workers affiliated in 1997. But while the party's intention to organize and represent working-class Americans is admirable, so far it has been little more than a debating society and occasional pressure group. At the party's first constitutional convention, held in Pittsburgh in mid-November 1998, which I attended, the fourteen hundred delegates there voted to allow Labor Party candidates to seek office, but only under very stringent conditions. Prospective candidacies would have to show a realistic chance of winning and could not go forward without approval from the party's national council. No protest candidacies or "fusion" efforts would be sanctioned. As a result, the Labor Party has yet to enter electoral politics. Supporters of the policy compared it to how a union organizes to win a certification fight—one doesn't seek a vote until victory is certain or very likely. Opponents said the policy would retard the party's growth, which it has. In 2000, major affiliates of the Labor Party, including the United Electrical Workers union and the California Nurses Association, acted on their own and publicly endorsed Ralph Nader's presidential bid. David Bacon, "Will the Labor Party Work?" *The Nation*, July 8, 1996. For another perspective on the party's slow development, see Sean Sweeney, "The Labor Party: A New Political Architecture," *New Politics*, summer 1999.

20. Peter Argesinger, "A Place on the Ballot: Fusion Politics and Antifusion Laws," *American Historical Review* 287 (1980), pp. 288–89. Interestingly, New Party advocates always cited Argesinger on this exact point but left out the first part of his statement, where he says that "fusion sometimes helped destroy individual third parties" because the major parties often used it to their ends. This elision might be attributed to a certain "optimism of the will."

21. Ibid., p. 289.

22. Ibid., p. 296. See also note 75 below on the state-by-state effort to defang the People's Party, the electoral voice of the Populist movement.

23. Frances Fox Piven and Richard Cloward, *Why Americans Still Don't Vote* (Boston: Beacon Press, 2000).

24. Brief of the Conservative Party of New York and Liberal Party of New York as Amici Curiae in Support of Respondent, *McKenna v. Twin Cities Area New Party*, pp. 13–15, August 30, 1996.

25. Daniel Cantor and Juliet Schor, *Tunnel Vision: Labor, The World Economy and Central America* (Boston: South End Press, 1987).

26. Phone interview with Joel Rogers, March 21, 2001.

27. Daniel Cantor and Joel Rogers, "Party Time," May 1990 memo, pp. 1–2.

28. In so explicitly aligning the New Party with unions, Cantor and Rogers astutely anticipated the opening in the AFL-CIO that took place in 1995 with the election of John Sweeney and his slate of activist leaders.

29. Daniel Cantor and Joel Rogers, "Time for a New Party?" May 1990 memo, p. 1.

30. Phone interview with Joel Rogers, March 21, 2001.

31. Marcia Coyle, "This Team Hopes to Revolutionize Politics," *National Law Journal*, December 2, 1996.

32. Daniel Cantor and Joel Rogers, "Sue!" May 1990 memo.

33. "The parent internationals of these unions [CWA, 1199, and DC 37] spent several million dollars to elect their members as delegates to the 1988 Democratic Convention, and the net result was almost less than zero. For a much smaller investment the NP offers real returns." Daniel Cantor and Joel Rogers, "Getting Started," May 1990 memo, p. 7.

34. Daniel Cantor and Joel Rogers, "Getting Started," May 1990 memo, p. 1.

35. Interview with Bob Master in New York City, April 5, 2000.

36. Interview with Daniel Cantor in New York City, August 20, 1999.

37. Justices Ripple, Posner, and Easterbrook, cited in Steve Cobble and Sarah Siskind, *Fusion: Multiple Party Nomination in the United States* (Madison, Wis.: Center for a New Democracy, 1993), p. 5.

38. Memo to New Party Penguins from Daniel Cantor and Sandy Pope, August 31, 1992, http://www.new-party.org/up9208.html.

39. Phone interview with Sandy Morales Pope, April 2, 2001.

40. Phone interview with Tom Hucker, August 19, 1999.

41. Joel Rogers, "Reviving American Politics: A Debate on the New Party," *Boston Review*, January/February 1993.

42. *New Party News*, summer 1995.

43. *New Party News*, spring 1996.

44. Interview with Daniel Cantor in New York City, April 15, 1998.

45. *New Party News*, spring 1996.

46. Interview with Daniel Cantor in New York City, April 15, 1998.

47. The Hotel and Restaurant Employees union provided crucial infrastructure to the Missoula chapter, which was also supported heavily by the Montana People's Action, an ACORN-style community organization, and Women's Opportunity Resource Development, a feminist group with a strong community service orientation. E-mail to author from Bill Chaloupka, a member of the Missoula New Party Steering Committee, November 13 and 20, 1998; Phone interview with Secky Fascione, April 3, 2001. In Maryland, the chapter had early support from a large National Education Association local, along with locals representing public employees,

hotel and restaurant workers, parking attendants, train and bus drivers, and food and commercial workers. Local churches, Latino groups, and a chapter of the Rainbow Coalition were also involved. Phone interview with Tom Hucker, August 19, 1999.

48. In other parts of the country, similar feelers from New Party organizers proved fruitless. Meetings with interested organizers in the Oregon Alliance for Progressive Policy, and the Northern Plains Resource Council went nowhere. In Connecticut, where there was already a progressive electoral coalition called LEAP, the Legislative Electoral Action Program, a group with more of a focus on progressive policy coordination and less on membership development, the New Party was asked to steer clear.

49. This was commendable, considering that the very first strategic planning meetings, held in Joel Rogers's home, were among an all-white group of men—Rogers, Cantor, Wade Rathke, and Steve Cobble—plus Sarah Siskind. The party's chapters and overall membership were remarkably well-integrated by race and gender, and as chapters elected leaders to sit on the party's interim executive committee, that body diversified as well. But key strategic discussions still tended to center on a core group that was white and male (Cantor, Rogers, Rathke, Polett, Steve and Jon Kest of ACORN, Cobble in an advisory role), plus Sandy Morales Pope (for the first eighteen months), Harriet Barlow and Barbara Dudley. Said Cobble, "The party actually did a pretty remarkable job in attracting black and Hispanic party members, considering that the first meetings were four or five whites in Madison, Wisconsin. Its membership, chapters, and board were all pretty integrated, certainly more than any other party that I know of. Does that mean that the strategic decisions were made by people of color? Probably not. But it's hard to say that this wasn't better than not having that. The Greens have never come close to that. There just aren't meetings of the Greens that are that integrated. A few cases, maybe. The New Party rooms were not all-white."

Sandy Morales Pope concurred with Cobble's view, saying, "We didn't have any African Americans or Latinos at the top in the initial years. I know some women leaders later on complained about [how few women there were]. I don't know if that was due to sexism, or just an unconscious attitude that 'this is our baby and you're not going to tell us what to do.'"

And Secky Fascione, one of two women now co-chairing the party, agreed that the makeup of the party's core leadership was an issue. "There's no question that the group you listed, some of the visionary founding staff, were and still are white men. But the chapter leadership was integrated and saw the need to change the makeup of the staff. Our field staff has always been more mixed. Both locally and on the Interim Executive Committee, the leadership has been really mixed, in terms of race and gender. In 1997, we decided to move to having national co-chairs to balance that leadership picture. Currently Rosa Fenton, a Latina woman from New York, and I are co-chairs."

Cantor said, in response, "There's no denying the fact that Joel and I were and are definitely still white men." But he pointed out that the very first meeting held to propose starting the New Party included black organizers Gerry Hudson and Gary Delgado, along with labor activists Sam Pizzigati and Tony Mazzochi. Anthony Thigpen, a prominent African-American organizer in Los Angeles, was another leader he courted early on. "But while these folks were always friendly to the New Party concept, they didn't want to play a leadership role," Cantor said. He also suggested that many black leaders in particular didn't want to alter their important role in local Democratic Party politics. "The political talent in the black community is still in the Democratic Party and not willing to break with it." The result of this, he said, is that the New Party was always hindered in its ability to reach out to people beyond its own networks. "A problem of omission, not commission," he called it. Phone interviews with Steve Cobble, April 2, 2001; Sandy Morales Pope, April 2, 2001; Secky Fascione, April 3, 2001; Daniel Cantor, April 9, 2001.

50. Indeed, Shapiro and his wife deliberately chose to live in Brentwood, a town that was more working class and racially integrated. Shapiro served on the town council, and in 1998 was elected to the county council, with the support of the New Party's Progressive Montgomery chapter. Interview with Peter Shapiro in College Park, Maryland, June 12, 1998.

51. Phone interview with Becky Glass, March 22, 2001.

52. Phone interview with Daniel Cantor, March 19, 1998.

53. "The real oddity about the Perot phenomenon, from my end," Joel Rogers later said, "is that they could not see the real importance of fusion for their own effort. They joined us on the Supreme Court case with an amicus brief, but it was pretty desultory." Phone interview with Joel Rogers, March 21, 2001. Rogers-Verney conversation is from Rogers, cited in Micah L. Sifry, "United He Stands: Perot's Party Politics," *The Nation*, April 15, 1996.

54. Pope added, "In New Jersey we didn't have an organized base. We certainly had little groupings of people in certain communities. But it's a very densely populated state. In order to win even a lower-level office, you have to get a ton of votes. Doing it on your own as a third party running for county level office is incredibly hard. We should have been focusing on winning lower-level office first. In fact [the candidates we worked with] did

later. One guy almost unseated his mayor. Another ended up getting elected to his town council." Phone interview with Sandy Morales Pope, April 2, 2001.

55. E-mail from Daniel Cantor to author, June 8, 1998.

56. Daniel Cantor, "Status Report #4," April 13, 1993, memo, http://www.newparty.org/up9304.html.

57. Letter from Thomas Leighton to the editors of *The Nation*, April 29, 1993.

58. Doug Henwood, "Old Party, New Bottle," *Left Business Observer*, 58, April 26, 1993 (unpulbished).

59. Phone interview with Daniel Cantor, March 26, 2001.

60. New Party Progress Report #5, April 1994.

61. *New Party News*, summer 1995.

62. New Party November 1995 Update, http://www.newparty.org/up9511.html.

63. Cantor described Bruce Colburn as "the person who disciplined everybody from the fractious ACT-UP crowd to the Latino housing activists," and compared his leaving the Milwaukee New Party chapter to "the [New Mexico] Greens losing Cris Moore." Phone interview with Daniel Cantor, November 10, 1998. Colburn said the problems ran deeper. First was the issue of training and recruiting candidates, which got harder after the first wave of Progressive Milwaukee activists who wanted to run either got elected or exhausted their ambitions. "Being able to find candidates that you can proactively move, so you don't get caught between the unions and the community groups, each with their own set of demands, was very hard." The chapter was also buffeted by unresolved differences about how much electoral work it should do, and by differences between the mostly white unionists and black neighborhood activists who joined it, especially over the issue of school choice and vouchers. "It wasn't that easy to get people to work together either. That's why the second phase is so important. We showed that you can get into the game of politics. We won some county board seats, an aldermanic seat, some on the school board. But we didn't have an agenda past that." Phone interview with Bruce Colburn, May 7, 2001.

64. At the same time, the party's interim executive council made an explicit decision to stay away from the 1996 presidential election, taking a hard look at what it would take to raise $5,000 in twenty states—the minimum needed to qualify for federal matching funds—and agreeing that it would be a massive diversion away from the party's "grow local" strategy.

65. "We never actually filed organizing petitions," Johnson recalled. "But we did put forth to [national] that we were considering it as an option. I pretty much dropped it when it became evident to me that the other organizers didn't have their chapter's support or they were in an ACORN environment that wouldn't support that approach." Johnson's complaint was confirmed by a member of the Progressive Milwaukee board who did not want to be identified. Phone interviews with Tammy Johnson, March 30 and April 16, 2001.

66. Phone interview with Tammy Johnson, March 30, 2001.

67. The following narrative is drawn from interviews with Chicago New Party members Luis Flores, Cora Coleman, Nelson Soza, and head organizer Jonathan Green, October 9, 1998; and Carl Davidson, "Independent Electoral Politics Today: Lessons from the New Party in Chicago," *dialogue & initiative* 12, summer 1996.

68. They also dismissed concerns the state's lawyers raised about cross-endorsement leading to voter confusion or an overcrowded ballot, noting that multiple party nomination would increase the amount of information voters could learn about candidates, and that existing rules restricting access to the ballot to candidates with a demonstrated level of support would take care of the latter problem. United States Court of Appeals, Eight Circuit, *Twin Cities Area New Party vs. McKenna*, January 5, 1996.

69. "Hot Fusion? Labor, Independent Politics, and Post-1996 Organizing," *New Party News*, fall 1996.

70. Coyle, "This Team Hopes to Revolutionize Politics."

71. These were not small matters, since there was the danger that states would technically legalize fusion but make it almost impossible to use in practice. "God is in the details," said a September 26, 1996, confidential memo from Cantor to the members of the party's interim Executive Committee. He outlined plans to lobby key institutional supporters of the Democratic Party, particularly in the labor and minority communities, to enlist the support of Ross Perot and the Reform Party (which would be a major winner if fusion was legalized) and with secretaries of state to suggest fusion-friendly ballot designs. Some state parties, like the Arkansas Democratic Party, actually had an internal rule preventing its candidates from accepting the nomination of another party— even though fusion was already legal there. Cantor knew the New Party had to head off similar decisions by Democrats in other states, having just tried and failed to get incumbent Democratic Senator Paul Wellstone of Minnesota to accept the cross-endorsement of the New Party's affiliate there.

72. Phone interview with Daniel Cantor, November 21, 1996.

73. An audio recording of the oral argument can be found at *The Oyez Project* of Northwestern University, http://oyez.nwu.edu/cases/cases.cgi?command=show&case_id=830.

74. There appeared to be no political motive for the Republican National Committee to support the New Party's case, other than a desire to support the First Amendment rights of political parties in general (which for

GOP legal strategists is linked to its desire to be able to raise and spend unlimited amounts of money on behalf of its candidates). In its amicus brief, the Republican panel supported the crucial right of a party to speak to the public through its nomination process and ballot endorsement. "Because the nomination process is so central to the party's function, merely speaking out on behalf of another candidate without actually seeing the party's endorsement on the ballot robs the party of its legitimacy. While the party can still speak out on behalf of that candidate, its speech as a party ultimately must take place *on the ballot*. Any other speech is hollow in comparison." [Emphasis in original.] Brief for the Republican National Committee as Amicus Curiae in Support of Respondent, *McKenna v. Twin Cities Area New Party*, August 19, 1996.

75. Bans on fusion, coupled with restrictions of suffrage and ballot access, wiped out the populist People's Party, which had risen in 1891. "In every setting in which the Populists threatened success, the party in power (Democrats in the South, Republicans in the Midwest) moved to narrow the electorate and erect barriers to effective opposition. In the election of 1896, William Jennings Bryan, the Populist-Democratic presidential candidate, stumbled badly in anti-fusion states and did well where the practice was still legal and common. Indeed, the election was so instructive that Republican legislatures hurriedly passed anti-fusion laws in Illinois, Indiana, Iowa, North Dakota, Pennsylvania, Wisconsin, and Wyoming in 1897; in California and Nebraska in 1899; in Kansas, Minnesota, and South Dakota in 1901; in Idaho in 1903, and in Montana in 1907." Brief Amici Curiae of Twelve University Professors and Center for a New Democracy in Support of Respondent Twin Cities Area New Party, *McKenna v. Twin Cities Area New Party*, August 30, 1996.

76. "Justices Reveal Bias at Fusion Hearing," *Ballot Access News*, December 12, 1996.

77. Hindsight suggests that Rogers and Siskind, who had developed the party's legal strategy from the very beginning, might have been more forceful advocates before the High Court that December morning. But had they insisted in handling the case rather than Tribe, who had more experience in oral argument, and the party still lost, Rogers would probably have been unfairly blamed by some party members who resented his prominent role.

78. In an e-mail that Cantor sent to New Party members and supporters a few days after the oral arguments, he was more optimistic. "Yankees in 6," he predicted, jokingly. "(Actually, I think we're going to win.)"

79. Souter also made clear that he did not necessarily disagree with the need to protect the two-party system but that he dissented on that point solely because the state had failed to raise it.

80. Rehnquist also accepted the state's assertion that minor parties might use fusion to cash in on the popularity of another party's candidate in order to get the votes it needed to maintain its access to the ballot. This despite the fact that the state could prevent that from happening by counting only the votes cast on the minor party's line toward its ballot access requirements.

81. Justice Rehnquist, Bench Opinion, *Timmons v. Twin Cities Area New Party*, No. 95–1608, April 28, 1997, pp. 6, 7, 9, 11, 13, 15; Justice Stevens, Dissent, pp. 4–6, 8.

82. Richard L. Hasen, "Entrenching the Duopoly: Why the Supreme Court Should Not Allow the States to Protect the Democrats and Republicans from Political Competition," 1997 *Supreme Court Review* 331.

83. *Ballot Access News*, May 5, 1997.

84. "Cold Fusion," *New Party News*, spring 1997, p. 11.

85. Cantor's description of their meeting with the AFL's Committee on Political Education with about forty union political directors along with another sixty State Federation presidents and communications staff was revealing. "Several unions held the view that an independent, labor-friendly formation could tremendously increase union leverage vis-à-vis the Democrats. Interestingly, some folks also felt that it would allow them to reach members who are alienated from the Democrats but who retain economic populist views. Speaking against experimentation with independent structures were those who feel that 'it's already hard enough to get our members out to vote, let alone vote on a new line.' The overall reaction of those who spoke leaned slightly to the positive side, but only slightly. The majority of people didn't say anything, so we have our work cut out for us." *New Party Online News #9*, April 2, 1997; phone interview with Joel Rogers, November 26, 1996; interviews with Daniel Cantor, December 3, 1996, and January 10, 1997.

86. Phone interview with Secky Fascione, April 3, 2001.

87. Interview with Daniel Cantor in New York City, August 20, 1999.

88. Letter from Daniel Cantor to Katrina vanden Heuvel, editor of *The Nation*, October 9, 1997.

89. In the spring of 1998, the national New Party made a big push to hire twenty full-time organizers. Several were sent to Chicago, with a couple each going to the Twin Cities, Little Rock, and Montgomery County (Maryland). The only new organizing site was Portland, Oregon. "We're trying to deepen what we have where we are," Cantor told me in the spring of 1998. "It's a direct result of the *Timmons* decision." Phone interview with Daniel Cantor, March 19, 1998.

90. Roberto Rivera, presentation at the Community Action School, University of Maryland, June 13, 1998; Jonathan Green, "Building the People's Machine in the 35th Ward," New Party e-mail update, March 18, 1998.

91. This fact was very important, particularly to ACORN members who had earlier boosted community activist Michael Chandler into office. "Though Chandler would ask community residents where they stood on issues from time to time, for the most part community people felt they had to push their way in to see him," reported Keith Kelleher of Local 880 and Madeline Talbot of ACORN (both are lead organizers of their groups). "When they took a stand on an issue and were very clear about it, they could count on Chandler to vote their way. . . . But it was never as easy and natural as ACORN members had expected it would be. Over the years, Chandler moved further and further away from the people who had worked so hard to put him in. He became a very visible symbol of what ACORN members did not want in an elected community leader." Kelleher and Talbot, "The People Shall Rule: Holding Public Officials Accountable in Chicago," *Shelterforce Magazine*, November/December 2000.

92. New Party e-mail update, August 30, 1998; Jonathan Green, "Score One for the People's Machine: NP Chair Elected to Chicago City Council," New Party e-mail update, June 15, 1999; Jonathan Green, "Setting the Agenda in the 15th Ward," New Party e-mail update, August 31, 1999.

93. John Nichols, "After Fusion: The New New Party," *In These Times*, March 22, 1998; Ted Kleine, "Where's the Party? For the New Party, All Politics Is Local," *In These Times*, November 14, 1999.

94. Phone interview with Secky Fascione, April 3, 2001.

95. Phone interview with Tom Hucker, August 19, 1999.

96. Phone interview with Zach Polett, March 23, 2001.

Chapter Ten

1. Interview with Bob Master in Manhattan, April 5, 2000.

2. Phone interview with Daniel Cantor, February 26, 1999.

3. Memo from Bob Master and Daniel Cantor to the WFP Steering Committee, December 2, 1998

4. "The fact that the Communications Workers and the United Auto Workers took the lead in getting this going totally changed the dynamic," said Karen Scharf, executive director of Citizen Action New York. Presentation on third party politics at Northeast Action regional conference, February 27, 1999.

5. Interview with Richard Schrader in Manhattan, June 6, 1998.

6. This was the Majority Coalition for a New New York, backed by Local 1199.

7. Interview with Bob Master, April 5, 2000.

8. Doug Ireland, "Labor's Time to Party?" *The Nation*, July 20, 1998.

9. Interview with Bob Master, April 5, 2000.

10. Speech at the Working Families Party state convention in Albany, March 26, 2000.

11. David Halbfinger, "Hempstead Democrats Perk Up, Winning 2 Trustee Races," *New York Times*, March 18, 1999; phone interview with Daniel Cantor, March 23, 1999.

12. While open to running against Democrats at the local level, Feiner was more cautious about national races. "You can't be a pain in the ass with the president—the guy picks the Supreme Court," he said. Interview with Irv Feiner in Albany, March 25, 2000.

13. Interview with Ericka Bozzi Gomez in Spring Valley, March 2, 2000.

14. Phone interview with Tom Stoner, October 16, 2000.

15. Upon hearing this, I asked Lewis, "Aren't we hoping to get to a time where there are no sharks?" Everyone laughed. "That's a fairytale world," she answered. Waldron later handed me a short essay she had written that made clear she indeed wanted a better world for all. It began, "What if we all agreed to be our brother's keeper, recognizing that the same pain and problems that befall one, befalls the other." Waldron was elected president of New York ACORN in the spring of 2001. Interview with Bertha Lewis, Gloria Waldron, Barbara Hunt, Fred Simmons, and Valerie Holder in Brooklyn, April 12, 2000.

16. Richard Perez-Pena, "Feeling Vulnerable, Albany Republicans Nudge Senate to the Left," *New York Times*, June 12, 2000.

17. Walter Karp, *Indispensable Enemies: The Politics of Misrule in America*.

18. Relations between the two major parties in New York have been so cozy that in 2000 the lobbying firm of one former Democratic House Speaker actually helped run several Senate Republicans' reelection campaigns. And, as pointed out by the *Village Voice*, "the dual majorities [House Democrats and Senate Republicans] have . . . created gargantuan slush funds [totaling many hundreds millions of dollars], concealed in the nooks and crannies of the state budget, that allow them to raid the state treasury to protect their marginal members." Wayne Barrett, "The Albany Glacier," *Village Voice*, December 5, 2000.

19. Weeks later, the same Republicans who had sought the WFP's endorsement retaliated by trying, futilely, to knock the party off the ballot altogether. E-mail from Daniel Cantor to WFP members and friends, "Re: Endgame on the Minimum Wage," June 27, 2000.

20. In the spring of 2001, the WFP signed on to an effort led by Assemblywoman Catherine Nolan, head of the labor committee that sought to restore the linkage between the state minimum wage and the restaurant workers' minimum. Andrew Hsiao, "Stiffed! State Legislature Slices Waiters' Minimum-Wage Raise," *Village Voice*, April 12–18, 2000.

21. Christopher Hitchens, *No One Left to Lie To* (New York: Verso, 1999), p. 135.

22. Interview with Bob Master, April 5, 2000.

23. Phone interview with Ericka Bozzi Gomez, October 17, 2000.

24. Interview with Irv Feiner, March 25, 2000.

25. The rally, led by Khalid Muhammed, the former Farrakhan aide who had made a specialty of anti-Semitic slurs and obscene remarks about whites, was a flop. But instead of giving participants time to disperse peacefully after their permit to demonstrate expired, the police moved in with what many observers called excessive force. Asked about the incident, Vallone went out of his way to say that the police "handled themselves very, very well." One WFP board member, Donald Shaffer of the Long Island New Party, pressed the party's board to make a public condemnation of Vallone's remarks. But the most the board would do is send the candidate a private letter. Later, when Rev. Al Sharpton organized a series of daily protests at police headquarters, culminating in the arrests of hundreds of prominent New Yorkers engaged in nonviolent civil disobedience, the WFP was a willing and eager participant. Abby Goodnough, "Giuliani and Organizers Clash over Rally," *New York Times*, September 7, 1998.

26. Interview with Bob Master, April 5, 2000.

27. Interview with Bertha Lewis, April 12, 2000.

28. Phone interview with Daniel Cantor, April 9, 2001.

29. Phone interview with Ericka Bozzi Gomez, October 17, 2000.

30. In terms of institutional support, the Rockland WFP had the help of a CWA local, which lent it office space and allowed the chapter to use its phone banks. But the chapter had few college-age volunteers, since the county lacked a major university. Most members were either union members, ideologically motivated progressives, or people of color (predominantly women).

31. Phone interview with Tom Stoner, April 3, 2001.

32. Cantor credibly blamed the usual snafus that plague New York elections for costing the party some unknown number of votes. "[D]espite broken WFP levers on literally SCORES of machines ('Oh, just vote on the Democratic line,' said the poll commissioners, 'it doesn't matter!'), despite an absurd and confusing ballot position that cost us votes upstate and downstate ('I wanted to vote on your line, but I saw Buchanan in the same column and was confused'), despite incredible hostility in a few counties (and the arrests of 3 high school students and a postal worker in Broome County) . . . despite all this, we got our votes." E-mail from Daniel Cantor to wfp-update@topica.com, November 10, 2000.
For anyone newly sensitized to the obscene vagaries of vote counting in the wake of the Florida tally in the Bush/Gore race, it's worth noting that the proportion of "blank, void, and scattered" ballots that went uncounted was three times as high in New York City than in the rest of the state, 3.6 percent to 1.2 percent.

33. Al Gore got 3,942,215 Democratic votes, 88,395 WFP votes, and 77,087 Liberal votes. George Bush got 2,258,577 Republican votes and 144,797 Conservative votes. The Independence Party got a paltry 24,361 votes for its endorsed candidate, John Hagelin, while Pat Buchanan got 25,175 votes on the Right to Life line and just 6,424 on the Buchanan Reform line. (Or at least these were the numbers of votes counted.)

34. The party reported recruiting 676 "workplace captains" who distributed four sets of fliers to an average of one hundred co-workers each, touting their union's endorsement of Clinton on the WFP line. It also claimed to have developed 118,244 "friends and neighbors" contacts, which it used for targeted personalized mailings, and expanded its e-mail list from seven thousand to sixteen thousand. Working Families Party Election 2000, Campaign Summary and Analysis, undated.

35. The Conservative Party went from 348,727 votes for governor in 1998 to just 191,141 for senator in 2000, a drop of 55 percent. The Independence Party got only 12 percent of its 1998 vote. The Greens went from 52,533 voting for "Grandpa" Al Lewis in 1998 to 40,991 for organic farmer Mark Dunau. Only the Liberal Party showed an upswing, from 77,915 to 82,801.

36. In assembly district (AD) 54, the WFP went from 134 to 825 votes; in AD 40 it jumped from 280 to 1,723.

37. In several upstate counties targeted by the WFP, the party did much better than its statewide average. In Erie and Albany counties, it got 1.8 percent of the total Senate vote; in Broome it got 2.1 percent.

38. Overall, the percentage of WFP votes coming from progressive districts dropped from 30.2 percent in 1998 to 19.4 percent in 2000. This was most dramatic in New York City, where 50 percent of the party's vote in 1998 had come from assembly districts comprising Park Slope, the Upper West Side, the West Village, the Lower East Side, SoHo, and Chelsea. In 2000, these areas supplied just 36 percent of the WFP's total vote in the city; the party made up the difference with healthy jumps in neighborhoods that were more than 70 percent minority and in white working class districts. Working Families Party Election 2000, Campaign Summary and Analysis, undated.

39. "If the makeup of the party is the same five years from now, then we've failed. If we still get 60 percent of our vote from ideological progressives, that's not a way to grow. We need East New York and Crown Heights, not just Park Slope," Cantor added. Interview, August 20, 1999.

Chapter Eleven

1. Parties autonomous in just one state were, as of 2001, the Alaskan Independence Party; Aloha Ina Party of Hawaii; the Republican Moderate Party of Alaska; the Conservative parties of New York and New Jersey; the Consumer Party of Pennsylvania; the Cool Moose Party of Rhode Island; the Independence parties of Minnesota, New York, Delaware, and Connecticut; the Independent American Party of Utah; the Liberal Party of New York; the Mountain Party of West Virginia; the Peace and Freedom Party of California; the Right-to-Life Party of New York; the Liberty Union Party of Vermont; the Grassroots Party of Vermont; the Progressive Party of Vermont; and the Working Families Party of New York.

2. The sectarian parties include the Anarchists, the Communist Party, the Constitution Party (formerly known as the U.S. Taxpayers Party), the Natural Law Party, the National Socialist White Peoples Party (successor to the American Nazi Party), the Progressive Labor Party, the Prohibition Party, the Revolutionary Communist Party, the Socialist Equality Party, the Socialist Labor Party, the Socialist Party, the Socialist Workers Party, and the Workers World Party.

3. Jonathan D. Salant, "Buchanan Vote May End Reform Party," Associated Press, November 7, 2000; Carolyn Barta, "Verney's Exit Could Signal End of Reform Party," *Dallas Morning News*, April 19, 2001.

4. Not only do Americans want more choices, they instinctively oppose efforts to unfairly restrict access to the ballot as fundamentally undemocratic. In 1998, Floridians got a chance to prove their interest in a level-playing field when they voted overwhelmingly in favor of an amendment to the state constitution providing for equalized access to the ballot for all parties. A poll commissioned by the Florida Constitution Revision Commission that pushed for the change showed that 66 percent of voters favored eliminating the requirement that minor-party and independent candidates collect huge number of petition signatures, while major-party candidates were allowed to pay a modest filing fee. When those voters were told specifically that the revision would make it easier for independent candidates to get on the ballot, 82 percent said that fact would make them be more likely to vote for it. Deborah O'Neil, "Minor Parties Push for Equal Access to Ballot," *St. Petersburg Times*, August 3, 1998.

5. In 1996, the Libertarian Party spent about 10 percent of its national campaign budget to get its presidential candidate on the ballot, compared to 30 to 35 percent in 1980, according to party officials in charge of petition drives. By 2000, it projected having to spend only about 1 percent, according to Steven Dasbach, the party's national director. "Most of the state Libertarian parties are strong enough to do it themselves," he told me. Phone interview with Eric O'Keefe, former national director of the Libertarian Party, August 28, 1998; Interview with Steven Dasbach at the Washington College of Law conference on "The Two-Party System and Its Discontents," May 13, 1999.

6. On July 9, 1999, the *New York Times* published the following letter to the editor complaining about the practice:

> To the Editor:
> Hillary Rodham Clinton's "listening tour" (news article, July 7) of New York State comes to Albany on July 9. Mrs. Clinton's appearance is advertised as support for Representative Michael R. McNulty's re-election campaign. I wanted to attend to hear a potential United States senator and Mr. McNulty, who is my Congressman. When I called the number listed in a local newspaper advertisement, I was told that the minimum admission for a retired senior citizen is $50 and that Mr. McNulty had lowered the entry fee so as not to drain constituents. Other tickets are available for $200 and $500. No other appearance in the Albany region is planned at this time. For the state capital's part of "the listening tour," only money talks.
> We need campaign finance reform.
> Francis W. Rodgers, Rensselaer, N.Y., July 7, 1999.

7. These included "reform of absentee voting procedures, ballot design, voter registration and purging of voter lists, recount procedures and standards for counting votes to poll worker training, voter education, restrictions on exit polling and media predictions, procedures for appointing electors, and the establishment of funding, standards or procedures for updating voting technology." Testimony of Martin R. Stephens, Utah House Speaker, and John A. Hurson, majority leader of the Maryland House of Delegates, before the U.S. House Administration Committee, April 25, 2001.

8. The Florida bill, which was swiftly praised by the *New York Times* and other newspapers, also failed to address other problems. It did not extend voting hours past 7:00 P.M., despite many reports of overcrowded polling sites. Nor did it require that top election officials be nonpartisan, a basic rule that American officials always apply when they act as observers of foreign elections. The bill did ban the use of punch cards and clarified the use of manual recounts and provisional ballots, important technical improvements. It also called for better voting hardware and training of poll workers, without providing sufficient funding for these goals. Dan Hendrickson, "Florida's Electoral Reform Act: A Long List of (Deliberately) Missed Opportunities," *The Pelican* (Sierra Club Florida newsletter), summer 2001, Vol. 33, No. 2.

9. After the California State Assembly passed a bill allowing same-day voter registration, Governor Davis's press spokesman said he was opposed to it. "The governor thinks an effort should be made all year long leading up to an election to register people," Michael Bustamante said. "It shouldn't be left up to the last day." Lynda Gledhill, "Assembly OKs Looser Rules for Voting," *San Francisco Chronicle*, June 3, 1999.

10. Phone interview with Patrick Caddell, November 5, 1998. Caddell was on MSNBC Election Night, 1998.

11. Micah L. Sifry, "Body Slam," *Salon.com*, November 6, 1998, http://www.salon.com/news/1998/11/06newsb.html.

12. "It is a place for malcontents and disconnects, third-rate politicians and pamphleteers with bleeding ulcers. It is a big teepee, with no flap—where Patriot party members smoke the peace pipe with neo-Marxist New Alliance loyalists," wrote Matt Labash in the *Weekly Standard* ("Body Slam: Jesse Ventura, Ross Perot, and the Lunacy of the Reform Party," August 9, 1999). "The crazy aunts have come out of the basement," wrote Dana Milbank in the *New Republic* ("Amateur Night," August 16, 1999), describing some of the strange characters seeking the Reform Party's presidential nomination. He ended his article by noting Gargan's election and saying that would carry on "at least part of the Perot legacy. The new chairman, I notice at Gargan's press conference, has enormous ears."

One wishes that such talented journalists would feel as free to turn their poison penmanship at the truly powerful in America, as opposed to those average citizens who simply dream about opening up the political system to a little change. But such writing about the powerful is rare, for all sorts of obvious reasons.

13. "Who Will Be a Third-Party Presidential Candidate in 2000?" *Crossfire* transcript, July 13, 1999.

14. Editorial, "Mr. Nader's Misguided Crusade," *New York Times*, June 30, 2000.

15. Editorial, "Stop Arguing and Start Debating," *New York Times*, August 22, 2000.

16. Editorial, "Exclusionary Politics in New York," *New York Times*, January 29, 2000.

17. Editorial, "Third Parties in Pennsylvania," *New York Times*, July 5, 1997.

18. Jamin Raskin, "The Debate Gerrymander," *Texas Law Review*, June 1999, Vol. 77, No. 7.

19. Phone interview with Dean Barkley, April 30, 2001.

20. Phone interview with Phil Madsen, May 1, 2001.

21. See chapter 2.

22. Terry Bouricius, *Building Progressive Politics: The Vermont Story* (Madison: Center for a New Democracy, 1993); Greg Guma, *The People's Republic: Vermont and the Sanders Revolution* (Shelburne, Vt.: New England Press, 1989); Bernie Sanders (with Huck Gutman), *Outsider in the House* (New York: Verso, 1997).

23. Phone interview with Ellen David-Friedman, June 4, 2000.

24. Proof that the Progressives had developed a secure base in Burlington came from the fact that Bouricius was essentially able to hand his seat to a fellow Progressive, not fearing that if he left elective office, the seat would fall back into major party hands.

25. Phone interview with Ellen David-Friedman, May 1, 2001.

26. Phone interview with Terry Bouricius, April 30, 2001.

27. Press release, "Working Families Party Statement on the Presidential Election," December 15, 2000.

28. Phone interview with Bob Master, April 27, 2001.

29. Phone interview with Zach Polett, March 23, 2001.

30. E-mail from Zach Polett to author, March 21, 2001.

31. Among the groups interested in spreading the New Party model, according to party director Jim Fleischmann were "ACORN, HERE [the hotel and restaurant employees union], the unions affiliated with the WFP that are

having a positive experience with it like the CWA and UAW. In Oregon we have the postal carriers, the CWA, and the SEIU. In Arkansas, it's a lot of folks from SEIU In Montana, it's groups like Montana People's Action and the Women's Opportunity Resource Development [a feminist group]." Phone interview with Jim Fleischmann, April 16, 2001.

32. Joel Rogers, the group's founding chair, stepped down in 1998 and said he was out of the third-party business. After Daniel Cantor moved to New York to help build the WFP in early 1998, the New Party went without an executive director until the middle of 2001. That was when Fleischmann, a veteran organizer who had previously run the Montana People's Alliance and Oregon Action, came on board. In the interim, the party's website stagnated, its national newsletter stopped appearing, and membership dropped to about six thousand, according to Zach Polett.

33. Phone interview with Secky Fascione, April 3, 2001.

34. L. Neil Smith, "Target G.O.P.: At Last, a Libertarian Party Strategy," *Libertarian Enterprise*, June 1, 1997.

35. John Miller and Ramesh Ponnuru, "The GOP's Libertarian Problem," *NationalReview.com*, March 19, 2001, http://www.nationalreview.com/daily/nrprint031901.html.

36. Libertarian Party press release, October 23, 2000.

37. Libertarian Party press release, February 25, 1997.

38. Here is Ventura being interviewed by Fox News' Catherine Crier:

Crier: "Is it fair to call you a libertarian, or do you have a place you establish yourself?"

Ventura: "Libertarian would be pretty close. You know, if you meet libertarian people, I don't know if you've ever met them, Catherine, they all have these cards that [have] 10 questions they give you and they rate you 30, 20, and 10 points. I've scored perfect on it before."

Crier: "I've got a label for you, then."

Ventura: "What's that?"

Crier: "Libertarian."

Ventura: "Oh, yes and no. I mean libertarian. I suppose, it's not a bad label. You know, I'll accept that."
CNN, *The Crier Report*, December 14, 1998.

39. James Foster, "Jesse Ventura: The Good (and Bad) News," LP News, January 1999.

40. Blois Olson and David Erickson, "Cato This," MN-Politics.com, April 16, 1999.

41. Ventura also called Libertarians "anarchists," saying, "They're against everything, virtually, that government—you know they don't think there should be gov[ernment]—that's why I call them anarchists now." Blois Olson and David Erickson, "The Political Education of a Governor," MN-Politics.com, May 21, 1999.

42. Phone interview with Cisco McSorley, July 31, 1998.

43. Suzanne Dougherty, "Green Party's Red Light Could Affect N.M. House Race," *Washington Post*, February 16, 2000; Gilbert Gallegos, "Green Party Struggles to Maintain Strength, Credibility In 2-Party System," *Albuquerque Tribune*, June 6, 2000; Dennis Domrzalski and Valerie Yarberry, "Thunder Dan," *Weekly Alibi*, November 2–8, 2000.

44. Phone interview with David Cobb, February 9, 2001.

45. In fact, this very idea was suggested to him by Steve Cobble.

46. Actually, Medea Benjamin tried valiantly to express support for the people protesting the violation of their voting rights but was physically barred from several public meetings organized by Democrats.

47. Phone interview with Steve Cobble, February 6, 2001.

48. Phone interview with Tom Sevigny, April 12, 2001.

49. Phone interview with Tom Linzey, April 12, 2001.

50. Phone interview with Ralph Nader, April 13, 2001.

51. Phone interview with Carl Mayer, March 27, 2001.

52. Phone interview with Greg Kafoury and Mark McDougal, February 22, 2001.

53. Phone interview with Greg Kafoury, March 8, 2001.

54. Phone interview with Ralph Nader, April 13, 2001.

55. John Berg, "Historical Perspective on Ralph Nader's Campaign," November 12, 2000, http:// world.std. com/~jberg.

56. Justice William O. Douglas, concurring in *Williams v. Rhodes*, 1968.

Index